Creating Value through
corporate
restructuring

Founded in 1807, John Wiley & Sons is the oldest independent publishing company in the United States. With offices in North America, Europe, Australia and Asia, Wiley is globally committed to developing and marketing print and electronic products and services for our customers' professional and personal knowledge and understanding.

The Wiley Finance series contains books written specifically for finance and investment professionals as well as sophisticated individual investors and their financial advisors. Book topics range from portfolio management to e-commerce, risk management, financial engineering, valuation and financial instrument analysis, as well as much more.

For a list of available titles, please visit our Web site at www.WileyFinance.com.

Creating Value through corporate restructuring

Case Studies in Bankruptcies,
Buyouts, and Breakups

STUART C. GILSON

John Wiley & Sons, Inc.
New York • Chichester • Weinheim • Brisbane • Singapore • Toronto

Published by John Wiley & Sons, Inc.

Published simultaneously in Canada.

This publication is designed to provide accurate and authoritative information in regard to the subject matter covered. It is sold with the understanding that the publisher is not engaged in rendering professional services. If professional advice or other expert assistance is required, the services of a competent professional person should be sought.

Designations used by companies to distinguish their products are often claimed by trademarks. In all instances where the author or publisher is aware of a claim, the product names appear in Initial Capital letters. Readers however, should contact the appropriate companies for more complete information regarding trademarks and registration.

Library of Congress Cataloging-in-Publication Data:

Gilson, Stuart C.
    Creating value through corporate restructuring : case studies in bankruptcies, buyouts, and breakups / Stuart C. Gilson.
        p.   cm.
    Includes bibliographical references and index.
    ISBN 0-471-40559-0 (cloth : alk. paper)
    1. Corporate reorganizations—Management—Case studies.   2. Consolidation and merger of corporations—Management—Case studies.   3. Leveraged buyouts—Management—Case studies.   4. Bankruptcy—Management—Case studies.   I. Title.
    HD58.8 .G555   2001
    658.1'6—dc21   2001023753

Printed in the United States of America.

10   9   8   7   6   5   4   3   2   1

To my parents

preface

Over the past 10 years, as global markets have grown increasingly competitive, the world has seen record numbers of companies dramatically restructure their assets, operations, and capital structures. For these companies, restructuring is a means to improve financial performance, exploit new strategic opportunities, and gain credibility with the capital market. When the competitive stakes are high, restructuring can make the difference in whether a company survives or dies.

Each day brings new announcements of corporate bankruptcy reorganizations, equity spin-offs, tracking stock issues, divestitures, buyouts, mergers, and corporate cost-cutting/downsizing programs. Many thousands of other companies are affected by this activity as competitors, customers, or suppliers of companies that are restructured. Once considered a rare event, restructuring has become an important part of everyday business practice. In this new competitive landscape, every manager can benefit from understanding how corporate restructuring can be used to advance the firm's business goals, gain competitive advantage, and create value for shareholders.

Despite the expanding impact and reach of corporate restructuring, however, much of what transpires in a restructuring is typically hidden from public view. As a result, many of those directly affected by a restructuring—managers, directors, employees, and investors—may have little in the way of experience or training to prepare them for the critical decisions and challenges they will face.

This book bridges that gap, by rigorously analyzing the actual decision-making process that was followed inside 13 major company restructurings. Each of these situations is presented as a case study, letting the reader view the restructuring process through the eyes of management. The case studies were developed over an eight-year period for a course that I teach at Harvard Business School called "Creating Value through Corporate Restructuring." Drawing on extensive interviews with managers, consultants, bankers, attorneys, and others directly involved in these cases, this book provides readers with a unique inside perspective on corporate restructuring that has never before been available to the general public. The cases include some of the most innovative and controversial restructurings of the past decade. The situations have been picked to represent a wide range of restructuring techniques and strategies, and an equally wide range of management problems and challenges.

Each case study presents readers with the facts and data on which management had to rely in making its own decisions. These decisions include choosing *whether* to restructure, as well as *how* to restructure when several alternative restructuring options are available. Equally important are the many decisions that have to be made when *implementing* a restructuring strategy. (For example, in a corporate downsizing program, over what time frame should employees be laid off? In a distressed debt restructuring, how much of the firm's equity should be given to creditors?) By providing readers with a specific decision context, the cases in this book are designed to stimulate discussion of how a corporate restructuring actually gets done.

The case studies are informed by my own scholarly research on corporate restructuring. They also draw on insights that I have gained over the years while consulting to companies that have been involved in various kinds of restructuring. This has included teaching my case studies to corporate executives who are themselves grappling with the same difficult issues and challenges highlighted in this book. In the course of these interactions I realized there is widespread interest among general managers and business practitioners in understanding what corporate restructuring implies for them in real-world, practical terms. With this in mind, I wrote this book with the goal of helping managers make better decisions and choices when confronted with a restructuring situation.

This book is also intended to appeal to business students who wish to learn more about the practical challenges posed by corporate restructuring. As a textbook, it can be useful in teaching students about the difficult issues and choices that companies face when unexpectedly large changes in their economic fortunes make it necessary to restructure. More generally, the book offers practical guidance about corporate deal making, and how a deal should be structured and negotiated to create maximum value. To get the most out of the case studies, students should have an understanding of basic accounting and financial analysis. Some familiarity with discounted cash flow valuation methods is also helpful; Appendix B of this book provides a technical overview of these methods. To provide a broader context for interpreting the cases, each of the three main sections of this book—focusing on the restructuring of creditors', shareholders', and employees' claims, respectively—contains an introductory chapter that summarizes relevant academic research in the area. In a separate instructor's manual, I provide recommended classroom teaching plans for all of the cases.

ACKNOWLEDGMENTS

I owe many thanks to the people who have commented on the case studies in this book, or otherwise influenced how I study and teach the subject of corporate restructuring: Jay Alix, Ed Altman (who also encouraged me to work on this book), Bob Bruner, Dwight Crane, Harry DeAngelo, Linda DeAngelo, Steve Fenster, Martin Fridson, Bill Fruhan, Max Holmes, Michael Jensen, Paul Kazarian, Carl Kester, Jay Light, Lynn LoPucki, Ron Masulis, James McKinney, Harvey Miller, Ron Moore, Arthur Newman, Andre Perold, Tom Piper, Hank Reiling, Richard Ruback, Sanford Sigoloff, Peter Tufano, Elizabeth Warren, Jay Westbrook, and Karen Wruck. I owe a huge debt of gratitude to the many executives and practitioners who candidly spoke to me about their companies and experiences. They are too many to list by name, but their contributions were profound and are deeply appreciated. The case studies have also benefited tremendously from the insightful comments that I have received from my students over the years. A number of people were key collaborators in researching and writing these cases, including Roy Burstin, Jose Camacho, Cedric Escalle, Perry Fagan, Fritz Foley, Samuel Karam, Matthias Vogt, and, especially, Jeremy Cott. Superb editorial, administrative, and research support was provided by Dale Abramson, Chris Allen, Audrey Barrett, Sarah Eriksen, Jennifer MacDonald, Tracey Perriera, and Sarah Woolverton. The Harvard Business School Division of Research generously funded this research. Thanks go to Mary Daniello, for handling the production on this book. I owe a special thanks to Pamela van Giessen, my editor at Wiley, for expertly guiding me through this process. Finally, my wife Susan was a constant source of support and encouragement during the many years that the materials in this book were being developed; for this, as for so much else, I am ever grateful.

STUART C. GILSON

Boston, Massachusetts
June 2001

contents

Corporate Restructuring: Challenges and Opportunities

As the new century begins, businesses around the world face more competition in their markets than ever before. Significant reductions in import tariffs and other trade barriers have exposed inefficient high-cost firms to the discipline of the global marketplace. Large pools of capital now move easily through the world's financial markets, seeking the highest return. And revolutionary advances in technology have dramatically reduced the costs of producing many goods and services. In this highly competitive environment, corporate managers find themselves under ever increasing pressure to deliver superior performance and value for their shareholders. Companies that do not successfully respond to these challenges risk losing their independence, or becoming extinct.

In response to these developments, during the past twenty years record numbers of companies have dramatically restructured themselves in an effort to cut expenses, improve internal incentives, and regain their market advantage. This has meant rewriting or renegotiating the contractual relationships that exist between the firm and its key claimholders, including shareholders, creditors, employees, and suppliers. Sometimes the decision to restructure is forced upon a company—for example, by a financial crisis or hostile takeover threat. But other times the decision is preemptive. In either case, the impact on corporate claimholders is often enormous.

Of the developed economies, the United States arguably has the most experience with corporate restructuring. And the statistics suggest that the impact of restructuring within the United States has been very widely felt. Since 1980, more than 2,000 public companies, with nearly $700 billion of assets, have filed for Chapter 11 bankruptcy protection, while it is estimated that an equal number of companies have restructured their debt out

1

of court. During the same period, more than 1,500 companies have split themselves apart through equity spin-offs and carve-outs, or by issuing tracking stocks, creating over $700 billion in new publicly traded equity. And by some estimates, as many as 10 million employees have been laid off under corporate downsizing programs.[1] What may be surprising to many is that the level of restructuring activity in the United States has grown almost every year during this period, through both booms and busts in the economy.[2]

Despite the U.S. lead in restructuring, however, the rest of the world is quickly catching up. During the past five years, Europe and Asia have been overtaken by a wave of corporate restructuring activity. In Europe, with the establishment of the monetary union and the adoption of the euro, fewer high-cost companies can now hide behind devaluations of their home country currencies, or pass these costs along to consumers. An increasingly active market for corporate control means that managers of inefficiently run firms are now at risk of losing their jobs. And the explosive growth of the European high-yield public bond market has provided vast new financing for corporate acquisitions.

In Asia, meanwhile, the aftershocks of the 1997 currency crisis continue to be felt. The crisis exposed economic inefficiencies that ran deep throughout the Asian corporate sector. Many of the largest companies in Thailand, Korea, Indonesia, and Malaysia are going through painful restructurings in bankruptcy court. The end result of these proceedings is quite often the complete dismantling or liquidation of vast enterprises that once employed hundreds of thousands of people, and served as the primary engines of growth in their countries. In Japan, too, for the first time companies are being forced to reckon with their financial problems alone, with-

---

[1] All dollar figures have been converted into constant 1999 dollars, using the U.S. producer price index. The sources for these statistics and estimates include: *The Bankruptcy Yearbook & Almanac*; Securities Data Corporation; Stuart Gilson, Kose John, and Larry Lang, 1990, "Troubled Debt Restructurings: An Empirical Study of Private Reorganization of Firms in Default," *Journal of Financial Economics* 26: 315–353; Bureau of Labor Statistics (U.S. Department of Labor); Alan Downs, *Corporate Executions* (New York: American Management Association, 1995); and layoff data provided by Challenger, Gray and Christmas, Inc.

[2] The introductions to the three modules of this book report annual statistical trends for each category of restructuring.

out the support of an affiliated bank, customer, or supplier.[3] And as international product, capital, and labor markets continue to open up, economic pressures to restructure can be expected to spread throughout the rest of the world. This is evident already in South America and China.[4]

As the foregoing discussion makes clear, corporate restructuring is no longer a rare or episodic event that happens to someone else. It has become a common and significant event in the professional lives of many managers. The reach of corporate restructuring is far greater than this when one also considers the web of relationships between restructured companies and their customers, suppliers, lenders, employees, and competitors. And restructuring directly impacts the millions of investors who provide capital to these firms.

SCOPE AND ORGANIZATION OF THIS BOOK

In the modern economy, all managers can benefit from understanding the methods and best practices of corporate restructuring. But the issues, trade-offs, and conflicts that restructuring presents are complicated. Restructuring often involves difficult tax, legal, and accounting issues. Companies often have multiple restructuring options. There can be great uncertainty over how a restructuring will affect the firm's business or market value. And restructuring is often not a "positive sum game": Some claimholders, such as shareholders, may benefit from a restructuring, while others, like employees or suppliers, are made worse off. Thus any effort to restructure a company may encounter strong resistance.

Although there has been much academic research on the causes and consequences of corporate restructuring—for example, documenting how restructuring affects companies' stock prices—much less is known about the *practice* of restructuring. Put simply, how does a restructuring *get done*? Answering this question can be difficult because the issues involved are often politically or competitively sensitive. Many managers are reluctant to discuss the difficult decisions and choices that they had to make in

---

[3]For example, see Norihiko Shirouzu, "Leaner and Meaner: Driven by Necessity—and by Ford—Mazda Downsizes, U.S. Style," *Wall Street Journal* (January 5, 2000): A1; and Peter Landers, "Japan Drops Big Bailout Amid Public Outcry," *Wall Street Journal* (July 13, 2000): A18.

[4]For example, see *Financial Times* "Survey of Argentina," September 26, 2000; and Erik Eckholm, "Joblessness: A Perilous Curve on China's Capitalist Road," *New York Times* (January 20, 1998): 1.

these situations. Thus much of what has been written about corporate restructuring is based on publicly known facts and data. Although this literature provides valuable insights into the restructuring process, most of what transpires inside these companies is still a black box.

This volume is intended to fill this gap, by providing an intensive inside look at thirteen corporate restructurings that took place during the years 1992–2000. These case studies cover such varied topics as corporate bankruptcy reorganization and debt workouts, "vulture" investing, equity spinoffs, tracking stock, asset divestitures, employee layoffs and corporate downsizing, mergers and acquisitions, highly leveraged transactions, negotiated wage give-backs, employee stock buyouts, and the restructuring of employee benefit plans.

The cases were developed over an eight-year period for a course at Harvard Business School called "Creating Value Through Corporate Restructuring." The course attracts students who plan to pursue careers in investment or commercial banking, strategy consulting, corporate law, private equity investing, and general management. Over the years, these cases have also been used successfully in a number of executive programs at Harvard, and in graduate and undergraduate courses at many other business schools.

The cases are based on interviews with executives, investment bankers, attorneys, investors, and other key participants in the restructurings, and incorporate insights and data that have not been available to the general public. They represent a broad range of different restructuring techniques and company and industry contexts. The cases feature some of the most controversial and innovative restructurings of the past decade. Examples include the massive downsizing of Scott Paper Company under "Chainsaw" Al Dunlap, the employee buyout of UAL Corporation (parent of United Air Lines), USX Corporation's pioneering tracking stock offering, Continental Airlines' *second* trip through Chapter 11 bankruptcy court, and the merger of Chase Manhattan Corporation and Chemical Bank.

Although most of the cases in this book feature U.S. companies, reflecting this country's longer experience with restructuring (and U.S. managers' greater openness to discuss the subject), two cases highlight restructuring outside the United States. One of these concerns a German company's experience dealing with high labor costs; the other concerns a distressed Thai company that was the first to reorganize under Thailand's recently amended bankruptcy law, following the Asian currency crisis.

The cases show that restructuring can have a very large impact on market value—often in the billions of dollars. After Scott Paper Company furloughed over 11,000 employees, its industry-adjusted market value eventually increased by $2.9 billion, for a gain of more than 200 percent.[5] United Air Lines' market value increased by a similar amount after employees purchased a majority of its stock in exchange for significant wage and benefit concessions. (Appendix B of this book describes different techniques that can be used to estimate the impact of restructuring on companies' market values.)

The cases are organized in three modules, based on which of the following three key classes of corporate claimholders the restructuring targets: creditors, shareholders, or employees. Each module contrasts the different approaches that are available for dealing with a particular problem or challenge that confronts a company. For example, in the module on restructuring creditors' claims, firms deal with excess leverage and financial distress either by filing for Chapter 11 bankruptcy protection or by negotiating with their creditors out of court. The module on restructuring shareholders' claims includes case studies on corporate spin-offs and tracking stock as alternative approaches for dealing with undervalued common stock. And the module on restructuring employees' claims features different approaches companies can take to reduce their labor costs: layoffs, voluntary early retirement programs, and negotiated wage/benefit concessions.

LESSONS OF RESTRUCTURING

Although the case studies in this book span a wide range of companies, industries, and contexts, some common issues and themes emerge. Taken together, they suggest there are three critical hurdles or challenges that management faces in any restructuring program:

---

[5]This percentage appreciation is estimated as follows. At the beginning of Scott's restructuring, in April 1994, its common stock had a market value of $1.4 billion. At the end of the restructuring, marked by the acquisition of Scott by Kimberly-Clark in December 1995, the market value of Scott's common stock was $4.7 billion. This represents an increase of $3.3 billion (236%). Had Scott's common stock appreciated at the same rate as the Standard & Poor's (S&P) Paper and Forest Products Index, the increase in value would have been only $0.4 billion (29%). Note that this estimate represents the increase in the market value of Scott's common stock only; it does not factor in any gains or losses realized by other Scott claimholders and stakeholders, including employees, suppliers, customers, creditors, or the communities in which Scott's manufacturing facilities were located.

1. *Design.* What type of restructuring is appropriate for dealing with the specific challenge, problem, or opportunity that the company faces?
2. *Execution.* How should the restructuring process be managed and the many barriers to restructuring overcome so that as much value is created as possible?
3. *Marketing.* How should the restructuring be explained and portrayed to investors so that value created inside the company is fully credited to its stock price?

Failure to address any one of these challenges can cause the restructuring to fail.

Having a Business Purpose

Restructuring is more likely to be successful when managers first understand the fundamental business/strategic problem or opportunity that their company faces. At Humana Inc., which jointly operated a hospital business and a health insurance business, management decided to split the businesses apart through a corporate spin-off because it realized the businesses were strategically incompatible—the customers of one business were competitors with the other. Alternative restructuring options that were considered, including issuing tracking stock, doing a leveraged buyout, or repurchasing shares, would not have solved this underlying business problem.

Chase Manhattan Bank and Chemical Bank used their merger as an opportunity to both reduce operating costs and achieve an important strategic objective. Combining the two banks created opportunities to eliminate overlaps in such areas as back-office staff, branch offices, and computing infrastructure. Management of both banks also believed that larger and more diversified financial institutions would increasingly have a comparative advantage in attracting new business from corporate and retail customers. The merger was therefore also viewed as a vehicle for increasing top-line revenue growth. Internal cost cutting alone would not have enabled either bank to achieve this second goal.

Scott Paper's chief executive officer (CEO) decided to implement the layoffs quickly—in less than a year—to minimize workplace disruptions and gain credibility with the capital market. For some companies, however, strategic and business factors could warrant a more gradual approach to downsizing. For example, consider a firm that is shifting its strategic focus from a declining labor-intensive business to a more promising but less labor-intensive business. Ultimately this shift may necessitate downsizing the workforce. However, if the firm's current business is still profitable, the transition between businesses—and resulting layoffs—may be appropriately staged over a number of years. This situation could be said to characterize the mainframe computer industry during the 1980s, when business customers moved away from mainframes towards UNIX-based "open architecture" computing systems.[6]

Knowing When to Pull the Trigger

Many companies recognize the need to restructure too late, when fewer options remain and saving the company may be more difficult. Scott Paper's new CEO was widely criticized in the news media for the magnitude of the layoffs he ordered. However, such drastic action was arguably necessary because the company had taken insufficient measures before that to address its long-standing financial problems. Some research suggests that voluntary or preemptive restructuring can generate more value than restructuring done under the imminent threat of bankruptcy or a hostile takeover.[7]

Several companies featured in this book undertook major restructurings without being in a financial crisis. Compared to the rest of the U.S. airline industry, United Air Lines was in relatively strong financial condition when its employees agreed to almost $5 billion in wage and benefit reductions in 1994. And Humana was still profitable when it decided to do its spin-off.

What can be done to encourage companies to restructure sooner rather than later? In the case of United Air Lines, management in effect *created* a crisis that made employees more willing to compromise. Early in the negotiations, management threatened to break up the airline and lay off thousands of employees if a consensual agreement could not be reached. Management made the threat real by developing an actual restructuring

---

[6]The computing technology used in open architecture systems uses more standardized components than mainframe computing technology (e.g., microprocessors in personal computers). The manufacture of these components was easily outsourced to low-wage countries like Thailand and Indonesia, creating redundancies in the workforce at home. However, the mainframe business continued to be profitable due to a core group of customers that found it too costly to switch technologies, such as schools, governments, and churches.

[7]Gordon Donaldson, *Corporate Restructuring: Managing the Change Process from Within* (Boston: Harvard Business School Press, 1994).

plan, containing detailed financial projections and valuations. Moreover, United's CEO at the time had a reputation for following words with deeds, and he was not liked by the unions. (With hindsight, it is debatable whether he really intended to pursue the more radical restructuring plan; however, what matters is that the unions *believed* he would.)

In Humana's case, the company culture encouraged managers to constantly question the status quo and consider alternative ways of doing business. This sense of "organizational unease" was encouraged by Humana's CEO-founder, who twice before had shifted the company's course to a brand-new industry. As the company's integrated product strategy began to exhibit some problems—although nothing approaching a crisis—a small group of senior managers decided to investigate. This effort, which took place off-site and lasted several weeks, uncovered a serious flaw in the strategy itself, setting the stage for the eventual restructuring.

At each of these companies, there was a set of factors in place that made early action possible. However, some of these factors—a strong or visionary CEO, for example—are clearly idiosyncratic and company-specific. Thus it remains a question whether firms can be systematically *encouraged* to preemptively restructure. One approach that has been suggested is to increase the firm's financial leverage (so it has less of a cushion when the business begins to suffer); another is to increase senior managers' equity stake so they are directly rewarded for restructuring that enhances value. Such approaches are not widespread, however.[8]

---

[8]For an overview of these issues see Michael Jenson, 1993, "The Modern Industrial Revolution and the Challenge to Internal Control Systems," *Journal of Finance* 48: 831–880. Wruck shows how a company can deliberately increase its debt load to encourage the organization to restructure more quickly (Karen Wruck, 1994, "Financial Policy, Internal Control, and Performance: Sealed Air Corporation's Leveraged Special Dividend," *Journal of Financial Economics* 36: 157–192). However, other research suggests that most companies do not undertake significant restructuring unless they are confronted with a crisis, such as a takeover threat or bankruptcy. (See David Denis, Diane Denis, and Atulya Sarin, 1997, "Agency Problems, Equity Ownership, and Corporate Diversification," *Journal of Finance* 52: 135–160.) One reason equity incentives may not be used more widely is the risk of a public backlash, if managers appear to be profiting at the expense of those hurt by the restructuring (Jay Dial and Kevin Murphy, 1995, "Incentives, Downsizing, and Value Creation at General Dynamics," *Journal of Financial Economics* 37: 261–314).

The Devil Is in the Details

The decisions that managers have to make as part of implementing a restructuring plan are often critical to whether the restructuring succeeds or fails. In the language of economics, implementation is the process of managing market imperfections. The challenges that managers face here are many and varied.

In a bankruptcy restructuring, for example, one obvious objective is to reduce the firm's overall debt load. However, cancellation of debt creates equivalent taxable income for the firm. Flagstar Companies, Inc. cut its debt by over $1 billion under a "prepackaged" bankruptcy plan. In addition, if ownership of the firm's equity changes significantly, say because creditors exchange their claims for new stock, the firm can lose the often sizable tax benefit of its net operating loss carryforwards.[9] When Continental Airlines was readying to exit from Chapter 11, it had $1.4 billion of these carryforwards. However, to finance the reorganization, the company sold a majority of its stock to a group of investors—virtually guaranteeing a large ownership change.

Companies that try to restructure out of court to avoid the high costs of a formal bankruptcy proceeding can have difficulty restructuring their public bonds. If such bonds are widely held, individual bondholders may be unwilling to make concessions, preferring to free ride off the concessions of others. Thus it will be necessary to set the terms of the restructuring to reward bondholders who participate and penalize those who do not—all the while complying with securities laws that require equal treatment of creditors holding identical claims. This was the situation facing the Loewen Group Inc. as it stood at the crossroads of bankruptcy and out-of-court restructuring.

Before a company can divest a subsidiary through a tax-free spin-off, management must first decide how corporate overhead will be allocated between the subsidiary and the parent. The allocation decision can be complicated by management's understandable desire not to give away the best assets or people. It is also necessary to allocate debt between the two entities, which will generally entail some kind of refinancing. The transaction must meet certain stringent business purpose tests to qualify as tax-exempt. And if the two entities conducted business with each other before the

---

[9]There are some exceptions. For a description of tax issues in bankruptcy restructuring, see Stuart Gilson, 1997, "Transactions Costs and Capital Structure Choice: Evidence from Financially Distressed Firms," *Journal of Finance* 52: 161–196.

spin-off, management must decide whether to extend this relationship through some formal contractual arrangement. Humana's two divisions transacted extensively with one another before its spin-off, and abruptly cutting these ties risked doing long-term harm to both businesses.

Corporate downsizing also presents managers with formidable challenges. In addition to deciding how many employees should be laid off, management must decide which employees to target (e.g., white collar vs. factory workers, domestic vs. foreign employees, etc.) and set a timetable for the layoffs. It must also carefully manage the company's relations with the remaining workforce and the press. This process becomes much more complicated when management's compensation is tied to the financial success of the restructuring through stock options and other incentive compensation. And when layoffs are the by-product of a corporate merger, it is necessary to decide how they will be spread over the merging companies' workforces. This decision can significantly impact the merger integration process and how the stock market values the merger, by sending employees and investors a signal about which merging company is dominant.[10]

Bargaining Over the Allocation of Value

Corporate restructuring usually requires claimholders to make significant concessions of some kind, and therefore has important distributive consequences. Restructuring affects not only the value of the firm, but also the wealth of individual claimholders. Disputes over how value should be allocated—and how claimholders should "share the pain"—arise in almost every restructuring. Many times these disputes can take a decidedly ugly turn. A key challenge for managers is to find ways to bridge or resolve such conflicts. Failure to do so means the restructuring may be delayed, or not happen, to the detriment of all parties.

Inter-claimholder conflicts played a large role in Navistar International's restructuring. The company had amassed a $2.6 billion liability for the medical expenses of retired Navistar workers and their families, which it had promised—in writing—to fully fund. This liability had grown much faster than expected, to more than five times Navistar's net worth. Claiming imminent bankruptcy, the company proposed cutting retirees' benefits

---

[10]Many mergers that are publicly portrayed as "mergers of equals" often appear to end up as anything but. See Bill Vlasic and Bradley Stertz, *Taken for a Ride: How Daimler-Benz Drove Off with Chrysler* (New York: William Morrow & Co., 2000).

by over half. With billions of dollars at stake, the negotiations were highly contentious, and an expensive legal battle was waged in several courts.

FAG Kugelfischer also faced a major battle with its employees over the division of value. Kugelfischer's high labor costs—the average German worker earned over 40 percent more than his/her U.S. counterpart—had made it increasingly difficult for it to compete in the global ball bearings market. However, opposition from the company's powerful labor unions made cutting jobs or benefits very difficult. Moreover, under the German "social contract," managers historically owed a duty to employees and other corporate stakeholders as well as to shareholders. So any attempt to cut labor expense could well have provoked a public backlash—especially since at the time the company's home city of Schweinfurt had an unemployment rate of 16 percent.

Sometimes disputes over the allocation of value arise because claimholders disagree over what the entire company is worth. In Flagstar Companies' bankruptcy, junior and senior creditors were over half a billion dollars apart in their valuations of the company. Since the restructuring plan proposed to give creditors a substantial amount of new common stock, their relative financial recoveries depended materially on what the firm, and this stock, was ultimately worth.

To bridge such disagreements over value, a deal can be structured to include an "insurance policy" that pays one party a sum tied to the future realized value of the firm. This sort of arrangement sometimes appears in mergers in the form of "earn-out provisions" and "collars."[11] The terms of United Air Lines' restructuring included a guarantee that employees would be given additional stock if the stock price subsequently increased (presumably because of their efforts). And in some bankruptcy reorganization plans, creditors are issued warrants or puts that hedge against changes in the value of the other claims they receive under the plan.[12] Despite how much sense these provisions would seem to make, however, in practice they are relatively uncommon. The reasons for this are not yet fully understood.[13]

---

[11]When a merger is financed by swapping the stock of the bidder company for the stock of the target company, the target company shareholders face the risk that the stock they receive will subsequently lose value. A collar would directly compensate them for this loss.

[12]See Stuart Gilson, Edith Hotchkiss, and Richard Ruback, 2000, "Valuation of Bankrupt Firms," *Review of Financial Studies* 13: 43–74.

[13]See Micah Officer, 2000, "Collar Bids in Mergers and Acquisitions," University of Rochester Ph.D. dissertation paper.

Getting the Highest Price

For publicly traded companies, the success of a restructuring is ultimately judged by how much it contributes to the company's market value. However, managers cannot take for granted that investors will fully credit the company for all of the value that has been created inside.

There are many reasons why investors may undervalue or overvalue a restructuring. Many companies have no prior experience with restructuring, so there is no precedent to guide investors. Restructurings are often exceedingly complicated. (The shareholder prospectus that described United Air Lines' proposed employee buyout contained almost 250 pages of text, exhibits, and appendices). When it filed for bankruptcy protection in Thailand, Alphatec Electronics Pcl had over 1,200 different secured and unsecured creditors, located in dozens of countries. And restructuring often produces wholesale changes in the firm's assets, business operations, and capital structure.

So in most restructurings, managers face the additional important challenge of marketing the restructuring to the capital market. The most obvious way to do this is to disclose useful information to investors and analysts that they can use to value the restructuring more accurately.[14] However, managers are often limited in what they can disclose publicly. For example, detailed data on the location of employee layoffs in a firm could benefit the firm's competitors by revealing its strengths and weaknesses in specific product and geographic markets. Disclosing such data might also further poison the company's relationship with its workforce. In its public communications with analysts, United Air Lines' management could not aggressively tout the size of the wage/benefit concessions that employees made to acquire the airline's stock, since many employees entered the buyout feeling they had overpaid.

Management's credibility obviously also matters in how its disclosures

---

[14]Academic researchers have studied how discretionary corporate disclosures can increase firms' market values. For example, see Paul Healy and Krishna Palepu, 1995, "The Challenges of Investor Communication: The Case of CUC International, Inc.," *Journal of Financial Economics* 38: 111–140; and Paul Healy, Amy Hutton, and Krishna Palepu, 1999, "Stock Performance and Intermediation Changes Surrounding Sustained Increases in Disclosure," *Contemporary Accounting Research* 16: 485–520. Note that the idea of helping investors better understand the firm's market value is not inconsistent with the well-known efficient markets paradigm, which states that traded financial assets are correctly priced *on average*. This does not imply that every asset is always priced correctly, and so provides an opportunity for managers to correct mistakes in how their companies are valued.

are received. Many restructurings try to improve company profitability two ways, by both reducing costs *and* raising revenues. Scott Paper Company's restructuring was also designed to increase the firm's revenue growth potential by leveraging the brand name value of its consumer tissue products business. Management was quite open in declaring this goal. However, experience suggests that investors and analysts generally reward promises of revenue growth much less than they do evidence of cost reductions. In public financial forecasts of the merger benefits, Chemical and Chase management downplayed the size of the potential revenue enhancements, even though privately they believed the likely benefits here were huge.

When conventional disclosure strategies are ineffective in a restructuring, sometimes more creative strategies can be devised. As part of its investor marketing effort, United Air Lines began to report a new measure of earnings—along with ordinary earnings calculated under Generally Accepted Accounting Principles (GAAP)—that excluded a large noncash charge created under the buyout structure. The new earnings measure, which corresponded more closely to cash flows, was designed to educate investors about the buyout's financial benefits. Acceptance of this accounting innovation by the investment community was uneven at first, however.

Of course communicating with investors is relatively easy when the company is nonpublic and/or closely held. But having no stock price is a double-edged sword, as the case of Donald Salter Communications Inc. illustrates, since it is then harder to give managers incentives to maximize value during the restructuring.

THE FUTURE

The case studies in this volume represent some of the most important examples of corporate restructuring seen in the last decade. They also provide a model for thinking about how restructuring practices will likely evolve during the next decade. Corporate restructuring creates value by helping companies address poor performance, pursue new strategic opportunities, and attain credibility with the capital market. The environmental factors that create the need to restructure—advances in technology, competition, deregulation, financial innovation, taxes, macroeconomic shocks—will only become more important over time, as the world continues to become a more volatile place and change occurs more rapidly. The Internet's huge impact on traditional business is only the latest manifestation of this evolutionary process. Although the specific approaches that managers take to restructure their companies may change, what is clear is that in the years ahead, restructuring will play an increasingly important role in managers' quest to create value.

Restructuring Creditors' Claims

This module examines how financially distressed companies restructure their debt contracts. When a company is unable to meet its financial obligations to creditors, it has several options. Choosing the best option, and making it work, poses significant challenges. There are complicated legal, tax, and accounting issues to be considered. There may be substantial uncertainty over how competing options will affect the firm's market value. Management must be skillful in how it negotiates with creditors. And beyond any financial restructuring, there may be severe problems with the firm's business, which also require management's attention.

The five case studies in this module illustrate the range of approaches available for restructuring debt. Management's choices are mapped in Exhibit I1.2. The firm can either restructure its debt under the supervision of the bankruptcy court or attempt to restructure its debt out of court. In either case, the restructuring has two possible outcomes: The firm will be reorganized as a going concern, or it will be liquidated and all of its assets will be sold off for the benefit of creditors. In the United States, reorganization and liquidation of bankrupt firms takes place under Chapters 11 and 7, respectively, of the U.S. Bankruptcy Code.

MANAGEMENT CHALLENGES

Management's goal in a reorganization is to persuade creditors to swap their claims against the firm for a package of new claims. The pressure points in the negotiation typically concern how much value each class of creditors will receive (as a fraction of what they were owed), and what form (cash, new debt, new stock, etc.) this value will take. In the background of the negotiations, management must also be watchful that the new capital structure does not contain too much debt *in total*. And it needs to address any problems in the firm's business. These are often difficult challenges to meet.

Achieving agreement on a restructuring plan can be frustrated when, as often happens, there are conflicts among the creditors. Senior secured creditors may be much less interested in whether the firm remains in business than junior creditors. Creditors may disagree over what the reorganized firm, and the new claims they receive in the restructuring plan, are worth. And creditors who originally lent the firm money may take exception to the actions of so-called "vulture investors"—professional investors who purchase the claims of distressed or bankrupt companies. These investors often take an active role in the restructuring, but their goals can differ materially from those of the original or par lenders. Since vultures often purchase debt at a substantial discount to face value, they will generally settle for a lower recovery than par lenders. Vultures also generally have no interest in doing business with the firm after the restructuring, unlike banks or suppliers. (Chapter 6 of this book presents a comprehensive overview of this market, and discusses alternative strategies for investing in distressed companies.)

Management's responsibilities in a debt restructuring are further complicated by corporate governance issues. When a firm is near insolvency, do managers owe a fiduciary duty mainly to current shareholders or to creditors, who are essentially "shareholders in waiting"? Without some guidance on this question, managers' ability to make quick decisions may be compromised at an especially critical time for the company. And conflicts between shareholders and creditors may be exacerbated, producing costly delays. Currently in the United States, the courts have determined that when a firm is insolvent, managers are obligated to take actions that maximize the value of the *firm*—effectively weighting the interests of both creditors and shareholders.[1] However, holding managers to this standard can be difficult. And outside the United States, the rules are often very different. In Asia, for example, the bankruptcy laws of some countries have allowed managers to entrench themselves, to the detriment of creditors and outside shareholders.

In choosing an appropriate *financial* restructuring strategy for the firm,

---

[1] See John Coffee Jr., 1992, "Court Has a New Idea of Directors' Duty," *National Law Journal* (March 2): 18.

managers must also consider how this strategy impacts the firm's *business*. Chapter 11 is a legal process. It can slow down decision making, because it gives creditors the right to question management's actions in court. There are enforced waiting periods. The bankruptcy judge may be asked to rule on important business matters. And relative to out-of-court restructuring, professional fees are typically much higher in Chapter 11. Thus bankruptcy can impose a heavy cost burden on the firm.

On the other hand, Chapter 11 offers significant benefits for some businesses. It allows a company to reject unfavorable lease contracts, licensing agreements, and other "executory contracts." While a firm is in Chapter 11, it is excused from paying, or even accruing, interest on most of its debt. It has access to relatively cheap financing from new lenders who are granted "superpriority" over existing creditors. A reorganization plan can be approved without creditors' unanimous consent. It can be easier to sell assets. And Chapter 11 can help firms settle mass tort claims more efficiently (e.g., by consolidating many thousands of such claims into a single class). Over the years a number of companies have filed for Chapter 11 in response to mass asbestos litigation, for example.[2]

ACADEMIC RESEARCH

Academic research on bankruptcy has been concentrated in four main areas: corporate governance changes in bankruptcy; bankruptcy costs; the impact of bankruptcy on firms' stock prices and long-run performance; and bankruptcy resolution.[3]

Corporate Governance Changes

Researchers have documented significant changes in corporate governance for financially distressed firms. Gilson (1989, 1990) reports that over two-thirds of senior executives and corporate directors are replaced in firms that file for Chapter 11 or restructure their debt out of court.[4] Creditors

---

[2]Examples are Johns-Manville, Celotex, Owens Corning, and Armstrong World Industries.

[3]The purpose of this section is not to provide a comprehensive review of the literature, but rather to highlight selected areas of research that may be helpful for analyzing the case studies.

[4]Articles and books cited in the text are fully referenced in the list of readings at the end of this chapter.

initiate a high fraction of management changes. In addition, ownership of firms' common stock becomes significantly more concentrated around these events. Gilson and Vetsuypens (1993) show that the new chief executive officers who are brought in from outside to lead these firms receive a significant share of their pay in the form of stock options and other equity-linked compensation.

Bankruptcy Costs

Several studies have measured the costs of the reorganization process. Warner (1977) and Weiss (1990) conclude that the direct out-of-pocket costs of Chapter 11 (including professionals' fees, court filing fees, etc.) are less than 5 percent of corporate assets, on average. However, these costs are proportionately much higher for smaller firms. Altman (1984), Opler and Titman (1994), and Kaplan and Andrade (1999) attempt to measure the business losses caused by bankruptcy. (For example, potential customers or suppliers may be reluctant to do business with a bankrupt firm.) These costs are potentially much larger than out-of-pocket bankruptcy costs, but measuring them is difficult because business losses may be the cause, rather than the consequence, of bankruptcy. The studies conclude these additional costs average roughly 10 to 25 percent of firms' stock market values before bankruptcy and that highly leveraged firms suffer greater losses of business than less leveraged firms during industry downturns. Gilson, John, and Lang (1990) show that direct costs are significantly lower in out-of-court restructurings than in Chapter 11. This cost advantage gives most firms an incentive to restructure out of court if they can. An alternative restructuring option that has gained popularity recently is "prepackaged" Chapter 11, which allows firms to reorganize in Chapter 11 more quickly. Tashjian, Lease, and McConnell (1996) show that the costs of prepackaged Chapter 11 are midway between the costs of conventional Chapter 11 and out-of-court restructurings.

Stock Prices and Long-Run Performance

Aharony, Jones, and Swary (1980) show that when firms file for bankruptcy, their common stock prices decline significantly, on average (controlling for differences in firms' risk and market movements). Moreover, for up to five years before they enter bankruptcy, firms' stock prices significantly underperform the market. Gilson, John, and Lang (1990) document that when distressed firms successfully restructure their debt out of court, their risk-adjusted stock prices increase by over 40 percent, on average, from the time they first default on their debt. In contrast, firms that file for Chapter 11 suffer an average 40 percent stock price decline. This difference suggests that for most firms, it is significantly less costly to resolve financial distress out of court. Hotchkiss (1995) shows that after firms leave Chapter 11, they tend to be significantly less profitable than the average for their industries. Consistent with Hotchkiss, Gilson (1997) finds that roughly one in four companies that reorganize in Chapter 11 subsequently have to return to bankruptcy court (as so-called "Chapter 22s"), because they either continue to perform poorly or leave Chapter 11 with too much debt.

Bankruptcy Resolution

A number of studies have documented patterns in how financial distress is resolved. Several studies show that debt restructuring plans, both in and outside Chapter 11, exhibit strong deviations from the "rule of absolute priority"—for example, Franks and Torous (1989, 1994); Eberhart, Moore, and Roenfeldt (1990); Weiss (1990); LoPucki and Whitford (1993). This rule, which has to be followed in a liquidation, states that no creditor or shareholder can receive anything of value under a restructuring plan unless all more senior claimholders have been made whole. Absolute priority deviations typically mean that shareholders receive something of value in a restructuring, even though the firm is insolvent. This outcome is a by-product of the U.S. system, which encourages consensual reorganization of distressed firms. In other countries, where liquidation is more common or shareholders do not get to vote on the restructuring, absolute priority is more likely to be observed. As for how firms resolve financial distress, Gilson, John, and Lang (1990) find that most distressed large public companies are successfully reorganized—approximately half the time in Chapter 11 and half the time out of court. Firms that are able to restructure out of court typically have less complex capital structures, higher growth opportunities, and more bank debt. Finally, Gilson, Hotchkiss, and Ruback (2000) show that claimholders' relative recoveries in Chapter 11 strongly depend on how disputes over the firm's value are resolved.

CASE STUDIES

This module consists of five case studies. The first company, **The Loewen Group Inc.**, was a rapidly growing funeral home consolidator that borrowed heavily to defend itself against an unsolicited takeover offer from its chief rival. After being hit with a major legal judgment, and suffering a downturn in its markets, the company faced possible bankruptcy. Management had to decide what restructuring option was best for the company. The decision was complicated by the fact that the company was headquartered in Canada but 80 percent of its business was based in the United States. Thus if bankruptcy was chosen, it would be necessary to reconcile the different, sometimes conflicting, bankruptcy laws of the two countries.

National Convenience Stores Incorporated operated a large chain of combination convenience store–gas stations in the Southwest. It filed for Chapter 11 after its business was damaged by the Gulf War and a major economic recession. Management had to design a reorganization plan that was satisfactory to its claimholders, including banks, insurance companies, public bondholders, and suppliers. The situation was complicated by the involvement of a vulture investor, who had purchased a large block of the bonds. Further, senior managers sought 15 percent of the company's stock under the proposed plan, in the form of stock options with a below-market exercise price.

The **Continental Airlines** case relates the airline's second trip into Chapter 11. (The first time in, the company used Chapter 11 to reject its collective bargaining agreements with its workers.) When it filed in 1992, the U.S. airline industry was suffering the worst recession in its history. Fully a third of all U.S. airline capacity was operating in Chapter 11. In the second year of the bankruptcy, five investor groups, including four airlines, made bids to purchase a controlling stake in Continental. Competition among the groups produced a spirited auction for Continental's assets. Management's decision was complicated, however, by the need to consider various nonfinancial aspects of the bids. Further, with one of the oldest fleets of any U.S. airline, Continental had to spend billions of dollars over the next few years to replace most of its aircraft.

Flagstar Companies, Inc. was the holding company for several national low- to mid-priced restaurant chains, including Denny's and Hardee's. The firm was created in a leveraged buyout, then later recapitalized by the buyout firm Kohlberg Kravis Roberts & Co., which became the principal shareholder. The case describes the firm's attempt to restructure its debt in a prepackaged Chapter 11 reorganization. In principal, the "prepack" would allow the firm to restructure its publicly traded bonds more efficiently and quickly than a conventional out of court exchange offer. However, a valuation dispute between the senior and junior creditors threatened to undermine the restructuring. Each side hired an investment banking firm to produce expert valuation analysis that was presented to the court (and is reproduced in the case).

Finally, **Alphatec Electronics Pcl** describes the attempt by a Thai semiconductor manufacturer to reorganize under Thailand's new bankruptcy law. The company, which had significant U.S. dollar–denominated debt, was forced to restructure following the massive devaluation of the Thai baht in 1998. In addition, Alphatec's auditors alleged there were material misstatements in the company's financial statements. Under Thailand's previous bankruptcy law, it had been almost impossible for creditors to seize collateral or force a management change; companies could stay protected in bankruptcy for years. The new law incorporated a number of key features of U.S. Chapter 11, designed to address these problems. However, negotiations were complicated by the large number of creditors, conflicts between foreign and domestic lenders, and uncertainty over what the firm was worth due to the accounting irregularities.

READINGS

Academic Research

Aharony, Joseph, Charles Jones, and Itzhak Swary. 1980. "An Analysis of Risk and Return Characteristics of Corporate Bankruptcy Using Capital Market Data," *Journal of Finance* 35: 1001–1016.

Altman, Edward. 1984. "A Further Empirical Investigation of the Bankruptcy Cost Question," *Journal of Finance* 39: 1067–1089.

Altman, Edward. 1993. *Corporate Financial Distress and Bankruptcy* (New York: John Wiley & Sons).

Eberhart, Alan, William Moore, and Rodney Roenfeldt. 1990. "Security Pricing and Deviations from the Absolute Priority Rule in Bankruptcy Proceedings," *Journal of Finance* 45: 1457–1469.

Franks, Julian and Walter Torous. 1989. "An Empirical Investigation of U.S. Firms in Reorganization," *Journal of Finance* 44: 747–770.

Franks, Julian and Walter Torous. 1994. "A Comparison of Financial Recontracting in Distressed Exchanges and Chapter 11 Reorganizations," *Journal of Financial Economics* 35: 349–370.

Gilson, Stuart. 1989. "Management Turnover and Financial Distress," *Journal of Financial Economics* 25: 241–262.

Gilson, Stuart. 1990. "Bankruptcy, Boards, Banks, and Blockholders: Evidence on Changes in Corporate Ownership and Control When Firms Default," *Journal of Financial Economics* 26: 355–387.

Gilson, Stuart. 1997. "Transactions Costs and Capital Structure Choice: Evidence from Financially Distressed Firms," *Journal of Finance* 52: 161–196.

Gilson, Stuart and Michael Vetsuypens. 1993. "CEO Compensation in Financially Distressed Firms," *Journal of Finance* 48: 425–458.

Gilson, Stuart, Kose John, and Larry Lang. 1990. "Troubled Debt Restructurings: An Empirical Study of Private Reorganization of Firms in Default," *Journal of Financial Economics* 26: 315–353.

Gilson, Stuart, Edith Hotchkiss, and Richard Ruback. 2000. "Valuation of Bankrupt Firms," *Review of Financial Studies* 13: 43–74.

Hotchkiss, Edith. 1995. "Postbankruptcy Performance and Management Turnover," *Journal of Finance* 50: 3–21.

Kaplan, Steven and Gregor Andrade. 1998. "How Costly is Financial (Not Economic) Distress? Evidence from Highly Leveraged Transactions That Became Distressed," *Journal of Finance* 53: 1443–1493.

LoPucki, Lynn and William Whitford. 1993. "Patterns in the Bankruptcy Reorganization of Large, Publicly Held Companies," *Cornell Law Review* 78: 597–618.

Opler, Tim and Sheridan Titman. 1994. "Financial Distress amd Corporate Performance," *Journal of Finance* 49: 1015–1040.

Tashjian, Elizabeth, Ronald Lease, and John McConnell. 1996. "Prepacks: An Empirical Analysis of Prepackaged Bankruptcies," *Journal of Financial Economics* 40: 135–162.

Warner, Jerold. 1977. "Bankruptcy Costs: Some Evidence," *Journal of Finance* 32: 337–347.

Weiss, Lawrence. 1990. "Bankruptcy Resolution: Direct Costs and Violation of Priority of Claims," *Journal of Financial Economics* 27: 285–314.

Weiss, Lawrence and Karen Wruck. 1998. "Information Problems, Conflicts of Interest and Asset Stripping: Chapter 11's Failure in the Case of Eastern Airlines," *Journal of Financial Economics* 48: 55–97.

Management Books and Practitioner Resources

American Bankruptcy Institute Journal. Published monthly by the American Bankruptcy Institute, 44 Canal Center Plaza, Suite 404, Alexandria, VA 22314 (or online: www.abiworld.org).

Annual Current Developments in Bankruptcy & Reorganization. Published annually by Practicing Law Institute, 810 Seventh Avenue, New York, NY 10019.

The Bankruptcy Yearbook & Almanac. Published annually by New Generation Research, 225 Friend Street, Suite 801, Boston, MA 02114.

The Daily Bankruptcy Review. Published daily by Federal Filings, Inc., available online at www.fedfil.com/bankruptcy/dbrinfo.htm.

The Journal of Corporate Renewal. Published monthly by the Turnaround Management Association, Time & Life Building, 541 North Fairbanks Court, Suite 1880, Chicago, IL 60611 (or online: www.turnaround.org).

Rosenberg, Hilary. 2000. *The Vulture Investors (Second Edition)* (New York: Harper Business).

Troubled Company Reporter. Published daily by Bankruptcy Creditors' Service, Inc., 24 Perdicaris Place, Trenton, NJ 08618.

Turnarounds and Workouts. Published monthly by Beard Group, Inc., P.O. Box 9867, Washington, DC 20016.

Weil, Gotshal & Manges LLP. 2000. *Restructurings: Extracting Value from a Distressed Enterprise (Second Edition)* (London: Euromoney Books).

EXHIBIT I1.1 Business Bankruptcy Filings, United States, 1980–2000

Year	All Business Bankruptcies		Public Company Bankruptcies	
	Number of Chapter 7	Number of Chapter 11	Number of Chapter 11	Total Assets in Chapter 11 ($millions)
1980	249,136	6,348	62	$ 1,671
1981	260,664	10,041	74	4,703
1982	257,644	18,821	84	9,103
1983	234,594	20,252	89	12,523
1984	234,997	20,252	121	6,530
1985	280,986	23,374	149	5,831
1986	374,452	24,740	149	13,033
1987	406,761	19,901	112	41,503
1988	437,882	17,690	122	43,488
1989	476,993	18,281	135	71,371
1990	543,334	20,783	115	82,781
1991	656,460	23,989	125	83,202
1992	681,663	22,634	91	54,283
1993	602,980	19,174	86	16,752
1994	567,240	14,773	70	8,336
1995	626,150	12,904	84	23,471
1996	810,400	11,911	84	13,999
1997	989,372	10,765	82	17,245
1998	1,035,696	8,386·	120	28,940
1999	927,074	9,315	145	58,760
2000	870,805	9,835	176	94,786
Total	11,525,283	344,169	2,275	$692,311

Source: New Generation Research, Inc.

EXHIBIT I1.2   Management's Choices

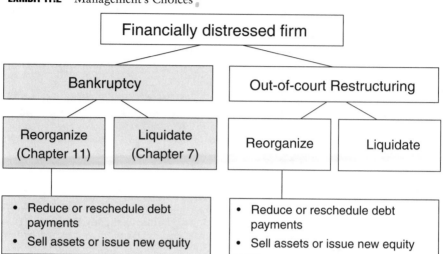

CHAPTER 1

The Loewen Group Inc.

Whatever you do, always save six for pallbearers.
—Max Shulman

On January 22, 1999, John Lacey, a renowned turnaround specialist, was appointed chairman of the Loewen Group Inc., the second largest death care company in North America. Headquartered in Burnaby, British Columbia, Loewen owned over 1,100 funeral homes and more than 400 cemeteries in the United States and Canada; it also owned 32 funeral homes in the United Kingdom. The company had come a long way since its modest beginnings in Canada, where Ray Loewen, the founder and, until recently, chairman and chief executive officer (CEO), started out helping his father run the family funeral business in the late 1950s. During the previous two decades Loewen Group had grown explosively, mainly by acquiring small independent funeral homes and cemeteries in densely populated urban markets; in recent years the company had also acquired several large established funeral chains. Over the prior five years alone, consolidated revenues had grown by nearly 30 percent a year on average, from $303 million to over $1.1 billion.

Despite its impressive growth, however, the company now faced a major financial crisis. For 1998 it would report a loss of $599 million, compared to earnings of $42 million the previous year. Loewen's ongoing acquisitions program had been aggressively financed with debt. At year-end 1998, total interest-bearing debt stood at more than $2.3 billion—more than *seven times* the amount outstanding five years earlier. Loewen's common stock, which was simultaneously traded on the New York, Toronto,

This case was prepared by Professor Stuart Gilson, assisted by Research Associate Jose Camacho. Copyright © 2000 by the President and Fellows of Harvard College. Harvard Business School case 201-062.

and Montreal stock exchanges, had ended the year at around $8 in New York, down from roughly $40 at the end of 1996.

Confronted with the company's mounting difficulties, the board of directors decided in October 1998 to replace Ray Loewen as CEO; soon thereafter, with the appointment of John Lacey, he was also replaced as chairman. The company also took some steps to raise profitability and cash flows. It consolidated various administrative functions at corporate headquarters and cut management overhead; it reviewed its pricing policies; and it hired investment bankers to explore various financing options, including asset sales, strategic partnerships, and outside capital investments in the company. However, the company's situation continued to worsen, and in mid-February Standard & Poor's downgraded Loewen's public bonds to B–, causing the stock price to drop by 38 percent in a day. In addition, certain covenants in Loewen's bank debt would be violated as a result of the company's 1998 financial performance, making it necessary to restructure the debt.

Loewen had not yet missed any payments on its debt, and had approximately $30 million of cash on hand. However, this would not be sufficient to meet several large interest and principal payments that were due over the coming months. A payment default would only make negotiations with creditors more difficult and increase the likelihood of bankruptcy. This possibility would no doubt weigh heavily on the managers' minds as they turned to the important task of restructuring the company's debts.

THE DEATH CARE BUSINESS

The primary activities of death care firms include the provision of funeral, burial, and cremation services, and related products like cemetery plots, caskets, urns, and grave site markers. Funeral services and cemetery plots can be sold either on an at-need basis (i.e., at the time of death) or on a prearranged or "pre-need" basis. In the latter case, payment for a funeral service or cemetery plot is made in advance, and the proceeds are either held in trust or invested in an insurance policy (that names the death care firm as beneficiary).

While traditional burials account for the majority of funeral services performed in the United States, cremations have been increasing in popularity in recent years. In 1998, almost 24 percent of all dispositions took place through cremation, compared to only 6 percent in 1975; analysts ex-

---

[1]Industry statistics in this section are derived from firms' annual reports and the Merrill Lynch industry report, "Post Life Services," by Fran Blechman Bernstein and Yasmine C. Nainzadeh, April 26, 1999.

pect this figure to reach 33 percent by 2010.[1] In 1998, approximately 26 percent of Loewen's funeral services were cremations. Although cremations generate relatively higher profit margins (35–40%) than traditional burials (30–35%), they contribute less to gross revenue. Cremations are much more common outside the United States, representing, for example, roughly 60 percent of dispositions in the United Kingdom.[2]

In 1999 the death care industry was highly fragmented, with approximately 22,000 funeral homes and 9,600 commercial cemeteries in the United States. Most of these were small family-owned concerns that served their local communities, where reputation and personal relationships were critically important in generating future business. (In a given geographic market, families generally used the same funeral home to care for their entire funeral needs over time.)

The largest firms in the industry were, like Loewen, publicly traded, and had achieved this scale by acquiring hundreds of independent funeral homes and cemeteries. Exhibit 1.1 lists the twelve largest North American death care companies. The largest firm, Service Corporation International (SCI), owned 3,442 funeral homes, 433 cemeteries, and 191 crematoria, spread across 20 countries. Loewen's other major competitors were Stewart Enterprises and Carriage Services Inc. At the end of 1998, the four largest firms collectively owned 2,986 funeral homes and 1,083 cemetery properties in the United States, but this represented only 13.5 percent and 11.3 percent, respectively, of each market.

Exhibit 1.2 presents Loewen's financial statements. Exhibits 1.3 and 1.4 present comparative financial, operating, and stock market data for Loewen and its three main competitors. Exhibit 1.5 reports acquisition premiums paid by Loewen and its competitors.

Aggregate revenues in the death care industry were relatively predictable. One reason was that death rates were largely driven by demographic factors that did not vary significantly from year to year. Since 1960, the number of deaths in the United States had increased at an annually compounded rate of 0.8 percent a year. Occasional large deviations from this rate were possible, however.[3] Another stabilizing influence on revenues was the historical lack of price competition in the industry. New entry into the funeral home business was extremely difficult, given how

---

[2]See Craig F. Schreiber and Benjamin C. Esty, "Service Corporation International," HBS Case No. 296–080 (July 24, 1996).

[3]For example, the number of deaths in the United States actually declined in 1981 and 1982—by 0.6 percent and 0.2 percent, respectively—but then increased by 2.3 percent in 1983 due to the sudden onset of HIV-related illnesses.

much weight most people placed on tradition and reputation when selecting a funeral home. (Most family-owned funeral homes in the United
States had been passed down through several generations.) New entry into
the cemetery business was often limited by regulation or by scarcity of
land. Further, in the case of at-need sales, bereaved family members were
rarely in a frame of mind to haggle over price.

Such industry stability was manifested in an exceedingly low business
failure rate among funeral homes. According to Dun & Bradstreet, the average annual failure rate for funeral homes and crematoria—8 out of every
10,000—was less than one-tenth the rate for all U.S. businesses.

Pre-Need Business

During the 1990s, pre-need sales of funeral services and cemetery plots had
come to represent an increasing share of the death care business. The segment
of the population that was most likely to buy on a pre-need basis—people
who were now in their 50s and 60s—was rapidly expanding. From the companies' perspective, pre-need sales provided a way to lock in sales growth and
market share. Companies also could earn an investment return on monies
that were paid to them in advance, and held in an insurance policy or trust.
As shown in Table 1.1, a large and increasing fraction of Loewen's revenues
was derived from pre-need sales, particularly of cemetery plots.

Service Corporation International was especially aggressive in marketing its pre-need business. At the end of 1998, SCI had a pre-need funeral
backlog of $3.7 billion, compared to $410 million for Loewen, $819 mil-
lion for Stewart Enterprises, and $225 million for Carriage Services.[4] (The
backlogs represented the total value of insurance policies outstanding that
had been taken out to cover the costs of providing future services and
products under pre-need sales contracts.) It was estimated that the total
pre-need market in the United States was between $20 billion to $50 billion in size, measured by current backlogs.[5]

Accounting for Pre-Need Sales   Accounting for pre-need sales was complicated.[6] For funerals, the company received cash when the pre-need con-

---

[4]See Bernstein and Nainzadeh, "Post Life Services."

[5]Data from the National Funeral Directors Association.

[6]A detailed discussion of corporate accounting for death care companies appears in
David Gallo, Ian Reynolds, and Collin Roche, 2000, "The Loewen Group: An Au-
topsy of a Chapter 11 Death Care Company," Harvard Business School, and Bernstein and Nainzadeh, "Post Life Services."

TABLE 1.1   Loewen Group's Pre-Need Sales

	Funeral Services		Cemeteries	
	Pre-Need Sales ($millions)	Pre-Need as Percent of Total	Pre-Need Sales ($millions)	Pre-Need as Percent of Total
1995	$ 97	22%	$ 88	61%
1996	$190	35%	$189	66%
1997	$267	44%	$325	77%
1998	$258	41%	$306	75%

Source: Company annual reports.

tract was purchased, but the costs of providing the funeral were mostly incurred when the customer died. On average, it took about twelve years for the contract to convert to at-need. The standard industry practice was to defer the recognition of revenue from the contract to when the funeral was performed (and the associated costs were incurred).

In the interim period, the company had two options for dealing with the initial cash payment from the customer. One option was to invest the cash in an income-earning trust and report the amount held in the trust, including any accrued investment income, as deferred revenue (i.e., a liability). When the customer eventually died the revenue was fully recognized, and the cash was withdrawn from the trust to pay for the costs of providing the funeral.[7]

A second option was to use the cash to purchase a life insurance policy in the customer's name, with the company as beneficiary. When the customer died, proceeds from the policy would pay for the funeral. Prior to this event, the insurance policy was treated as an off–balance sheet asset.[8] Loewen funded 57 percent of its pre-need funeral sales with insurance poli-

---

[7]Some state laws allowed companies to keep a specified fraction of the initial cash payment outside of the trust to pay for administrative costs. Such "retainage" was typically 10 to 15 percent of the contract sales price. Loewen accounted for retainage as current revenue at the time the pre-need contract was signed. It was the policy of all other companies to defer recognizing retainage as revenue until the funeral services were actually delivered.

[8]Upon purchasing the insurance policy, the death care company would receive a cash sales commission back from the insurance company, which would be immediately recognized as income.

cies (as opposed to trusts). The company currently operated three insurance subsidiaries that specialized in selling these policies.

A different approach was used to account for pre-need sales of cemetery plots. Customers were generally expected to make a down payment (of up to 20 percent of the total price) and pay the balance in four or five annual installments. The practice followed by Loewen and the other death care companies was to book the entire purchase price as current period revenue, showing future installment payments as long-term receivables.[9] To ensure matching of revenues and expenses, all current and future costs that would be incurred as a result of the sale were immediately expensed.[10]

Sales commissions paid to Loewen staff at the time of pre-need sales— whether sales of funerals or cemetery plots—were capitalized, and written off over time. Most companies, including SCI, used a twenty-year amortization period; Loewen used ten years.

GROWTH THROUGH CONSOLIDATION

Loewen Group and the other large public death care companies employed a dramatically different business model than traditional family-owned funeral homes. Traditional businesses historically had to contend with high fixed operating costs, which limited profit margins. Fixed costs were high because a funeral home might typically perform only one or two services a week, yet have to employ an office receptionist and various back-office staff full time. Similarly, essential assets like hearses and embalming equipment would sit around most of the time unused, tying up capital.

In the 1960s, Robert Waltrip, founder of Service Corporation International, recognized the potential to realize enormous cost savings in the industry by buying up funeral properties in concentrated geographic areas and eliminating redundant assets and overhead expenses. A cluster of funeral homes formed this way would only have to employ a single receptionist, for example, and could share hearses and other fixed assets. A typical cluster might include ten to twenty properties, located within a thirty- to sixty-mile radius. It was estimated that in an SCI-owned funeral home, fixed costs represented 54 percent of revenues on average, compared

---

[9]A reserve was established for uncollectible accounts and cancellations.
[10]Typically some of the cash down payment was placed in a trust, to cover future expenditures on cemetery-related merchandise. Another small portion of the down payment would be placed in a separate "perpetual care" trust to fund future maintenance of the property.

to 65 percent for the rest of the industry (although SCI homes were typically somewhat larger than average).[11] Clearly the cluster strategy was more appropriate for concentrated urban markets, where the properties were closer to one another; the strategy worked less well in rural areas. To avoid alienating local communities, SCI tried as much as possible to avoid altering the appearance of the acquired businesses. Most of these businesses continued to operate under the same name; no "SCI" sign or logo was displayed.

SCI's consolidation strategy had two other potential benefits. First, through increased buying power, the company might be able to obtain price concessions from suppliers (e.g., for caskets and embalming chemicals). In addition, managers of the acquired businesses would gain access to SCI's considerable financial resources and professional management practices. Thus SCI-owned funeral homes were also able to lower their variable costs, which were estimated to be 15 percent of revenues, versus 23 percent for the average U.S. funeral home.[12]

The consolidation strategy had its critics, however. Over the years there had been recurring accusations in the news media that SCI and other funeral home consolidators eliminated competition and charged excessive prices.[13]

RAY LOEWEN'S WAY

In the late 1960s, SCI, which was based in Texas, began to acquire properties in Canada. Ray Loewen's entry into the funeral home consolidation business effectively began in 1969, when he purchased a funeral home in British Columbia after learning that the home's owner was thinking of selling out to SCI. At the time, Loewen owned a single funeral home in Ontario, having sold the family business to his brother several years before.

Loewen foresaw that increasing numbers of funeral home directors, many of them in their 20s or 30s who had inherited the business from their parents, would be receptive to selling out to pursue alternative careers for financial or lifestyle reasons. Others might decide to sell because a dispro-

---

[11]See Schreiber and Esty (based on data reported by SCI).

[12]Ibid.

[13]For example, see Bruce Mohl, "Growth of Chains Has Led to Rise in Funeral Prices," *Boston Globe*, August 28, 1995, p. 1. In 1998, the CBS investigative news program *60 Minutes* ran a report investigating allegations of overcharging by SCI.

portionate fraction of their wealth was tied up in the business, even though they were satisfied in their current jobs.

As he expanded his holdings within Canada, Loewen approached the consolidation process differently from SCI. The few Canadian funeral directors who had sold their businesses to SCI thus far appeared to be unhappy with SCI's approach of managing "from afar."[14] Loewen's approach, in contrast, was to take a majority ownership stake in each acquired business, but to retain the same managers if possible and to give them relative autonomy. He would say:

> *You can't have a group of MBAs in a head office telling funeral directors how to work. They feel they know their craft and their community. So let's stress local management. If a man wants to retire—or do some estate planning—and he has a good operation, number one in his community, let's give him a good deal, allowing him to live well, ease up a bit, but remain with the firm that carries the family name.*[15]

The seller would often retain a small minority stake in the business. SCI, in contrast, had a policy of acquiring full ownership of acquired properties, although the previous owners might be kept on in management roles.

After acquiring a business, Loewen Group would often inject much needed new financing for capital improvements and increased merchandising. However, the company eschewed aggressive sales tactics, the use of telemarketing, and negative advertising that was critical of competitors. Loewen believed such tactics undermined the industry's credibility. About his main competitors at the time—SCI and Arbor Capital, a Canadian firm—he said: "Their aggressive approach hurts us all, because it reflects badly upon funeral service."[16] Loewen also was highly critical of Arbor Capital's practice of building funeral homes directly on cemetery properties; he believed each business required a distinct type of management.

As Loewen Group continued to grow through acquisitions during the 1970s and 1980s, its demand for capital increased, and in mid-1987 it listed its shares on the Toronto Stock Exchange. (Three years later it also acquired a U.S. listing on Nasdaq.) In August 1987, Loewen made its first acquisition in the United States, the Chapel of the Valley funeral home in

---

[14]Kenneth Bagnell, "A Profitable Undertaking," *Globe and Mail*, October 21, 1988, p. 128.
[15]Ibid.
[16]Ibid.

Sacramento, California. The owner was paid $1.8 million, and required to stay on as manager for three years. "It was made clear," the owner said, "that if I did not wish to work, they did not wish to buy."[17] At the time, SCI faced no meaningful competition in the United States. Shortly thereafter, Loewen acquired a small local chain of funeral homes in Fresno, California. The seller later commented: "In less than a year our calls are well up, so are our revenues. All because of Loewen. We thought we knew this business. But this Canadian makes us look like schoolboys. He's a genius in marketing."[18]

Having achieved a foothold in the giant U.S. market, Loewen Group's growth escalated. Dozens, later hundreds, of new properties were added every year. By 1998, the company had properties in forty eight U.S. states and eight Canadian provinces. (See Exhibit 1.6 for a ten-year summary of Loewen's financial position.) Ray Loewen apparently spared no expense in courting independent funeral home and cemetery owners. One cemetery owner from Indiana described his experience:

> *Mr. Esterline . . . says he and his wife were flown first-class to Vancouver, where they joined about 50 other owners of private cemeteries at the elegant Pan Pacific Hotel. The next day, they were all shuttled by seaplane to the Queen Charlotte Islands off the western coast of Canada. "Ray Loewen and his wife were greeting each of us as we got off," Mr. Esterline recalls. Nearby was Mr. Loewen's 110-foot yacht, the Alula Spirit, with a helicopter on deck.*
>
> *The fishing was first-rate. Guides led them aboard smaller boats, and everyone got a wet suit. Another boat cruised nearby, serving hot coffee. Others took helicopter rides, hopping to different islands for eagle watching. At night, the prospects stepped aboard the Alula Spirit for cocktails with company officials, who laid out bold expansion plans.*
>
> *The hospitality was soothing. "It made us feel good about" a sale to Loewen, remembers Ann Taylor, Mr. Esterline's sister and a co-owner of the cemetery.[19]*

---

[17]Ibid.

[18]Ibid.

[19]Dan Morse and Mark Heinzl, "Laid Low: Funeral Home Operators Discover the Downside of Sale to Consolidator," *Wall Street Journal*, September 17, 1999, p. A1.

SCI'S HOSTILE TAKEOVER OFFER

Described in the news media as "fierce competitors" and "arch rivals," Loewen Group and SCI increasingly found themselves competing for properties in the same markets. In 1994, the two companies collided in the United Kingdom, where both sought to acquire the large British funeral company, Great Southern Group. SCI ultimately prevailed, paying almost $200 million.[20]

During 1996 SCI had made several informal acquisition proposals to Loewen, but all were declined. On September 17, 1996—the very day that Loewen's stock began trading on the New York Stock Exchange—SCI announced a formal offer to acquire all Loewen common stock for $43 a share. The offer was addressed to Ray Loewen personally, in a letter from SCI's president (Exhibit 1.7).[21]

Loewen's board of directors promptly rejected the offer. Ray Loewen believed the company's stock, which only two weeks earlier had traded around $30 a share, was significantly undervalued. He portrayed SCI's action as an attempt to eliminate an important, and more successful, competitor. In a letter to shareholders, he expressed his confidence in the company's long-run business plan, noting that "during the past five years, Loewen's revenue and earnings have experienced the highest growth rates of public companies in our industry, 41.5% and 36.8%, respectively."[22] Although within two weeks of its initial offer SCI increased its bid to $45 a share—and redirected its offer to Loewen's shareholders directly—Ray Loewen said the company's stock was worth at least $52 a share.

The stock price was depressed, he argued, because of a recent unfavorable jury verdict against the company in Mississippi. A funeral home operator had accused Loewen Group of reneging on an agreement to purchase two of his homes, plus certain insurance services. Although the properties were worth only a few million dollars, in November 1995 the jury found the company liable for damages of $500 million, including $400 million in punitive damages. Loewen's stock price fell by 15 percent on the day the verdict was announced, and its bonds were soon downgraded to specula-

---

[20]Rachel Bridge, "SCI Set to Tie Up Southern Deal," *Evening Standard*, August 8, 1994, p. 1.
[21]SCI also jointly offered to acquire all of Loewen's Series C preferred stock outstanding for $29.51 per share, to be paid in SCI common stock.
[22]The Loewen Group Inc., Form 8-K, September 26, 1996.

tive, or "junk," status.[23] An expert witness for the company would later argue that the verdict resulted from the "ruthless and blatant working up of both racial and nationalistic prejudice, particularly against Canadians."[24] To appeal the verdict, under Mississippi law the company would have had to post a bond equal to 125 percent of the award, or $625 million. In early 1996, it settled the suit for $85 million.[25]

The company responded to SCI's offer in several ways. It filed an antitrust lawsuit in U.S. federal court against SCI; soon thereafter a number of states, as well as the Canadian government, started their own antitrust investigations of the proposed acquisition. It also adopted lucrative severance packages, or "golden parachutes," for more than seventy of its senior executives.[26] And, perhaps most significantly, it accelerated its acquisition program.

In late August, Loewen, in partnership with The Blackstone Group, had acquired the fourth-largest funeral service provider in the United States, Prime Succession Inc. (Blackstone was an investment bank in New York that specialized in advisory work, and also made proprietary private equity investments.) The total purchase price was $320 million, financed with $190 million of bank and public high-yield debt. A few months later, in a similar transaction, Loewen and Blackstone acquired Rose Hills cemetery, the largest cemetery in North America, for $285 million ($155 million of this deal was financed with debt as well). In each transaction, after four years Loewen would have the option to buy Blackstone's equity stake at a specified price; after six years, Blackstone would have the option to sell its stake to Loewen, also at a specified price. (Exhibit 1.8 summarizes the terms of the two acquisitions.)

During all of 1996, Loewen acquired 159 funeral homes, 136 cemeteries, and 2 insurance companies, for total consideration of $620 million. By the beginning of 1997, it had entered into agreements to purchase $222 million of additional properties.

---

[23]Junk bonds, also known as *high-yield* or *below investment grade* bonds, are bonds that receive less than a BBB– credit rating by Standard & Poor's, or less than a Baa3 rating by Moody's Investors Service.

[24]Tamsin Carlisle, "Canada's Loewen Group, Founder Seek $725 Million from the U.S.," *Wall Street Journal*, January 13, 1999, p. B8.

[25]Loewen Group later hired the attorney who had represented the plaintiff in the case, to make sure he would not be retained in future lawsuits against the company. See John Schreiner, "Ray Loewen Looks Back from the Brink," *Financial Post*, February 17, 1993, p. 3.

[26]Loewen already had a "poison pill" shareholder rights plan in place before SCI made its offer.

A relatively high percentage of the financing for these acquisitions came from issuing debt. The company's stated policy on debt financing was to try to maintain its long-term debt/equity ratio in the range of 1.0:1 to 1.5:1.[27] It expected that this ratio would move towards the top of the target range when it made more acquisitions, but it would endeavor to bring the ratio back down eventually through equity issues. At the end of 1996 Loewen's debt/equity ratio was 1.4:1.

In the first week of 1997, SCI suddenly announced that it was dropping its bid for Loewen. In addition to concerns over the antitrust suit and Loewen's various takeover defenses, SCI cited Loewen's high debt financing costs as a major deterrent to proceeding with the offer. Special mention was made of the Prime Succession and Rose Hills transactions. Later, a Loewen spokesman would say that the company had taken on enough debt "to make it impossible for a sensible company to take it over."[28]

FINANCIAL DISTRESS

Loewen continued its aggressive growth strategy in 1997, acquiring 138 funeral homes, 171 cemeteries, and an insurance company, paying a total of $546 million. The year also marked the company's entry into the United Kingdom, where it acquired thirty two funeral homes. Debt again played an important role in financing this growth, and for the full year, interest expense on long-term debt was $132 million, up from $93 million in 1996.

Loewen's businesses, however, performed less well than expected. The company attributed this in part to a decline in death rates, which negatively impacted all death care companies. Although Loewen's total funeral revenues increased by 9.5 percent during the year, its established funeral homes (i.e., those not acquired during the year) performed 3.2 percent fewer services than in 1996, and the gross margin earned by these properties declined from 40.8 percent to 38.7 percent. The company attributed most of the margin decline to an increase in reserves for doubtful accounts. The gross margin earned by Loewen's cemetery business also declined in 1997, from 31 percent to 28.2 percent. The company said this decline occurred in part because it reversed $3.7 million of sales (and $1.2 million of related costs) that it had reported in 1996 for transactions that were supposed to take place in 1997, but were never consummated. In addition, it took a $2.1 million write-down for cemetery accounts receivable.

---

[27]The Loewen Group Inc., Form 10-K, December 31, 1996.
[28]Morse and Heinzl, "Laid Low."

These trends worsened in 1998. Revenues and profits for the company's established funeral services and cemetery businesses continued to fall. In August the company announced that second-quarter earnings were 56 percent lower than the previous year. And in early October, it announced that earnings for the third quarter would likely be more than 30 percent below what analysts had forecasted—causing Loewen's stock price to fall 15 percent in a single day. Management blamed the shortfall on declining death rates, difficulties in integrating newly acquired assets, and problems in the cemetery business. (In 1998 Loewen's cemetery business had a gross margin of 12.6 percent, compared to 28.2 percent the previous year.) By the end of 1998 Loewen's stock price had fallen to $8, from $26 at the start of the year.

New Management

In the second half of 1998, Loewen took a number of steps to address its problems. It severely cut back the pace of acquisitions. (During all of 1998 it acquired only 89 funeral homes and 65 cemeteries, paying $278 million.) It hired investment bankers to explore different options for raising cash and improving profitability. It sold one of its insurance subsidiaries for $24 million.

In October, following the company's third-quarter profit warning, Ray Loewen resigned as chief executive officer, and three months later he was also replaced as chairman. Loewen had recently owned more than 18 percent of the company's common stock, but he had been forced to surrender almost his entire stake to the Canadian Imperial Bank of Commerce to settle a personal loan. Now the company's largest shareholder, the bank nominated John Lacey as Loewen Group's new chairman.

A graduate of Harvard Business School, John Lacey had built a reputation as a successful turnaround specialist. On the day that his appointment was announced, Loewen's stock price increased by 20 percent on the Toronto Stock Exchange. In previous assignments, Lacey had shown an ability to raise large amounts of cash through asset sales. For example, while at Oshawa Group, a Canadian grocery store chain, he negotiated the sale of the entire company for $1.5 billion. Following his appointment to Loewen, however, Lacey said: "My role over the last five or six years has been one of maximizing shareholder value. . . . I think what I do is look for opportunities to deliver value to the shareholders."[29]

---

[29]Drew Hasselback, "Lacey Joins Loewen for Another Selloff," *Financial Post*, January 25, 1999, p. C2.

Company Debt

By the end of the year, Loewen Group's long-term debt was the highest it had ever been, at $2.3 billion (including debt due within a year). The debt structure was complicated (see Exhibit 1.9). It owed approximately $540 million to a consortium of 25 Canadian and U.S. banks, led by the Bank or Montreal. It also had over $1.5 billion of senior guaranteed notes outstanding, most of which were publicly traded ($300 million of this debt came due on October 1).

Almost all of the debt was secured, or collateralized, by various assets of the company. If Loewen were ever liquidated, secured creditors would be legally entitled to receive the cash generated from the sale of the assets that secured their debt. In 1996, the banks and the note holders had agreed to share most of their security on a pari passu basis (i.e., in the event of liquidation, the two groups of creditors would have equal claim to the resulting cash proceeds).[30]

Loewen also had large contingent and other liabilities outstanding. This amount included $87.8 million owed to former owners of certain funeral and cemetery properties that Loewen had acquired. For tax reasons, the sellers had chosen to be paid in installments over several years.[31] In return, they had signed contracts promising not to compete against Loewen during the life of the payments ("noncompetition agreements").

The company's bank and public debt contained numerous restrictive covenants. Among other things, the covenants specified precise limitations on the amount of debt that the company could have, the amount of dividends that it could pay, and the amount of new preferred stock that it could issue. Other covenants restricted the company's ability to sell assets, or required that when assets were sold the proceeds be used to retire debt. A covenant in Loewen's bonds stated that if ownership of the company's

---

[30]The security consisted of accounts receivable and any related rights to receive payment, the capital stock of substantially all of Loewen's majority-owned subsidiaries, and a guarantee by each subsidiary that had pledged its stock.

[31]As of December 31, 1998, the amounts owed over time were as follows (in $millions):

1999:	$13.8
2000:	$14.5
2001:	$11.6
2002:	$10.6
2003:	$8.9
Thereafter:	$28.4

stock changed significantly, it would have to offer to repurchase the bonds for 101 percent of their face value.

If Loewen was ever found to be not in compliance with a covenant, or it missed a scheduled interest or principal payment, an event of default would be declared. Creditors would then, after 30 days, have the right to accelerate their claims (i.e., all principal and accrued interest would become immediately due and payable). "Cross default" covenants in the debt ensured that if any one debt contract went into default, all other contracts would be considered in default as well.

In early 1999 Loewen was not in compliance with certain covenants in its bank debt. If it could not persuade its banks to waive the defaults or renegotiate the covenants, the company might have no choice but to file for bankruptcy.

Bankruptcy

Corporate bankruptcy in the United States is governed by the U.S. Bankruptcy Code. Chapter 11 of the Code deals with reorganizations. If a company files for Chapter 11, it is allowed to conduct its regular business and propose a financial restructuring plan without interference from creditors (e.g., secured creditors cannot seize its collateral). A central presumption of the Code is that the firm would be worth more as a going concern than if shut down.[32] The bankruptcy case is overseen by a judge, who can hear appeals from creditors if they believe they are being unfairly treated. Creditors are also allowed to form committees to represent their interests in the case. Such committees can hire their own legal and financial advisors and charge all professional fees to the company. The company also hires its own advisors.

To emerge from bankruptcy, management of the firm (the "debtor") proposes a plan of reorganization to the creditors. The plan divides the firm's creditors and other financial claimholders into classes, and each class is asked to exchange its claims for new claims. Each class votes separately on the proposed plan. If each class approves the plan by at least one-half in number and two-thirds in value, the judge would approve, or "confirm," the plan and the firm would exit from Chapter 11. Minority

---

[32]In some countries, such as the United Kingdom, bankruptcy generally means that the firm is liquidated or sold, and the proceeds are paid to creditors from most senior to most junior. In these countries, shareholders would receive anything only if there is enough value to make all creditors whole—which rarely happens.

creditors who voted against the plan would have to accept the will of the majority. The judge would in addition have to determine that the reorganization plan would leave the firm with a sensible new capital structure that is not overleveraged.

Management has the exclusive right to propose the first plan. The law states that a plan has to be proposed within 120 days of the bankruptcy filing and confirmed within an additional 60 days. After this date the judge can allow other interested persons to file alternative plans. Most judges are willing to grant management extensions to the deadline, however. In practice, multiple extensions are often granted, and large, complex cases might run for two or three years before an initial vote is taken.

In addition to being protected from creditors, firms benefit in other ways while they are in Chapter 11. They do not have to pay interest on their debt.[33] They can cancel leases and other so-called "executory contracts." (An executory contract is a contract where both parties to the contract are still obligated to perform future services.) And they can borrow on favorable terms from new lenders through "debtor-in-possession financing," based on a provision of Chapter 11 that gives any new lenders to a bankrupt firm higher priority than the firm's prebankruptcy lenders.

If Loewen were to file for Chapter 11, its situation could be complicated by the fact that roughly 10 percent of its business was conducted in Canada.[34] A U.S. bankruptcy filing would almost certainly trigger a simultaneous bankruptcy filing in Canada. Canadian bankruptcy law is governed by the Companies' Creditors Arrangement Act (CCAA), which differs in some important ways from Chapter 11. Like Chapter 11, CCAA initially gives operating control of the company to management; however, it is generally easier for creditors to remove management than in the United States. In addition, management has only one chance to present a reorganization plan. If the plan fails to pass, or was not submitted within the allotted time, under the "guillotine rule" the firm would be liquidated. There is no provision for debtor-in-possession financing as in the United

---

[33]A Chapter 11 debtor does not even have to *accrue* interest on its unsecured debt. At the end of a case the firm would owe unsecured creditors the same face value of debt that it had owed at the beginning of the case. Interest can continue to accrue on the firm's secured debt, but the amount is limited by the value of the underlying security.

[34]Loewen's U.S. assets were owned and operated by Loewen Group International Inc., which was a wholly owned subsidiary of the Canadian parent company.

States.[35] If Loewen filed for bankruptcy in both countries, some kind of administrative protocol would have to be established for resolving potential conflicts between the two courts.

THE COMPANY'S OPTIONS

John Lacey had relatively little time to develop a plan for dealing with the growing crisis. The company had $42 million of debt payments coming due in the first two weeks of April, and in early March it still had not reached an agreement with its banks on how to restructure their loans. Although a few months earlier the company had found a buyer for its insurance subsidiary, raising large amounts of cash through asset sales could be difficult. The death care industry in general was feeling the effects of lower death rates, so there might be limited demand for Loewen's properties. Further, piecemeal sales of assets could take a long time, given the company's organizational complexity (it had over 850 U.S. and 100 Canadian subsidiaries).

On a different front, the company had recently filed a lawsuit against the U.S. government seeking $725 million in damages related to the 1995 settlement in Mississippi. Alleging significant "anti-Canadian" bias by the Mississippi court, the company was arguing that the court's behavior violated a provision of the North American Free Trade Agreement (NAFTA), which bars discrimination against foreign investors. It was unclear whether Loewen would win the suit, however, and even if it did, years could pass before it received any payment.

Making a difficult situation even worse, regulators had recently suspended the licenses of sixteen of Loewen's funeral homes in Florida after discovering certain accounting violations. Whether the full extent of the problem had been discovered remained to be determined.

---

[35]Voting takes place similarly under CCAA as under Chapter 11. Under CCAA, three-quarters in value and one-half in number of the holders in each class of claims are required to approve the plan. In the United States, if one or more classes do not approve a plan, the judge can either order the parties to modify the plan and vote again, or "cram down" the plan over the objections of the dissenting classes. In Canada there is no equivalent of the cram-down.

EXHIBIT 1.1   Twelve Largest North American Death Care Companies by Revenues, 1998

Company	Country	Revenues (US$millions)	Number of Employees
Service Corporation International	U.S.	$2,875	27,266
Loewen Group Inc.	Canada	1,136	16,700
Stewart Enterprises	U.S.	756	11,200
Carriage Services Inc.	U.S.	117	940
Arbor Memorial Services	Canada	97	1,620
Federated Funeral Directors	U.S.	34	200
Gatlings Chapel	U.S.	21	125
Trillium Funeral Service Corp.	Canada	15	100
Forest Lawn–Ocean View	Canada	15	100
Woodlawn Memorial Funeral Home	U.S.	15	90
Doane Beal & Ames Inc.	U.S.	10	90
Fairlawn Mortuary	U.S.	9	50

Source: One Source Global Business Report.

EXHIBIT 1.2 Loewen Group's Financial Statements (Dollars in US$millions)

Loewen Group, Consolidated Income Statement	1996	1997	1998
Revenue			
Funeral	$549.8	$ 602.1	$ 631.2
Cemetery	286.7	422.0	408.5
Insurance	71.9	90.0	96.5
	$908.4	$1,114.1	$1,136.2
Cost and expenses			
Funeral	326.9	374.2	407.3
Cemetery	197.8	303.0	357.2
Insurance	54.7	73.3	80.0
	$579.4	$ 750.5	$ 844.5
	$329.0	$ 363.6	$ 291.7
Expenses			
General and administrative	71.2	112.8	133.3
Depreciation and amortization	53.1	65.4	88.5
Asset impairment[a]	—	—	333.9
Restructuring costs	—	33.4	—
	$124.3	$ 211.5	$ 555.7
Earnings (loss) from operations	204.7	152.1	(264.0)
Interest on long-term debt	93.0	132.3	182.3
Investment impairment and contingent loss[b]	—	—	315.2
Loss on early extinguishment of debt	—	7.7	—
Gain on sale of investment	—	(24.1)	—
Finance and other costs related to hostile takeover proposal	18.7	—	—
Earnings (loss) before undernoted items	93.0	36.3	(761.5)
Dividends on preferred securities of subsidiary	7.1	7.1	7.1
Earnings (loss before income taxes and undernoted items	85.9	29.2	(768.6)
Income taxes			
Current	22.5	34.2	23.1
Future	0.9	(33.4)	(187.6)
	23.5	0.8	(164.5)
	62.4	28.4	(604.1)
Equity and other earnings of associated companies	3.6	13.4	5.1
Net earnings (loss) for the year	$ 66.0	$ 41.8	$(599.0)
Basic earnings (loss) per common share	$ 1.01	$ 0.48	($ 8.22)
Fully diluted earnings (loss) per common share	$ 1.00	$ 0.48	($ 8.22)

[a]Amount for 1998 represents a write-down of the book values of certain properties that the company is considering for possible sale, to reflect the properties' estimated current "fair value." The properties consist of 124 cemeteries, 3 funeral homes, and some other assets. Fair value is based upon the properties' estimated future operating cash flows, as well as anticipated proceeds from selling the properties.
[b]Amount for 1998 represents a write-down of the company's investment in Prime Succession and Rose Hills, reflecting the company's behalf that its option to purchase Blackstone's majority equity stake in each entity is significantly less likely to be exercised, while Blackstone's option to sell its stake to Loewen is significantly more likely to be exercised.

EXHIBIT 1.2 *(Continued)*

Loewen Group, Consolidated Balance Sheet

	December 31,	
	1997	1998
Assets		
Current assets		
Cash and term deposits	$ 36.8	$ 94.1
Receivables, net of allowances	251.0	221.7
Inventories	34.9	34.5
Prepaid expenses	11.1	8.9
	$ 333.8	$ 359.2
Long-term receivables, net of allowances	410.4	647.1
Cemetery property	553.7	1,235.8
Property and equipment	224.0	826.0
Names and reputations	305.6	748.7
Investments	957.8	3.4
Insurance invested assets	797.2	266.7
Future income tax assets	633.1	12.0
Prearranged funeral services	130.9	413.9
Other assets	156.6	161.1
	$4,503.2	$4,673.9
Liabilities and shareholders' equity		
Current liabilities		
Current indebtness	—	66.2
Accounts payable and accrued liabilities	160.2	170.1
Long-term debt, current portion	43.3	874.1
	$ 203.7	$1,110.5
Long-term debt, net of current portion	1,750.4	1,393.9
Other liabilities	308.9	399.3
Insurance policy liabilities	214.5	166.9
Future income tax liabilities	310.0	208.9
Deferred prearranged funeral services revenue	410.4	413.9
Preferred securities of subsidiary	75.0	75.0
Shareholders' equity		
Common shares	1,271.2	1,274.1
Preferred shares	157.1	157.1
Retained earnings (deficit)	98.4	(539.7)
Foreign exchange adjustment	13.6	13.9
	$1,540.2	$ 905.4
	$4,503.2	$4,673.9

EXHIBIT 1.2   *(Continued)*

Loewen Group, Consolidated Statement of Cash Flows			
	1996	1997	1998
Cash flows from operating activities			
Net earnings (loss)	$ 66.0	$ 41.8	$(599.0)
Items not affecting cash			
Depreciation and amortization	53.2	65.4	88.5
Amortization of debt issue costs	4.1	6.8	26.6
Asset impairment	—	—	333.9
Investment impairment and contingent loss	—	—	315.2
Gain on sale of investments	—	(27.2)	(6.8)
Future income taxes	0.9	33.4	(187.6)
Equity and other earnings of associated companies	(3.6)	(13.4)	(5.1)
Restructuring costs	—	15.7	—
Other, including net changes in other noncash balances	(167.4)	(216.4)	(90.2)
	$ (46.9)	$(160.7)	$(124.5)
Cash flows from investing activities			
Business acquisitions	(556.9)	(481.6)	(252.6)
Construction of new facilities	(17.7)	(32.4)	(19.2)
Investments, net	(148.4)	14.5	(1.4)
Purchase of insurance invested assets	(85.2)	(262.0)	(224.1)
Proceeds on disposition and maturities of insurance invested assets	71.9	252.6	180.2
Purchase of property and equipment	(54.9)	(52.8)	(43.5)
Proceeds on disposition of investments and assets	3.7	70.1	56.3
	$(787.5)	$(491.6)	$(304.4)
Cash flows from financing activities			
Issue of common shares, before income tax recovery	216.9	439.4	1.8
Issue of preferred shares, before income tax recovery	154.1	—	—
Increase in long-term debt	1,037.4	1,343.6	1,105.4
Repayment of long-term debt	(514.5)	(1,083.0)	(645.7)
Common share dividends	(6.7)	(12.3)	(14.7)
Preferred share dividends	(6.5)	(9.5)	(8.9)
Current not payable	—	—	71.7
Repayment of current note payable	(38.6)	—	(5.4)
Debt issue costs	(29.2)	(7.1)	(17.9)
	$ 813.1	$ 671.0	$ 486.3
Increase (decrease) in cash and cash equivalents during year	(21.3)	18.7	57.4
Effect of foreign exchange adjustment	(0.1)	0.0	(0.0)
Cash and cash equivalents, beginning of year	39.5	18.1	36.8
Cash and cash equivalents, end of year	$ 18.1	$ 36.8	$ 94.1

Source: Loewen Group Inc., Form 10-K, December 31, 1998.

EXHIBIT 1.3 Selected Data on Loewen Group and Its Main Competitors (Dollars in US$millions, except Per Share Items)

	Loewen Group		Service Corp. International		Stewart Enterprises		Carriage Services	
	Dec 97	Dec 98	Apr 97	Apr 98	Dec 97	Dec 98	Mar 97	Mar 98
Sales	$1,114.1	$1,136.2	$2,468.4	$2,875.1	$532.6	$648.4	$77.4	$116.8
Gross profit	370.7	291.7	812.8	879.3	175.1	217.1	27.2	45.8
Selling, general, and administrative expense	99.5	125.2	66.8	66.8	15.4	16.6	5.3	7.6
Depreciation and amortization	71.4	88.5	125.2	160.5	18.0	21.1	7.8	11.4
Operating profit	199.8	78.0	620.8	651.9	141.8	179.4	14.1	26.7
Interest expense	127.5	182.3	141.1	177.1	38.0	43.8	6.2	10.2
Taxes	2.7	(164.5)	205.4	176.4	36.7	23.1	3.7	7.5
Net income	42.7	(599.0)	333.8	342.1	69.7	41.9	3.6	8.9
Earnings per share (reported)	$ 0.48	($ 8.22)	$ 1.36	$ 1.34	$ 0.76	$ 0.43	$ 0.33	$ 0.67
Assets	$4,503.2	$4,673.9	$10,514.9	$13,266.2	$1,637.2	$2,048.9	$277.9	$466.1
Short-term debt	43.5	940.3	64.6	96.1	34.0	11.2	2.3	6.4
Long-term debt	1,750.4	1,393.9	2,634.7	3,764.6	524.4	913.2	126.0	216.2
Preferred stockholders' equity	232.1	232.1	—	—	—	—	14.0	1.7
Common stockholders' equity	1,383.1	748.3	2,726.0	3,154.1	819.6	839.3	98.6	200.4
Number of funeral homes	1,070	1,151	3,127	3,442	419	575	120	166
Number of cemeteries	483	550	166	151	131	141	20	27
Common stock beta[a]	1.15		0.74		1.05		0.85	

Source: Datastream and company annual reports.

[a]Beta is calculated using the most recent five years of monthly data, based on month-end closing prices (including dividends). The stock market index used is the Standard & Poor's 500.

EXHIBIT 1.4 Long-Run Stock Price History (stock prices in US$)

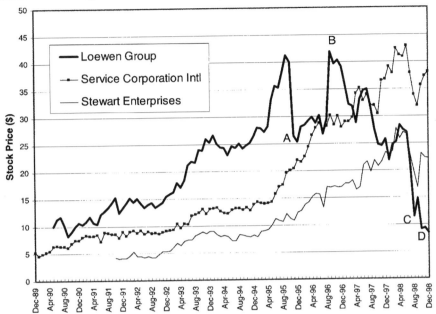

Selected key events:

A   Nov. 2, 1995   Loewen Group is hit with a $500 million civil damages award by a Mississippi jury in a breach of contract suit.

B   Sep. 17, 1996   Service Corporation International makes an unsolicited offer to acquire Loewen.

C   Aug. 6, 1998   Loewen discloses that second-quarter earnings were 56% lower than last year.

D   Oct. 8, 1998   Ray Loewen is removed as CEO of Loewen Group, following company's announcement on previous day that third-quarter earnings will be less than 13 cents a share, versus analysts' consensus estimate of 19 cents a share.

Casewriter note: Carriage Services first began trading publicly in August 1996, and is omitted from the figure for clarity.

Source: Datastream.

EXHIBIT 1.5 Acquisition Multiples

Acquirer	(1) Revenues of Acquired Companies (US$millions)			(2) Amount Spent on Acquisitions (US$millions)			Acquisition Multiple: (2) ÷ (1)		
	1996	1997	1998	1996	1997	1998	1996	1997	1998
Carriage Services	$ 28.6	$ 42.8	$ 51.9	$ 69.1	$ 118.3	$ 158.7	2.41x	2.77x	3.06x
Equity Corp.	30.9	49.0	56.8[a]	65.0	156.1	120.0[a]	2.11x	3.19x	2.12x
Loewen Group	251.5	187.6	29.1	620.0	546.0	278.0	2.47x	2.91x	9.55x
Service Corp. Intl.	180.0	260.0	296.0	363.0	643.0	784.0	2.02x	2.47x	2.65x
Stewart Enterprises	68.8	77.8	109.1	179.0	184.5	266.3	2.60x	2.37x	2.44x
Total	559.8	617.2	486.1[b]	1,296.2	1,647.9	1,487.0[b]	2.32x	2.67x	3.06x[b]

[a]For nine months ended September 30, 1998.
[b]Excludes Equity Corporation. Approximately 40% of Equity Corporation's stock is owned by Service Corporation International.

Source: Merrill Lynch industry report by Fran Blechman Bernstein and Yasmine C. Nainzadeh. "Post Life Services," April 26, 1999.

EXHIBIT 1.6 Loewen Group, Ten-Year Financial Summary (Dollars in US$millions, except Share Prices)

	1989	1990	1991	1992	1993	1994	1995	1996	1997	1998
Sales	$ 63.8	$117.6	$188.5	$231.5	$300.1	$ 417.5	$ 598.5	$ 899.4	$1,114.1	$1,136.2
Gross profit	25.5	47.2	72.2	87.4	114.5	159.0	225.4	328.6	370.7	291.7
Operating profit	17.7	31.0	44.4	52.0	66.6	94.6	131.9	195.1	199.8	78.0
Net income	6.2	11.1	16.5	20.5	27.9	38.5	(76.7)	63.9	42.7	(599.0)
Total assets	$163.4	$341.3	$446.1	$547.0	$748.5	$1,115.7	$2,263.0	$3,496.9	$4,503.2	$4,673.9
Total liabilities	108.0	238.3	275.5	343.0	472.3	829.8	1,977.1	2,728.0	3,291.9	5,000.7
Long-term debt due in one year	5.1	7.2	6.9	7.9	6.6	45.5	69.7	79.6	43.5	874.1
Long-term debt	79.7	172.1	217.0	251.5	334.4	471.1	864.8	1,428.6	1,750.4	1,393.9
Capital expenditures	$ 3.1	$ 8.6	$ 14.0	$ 12.6	$ 22.2	$ 39.8	$ 36.1	$ 72.6	$ 85.3	$ 62.7
Acquisition expenditures	36.0	159.7	78.4	87.3	147.6	265.6	487.9	619.6	546.5	252.6
Proceeds from issuance of common and preferred stock	33.9	53.5	46.0	33.7	54.4	53.4	203.1	454.7	462.4	1.8
Proceeds from issuance of long-term debt	14.0	91.7	197.5	34.3	92.9	187.4	396.5	1,128.4	1,385.4	1,105.4
Market value of common stock[a]		$301.6	$438.1	$550.8	$980.7	$1,086.9	$1,219.2	$2,310.6	$1,903.2	$ 624.9
Book value of common stock		134.2	197.1	245.7	324.8	411.1	614.7	891.1	1,383.1	748.3
Year-end stock price		$ 10.88	$ 13.38	$ 15.50	$ 25.38	$ 27.00	$ 25.31	$ 39.13	$ 25.75	$ 8.44

[a]Loewen Group's common stock was first traded in a U.S. market in 1990.
Source: Datastream United States database.

EXHIBIT 1.7   Letter to Raymond Loewen from William Heiligbrodt, SCI's President and Chief Operating Officer

September 17, 1996

Mr. Raymond L. Loewen
Chairman of the Board and Chief Executive Officer
The Loewen Group Inc.

Dear Mr. Loewen:

As you know, I have tried to reach you several times since September 11. While your office has assured me that you received my messages, my calls have not been returned. In view of that, and in view of the importance of this matter, I am sending this letter.

I would like to discuss with you a combination of our two companies. The combination would involve a stock-for-stock exchange accounted for as a pooling which values Loewen Group at US$43 per share. We believe that this transaction can be structured in a manner that is tax-free to both companies. . . .

I think you and your Board and stockholders would agree that our proposal is a generous one, resulting in the following premiums for Loewen Group stockholders:

- 48.9% above the price at which Loewen Group stock traded 30 days ago;
- 39.3% above the price at which Loewen Group stock traded one week ago; and
- 27.4% above the price at which Loewen Group stock is currently trading.

This represents an opportunity for your stockholders to realize excellent value, by any measure, for their shares. In addition, and importantly, since your stockholders would be receiving stock, they would continue to participate in Loewen Group's business as well as share in the upside of our business.

Thus, in essence, your stockholders would:

- continue their investment in our industry;
- get an immediate, and very significant, increase in the market value of their investment;
- get that immediate and substantial increase on an essentially tax-free basis; and
- diversify their risk by participating in a much larger number of properties.

This is a "win-win" situation for you and your stockholders.

Finally, with respect to consideration, I would note also that our proposal is based on public information. After a due diligence review, we may be in a position to increase the consideration that your stockholders would receive. . . .

I would very much like to discuss any and all aspects of our proposal directly with you and your Board of Directors. We believe you and they will recognize the tremendous benefit to your stockholders of our proposal. Our proposal is conditioned upon approval of our Board and upon negotiation of mutually satisfactory agreements providing for a combination on a pooling basis.

We hope that after you meet with us, you will similarly determine that the transaction should be pursued. We look forward to hearing from you.

In view of the importance of this matter, we are simultaneously releasing this letter to the press.

Sincerely,

William Heiligbrodt
President and Chief Operating Officer
Service Corporation International

Source: "Service Corporation International Announces a Proposed Business Combination with the Loewen Group Inc.," PR Newswire, September 17, 1996.

EXHIBIT 1.8 Summary of Prime Succession and Rose Hills Acquisitions

Prime Succession

Under the transaction, all of the outstanding common stock of Prime Succession Inc. was acquired by a special-purpose entity, Prime Succession Holdings, Inc. (PSHI). The total purchase price, including transaction and financing costs, was $320 million. The excess of the purchase price above the fair value of the acquired assets (estimated at $230 million) would be reported as goodwill, and amortized over 40 years.

The purchase price was financed with $190 million of debt, $62 million of 10% payment-in-kind preferred stock, and $68 million of common stock—all issued by PSHI. The debt included a $90 million bank term loan from a group of institutions led by Goldman, Sachs & Co., and a $100 million public issue of 10.75% senior subordinated notes, with Smith Barney Inc. as lead manager of the offering. In addition, the Bank of Nova Scotia provided a $25 million revolving credit facility.

All of the preferred stock and $16 million of the common stock (23.5%) were purchased by Loewen Group. Blackstone Group purchased the remaining $52 million of common stock. Blackstone and Loewen would have the right to designate five and three nominees, respectively, to PSHI's board of directors. Two former executives of Loewen would manage PSHI, but Blackstone would control the strategic, operating, financial, and investment policies of the firm. Neither party would be allowed to sell its shares to an unaffiliated party without the consent of the other.

Loewen would account for its investment in PSHI using the equity method of accounting, reporting its proportional share of the net earnings (or losses) of PSHI, after deducting the payment-in-kind dividend.

Between the four- and six-year anniversary of the transaction, Loewen would have the option to "call" or purchase Blackstone's PSHI common stock at a specified price. This price was determined by a complicated formula. In general, the price paid to Blackstone increased as the estimated value of PSHI's common stock (V, defined below) passed certain thresholds. Regardless of what V was, however, Loewen could not exercise its option unless Blackstone received at least a 24.1% compound annual return on its initial investment of $52 million. If the option was exercised after four years, for example, Loewen would have to pay Blackstone at least $123.5 million.[a]

Between the six- and eight-year anniversary of the transaction, Blackstone would have the option to "put" or sell its PSHI common stock back to Loewen at a specified price. This price was also determined by a complicated formula. As with the call option,

(Continued)

---

[a]This calculation is based on analysis reported in Gallo, Reynolds, and Roche, "The Loewen Group" (unpublished student manuscript, 2000).

EXHIBIT 1.8   *(Continued)*

Blackstone's dollar return from exercising the put would in general increase with V. V was estimated as the difference between the estimated value of PSHI's assets and all debt and preferred stock outstanding (including accreted payment-in-kind dividends). The value of PSHI's assets was in turn estimated by multiplying PSHI's EBITDA (earnings before interest, taxes, depreciation, and amortization) for the latest twelve months by a multiple. This multiple was the ratio of the original transaction price ($320 million) to PSHI's average EBITDA for the first two years following the acquisition.

Rose Hills

This transaction was structured essentially the same way as the Prime Succession acquisition.

A special-purpose entity, Rose Hills Holding Corp. (RHHC), was formed to acquire the cemetery and mortuary operations of The Rose Hills Memorial Park Association, for total consideration of $285 million. This amount was financed with $155 million of debt from banks and other institutional investors, $86 million of 10% payment-in-kind preferred stock, and $44 million of common stock. Loewen purchased the entire issue of preferred stock. Blackstone purchased 79.5% of the common stock, and Loewen purchased 20.5%.

Blackstone would control the board of directors, and the strategic, operating, financial, and investment policies of the firm. Loewen would account for its investment in RHHC using the equity method of accounting.

The transaction terms also included a call/put agreement that was similar to the one in the Prime Succession deal.

Source: The Loewen Group Inc., Form 8-K dated August 29, 1996, and Form 10-K dated December 31, 1996.

EXHIBIT 1.9 Loewen Group's Long-Term Debt, Including Amounts Due within One Year, December 31, 1998 (Dollar Amounts in US$millions)

Bank credit agreement	$ 330.0
Management Equity Investment Plan bank term credit agreement due in 2000	97.3
9.62% Series D senior amortizing notes due in 2003	42.9
6.49% Series E senior amortizing notes due in 2004	42.9
7.50% Series 1 senior notes due in 2001	225.0
7.75% Series 3 senior notes due in 2001	125.0
8.25% Series 2 and 4 senior notes due in 2003	350.0
6.10% Series 5 senior notes due in 2002 (Canadian $200)	130.7
7.20% Series 6 senior notes due in 2003	200.0
7.60% Series 7 senior notes due in 2008	250.0
6.70% PATS senior notes[a]	300.0
Present value of notes issued for legal settlements discounted at an effective interest rate of 7.75%	38.2
Present value of contingent consideration payable on acquisitions discounted at an effective interest rate of 8.0%	19.8
Other, principally arising from vendor financing of acquired operations or long-term debt assumed on acquisitions, bearing interest at fixed and floating rates varying from 4.8% to 14.0%, certain of which are secured by assets of certain subsidiaries	116.4
Total	$2,268.0

[a]These notes are due in 2009, but are redeemable in full at the holder's option on October 1, 1999. If the option is not exercised by this date, the interest rate on the notes is reset at a fixed rate tied to then-current credit spreads.

Source: Loewen Group Inc. Form 10-K, December 31, 1998.

Note: Long-term debt matures as follows ($millions):

1999	$874.1
2000	23.3
2001	370.1
2002	144.1
2003	563.1
Thereafter	293.3

In addition to long-term debt listed above, $66,222,000 is outstanding under a revolving receivables finance facility with a bank. The facility is an obligation of a wholly owned company subsidiary, and is secured by cemetery receivables. No additional borrowings are permitted under the facility, based on the value of eligible receivables. The facility bears interest at a floating rate based on commercial paper rates (5.51% at December 31, 1998).

CHAPTER 2

National Convenience Stores Incorporated

INTRODUCTION

On a hot summer day in 1992, V.H. ("Pete") Van Horn, president and chief executive officer (CEO) of National Convenience Stores (NCS), was chairing a meeting with representatives of the company's creditors. The company had been operating under Chapter 11 of the Bankruptcy Code since December 9, 1991. Van Horn and his management group were explaining to the creditors that each day they were in bankruptcy they were losing opportunities. He reminded them that NCS had to greatly downsize its store modernization program following the Chapter 11 filing and that they were paying more for gasoline, which represented approximately 40 percent of sales, because as a Chapter 11 company they could not avail themselves of the cheapest way of buying gasoline.

To come out of Chapter 11 and resume life as a normal company, NCS had to complete a plan of reorganization and have it approved by its creditors. The plan would set forth how the company would be managed after Chapter 11. It would describe the company's strategy and attempt to quantify the results with financial projections. In turn, these projections would define the size of the pie that could be provided to creditors.

During the meeting, Van Horn distributed to the creditors the company's "blue book," a presentation containing management's first round of projections for a reorganized NCS. Representatives of the creditors knew the importance of Pete Van Horn's presentation. They were determined to

This case was prepared by Professors Steven Fenster and Stuart Gilson, assisted by Research Associate Roy Burstin. Copyright © 1994 by the President and Fellows of Harvard College. Harvard Business School case 294-068.

pay careful attention and to try to shape NCS's conclusions to a form that would benefit their group.

BACKGROUND OF NCS

At the time of its bankruptcy filing, NCS was one of the twenty largest operators of convenience stores in the United States. It now operated 725 specialty convenience stores in six cities in three Sunbelt states under the name Stop N Go. NCS was the largest convenience store operator in the Houston and San Antonio areas. The locations of the company's stores are set forth in Table 2.1.

NCS's convenience stores were extended-hour retail facilities, emphasizing convenience to the customer. Virtually all of the stores were open every day of the year, and over 95 percent operated 24 hours a day. Typically, NCS's stores were located in residential areas, on main thoroughfares, in small shopping centers, or on other sites selected for easy accessibility and customer convenience. The stores offered a diverse range of over 3,000 high-traffic items including fast foods, fountain beverages, beer and wine, soft drinks, candy, snacks, groceries, health and beauty aids, magazines and newspapers, automotive products, seasonal and promotional items, school supplies, and self-serve gasoline. The company sold lottery tickets in all of its California stores and, commencing in May 1992, in all of its Texas stores. In addition, nearly all of NCS's stores sold money orders prior to filing Chapter 11 and were expected to continue doing so following a reorganization. The company's customers were typically lunchtime customers, early and late shoppers, weekend and holiday shoppers, and people needing only a few items at a time and desiring rapid service.

As was the norm in the convenience store industry, prices on most

TABLE 2.1   Location's of NCS's Stores (as of July 31, 1992)

Location	Number of Stores
Houston, Texas	374
San Antonio, Texas	144
Dallas–Fort Worth, Texas	95
Austin, Texas	29
Los Angeles, California	54
Atlanta, Georgia	29
Total	725

items were somewhat higher than in supermarkets and certain other retail outlets. However, the value placed by the customer on easy accessibility and convenience enabled NCS to receive premium prices for its products. Operating under the Stop N Go name, NCS's stores were well recognized among customers in its markets. NCS estimated that its stores served, on average, an aggregate of approximately 700,000 customers a day. The company prioritized the use of floor space in its stores by allocating it to products based on sales performance. Substantially all store sales were made in cash, although NCS accepted most major credit cards.

Table 2.2 sets forth certain statistical information regarding the company's sales for the periods indicated.

HISTORICAL FINANCIAL PERFORMANCE

The company's most successful year in its history was in fiscal 1984; however, several events, notably the severe economic recession in Texas, began to negatively impact its operations in fiscal year (FY) 1985. During this year, the Texas real estate markets suffered a collapse, causing the loss of thousands of construction and other related jobs directly affecting NCS's core customer base. Reacting to the rapidly deteriorating economic environment, and foreseeing an increase in competition from oil companies and independent operators, commencing in 1986 Pete Van Horn and his management group adopted a strategy of increasing store concentration in key markets while selling stores in markets where the

TABLE 2.2   Composition of NCS's Sales

	Year Ended June 30		
	1992	**1991**	**1990**
Sales ($millions)	$958.5	$1,073.9	$1,062.2
Percentage of sales contributed by:			
Gasoline	40.5%	45.7%	42.7%
Alcoholic beverages	15.2	13.6	13.0
Tobacco products	14.9	11.1	11.5
Other categories not individually contributing more than 10%	29.4	29.6	32.8
	100.0%	100.0%	100.0%

company had a limited presence. Thus NCS reduced its geographic markets of operation from 21 in 1985 to 7 in 1991, while decreasing its store count only slightly. By repositioning a significant percentage of its stores through several dispositions to and acquisitions from major competitors, NCS became the largest convenience store operator in the Houston and San Antonio areas. For management, market concentration meant more value per advertising dollar and enhanced operating and merchandising performance due to economies of scale in product acquisition and managerial overhead. Table 2.3 provides selected financial data for the periods indicated.

SHIFTS IN MARKETING STRATEGY

In the fall of 1989, Van Horn and his management team decided to update the company's merchandising strategy by introducing a variety of new quality-branded products, including bottled water, low-calorie products, fresh foods, gourmet chips and cookies, and frozen foods, as well as some new nonfood items. This shift in strategy was based on the assumption that customers preferred and therefore were willing to pay higher prices for quality products and shopping convenience. NCS's CEO hoped that the sale of superior products in geographic areas where the company was the largest operator would allow it to increase its sales and achieve higher gross margins.

During this period, NCS also embarked on an effort to update the Stop N Go store image, by remodeling the interior of selected stores around one of three basic demographic groups: upscale, Hispanic, and core customer. Emphasis was placed on new product displays, modern appearance, fresh foods, and selected new products to match the stores' demographics. This targeting strategy stood in contrast with that of most of NCS's competitors, who generally offered the same mix of products throughout their chains. Van Horn anticipated that these measures would help reverse a trend of declining same-store merchandise sales that had begun in 1987. By January 1990, NCS had completed the implementation of this new strategy in its 100 highest-volume stores with rather promising results. However, the company's worsening financial condition, eventually leading to its Chapter 11 filing, forced NCS to suspend store remodeling activities. Hoping that this initiative could be resumed following a successful reorganization, Van Horn had made some provisions for store remodeling in the company's "blue book" projections for capital expenditures.

TABLE 2.3 Selected Financial Data

	Year Ended June 30							
	1984	1985	1986	1987	1988	1989	1990	1991
Net earnings (loss) ($millions)	18.5	15.5	3.6	(5.4)	6.8[a]	(8.9)	5.0[b]	(10.5)
Total long-term debt ($millions)	182.3	241.0	239.9	274.3	344.0	280.5	204.9	191.6
Debt-to-equity ratio	2.1	2.5	2.7	3.7	4.6	4.4	2.5	2.7
Number of stores	1,081	1,130	958	950	1,119	1,142	1,090	988
Number of geographical markets	21	21	12	11	10	10	9	7
Stock price: High $	17.60	18.50	13.63	11.13	12.38	10.00	9.00	5.63
Low $	11.20	10.50	9.00	8.13	6.00	7.63	4.00	2.88

[a]Includes $6.5 million gain related to the cumulative effect of an accounting change as a result of the company's implementation of SFAS No. 96, "Accounting for Income Taxes."

[b]Includes $3.4 million related to the gain on the sale of the company's Nashville, Tennessee, market and $6.6 million related to an extraordinary gain realized on a preferred stock-for-debt exchange.

Besides adopting the "neighborstore" concept and introducing higher-quality products in some of its stores, NCS management continued to design opportunities to stimulate sales increases. In 1991, the management group began the introduction of its "eateries" concept: in-store food kiosks preparing and selling branded take-out food such as Pizza Hut and Taco Bell. NCS also pioneered its own line of fresh foods, including made-fresh-daily salads and sandwiches, which it distributed to its stores through its Corporate Kitchen's in-house distribution operation. By addressing customers' preference for fresh food, this concept sought to boost store traffic as well as attract a new target customer base. By June 30, 1991, the company had installed "eateries" in five of its Houston stores with marked success. These stores posted sales increases of between 30 percent and 50 percent over prior-year levels. Enthusiastic about these results, Van Horn made plans to introduce more "eateries" in NCS stores as funds became available.

In June 1991, NCS adopted a value pricing strategy on certain core products in key geographical markets where it was difficult for its competitors to follow. This strategy, applied initially to cigarettes, also aimed at increasing customer traffic and thereby augmenting the potential for multiple item purchases. As management had expected, the initial effect of value pricing on cigarettes was a decrease in gross profit margins of approximately 4 percent. It was not until October 1991 that the combined effects of the fresh foods program and the value pricing strategy began to show positive results by gradually increasing the company's level of gross margin dollars.

LIQUIDITY CRISIS LEADS TO BANKRUPTCY FILING

Since its strategic shift in 1985, several of the company's expense categories, namely workers' insurance, rent, and interest expenses, had been growing at a rapid pace. Table 2.4 traces the growth of these expenses over the time periods indicated.

NCS had financed its asset repositioning strategy between 1985 and 1988 with a number of term loans that had significantly increased the company's leverage. NCS's debt-to-equity ratio had grown from 2.5× in 1985 to 4.6× in 1988. Accordingly, its interest cost burden had increased substantially during this period, peaking at $34.8 million in 1989—a 56 percent increase over the 1985 level. NCS sought to remedy this situation between fiscal 1989 and 1991 by using proceeds from asset sales and sale/leaseback transactions to pay down debt. These measures allowed

TABLE 2.4   Historical Interest, Rent, and Insurance Expenses ($ in millions)

	Year Ended June 30						
	1985	**1986**	**1987**	**1988**	**1989**	**1990**	**1991**
Interest[a]	$22.3	$25.9	$26.7	$31.5	$34.8	$27.5	$23.9
Rent[b]	11.2	13.7	15.7	17.0	20.7	28.6	31.1
Insurance[c]	7.9	10.6	11.6	12.7	13.4	16.9	25.4
Total	$41.4	$50.2	$54.0	$61.2	$68.9	$73.0	$80.4
Interest expense as a % of EBITDA	27%	44%	55%	50%	68%	57%	118%

[a]Excludes capitalized interest.
[b]Rent under operating leases.
[c]Includes policy costs, workers' compensation, general liability, and employee health.

NCS to meet its debt repayment schedule on time and reduce its debt-to-equity ratio to 2.7× (NCS paid down $125 million in long-term debt during this period). However, the partial reduction in interest expense between 1989 and 1991 was offset by substantially higher rent expenses resulting from the aforementioned sale/leaseback transactions.

Also of concern was the spiraling growth of the payments for workers' compensation that NCS had to make as a participant in the State of Texas Workers' Compensation program. Van Horn believed that an in-house workers' compensation program could be managed more efficiently and therefore result in significant cost savings. Accordingly, in February 1991, Van Horn withdrew the company from the state-managed program. Although his management group believed this move would yield savings in the range of 50 to 70 percent of current costs, Van Horn had expected that in the short term NCS would continue to be burdened by a large number of old claims arising out of the state-managed program.

The unfavorable combination of slow sales growth, swelling expenses, and ongoing operating losses was magnified by a sequence of unusual events that considerably exacerbated the company's financial condition. The outbreak of the Gulf War in January 1991 substantially decreased customer traffic in NCS stores as the American public stayed at home tuned in to the televised news coverage. This was followed by an intense gasoline price war between two major oil companies operating gas station/convenience stores in the company's markets. The result was a 30 percent reduction in gasoline sales volume and a profit margin of 5 cents per gallon, compared with a historical average of 11 cents per gallon. Lastly, heavy rainfall in the third quarter, twice the normal level, also contributed to the company's difficulties since a large part of its product mix was concentrated in items consumed during periods when leisure-time activities were more prevalent. As a result, the modest profits that NCS had reported during the first half of FY 1991 were wiped out.

Subsequently, the deepening recession in the United States further constricted NCS's cash flows. Earnings before interest, taxes, depreciation, and amortization (EBITDA) levels per store fell by more than half—from $42,626 in 1990 to $19,190 in 1991. Because over the years Van Horn had developed a good relationship with the company's principal lender, NCNB Texas, his management group was able to renegotiate NCS's credit agreement several times. The amendments to the agreement were needed to cure defaults of various financial ratio coverage tests. Borrowing levels and repayment schedules were repeatedly adjusted to terms that Van Horn and his team believed they could meet based on their financial projections. As part of each rescheduling, NCS had to pledge additional collateral to its bankers. By the time the company was forced to file for bankruptcy, substantially all of its assets, including gasoline and merchandise inventories, had been pledged as collateral.

Searching for a shot-in-the-arm solution to what he considered to be a manageable liquidity crunch, Van Horn sought to raise some funds through the sale of one of the company's noncore markets. However, no buyers could be found when he tried to sell the California stores. His efforts to find strategic partners that could provide an equity infusion were also unsuccessful. Not being able to meet its projections, beginning in August 1991 NCS was forced to arrange with NCNB Texas for the repeated deferral of certain principal payments.

In mid-November 1991, with no relief in sight and in preparation for the third quarter, in which NCS typically recorded substantially negative cash flows, Van Horn decided to adopt a cash conservation program that called for the suspension of dividends on NCS's preferred stock and a moratorium on principal payments on the company's term loan used to finance the purchase of NCS stock by the company's employee stock ownership plan (ESOP), certain mortgages, and interest payments on subordinated debentures. The negative coverage in the financial press of this measure resulted in the elimination of the company's gasoline trade credit. Moreover, when NCS failed to make a scheduled mortgage debt payment on December 1, it triggered a technical default on $170 million in debt and the requirement to cash collaterize letters of credit in the amount of $30 million. The ensuing uncertainty surrounding the company's situation caused a significant number of its vendors to withdraw their credit. Since trade credit was critical to the company's financing needs, Van Horn found himself with no other option than to file for protection under Chapter 11 of the Bankruptcy Code on December 9, 1991.

STRATEGIC REVIEW OF THE COMPANY

Despite intense last-minute efforts, Van Horn and his management group had not been able to obtain debtor-in-possession financing prior to the Chapter 11 filing. As a result, the withdrawal of vendor credit forced them to make some quick decisions in order to keep the stores in operation. With an inventory turnover rate of 11 to 12 times per year on most merchandise products and rates two to four times that high for perishable foods, dairy products, and gasoline, it was clear that NCS would not be able to stock all of its stores in the weeks immediately following its bankruptcy filing. To make matters worse, inventories were already at a low level. Accordingly, Pete Van Horn's framework in making the initial decisions as to how to operate the company was defined by the need to maximize NCS's cash flow generating capability. It was not until December 20, 1991 that the bankruptcy court signed an order approving debtor-in-possession financing for NCS. The company obtained an $8 million line of credit from NCNB North Carolina and NCNB Texas.

Prior to the Chapter 11 filing, Van Horn and his management group had been performing a strategic review of NCS's operations and the performance of each of its convenience stores. Once in bankruptcy, they used this review to formulate an aggressive store closure and lease rejection program. In selecting the stores to be closed, Van Horn took into consideration factors such as historical and projected cash flows, lease or ownership terms, age and condition of the property, the nature and amount of insurance claims, competition, and the potential for future changes to any of the foregoing. Unprofitable stores were closed immediately and their inventories were used to stock those stores which management had decided to keep.

The result was a 26 percent downsizing of the company's convenience store operations from a 986-store base as of the Chapter 11 filing date to the 725 convenience stores the company was currently operating. The downsizing had been accomplished pursuant to the Bankruptcy Code, which gives a debtor the right to assume or reject executory contracts, including any unexpired leases.[1] The closure of these 261 stores resulted in pretax savings of $4.4 million, including field management and administrative costs. In addition, NCS rejected the leases on 188 stores that had been previously closed. Prior to the filing, the company had been unable to reject these leases, which cost $7.4 million in annual operating expenses. In the process of assuming the leases of the stores it had decided to keep, the management group achieved an additional $3.2 million in cost savings by renegotiating the terms of many of its store and equipment leases.[2] The reduction of the company's store base also resulted in the downsizing of NCS's workforce from approximately 6,500 employees prior to the filing to approximately 4,800 employees.

NCS management also took a number of other cost cutting measures, some of which were made available to the company by the bankruptcy process. NCS closed its Corporate Kitchen distribution system and contracted for the distribution of its fresh food items with its grocery vendors. This measure eliminated $4.8 million in yearly corporate expenses. Corporate staff reductions (33 percent of the officer group and 27 percent of corporate staff) and the renegotiation of the lease of the company's headquarters resulted in additional savings of $2 million and $1.5 million, respectively. Write-offs on the book value of closed stores and nonoperating properties reduced ongoing depreciation and amortization charges by $3.2 million. Lastly, the management group calculated that its private job-related injury insurance program would save the company $7 million annually. The combined effects of these restructuring measures had been to reduce net operating expenses by over $30 million per year below fiscal 1991 amounts. In connection with this strategic review, NCS recorded $168.1 million of restructuring and other special charges in fiscal 1992. (See Exhibit 2.1.) All these measures

---

[1]If a lease is rejected in Chapter 11 proceedings, the debtor is obliged to surrender the premises and is relieved of the obligation to continue paying rent under the lease agreement. The rejection of a lease creates a prepetition, general unsecured claim. The bankruptcy court imposes a limit on the amount of a landlord's general unsecured claim arising from the lease rejection so that it may not exceed the greater of a year's rent without acceleration or 15 percent of the remaining rent reserved in the lease, not to exceed three years' rent.

[2]Since a company in Chapter 11 has the ability to reject leases, a landlord with above-market leases becomes vulnerable to renegotiation.

were achieved relatively early in the company's bankruptcy process, leading Van Horn to believe that they would help set the tone for a quick restructuring.

SHIFT IN MARKETING STRATEGY

In addition to eliminating certain operating expenses, NCS management made some adjustments to its marketing strategy. The previous assumption that the sale of higher-quality products would support a pricing strategy leading to higher gross margins had been disproved by market studies revealing the increasing importance of value for the customer. This was particularly accurate in light of the changed economic environment of the early 1990s. In response, Van Horn planned to reduce the company's gross profit margins and extend the value pricing strategy to other high-volume items such as alcoholic beverages and fountain drinks (the latter accounted for approximately 9 percent of total merchandise sales). He thought that a higher turnover and reduced operating costs would more than offset the effect of lower gross margins. This strategic shift, bolstered by the resumption of NCS's store modernization program and the expansion of the "eateries" concept to include more name brands (such as Burger King) in more stores would, he hoped, make a reorganized NCS a viable and competitive company. In turn, this meant that creditors and shareholders were more likely to achieve higher recoveries from a reorganized NCS than from the liquidation of its businesses. To illustrate this point, Van Horn had asked his management team to prepare a liquidation analysis that would ultimately be included in the company's disclosure statement on its plan of reorganization. Exhibit 2.2 summarizes the results of this analysis of liquidation proceeds.

FINANCIAL PROJECTIONS

Having accomplished a good deal of the repositioning of NCS, Pete Van Horn had felt prepared to set forth the results he thought could be accomplished. His colleagues recalled how he had emphasized that "he wanted realistic projections. He wanted projections that could be met, yet reflected the improvements that had been made in the business." He had often remarked to them that "Chapter 11 was enough of a nightmare that he had no intention of landing there a second time." Although

NCS had posted a 12 percent increase in same-store sales in FY 1992 (despite inventory stockouts during the first month of bankruptcy), Van Horn was concerned about being overly optimistic in projecting the company's outlook.

Van Horn also knew that the capitalization of a reorganized NCS would be a subject of heated discussion among the company's creditors. This decision, together with the value placed on the reorganized company, would directly affect the creditors' recoveries and the nature of the consideration they would receive. At the same time, NCS's CEO was aware that the company could accept only a certain amount of leverage for the reorganization to be successful. Van Horn thought that a reorganized NCS could handle debt in an amount between 3.5× and 4.5× the company's projected FY 1993 EBITDA. Furthermore, he knew that in order to meet the bankruptcy court's feasibility standard for the approval of a plan of reorganization, NCS would have to demonstrate that it would be able to generate the funds necessary to make the payments to creditors prescribed by the plan. As a benchmark for meeting this feasibility test, financial advisors in Chapter 11 situations often recommend a capitalization reflecting the industry average. Exhibit 2.3 sets forth the capitalization of NCS prior to the bankruptcy and as a Chapter 11 company.

Exhibit 2.4 sets forth the projections of NCS. These were the projections included in the "blue book" that Van Horn and his team had prepared for discussion with creditors. The projections would be used to develop a restructuring plan for NCS. The plan would, among other things, spell out which creditors and equity holders would realize consideration in the reorganized company and what form that consideration would take. The projections would be part of the disclosure statement that NCS would send out to its creditors and equity holders.

For valuation purposes, Van Horn also submitted a comparison of certain statistics for companies considered comparable to NCS. The companies selected and the statistics were done by NCS' financial advisor. See Exhibit 2.5 for the comparable companies analysis, and Exhibit 2.6 for capital market data relevant for valuing NCS as a going concern.

PARTICIPANTS IN THE REORGANIZATION

Pete Van Horn knew that each class of claimants would examine the projections with a microscope to anticipate the effect they would have on the nature of the offer that would be made to each class. In his mind, there were four principal classes.[3]

1. Secured Claims. These included claims secured by a range of assets, including real estate and inventories. While the particular security of each claim was often different, Van Horn thought that as a first approximation it was possible to treat these claims as a single group. These claims totalled $159 million of which approximately $90 million were represented by claims held by the company's banks, including NCNB Texas ($57 million credit line), NCNB North Carolina ($25 million ESOP loan), and Bank of America ($8 million letters of credit). Insurance companies and other lenders together held the bulk of the balance of these claims in the form of mortgage loans. Van Horn was aware that NCNB Texas had exposure in at least two of NCS's competitors that were also undergoing Chapter 11 restructurings. He knew that this exposure, and the bank's somewhat pessimistic views on NCS's and the industry's prospects, would influence NCNB Texas's attitude in the upcoming negotiations.

2. Unsecured Claims. These consisted of two subgroups—senior unsecured claims and subordinated unsecured claims. The claim amounts were $88.7 million and $60.2 million, respectively, for a total of $148.9 million. The U.S. trustee for the bankruptcy court had appointed a nine-member Official Committee of Unsecured Creditors to represent all unsecured claims. Although Van Horn expected these claimants to negotiate as a group, he suspected that some of the Committee's members would have different priorities. One-time trade creditors, various insurance companies, parties to rejected leases, and others represented $69 million of senior unsecured claims. An additional $19 million of senior unsecured claims were held by trade creditors who had tentatively agreed to continue to provide credit to NCS post-reorganization. The subordinated unsecured claims included the company's subordinated 12.5 percent debentures in the amount of $40 million, and its subordinated 9 percent debentures in the amount of $19 million. A portion of the 12.5 percent debentures (approximately $16 million) had been purchased by Smith Management Co. following the company's bankruptcy filing. Smith had acquired these securities at a substantial

---

[3]Excluded from Van Horn's categories were administrative and priority claimants that would be paid cash in full on the date of the plan's consummation.

discount (possibly 80 to 85 percent of their face value). Because of their varying interests, Van Horn expected these groups to argue extensively among themselves, especially in regard to the effect that the subordination provisions would have on their respective recoveries.[4]

3. *Equity.* In this group was the preferred and common stock. While the preferred stock had some modest seniority advantages compared to the common stock, Van Horn assumed the equity would negotiate as a group against the other groups and then negotiate among themselves, assuming they realized something from the reorganized company. The bulk of the company's preferred shares had been originally issued in 1990 in an exchange offer for certain of NCS's 9 percent debentures. To the extent that participants in this exchange continued to be holders of preferred stock, Van Horn expected this group to be particularly disgruntled. Although they were in the rear of the seniority queue, he thought they would try hard to get something out of the restructuring. Van Horn also expected common shareholders to play a role in the restructuring, particularly since the company's two largest shareholders, a private investor and NCS's ESOP, held 18 percent and 15 percent, respectively, of all outstanding shares. He knew that the fate of the ESOP claim would affect employee relations. This posed a delicate issue for Van Horn, since a successful reorganization would, to a large extent, depend on the efforts and morale of the workforce. This concern also extended to the company's management which, as a holder of 6 percent of NCS's shares, had also lost a good deal in the bankruptcy.

4. *Management.* Van Horn believed that the success of a reorganized NCS would depend heavily on management's efforts post-confirmation. Thus, he believed it appropriate that management be given incentives commensurate with these efforts.

Having worked with the creditor and equity groups since December 1991, Van Horn knew his submission of these projections would lead to multiple attacks. He thought the projections had been prepared in good faith and he looked forward to debating them and their implications with the various groups. He was optimistic that the new NCS could be successful and hoped the various groups would see this and work in the

---

[4]This was particularly true since there was some ambiguity concerning the provisions of the unsecured debt with respect to subordination issues.

larger interest of NCS. Bringing the different creditor groups together would require a lot of work. In the worst-case scenario, however, Van Horn knew he could force the creditors to compromise by using the threat of a cram-down in the bankruptcy court.[5]

As he surveyed the room, Van Horn turned to his colleague A. J. Gallerano, the company's general counsel, with whom he had worked closely since the filing, and said, "It's going to get interesting now."

---

[5]The bankruptcy court can confirm a plan of reorganization at the request of the debtor if the plan meets the principal requirements of the Bankruptcy Code, including the requirement that at least one class of claims that is impaired under the plan has accepted the plan and, as to each impaired class that has not accepted the it, the plan "does not discriminate unfairly" and is "fair and equitable." A plan of reorganization does not discriminate unfairly within the meaning of the Bankruptcy Code if no class receives more than it is legally entitled to receive for its claims or equity interests. "Fair and equitable" with respect to an unsecured claim means either that each impaired unsecured creditor receives or retains property of value equal to the amount of its allowed claim, or that the holders of claims and interests that are junior to the claims of the dissenting class will not receive any property under the plan.

Note: NCS and the Harvard Business School have discussed the description of the reorganization, and each recognizes that this case represents a simplification, and therefore is not a complete description of the facts and issues applicable to the company and its reorganization.

EXHIBIT 2.1   Restructuring and Other Special Charges

In connection with the Chapter 11 filing, NCS management performed a comprehensive strategic review of company and store operations, which resulted in the recording of restructuring and other special charges of $168.1 million in December 1991. The charges are summarized as follows ($in thousands):

Restructuring charges:	
Write-off of net book value of closed stores and rejected leases and record reserves for anticipated market divestitures and nonperforming leaseholds	$ 44,438
Write-down of nonoperating properties to fair market value	12,602
Write-off of net book value of goodwill	21,357
Write-off of net book value of debt issue costs and other deferred charges	9,435
Other write-offs and reserves associated with the Chapter 11 filing	13,201
Total restructuring charges	$101,033
Other special charges:	
Change in the method of estimating insurance reserves	46,632
Reserve for environmental costs	12,822
Other	7,619
Total other special charges	$ 67,073
Total	$168,106

Source: National Convenience Stores Incorporated, annual report on Form 10-K, 1992, p. 57.

EXHIBIT 2.2 Schedule of Assets and Liquidation Proceeds

The following schedule represents, to the best of management's belief, the estimated cash receipts of selling NCS's assets and the resulting estimated cash disbursements to its creditors in a Chapter 7 liquidation ($in thousands):

	Estimated Book Value as of June 20, 1992	Estimated Recovery Nearest Percent	Estimated Liquidated Recovery
Estimated cash balances	$ 32,723	100%	$ 32,723
Accounts and notes receivable	2,396	65	1,566
Inventories	40,069	81	32,381
Prepaid expenses	9,798	47	4,620
Land and buildings	89,548	51	45,347
Furniture, fixtures, and equipment	56,017	25	13,756
Leaseholds and improvements	18,030	0	0
Capital leases	5,539	0	0
Property held for future development	5,151	48	2,490
Liquor licenses	951	75	713
Vendor deposits	3,481	0	0
Other assets	4,798	0	0
Total assets	**$268,501**	**50%**	**$133,596**
Less: cash trust funds			15,475
Net proceeds after cash trust funds			118,121
Less:			
Corporate operating expenses during liquidation			$ 28,167
Trustee fees			3,544
Chapter 7 professional fees			2,800
Total costs associated with liquidation			$ 34,511
Net estimated liquidation proceeds available for allocation to creditors			$ 83,610

Source: National Convenience Stores, Third Amended Disclosure Statement, October 6, 1992, Exhibit C, p. 1.

EXHIBIT 2.3   Capital Structure

The capital structure of NCS, as of June 30, 1991, the last-year end date prior to the filing of Chapter 11, was:

	($in '000s)
Revolving credit agreement[a]	$ 36,089
Mortgage note on real estate due through 2003	71,600
12½% senior subordinated debentures due 1996, net of discount	39,626
ESOP loan due 1995[a]	23,167
Other	159
Capital lease obligations	11,640
9% convertible subordinated debentures	17,932
	$200,213
Stockholders' equity	70,098
Total capitalization[b]	$270,311

Source: National Convenience Stores Incorporated, annual report on Form 10-K, 1992, pp. 46, 59.

[a]Borrowing under the Revolving Credit Agreement, the ESOP loan and outstanding letters of credit (see below) are collectively secured by all assets of the company not otherwise pledged.

[b]NCS had $23 million in undrawn letters of credit supporting, for the most part, prior-year obligations on the company's worker's compensation program. These letters of credit were subsequently capitalized as liabilities subject to compromise in Chapter 11 proceedings.

In terms of the claims following the Chapter 11 filing, the principal additions to the figures above, as of June 30, 1992 are:

	($in '000s)
General unsecured claims	$110,542[a]
Postpetition interest on secured debt	3,369[b]
Letter of credit drawn	9,223[c]
	$123,134

Source: National Convenience Stores Incorporated, annual report on Form 10-K, 1992, p. 55.

[a]General unsecured liabilities include trade payables, insurance claims not settled through letter of credit draw downs subsequent to the petition date, and lease rejection obligations generated as a result of the strategic review of the company's operations.

[b]The company has taken the position that only the mortgage notes are fully secured, and thus post-petition secured interest relates to these obligations only.

[c]Certain letters of credit were outstanding as of the filing of the Chapter 11 petition and were funded. The provider of the letter of credit has a senior debt claim secured by all assets of the company not otherwise pledged.

EXHIBIT 2.4   Projections: Fiscal 1994–2003 ($in thousands)

	Before Reorganization			Projected after		
Income Statement	As Reported FY 1990	As Reported FY 1991	As Reported FY 1992	Plan FY 1993	Plan FY 1994	Plan FY 1995
Sales:						
Merchandise	$462,599	$466,328	$506,219	$491,487	$511,150	$531,597
Gasoline	400,728	380,325	361,102	387,019	396,695	406,612
Other	6,709	6,020	7,025	10,025	11,649	11,776
	$870,036	$852,673	$874,346	$888,531	$919,494	$949,985
Cost of sales:						
Merchandise	284,303	299,125	343,193	329,248	342,641	356,574
Gasoline	358,636	333,149	322,909	358,095	364,024	370,255
	$642,939	$632,274	$666,102	$687,343	$706,665	$726,829
Gross profit:						
Merchandise	178,296	167,203	163,026	162,239	168,509	175,023
Gasoline	42,092	47,176	38,193	28,924	32,671	36,357
Other	6,709	6,020	7,025	10,025	11,649	11,776
	$227,097	$220,399	$208,244	$201,188	$212,829	$223,156
Labor	64,516	64,953	67,145	61,339	63,741	66,291
Shrinkage	8,207	8,406	7,448	6,941	7,556	7,857
Utilities	16,706	16,358	16,207	15,055	15,978	16,617
Other	8,677	9,887	9,055	8,048	8,413	8,749
Controllable expenses	$ 98,106	$ 99,604	$ 99,855	$ 91,383	$ 95,688	$ 99,514
Rent	18,174	20,636	20,588	15,518	15,792	16,069
Depreciation and amortization	20,043	20,403	17,358	16,191	17,702	18,555
Insurance	10,986	22,159	24,040	15,380	15,765	16,339
Maintenance	8,213	8,446	7,958	7,827	8,218	8,425
Advertising	9,240	6,311	3,689	3,614	3,703	3,796
Taxes, licenses and other	6,074	6,932	7,130	6,445	6,542	6,640
General expenses	$ 72,730	$ 84,887	$ 80,763	$ 64,975	$ 67,722	$ 69,824
Total operating expenses	$170,836	$184,491	$180,618	$156,358	$163,410	$169,338
Field overheads	11,700	11,385	10,456	10,045	10,043	10,043
Closed stores	4,444	8,799	12,392	(240)	(240)	(167)
Corporate overhead	22,204	21,068	15,615	18,338	20,324	20,845
Commissary	1,203	4,518	2,387	(624)	(630)	(646)
Total overhead expenses	$ 39,551	$ 45,770	$ 40,850	$ 27,519	$ 29,497	$ 30,075
Total expenses	$210,387	$230,261	$221,468	$183,877	$192,907	$199,413
Operating profit (loss)	16,710	(9,862)	(13,224)	17,311	19,922	23,743
Interest Income	0	0	0	1,023	1,071	1,120

Reorganization

Plan FY 1996	Plan FY 1997	Plan FY 1998	Plan FY 1999	Plan FY 2000	Plan FY 2001	Plan FY 2002	Plan FY 2003
$552,860	$ 574,974	$ 597,973	$ 621,892	$ 646,767	$ 672,638	$ 699,543	$ 727,525
416,777	427,197	437,877	448,823	460,044	471,545	483,334	495,417
11,907	12,041	12,179	12,483	12,795	13,114	13,441	13,777
$981,544	$1,014,212	$1,048,029	$1,083,198	$1,119,606	$1,157,297	$1,196,318	$1,236,719
371,069	386,149	401,839	418,163	435,144	452,813	471,193	490,315
376,734	387,154	397,834	407,766	417,948	428,384	439,082	450,046
$747,803	$ 773,303	$ 799,673	$ 825,929	$ 853,092	$ 881,197	$ 910,275	$ 940,361
181,791	188,825	196,134	203,729	211,623	219,825	228,350	237,210
40,043	40,043	40,043	41,057	42,096	43,161	44,252	45,371
11,907	12,041	12,179	12,483	12,795	13,114	13,441	13,777
$233,741	$ 240,909	$ 248,356	$ 257,269	$ 266,514	$ 276,100	$ 286,043	$ 296,358
68,942	71,700	74,568	77,550	80,653	83,879	87,234	90,723
8,172	8,499	8,839	9,192	9,560	9,942	10,340	10,754
17,282	17,973	18,692	19,440	20,217	21,026	21,867	22,742
9,100	9,464	9,842	10,235	10,645	11,071	11,514	11,973
$103,496	$ 107,636	$ 111,941	$ 116,417	$ 121,075	$ 125,918	$ 130,955	$ 136,192
16,349	16,633	16,918	17,341	17,774	18,218	18,674	19,141
19,626	20,927	22,066	23,027	24,029	25,074	26,162	27,295
16,912	17,581	18,059	18,510	18,974	19,448	19,933	20,432
8,637	8,856	9,082	9,308	9,541	9,779	10,024	10,275
3,891	3,988	4,088	4,190	4,295	4,403	4,513	4,626
6,740	6,841	6,944	7,118	7,295	7,477	7,664	7,855
$ 72,155	$ 74,826	$ 77,157	$ 79,494	$ 81,908	$ 84,399	$ 86,970	$ 89,624
$175,651	$ 182,462	$ 189,098	$ 195,911	$ 202,983	$ 210,317	$ 217,925	$ 225,816
10,043	10,043	10,043	10,294	10,552	10,816	11,086	11,363
(15)	225	535	928	1,259	1,472	1,652	1,750
21,476	21,918	22,271	22,835	23,414	24,006	24,614	25,237
(662)	(679)	(695)	(713)	(731)	(749)	(768)	(787)
$ 30,842	$ 31,507	$ 32,153	$ 33,344	$ 34,494	$ 35,545	$ 36,584	$ 37,563
$206,493	$ 213,969	$ 221,251	$ 229,255	$ 237,477	$ 245,862	$ 254,509	$ 263,379
27,248	26,940	27,105	28,014	29,037	30,238	31,534	32,979
1,167	1,168	1,181	1,182	1,018	862	858	987

(Continued)

EXHIBIT 2.4 *(Continued)*   Projected Consolidated Balance Sheets (Unaudited) ($in thousands)

| | Before Reorganization | | | | |
Balance Sheet	Reported FY 1990	Reported FY 1991	Reported FY 1992	Estimated FY 1993	Plan FY 1994
Assets					
Current assets					
Cash and cash equivalent	$ 7,251	$ 18,699	$ 32,724	$ 34,559	$ 34,968
Accounts and notes receivable	6,680	9,988	2,288	3,618	3,507
Inventory	67,845	49,609	41,022	37,112	37,086
Prepaid expenses	6,853	7,344	8,845	4,672	5,207
Total current assets	$ 88,629	$ 85,640	$ 84,879	$ 79,961	$ 80,768
Net property and equipment	255,860	226,210	169,605	185,601	181,299
Total other assets	54,355	52,479	14,017	6,503	5,631
Total assets	$398,844	$364,329	$268,501	$272,065	$267,698
Liabilities					
Current liabilities					
Accounts payable and accrued expenses	$ 72,699	$ 76,104	$ 39,472	$ 50,883	$ 50,858

Note: The actual balance sheets in the disclosure statement were complete since they assumed a capital structure proposed by the company and detailed in the balance sheet.

	Projected after Reorganization							
Plan FY 1995	Plan FY 1996	Plan FY 1997	Plan FY 1998	Plan FY 1999	Plan FY 2000	Plan FY 2001	Plan FY 2002	Plan FY 2003
$ 37,012	$ 37,335	$ 37,082	$ 37,944	$ 37,158	$ 29,758	$ 29,365	$ 29,558	$ 35,793
3,551	3,596	3,643	3,690	3,782	3,876	3,972	4,070	4,171
38,391	40,715	43,174	44,723	46,391	48,120	49,916	51,781	53,718
5,249	5,292	5,336	5,381	5,487	5,596	5,708	5,823	5,940
$ 84,203	$ 86,938	$ 89,235	$ 91,738	$ 92,818	$ 87,350	$ 88,961	$ 91,232	$ 99,622
178,704	181,318	185,461	186,035	186,218	185,977	185,275	184,077	182,387
5,259	4,887	4,515	4,643	4,371	4,203	4,307	4,414	4,525
$268,166	$273,143	$279,211	$282,416	$283,407	$277,530	$278,543	$279,723	$286,534
$ 53,287	$ 56,086	$ 60,556	$ 64,544	$ 66,135	$ 67,779	$ 69,477	$ 71,229	$ 73,040

EXHIBIT 2.4 *(Continued)*   Projected Cash Flow Statement (Unaudited) before Reorganization ($in thousands)

Cash Flow Statement	Reported FY 1990	Reported FY 1991	Estimated FY 1992
Cash flow from operating activities			
Net earnings (loss)	$ 4,963	($10,465)	($185,438)
Depreciation and amortization	28,892	28,775	22,702
Deferred income taxes	1,498	(9,114)	(11,271)
Restructuring and other special charges	0	0	168,106
Gain on sale of assets	(5,393)	(13,046)	0
Nonrecurring charges	0	0	0
Extraordinary gain on debt exchange	(9,980)	0	0
Changes in operating assets and liabilities			
(Increase) decrease in accounts and notes receivable	(1,887)	(352)	26
Decrease (increase) in inventory	(7,857)	15,810	6,052
Increase (decrease) in accounts payable and accrued expenses	(844)	3,745	28,409
Increase (decrease) in income taxes	108	(285)	175
Other, net	(2,796)	(78)	(284)
Net cash provided by operating activities	$ 6,704	$14,990	$28,477
Cash flows from investing activities			
Capital expenditures	(10,013)	(13,418)	(3,557)
Proceeds from sale of assets/other reductions	53,896	33,893	2,900
Debt issue costs	(1,619)	(1,599)	(2,629)
Vendor deposits	0	0	(3,481)
Other	866	(838)	(748)
Net cash used in investing activities	$43,130	$18,038	$ 7,515

(Continued)

EXHIBIT 2.4 *(Continued)* Projected Cash Flow Statement (Unaudited) after Reorganization ($in thousands)

Cash Flow Statement	Plan FY 1993	Plan FY 1994	Plan FY 1995	Plan FY 1996
Cash flow from operating activities				
Operating profit (loss)	$17,311	$19,922	$23,743	$27,248
Interest income	1,023	1,071	1,120	1,167
Income taxes[a]	(6,271)	(7,180)	(8,503)	(9,718)
Depreciation and amortization	16,191	17,702	18,555	19,626
Deferred income taxes	0	0	0	0
Restructuring and other special charges	0	0	0	0
Gain on sale of assets	0	0	0	0
Nonrecurring charges	0	0	0	0
Extraordinary gain on debt exchange	0	0	0	0
Changes in operating assets and liabilities				
(Increase) decrease in accounts and				
notes receivable	(1,330)	111	(44)	(45)
Decrease (increase) in inventory	3,910	26	(1,305)	(2,324)
Increase (decrease) in accounts payable				
and accrued expenses	11,411	(25)	2,429	2,799
Increase (decrease) in income taxes	0	0	0	0
Other, net	4,173	(535)	(42)	(43)
Net cash provided by operating activities	$45,419	$31,092	$35,953	$38,710
Cash flows from investing activities				
Capital expenditures	(9,800)	(13,400)	(15,960)	(22,240)
Proceeds from sale of assets/other				
reductions	0	0	0	0
Debt issue costs	0	0	0	0
Vendor deposits	3,481	0	0	0
Other	3,757	(1,128)	(1,628)	(1,628)
Net cash used in investing activities	($ 2,562)	($14,528)	($17,588)	($23,868)

[a]Assumes a pro forma tax rate of 34.2%.

Plan FY 1997	Plan FY 1998	Plan FY 1999	Plan FY 2000	Plan FY 2001	Plan FY 2002	Plan FY 2003
$26,940	$27,105	$28,014	$29,037	$30,238	$31,534	$32,979
1,168	1,181	1,182	1,018	862	858	987
(9,613)	(9,674)	(9,985)	(10,279)	(10,636)	(11,078)	(11,616)
20,927	22,066	23,027	24,029	25,074	26,162	27,295
0	0	0	0	0	0	0
0	0	0	0	0	0	0
0	0	0	0	0	0	0
0	0	0	0	0	0	0
0	0	0	0	0	0	0
(47)	(47)	(92)	(94)	(96)	(98)	(101)
(2,459)	(1,549)	(1,668)	(1,729)	(1,795)	(1,865)	(1,937)
4,470	3,988	1,591	1,644	1,698	1,752	1,811
0	0	0	0	0	0	0
(44)	(45)	(106)	(109)	(112)	(115)	(117)
$41,342	$43,025	$41,963	$43,517	$45,233	$47,150	$49,301
(25,070)	(22,640)	(23,210)	(23,788)	(24,372)	(24,964)	(25,605)
0	0	0	0	0	0	0
0	0	0	0	0	0	0
0	0	0	0	0	0	0
(1,628)	(2,128)	(1,363)	168	(104)	(107)	(111)
($26,698)	($24,768)	($24,573)	($23,620)	($24,476)	($25,071)	($25,716)

(Continued)

EXHIBIT 2.4 *(Continued)*   List of Assumptions

A. Store Count   The projections are based on an open store count of 725 stores, 622 of which sell gasoline.

B. Merchandise Sales and Margins:
1. Merchandise sales are projected to grow at 4% per year. This is comprised of a 1.5% real growth component and a 2.5% inflationary component.
2. Merchandise margin (after vendor discounts and allowances) is projected to be 32.9% over the projection period, which is consistent with recent historical rates and lower than previous historical rates; the recent historical decrease in the merchandise margin is attributed principally to a value pricing strategy on cigarettes and other products.

C. Gasoline Sales Volume and Margins:
1. Gasoline sales volumes are expected to remain at 368 million gallons annually, representing approximately a 6% increase on a same store basis over 1991. The increase in sales volumes is attributable to a volume growth strategy adopted in January 1992. The volume growth strategy has recently begun to produce sales volumes consistent with the volumes used in the projection model.
2. Gasoline profit margins are assumed as follows:

	1993	1994	1995	1996	1997	1998–2003
Gasoline margins (in cents per gallon)	8	9	10	11	11	11

The profit margins used in the Plan are lower than the Company's five-year historical average of 11.0 cents per gallon principally due to the new volume growth strategy, the inability since the bankruptcy filing of the Company to purchase gasoline on the national exchange level, and recent short-term market factors. The growth in margins in future years is attributed to management's belief that it can resume its gasoline purchases on the national exchange level, which affords the Company substantial economies of scale.

D. Other Revenues   Other revenues are composed of revenues associated with pay phones, amusement games, and money order sales, which were projected on per store historical rates adjusted for inflationary increases. Also included in this category are revenues from lottery tickets sold in the Company's California and Texas stores.

E. Operating Expenses   Operating expenses include direct store operating expenses (identified as Controllable Expenses), insurance, advertising, rents, taxes, and depreciation. The expenses were generally projected by management based on historical per store expenses, adjusted for inflation. Depreciation expense was

EXHIBIT 2.4 *(Continued)*

increased in future years as a result of the net increase in property and equipment due to the capital expenditure budget. Additionally, depreciation expense is increased by $2 millon per year as a result of accounting adjustments required for companies coming out of Chapter 11.[a] Certain expenses, notably inventory shrinkage and insurance, were further adjusted for anticipated improvements in operating procedures and personnel. Rent expense was reduced by approximately $3 million from current annual rates to reflect lower expected expenses resulting from renegotiated store lease expenses which the Company has achieved.

F. Overhead Expenses   Overhead expenses include Field Overhead expenses and Corporate Expenses. These expenses were estimated based on historical rates for each of the field and corporate functions, after adjustment for the reduced scope of operations, inflation, and for additional reductions in personnel and occupancy costs.

G. Interest Income   Assumed to be 4% on cash balances, excluding store cash and other non-earning cash balances, totalling $8.0 million.

H. Income Tax Assumptions   The projections assume a 34.2% rate is paid once the NOLs are exhausted. The projections assume $80 million of NOLs.[b]

I. Cash   Minimum cash necessary to operate the business is assumed to be $27.3 million.

J. Accounts and Notes Receivable   NCS's business is basically a cash business although credit cards are accepted. The projection for Accounts and Notes Receivable consists primarily of amounts due from the Texas Superfund for environmental remediation and discounts and allowances receivable from vendors.

K. Inventory   The inventory balances are projected from historical data concerning both merchandise and gasoline.

L. Prepaid Expenses   These are projected based on historical data.

M. Capital Expenditures   The Company projects the following capital expenditures over the Plan period:

---

[a] Companies emerging from Chapter 11 are, in general, required to adopt "fresh-start reporting," as set forth in American Institute of Certified Public Accountants' Statement of Position 90-7, "Financial Reporting by Entities in Reorganization Under the Bankruptcy Code." In effect, a company is viewed as "sold" at the enterprise value that is assumed in the negotiation of a Chapter 11 plan. This, in turn, requires some adjustment to asset and liability values to bring them to fair market value. In the case of NCS, fixed assets were increased by $22.4 million which created an additional depreciation charge of $2 million annually for financial reporting purposes. This "extra" depreciation is not deductible for tax purposes.
[b] This statement is a simplified form of the assumptions stated in NCS's projections set forth in the Disclosure Statement.

(Continued)

EXHIBIT 2.4 *(Continued)*   Schedule of Capital Expenditures ($in thousands)

	1993	1994	1995	1996	1997	1998
General maintenance	$ 3,200	$ 3,200	$ 3,200	$ 3,200	$ 3,200	$ 3,200
Environmental expenditures	3,000	3,000	3,000	3,000	3,000	3,000
Stage II vapor recovery—high volume	0	1,800	1,800	0	0	0
Stage II vapor recovery—low volume	0	0	0	5,400	5,400	0
Store remodeling	4,600	4,600	4,600	4,600	4,600	4,600
Gasoline equipment refurbishment	1,000	1,000	1,000	1,000	1,000	1,000
Major gas remodels	0	1,800	1,800	1,800	1,800	1,800
Store relocations to new facilities	0	0	2,560	5,240	8,070	11,040
General corporate, other	1,000	1,000	1,000	1,000	1,000	1,000
Total capital expenditures	$12,800	$16,400	$18,960	$25,240	$28,070	$25,640

Estimated capital expenditures for 1999–2003 were as follows (in thousands of dollars):

1999	2000	2001	2002	2003
$23,210	$23,788	$24,372	$24,964	$25,605

Environmental expenditures (largely related to the gasoline business) are not reflected in the Property and Equipment Account on the Balance Sheet. Of the $3.0 million annual expenditures, $2.0 million is charged against other Liabilities and $1.0 million is reimbursed from the Superfund.

N. Other Assets   Projected based on historical experience.

O. Accounts Payable and Accrued Expenses   Accounts payable are based on the assumption that after the reorganization 12-days' merchandise terms will be outstanding at any time. Accrued salaries, wages, and insurance expenses are based on historical patterns.

P. Other Liabilities and Deferred Revenue   This category amounted to $21.360 million as of June 30, 1992. Included in this account is $12 million of environmental remediation reserve, ESOP reserve of $5.576 million, and reorganization expense accruals of $2.149 million. The $12 million environmental remediation reserve is assumed to be depleted at a rate of $2 million per year. It is expected that the remaining bankruptcy related accruals will be eliminated at the Effective Date. The ESOP is cancelled under the Plan. Therefore, all allocated ESOP reserves are eliminated at the Effective Date and no further amortization is required.

EXHIBIT 2.5 Comparable Company Analysis (as of October 15, 1992) (Dollars in Millions, Except Per Share Amounts)

Company Name	Circle K[a]	General	Casey's Dairy Mart	Sunshine Jr.	Uni-Mart
Ticker Symbol	CKP	CASY	DMCV	SJS	UNI
TEV/EBITD[b,c]	15.3	6.3	3.8	5.0	4.6
TEV/EBIT[b,c]	39.4	10.0	7.7	36.3	8.9
Price/latest 12 months EPS	NA	14.8	7.8	NA	10.5
Equity beta	NA	0.56	1.05	0.05	0.31
Market value of common equity	$ 0.0	$178.6	$ 30.6	$ 6.8	$ 17.1
Total debt and preferred	1,488.1	68.2	77.3	14.5	49.8
Minority interest	0.0	0.0	0.0	0.0	0.0
Less: Cash and equivalents	41.3	4.4	4.3	0.5	2.9
TEV (E)	$1,446.8	$242.4	$103.6	$ 20.8	$ 63.9
Stock price @ 10/15/92	(b)	$ 16.125	$ 5.625	$ 4.000	$ 2.500
Shares outstanding (millions)	45.3	11.1	5.4	1.7	6.8
Market value of common equity	$ 0.0	$178.6	$ 30.6	$ 6.8	$ 17.1
Latest 12 months					
Sales	$2,946.6	$624.0	$565.9	$222.5	$324.3
COGS	2,359.8	504.3	410.4	176.9	245.7
Gross profit	$ 586.8	$119.7	$155.5	$ 45.5	$ 78.7
SG&A	550.1	95.4	142.0	45.0	71.5
EBIT	$ 36.7	$ 24.3	$ 13.5	$ 0.6	$ 7.1
Depreciation and amortization	58.1	14.3	13.5	3.6	6.6
EBITDA	$ 94.8	$ 38.6	$ 27.0	$ 4.1	$ 13.8
Net Income	($ 199.1)	$ 12.1	$ 3.9	$ (0.4)	$ 1.6
CAPEX	27.1	43.9	18.9	1.9	6.3
EBITDA-CAPEX	$ 67.7	$ (5.3)	$ 8.1	$ 2.2	$ 7.5
Latest 12 months earnings per share	$ (4.40)	$ 1.09	$ 0.72	$ (0.24)	$ 0.24
Capitalization					
Short-term debt	$ 5.1	$ 2.1	$ 6.6	$ 11.2	$ 4.0
Long-term debt	1,433.0	66.1	70.7	3.3	45.8
Preferred stock	50.0	0.0	0.0	0.0	0.0
Minority interest	0.0	0.0	0.0	0.0	0.0
Common equity	0.0	178.6	30.6	6.8	17.1
Total capitalization	$1,488.1	$246.9	$107.9	$ 21.3	$ 66.9
Intangible assets	$ 0.0	$ 2.8	$ 20.4	$ 0.0	$ 8.9
Tangible book value (Incl. Min. Int.)	$ 0.0	$175.9	$ 10.2	$ 6.8	$ 8.2
Most recent fiscal year-end	4/30/92	4/30/92	2/1/92	12/26/91	9/30/92
Most recent quarter-end	7/31/92	7/31/92	8/1/92	9/24/92	9/30/92
52-week high	$ 1.00	$ 17.25	$ 10.25	$ 5.50	$ 4.88
52-week low	$ 0.22	$ 12.13	$ 5.63	$ 2.88	$ 2.25
Margins					
Gross profit	19.9%	19.2%	27.5%	20.5%	24.3%
EBIT	1.2%	3.9%	2.4%	0.3%	2.2%
EBITDA	3.2%	6.2%	4.8%	1.9%	4.3%

[a]Circle K was in the process of bankruptcy reorganization.
[b]Total enterprise value = Market value or equity + Net debt (using face value of debt).
[c]TEV, i.e., Total Enterprise Value as calculated (using face value of debt) is unlikely to reflect actual enterprise value for Circle K as it is in bankruptcy.

EXHIBIT 2.6 Interest Rate Environment and NCS Asset Beta

Listed below are the yields of fixed income securities as of June 30, 1992:

U.S. Government Securities

Maturity	Yield
1-Year	4.04%
5-Year	5.30%
10-Year	7.12%
30-Year	7.78%

Corporate Bonds

S&P Rating	Yield
AAA	8.45%
AA	8.63%
A	9.18%
BBB	9.20%
BB	10.69%
B	11.59%

Asset Beta

NCS's asset beta was estimated at 0.72.

CHAPTER 3

Continental Airlines—1992

This business is intensely, vigorously, bitterly, savagely competitive.

—Robert Crandall
CEO of American Airlines, 1992

On the evening of Thursday, November 5, 1992, Bob Ferguson, president and chief executive officer (CEO) of Continental Airlines Holdings, Inc. ("Continental Holdings"), sat in his Houston office and reflected on recent events. Since December 1990, Continental Holdings and its subsidiaries (including its principal operating subsidiary, Continental Airlines) had been operating under Chapter 11 of the U.S. Bankruptcy Code. Ferguson was greatly concerned about the negative impact that the bankruptcy was having on Continental Holdings' financial resources and competitive position. Legal fees and other bankruptcy-related expenses incurred to date totaled more than $30 million and were growing by $1 million each additional month that the company remained in bankruptcy court. Moreover, many travel agents were reluctant to book customers on flights offered by bankrupt carriers; this problem was magnified by the public's perception that bankrupt airlines scrimped on service and safety to conserve scarce cash.

The recent financial performance of the company had not been encouraging. After having reported positive net income of $73 million for 1986, Continental Holdings reported annual losses for each of the next four years, with a record loss of $2.3 billion for 1990. Nor did the future seem

---

This case was prepared by Professor Stuart Gilson, assisted by Research Associate Samuel Karam. Copyright © 1993 by the President and Fellows of Harvard College. Harvard Business School case 294-058.

to hold much hope. During the past two years the commercial airline industry had lost a total of $6 billion, more than the total amount it had earned since it came into existence. At the start of 1992, almost 20 percent of industry capacity was operated by bankrupt airlines. If Continental Holdings could not soon be returned to profitability, it risked the same fate as Pan American World Airways and Eastern Airlines (the latter until April 1990 a wholly owned subsidiary of Continental Holdings), both of which had been unable to leave Chapter 11 and were ultimately liquidated.

Just as its options seemed to be running out, the company received five proposals from outside investors during the summer of 1992 to infuse it with new capital. Now, only three days remained until the company had to go before the bankruptcy judge and present a reorganization plan. Any outside investment in the company would have to be included as part of the plan and obtain the approval of Continental Holdings' creditors. Although the company could ask for an extension of its right to file a reorganization plan, any further delay carried the risk that some or all of the bidders might withdraw their offers.

THE COMPANY

The company that would eventually become known as Continental Airlines was established in 1934 to provide mail service between Colorado and western Texas. Over the next forty years, the company grew to become one of the world's largest carriers, flying to hundreds of destinations in the United States and abroad, and operating a fleet of several hundred aircraft. In many ways, the current problems of Continental and the rest of the airline industry could be traced back to 1978, when the U.S. airline industry was deregulated. Following deregulation, the airlines had been free to set their own fares and routes. Prompted in part by competition from no-frills carriers like Southwest Airlines and People Express, the major airlines frequently engaged in aggressive fare discounting (especially in the first and fourth calendar quarters when travel demand was weakest), and competed indirectly on price by offering generous frequent flier programs. Such competition put increasing downward pressure on airline passenger yields.[1]

---

[1]The *yield* is defined as total revenue divided by total revenue passenger miles flown, where one *revenue passenger mile* (RPM) equals one passenger flown one mile. One *available seat mile* (ASM) equals one seat on an aircraft flown one mile, whether or not it is occupied. The *load factor* is a measure of capacity utilization, equal to total RPMs divided by total ASMs.

In late 1980, a financially weakened Continental became the object of a hostile tender offer by Texas Air Corp., an airline holding company controlled by Frank Lorenzo. Over the bitter objections of Continental's unionized employees, Texas Air ended up acquiring a 51 percent interest in the company. About three years later, on September 24, 1983, Continental filed for Chapter 11 bankruptcy protection. Within days, the airline abrogated its union contracts, shed 65 percent of its workforce, and resumed flying on a much-reduced network of routes. Continental returned to profitability within a year and emerged from bankruptcy in 1986.

In the latter half of the 1980s, Texas Air embarked on an ambitious growth strategy that involved buying up other airlines. In 1985 it bid unsuccessfully for Trans World Airlines (losing to Carl Icahn) and Frontier Airlines (losing to People Express Airlines). But in 1986 it successfully acquired both People Express (including its Frontier subsidiary) and Eastern Airlines. In 1987 Texas Air acquired all of the remaining outstanding shares of Continental Airlines in a merger. The airline operations of Texas Air were conducted mainly through its Continental Airlines and Eastern Airlines subsidiaries. Continental Airlines was also assigned ownership of all of Texas Air's other airline assets. In June 1990 Texas Air changed its name to Continental Airlines Holdings.

The company's growth over the latter half of the decade was truly impressive. Between fiscal years 1984 and 1989, annual consolidated revenues of Continental Holdings/Texas Air increased from $1.4 billion to $6.7 billion, and total assets went up from $1.3 billion to $7.7 billion. By the end of the decade, Continental Airlines had become the fifth-largest U.S. carrier (after American, United, Delta, and Northwest). Exhibit 3.1 presents a map of the domestic and international routes served by Continental Airlines.[2]

Unfortunately, rapid growth and external events placed the company under increasing financial strain. It had relied heavily on high-yield, non-investment-grade debt in financing its acquisition program. Over the period 1984–1989 Continental Holdings' long-term debt increased from $0.8 billion to $5.2 billion. Since it emerged from bankruptcy in 1986, debt as a percentage of total capitalization had remained well above 80

---

[2]Continental, like most major airlines, operated under a hub and spoke system. Under this system, the airline's network of routes resembled a bicycle wheel, with a "hub" airport located at the center. Continental was the dominant carrier at three of its four hubs, offering (at year-end 1991) 75% of all flights in and out of Houston, 48% at Newark, 47% at Cleveland, and 37% at Denver.

percent, versus an industry average of under 60 percent. And in 1988 and 1989 the company posted industry-record losses of $719 million and $886 million.

Lorenzo's efforts to cut costs met with particular resistance at Eastern Airlines, where union resentment of his tactics in Continental's 1983 bankruptcy still ran high. In March 1989 Eastern's unions struck the company, and a few days later it filed for Chapter 11. In April 1990 the judge in the Eastern bankruptcy case appointed a trustee to run the company. From this point onward Eastern was removed from Continental Holdings' control. Eastern ultimately eased operations in January 1991.

Continental Holdings' management also responded to the crisis by attempting to sell off assets and place new securities with outside investors. In 1988 Eastern Airlines (then a subsidiary of Continental Holdings) sold its profitable northeast shuttle to Trump Shuttle for $365 million, and in 1989 it sold $471 million of assets (including its Latin American routes) to American Airlines. During 1989 and 1990, Scandinavian Airlines System (SAS) bought a 18 percent equity stake in Continental Holdings (including stock owned by Lorenzo and another company officer), and received three seats on the board.

These actions were not sufficient to alleviate the company's financial crisis. In August 1990 the situation turned critical when Iraq's invasion of Kuwait caused airline fuel costs to double within three months, increasing the company's monthly fuel costs in the fourth quarter of 1990 by more than $60 million. Declining passenger traffic stemming from the worsening U.S. recession and heightened fears of international travel made it impossible for the airlines to cover these higher costs by raising fares. Restructuring Continental Holdings' debt out of court was not considered feasible because the company's capital structure was exceedingly complex, involving thousands of creditors and lessors and numerous interconnected debt agreements. On December 3, 1990, Continental Holdings and its 52 subsidiaries (including Continental Airlines) filed for Chapter 11 bankruptcy protection in Wilmington, Delaware, listing total assets of $4.8 billion and total liabilities of $5.9 billion.

THE BANKRUPTCY

When Continental Holdings filed for bankruptcy in December 1990, Bob Ferguson was the company's chief financial officer (CFO). (Frank Lorenzo had been replaced as CEO a few months earlier by Hollis Harris, who had formerly worked for Delta Airlines.) Ferguson recalled vividly that the decision to file had not been easy. Management was concerned that a bankruptcy would further weaken the airline's operations. For one thing, bankruptcy was a complex legal process in which management had limited expertise. For a company of Continental Holdings' size, this would mean having to hire possibly scores of lawyers, investment bankers, and other financial advisors to guide the firm through its bankruptcy. These advisors often charged by the hour or month, and the process often took two or three years to complete. In addition, any business decision taken by a firm in Chapter 11 (such as selling off assets) had to be approved by the bankruptcy judge in the case and could be appealed by creditors. This had the potential to produce lengthy delays and distract management from the important task of turning around the business. Finally, the stigma of bankruptcy could make it more difficult for the firm to do business with suppliers or to attract travelers who had concerns over safety and service.

During 1991, the company had taken several actions to reduce its costs and improve the profitability of its airline operations. These included cutting back on flights in the off-peak season, laying off nonessential personnel, cutting or deferring capital expenditures, and putting off all scheduled wage and salary increases until the following May (the latter action produced annual savings of over $100 million). The company also considered selling off various assets to raise cash. By year-end Ferguson's turnaround strategy started to be reflected in the company's bottom line. Continental Airlines' operating losses for the fourth quarter of 1991 represented a $243 million improvement over the previous year's fourth-quarter results. For 1991, Continental Holdings reported a loss of $306 million, compared to the $2.3 billion loss it posted in 1990. Exhibit 3.2 presents Continental Holdings' 1989–1991 consolidated financial results.

Certain features of Chapter 11 gave the company additional financial breathing room. First, it did not have to pay or accrue interest on its unsecured debt (or on any portion of its secured debt that was undercollateralized). By the end of 1991 this saving amounted to $154 million. Second, it could avail itself of debtor-in-possession (DIP) financing. Under Chapter 11, a bank or other financial institution that lends money to a bankrupt company can be granted a senior claim that ranks ahead of the firm's other outstanding debts. In the absence of this provision, bankrupt firms would find it considerably more difficult to obtain new financing. In July 1991, the company negotiated a $120 million secured DIP facility with Chase Manhattan Bank, N.A., bearing interest at prime plus 2.5 percent.

Finally, Chapter 11 allows a company to reject executory contracts, which for Continental consisted mainly of rental and lease agreements.

Airlines often lease rather than own the planes they fly.[3] At year-end 1989, Continental's fleet consisted of 329 aircraft, 231 (71%) of which were leased. This meant that a substantial portion of the airline's liabilities (excluding capitalized leases) were off balance sheet. At the end of 1989, the present value of all future lease payments owed by Continental Holdings or its subsidiaries under capital leases was $1.1 billion while the (undiscounted) sum of all future lease payments it owed under operating leases was $8.8 billion (largely representing rental of airport and terminal facilities, maintenance facilities, and offices). In contrast, total interest expense for the company for 1989 came to only $664 million.

Under Section 365 of the U.S. Bankruptcy Code, Continental had the right to accept or reject its executory contracts within sixty days of its bankruptcy filing. If a lease was rejected, the lessor's economic loss would become a general unsecured claim on the company's estate. This gave a company considerable leverage to negotiate more favorable terms under its leases.

Unfortunately for Continental, a special set of rules applied to aircraft lessors. Under Section 1110 of the code, such lessors would be able to repossess their planes within sixty days if Continental stopped making payments under the original lease contracts. Nevertheless, the company challenged this rule in court and reached a settlement with its aircraft lessors under which it was able to defer $164 million in lease payments that would otherwise have been due during 1991 and the first half of 1992. In addition, the lessors agreed to reduce lease payments by $3.3 million per month and extend Continental $91 million in additional financing to refurbish its aircraft.

By the end of 1991, Ferguson (who had become CEO in August) saw the company's operations begin to turn around. Over the two fiscal quarters ending on March 31, 1992, Continental reported the second-best financial results of any major U.S. carrier. Ferguson and the board believed that it was time to start planning for life after Chapter 11. It was decided that the company would propose a reorganization plan in the spring. The plan would assign the company's various claimholders to various classes

---

[3]Leases are often entered into under a sale-leaseback arrangement. Under this arrangement, a company can raise funds by selling an asset that it already owns to a third party and immediately lease it back from that same party. In 1989, Continental Airlines raised $252 million by selling and leasing back 21 of its aircraft, and cumulatively over a four-year period had sold and leased back in excess of $750 million worth of aircraft (primarily older, Stage 2 type aircraft).

and propose a separate exchange of new securities for those currently held by each class. It was expected that large amounts of new common stock would be issued, significantly diluting, if not entirely eliminating, the ownership of the existing stockholders. Exhibit 3.3 lists the different claims that were outstanding when the first reorganization plan was proposed in February 1992.

For the plan to be confirmed by Continental Holdings' bankruptcy judge, it was necessary for a majority (two-thirds in value and one-half in number) of the claimholders in each class to vote for the plan. The plan also had to satisfy the "best interests of creditors" test, which meant the market value of new securities distributed to each class had to be at least equal to what that class would receive in a liquidation. In the latter event, each claimholder class would be paid off under the rule of absolute priority: No class could receive anything under the plan unless all more senior classes were paid in full. Exhibit 3.4 presents a liquidation analysis of Continental Holdings' assets as of June 30, 1992. Finally, the judge had to ensure that the plan was "feasible," meaning it was unlikely that a future financial restructuring or bankruptcy would be necessary. The fact that Continental had already been through Chapter 11 once before meant that the judge would probably pay special attention to this last criterion.

Continental Holdings filed its first reorganization plan on February 6, 1992. Under the plan, long-term debt would be slashed to $1.7 billion and almost all stock in the reorganized firm would be given to nonsubordinated creditors; the prepetition common and preferred stockholders would receive nothing. Even though it was necessary to hold a vote, the plan already had the approval of the Official Committee of Unsecured Creditors, and Ferguson and the board believed that plan confirmation was possible by July 1, 1992.

The plan was never put to a vote. On April 9, American Airlines announced that it was substantially reducing fares on its domestic flights (38 percent on average for full fares and 12 percent for leisure fares). This was followed by a systemwide, 50 percent off sale (from already low fares) launched by American in late May in reaction to a more limited fare action by Northwest Airlines. Continental, like the other major airlines, had to match these initiatives to remain competitive. The company estimated that American's fare actions would cost it at least $29 million a month in lost net revenue; for the second quarter of 1992, total revenues for the airline subsidiary were fully $134 million below projections. Clearly, reorganization under the original plan terms was no longer feasible. Ferguson and the other board members had to quickly search for other options.

THE AUCTION

Dating back to before the bankruptcy filing, Continental Holdings had been informally approached by several outside investors interested in buying a stake in the company. Rumored suitors had included British Airways, the Bass family of Texas, Los Angeles investor Marvin Davis, and Ross Perot, Jr., among others, but none of these initial inquiries had resulted in a firm offer. Now recent events had made it essential for the company to obtain outside financing to complete its reorganization. This need for capital was also known outside the firm, and over the period from July to September the company received five formal offers to provide it with new financing.

MAXAIR

The first of these offers came on July 9, 1992, from the investment group MAXAIR, led by Maxxam Inc., a Houston-based natural resources company that had interests in forestry, mining, and various commercial and residential real estate operations. The founder and CEO of Maxxam was Charles Hurwitz, who had gained a reputation (and considerable fortune) in the 1980s as a corporate raider. Maxxam had reported net income for 1991 of $57.5 million on sales of $2.2 billion. Also included in the group were two investment banking firms, Kidder Peabody and Donaldson, Lufkin & Jenrette. The group's initial offer called for an investment of $350 million, to consist of $325 million in secured notes and $25 million of a new class of common stock having three votes per share (class B stock). The notes would be callable, amortizing, and mature in seven years. In addition, the group was to receive warrants to purchase 130 million shares of normal class A common stock. With the remaining shares and warrants to be owned by the company's unsecured creditors and management, the investor group would own 72 percent of the firm's equity (and 82 percent of the votes) on a fully diluted basis (i.e., assuming full exercise of the warrants). After leaving bankruptcy, the investor group would be given thirteen of fifteen seats on Continental Holdings' board of directors (with the two remaining seats going to the unsecured creditors). The company also agreed not to entertain any competing offers for less than $385 million ($35 million above the Maxxam group's offer), and to pay the investor group a breakup fee of $8 million to $12 million if the deal did not go through.

Houston Air

On August 7, a second offer was submitted by Houston Air, an investment group headed by Alfredo Brener, a 40-year-old Mexican entrepreneur who lived in Houston and whose family owned a sizable stake in Mexicana Airlines. Brener proposed investing $385 million in the company—$325 million in debt and $60 million in new common stock. Like the first investor group, he would also receive warrants for 130 million new shares, giving him a 72 percent equity stake on a fully diluted basis. The proposed terms for the debt securities and warrants were virtually identical to those specified in the first offer, except the warrants would carry a slightly higher exercise price ($2.60 instead of $2.50) and would be immediately callable. One potentially serious drawback to this offer was that under U.S. law, foreign equity ownership in a domestic airline could not exceed 49 percent (25 percent on a control basis). Thus the Brener group would have to either bring in a significant U.S. partner or reduce the size of its equity investment. The press speculated that Brener might even apply for U.S. citizenship. Advising Brener on the deal were Chemical Bank and the investment banking firm of Wasserstein Perella & Co.

Air Canada/Air Partners

The third investment offer came on August 27 from a group consisting of Air Canada and Air Partners. Air Canada was the larger of Canada's two national airlines, with 1991 operating revenues of $3.6 billion (Cdn.). In terms of total revenue passenger miles (RPM) service in 1991, Air Canada was the twentieth-largest airline in the world (Continental was ranked sixth). In 1988–89 the Canadian government sold off its 100 percent ownership of Air Canada stock, which was now listed on various Canadian stock exchanges. The CEO of Air Canada was none other than Hollis Harris, until a year earlier the CEO of Continental Holdings. Air Partners was a company formed by Fort Worth investors David Bonderman and James Coulter, two longtime advisors to financier Robert Bass. The group proposed investing $400 million in the company in return for $100 million in new common stock and $300 million in secured notes (the notes would carry roughly the same terms as the MAX-AIR notes). It would also receive two classes of warrants that would enable it to buy an additional 11 million shares at a weighted average exercise price of $20. If the warrants were fully converted, Air Canada/Air Partners would also own 72 percent of the company's equity. To comply with foreign ownership restrictions, Air Canada alone would receive securities representing a 24 percent voting interest and 29 percent equity interest. The group would also be allowed to designate ten of the company's sixteen directors (the remaining board seats would be shared by unsecured creditors, management, and independent outside directors). The group's financial advisors included Lehman Brothers, Merrill Lynch, and the Canadian firm of RBC Dominion Securities.

Lufthansa/Davis

On September 16, a fourth bidder emerged for the company. The German airline Deutsche Lufthansa AG and the California investor Marvin Davis jointly offered to buy or place $100 million of common stock and $300 million of debt in Continental Holdings, matching the previous offer by Air Canada/Air Partners. Davis had recently tried (unsuccessfully) to acquire two other major airlines, Northwest and United. Lufthansa was one of the leading European carriers with $9 billion in annual revenues and had a reputation for providing superior service and reliability. It was also 51 percent owned by the German government. In 1991 it was the world's eleventh-largest airline ranked by total revenue passenger miles. Lufthansa's interest in Continental reflected a growing interest among European carriers in gaining a foothold in the U.S. market. For example, British Airways was currently exploring a possible alliance with USAir, and KLM Royal Dutch Airlines had recently acquired a major stake in NWA, the parent of Northwest Airlines. Lufthansa's 49 percent share of the $100 million in equity would be paid for in surplus aircraft from its own fleet rather than cash. As with the competing offers by MAXAIR and Air Canada/Air Partners, at least $150 million of the new debt would be secured by the assets of Continental Holdings' Air Micronesia division.

Benefits Concepts of New York Inc.

The fifth and final bid for the company was made on September 30 by Benefits Concepts of New York Inc., a company led by Jack Robinson, the 32-year-old president of Florida Air and a former Eastern and Continental middle-level manager, and Dan Carpenter, chairman of Florida Air. The offer was for $425 million, to consist of $25 million in equity and $400 million in debt. In addition, 52 percent of the stock in the reorganized company was to be placed in an employee stock ownership plan.

Competition Among the Bidders

From the perspective of the five bidders, Continental Holdings represented a highly desirable acquisition opportunity. For one thing, its airline operations enjoyed one of the lowest cost structures in the industry. For 1991, Continental's operating cost per available seat mile was only 8.2 cents, compared to an average of 9.6 cents for the other major airlines. A major contributing factor was the fact that 82 percent of the company's employees were nonunionized, putting its labor costs at 75 percent of the industry average. Exhibit 3.5 presents a cost breakdown for the U.S. airline industry, and Exhibit 3.6 compares various operating statistics for Continental and the other major carriers.

In addition, Continental's four major hubs (in Houston, Newark, Cleveland, and Denver) were located at highly desirable low-density airports, where air traffic was relatively less congested. Concerns over safety and service had recently led to calls for more regulation of high-density airports like John F. Kennedy International Airport (JFK), La Guardia Airport, O'Hare International Airport, and Washington National Airport. New regulations being considered by the Federal Aviation Administration would reduce the number of flights at these airports and limit the airlines' ability to freely buy and sell takeoff and landing slots.

Continental also had a number of other desirable assets, including System One, the fourth-largest computer reservation system (CRS) in the country. CRSs are leased to travel agencies, which use them to book flights for their customers. Airlines that do not have their own CRSs are forced to pay a fee to list their flights on systems operated by competing airlines (the two most widely used CRSs are Sabre and Apollo, owned by American Airlines and United Air Lines, respectively). Continental also had a profitable joint venture agreement with Air Micronesia, a small carrier that provided service from the Micronesian Islands (including Guam and Saipan) to Japan, Hawaii, and the Philippines. In 1991, this business accounted for over $400 million of Continental's net operating revenues. Under the reorganization plan, Air Micronesia would become a wholly owned subsidiary of Continental.

Competition among the first four bidders was intense (the fifth bid by Benefits Concepts of New York was never considered credible by Continental's board and was ultimately withdrawn). By the first week of October, MAXAIR had increased the total value of its offer to $400 million, and had taken on a Mexican airline, Aerovias de Mexico S.A. de C.V. ("Aeromexico"), as a partner. Under its revised offer, MAXAIR would increase its equity investment to $30 million, and Aeromexico would pay $100 million in cash for a new class of convertible preferred stock. In response, Air Canada/Air Partners raised its bid to $425 million by increasing the debt portion of the offer to $325 million from $300 million. The

Lufthansa/Davis group stayed put at its original offer but argued that it was still superior to the other offers because it contained the largest commitment of new equity ($100 million of common stock) and represented the best strategic fit with Continental. Houston Air claimed that it was being joined in its bid by Scandinavian Airlines System (SAS), which already owned 18 percent of Continental Holdings' equity and had three seats on the board.

On October 14, at the request of Continental Holdings' board, Bankruptcy Judge Helen Balick issued an order that set November 2, 1992, as the deadline for the submission of additional or revised bids to invest in the company. Although not publicly known at the time, by the close of business on November 2 only two bids remained on the table: those of MAXAIR and Air Canada/Air Partners. The terms of these two offers are summarized in Exhibit 3.7. It was decided that the directors of Continental Holdings and Continental Airlines would meet with the two finalists on Friday, November 6, and announce a winner the following Monday.

THE DECISION

On the night before he was to meet with MAXAIR and Air Canada/Air Partners, Bob Ferguson considered his options. Competition among the various bidders had dramatically increased the amount being offered for the company. To help management evaluate the alternative bids, the company's financial advisors had put together the set of financial forecasts shown in Exhibits 3.8 and 3.9. Exhibit 3.10 reports various market interest rates that obtained at the beginning of November 1992, and Exhibit 3.11 presents financial information for Continental's principal competitors. A number of other important factors to consider were more difficult to quantify. First, many industry insiders believed that the future of commercial aviation belonged to those carriers that could operate on an expanded global scale and effectively serve the entire world market. Although Continental operated hundreds of flights outside the United States, access into foreign markets was still relatively restricted. Linking up with a foreign carrier was a way of getting around these restrictions. This made Ferguson wonder whether he should somehow try to get Lufthansa back into the bidding, given the enormous opportunities presented by the European market. Forming an alliance with Lufthansa also made sense because Lufthansa currently served both Newark and Houston; each airline could therefore feed connecting passengers from its own flights onto flights offered by the other carrier, thus increasing both airlines' load factors. This arrangement would be facilitated by the practice of "code sharing."[4]

Ferguson also had to consider the value of possible operating and financial synergies from combining with another airline. In a presentation to Continental's board in early October, Air Canada/Air Partners had estimated that Continental would realize $401 million in cost savings through 1997 as a result of increased efficiency in traffic flow, aircraft maintenance, information systems, fleet planning, and elimination of operational redundancies. In a similar presentation, Lufthansa/Davis estimated synergies to Continental of between $200 million and $350 million a year. MAXAIR also stressed possible synergies available through the involvement of Aeromexico, including the feed-through of passengers at Continental's Houston hub.

Another major concern of Ferguson's was that Continental be allowed to undertake planned capital expenditures on aircraft and airport facilities, which he believed were crucial to the company's long-term competitive viability. The average age of Continental's fleet (including both leased and owned aircraft) was about 14 years, compared to an average of about 12 years for the other U.S. major airlines (Exhibit 3.12). In addition, 49 percent of Continental's fleet consisted of noisier Stage 2 aircraft, which under new federal regulation had to be removed from service by the year 2000. Both factors necessitated huge investments in new aircraft. In 1989 and 1990, Continental had entered into agreements with the Boeing Company and the European Airbus consortium to purchase 196 new aircraft for over $10 billion.[5] Under one plausible scenario, the company would reduce the average age of its fleet to that of the industry by 1995 or 1996.

The company expected to spend an additional $125 million on collision and wind shear avoidance systems to comply with new federal rules taking effect over the next decade. It was also planning to extensively up-

---

[4]Under code sharing, two airlines operate as independent entities but share the same flight codes on connecting flights. Thus, a passenger booking from Frankfurt to Los Angeles with a connection in Newark would have a single flight number for the entire trip. Such flights are typically given a higher priority on CRS screens, making it more likely that passengers will book with these rather than other connecting flights that have different codes.

[5]About half of these orders represented nonbinding options to purchase new aircraft. Under Chapter 11, Continental was not required to assume these agreements (firm commitments as well as options to purchase) and was currently in discussions with both aircraft manufacturers over renegotiating the terms of the earlier agreements.

grade the interior of its airplanes in order to attract a greater share of higher-margin business passenger traffic. Finally, it might be necessary to construct a new aircraft maintenance facility to replace the company's current facility at Denver's Stapleton Airport, which was scheduled to be closed down in 1993. Ferguson wanted to be sure that any new outside investor would be both willing and able to support Continental's planned capital expenditure program. He was therefore concerned that both Air Canada and Lufthansa had recently reported large operating losses, although Air Canada had forecast that it would have access to $972 million in cash at year-end 1992 (including $400 million in unused lines of bank credit).[6]

Finally, it was important that the deal be structured in such a way as not to jeopardize Continental Holdings' accumulated net operating loss carryforwards (NOLs). At the end of 1991, the company's NOLs amounted to $1.9 billion. These NOLs would expire over 1995–2006 (a company could use its NOLs only to offset positive taxable income going three years back and fifteen years forward from the year in which the loss was incurred). In addition, the company's ability to use its NOLs could be severely limited if ownership of its common stock changed significantly once it left Chapter 11. Ferguson therefore wanted to be sure that the firm would not have to issue large amounts of new equity in the future.

Any outside investment in Continental Holdings would have to be incorporated in the company's reorganization plan. It was anticipated that its existing shareholders and subordinated lenders would receive nothing under the plan and that about $1.4 billion in long-term debt would be outstanding after the company emerged from bankruptcy (exclusive of any new debt issued to the outside investors).

Bob Ferguson sat back in his chair and considered what he would recommend to the board.

---

[6]For the most recent fiscal year, Air Canada had reported a net loss from continuing operations of $211 million (Cdn.), while Lufthansa reported its worst-ever annual loss of DM1.2 billion, or $800 million (U.S.).

EXHIBIT 3.1 Continental Airlines Domestic and International Route Systems

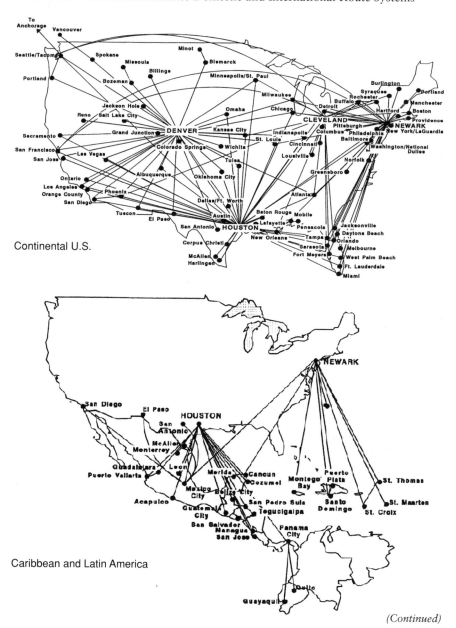

Continental U.S.

Caribbean and Latin America

(Continued)

EXHIBIT 3.1 *(Continued)*

North Atlantic

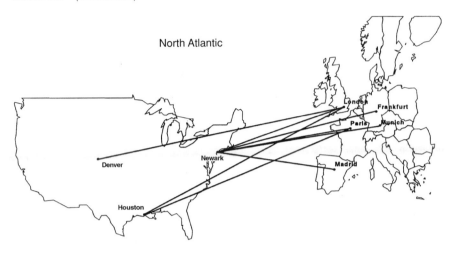

Pacific

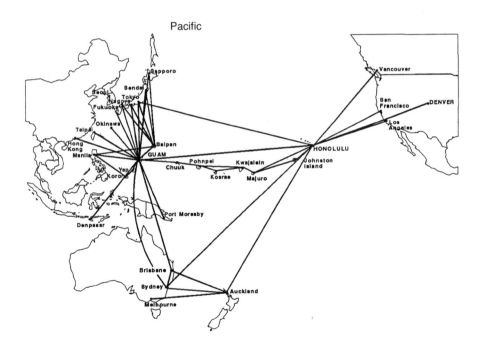

EXHIBIT 3.2 Texas Air Corp./Continental Airlines Holdings, Inc., Consolidated Annual Financial Statements ($millions)

	Twelve Months Ended December 31		
	1991	**1990**	**1989**
Operating revenues			
Passenger	$4,656.5	$5,165.6	$5,705.1
Cargo, mail, and other	894.5	1,064.9	944.8
Total operating revenues	$5,551.0	$6,230.5	$6,649.9
Operating expenses			
Wages and salaries	$1,456.2	$1,728.7	$1,982.4
Aircraft fuel	868.9	1,129.7	996.0
Rentals and landing fees	786.3	833.3	882.3
Commissions	546.8	543.5	593.4
Depreciation and amortization	231.5	351.9	552.4
Other	1,880.2	2,070.0	2,280.7
Total operating expenses	$5,769.9	$6,657.1	$7,287.2
Operating income (loss)	$ (218.9)	$ (426.6)	$ (637.3)
Other income (expense)			
Interest	$ (162.3)	$ (338.5)	$ (580.6)
Gain on disposition of assets	148.7	100.2	612.3
Preferred stock dividends of Eastern	0.0	(28.0)	(46.1)
Eastern pension-related adjustments	0.0	(575.5)	(118.0)
Eastern liquidation-related adjustments	0.0	(797.5)	0.0
Chapter 11–related charges	(65.2)	(440.7)	0.0
Expenses relating to Eastern bankruptcy	0.0	(9.8)	(36.9)
Provision for Eastern pilot back pay award	0.0	0.0	(65.5)
Other	(6.7)	116.4	(33.0)
Total other income (expense)	$ (85.5)	$(1,973.6)	$ (267.8)
Net profit (loss) before taxes and extraordinary items	$ (304.4)	$(2,400.2)	$ (905.1)
Income tax (credit) provision	1.3	2.7	0.6
Extraordinary items	0.0	59.0	20.1
Net profit (loss)	$ (305.7)	$(2,343.9)	$ (885.6)

(Continued)

EXHIBIT 3.2 *(Continued)*

	Twelve Months Ended December 31		
	1991	1990	1989
Assets			
Current assets			
Cash and cash equivalents	$341.2	$197.8	$1,271.5
Accounts receivable	513.5	489.7	745.0
Inventories of spare parts and supplies	212.1	219.2	444.5
Prepayments and other	83.9	107.3	99.0
Total current assets	$1,150.6	$1,014.0	$2,560.1
Property and equipment			
Flight equipment	$2,135.4	$2,050.5	$3,271.3
Other	768.0	779.1	1,334.9
Less: accumulated depreciation	(1,003.0)	(856.6)	(1,102.6)
Property and equipment under capital leases			
Flight equipment	492.0	427.4	1,088.7
Other	8.5	58.2	81.7
Less: accumulated depreciation	(185.0)	(161.8)	(351.1)
Other assets	156.4	158.0	773.0
Total assets	$3,522.9	$3,468.7	$7,656.1
Liabilities and Shareholders' Equity			
Current liabilities			
Current maturities of long-term debt and capital leases	$ 185.4	$ 0.0	$ 283.0
Accounts payable	569.4	316.8	769.6
Air traffic liability	478.3	487.4	426.5
Other	273.0	244.3	546.5
Total current liabilities	$1,506.1	$1,048.5	$2,025.6
Estimated liabilities subject to Chapter 11 proceedings	$4,225.8	$4,352.0	$3,024.4
Long-term debt	81.2	0.0	2,229.4
Capital leases	0.0	0.0	366.5
Deferred credit related to Eastern	1,056.5	1,056.5	624.4
Other liabilities	291.8	344.3	
Minority stockholders' equity in subsidiaries	0.0	0.0	8.5
Preferred stock	102.2	102.7	483.5
Common stock—$0.01 par value; 200,000,000 shares authorized; 46,745,170 shares issued (year-end 1991)	0.5	0.4	0.6

EXHIBIT 3.2   *(Continued)*

	Twelve Months Ended December 31		
	1991	1990	1989
Additional paid-in capital	1,094.8	1,094.3	1,085.6
Retained deficit	(4,823.7)	(4,518.0)	(2,171.4)
Common treasury stock	(12.0)	(12.0)	(21.1)
Total shareholders' equity	$(3,638.0)	$(3,333.0)	$ (614.3)
Total liabilities and shareholders' equity	$ 3,522.9	$ 3,468.7	$7,656.1

Note: Financial results for all of 1989 and the first three and one-half months of 1990 include revenues, expenses, and operating losses of Eastern Airlines.
Source: Continental Airlines Holdings, Inc., 10-K reports.

EXHIBIT 3.3   Claims Against Continental Airlines Holdings, Inc., in February 1992 Reorganization Plan

Claim Type	Amount ($millions)	Number
Administration and priority claims		
Chase DIP loan agreement	$120	1
Capital expenditure financing	8	15
Rent deferral agreement	131	27
Administration claims	7	163
Priority tax	43	1,243
Priority plan contribution	0	0
Priority wage	0	0
Other priority and superpriority	Contingent	3
Secured classes	1,472	128
Claims relating to pension plans		
Eastern-related	Contingent	1
Continental	Contingent	1
System One	Contingent	1
Frontier I trust claims	9	328
General unsecured	3,484	27,218
Subordinated claims	365	25,706
Equity interests	nil	nil

Source: Continental Airlines Holdings, Inc.

EXHIBIT 3.4   Continental Airlines Holdings, Inc., Liquidation Analysis as of June 30, 1992 ($millions)

	Current Estimate Market Value	Liquidation Value
Current assets		
Cash and temporary investments	$ 355.1	$ 355.1
Air Micronesia escrow	35.0	35.0
Accounts receivable, less doubtful accounts	573.0	358.8
Inventories	34.1	20.9
Prepayments	73.6	20.8
Total current assets	$1,070.8	$ 790.6
Property and equipment		
Owned flight equipment	1,218.8	1,030.3
Leased flight equipment—positive equity	173.0	24.5
Total property and equipment	$1,391.8	$1,054.8
Routes		
Air Micronesia (to be sold)	0.0	0.0
South Pacific	15.0	0.0
North Pacific	85.0	55.3
Europe	135.0	67.5
Madrid/Barcelona	40.0	20.0
Central America	7.5	2.3
Mexico	65.0	15.0
Canada	1.0	0.0
Caribbean	20.0	0.0
Total routes	$ 368.5	$ 160.1
Slots:		
LGA/DCA slots (to be sold)	0.0	0.0
Remaining 44 slots at LGA	22.0	13.2
36 slots at ORD	35.0	26.3
42 slots at DCA	30.0	15.0
Total slots	$ 87.0	$ 54.5
Gates and hubs:		
Three gates at ORD	21.0	18.9
Two gates at LAX	14.0	12.6
Newark	125.0	62.5
Total gates and hubs	$ 160.0	$ 94.0
Aircraft orders	57.3	57.3
Simulators	17.3	6.9
Pledged spare parts	357.3	178.7
Pledged assets	24.6	15.8
Air Micronesia preferred stock	20.0	5.0
CRS franchise and software	60.0	40.0
Other	261.6	92.1
Total assets	$3,876.2	$2,549.8

Source: Continental Airlines Holdings, Inc.

Casewriter's note: Difference between current market value and liquidation value represents the estimated loss in value that would occur if Continental Holdings' assets were sold off piecemeal rather than as a single unit.

EXHIBIT 3.5 Cost Breakdown for Major and National U.S. Carriers (Percent of Total Expenses Excluding Depreciation and Taxes)

	Labor	Fuel	Travel Agent Commissions	Passenger Meals	Interest	Landing Fees	Advertising Promotion	Other[a]
1978	42%	20%	4%	3%	3%	2%	2%	24%
1980	35	30	5	3	3	2	2	21
1985	35	22	7	3	4	2	2	25
1990	33	18	10	4	3	2	2	28
1991	34	15	11	4	2	2	2	30

Source: Air Transport Association of America.
[a]Includes aircraft and facility rental leases.

EXHIBIT 3.6 Operating Statistics of Major Airlines, 1991

	Continental	Average for All Other Major Carriers
Revenue passengers enplaned (thousands)	36,969	54,041
Revenue passenger miles (millions)	41,400	56,999
Available seat miles (millions)	65,900	92,670
Passenger mile yield (cents)	11.14	13.12
Passenger load factor (%)	62.80	62.82
Breakeven passenger load factor (%)	68.80	67.49
Average fuel price per gallon (cents)	69.38	70.53
Available seat miles per fuel gallon	51.77	50.24
Cost per available seat mile (cents)	8.20	9.58
Pay per employee as percent of industry average	76.30	—
Number of employees	36,300	60,422

Source: Airlines' annual reports; Air Transport Association of America.

EXHIBIT 3.7 Bids for Continental Airlines Holdings, Inc., as of November 6, 1992: Basic Financing (in Thousands of Dollars Except Where Indicated)

	MAXAIR Holdings, Inc.	Air Canada/ Air Partners, L.P.
Equity investment		
Common equity	$ 45,000	$110,000
Preferred equity	100,000	30,000
Debt investment		
Notes secured by:		
Air Micronesia subsidiary	175,000[a]	160,000[b]
Unencumbered assets of Continental Airlines	90,000[c]	150,000[d]
Total initial investment	$410,000	$450,000
Total committed financing	325,000[e]	450,000
Total primary shares outstanding (000s)	136,900	18,210
Total fully diluted shares outstanding (000s)	270,000	30,580
First-tier warrant exercise price ($)	$ 2.00	$ 15.00
Shares exercisable (000s)	70,200	7,413
Second-tier warrant exercise price ($)		$ 30.00
Shares exercisable (000s)		3,707
Total warrant proceeds	$140,400[f]	$222,400[g]
Total investment with warrants	$550,400	$672,400

Source: Continental Airlines Holdings, Inc.

[a]Kidder and DLJ will attempt a private placement of the Air Micronesia notes. If the private placement is unsuccessful, $150.0 million is currently committed to by GECC; $25.0 million has been committed as Air Micronesia Senior Subordinated Notes by DLJ, with an "equity kicker" of 20% of Air Micronesia common stock in the form of "nominally priced" warrants.

[b]$150 million has been committed by GECC. If more than $150 million but less than $160 million is placed, Air Partners will fund the difference up to $160 million. If more notes can be placed, Air Micronesia will issue additional notes up to $225 million.

[c]DLJ has committed to purchase $25 million of the CAL notes. DLJ, Kidder, and MAXAIR have committed to purchase $5 million, subject to payment of their fees.

[d]Air Canada has committed to purchase the CAL notes.

[e]Excluding the $25 million of DLJ-committed Air Micronesia senior subordinated notes.

[f]Excluding proceeds from conversion of creditor warrants of $28.9 million, representing 8.90 million shares at an exercise price of $3.25.

[g]Excluding proceeds from conversion of creditor warrants of $37.5 million, representing 1.25 million shares at an exercise price of $30.

EXHIBIT 3.8   Forecasted Operating Performance of Continental Airlines Holdings, Inc., as of September 15, 1992 ($millions)

	1992	1993	1994	1995
Passenger revenue				
Mainland	$3,358.9	$3,852.5	$4,510.8	$4,982.5
International	1,377.9	1,559.0	1,869.9	2,197.2
Cargo	254.9	279.4	299.5	318.0
Other	187.7	184.1	202.4	223.0
Total operating revenues	$5,179.4	$5,875.0	$6,882.6	$7,720.7
Operating expenses	$5,346.8	$5,727.7	$6,543.3	$7,149.7
Operating income (loss)	$(167.4)	$147.3	$339.3	$571.0
Interest expense	(131.3)	(175.4)	(168.3)	(145.4)
Other	19.3	24.2	28.2	39.2
Equity in subsidiaries	9.9	5.4	17.7	26.6
Total nonoperating income (expense)	$ (102.1)	$ (145.8)	$ (122.4)	$ (79.6)
Net profit (loss) before reorganization related charges	(269.5)	1.5	216.9	491.4
Reorganization-related charges	(15.6)	0.0	0.0	0.0
Net profit (loss) before taxes	(285.1)	1.5	216.9	491.4
Operating Statistics				
RPMs (millions)	43,565	44,311	48,539	51,396
ASMs (millions)	68,168	67,497	71,550	74,898
Load factor	63.9%	65.6%	67.8%	68.6%
Break-even load factor	67.9%	66.0%	66.0%	64.6%
Net yield per RPM (cents)	10.87	12.21	13.15	13.97
Break-even yield per RPM (cents)	11.56	12.28	12.79	13.14
Total revenue per ASM (cents)	7.60	8.70	9.62	10.31
Operating expense per ASM (cents)	7.84	8.49	9.15	9.55
Fuel cost per gallon (cents)	64.24	64.91	66.84	68.94
Enplanements	38,916	40,088	43,269	45,212
Block-to-block hours	1,136,672	1,146,921	1,198,446	1,246,133
Departures	490,407	495,648	518,554	541,298

Source: Continental Airlines Holdings, Inc.
Assumes:
- Emergence from bankruptcy, through a confirmed plan of reorganization, on December 31, 1992.
- Continuation throughout 1992 of the approximate 10% pay reduction implemented July 1, 1992 (estimated payroll savings of $98.7 million per year, of which $54 million occurs in 1992), to be phased out by July 1, 1993.
- Assets of Air Micronesia division are not sold; assets are instead used as collateral for a $200 million loan.
- The Denver maintenance base will be closed at the end of 1993, and a new major maintenance base will not be available until the beginning of 1995. The loss of this facility will increase maintenance costs about $9 million in 1994. The opening of the new facility will add $40 million per year in facility-related costs but will provide cost reductions estimated at $30 million in 1995 and higher in following years.
- Approximate $91.5 million reduction in other expense in 1992.
- Implementation of Fleet Plan 17, which assumes the following aircraft changes:

	Narrowbodies	Widebodies	Deletions	Net
1993	29	2	31	0
1994	41	2	27	16
1995	26	6	16	16

EXHIBIT 3.9 Forecasted Sources and Uses of Cash of Continental Airlines
Holdings, Inc., as of September 15, 1992 ($millions)

	1992	1993	1994	1995
Beginning cash balance	$280.2	$460.9	$ 478.2	$ 670.2
Cash generated				
Net income before gains	(285.1)	1.0	134.5	304.7
Depreciation and amortization	207.0	199.0	233.6	256.5
New aircraft financing	0.0	383.4	1,352.4	1,403.5
Capital expenditure financing	56.2	69.4	95.6	57.0
Exercise of warrants	0.0	0.0	325.0	0.0
Plan-related transactions	281.8	0.0	0.0	0.0
Total sources	$259.9	$652.8	$2,141.1	$2,021.7
Cash used				
Scheduled debt repayment	$112.8	$ 96.0	$ 343.6	$ 278.8
Stayed interest on non-Section 1110	(39.8)	0.0	0.0	0.0
Lease payment deferrals	(140.6)	(64.3)	0.0	0.0
Deferred interest	(7.8)	(80.5)	0.0	0.0
Capital expenditures	231.3	271.2	264.1	221.7
New aircraft purchases	0.0	383.4	1,352.4	1,403.5
Net predelivery deposits	0.0	29.2	5.5	9.3
Other uses (sources)	(76.7)	0.5	(16.5)	(70.1)
Total uses	$ 79.2	$635.5	$1,949.1	$1,843.2
Net sources/(uses)	180.7	17.3	192.0	178.5
Ending reportable cash balance	$460.9	$478.2	$ 670.2	$ 848.7
Less restricted cash	$ (92.7)	$ (93.4)	$ (100.0)	$ (100.0)
Investable cash	$368.2	$384.8	$ 570.2	$ 748.7

Source: Continental Airlines Holdings, Inc.
Assumes:
- Continental emerges from bankruptcy protection on December 31, 1992, by way of
  a nontaxable transaction.
- Capital expenditures represent total anticipated capital spending, including rotables
  and expendables related to new jet aircraft. Capital expenditures in January 1993
  include a one-time payment of $12.5 million to USAir for leasehold improvements at
  La Guardia. An additional $14.5 million may be expended during the second and
  third quarters of 1993.
- Noncommuter subsidiaries reflects the net cash flow contribution of System One,
  taking into consideration its cash flow from operations, debt amortization, and
  nonfinanced capital expenditures. Also included is the receipt of $35.0 million, in 12
  consecutive monthly installments, from the sale of the Airline Services Division to
  EDS, commencing in January 1993.
- Net predelivery deposits includes net progress payments anticipated to be required
  by Boeing related to Continental's 737-300 purchase contract. Predelivery deposit
  requirements due during first quarter 1993 for Boeing 737-300s are assumed to be
  deferred and paid over 18 months beginning April 1993. Predelivery deposits
  required for 757-200s, 200-seat and 300-seat aircraft are assumed to be 100%
  financed by manufacturers.
- Aircraft included in "new aircraft purchases" are 100% lease financed.
- "Other uses (sources)" includes a $5 million per year increase in net working capital.

EXHIBIT 3.10   Market Interest Rates during First
Week of November 1992 (Expressed on a Bond
Equivalent Yield Basis)

Treasury Securities	
3-month	3.06%
6-month	3.28
1-year	3.47
5-year	5.91
10-year	6.85
30-year	7.69
Long-Term Corporate Bonds (industrial average)	
AAA-rated	8.30%
AA-rated	8.48
A-rated	8.95
BBB-rated	9.22
BB-rated	10.00
B-rated	11.46

Source: Moody's Bond Survey and Standard &
Poor's Statistical Service.

EXHIBIT 3.11 Principal U.S. Competitors of Continental Airlines

	1991	1990	1989
AMR Corp. (American Airlines)			
Beta = 1.45			
Operating revenues ($millions)	$12,887	$11,720	$10,480
Operating expenses ($millions)	12,882	11,596	9,736
Capital expenditures ($millions)	3,536	2,901	2,395
Depreciation ($millions)	883	723	613
Long-term debt ($millions)[a]	5,879	3,272	2,306
Net worth ($millions)	3,794	3,727	3,766
Net income (loss) ($millions)	(240)	(40)	455
Earnings per share ($)	(3.54)	(0.64)	7.16
Dividends per share ($)	Nil	Nil	Nil
Common stock price range ($) High/Low	71.1/44.3	70.3/39.8	107.3/52.1
Shares outstanding (millions)	68.36	62.31	62.24
Delta Air Lines			
Beta = 1.10			
Operating revenues ($millions)	$ 9,171	$ 8,582	$ 8,090
Operating expenses ($millions)	9,621	8,163	7,411
Capital expenditures ($millions)	2,145	1,690	1,481
Depreciation ($millions)	522	459	393
Long-term debt ($millions)[a]	2,059	1,315	703
Net worth ($millions)	2,506	2,618	2,620
Net income (loss) ($millions)	(324)	303	461
Earnings per share ($)	(7.73)	5.28	9.37
Dividends per share ($)	1.20	1.70	1.20
Common stock price range ($) High/Low	78.8/55.5	80.9/52.5	85.8/48.8
Shares outstanding (millions)	49.40	46.09	49.27
UAL Corp. (United Airlines)			
Beta = 1.25			
Operating revenues ($millions)	$11,663	$11,038	$ 9,794
Operating expenses ($millions)	12,157	11,074	9,329
Capital expenditures ($millions)	2,122	2,576	1,568
Depreciation ($millions)	604	560	517
Long-term debt ($millions)[a]	2,423	1,238	1,321
Net worth ($millions)	1,598	1,672	1,566
Net income (loss) ($millions)	(332)	96	324
Earnings per share ($)	(14.31)	4.33	14.96
Dividends per share ($)	Nil	Nil	Nil
Common stock price range ($) High/Low 294.0/105.3	161.5/109.0	171.0/84.3	
Shares outstanding (millions)	23.76	21.89	21.83
USAir Group			
Beta = 1.65			
Operating revenues ($millions)	$ 6,514	$ 6,559	$ 6,252
Operating expenses ($millions)	6,688	7,060	6,230
Capital expenditures ($millions)	306	730	683
Depreciation ($millions)	295	287	254
Long-term debt ($millions)[a]	2,115	2,263	1,468
Net worth ($millions)	1,676	1,792	2,251
Net income (loss) ($millions)	(305)	(455)	(63)
Earnings per share ($)	(7.62)	(10.89)	(1.73)
Dividends per share ($)	Nil	0.06	0.15
Common stock price range ($) High/Low	24.5/7.0	33.8/12.6	54.8/30.6
Shares outstanding (millions)	46.60	45.50	44.20

Source: Airlines' annual reports.
[a]Includes capital lease obligations.

EXHIBIT 3.12   Average Age of Major Carrier Fleets as of December 1991

	Average Age (Years)
U.S. airline fleets	
American Airlines	9.0
Continental Airlines Holdings	14.0
Delta Air Lines	9.1
Northwest Airlines (estimate)	16.5
Trans World Airlines	18.0
United Airlines	10.8
USAir	9.0
U.S. Industry Average	12.3
Other airline fleets:	
Air Canada	12.2
Lufthansa	5.4

Source: Airlines' annual reports and Continental Airlines Holdings, Inc.

CHAPTER 4

Flagstar Companies, Inc.

In early June 1997 the management of Flagstar Companies, Inc. sent a detailed prospectus to holders of $1.5 billion of its debt securities, as well as holders of all of its preferred and common stock, in a solicitation of votes on a prepackaged plan of reorganization. Flagstar was one of the largest restaurant companies in the United States, operating—either directly or through franchisees—over 3,200 low- to moderately priced restaurants. It had lost money, however, almost every year since its leveraged buyout in 1989 by Coniston Partners, one of the most aggressive takeover firms in the United States. (Exhibit 4.1 shows selected financial data for Flagstar from 1988 through 1996.) Flagstar management was now hoping to be able to restructure the company quickly. It was apparent, however, that there might be problems in doing so: The company's various claimants—particularly the senior subordinated debt holders, the junior subordinated debt holders, and the common stockholders—had conflicting views about what the company could and should be doing and were evidently prepared to defend their positions by exercising whatever legal options they had.

INDUSTRY BACKGROUND

The U.S. restaurant industry as a whole was a mature industry. Since the early 1970s, it had grown significantly due in part to population growth, but even more to demographic and lifestyle changes, including the sharp

This case was prepared by Research Associate Jeremy Cott and Professor Stuart Gilson. Copyright © 1998 by the President and Fellows of Harvard College. Harvard Business School case 299-038.

increase in the number of two-income households, which gave people less time to prepare food at home as well as more income to pay for eating out. In 1996 American consumers spent almost 45 cents of every food dollar on meals prepared or served away from home, up from 38 cents only ten years earlier. That kind of growth, however, was not expected to continue, and, for most large companies, sales gains were expected to come largely at the expense of competitors.

The restaurant industry as a whole generated $217 billion in sales in 1996. There were about twenty publicly traded restaurants with annual, systemwide sales of over $1 billion each (including sales at both company-owned sites and franchised sites). In its annual reports, Flagstar divided the industry into three main categories:

1. The *quick service* segment was dominated by large national fast-food chains like McDonald's and Pizza Hut. The average check in this segment was $3 to $5 per person. Flagstar's own restaurants in this category were Hardee's, of which it was the largest franchisee in the country, and El Pollo Loco, a chain of Mexican-themed chicken restaurants centered in southern California.
2. The *midscale* segment—moderately priced restaurants with table service—included a much smaller number of national chains, many local and regional chains, and thousands of independent operators. The average check in this segment was $4 to $7. Flagstar's own restaurants in this category were Denny's, which was the largest chain of such restaurants in the country; Coco's and Carrows, which it had acquired in May 1996; and Quincy's, a steak house chain.
3. The *upscale* segment consisted of higher-priced restaurants, mostly small independents. Flagstar had no restaurants in this category.

Restaurant chains generally operated with negative net working capital. That was because virtually all sales were made in cash or quasi-cash (like credit cards) and inventory turned over quickly, but most supplies were purchased on credit. On the other hand, capital expenditure needs were fairly significant. For the chain restaurants, capital expenditures involved primarily the development of new sites, remodeling of existing sites, and the upgrading of computer systems.

Although the economic fortunes of high-priced restaurants were fairly closely tied to the business cycle, the low- to moderate-priced segments of the industry were not particularly cyclical because eating out in them had become such a common practice.

COMPANY HISTORY

Flagstar's business consisted of six restaurant chains or "concepts"—four in the full-service segment of the industry, two in the quick-service segment. The company said in its June 1997 prospectus that its restaurants "benefit from a single management strategy that emphasizes superior value and quality, friendly and attentive service, and appealing facilities."[1]

The company had evolved through an elaborate series of mergers and divestitures. Originally it was part of Trans World Corp., a holding company whose properties included Trans World Airlines (TWA), the Hilton hotel chain, two restaurant chains, a contract food services company, a nursing home business, and a real estate company. In the mid-1980s, in an effort to streamline its operations, it spun off TWA to its shareholders and sold the real estate company and Hilton hotels. It acquired two more restaurant chains—Denny's and El Pollo Loco—and it changed its name to TW Services. The company paid $850 million to acquire Denny's, including the assumption of $625 million in debt. (Exhibit 4.2 shows selected historical financial and operating data for Denny's.)

Leveraged Buyout

In late 1988 TW Services attracted the attention of Coniston Partners, one of the most aggressive takeover firms of the 1980s. In 1989, after a contentious, nine-month proxy fight, Coniston acquired the company for $1.7 billion, including $1.4 billion in new debt. Coniston owned 52 percent of the stock of the new company.[2] Soon afterward, the company sold its nursing home operation for $90 million ($39 million less than it had paid), as well as a few other nonrestaurant businesses.

The investment was risky, but, in the first half of 1990, it was viewed favorably by various parties. For example, an equity analyst at Kemper Se-

---

[1]Flagstar prospectus, June 5, 1997.

[2]In connection with the acquisition, the company agreed to pay an annual advisory fee of $1 million to Gollust, Tierney and Oliver (GTO), the principals of Coniston. In 1989 it also paid $35 million to GTO for "various fees and dividends" and $55 million to Donaldson, Lufkin & Jenrette (DLJ) "for assistance in the financing of the acquisition." In 1989 it also sold $150 million in senior notes to GTO and DLJ, most of which they later sold to third parties. Interest paid by the company to GTO and DLJ totaled $18 million in 1990 and $9 million in 1991.

curities said that she thought the company's stock could double in the next twelve to eighteen months, and double again by the end of 1992. An equity analyst at Salomon Brothers said that he thought the stock was worth twice its current price.[3]

In its first annual company report in early 1990, new management indicated some of its plans for Denny's restaurants. It intended to use franchising as the primary means of growing the chain, which would allow it to gain market share without significant capital investment. It also launched an accelerated remodeling program for Denny's. In 1989, it remodeled 98 restaurants, and planned to remodel another 600 during the next four years. Each remodeling, it said, cost about $160,000.[4]

Recapitalization

In every year since the buyout the company had lost money, and in late 1992 it undertook a huge recapitalization.

As part of the recapitalization, the buyout firm of Kohlberg Kravis Roberts (KKR) invested $300 million in the company, receiving 100 million new shares of common stock and warrants for another 75 million shares (exercisable after December 31, 1994, for $3.50 a share). Exhibit 4.3 summarizes changes in the ownership of Flagstar's common stock over time. KKR also gained six of the ten seats on the board of directors; also represented on the board were Donaldson, Lufkin & Jenrette (DLJ), Coniston, and Flagstar's chief executive officer (CEO). The day before KKR's investment was announced (June 25), the company's stock closed at an ask price of $3.06. Between June 1 and June 24, the closing ask price had averaged $3.26. Henry Kravis, founding partner of KKR, said: "We believe the company, which has very fine operating franchises and terrific

---

[3]*Nation's Restaurant News*, June 11, 1990; *Business Week*, May 14, 1990; *Business Week*, July 2, 1990.

[4]In 1990, 1991, and 1992 the company remodeled 142, 121, and 125 Denny's restaurants, respectively. At the end of 1992 it said that company-owned Denny's restaurants would be remodeled on a seven-year cycle, and that each remodeling would cost about $195,000. By the end of 1993 it had remodeled another 41 Denny's restaurants, and said that each remodeling would cost about $265,000. In late 1996, Donaldson, Lufkin & Jenrette stated that Denny's sites were generally older than those of competitors; 72 percent of them, it said, were built before 1980 (DLJ, "Analysis of Denny's," U.S. Bankruptcy Court for the District of South Carolina, 1997).

management, will benefit greatly from the new source of long-term equity capital we can provide."[5]

The company also changed its debt structure (Exhibit 4.4). It established a new bank credit facility with less restrictive covenants. From year-end 1991 to year-end 1992, it reduced its outstanding bank debt by $220 million, and it retired another $150 million bank loan with proceeds from a new issue of convertible preferred stock. The company also refinanced most of its public debt to take advantage of favorable market interest rates. This debt included $150 million (face value) of 14.75 percent senior unsecured notes, $520 million of 17 percent senior subordinated discount debentures, and $200 million of 15 percent senior subordinated debentures. The company also had $100 million in 10 percent junior subordinated debentures outstanding, but these were not affected by the recapitalization.

The deal was finalized in November 1992. The following year, the company changed its name to Flagstar, and it issued $275 million of additional unsecured senior notes and $125 million of senior subordinated debt. It also reduced its outstanding bank loan by another $400 million.

In connection with the recapitalization, the company also loaned $13,922,000 to its chairman and chief executive officer, Jerry Richardson. Richardson used the proceeds of this loan to repay a bank loan he had taken out in 1989 to finance the purchase of company stock. Interest on the new loan accrued at 5.6 percent a year, and was payable in full when the loan came due in November 1997.

Ongoing Management

Flagstar's CEO, Jerry Richardson, had a long association with the company. A former professional football player, Richardson had started out in business in the 1960s as a manager of restaurant franchises. He acquired a good many and eventually sold them to Trans World in 1979. In 1989, af-

---

[5]*New York Times*, June 26, 1992. Under the preliminary terms of the deal, the company agreed to reimburse KKR for any out-of-pocket expenses and to pay the firm a fee of $10 million if the recapitalization was not consummated. After the deal went through, the company paid KKR $15 million for "financial advisory services," and agreed to pay an additional $1.25 million advisory fee in 1993. The company later said that KKR had assisted Flagstar in getting the most favorable bank interest rates for the recapitalization ("Debtors' Response to Objections . . . ," U.S. Bankruptcy Court for the District of South Carolina, November 3, 1997).

ter Coniston Partners bought the company, he was named its president and chief executive. After KKR took control in 1992, he also became chairman.

Even with the infusion of cash from KKR, the company still owed $2.4 billion in debt. Richardson said at the time: "I wake up knowing we have to earn $900,000 every day just to pay the interest." He demonstrated how the debt feels to him by standing over a companion seated in a chair and pressing hard on the man's shoulders until the man squirmed.[6]

Charges of Discrimination   Soon after the recapitalization, Richardson was faced with a number of incidents involving allegations of racial discrimination at Denny's restaurants. Media accounts of one such incident in northern California came to Richardson's attention in January 1992. Affidavits were later filed by many people—customers and employees, blacks and whites—that racial discrimination had been fairly common practice at Denny's restaurants for years.

In October 1992, the U.S. Justice Department informed Denny's that it was planning to file a lawsuit against the company alleging discriminatory practices in restaurants in northern California. Richardson publicly insisted that the alleged incidents were isolated incidents, and the company formed a crisis team to deal with the issue. In March 1993, the company announced a consent agreement with the Justice Department, which required it to implement various changes in policy and employee training to prevent discrimination in the future. A week later, six black Secret Service officers, in full uniform, responsible for guarding the president of the United States, were refused service in a Denny's restaurant in Maryland—even as their white counterparts nearby were served. Eventually thousands of people joined two class-action lawsuits against the company. In August 1994, without publicly acknowledging any guilt, the company settled the suits, agreeing to pay $54 million in damages. It was said to be the largest case ever filed in the history of the public accommodations section of the 1964 Civil Rights Act.

Flagstar's financial difficulties, however, continued. From 1992 to 1993, average customer traffic in Denny's restaurants declined over 4 percent. The largest franchisee of Denny's restaurants—a company named DenAmerica—reported that it "experienced a decline in traffic and restaurant sales in certain of its Denny's restaurants as a result of the negative publicity that arose in 1993 relating to claims of alleged racial discrimination against customers in certain Denny's, Inc. restaurants."

---

[6]*New York Times*, November 6, 1994.

Shortfalls and Write-Downs   Beginning in 1993 the company indicated that its revenues and earnings were falling short of the levels projected at the time of the 1989 acquisition. It attributed the shortfall to "increased competition, intensive pressure on pricing due to discounting, declining customer traffic, [and] adverse economic conditions."[7] In the fourth quarter of 1993, the company wrote off $1,475 million of goodwill and recorded a restructuring charge of $192 million. Most of the restructuring charge reflected the write-down of assets in 240 of the company's restaurants. In 1995 the company announced further asset write-downs and a restructuring charge of $67 million.

New CEO

In January 1995 Jerry Richardson resigned as CEO of the company and was replaced by James Adamson, who had experience in both the restaurant and retail industries. (He was previously CEO of Burger King.) Richardson had, in 1993, entered the competition to win a National Football League franchise; he had been awarded the franchise and now said he needed to give more time to it.[8]

In his first meeting with employees after he became CEO, Adamson told employees that he was "going to do everything possible to provide better jobs for women and minorities. And I will fire you if you discriminate." Adamson replaced a lot of the senior executives. One of the new executives was African-American; another was Hispanic. A new director of purchasing began buying from minority vendors.

He also continued a process that Richardson had begun in 1994 to sell off nonrestaurant businesses. In the first half of 1994, Flagstar sold its institutional food contract and vending business for $447 million, recognizing a gain of $399 million, net of tax. Then, in 1995, it sold a stadium concessions business and a food distribution business. In 1996 it sold two food processing operations.

---

[7]For example, 10-Ks for 1993, 1994, and 1995.

[8]Two years later, in January 1997, the company said it "settled its . . . loan receivable from" Richardson that was "previously scheduled to mature in November 1997. The company received net proceeds of $8.2 million and recorded a net charge of approximately $3.5 million" (1996 10-K). The company had been showing this loan receivable as a specific item on its balance sheet. The amount shown was $14.0 million at year-end 1992, $14.8 million at year-end 1993, $15.7 million at year-end 1994, and $16.5 million at year-end 1995.

In May 1996 the company acquired, for $313 million, two restaurant chains, named Coco's and Carrows, consisting of about 350 company-owned units in the United States and about 280 franchised units overseas. The company made the acquisition, it said, in order to increase the synergies among its restaurant chains. The domestic sites for Coco's and Carrows were primarily in California, where many of the Denny's restaurants were also located, and they occupied roughly the same segment of the restaurant industry as Denny's.[9] The acquisition cost of $313 million was financed by existing cash balances, new borrowing, and the assumption of debt. Under the terms of the acquisition debt, cash flows from Coco's and Carrows could only be used to service that debt.

PREPACKAGING A CHAPTER 11

In early December 1996 Flagstar began discussions with the investment banking firm Donaldson, Lufkin & Jenrette about possible restructurings, and DLJ submitted an initial restructuring proposal to Flagstar on December 23. It involved pursuing a prepackaged Chapter 11 bankruptcy reorganization.

In a prepackaged Chapter 11, or "prepack," the firm simultaneously files for bankruptcy *and* files a reorganization plan with the court. The requirements for voting on and confirming a prepack Chapter 11 plan are largely the same as in regular Chapter 11 (see the Appendix in Chapter 6). The key difference is that the firm negotiates with creditors and solicits their votes in advance of filing for bankruptcy.[10] In principle, a prepack can be completed in one to two months; regular Chapter 11 cases can last several years.

---

[9]The investment banker representing the seller of Coco's and Carrows in the deal was DLJ, while KKR served as Flagstar's investment banker. KKR was paid about $4 million for its work on this deal.

[10]The Bankruptcy Code allows firms to make prebankruptcy solicitations to creditors as long as they provide creditors with as much information as they would be entitled to under relevant nonbankruptcy law. So, for example, prebankruptcy disclosures to holders of publicly traded bonds must comply with federal and state securities laws, including the Securities Act of 1933 and the Securities Exchange Act of 1934. If no comparable nonbankruptcy laws exist, the firm must meet the minimum acceptable level of disclosure set by bankruptcy law (i.e., as if it were operating inside Chapter 11). What constitutes minimum acceptable disclosure inside Chapter 11 is not precisely specified in the Code, however, and is determined by case law.

Flagstar and DLJ decided to approach an ad hoc committee of senior subordinated debt holders first because they saw that the "enterprise value" of the company ran out at that class, and it would probably have to be allocated most of the new common equity. ("Enterprise value" means the estimated market value of equity plus debt, minus cash and cash equivalents on hand.)

The company's first proposal to the senior subs (holders of senior subordinated debentures) in late February 1997 had them getting 85 percent of the new common stock and the existing common stockholders getting 5 percent, along with warrants. The remaining 10 percent of the new common stock was to be divided between the junior subs and the preferred stockholders. The senior subs strongly rejected this proposal, and negotiations continued. On March 17, the company announced the principal terms of a plan of reorganization, and a few days later the ad hoc committee of senior sub debt holders formally agreed to vote in favor of it. On March 24 Flagstar filed the plan with the Securities and Exchange Commission (SEC) for its review and approval. Finally, on June 5, it issued a formal prospectus and solicitation of votes on the plan to its creditors and shareholders. In the prospectus the company set a voting deadline of July 7, and indicated that it would file for Chapter 11 a few weeks later. It anticipated exiting from Chapter 11 after only forty-five to sixty days.

"The company's position," as a senior managing director of DLJ later said, "was that they wanted a consensual Plan of Reorganization because they [believed] that was the best way to preserve value and minimize the damage to the corporation, which would accrue to the benefit of all of its constituencies."[11] In April 1997, however, a representative for holders of about 44 percent of the 10 percent junior subordinated bonds informed the company that they would vote against the plan.

Exhibit 4.5 summarizes the proposed treatment of Flagstar's claimholders under the plan. Several classes of Flagstar's debt would be "unimpaired"—bank and other secured debt, priority administrative claims, and trade claims. Their vote, therefore, was not even being solicited. The only classes whose vote was being solicited, because their claims *were* deemed to be impaired, were the senior notes, the senior sub debt, the junior sub debt, the preferred stock, and the common stock.

The ballot sent to senior sub debt holders also asked them to approve a formal amendment to their security's indenture that would grant

---

[11]Testimony of senior managing director of DLJ, bankruptcy court proceedings, September 25, 1997.

the proposed consideration to the preferred and common stockholders even if the junior sub debt holders voted against the plan. This proposed amendment had nothing to do with bankruptcy law. It would be a voluntary concession by the senior sub debt holders to the company's equity holders.

The company also said that if it did not receive sufficient acceptances of the plan in the vote, it would consider other options, including filing for Chapter 11 without a preapproved plan of reorganization. The company reserved the right, in any case, to have the plan "crammed down" on dissenting classes of claims (see Appendix in Chapter 6). The company stated that in the event of a cram-down, the junior subs would receive *less* value than they were being offered in the present plan.

The prospectus described certain risk factors with the proposed plan. Among them was the extremely competitive nature of the restaurant industry. Exhibit 4.6 shows recent financial data for seventeen companies that DLJ believed offered "products and service that are comparable to or competitive with the Company's various operating concepts."

THE "BEST INTERESTS" AND "FEASIBILITY" TESTS

The "best interests" test of bankruptcy law (Section 1129) requires that, in a Chapter 11 reorganization, all holders of impaired claims receive property with a value no less than what they would receive if the company were liquidated. So, in its June 5 prospectus, Flagstar also provided a liquidation analysis (summarized in Exhibit 4.7).

The analysis assumed that the individual restaurant chains would, with one limited exception, be sold separately as going concerns. The "going concern" values of the individual businesses were estimated by applying cash flow multiples to the cash flow—defined as earnings before interest, taxes, depreciation, and amortization (EBITDA)—that each of the operations was expected to achieve in fiscal year 1997. The cash flow multiples were derived from multiples of publicly traded companies in each of the relevant restaurant industry segments as well as from recent acquisitions in the restaurant industry.

For a Chapter 11 reorganization plan to be confirmed by the judge, it is also necessary to show that the firm will be able to repay its debts as they come due after the reorganization (i.e., that the plan is "feasible"). Thus the description of a Chapter 11 reorganization plan given to creditors generally includes a set of pro forma financial projections. Exhibit 4.8 summarizes the financial projections that Flagstar included in its June 5 prospectus.

ESTIMATING FLAGSTAR'S ENTERPRISE VALUE

Estimating the enterprise value of the reorganized company was critical because it would determine how much the company's various claimants would recover. In fact, Flagstar's valuation as a reorganized entity became an extremely contentious issue, and specific details of it became the subject of heated questioning in bankruptcy court proceedings in the summer of 1997.

Both Flagstar and the junior sub debt holders had outside financial advisors do formal valuations of company. Flagstar had this work done by Donaldson, Lufkin & Jenrette. The junior creditors had this work done by Jefferies & Co.

DLJ's Valuation on Behalf of the Company

DLJ based its valuation primarily on a "comparable companies" analysis. It did not use a discounted cash flow analysis as a formal valuation technique because of what it saw as the significant uncertainty of Flagstar's future cash flows. DLJ believed this would be particularly problematic for cash flows several years out, which would serve as the basis for a terminal or exit value. "Comparable companies" analysis was better, it said, because it incorporated current market assessment of similar companies, including their future prospects.

Exhibit 4.9 provides a summary of DLJ's valuation of Flagstar. Exhibit 4.10 shows the comparable companies that DLJ used in valuing each of Flagstar's businesses. DLJ claimed that Flagstar's total enterprise value was between $1,626 million and $1,770 million. It used the midpoint of this range, $1,698 million, as a point of reference—of which $1,319 million would consist of debt and $379 million of which would be the residual value attributable to shareholders' equity.

All of the pro forma financial statements in Flagstar's prospectus were based on the valuation work that DLJ had done. Exhibit 4.11 shows historical and pro forma balance sheets for Flagstar, reported in the June 1997 prospectus. In accordance with generally accepted accounting principles, the pro forma balance sheet was prepared using "fresh-start accounting" (Exhibit 4.12).

Flagstar's lawyers asserted that "substantial other evidence" corroborated the validity of DLJ's valuation.[12] First, they noted that "the DLJ valu-

---

[12]"Debtors' Response to Objections to the Debtors' Joint Plan of Reorganization and Disclosure Statement," U.S. Bankruptcy Court for the District of South Carolina, November 3, 1997.

ation was verified with the merger and acquisition comparables method." DLJ assembled data on recent mergers and acquisitions in the restaurant industry (Exhibit 4.13). Second, the lawyers noted that "independent financial analysts reached the same conclusions regarding valuation as DLJ." These other valuations were contained in recent analyst reports on Flagstar by Lazard Freres, Dillon Read, and J.P. Morgan.

Lazard Freres's Report The Lazard Freres report, dated March 19, stated that its valuation of Flagstar was "based on comparable companies," and that "the appropriate multiple of consolidated EBITDA for Flagstar is 5.6× 1997 EBITDA, roughly in the same area as well-diversified restaurant companies such as Darden, Shoney's, and Brinker." Lazard Freres and DLJ both regarded Shoney's as the best comparable to Denny's.

Dillon Read's Report In a report dated March 13, Dillon Read estimated Flagstar's value based on an analysis of 11 comparable companies. In Dillon Read's analysis, the average multiple of enterprise value to EBITDA for companies comparable to Flagstar was 7.9 (based on latest 12-month EBITDA figures). It said: "We believe that Flagstar should be valued at the lower end of the range and believe that multiples of 5.5 to 6.0 are appropriate." Dillon Read also considered Shoney's a close comparable to Flagstar. Exhibit 4.14 details how DLJ, Lazard Freres, and Dillon Read calculated the enterprise value/EBITDA multiple for Shoney's.

J.P. Morgan's Report J.P. Morgan's report on Flagstar was dated May 14, and proposed valuation multiples of 5.5 to 6.0 times estimated 1997 EBITDA. The bank did not indicate how it arrived at these multiples, however.

Jefferies' Valuation on Behalf of the Junior Creditors

Jefferies based its valuation primarily on a discounted cash flow analysis (summarized in Exhibit 4.15). Jefferies' analysis incorporated some key aspects of the company's financial projections (summarized in Exhibit 4.8), such as projected EBITDA for the restaurant divisions, and total revenues. Jefferies' projections differed from the company's in certain other ways, however.

Jefferies claimed that Flagstar's total enterprise value was $2,317 million. It disagreed with DLJ's approach to valuing Flagstar, arguing that using estimated 1997 operating results as the primary basis for valuing the company was unsound because all the restructuring work going on was a distraction to people in the company and would therefore make operating results lower than they would normally be.

DLJ disagreed. Responding to Jefferies' argument in court, a senior managing director of DLJ testified that, first of all, he had "normalized" estimated results for 1997 by excluding one-time costs related to the restructuring. Moreover, he said:

> *I don't think the use of [a different year's earnings] would make a material difference [to the valuation]. If you use a future year, you'd have to discount to the present, which I think would offset any perceived improvement in earnings. I also ... don't believe the company has been materially adversely affected by the restructuring process. ... [For example,] people are still going to Denny's and buying breakfast. They don't even know what Flagstar is.*[13]

Jefferies estimated Flagstar's terminal value in 2001 (the last year of the projections) using a comparable companies analysis, similar to the approach DLJ used to value the entire company. Exhibit 4.16 lists the companies that Jefferies treated as "comparable" to Flagstar's Denny's and Coco's/Carrows restaurant chains. Three of the companies that Jefferies considered comparable to Denny's were excluded altogether from DLJ's analysis: DenAmerica, Apple South, and Applebee's.

Exhibit 4.17 shows historical betas and other relevant financial information for Flagstar, the S&P 500, and all 14 companies that both Jefferies and DLJ treated as comparable to one or more of Flagstar's businesses.

Possible Vulture Investing in Debt

Valuation was also an important issue to investors who had been acquiring portions of the company's debt in the public market. These "vulture" investors could profit by buying the claims for less than their ultimate recovery or by using their ownership stake to influence the outcome of the case. Exhibit 4.18 shows the market prices, yields to maturity, and ratings of Flagstar's five unsecured, publicly traded debt issues from early 1995 through the first half of 1997.

Dillon Read's March 13, 1997, report on Flagstar provided a sensitivity analysis of the value of Flagstar's public debt securities. Using a "conservative" valuation, it concluded that the secured debt and the senior unsecured notes would most likely be completely covered in the restructuring. It also did an analysis of possible returns from purchase of the senior

---

[13]Testimony of senior managing director of DLJ, September 25, 1997.

subordinated debt. The present value of the estimated recoveries would depend on when the new securities were actually distributed and on the appropriate discount rate. Dillon Read therefore put together a grid that summarized a range of possible recoveries for the senior subordinated debt (Exhibit 4.19).

OTHER OBJECTIONS OF THE JUNIOR CREDITORS

Holders of Flagstar's junior subordinated debentures strongly objected to other provisions of the company's plan, in addition to the proposed claimholder recoveries and enterprise valuation.

Subordination

One especially contentious issue concerned the priority status of the junior subordinated debentures—specifically, whether they were really subordinate to the "senior subordinated" debentures. The junior debt holders argued that they were not subordinate; the senior debt holders and the company argued that they were. A hundred million dollars—the face value of the junior debt—was potentially at stake.

The junior subordinated debentures had been issued in 1989. The indenture for the bonds specified that this new junior debt was subordinate to all "senior indebtedness," defined as:

(i) *the existing bank debt or any refinancing of it; the existing 14.75% senior notes, due 1998, with a principal amount of $150 million, or any refinancing of them not to exceed $150 million,*

(ii) *any interest rate protection agreements (e.g., interest rate "swaps"),*

(iii) *the existing 17% senior subordinated discount debentures, due 2001, with a principal amount of $722 million and*

(iv) *the existing 15% senior subordinated debentures, due 2001, with a principal amount of $200 million.*

In the company's 1992 recapitalization, the 17 percent senior subordinated discount debentures and the 15 percent senior subordinated debentures were refinanced with new public debt carrying interest rates of approximately 11.5 percent. The junior subordinated debt was left alone. At the time, however, the company realized that the original indenture was unclear as to whether the junior debt was subordinate to any debt that might *replace* the 17 percent and 15 percent senior subordinated debentures.

The company therefore decided to issue a "supplemental indenture" for the junior sub debt that would modify some of the original indenture wording. Section 9.01 of the indenture authorized the company and the bondholders' trustee to "amend [the] Indenture, . . . without the consent of [the] Holder, [in order] to cure any ambiguity, defect, or inconsistency" so long as that "does not adversely affect the legal rights . . . of any Holder."

The supplemental indenture, executed on August 7, 1992, expanded the definition of senior indebtedness to include the following clause:

> (v) all other Indebtedness created, incurred, assumed or guaranteed by the Company after the date of this Indenture which is expressly stated to be senior in right of payment to, and is not expressly subordinated to, or pari passu with, the Securities.

During the summer of 1996, the junior sub debt holders argued that the supplemental indenture was invalid. The company countered that it had fully complied with Section 9.01. It noted that on August 10, 1992—several months before the recapitalization became effective—Flagstar's lawyers had issued an "opinion" that the supplemental indenture was legally valid.

The company also noted that the indenture obligated it to offer to repurchase the bonds at 101 percent of face value, plus accrued interest, in the event there was a "change of control." The indenture also gave the company the option to redeem the bonds (also at a premium to face value) if there was a change of control at any time prior to November 1, 1992.[14] KKR's agreement to invest in the company was signed on August 11, 1992, and on November 16, at a special meeting, KKR representatives obtained a majority of seats on Flagstar's board. On February 19, 1993, the company sent the junior sub debt holders a formal "Notice of Change of Control Offer." Fully 99 percent of the junior sub debt holders declined the company's offer, however. In the 1997 court proceedings, the company argued that junior sub debt holders' willingness to hold onto their bonds was evidence they had not been harmed by the indenture amendment.

---

[14]The provision stated that "[if] a Change of Control occurs, the Company may redeem all or any portion of the Securities, at the redemption prices (expressed in percentage of principal amount) set forth below plus accrued interest to the redemption date if redeemed during the 12-month period beginning November 1 of the years indicated below:"

Year	Percentage
1989	110.000%
1990	109.167%
1991	108.333%

At the end of January and February 1993, the junior bonds had traded at 105 percent and 106.25 percent of face value.

Executive Compensation

Junior creditors also objected to senior management's compensation, which they regarded as excessive. They noted that "in 1997, the year the company commenced this bankruptcy proceeding, wage increases for eight members of the management committee averaged over 14%, with certain members receiving pay increases of up to 24%."

They also noted that the company had paid CEO Adamson a retention bonus of $1.5 million in January 1997 and agreed to pay him retention bonuses of $2 million and $3 million in January 1998 and January 1999, respectively, provided he was still employed by the company on those dates, or if, prior to those dates, he was terminated without "cause." In aggregate, about $18 million in retention bonuses was to be paid to 56 company managers in 1997 through 1999. The bonuses were not related to the company's operating performance.

Finally, the junior creditors objected to certain "change of control" rights that the company had awarded Adamson and nine other senior managers. If a "change of control" occurred during the next few years, Adamson and the other managers could resign from the company, and they would be paid a lump sum amounting to roughly three times their base salary.[15]

The junior creditors argued that management's proposed compensation violated bankruptcy law (e.g., section 1129(a)(4)), which requires that any payments made by the debtor for expenses in the case be "reasonable." Citing court rulings in other cases, the junior creditors argued that

> . . . *in bankruptcy cases . . . monies paid to corporate officers in the operation of a debtor's business . . . are not purely private agreements— each dollar correspondingly depletes the fund available to creditors, and excessive expenses could jeopardize the debtor's rehabilitation.*

---

[15]A short time before the June 1997 prospectus was issued, the company reached an agreement in principle with the ad hoc committee of senior sub debt holders regarding certain modifications to senior management's compensation contract. When the company emerged from bankruptcy, 10 percent of its common stock would be reserved for a new management stock option plan. In addition, CEO Adamson would be given $3.75 million worth of its common stock (to be purchased by the company on the open market).

The junior creditors argued that Flagstar's operating performance hadn't improved since Adamson and other senior managers had come on board in 1995, and that their high compensation was therefore undeserved, and smacked of "fraudulent" or "preferential" transfers.

Flagstar's lawyers disputed these arguments. They argued that the company was in a bad situation, Adamson and the other managers were well regarded, and the company simply couldn't afford to lose them. In court testimony, one of the KKR partners conceded that the company's operating cash flow (or EBITDA) hadn't increased since Adamson came on board, but that, he said, was largely due to problems with its Hardee's restaurants, of which Flagstar was only a franchisee.

Legal Releases

Another provision of the plan that junior creditors found highly objectionable was the granting of broad legal "releases" to officers, directors, shareholders, attorneys, members of the ad hoc creditors committees, bond indenture trustees, and other parties in interest. The only actions not covered by these releases were those based on willful misconduct or gross negligence.

Flagstar's lawyers argued that these releases were an essential part of the plan. Since Flagstar fully indemnified its management, any suit brought against managers, they argued, would in effect be a suit against the company, and that could cost it a lot of time and money ("deplete its assets").

The junior creditors' lawyers countered that Flagstar did not have the legal right to grant such releases. They cited a district court ruling that prohibiting suits against "nondebtor third parties" would allow those parties "to use the Bankruptcy Court and its power as a shield [against their] legal obligations, a purpose never intended by the Code or Congress."[16] For example, the juniors claimed that, since 1992, Flagstar had been technically insolvent and that therefore "the Board breached a fiduciary duty to creditors by approving certain transactions and acquisitions" (e.g., the acquisition of Coco's/Carrows in 1996). The juniors also argued that there had probably been fraudulent transfers to KKR (e.g., the $15 million fee paid to KKR in the 1992 recapitalization).

Flagstar's lawyers countered that the board relied in good faith on the records of the corporation and that there were other indicators of its solvency as well (e.g., the "positive trading value of the [common] stock" and the "high trading value of the debt"). They also argued that the fees paid

---

[16] "Official Committee's Objection . . . ," September 25, 1997.

to KKR were all "standard rates," and that KKR's $300 million equity investment "could have just as easily been structured as a $285 million financing without the advisory fees."[17]

THE COMPANY'S OPTIONS

Disagreements among Flagstar and its junior creditors would have to be addressed somehow before a consensual reorganization would be possible. If a compromise could not be reached, the company's attempt to negotiate a prepackaged bankruptcy could unravel, resulting, as the company put it, in "a nonprepackaged Chapter 11 [that] would likely be lengthier, involve more contested issues with creditors and other parties in interest, and result in significantly increased Chapter 11 expenses."[18] Another possibility was a Chapter 11 cram-down on junior creditors. As Flagstar's lawyers viewed things, the junior creditors' objections were "the gripes of litigious malcontents seeking leverage."[19]

---

[17]"Debtor's Response to Objections . . . ," November 3, 1997, Exhibit 1.
[18]Flagstar prospectus, June 5, 1997.
[19]"Debtor's Response to Objections . . . ," November 3, 1997.

EXHIBIT 4.1 Flagstar: Selected Financial Data ($000)

	"Predecessor Company"		"Successor Company"						
	1988	1989	1990	1991	1992	1993	1994	1995	1996
Assets	$2,040	$3,632	$3,496	$3,385	$3,396	$1,797	$1,587	$1,508	$1,687
Liabilities	1,539	3,425	3,356	3,308	3,101	3,220	2,650	2,639	2,915
Debt	1,047	2,440	2,414	2,421	2,290	2,394	2,099	2,035	2,242
Shareholders' equity	502	208	139	77	295	(1,423)	(1,063)	(1,131)	(1,228)
Operating revenues	3,313	3,485	3,627	3,618	3,720	3,970	2,666	2,571	2,542
Operating income (EBIT)[a]	240	233	238	224	246	(1,461)	211	98	156
Depreciation and amortization expense	134	166	210	218	227	247	130	133	130
Interest expense	109	177	314	309	304	266	233	233	262
Income from continuing operatings, after tax	51	(56)	(68)	(68)	(52)	(1,648)	(17)	(133)	(85)
Purchase of property	(145)	(156)	(136)	(109)	(139)	(165)	(154)	(124)	(55)
Proceeds from disposition of property	40	18	53	9	11	36	20	26	14
Acquisition of business	0	(1,291)	0	0	(16)	(33)	0	0	(127)
Proceeds from sale of business	0	0	0	0	0	0	447	295	63
Common stock price[b]									
High			29.69	22.19	21.88	20.63	12.50	7.88	4.81
Low			12.81	10.94	13.75	8.75	5.75	3.00	1.06
Average			18.67	15.57	17.98	13.43	9.11	5.36	2.89

[a]"Operating income" includes the following unusual charges: $25 million in 1988 for write-downs and special legal fees; $100 million in 1989 for merger-related costs; $1,475 and $192 million in 1993 for write-off of goodwill and restructuring charges, respectively; and $67 million in 1995 for restructuring charges.

[b]Stock prices are adjusted for 1-for-5 reverse split in June 1993. When the Coniston-led takeover took effect in December 1989, the stock began trading at 21.25.

Source: Company 10-Ks; Bloomberg.

EXHIBIT 4.2 Denny's: Selected Financial and Operating Data

	1988	1989	1990	1991	1992	1993	1994	1995	1996
Owned restaurants									
Number	1,001	1,001	992	996	1,013	1,024	978	933	894
% of total	81%	79%	77%	75%	73%	71%	66%	61%	57%
Average annual unit sales ($ thousands)	$1,090	$1,117	$1,209	$1,232	$1,231	$1,233	$1,248	$1,283	$1,313
Franchised restaurants									
Number	233	273	302	326	378	427	512	596	677
% of total	19%	21%	23%	25%	27%	29%	34%	39%	43%
Average annual unit sales ($ thousands)	$ 834	$ 865	$ 949	$1,040	$1,065	$1,057	$1,060	$1,086	$1,090
Total revenues ($ millions)	$1,216	$1,284	$1,407	$1,429	$1,449	$1,546	$1,548	$1,491	$1,257
EBITDA ($ millions)	$ 142	$ 155	$ 186	$ 203	$ 212	($ 537)	$ 191	$ 167	$ 165
EBITDA as percent of sales (excluding unusual items)	11.7%	12.1%	13.2%	14.2%	14.6%	11.6%	12.3%	13.1%	13.1%

Notes:
- Revenue and EBITDA figures include, through part of 1995, a food distribution operation, which was then sold. Revenue and EBITDA figures include, through part of 1996, a food processing operation, which was then sold.
- EBITDA figures exclude corporate expenses.
- EBITDA figure for 1993 includes write-offs and restructuring charges of $716 million. EBITDA figure for 1995 includes write-offs and restructuring charges of $29 million.

Source: Company 10-Ks.

EXHIBIT 4.3   Largest Owners of Common Stock (Percentages of Total Shares Outstanding)

	As of March						
	1990	1991	1992	1993	1994	1995	1996
KKR Associates	—	—	—	47.2%	47.2%	60.9%[a]	60.9%[a]
Gollust, Tierney and Oliver (principals of Coniston Partners)	52.1%	52.1%	50.3%	26.6%	26.6%	11.4%	5.2%
Donaldson, Lufkin & Jenrette	15.3%	15.3%	14.6%	7.2%	7.2%	7.2%	5.2%
Jerome Richardson	3.7%	3.7%	3.9%	1.9%	2.2%	2.5%	2.8%
Kemper Financial Services	—	5.7%	—	—	—	—	—
Ryback Management	—	—	—	—	—	—	5.3%
TCW Management Company	—	—	—	5.1%	—	—	—

[a]Percentage figures for KKR for 1995 and 1996 include the significant number of warrants that KKR acquired as part of the 1992 recepitalization. Flagstar's proxy statement for 1995 included them for the first time in its calculation of KKR's equity ownership, evidently because the warrants became exercisable on March 31, 1995.
Source: Company 10-Ks and proxy statements.

EXHIBIT 4.4 Change in Outstanding Debt as a Result of KKR Recapitalization ($millions)

	As of December 31		
	1991	**1992**	**1993**
Bank loans			
Working capital facility			$ 93
Term loan (variable interest rate; 7.1%, 6.4%, and 5.9% @ year-end 1991, 1992, 1993)	$ 792	$ 573	171
Term loan (variable interest rate; 8.6% @ 12/31/91)	150	—	—
Note payable to holding company (for proceeds from new issue of preferred stock), 9%[a]	—	150	150
Notes and debentures			
14.75% senior notes, due 1998	150	—	—
10.875% senior notes, due 2002	—	300	300
10.75% senior notes, due 2001	—	—	275
17% senior sub discount debentures (net of discount of $263 and $200 at 12/31/91 and 11/1/92, respectively); pays cash interest @ 17% beginning 11/1/94), due 2001	449	—	—
15% sub debentures, due 2001	200	—	—
11.25% senior sub debentures, due 2004	—	722	722
11.375% senior sub debentures, due 2003	—	—	125
10% convertible junior sub debentures, due 2014	100	100	99
Mortgage notes (secured)			
10.25% bonds, due 2000	222	211	209
11.03% notes, due 2000	160	160	160
10.51% note, due 1993	12	11	—
Other notes, with varying maturities	28	28	25
Capital lease obligations	122	141	191
Other (mostly secured)	1	5	23
Totals	$2,386	$2,401	$2,543
Less current maturities	(125)	(72)	(42)
	$2,261	$2,329	$2,501

[a]This security was first listed as debt to the holding company but then restated as preferred stock.
Source: Company 10-Ks.

EXHIBIT 4.5 Summary of Proposed Recoveries in Plan of Reorganization

Class	Description	Face Value of Debt on 4/2/97 ($millions)	Proposed Recovery	Percentage of New Security to Be Received
1	Bank claims	$ 46	Unimpaired; will be paid in full; therefore deemed to accept the plan	
2	Other secured claims	685	Unimpaired; will be paid in full; therefore deemed to accept the plan	
3	Priority ("administrative") claims		Unimpaired; will be paid in full; therefore deemed to accept the plan	
4	Senior unsecured claims (old senior notes) 10.875% senior notes due 2002 10.75% senior notes due 2001	280 } 270	Impaired; will get 100% recovery in the form of the following new security: 11.25% senior notes due 2007	100.00%
5	Senior subordinated claims 11.25% senior subordinated debentures due 2004 11.375% senior subordinated debentures due 2003	722 } 125	Impaired; will get approximately 43% recovery in the form of new common stock	95.50%
6	Junior subordinated claims 10.0% junior subordinated debentures dues 2014	100	Impaired; will get approximately 12% recovery in the form of new common stock	3.25%
7	General unsecured claims (e.g., trade creditors, rejected executory contracts)		Unimpaired; will be paid in full; therefore deemed to accept the plan	
8	Preferred stock		Impaired; will get approximately 3% recovery in the form of new common stock	1.25%
9	Common stock		Impaired; will receive warrants to purchase new common stock representing 7% of the common stock on a fully diluted basis; exercisable for five years @ $21.19	100.00%
	Total	$2,228		

Source: Company prospectus, June 5, 1997.

EXHIBIT 4.6   Financial Data for Comparable Companies

	Latest 12 Months ($millions)			Three-Year Average, as Percent of Sales		
	Revenues	EBITDA	Interest Expense	EBIT	EBITDA	Capex
Shoney's	$1,100	$126	$38	8.3%	12.3%	6.5%
Perkins Family Restaurants	251	32	5	7.7	13.3	10.0
International House of Pancakes	190	51	12	21.8	25.8	25.6
Bob Evans Farms	812	83	—	10.3	13.7	9.9
Cracker Barrel Old Country Store	981	151	—	13.1	16.4	15.3
CKE Restaurants	614	69	10	5.0	9.7	7.6
DavCo Restaurants	210	23	4	7.9	12.0	7.3
Foodmaker	1,062	107	46	4.2	7.8	4.8
Rally's Hamburgers	163	14	9	0.2	7.1	4.7
Ryan's Steak House	565	70	3	10.8	15.1	14.9
Piccadilly Cafeterias	301	28	4	5.0	9.1	6.3
Buffets	751	129	4	7.3	12.3	16.3
Luby's	464	81	2	14.4	18.1	7.9
Pollo Tropical	64	6	1	7.5	10.6	23.0
Taco Cabana	132	13	1	5.3	11.8	16.2
Vicorp Restaurants	343	28	4	1.2	7.4	4.3
Brinker International	1,182	161	5	9.8	15.4	15.8
Mean	$ 540	$ 69	$10	8.2%	12.8%	11.6%

Notes:
• The above companies represent all seventeen publicly traded, predominantly restaurant companies that DLJ analyzed for comparative purposes.
• EBIT and EBITDA figures exclude unusual items.
• Dashes mean that the relevant figure is less than $1 million.
• None of the above companies had any material amount of preferred stock outstanding.
• Latest twelve months data are through late 1996 or early 1997.

Sources: Donaldson, Lufkin & Jenrette, "Valuation Analysis," February 19, 1997, later submitted to U.S. Bankruptcy Court; company 10-Ks; some modifications and calculations by casewriter.

EXHIBIT 4.7A   Liquidation Analysis (Estimate as of October 1, 1997) ($000)

	Book Value	Estimated Percentage Recovery	Estimated Liquidation Value
Corporate assets			
Cash and cash equivalents			
Other current assets	$ 1,148	100.0%	$ 1,148
Equipment	6,357	25.0%	1,590
Other assets[a]	32,500	0.0%	
Total corporate assets	$ 40,005	6.8%	$ 2,738
Restaurant operations and real property			
Restaurant current assets	$ 110,236		
Property	1,119,522		
Goodwill and other intangible assets	226,866		
Other restaurant assets	56,308		
Total restaurant operations	$1,512,932	91.4%	$1,382,843
Other real property interest[b]	34,550	37.9%	13,100
Total restaurant operations and real property	$1,547,482	90.2%	$1,395,943
Total assets	$1,587,487	88.1%	$1,398,681

[a]The assets of the corporate parent consist of cash, equipment, and other assets. "Other assets" consist of deferred financing costs and receivables from subsidiaries, which would not be realized in the event of liquidation.

[b]"Other real property" consists of corporate headquarters and other miscellaneous real estate.

Source: Flagstar prospectus, June 5, 1997.

EXHIBIT 4.7B Liquidation Analysis: Application of Proceeds to Claims and Interests (Estimated as of October 1, 1997) ($000)

	Estimated Amount of Claims	Proceeds Available to Satisfy Claims	Liquidation Percentage
Total estimated liquidation proceeds available for distribution		$1,398,681	
Less: FRD indebtedness[a]		(237,999)	
Net estimated liquidation proceeds available for distribution		$1,160,682	
Secured debt			
Revolver debt	$ 9,200	($ 9,200)	100.0%
Mortgage notes	368,305	(368,305)	100.0%
Capital lease obligations	148,000	(148,000)	100.0%
Available to pay bankruptcy expenses and unsecured claims		$ 635,177	
Bankruptcy expenses and tax liabilities			
Chapter 7 expenses (trustee's and other professional fees, operating costs)	$ 46,055	($ 46,055)	100.0%
Chapter 11 expenses	5,000	(5,000)	100.0%
Tax liabilities[b]	10,000	(10,000)	100.0%
Available to pay unsecured claims		$ 574,122	
Unsecured claims			
Old senior notes and trade payables	$ 750,025	($ 574,122)	76.5%
Senior subordinated debentures	847,411		0%
Junior subordinated debentures	99,259		0%
Interests			
Old preferred stock			0%
Old common stock			0%
Old warrants			0%
Total claims	$2,283,255		

[a]"FRD" is the name of the acquisition subsidiary that Flagstar established specifically to acquire two restaurant chains, Coco's and Carrows, in May 1996. Legally, the first use of any cash flows generated by that subsidiary had to be to service the debt issued to make that acquisition.

[b]Based on the estimated liquidation proceeds and existing NOLs, the liquidation would not result in any income tax liabilities. Management estimated, however, that there would be about $10 million in other tax liabilities having to do with nonincome items and other tax assessments.

EXHIBIT 4.8 Flagstar's Financial Projections: Summary ($millions)

	Projected Three Months Ended 12/31/97	Projected Fiscal Year Ended December			
		1998	1999	2000	2001
Operating revenues	$685	$2,768	$2,816	$2,876	$2,946
Operating expenses	634	2,567	2,590	2,624	2,665
Amortization of excess reorganization value	43	172	172	172	172
Operating income	$ 8	29	55	80	110
Net interest expense	38	149	141	132	128
Other expenses	1	4	4	4	4
Pretax earnings	($ 31)	($ 124)	($ 90)	($ 55)	($ 22)
Provision for income taxes[a]	7	21	34	47	59
Net income (loss)	($ 38)	($ 145)	($ 124)	($ 102)	($ 81)
EBITDA					
Denny's	52	193	206	219	233
Hardee's	17	65	65	65	65
Quincy's	5	20	22	23	25
El Pollo Loco	6	23	25	28	32
Coco's and Carrows	15	70	79	87	96
Corporate general and administrative and other	(10)	(38)	(39)	(40)	(41)
Total	$ 85	$ 332	$ 358	$ 381	$ 410
Depreciation and amortization[b]	33	131	131	129	128
Decrease (increase) in net working capital	23	3	0	41	7
Capital expenditures	(21)	(83)	(84)	(86)	(88)
Other sources (uses) of cash	(1)	(9)	(17)	(8)	(5)

[a]Projected income taxes are based on assumed federal tax rate of 35%, a blended state income tax rate of 5%, and roughly $1.5 million a year in foreign taxes. When the projections were issued Flagstar had approximately $63 million in accumulated net operating losses (NOLs).

[b]Excludes amortization of excess reorganization value. As described in Exhibit 4.12, amortization of excess reorganization value must be recognized as an expense for financial accounting purposes, but it is not tax deductible.

Source: Flagstar prospectus, June 1997.

EXHIBIT 4.9 DLJ's Valuation: Summary ($millions)

Business	Projected 1997 EBITDA	Multiple of 1997 EBITDA		Enterprise Valuation Range, December 31, 1997	
		Low	High	Low	High
Denny's	$165.2	5.8	6.2	$ 958.2	$1,024.2
Hardee's	61.6	5.0	5.5	308.0	338.8
Quincy's	15.7	4.0	5.0	62.8	78.5
El Pollo Loco	19.0	7.0	8.0	133.0	152.0
Coco's/Carrows	52.1	6.0	6.5	312.6	338.7
Corporate G&A and other	(26.3)	5.7	6.2	(148.8)	(162.0)
	$287.3	5.7	6.2	$1,625.8	$1,770.2

Notes:
• EBITDA for each business excludes special, nonrecurring items.
• The multiples used for "Corporate G&A and other" are weighted averages of the multiples for the individual businesses.

Source: DLJ, "Valuation Summary," submitted to U.S. Bankruptcy Court for the District of South Carolina, 1997.

EXHIBIT 4.10   DLJ's Multiples for Comparable Companies

	Total Enterprise Value as Multiple of EBITDA	"Selected Multiple Range"	Summary of DLJ's Valuation Considerations
Denny's			
Shoney's	6.0		*Market segment generally*
Perkins Family Restaurants	6.4		Low growth prospects.
International House of Pancakes	7.6		
Bob Evans Farms	7.6		
Cracker Barrel	11.6		
Average	7.2	5.8–6.2	*Denny's specifically*
High	11.6		Strong breakfast brand; 24-hour operations; market share leader.
Low	6.0		Below-average ranking in food quality and service.
(Average excludes high and low.)			
Hardee's			
CKE Restaurants	12.0		*Market segment generally*
DavCo Restaurants	5.2		Low growth prospects; dominant players
Foodmaker	7.7		(McDonald's, Burger King, Wendy's)
Rally's Hamburgers	15.9		continue to open net sites aggressively.
Average	9.9	5.0–5.5	*Hardee's specifically*
High	15.9		Good locations.
Low	5.2		As franchisee, suffering from franchisor mismanagement; brand somewhat weak; same-store sales declines.
(Average excludes high and low.)			
Quincy's			
Ryan's Family Steak Houses	6.0		*Market segment generally*
Piccadilly Cafeteria	4.7		Long-term decline in "family" steak
Buffets	3.9		segment (which is Quincy's segment);
Luby's	7.1		"casual" steak segment stronger.
Average	5.3	4.0–5.0	*Quincy's specifically*
High	7.1		Good real estate.
Low	3.9		Deterioration of chain due to recent efforts to sell it.
(Average excludes high and low.)			

EXHIBIT 4.10   *(Continued)*

	Total Enterprise Value as Multiple of EBITDA	"Selected Multiple Range"	Summary of DLJ's Valuation Considerations
El Pollo Loco			
Pollo Tropical	7.6		*Market segment generally*
Taco Cabana	5.7		Chicken and Mexican food are fast-
Average	6.6		growing segments.
High	7.6	7.0–8.0	*El Pollo Loco specifically*
Low	5.7		Strong increases in same-store sales and
			EBITDA margins; trong brand appeal
			samong Hispanics.
			Comparable companies scarce.
Coco's/Carrows			
Vicorp Restaurants	5.1		*Market segment generally*
Cracker Barrel	11.6		Same as Denny's.
Bob Evans Farms	7.6		
Brinker International	6.4		
Perkins Family			
Restaurants	6.4		
Shoney's	6.0		
Average	6.6	6.0–6.5	*Coco's/Carrows specifically*
High	11.6		Above-average ranking in food quality and
Low	5.1		service; recent uptick in same-store sales;
(Average excludes			good international growth prospects.
high and low.)			Lack of uniform brand image.

Source: Bankruptcy Court Documents.

EXHIBIT 4.11 Flagstar: Recent Historical and Pro Forma Balance Sheets ($millions)

Assets	Historical 12/31/96	Historical 4/2/97	Pro forma 4/2/97
Current assets			
Cash and cash equivalents	$ 92.4	$ 31.8	$ 15.0
Receivables	17.8	10.5	10.5
Supply inventories	31.5	30.6	30.6
Other	48.9	41.9	42.0
	$ 190.6	$ 114.8	$ 98.1
Property			
Property owned, net	1,051.8	1,034.6	1,034.6
Property held under capital leases, net	116.8	118.8	118.8
	$1,168.6	$1,153.4	$1,153.4
Other assets			
Goodwill	205.4	204.2	0.0
Other intangible assets	27.6	26.8	26.8
Deferred financing costs	64.2	61.5	9.8
Other	31.0	31.1	31.1
Reorganization value in excess of amounts allocable to identifiable assets			885.5
	$ 328.2	$ 323.6	$ 953.2
Total assets	$1,687.4	$1,591.8	$2,204.7

Liabilities	Historical 12/31/96	Historical 4/2/97	Pro forma 4/2/97
Current liabilities			
Accounts payable	$ 160.4	$ 108.4	$ 108.4
Accrued salaries, insurance, taxes	136.2	137.5	137.6
Accrued interest	47.7	73.9	28.2
Other	76.1	82.8	82.8
Current maturities of long-term debt	62.9	1,001.0	54.3
	$ 483.3	$1,403.6	$ 411.3
Long-term liabilities			
Debt, less current portion	2,179.4	1,226.7	1,264.5
Deferred income taxes	16.4	16.0	(80.2)[a]
Liability for self-insured claims	57.7	57.5	57.5
Other	178.2	167.2	172.5
	$2,431.7	$1,467.4	$1,414.3
Stockholders' equity			
Preferred stock	0.6	0.6	0.0
Common stock	21.2	21.2	0.4
Paid-in capital	724.9	724.9	378.7
Deficit	(1,973.4)	(2,025.0)	0.0
Other	(0.9)	(0.9)	0.0
	($1,227.6)	($1,279.2)	$ 379.1
Total liabilities and stockholders' equity	$1,687.4	$1,591.8	$2,204.7

[a]The projection of a minus 80 figure, which represented a deferred tax asset, had to do primarily with an expected increase in the usability of NOLs.
Source: Company 10-Ks and June 5, 1997, prospectus.

EXHIBIT 4.12 "Fresh-Start Accounting"

The accounting standards for businesses emerging from Chapter 11 are quite different from what businesses normally use. These standards are described in Statement of Position (SOP) 90-7, "Financial Reporting by Entities in Reorganization under the Bankruptcy Code," issued by the American Institute of Certified Public Accountants in November 1990. These standards constitute what is called "fresh-start accounting." Flagstar referred explicitly to these standards in its June 5, 1997, prospectus and prepared its pro forma balance sheet in accordance with them (Exhibit 4.11).

To qualify for fresh-start reporting, the following three conditions must hold:

1. The company must reorganize in Chapter 11. Companies undertaking an informal out-of-court "workout" do not qualify for these accounting standards.
2. There must be a true loss of equity control. The holders of common, voting shares prior to confirmation in Chapter 11 must end up with less than 50 percent of the common stock of the entity emerging from Chapter 11.
3. The business must be technically insolvent. That is, what the business is judged to be worth as a going concern must be less than the face value of its total liabilities before any restructuring of them takes place.

What the business is worth as a going concern is the fair market value of its assets—what this accounting statement calls its "reorganization value." This is different from the historical cost basis of assets. "Reorganization value" is implicit in every Chapter 11 reorganization. It represents the amount of value assignable to all of people who have some financial claim on the company—that is, everyone on the right-hand side of the balance sheet (holders of interest-bearing claims, holders of non-interest-bearing claims, plus equity interests).

A business's "reorganization value" is not the same thing as its "enterprise value." Enterprise value is the market value of outstanding equity plus interest-bearing debt, minus cash and cash equivalents. This number is necessarily lower than a company's reorganization value.

A key objective of fresh-start accounting is to record the firm's assets at their presumed market values. This is accomplished by allocating the firm's overall reorganization value to specific assets on the balance sheet. At the end of this process, any residual reorganization value that cannot be attributed to specific, identifiable assets is assigned to an intangible asset called "reorganization value in excess of amounts allocable to identifiable assets." This asset is very much like "goodwill." It must be amortized over time (in theory up to 40 years), and the annual charge must be recognized as an ordinary expense, thus reducing the firm's reported earnings. Like amortization of goodwill, however, this charge is not tax deductible. Fresh-start accounting is therefore very similar to "purchase" accounting, which is used when one company acquires another company for an amount of money that exceeds the latter's book value.

Naturally, restating assets at their market value also involves restating liabilities and equity at their market value. For a company coming out of Chapter 11, this means reducing liabilities to whatever the company's creditors have agreed in Chapter 11 to accept—and increasing equity to whatever the various parties in Chapter 11 now think it's worth.

An aspect of fresh-start accounting that is very attractive to a restructuring company is that the large deficit that has usually built up in the stockholders' equity section of its balance sheet (representing its cumulative losses) is eliminated. The company emerging from Chapter 11 starts off with a retained earnings balance of zero—hence the term "fresh start."

EXHIBIT 4.13   Analysis of Mergers and Acquisitions in the U.S. Restaurant
Industry, 1990–1996

	Purchase Price as a Multiple of		
	Revenue	**EBIT**	**EBITDA**
High	2.3	41.1	13.5
Low	0.4	9.0	5.0
Median	0.8	14.2	7.3
Mean (excluding high and low)	0.9	16.3	7.9

Notes:
• "Purchase price" equals the price paid for equity plus the amount of debt assumed.
• Figures for revenue, EBIT, and EBITDA are for the latest 12 months for each transaction.
• Based on 12 transactions with meaningful data.

Source: Donaldson, Lufkin & Jenrette, "Valuation Analysis," February 19, 1997, later submitted to U.S. Bankruptcy Court.

EXHIBIT 4.14 Data for Shoney's ("Best Comparable to Denny's": DLJ; "Most Direct Competitor of Denny's": Lazard Freres) (in $millions, Except Stock Price)

Data per Most Recent 10-K

	12 Months Ended 10/27/96
Revenues	$1,099.7
Food and supplies	440.5
Restaurant labor	270.1
Operating expenses	240.9
	$ 951.5
General and administrative expenses	68.2
Interest expense	38.0
Total expenses	$1,057.7
Pretax income from continuing operations	$ 42.0
Provision for income taxes	16.0
	$ 26.0
Discontinued operations, net of tax	$ 0.4
Gain on sale of discontinued operations, net of tax	$ 22.1
Net income	$ 48.5

- Cash flow statement indicated that total depreciation and amortization during the year was $46.4.
- There were no unusual, material items in operating expenses.

	As of 10/27/96
Cash	$ 14.0
Long-term debt	$ 510.3
Preferred stock	$ 0.0
Common stock	

During the last three months of 1996 and the first three months of 1997, there were 48.5 million shares outstanding

Prices of common stock

1/22/97 (day after 10-K announcement)	$ 7.750
2/13/97 (date selected by DLJ)	$ 7.500
3/6/97 (date selected by Dillon Read)	$ 8.125
3/17/97 (date selected by Lazard Freres)	$ 5.250

DLJ's Presentation of Data

Fiscal year-end	10/96
Last financial statement used	10/96
Current stock price (as of 2/13/97)	$ 7.50
Shares outstanding	48.5
Market value	$ 363.8
Enterprise value	$ 860.4
Revenues	$1,318.3
EBITDA	$ 142.7
Enterprise value/revenues	0.7
Enterprise value/EBITDA	6.0

Lazard Freres' Presentation of Data

Fiscal year-end	10/96
Financial statements used	
Balance sheet	5/12/96
Income statement	1997 est.
Current stock price (as of 3/17/97)	$ 5.25
Shares outstanding	48.5
Market value	$ 254.6
Enterprise value	$ 766.0
Revenues	$1,322.0
EBITDA	$ 153.0
Enterprise value/revenues	0.6
Enterprise value/EBITDA	5.0

Dillon Read's Presentation of Data

Fiscal year-end	10/96
Last financial statement used	10/96
Current stock price (as of 3/6/97)	$ 8.125
Shares outstanding	42.7
Market value	$ 346.9
Enterprise value	$ 857.1
Revenues	$1,099.7
EBITDA	126.3
Enterprise value/revenues	0.8
Enterprise value/EBITDA	6.8

Source: Company 10-K and 10-Q; Bloomberg; bankruptcy court documents.

EXHIBIT 4.15   Jefferies' Valuation: Summary ($millions)

	1998	1999	2000	2001	EBITDA Exit Multiple	Exit Value	Total Enterprise Value
Total revenues	$2,768	$2,816	$2,876	$2,946			
EBITDA							
Denny's	193	206	219	233	7.5	$1,748	
Hardee's	65	65	65	65	6.0	390	
Quincy's	20	22	23	25	4.5	113	
El Pollo Loco	23	25	28	32	6.0	192	
Coco's and Carrows	70	79	87	96	7.0	672	
	$ 371	$ 397	$ 422	$ 451		$3,114	
Less							
Corporate G&A and other	(56)	(57)	(58)	(59)	6.0	(352)	
Capital expenditures	(89)	(91)	(76)	(76)			
Changes in working capital	3	0	41	7			
Other changes	1	(8)	2	2			
Interest tax shield	(60)	(56)	(53)	(51)			
Taxes	(8)	(19)	(35)	(51)			
	($ 209)	($ 231)	($ 179)	($ 228)		($ 352)	
Net cash flows (unlevered)	$ 162	$ 166	$ 243	$ 223		$2,762	
Discounted @ 12.4%	$ 144	$ 131	$ 171	$ 140		$1,730	$2,317

Note: Jefferies' analysis assumed that the effective tax rate was 40%, the average cost of debt was 10%, the cost of equity was 35%, the WACC was 12.4%, and the capitalization would be as follows:

Total debt	$1,319	78%
Implied equity value	373	22
Total market capitalization	$1,692	100%

Source: Jefferies, "Discounted Cash Flow," submitted to U.S. Bankruptcy Court for the District of South Carolina, 1997; Flagstar prospectus.

EXHIBIT 4.16A Jefferies' "Comparable Companies"

Companies That Jefferies Treated as Comparable to Denny's	Companies That Jefferies Treated as Comparable to Coco's/Carrows
Bob Evans Farms, Inc.	Bob Evans Farms, Inc.
Perkins Family Restaurant, LP	Perkins Family Restaurant, LP
Cracker Barrel Old Country Store	Cracker Barrel Old Country Store
Shoney's	Shoney's
International House of Pancakes	Vicorp Restaurants
DenAmerica Corp.	Brinker International
Applebee's International	
Apple South	

Note: DenAmerica, Applebee's, and Apple South were treated as comparable to Denny's by Jefferies but not by DLJ.
Source: Bankruptcy court documents.

EXHIBIT 4.16B Denny's, DenAmerica, Applebee's, and Apple South: Descriptive Information

Company (Largest Restaurant "Concept")	Average Customer Check at Largest "Concept" in 1996	Summary Description of Largest "Concept" (Quotations from Companies' 10-Ks)
Flagstar (Denny's)	$5.03	"Full-service," "moderately priced," "family" dining, diverse menu
DenAmerica (Denny's, as franchisee)	$5.18	"Full-service," "family" oriented, diverse menu; largest franchisee of Denny's; operates other, company-owned restaurants as well
Applebee's (Applebee's)	Not given	"Table service," "moderately priced," "family" oriented, diverse menu; serves alcohol
Apple South (Applebee's, as franchisee)	$6.40[a]	"Full-service," "moderately priced," diverse menu, largest franchisee of Applebee's; serves alcohol

[a]Casewriter's estimate.
Source: Company 10-Ks and press reports.

EXHIBIT 4.16C   DenAmerica, Applebee's, and Apple South: Excerpts from Income Statements, Balance Sheets, and Market Data ($millions, Except Stock Price)

	DenAmerica	Apple South	Applebee's
Most recent fiscal year-end	12/27/95	12/31/95	12/31/95
Most recent quarter end	10/2/96	9/29/96	9/29/96
Revenues	$184.7	$525.1	$403.0
EBITDA	$ 15.4	$ 80.8	$ 76.2
Cash	$ 0.0	$ 2.2	$ 10.2
Long-term debt	$101.6	$188.7	$ 26.0
Preferred stock	$ 0.0	$ 0.0	$ 0.0
Common stock			
Number of shares outstanding (millions)	13.4	38.3	31.3
Market price on 2/13/97	$ 3.31	$14.00	$27.00

Notes:
• Revenue and EBITDA figures are for the latest 12 months, and EBITDA excludes unusual items.
• Long-term debt includes capital leases and current portion of long-term debt.
Source: Company 10-Ks and 10-Qs.

EXHIBIT 4.17 Betas and Stock Returns for Comparable Companies

	Ticker	Date (10-Q or 10-K)	Debt in $millions		Market Price of Common Stock (as of One Day after Release of Most Recent 10-Q or 10-K)			Beta	Total Stock Return during Period
			Long-Term	Short-Term	Number of Shares	Price	Total ($millions)		
Shoney's	SHN	5/11/97	$ 417	$ 87	48.57	$ 5.75	$ 279	1.14	−71%
Perkins Family Restaurants	PFR	3/31/97	$ 58	$ 7	10.48	$13.50	$ 141	0.81	9%
International House of Pancakes	IHOP	3/31/97	$ 140	$ 6	9.52	$25.25	$ 240	1.46	63%
Bob Evans Farms	BOBE	4/25/97	$ 2	$ 69	42.64	$13.13	$ 560	0.84	−25%
Cracker Barrel Old Country Store	CBRL	5/2/97	$ 63	$ 4	60.95	$28.00	$1,707	1.24	25%
CKE Restaurants	CKR	5/19/97	$ 80	$ 6	33.44	$21.70	$ 726	1.51	375%
DavCo Restaurants	DVC	3/29/97	$ 28	$ 15	6.43	$ 9.63	$ 62	0.08	−27%
Foodmaker	FM	4/13/97	$ 396	$ 1	38.98	$10.38	$ 404	0.92	−47%
Rally's Hamburgers	RLLY	3/30/97	$ 67	$ 1	20.55	$ 3.63	$ 74	1.37	−58%
Ryan's Steak House	RYAN	4/2/97	$ 93	$ 45	47.41	$ 7.94	$ 376	0.46	−27%
Luby's	LUB	2/28/97	$ 95	$ 0	23.41	$20.38	$ 477	0.49	60%
Pollo Tropical	POYO	3/30/97	$ 10	$ 0	8.13	$ 5.00	$ 41	1.80	−89%
Vicorp Restaurants	VRES	4/30/97	$ 22	$ 1	9.08	$11.50	$ 104	0.77	−29%
Brinker International	EAT	3/26/97	$ 103	$183	67.47	$12.63	$ 852	1.50	−4%
Flagstar	FLSTQ	4/2/97	$2,228	$ 0	42.43	$ 0.60	$ 25	0.07	−94%
S&P 500	SPX							1.00	103%

Notes:
- The above companies respresent all 14 publicly traded, predominantly restaurant companies that both DLJ and Jefferies regarded as "comparable" to one or more of the restaurant chains that Flagstar owned.
- None of the above companies had any material amount of preferred stock.
- The time period used for the calculation of betas and total returns is approximately five years.

Sources: Company 10-Ks and 10-Qs; Bloomberg.

EXHIBIT 4.18 Flagstar's Unsecured, Publicly Traded Debt: Changes in Market Value (as of Month-End)

	3/95	6/95	9/95	12/95	3/96	6/96	9/96	12/96	1/97	2/97	3/97	4/97	5/97	6/97
10.75% senior notes, due 2001 ($270 million)														
Price	95.75	93.50	93.88	91.75	90.75	87.00	88.75	91.50	96.75	97.00	98.50	99.50	99.25	101.50
YTM	11.70	12.27	12.22	12.82	13.18	14.36	13.97	13.22	11.67	11.61	11.18	10.89	10.96	—
10.875% senior notes, due 2002 ($280 million)														
Price	96.75	92.75	93.00	90.00	90.63	87.25	86.75	91.00	96.50	96.75	98.50	98.75	99.00	101.50
YTM	11.72	12.39	12.37	13.11	13.01	13.94	14.16	13.10	11.71	11.66	11.23	11.18	11.12	—
11.25% senior sub debs, due 2004 ($722 million)														
Price	83.00	79.00	77.25	71.00	73.25	65.50	60.00	40.00	40.00	39.00	44.75	45.00	42.50	41.00
YTM	14.59	15.58	16.09	17.89	17.34	19.87	22.05	—	—	—	—	—	—	—
11.375% senior sub debs, due 2003 ($125 million)														
Price	84.50	77.75	77.00	72.25	74.50	65.50	65.00	40.00	39.50	38.38	44.75	45.00	42.00	40.00
YTM	14.62	16.39	16.70	18.19	17.65	20.80	21.21	—	—	—	—	—	—	—
10% convertible junior sub debs, due 2014 ($100 million)														
Price	72.75	70.50	72.00	54.00	58.50	56.88	32.88	28.88	24.50	15.25	15.38	17.50	16.00	16.00
YTM	14.13	14.60	14.31	19.05	17.65	18.16	—	—	—	—	—	—	—	—

Standard & Poor's average YTM on five-year industrial bonds

B rating	9.99	9.86	9.63	9.93	10.10	10.05	9.85
BB/BB– rating	8.79	8.67	8.36	8.70	8.84	8.85	8.66
BB+ rating	7.48	7.72	7.49	7.81	7.92	7.90	7.53

Standard & Poor's ratings of Flagstar's debt	Rating	Last Change	Rating	Last change	Rating	Last Change
10.75% senior notes, due 2001 ($270 million)	B	4/94	B–	5/95	CCC	2/97
10.875% senior notes, due 2002 ($280 million)	B	4/94	B–	5/95	CCC	2/97
11.25% senior sub debs, due 2004 ($722 million)	CCC+	4/94			CCC–	2/97
11.375% senior sub debs, due 2003 ($125 million)	CCC+	4/94			CCC–	2/97
10% convertible junior sub debs, due 2014 ($100 million)	NR					

Source: Standard & Poor's, *Bond Guide,* and *CreditWeek.*
Note: "Price" represents percent of par; "YTM" represents the yield-to-maturity. All prices indicated are approximate "bid" prices.

EXHIBIT 4.19 Dillon Read's Valuation Grid for Flagstar's Senior Subordinated Debt (as of Early March 1997) ($millions)

EBITDA (1996 actual)	$ 286	$ 286	$ 286
Possible multiples	5.5	6.0	6.5
Enterprise values per different multiples	$1,573	$1,716	$1,859
Less: senior debt	($1,295)	($1,295)	($1,295)
Available for all subordinated debt and equity claims	$ 278	$ 421	$ 564
Face value of senior subordinated debt ($722 + $125)	$ 847	$ 847	$ 847
Residual value as % of face value of senior sub debt	32.8%	49.7%	66.6%
Present value of senior subordinated debt assuming:			
6 months to emergence from Chapter 11			
@ 15% discount rate	30.5%	46.2%	61.9%
@ 20% discount rate	30.0%	45.4%	60.8%
@ 25% discount rate	29.4%	44.5%	59.6%
12 months to emergence from Chapter 11			
@ 15% discount rate	28.5%	43.2%	57.9%
@ 20% discount rate	27.4%	41.4%	55.5%
@ 25% discount rate	26.3%	39.8%	53.3%
18 months to emergence from Chapter 11			
@ 15% discount rate	26.8%	40.6%	54.4%
@ 20% discount rate	25.2%	38.2%	51.2%
@ 25% discount rate	23.9%	36.1%	48.4%

Source: Dillon Read "High-Yield Research" report, March 13, 1997; some modifications by casewriter for simplification.

CHAPTER 5

Alphatec Electronics Pcl

It is better to eat dogs' dung than to go to court.
—Thai saying[1]

On the morning of July 28, 1997, Robert Mollerstuen, president and chief operating officer (COO) of Alphatec Group, received a call from the Alphatec Electronics Public Company Limited (ATEC) board of directors asking him to take over as interim chief executive officer (CEO). Based in Thailand, ATEC was part of the Alphatec Group, a sprawling network of technology-intensive businesses ranging from semiconductors to telephones, plastics, and life insurance. ATEC had been a high-tech pioneer in Thailand, starting out as a subcontract semiconductor packager with assembly and test operations in Bangkok, Shanghai, and two locations in the United States. At an emergency session of ATEC's board, Charn Uswachoke, ATEC's charismatic founder and CEO, had resigned after a Price Waterhouse (PW) financial review uncovered several years of falsified financial statements and unauthorized disbursements to other companies controlled by him. Three weeks earlier Thailand had let its currency float, triggering a devaluation that set off a financial crisis across Asia.

The transactions PW discovered masked widening operating losses at

This case was prepared by Research Associate Perry Fagan, Ph.D. Candidate C. Fritz Foley, and Professor Stuart Gilson. Copyright © 2001 by the President and Fellows of Harvard College. Harvard Business School case 200-004.
[1]William Gamble, "Restructuring in Asia—A Brief Survey of Asian Bankruptcy Law," *Emerging Market*, vol. 3, no. 1, January 25, 1999.

ATEC, which left the company unable to service its $373 million debt. After it missed payments on two of its bond issues, a restructuring effort was launched in June 1997 under the direction of ATEC's management and creditors. An initial attempt at restructuring failed when Charn, ATEC's largest shareholder, rejected a plan that would have significantly diluted his ownership interest in the firm.

The failure of ATEC's first attempt at restructuring coincided with an April 1998 amendment to the Thai bankruptcy code that for the first time offered debtor companies like ATEC the option to seek reorganization under the Thai equivalent of Chapter 11 protection found in U.S. bankruptcy law. The prior law had provided only for the liquidation of distressed companies. Creditors could spend as long as fifteen years in court arguing their rights, and their prospects for significant recovery were dim. As a result, creditors were reluctant to seek the intervention of the courts.

In the wake of Charn's refusal to approve the first restructuring plan, ATEC and its creditors initiated bankruptcy proceedings under the new law. Under court supervision creditors devised a second plan to restructure the company, one that did not require shareholder approval.

However, certain key creditors voted down this plan because of the large write-off involved and because they believed it would not guarantee their right to pursue legal action against Charn and ATEC's former auditors, KPMG Peat Marwick Suthee Ltd. (KPMG). Negotiations over a revised plan commenced between ATEC's creditors steering committee, two potential equity investors, the court appointed planner, and ATEC management. A final vote on the plan was scheduled for February 2, 1999.

For Mollerstuen, a "yes" vote would prove his long-standing faith in ATEC's underlying business, and would allow ATEC to emerge as the first firm to be reorganized under Thailand's amended bankruptcy code. A rejection by creditors would lead to further delays and risk the defection of the plan's two equity investors, who had agreed to inject $40 million of fresh capital into the cash-starved company.

For over 18 months Mollerstuen had served as ATEC's head cheerleader (with bodyguards for protection), confronting anxious creditors, angry shareholders, and impatient customers against the backdrop of Thailand's economic collapse. He felt strongly that with the new business plan the company could roar out of bankruptcy and could be profitable enough to go public within five years. With the vote less than one week away, he reflected on the events surrounding ATEC's bankruptcy and wondered what more he could do to end the protracted crisis.

HISTORY OF ALPHATEC ELECTRONICS AND THE ALPHATEC GROUP

Born to a middle-class ethnic Chinese family in Bangkok, Thailand (see Exhibit 5.1 for a map of Thailand), Charn Uswachoke graduated from North Texas University. After graduating, he joined Honeywell in the United States, and soon returned to Thailand to work for a division of the company. Thailand's economy was booming, and Charn wanted to set out on his own. When Philips Electronics N.V. decided to sell a portion of an integrated circuit (IC) packaging plant, Charn borrowed money to make the purchase from Philips and build a new factory in Chachoengsao province (about forty kilometers southeast of Bangkok) in 1989. As part of the deal, Philips agreed to purchase 90 percent of the output for the next five years.

The company, named Alphatec Electronics, began production in 1991. ATEC's objective was to provide fully integrated "turnkey" IC packaging and testing services at competitive rates and high quality. Packaging involved the sealing of an IC in a plastic or ceramic casing. Packaged ICs were then tested to meet customer specifications. The company hoped to develop long-term strategic relationships with leading semiconductor manufacturers and offer a broad mix of packaging services. Some important early customers included Cypress Semiconductor Corporation and Microchip Technology, Inc.

Charn hoped to capitalize on two significant trends in the semiconductor industry. First, more semiconductor companies worldwide were subcontracting some or all of their packaging and testing operations to independent companies such as ATEC. Independents could offer significant cost savings due to their longer production runs and superior operating flexibility (e.g., they were better able to extend the useful lives of their equipment by migrating older machines to the testing of less complex products). Second, Southeast Asia was an increasingly attractive place to locate IC packaging and testing, due to the region's low operating costs and the heavy local concentration of high-tech manufacturing.

Nineteen ninety-three was a pivotal year in the company's development. The company went public in Thailand through an initial public offering (IPO), and in the process increased its borrowings from banks and public debt markets. Charn acquired a major semiconductor assembly and test plant from National Semiconductor, as well as telephone assembly and testing plants from AT&T Corp. He also entered the tool and plastic die industry.

The following year Charn began pursuing a longer-term strategy of developing a competitive cluster in the IC industry. He wanted to do design work, wafer fabrication, IC assembly and testing, and product manufacturing and marketing. His first major act under this expanded growth strategy was to launch a $1.1 billion venture called Submicron that would become Thailand's first state-of-the-art wafer fabricator. The project's initial financing included $350 million of debt with twenty six local banks and finance companies.

The fabrication industry had played a significant role in the development of fellow Asian tiger countries Taiwan and Singapore, but it required reliable sources of water and power. Since these were generally wanting in Thailand, Charn decided to develop AlphaTechnopolis, a 4,000-acre high-tech industrial park that would be located nine kilometers from Alphatec Electronics. This park was intended to include Alpha Power, a $400 million 400-megawatt power facility, a $150 million water plant, and $200 million in other assets. Long-range plans called for the development of housing and retail establishments, a hospital and school, a research and development center, and a technical university.

A string of acquisitions and investments followed during 1994–1996. These included a joint venture with China's state-owned Shanghai Industrial and Electronic Holding Group Co. (SIEHGC) and Microchip Technology of Arizona to produce high volumes of low-tech chips (named Alphatec Shanghai). Charn purchased the U.S. firm Indy Electronics for $30 million (renamed Alphatec Electronics USA). He founded several new businesses, including two life insurance companies, an equipment leasing company, and a telephone equipment company. He took a majority equity stake in Alpha Memory Co. Ltd., a joint venture between Texas Instruments (TI) and Acer that would provide assembly and testing services for semiconductor memory products and would require $100 million in capital expenditures. And in late 1995 he and TI broke ground on a new $1.2 billion semiconductor manufacturing facility at AlphaTechnopolis, even though little progress had been made in completing the Submicron plant.

"Mr. Chips"

Although Charn was a significant shareholder in all the companies he founded or acquired, he kept the businesses separate legal entities. Each company had its own board of directors and reported separate financial information. Many of Charn's family members supported his efforts to build a competitive integrated circuit (IC) group of companies in Thailand, and they had important management positions at AlphaTechnopolis, Alpha-Comsat, and other group affiliates.

To manage all of his operations effectively, Charn united Alphatec Electronics and all of the other companies in which he held major stakes into what became known as the Alphatec Group (see Exhibit 5.2). The

Group was an informal entity without any legal basis. Charn ran this centralized management group from ATEC headquarters in downtown Bangkok. Group managers were split across several departments, including public relations, finance, and operations. Charn had the financial organizations in each company report directly to himself.

The operations department was actively involved in improving the efficiency of Charn's various businesses. Mollerstuen was an important member of this group. He was an American with more than thirty years of experience in the computer industry in both the United States and Asia, and had held top-level operational management positions at National Semiconductor and Philips Semiconductor. As chief operating officer he was responsible for all group assembly and test operations. He also had a significant role in building and maintaining ATEC's customer base. Working closely with Mollerstuen was Willem de Vries, executive vice president for production. De Vries had previously been the managing director of Philips Semiconductor Thailand, and also had more than thirty years of industry experience, working in England, the Philippines, Germany, France, Brazil, and the United States.

The ATEC board of directors was headed up by Waree Havanonda, a former deputy governor of the Bank of Thailand (BOT) and Charn's former finance professor. She countersigned for all of the major ATEC checks written by Charn. The eleven-member board included, in addition to these two, six bankers, the chairman of a trading company, the vice president of Bangkok Coil Center Co., Ltd., and the dean of the Institute of Industrial Technology at Suranaree University. "At that time the board had a bunch of bankers on it," Mollerstuen recalled. "They did not know the electronics industry well and relied on Charn for a lot of guidance. People in operations and from the factory were never allowed to attend meetings. Charn insisted that the meetings be conducted in Thai." As a result, Mollerstuen, de Vries, and other expatriate executives in the operations department had very little interaction with the directors.

By the mid-1990s ATEC had won much praise for its financial management practices and performance. Charn was considered by many as a pioneer of Thailand's electronics industry, earning him the nickname "Mr. Chips." In 1995, Alphatec received the prestigious Financial Management Award from the Manila-based Asian Institute of Management, in a ceremony attended by the prime minister of Thailand. In 1996, *Electronic Business Asia* magazine named Charn one of Asia's top business executives,[2] and some observers compared him to Bill Gates. In 1996 ATEC employed over 1,700 workers

---

[2]*Bangkok Post*, December 20, 1996.

and accounted for roughly 1 percent of Thailand's total exports. By 1997, seven of the top ten North American integrated circuit producers were ATEC customers, including Advanced Micro Devices, Cypress Semiconductor, Microchip Technology, Philips Semiconductor, and Texas Instruments.[3]

ALPHATEC IN DISTRESS

In 1995, coinciding with a general slowdown in the global semiconductor industry, ATEC's profit fell by 35 percent, from 699 million baht to 452 million baht. (Historical financial statements appear in Exhibit 5.3.) The Group came under increasing pressure to raise new financing. The initial phases of investment in AlphaTechnopolis and the Submicron wafer fabrication plant had required large infusions of cash. However, businesses that could have provided positive cash flow for investment were slow in getting off the ground. For example, although Charn had hired a staff for his two life insurance companies, he had not yet been able to obtain licenses to operate them.

Charn turned to Lehman Brothers for advice on funding his numerous ventures. One proposal considered was to merge six of the group companies, including ATEC, and then raise money through an offering of American depository receipts. During the due diligence process, however, Lehman noted significant inconsistencies in ATEC's historical financial statements, and it terminated its relationship with Charn. Concerned by this development, ATEC's board hired Price Waterhouse to conduct a financial review of the company.

In March 1997 Charn made a proposal to the prime minister of Thailand asking the government to make investments in electronics companies, in a program similar to that used in Malaysia, Singapore, Taiwan, and Korea. On June 3 and June 10 the Thai cabinet issued proclamations confirming support of the electronics industry in general, and the Alphatec Group in particular. The cabinet committee appointed to study ATEC's request for funds said it felt the firm's debt was excessive and should be restructured. The committee appointed Krung Thai Bank (owned by the government and controlled through the Ministry of Finance) to work with ATEC on the restructuring. The envisioned restructuring would include write-offs, debt-to-equity conversions, and conversions from short-term to long-term debt.

In early May, Texas Instruments announced it was pulling out of two

---

[3]ATEC's contracts with semiconductor manufacturers were denominated in U.S. dollars, as were the majority of its direct material purchase contracts. Roughly 40 percent of factory spending was baht based. About 35 percent of ATEC's total debt was in U.S. dollars.

factory construction projects, Alphatec-TI and Alpha Memory. Although the factories were nearing completion, neither had the financing necessary to start production. "What was clear was that Charn was not infusing the capital he promised into the ventures," explained a spokesman for TI. "Nor was the area's infrastructure coming together."[4]

Later that month, ATEC failed to make a $34 million debt payment to a syndicate of banks led by ING Bank, and in late June it failed to come up with $45 million for a put option on its U.S. dollar-denominated euro convertible debentures. Under the company's loan covenants, any formal declaration of default on either claim would have placed its entire $373 million in debt in default.

In response to these developments, in August ATEC appointed a provisional creditors steering committee (CSC) to intermediate between the company and its various creditors. The group met multiple times per week in Bangkok and had twelve members representing more than 60 percent of the total loans outstanding. Members included Thai banks, Japanese and other foreign banks, bill of exchange holders, bondholders, and finance companies. Of ATEC's 1,277 listed creditors, 1,025 were company employees, 176 were trade creditors, 31 were bondholders, and 44 were financial institutions. Krung Thai Bank held the largest debt of 4.23 billion baht (32%), followed by Bangkok Bank with 1.47 billion baht (11%), and Union Bank of Bangkok with 390 million baht (3%). (See Exhibit 5.4 for a list of financial claims.)

The company's share price dropped from over 300 baht in early May to less than 100 baht in late June. "Even though the Alphatec Group was not a legal entity," Mollerstuen complained, "the press reported its collapse. People confused group problems with problems at ATEC, and this was very bad for our marketing efforts and employee morale."

The July 2, 1997, Currency Crisis

Nevertheless, Mollerstuen remained optimistic. "We believe the restructuring will work and by August it will be business as usual," he wrote in an update distributed to ATEC customers and employees on July 2. The very same day, the Bank of Thailand allowed the baht to float in international money markets. It had previously been tied to a basket of foreign currencies. By September, the baht had fallen by 25 percent, to 32.75 to the dollar (Exhibit 5.5), plunging firms with significant amounts of U.S. dollar–denominated debt into

---

[4]Crista Hardie Souza, "Alphatec Chairman Quits; Scandal Grows," *Electronic News*, vol. 43, August 4, 1997, p. 6(1).

financial distress. Foreign capital fled the country, causing an extreme liquidity crisis. Banks and finance companies suddenly found themselves burdened with huge numbers of nonperforming loans. The government directed sixteen finance companies to cease operations for thirty days and merge with stronger companies. Exhibits 5.6 and 5.7 provide data on Thailand's economic and stock market performance.

Price Waterhouse Audit

On July 24, 1997, PW issued its preliminary report to the ATEC board. The accounting firm raised two areas of concern. The first was that ATEC had maintained two distinct sets of financial records: a set of internal "management accounts," and a set of "financial accounts" for the public. Analysis of these accounts revealed that the company's reported profits and net assets had been overstated. PW concluded:

> *As at 24 May 1997 . . . our current best estimate is that the net assets of the company per the "financial accounts" were approximately Baht 3.6 billion higher than those per the "management accounts." In addition, our current best estimate is that reported profits of the company have been overstated by Baht 500 million in the first quarter of 1997, by Baht 1.8 billion in the year ended December 1996, by Baht 1.8 million in the year ended December 1995 and by lesser amounts in prior years. The company's reported profits in the first quarter of 1997 and in prior years should have been reported as significant losses.*

PW's second concern was that Charn had withdrawn money from ATEC without proper authorization. "From December 1994 to July 1997," the report stated, "amounts totaling Baht 3.95 billion have been paid out of the company to related persons apparently without the prior approval of the directors or the shareholders. A substantial portion of the payments have been initially recorded as being advanced to an executive director of the company, but subsequently recorded as transactions with companies under his control."

When ATEC's board questioned him about these accusations, Charn denied that he had used the money for personal gain. He told *The Bangkok Post* that he was "a determined guy who wanted to get things done quickly," and that was "one of the many reasons his ambitious project fell apart."[5]

---

[5]Busaba Sivasomboon, " 'Determined Guy' Runs into Storm Clouds," *Bangkok Post*, August 3, 1998.

On July 28 the Alphatec board issued a press release announcing that it had asked the Thai stock exchange (SET) to suspend trading in its shares. It also announced it had accepted Charn's resignation as CEO, although as ATEC's largest shareholder with over 13 percent of the firm's outstanding shares he remained a member of the board.[6] In the months following his resignation Charn remained secluded, out of sight of the press.[7] In a subsequent telephone interview with *The New York Times*, he was reported as saying that ATEC was a victim of Thailand's imploding economy.[8]

New Management Takes Charge

On the same day that Charn resigned, the board named Mollerstuen acting CEO (Exhibit 5.8 shows Alphatec's organization chart). When Mollerstuen arrived at headquarters the next day he found finance executives shredding documents. He barricaded them in a conference room and later suspended the whole financial management team. Mollerstuen had occupied the office next to Charn for years, and recalled the difficult situation he faced stepping in as acting CEO:

> As of August 1, 1997, the company had sales of about $50 million and debt of about $373 million. It was obvious that we needed to restructure. We put together a quick business plan and decided that $35 million was the most debt we could service. This meant that the banks would need to take more than a 90 percent write-off. They were shocked. The banks were facing their own liquidity problems because of the growing levels of nonperforming loans. Even though we tried to get them to help us to restructure, they were primarily focused on their own problems.

---

[6]Alphatec's board filed a complaint against Charn with Thai police, accusing him of damaging the company's finances. The police and the SET began an enquiry into doubtful accounting practices surrounding Alphatec's buying of land from its executives at above market prices, as well as at its procedures for acquiring foreign subsidiaries.

[7]The compound consisted of eight houses near the ATEC factory. According to an August 3, 1998, report in *The Bangkok Post*, in the months after the Alphatec crisis erupted Charn lost over 20 pounds due to stress. However, the press reported that "he never thought of escaping from the problems or committing suicide, something his secretaries and associates were concerned about." Soon thereafter reports surfaced in the press that Charn was hard at work trying to revitalize Submicron.

[8]Mark Landler, "No. 1 in Its Bankruptcy Class, a Company in Thailand Starts to Get Its Act Together," *The New York Times*, June 11, 1999.

In mid-August Crédit Agricole Indosuez filed a claim against ATEC in the Thai Civil Court for $8.2 million for failure to service an outstanding loan. "We wanted to assure our customers and creditors that this was an isolated claim," said Mollerstuen. "The provisional CSC had informed us that they continued to support us in our restructuring effort. We tried to convince the bank to withdraw its claim and participate with the other creditors under the umbrella of the CSC." Although the court ordered ATEC to pay the debt, the bank was persuaded to temporarily forbear.

In mid-September, Charn resigned from Alphatec's board of directors. He explained:

> *Now that I've fulfilled my responsibility to ensure the successful start to-ward implementation of the restructuring plan, I think it's time for me to leave the board. I'm very grateful that the bondholders and the credi-tors have supported Alphatec in its goal of restructuring. This company does have a very bright future, once the financial problems are solved.*[9]

In a company press release announcing Charn's departure, ATEC's board chairman stated, "Prior to his departure, we have been assured by Charn that it's his intention and his commitment to repay to the company all the moneys which were transferred out without the proper authority." On October 10, de Vries and Mollerstuen were appointed to ATEC's board of directors.

Running the Plant

Even though negotiating with creditors was an arduous, time-consuming process, Mollerstuen and de Vries faced the additional challenge of keeping the productivity and morale of the employees high.

"The first time most people at the plant knew there was a problem was when they read about the breakdown of the Alphatec Group in the news-paper," said Nonglak Phungsom, director of human resources at the Al-phatec Thailand plant. She continued:

> *People had viewed Alphatec as a great place to work. The stock price quickly went from the offering price of 10 baht to 400 baht. The situ-ation was very difficult for factory employees from a psychological*

---

[9]"Two Board Directors Resign from Alphatec," *Bangkok Post*, September 13, 1997.

perspective. Khun[10] Charn, whom most had looked up to, was being attacked in the press. Employees would read news stories that were sometimes only partially true. Employees were shocked and there was not much they could do. The average employee did not know that numbers in the annual report had been misstated.

Willem [de Vries] told us to remain calm, and that he would not lay people off so long as he was here. Since he is a European, and not an American, we thought that he would have a longer-term perspective, and we trusted him on this point. Finding another job during the crisis would have been difficult. Many employees just did not have outside opportunities. Also, if people left [voluntarily] during the crisis, it would have been a sign that they did not care, that they were ignoring the problems, or maybe even that they were guilty.

De Vries recalled: "I took over plant operations from the start and I was very open with people, even more so in this time of crisis. I told them that I would not leave, that I would be the last one to turn off the light. We lost some expatriates, but most people stayed on." De Vries and Mollerstuen believed that firing people at the plant would bring ATEC to its knees. Mollerstuen also explained that firing a worker in Thailand meant paying him or her six months' severance pay. Because he estimated that the restructuring would take five months, and that he would need to rehire people let go during the restructuring, he saw no point to firing people.

Nonglak described some of the actions taken at the plant during the restructuring:

The crisis forced us to learn new things. We were given the opportunity to challenge ourselves. We understood that we needed to make the factory more efficient if we wanted to survive. Our suppliers had stopped extending trade credit to us. We took a 20 percent salary cut at the management level. Employees were encouraged to find ways of saving cash and to write these up as suggestions. Many of their ideas were implemented. We started printing on both sides of each page. There was no more free coffee. We provided cheaper rice at the canteen. We carefully looked at all steps of the production process. We reduced the waste of gold wire and plastic compound. We consolidated the bus service lines that we provided to employees.

We began to give the employees all of the details about our cash position and our earnings. We never missed a payroll payment, but we came close. We tried to make it clear that we all needed to work together to survive.

---

[10]The term "Khun" is a polite form of address in Thailand.

During the restructuring, ATEC's Thailand plant was running at one-third its capacity. "During the slowdown at the plant, we tried to get QS 9000 and ISO 14000 certification so that we would be ready for the future," Nonglak explained. "This international quality standard would give us more credibility in export markets." Plant management also reduced cycle time from six to three days, and increased yield from 99 percent to 99.7 percent.

THE FIRST RESTRUCTURING PLAN

On February 2, 1998, the creditors steering committee and the ATEC board circulated the first formal restructuring plan.[11] The plan included a number of provisions that would enable the company to finance its short-term working capital requirements and make necessary capital improvements. First, cash could be raised through the prefinancing[12] of accounts receivable and a drastic reduction in receivables payment terms to less than ten days. Second, some of ATEC's creditors could form a trading company ("NewCo") to collect receivables, take customer orders, pay trade creditors, and supply materials on consignment to the existing Alphatec factory ("OldCo"). An extension of this proposal had NewCo also fund capital expenditures by financing and/or leasing equipment. Under this scenario NewCo would supply OldCo equipment on consignment or through operating lease, with service or lease payments remitted by OldCo to NewCo (see Exhibit 5.9).[13]

In the medium term, all lenders would participate as shareholders in a new private company that would take over the assets of the old ATEC. The existing liabilities would remain with the old ATEC, while the new company would become a platform for raising new debt and equity.

The plan also described alternative long-term scenarios for the company. Some of these proposed opening a new factory in early 1999 called "Alphatec II." Another proposed consolidating ATEC with another Group affiliate, NSEB, a subcontract IC packaging company (see Exhibit 5.10 for financial projections under the plan and Exhibit 5.11 for comparative

---

[11]In August 1997, ATEC had appointed a formal CSC comprised of eight financial institutions: ING Bank, Bangkok Bank, Bankers Trust, Dresdner Bank, Krung Thai Bank, Nakornthon Bank, Standard Chartered Bank, and Sumitomo Bank.

[12]Customers would send payment to one or more banks, which would extend a loan for the same amount to ATEC.

[13]No approval from ATEC's shareholders would be needed for this proposal. However, ATEC would need approval from 75 percent of shareholders in the event that the trading company controlled funds flowing into ATEC.

data).[14] The company claimed it had already cut corporate overhead by 50 percent by reducing head count in its Bangkok headquarters, and would realize additional cost savings by restructuring sales offices in Japan and the United States and by selling U.S.-based assembly and test operations, which had continued to be unprofitable.

The plan required that creditors convert 95 percent of their outstanding debt into equity, with senior unsecured creditors expected to receive 12 to 13 cents on the dollar.[15] The plan also proposed a $30 million equity infusion from two foreign investors. Equity would be invested in $6 million to $10 million tranches for agreed projects keyed to plan milestones.

The plan required the approval of 75 percent of the company's shareholders (by value) plus 100 percent creditors' approval. It also needed approval of 66 percent of bondholders (in number). The plan was contingent on ratification by shareholders of Price Waterhouse as the company's new auditor. Management believed ATEC's debt could be restructured by March 2. "We are getting close!" Mollerstuen wrote to customers. "The next few weeks will tell."

Negotiations Falter

Progress in the plan negotiations was interrupted when Price Waterhouse presented its year-end audit of ATEC's 1997 results to a meeting of shareholders on February 27, 1998. It recommended that ATEC record a net loss of 15.4 billion baht ($381 million) for the year—in dramatic contrast to the profit of 452 million baht reported in 1996. PW believed the company needed to take write-offs and write-downs totaling more than 11 billion baht against accounts receivable, loans to directors and related companies, unusable fixed assets, and falsified inventories.

Charn rejected both the report and the appointment of PW as ATEC's new auditor. According to *The Wall Street Journal*, shareholders believed "[PW's] assessment of how much of the company's assets should be written

---

[14]The IC contract assembly and test market was expected to grow at 28 percent in 1997; 29 percent in 1998; 30 percent in 1999; 35 percent in 2000; and 16 percent in 2001. ATEC's top five customers accounted for roughly 95 percent of revenues, including TI (37%), Cypress Semiconductor (30%), and Advanced Micro Devices (10%). It was estimated that a delay of one month during restructuring would delay anticipated production volumes by at least two months due to reduced customer confidence and qualification procedures.

[15]In contrast, creditors' returns from liquidation were estimated at between 20 and 25 percent for secured creditors, and zero for unsecured creditors.

off was too harsh."[16] Given the voting requirements of the plan, this meant that an out-of-court restructuring would not be possible under the current terms. Within a few days, Cypress Semiconductor announced that it was canceling its testing contract with ATEC.

On March 16, ATEC announced that it was "clearly insolvent" at the end of 1997. In a report to the ATEC board, PW expressed "substantial doubts" about ATEC's ability "to continue as a going concern."[17] According to Mollerstuen, the company had only enough cash to last into May, as it continued to reduce plant operating costs and sell excess equipment.

The next day Mollerstuen wrote to customers: "The word for today: Don't panic! Bankruptcy is our contingency plan. Bankruptcy is the way we want to go! We will come out of this a lot leaner and meaner—much better able to meet your ongoing cost requirements."

NEW THAI BANKRUPTCY LAW

For months the CSC and ATEC's management had been watching the slow progress of Thailand's government in amending the country's bankruptcy code. The existing law provided only for liquidation. After several delays, and under pressure from the International Monetary Fund, the new legislation was finally signed into law by Thailand's king on April 10, 1998.[18] By giving debtors and creditors more flexibility in renegotiating debt repayment and reorganizing troubled businesses, the government hoped to help the country's many ailing financial institutions and corporations. (See Exhibit 5.12 for a description of the new law.)

Under the new law, a creditor, debtor, or government agency could file a petition with the court to initiate the in-court restructuring process. A hearing would be scheduled to determine whether the court would issue an "order for business rehabilitation." During the hearing, the court would examine whether there was a reasonable way to rehabilitate the business. The petitioner also needed to establish that the company was insolvent. Insolvency required that the book value of assets be less than the book value of debt.

If granted, the order triggered an automatic stay on creditors' ability to seize assets. The new law also enabled firms to obtain working capital financing by granting certain lenders "preferential creditor" status, giving them first claim over other creditors. An official planner was selected by

---

[16]"Thai Alphatec Posts Massive Loss, Appears Headed for Bankruptcy," *Wall Street Journal*, March 17, 1998.
[17]Ibid.
[18]Amended bankruptcy laws were one requirement the IMF attached to its $17.2 billion bailout of the Thai economy.

creditors and approved by the court as part of the petition. The restructuring procedures gave the planner the control rights of the former managers and shareholders of the debtor. The planner had three months to submit a rehabilitation plan to the official receiver for a vote by creditors. Only two one-month extensions were allowed.

Once he or she had received the plan, the receiver would send copies to all creditors with voting ballots. The receiver would then convene a meeting of creditors and call for a vote on the plan. If approved by 50 percent of the creditors in number and 75 percent of creditors in value, the plan would be submitted to the court for approval. The law did not recognize different classes of creditors. Existing shareholders had no voice in the rehabilitation process. A final plan had to be approved by the court within five months of the original order for rehabilitation.

The company would then be placed under reorganization by the court. The company would have five years to implement the plan under the supervision of a plan executor. During implementation, the plan executor maintained the control rights of the managers of the debtor and the shareholders, but day-to-day management responsibilities were delegated to company executives. If the company did not meet targets established under the plan, the court could liquidate its assets, or creditors could attempt to restructure the company again.

ATEC FILES FOR BANKRUPTCY

On May 12, 1998, ATEC's management and creditors filed a petition for rehabilitation with the Bangkok Civil Court, the first such filing under the new law. On June 4, the petition was approved, and ATEC officially entered rehabilitation. The petition named Price Waterhouse Corporate Restructuring Ltd. (PWCR) as the official planner. Crédit Agricole Indosuez was named as international financial advisor to the creditors steering committee. The bank and PWCR would be responsible for securing additional equity investors and working capital for ATEC, advising the CSC on the soundness of the restructuring plan, and overseeing its implementation.

All Thai members of ATEC's board resigned, leaving de Vries and Mollerstuen as the only board members. All accounts payable were frozen. Payment of these amounts and other liabilities would be provided for in the rehabilitation plan. The company operated on a pay-as-you-go basis.

Rehabilitation Plan

Reaching agreement with creditors and potential equity investors on the terms of ATEC's rehabilitation proved difficult. After a one-month extension, PWCR filed the rehabilitation plan with the receiver on November 5.

Under the plan, assets of the old ATEC would be transferred to a new company, Alphatec Holding Co. Ltd. (AHC). AHC would own 99.9 percent of the equity of Alphatec Semiconductor Packaging Co. (ASP), which would be set up to take over ATEC's core business operations in Thailand. The holding company would also take over ATEC's 51 percent stake in the Alphatec Shanghai joint venture (ATES) and its 100 percent equity stake in Alphatec Electronics USA (renamed ATS).

The bankruptcy law of Thailand prohibited claims from being made if an application for the repayment of debt was not filed within a prescribed time period. However, the law did not cover overseas claims. Investors feared that such claims might arise and believed that the new organizational form would protect them. In addition, investors wanted to invest in a company that had a known history that could provide a "clean vehicle" for a future stock listing. Because AHC and ASP were newly incorporated companies, investors believed there would be no unpleasant surprises.

At that point ATEC had total debt of $373 million (15.4 billion baht) and book value of assets of $82.7 million (3.4 billion baht) (a current balance sheet is shown in Exhibit 5.13). ATEC owed $363 million of this debt to financial institutions, the rest mainly to trade creditors. Under the plan, the $363 million of institutional debt would be restructured as follows: $10 million would be converted into equity of AHC, $35 million would be converted into a new secured debt, $55 million would be converted into a non-interest-bearing "performance-linked obligation," and the rest would be written off or recovered through legal action against Charn and KPMG. The new secured debt and the performance-linked obligation would be claims against the assets of ASP, and were dominated in U.S. Dollars.[19]

Rather than hold the new equity and debt claims directly, ATEC's creditors would instead be given 99 percent of the equity in the reorganized

---

[19]The secured debt would consist of $20 million of senior debt and $15 million of junior debt. Both tranches of secured debt would mature in six years and pay interest at a premium above LIBOR or SIBOR, but would not pay any principal during the first three years. The performance-linked obligation had a ten-year maturity. On the tenth anniversary, the holder had the option to convert the obligation into either cash or new debt of ASP. However, the amount of the obligation that could be converted was tied to the profitability of ASP during the final three years of the obligation's life. If ASP's average annual net profits during this period were less than $40 million, the obligation could not be converted. If average profits exceeded $130 million, 100 percent of the obligation could be converted. The conversion percentage increased proportionately with profits between these extremes.

ATEC, which would in turn hold the new claims as its only assets. (Former ATEC shareholders would receive the remaining 1 percent of reorganized ATEC.) The reorganized ATEC would have no debt.

The plan also included a significant outside equity investment in AHC. Price Waterhouse announced that AIG Investment Corporation (Asia) Ltd. (part of insurance giant American Insurance Group) and Investor AB (the largest Swedish industrial holding company and parent of Ericsson) were finalizing negotiations for a large infusion of equity into AHC. Under the plan the investors would be required to inject an initial $20 million, followed by an additional $20 million to fund subsequent expansion of production capacity. AIG and Investor AB would own 80 percent of AHC, while creditors would own the remaining 20 percent. Like reorganized ATEC, AHC would be all-equity financed.

The company estimated that creditors would realize significantly higher recoveries under the plan than in a liquidation (see Exhibit 5.14). Financial projections for ASP are shown in Exhibit 5.15.

Krung Thai Balks

On December 14, 1998, ATEC's creditors voted down the rehabilitation plan. While the majority of creditors in number supported the plan, the necessary approval by value of 75 percent of creditors was not obtained.[20] The vote was swung by Krung Thai Bank, which voted against it. The bank believed that the plan did not protect its right to seek recovery from ATEC's former management (primarily Charn, who had personally guaranteed the loans) and KPMG. The bank feared that it would give up this right if it wrote down its debt.[21]

Creditors appointed a different division of PWCR as planner, and gave the firm forty-five days to present a modified plan. ATEC management forecasted that the company would deplete all available cash (including cash that had been reserved for traditional year-end employee bonuses) in mid-January 1999. As before, an offshore holding company would be created, AHC, and ATEC's assets would be transferred to a new Thai operating company, ASP.

Financial creditors of ATEC were offered an option in how they would hold their claims in the restructured company (see Exhibit 5.16). Creditors could opt to hold their claims in AHC and ASP indirectly through ATEC

---

[20]The vote was approximately 50 percent in favor and 50 percent opposed on a value basis.

[21]Under the amended Thai bankruptcy law, there was no legal recourse against alleged fraud involving personal guarantors if a rehabilitation plan was approved by the majority of creditors.

(as in the initial version of the plan), or hold the claims directly. If they decided to hold the claims directly, creditors would then have the option of taking a tax write-off for the difference between what they were originally owed and the value of the new claims received. However, if they elected to take this write-off and realize the associated tax benefits, they would give up the right to pursue their legal claims against Charn and KPMG.[22] Finally, AIG and Investor AB agreed to commit up to $5 million of their investment proceeds for working capital, if required. All other material aspects of the plan remained unchanged.

PWCR distributed the revised plan to creditors, and another vote was scheduled for January 27, 1999. "In the Planner's view," wrote PWCR "it is highly unlikely that Alphatec would be able to secure a more attractive restructuring alternative."

Another Deferral

On January 27, 1999, Krung Thai Bank asked fellow creditors to delay the vote while it considered its options. The receiver agreed to delay the vote by three working days. AIG and Investor AB also agreed to the delay, but said that if the decision were prolonged indefinitely, they would stop their plans to invest in ATEC, and would shift their investment to Malaysia.[23]

Meanwhile, Charn had resurfaced in the press. He claimed the creditors' plan to rehabilitate ATEC was unacceptable because it effectively established a new company and because it valued the company at only $40 million. He said the company's land, buildings, and machinery were worth more than $40 million, and that he was confident that the electronics industry would pick up by the fourth quarter of 1999 and would once again become profitable.[24] He was rumored to be considering taking legal action to stop the rehabilitation plan from proceeding.

In the event the revised rehabilitation plan failed, Mollerstuen and de Vries intended to pursue ATEC's restructuring through a management buy-out. "The company has managed to survive thanks to the efforts of employees, management, suppliers, and the loyalty and patience of customers," he said. "But time, patience, and cash are running out."[25]

---

[22]The plan executor would pursue these legal claims on behalf of the firm and the other creditors. Creditors who opted out could still share in these recoveries if they contributed to the costs of pursuing such claims, however.
[23]"Krung Thai Bank Defers Final Decision," *Bangkok Post*, January 28, 1999.
[24]Ibid.
[25]"Alphatec Creditors File Rehabilitation Plan," *The Nation*, May 13, 1998.

EXHIBIT 5.1   Map of Thailand

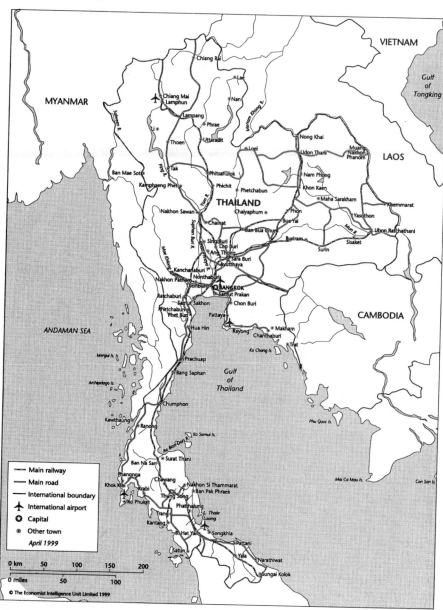

Source: Economist Intelligence Unit.

EXHIBIT 5.2 The Alphatec Group

The "Alphatec Group" consisted of over 11 companies, including ATEC, its subsidiaries, and Alphatec Shanghai. There was no legally recognized holding company, so the Alphatec Group was not a group of companies in the generally accepted sense of sharing a common parent. The companies were linked by a number of common shareholders, which together held a controlling interest in each of the Alphatec Group companies. The interests of individual common shareholders varied from company to company. (See chart showing the interrelationships of the companies within the group.)

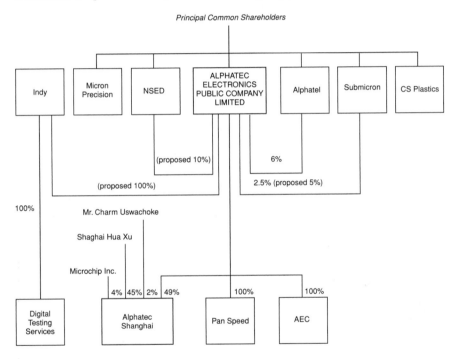

Source: Alphatec Electronics.

EXHIBIT 5.3   Alphatec Electronics Public Company Limited and Subsidiaries: Consolidated Balance Sheets, 1991–1996 (at December 31) (Million Baht)

	1991	1992	1993	1994	1995	1996
Assets						
Cash in hand and at banks	6.3	77.7	503.4	1,621.2	474.6	506.5
Short-term investment	—	1.0	1.0	4.3	3.7	3.2
Promissory notes—finance companies	—	—	—	—	2,167.0	1,927.0
Accounts receivable—other	3.5	512.3	1,109.3	610.0	1,359.8	2,004.9
Accounts receivable and loans to subsidiary companies	—	—	—	74.2	18.3	251.8
Inventories	745.1	1,034.0	1,100.4	1,216.7	1,423.1	2,203.4
Other current assets	74.5	58.8	42.4	15.2	48.3	101.7
Advances to employees	2.5	3.0	5.6	15.7	17.4	383.6
Investments in subsidiary and related companies	3.6	—	—	195.0	518.3	520.0
Deposits	—	—	—	250.4	805.3	1,094.5
Property, plant, and equipment—net	527.2	583.8	1,055.5	2,197.1	2,319.1	4,007.1
Other assets	93.9	449.5	574.4	780.2	937.6	577.7
Total assets	1,456.6	2,720.0	4,392.1	6,979.8	10,092.6	13,581.4
Liabilities						
Bank overdrafts and loans from banks	251.6	620.9	1,537.0	2,371.0	3,308.4	5,381.6
Short-term loans	118.6	203.4	690.4	901.0	201.9	798.2
Accounts payable	582.8	895.8	189.0	187.2	182.9	455.6
Current portion of long-term loans	122.1	283.4	18.4	150.3	160.2	630.8
Other current liabilities	22.6	286.6	349.3	154.5	197.8	435.7
Loans from directors	—	2.3	70.0	42.0	—	—
Long-term loans	193.8	80.8	329.6	394.7	320.7	556.7
Convertible debentures	—	—	—	1,101.6	1,101.6	1,101.6
Total liabilities	1,291.6	2,373.1	3,183.7	5,202.3	5,473.5	9,360.3
Shareholders' Equity						
Share capital—common shares at baht 10 par value:						
Authorized and fully paid up	150.0	220.0	300.0	300.7	369.7	369.7
Premium on share capital	—	19.6	587.6	620.2	3,094.2	3,094.2
Retained earnings						
Appropriated	—	—	30.0	54.0	74.0	100.0
Unappropriated	15.0	111.6	289.3	699.4	1,077.4	656.4
Foreign currency transaction adjustment	—	(4.4)	1.4	3.3	3.8	0.8
Total shareholders' equity	165.0	346.8	1,208.3	1,677.6	4,619.1	4,221.2
Total liabilities and shareholders' equity	1,456.6	2,720.0	4,392.1	6,979.8	10,092.4	13,581.4

Note: Consolidated financial statements since 1992 include Alphatec Shanghai and Alphatec Electronics USA, but not other Alphatec Group companies.

EXHIBIT 5.3 *(Continued)*   Alphatec Electronics Public Company Limited and Subsidiaries: Consolidated Income Sheets, 1991–1996 (for Year Ended December 31) (Million Baht)

	1991	1992	1993	1994	1995	1996
Sales and services	2,152.4	4,477.8	8,017.7	10,031.1	11,274.4	12,241.3
Other income	59.5	9.4	21.7	45.0	7.3	89.5
Total revenues	2,212.0	4,487.2	8,039.0	10,076.1	11,281.7	12,330.8
Cost of sales and services	2,070.9	4,090.5	7,318.4	8,910.7	9,825.5	10,891.3
Selling and administrative expenses	58.3	162.9	256.8	374.8	480.3	576.0
Interest expenses	67.8	135.0	201.4	300.8	274.0	445.7
Income tax	—	0.1	0.1	1.3	3.2	3.8
Total costs and expense	2,197.0	4,388.5	7,776.7	9,587.5	10,583.0	11,916.7
Income before extraordinary item	15.0	98.7	262.7	488.6	698.7	414.1
Add extraordinary item			—	—	—	125.5
Add net loss in subsidiary companies before acquisition date	—	—	—	—	—	60.7
Net result from investments in associated companies by equity method	—	—	—	—	—	(22.7)
Net profit for year	15.0	98.7	262.7	614.0	698.7	452.1

Alphatec Electronics Public Company Limited and Subsidiaries: Consolidated Cash Flow Statements for 1995 and 1996 (for Year Ended December 31) (Million Baht)

	1995	1996
Cash Flows from Operating Activities		
Net profit	698.7	452.1
Adjustment to reconcile net income to net cash provided by (used in) operating activities		
Depreciation and amortization	273.3	557.7
Allowance for obsolete goods	7.0	(6.4)
Loss on exchange rate	9.0	15.9
Change in assets and liabilities		
Foreign currency translation adjustments	.5	(3.0)
Increase in accounts receivable—others	(748.4)	(641.0)
Decrease (Increase) in accounts receivable and loans to related companies	57.0	(230.4)
Decrease (Increase) in advances to related company	(160.6)	163.5
Increase in inventories	(213.4)	(773.8)
Increase in other current assets	(33.1)	(53.4)
Increase in advances to directors and employees	(1.7)	(366.1)

(Continued)

EXHIBIT 5.3 *(Continued)*

	1995	1996
Decrease (Increase) in other assets	(74.2)	205.3
Increase (Decrease) in accounts payable—other	(5.4)	167.1
Increase in accounts payable—related companies	—	105.2
Increase in other current liabilities	43.4	223.5
Increase in other liabilities	—	14.4
Net loss in subsidiary companies before acquisition date	—	(60.7)
Net result from associated companies by equity method	—	22.7
Net cash provided by (used in) operating activities	(148.1)	(207.5)
Cash Flows from Investing Activities		
Decrease (Increase) in short-term investments	(.5)	.5
Decrease (increase) in notes receivable—financial companies	2,167.0	240.0
Decrease (Increase) in share subscriptions deposit	(444.7)	444.7
Increase in investments in associated and related companies	(159.8)	(127.2)
Cash received from (paid for) machinery deposits	(200.4)	(284.1)
Paid for land deposits	(310.6)	(450.0)
Increase in property, plant, and equipment	(291.4)	(2,091.1)
Land not used in operations	(187.0)	—
Paid for goodwill	—	(440.3)
Net cash used in investing activities	(3,360.8)	(2,707.5)
Cash Flows from Financing Activities		
Increase in bank overdrafts and loans from banks	925.1	2,057.5
Increase (Decrease) in short-term loans	699.1	594.7
Increase in current portion of long-term loans	10.0	470.6
Increase (Decrease) in long-term loans	(74.0)	230.9
Repayments on loans from director	(42.0)	—
Proceeds from share capital	2,543.1	—
Dividend paid	(300.7)	(406.7)
Net cash provided by financing activities	2,362.3	2,946.9
Net increase (decrease) in cash and cash at banks	(1,146.6)	31.9
Cash and cash at banks at January 1	1,621.1	474.6
Cash and cash at banks at December 31	474.6	506.5
Cash at banks under commitments	(50.0)	(80.9)
Cash and cash equivalents as at December 31	424.6	524.6
Supplemental disclosures of cash flows information:		
Cash paid during the years:		
Interest expenses	385.6	569.0
Income taxes	3.3	4.0

Source: Company annual reports.

EXHIBIT 5.4 List of Major Claims against ATEC

	Currency	Baht (Million)	U.S. Dollars (Million)
Financial Claims (Number)			
Claims for which amounts had been agreed (37)	USD and Baht	5,990.1	137.9
Convertible debentures (31)	USD	2,018.0	47.1
Claims for which amounts still had to be agreed (7)			
Bangkok Bank Plc	Baht	1,477.7	34.5
Bangkok Metropolitan Bank	Baht	853.1	19.9
GE Electric	USD	133.8	3.1
Krung Thai Bank	Baht	4,227.9	98.6
Nakornthon Bank	Baht	313.4	7.3
Pacific Finance & Securities Plc	Baht	128.2	3.0
Union Bank	Baht	390.7	9.1
Subtotal		7,524.7	175.6
Total		15,532.9	362.5
Employees (1,025)	Baht	63.5	1.5
Trade and other creditors (176)	Baht	548.9	12.8
Contingent liabilities (1)[a]	Baht	2,611.2	60.9

Note: 1 U.S. dollar = Baht 42.8613.

[a]Amount owed Custom Department and Revenue Department.

Source: Alphatec Electronics Public Company Limited Business Reorganization Plan, January 7, 1999. Based on American depository receipt (ADR) claim filings as part of ATEC's rehabilitation process.

EXHIBIT 5.5 Exchange Rate, Thai Baht to U.S. Dollar (January 1, 1990–January 1, 1999)

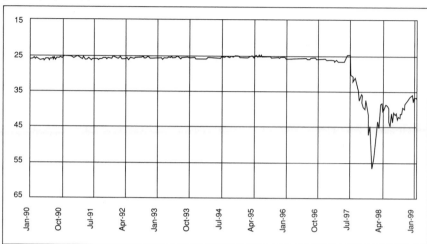

Note: Scale has been inverted to show the baht's decline.

Source: Datastream.

EXHIBIT 5.6 Selected Economic Indicators for Thailand
I. Comparative Indicators, 1998

	Thailand	Malaysia	Indonesia	United States	Japan
GDP ($billion)	116.1	71.1	88.3	8,511.0	3,782.7
GDP per capita	1,899	3,204	435	31,522	29,885
Consumer price inflation (average; %)	8.1	5.3	57.5	1.6	0.7
Current account balance ($ billion)	13.2	9.1	4.0	−233.7	121.0
% of gross domestic product (GDP)	11.4	12.8	4.6	−2.7	3.2
Exports of goods free on board (FOB) ($billion)	53.05	73.2	50.7	673.0	373.3
Imports of goods FOB ($billion)	−38.59	−58.3	−31.6	−919.0	−251.2
Foreign trade[a] (% of GDP)	78.9	185.0	93.2	18.7	16.5

Sources: Economist Intelligence Unit Country Profile of Thailand, 1999–2000.
[a]Merchandise exports plus imports.

II. Stockmarket Indicators

	1994	1995	1996	1997	1998
Number of quoted companies	389	416	454	431	418
Total capitalization at market value (baht billion)	3,300.8	3,564.5	2,559.5	1,133.3	1,268.1
Daily average turnover (baht million)	8,628.0	6,239.7	5,340.7	3,763.5	3,504.8
SET index (year-end)	1,360.1	1,280.8	831.6	372.7	355.8

Source: Bank of Thailand, *Key Economic Indicators*, as reported in Economist Intelligence Unit Country Profile of Thailand, 1999–2000.

III. Nonperforming Bank Loans (Baht Billion)

	December 1998	
	NPLs	Percent of Total credit
Commercial banks	2,356.08	43.0
Eight private banks	1,245.15	40.7
State-owned banks	1,036.69	62.5
Foreign banks	74.24	9.8
Finance companies	2,681.45	45.1

Source: Bank of Thailand, as reported in Economist Intelligence Unit Country Report on Thailand, second quarter, 1999.

EXHIBIT 5.7   Daily Closing Prices for Bangkok SET Index and Thailand SE
Electric Products/Computer Indices, January 1, 1990–January 1, 1999

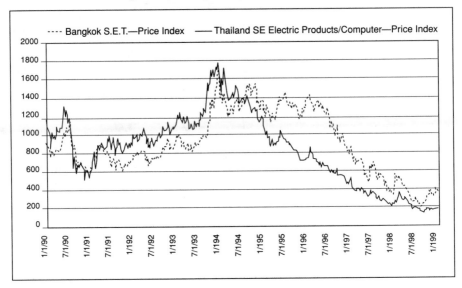

Source: Datastream.

EXHIBIT 5.8 Alphatec Organization Chart at November 25, 1997

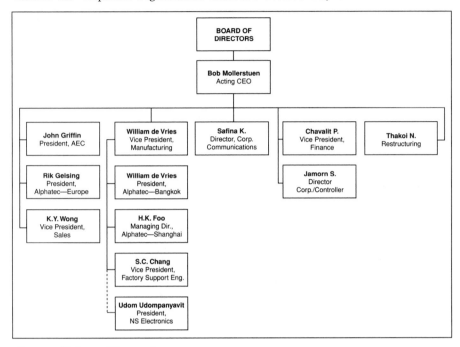

Source: Alphatec Electronics.

EXHIBIT 5.9   Proposals for a New Alphatec at November 25, 1997

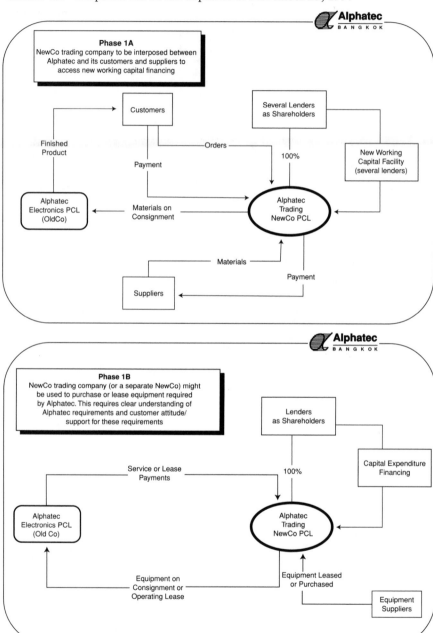

EXHIBIT 5.9 *(Continued)*

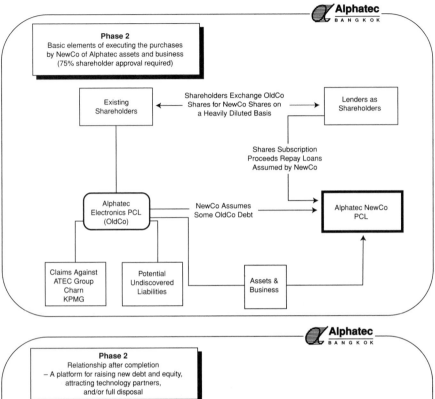

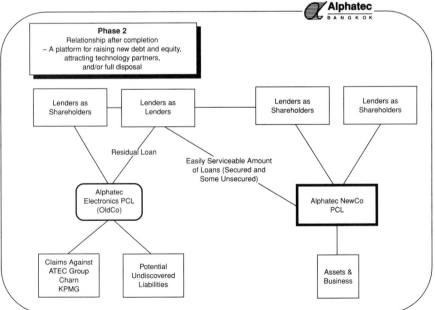

EXHIBIT 5.10   First Restructuring Plan Financial Projections (US$000s)

Totals, 1998–2002	Alphatec I	Alphatec I and II	Alphatec I and II and Alphatec Shanghai	Alphatec I and II, Alphatec Shanghai, and NSEB
Volume (units)	$1,529,468	$1,877,218	$4,982,418	$11,259,091
Revenue	668,776	1,799,366	2,162,313	3,212,063
EBIT	139,425	399,721	492,003	717,949
Cumulative depreciation	67,432	NA	NA	NA
EBITDA	206,856	543,600	683,332	1,029,707
Capex	(66,318)	(375,318)	(471,927)	(485,623)
Free cash flow	140,538	186,282	229,405	438,845

Note: The restructuring plan valued businesses of this type at multiples of 1× revenue, 6× free cash flow, and 10× EBIT.

EXHIBIT 5.11   Comparative Data for Selected Integrated Circuit Packagers (US$million)

Fiscal Year Ended	Net Sales	Depreciation and Amortization	Net Income	Net Cash from Operations	Total Assets	Long-Term Debt	Market Value of Common Stock
Amkor Technology Ltd. (USA)							
Dec. 1995	$ 932	$ 27	$ 62	$ 53	NA	NA	NA
Dec. 1996	1,171	58	33	9	$ 805	$167	NA
Dec. 1997	1,456	82	43	250	856	197	NA
Dec. 1998	1,568	119	75	238	1,004	15	$1,275
Advanced Semiconductor Engineering (ASE) (Taiwan)							
Dec. 1995	$ 595	$ 41	$ 85	$ 59	$ 744	$ 94	$ 967
Dec. 1996	649	63	72	170	844	130	1,405
Dec. 1997	586	71	227	156	1,387	365	3,575
Dec. 1998	645	101	50	NA	1,460	380	2,984
ST Assembly Test Services (Singapore)							
Dec. 1995	NA	NA	NA	NA	NA	NA	NA
Dec. 1996	$ 32	$ 12	($ 7)	$ 13	NA	NA	NA
Dec. 1997	88	25	(9)	10	$ 225	—	NA
Dec. 1998	114	42	(1)	48	237	$ 54	NA

Source: Global Access, Datastream.

Note: Amkor was the world's largest independent provider of semiconductor packaging and test services. It was also a leading developer of advanced semiconductor packaging and test technology. ASE was the largest independent IC packaging company in Taiwan, and one of the largest IC packagers in the world, with operations in Taiwan and Malaysia. ST Assembly Test Services was a Singapore-based independent provider of a full range of semiconductor test and assembly services.

EXHIBIT 5.12 Thai Bankruptcy Process

Procedures to Resolve Distress

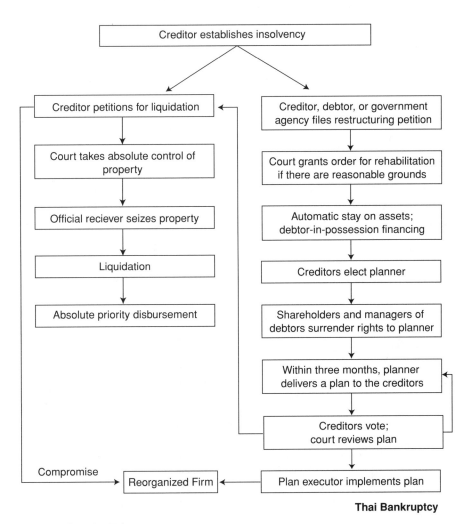

Thai Bankruptcy

Source: C. Fritz Foley.

EXHIBIT 5.13   ATEC Financial Position at June 4, 1998 (Baht Millions)

	Submitted to Court	Unaudited Management Accounts	Note
Current Assets			
Cash and deposits	61	61	
Investments	8	8	1
Accounts receivable—trade (net)	125	125	2
Accounts receivable, loans to related parties (net)	114	114	3
Inventory	210	210	
Other current assets	61	61	4
Total current assets	579	579	
Investments in subsidiaries and related companies (net)	234	234	5
Property, plant, and equipment (net)	2,355	2,355	6
Other assets (net)	234	234	7
Total assets	3,402	3,402	
Liabilities			
Loans from financial institutions	14,593	14,654	8
Accounts payable	314	314	8
Other current liabilities	446	446	8
Investment in subsidiary	0	183	9
Total liabilities	15,353	15,597	
Net deficiency	(11,951)	(12,195)	10
Contingent liabilities	314		11

Notes:

(Assume US$1.00 = Baht 41.16)

1. Comprise short-term deposits and investments in marketable securities, adjusted by management to reflect market prices.
2. Includes amounts owned by existing customers of Alphatec, in addition to a net amount of approximately Baht 1.4 billion owed by Pan Speed Limited, a wholly owned subsidiary of Alphatec, which has been fully provided against. It has subsequently been discovered that this amount was overstated by approximately US$750,000 as a result of bona fide price adjustments agreed with a customer that had not been reflected against recent invoiced amounts.

EXHIBIT 5.13 *(Continued)*

3. Comprises as follows:

	Baht Millions
Alphatec Electronics USA	27
Alphatec Shanghai	11
AlphaTechnopolis Company Limited	553
NS Electronics Bangkok (1993) Limited	73
Micron Precision Company Limited	130
Micron Archin Company Limited	435
Other related companies	62
	1,291
Less: Allowance for doubtful accounts	(1,177)
Total	114

4. Primarily consists of prepayments.
5. Comprises as follows:

	Baht Millions	Baht Millions
Subsidiaries		
Alphatec Electronics USA		17
Alphatec Shanghai		214
Pan Speed Limited (registered in Hong Kong)	139	
Less: Allowance for diminution in value of investment	(139)	
	0	231
Investments in Other Companies		
C.N.C. Building Company Limited	4	
Alphasource Manufacturing Solutions Public Company Limited	174	
Submicron Technology Public Company Limited	50	
	228	
Less: Allowance for diminution in value of investment	(228)	
Bangkok Club Co., Ltd.		3
Total	0	234

(Continued)

EXHIBIT 5.13   *(Continued)*

6. Comprise the land and buildings occupied by Alphatec at Chachoengsao, Thailand, and all machinery and equipment owned by Alphatec. Amounts represent book value. Valuations of land, buildings, machinery, and equipment indicate that book value exceeds the current market value of these assets.
7. Other assets (net) were:
   - Freehold vacant land located adjacent to land and buildings occupied by Alphatec at Chachoengsao (at purchase price): 201 baht million.
   - Refundable deposit: 26 baht million.
   - Advance and loan to directors and employees: 7 baht million.
8. Includes both secured and unsecured creditors, and convertible debentures.
9. At March 31, 1998, Alphatec Electronics USA, Inc., a wholly owned subsidiary of Alphatec, had a capital deficiency of US$4.4 million. Alphatec accounts for this as a negative investment under the equity method.
10. Indicates there is a substantial deficiency in shareholders' equity.
11. Consist of outstanding purchase orders issued by Alphatec, against which materials or services had not been provided as of June 4, 1998.

Note on Contingent Assets: Contingent assets of Alphatec include claims against certain parties as follows:
   - A civil lawsuit was filed in the Central Labour Court on July 17, 1998, in the amount of approximately Baht 14 billion against the former CEO, certain former employees of the company, and other companies in respect to alleged misappropriation of Alphatec funds, falsification of company records, and other actions causing detriment to Alphatec.
   - A lawsuit filed in the Civil Court on July 23, 1998, in the amount of approximately Baht 20 billion against the previous auditors of Alphatec up to the time that the financial irregularities were discovered in July 1997, in respect to alleged damages suffered by the company as a result of a failure to detect and report on the misstated financial position of the company.

Source: ATEC Rehabilitation Plan, January 7, 1999.

EXHIBIT 5.14 Estimated Realizations from Alternative Strategies under the Rehabilitation Plan (US$millions)

	Amount Outstanding	Restructured	Percent	Liquidation	Percent	Note
Financial creditors						
Interest in Alphatec's						
• Senior secured debt	$178	$20		$20		1
• Junior secured debt	185	15		8		2
• Shares in Holdco	—	10		—		
• Performance-linked obligation	—	Not known		—		3
Noncore assets	—	Not known		Not known		4
Legal claims	—	Not known		Not known		4
Total	$363	$45	12	$28	8	
Employee creditors	1	1	100	—	—	2
Trade and other unsecured creditors	9	3	33	1	10	2
Total	$373	$49	13	$29	8	

Notes:
1. In addition to the secured portion of senior secured debt, approximately US$2.6 million (liquidation value) of noncore assets can be realized for the benefit of secured creditors.
2. The liquidation value of unencumbered assets approximates US$10 million based on a valuation received in July 1998. In the event of liquidation, this amount would be shared among unsecured financial creditors, trade creditors, and employees.
3. In the plan, financial creditors will receive a performance-linked obligation with a face value of US$55 million. However, as this does not mature for 10 years and is contingent on future profit performance, realization from this instrument is not included in the above analysis.
4. Recoveries from noncore assets and legal claims are not possible to estimate with any certainty at this time.

Source: ATEC Rehabilitation Plan, January 7, 1999.

EXHIBIT 5.15   Financial Projections Contained in the Rehabilitation Plan

The financial projections prepared by management for distribution to potential investors indicated the following for the Thailand operations (in US$millions):

	1999	2000	2001	2002	2003	2004	2005	2006	2007	2008
Revenue	$73	$164	$241	$303	$332	$381	$439	$505	$580	$668
Cost of sales	(36)	(84)	(123)	(156)	(174)	(194)	(220)	(255)	(299)	(355)
Gross profit	37	80	118	147	158	187	219	250	281	313
Net profit	2	12	30	57	72	102	138	116	134	151
Capital expenditures	62	71	54	22	20	40	40	40	404	40

The results of work undertaken by Crédit Agricole Indosuez in seeking additional equity investment indicated that, given the existing state of the semiconductor market, potential investors were willing to invest significantly less than the amounts originally sought by ATEC to fund more conservative growth projections. Revised financial projections were prepared . . . based on a lower level of initial investment and lower capital expenditure levels going forward. The more conservative projections for Thailand operations indicated the following (in US$millions):

	1999	2000	2001	2002	2003	2004	2005	2006	2007	2008
Revenue	$36	$66	$102	$120	$131	$135	$140	$145	$153	$163
Cost of sales	(19)	(37)	(57)	(68)	(75)	(78)	(81)	(84)	(89)	(96)
Gross profit	17	29	45	52	56	57	59	61	64	67
Net profit	—	4	13	14	13	18	15	15	18	20
Capital expenditures	14	20	17	19	11	8	8	10	10	10

Notes:
- Includes royalty from Alphatec Shanghai (ATES) and Alphatec Electronics USA (renamed ATS).
- Management believed these projections were conservative, particularly for 2000 onwards; however, these revised projections formed the basis for the restructuring assumptions included in the second plan.
- Working capital requirements were estimated as follows (US$millions):
  1999 10
  2000 10
  2001 14
  2002 17
  2003 19

Source: ATEC Rehabilitation Plan, January 7, 1999.

EXHIBIT 5.16   Transaction Structure under the Revised Rehabilitation Plan

Under the terms of the original rehabilitation plan, each creditor was to have received directly its portion (the "entitlements") of restructured debt, performance-linked obligation, and shares in Holdco. In the revised plan, each creditor would have the option of (1) receiving its entitlement via a distribution such that it held its entitlement directly, or (2) retaining its entitlement via a continuing stake in ATEC:

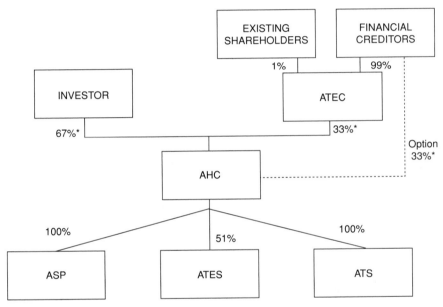

*Percentage ownership following the investor's initial investment of US$20 million. Once the investor made its subsequent US$20 million investment, the percentage ownership applicable to the investor and financial creditors would be 80% and 20%, respectively.

Source: ATEC Rehabilitation Plan, January 7, 1999.

CHAPTER 6

Investing in Distressed Situations

A Market Survey

The practice of investing in distressed companies is popularly known as "vulture" investing. The risks of investing in this market are highly firm specific and idiosyncratic. Investors who are adept at managing these risks, who understand the legal rules that must be followed in corporate bankruptcy, and who are skilled at identifying or creating value in a distressed situation consistently earn the highest returns in this market.

During the past ten years, the number of bankruptcy filings, debt restructurings, and junk bond defaults by U.S. public companies reached record levels. One of the most important and enduring legacies of this period has been the development of an active secondary market for trading in the financial claims of these companies. The participants in this market include many mainstream institutional investors, money managers, and hedge funds, as well as certain individuals—known as "vultures"—who specialize in trading distressed claims.

The strategies these investors use are as diverse as the claims they trade and the companies they target. Some investors prefer to acquire the debt

---

claims of a company while it tries to reorganize under Chapter 11 so they can either influence the terms of the reorganization or wait until the company's debt is converted into a major equity stake that can be used to influence company policy. Some investors prefer to purchase senior claims, others prefer junior claims, and still others spread their purchases throughout the entire capital structure. Some investors choose to take a passive role, seeking out undervalued claims, "hitching their wagons" to that of a more active vulture investor, or holding distressed securities as part of a broadly diversified portfolio.

The business of trading in distressed debt is not new. In the chaos that immediately followed the American Revolution, Treasury Secretary Alexander Hamilton proposed to restore confidence in the financial system by redeeming, at face value, the bonds the American states had issued to finance the war. On the heels of this proposal, speculators acquired large quantities of the bonds, which had fallen greatly in value under the weight of high inflation and the massive war debt, in the hope that Hamilton's program would be completed.[1]

What is unique about today's distressed debt market is its size and scope. There is a market for virtually every kind of distressed claim: bank loans, debentures, trade payables, private placements, real estate mortgages—even claims for legal damages and rejected lease contracts. It is only a slight exaggeration to suggest that anything that is not nailed down will be traded when a firm becomes financially distressed. Two and a half years into the Chapter 11 bankruptcy of R. H. Macy, 728 of the firm's claims had traded for a total dollar value of $510 million. In the recent bankruptcy of Hills Department Stores, more than 2,000 claims exchanged hands.

The market for distressed claims is also quite large. In 1992, coming off the peak of the most recent bankruptcy cycle, one estimate placed the total amount of U. S. corporate debt that was either distressed or in default at $159 billion (face value).[2] In 1993, *Investment Dealer's Digest* identified 27 major investment funds that specialized in buying distressed claims, managing total assets of more than $20 billion. (To put this figure in context, the total amount of money under management in U.S. venture capital

---

[1] See John Steele Gordon, *The Scarlet Woman of Wall Street* (New York: Weidenfeld & Nicolson, 1988).

[2] See Edward Altman, "The Market for Distressed Securities and Bank Loans" (Los Angeles: Foothill, 1992). This figure jumps to $284 billion if one adds debt that is not currently in default but that carries a yield of more than 1,000 basis points above long-term Treasury securities.

funds in 1993 was approximately $27 billion.)[3] Also in 1993, the annual volume of trading in distressed bank debt alone approached $10 billion.[4]

The level of financial distress in the economy, hence the supply of distressed debt, is of course highly cyclical. As Exhibit 6.1 shows, the past few years have seen fewer opportunities to invest in distressed situations, as measured by the number or size of publicly held firms that filed for Chapter 11 (although this group represents only part of the market). In part, this trend reflects the final weeding out of poorly structured deals for the 1980s. In part, the downtrend is the result of recent improvements in the economy. The supply of distressed debt, however—both within the United States and abroad—is certain to rise again. Exhibit 6.1 also shows that the market for distressed debt has historically provided more investment opportunities than other corporate restructuring transactions that have traditionally attracted the interest of investors, including hostile tender offers, leveraged buyouts (LBOs), and spin-offs.

This article surveys the theory and practice of investing in distressed situations. Trading practices in the market for distressed claims have become more sophisticated and institutionalized as the volume of activity has grown. To investors who are unfamiliar with this market, these methods may seem arcane and complex. One goal of this survey is to show that the core strategies for realizing value in distressed situations are relatively straightforward. Another goal is to describe and analyze the various risks—most of them highly firm specific and idiosyncratic—that one faces when purchasing distressed claims. Understanding how to manage these risks is key to earning superior returns in this market. I conclude by discussing future opportunities in distressed situation investing.

BASIC RESTRUCTURING OPTIONS

Investing in distressed situations involves purchasing the financial claims of firms that have filed for legal bankruptcy protection or else are trying to avoid bankruptcy by negotiations and out-of-court restructuring with their creditors. In the United States, corporate bankruptcy reorganizations take place under Chapter 11 of the U.S. Bankruptcy Code. Firms that liquidate

---

[3]This figure is the ten-year sum of the annual amounts raised by venture capital funds during the 1983–1994 period, assuming an average ten-year fund life. I am grateful to Joshua Lerner for providing me these data.
[4]This figure reflects trading by dealers only and excludes trading through brokers (source: Loan Pricing Corporation).

file under Chapter 7. In practice, most firms—more than nine in ten—first try to restructure their debt out of court and only when this fails do they file for bankruptcy. A recent academic study found that approximately 50 percent of all U.S. public firms that experienced financial distress in the 1980s successfully dealt with their problems by restructuring their debt out of court.[5]

An out-of-court restructuring can almost always be accomplished at much lower cost than a court-supervised reorganization. Part of this difference reflects savings in legal and other administrative costs. More importantly, Chapter 11 generally imposes a much heavier burden on the business because of the greater demands placed on management's time and costly delays engendered by litigation. Consistent with this cost differential, Gilson et al. found that firms that successfully restructure their debt out of court experience significant increases in their common stock price (approximately 30 percent, on average, after adjusting for risk and market movements) from the time they first experience financial distress to when they complete their restructuring. Over a corresponding interval, firms that try to restructure out of court but fail experience significant average stock price declines (also on the order of 30 percent).

Chapter 11, however, also provides certain benefits to a distressed firm. While in Chapter 11, the firm does not have to pay or accrue interest on its unsecured debt (and it only accrues interest on its secured debt to the extent the debt is overcollateralized). Chapter 11 also allows the firm to reject unfavorable lease contracts and to borrow new money on favorable terms by granting lenders superpriority over existing lenders ("debtor-in-possession" financing). Moreover, a reorganization plan in Chapter 11 can be passed with the approval of fewer creditors than a restructuring plan negotiated out of court (which generally requires creditors' unanimous consent).

From an investor's perspective, Chapter 11 can also be attractive because the firm is required to file more financial information with the court (e.g., monthly cash flow statements) than is generally available in an out-of-court restructuring.

Lately, in an attempt to realize the benefits of both out-of-court and

---

[5]See Stuart Gilson, Kose John, and Larry Lang, "Troubled Debt Restructurings: An Empirical Study of Private Reorganization of Firms in Default," *Journal of Financial Economics*, vol. 27, no. 2 (October 1990): 315–353; and Stuart Gilson, "Managing Default: Some Evidence on How Firms Choose Between Workouts and Chapter 11," *Journal of Applied Corporate Finance*, vol. 4, no. 2 (Summer 1991): 62–70.

court-supervised reorganization, an increasing number of distressed firms have made "prepackaged" Chapter 11 filings. Since 1989, about one in four bankruptcy filings by public firms has been of this kind. In a "prepack," the firm simultaneously files for bankruptcy and presents its claim holders with a formal reorganization proposal for a vote (having already solicited creditors' approval for the plan). As a result, the bankruptcy usually takes much less time. Trans World Airlines (TWA) recently completed a prepack in only three months. Prepacks work best for firms whose problems are more financial than operational in nature and that have relatively less trade and other nonpublicly traded debt outstanding.

STRATEGIES FOR CREATING VALUE

The Bankruptcy Code does not explicitly regulate trading in distressed claims. As a general legal principle, an investor who purchases a distressed claim enjoys the same "rights and disabilities" as the original claim holder. Thus, with some exceptions, the investor can assert the claim's full face value in a bankruptcy or restructuring, regardless of how much he or she paid to acquire it.

A plan of reorganization—whether negotiated in or out of court—is essentially a proposal to exchange the firm's existing financial claims for a new basket of claims (possibly including cash). The firm's immediate objective is to reduce the total amount of debt in the capital structure. In Chapter 11, the management of the firm (the "debtor") has the exclusive right to propose the first reorganization plan for 120 days following the bankruptcy filing. This period is routinely extended in many bankruptcy jurisdictions.

In deciding whether to vote for a plan, claimholders need to consider the total value, as well as the type, of new claims they are to receive under the plan. The treatment that a particular claim receives in either Chapter 11 or an out-of-court restructuring is not prescribed by formula. Under the "rule of absolute priority," no claimholder is entitled to receive any payment unless all more-senior claims have been made whole. This rule must be followed in a Chapter 7 liquidation. In Chapter 11, certain claims are given a higher priority to receive payment than others (see Exhibit 6.2), but absolute priority does not have to be followed exactly. Small deviations from absolute priority are in fact routine in Chapter 11 cases, as senior claimholders willingly leave some consideration on the table for more-junior claimholders to ensure passage ("confirmation") of the reorganization plan. (The precise legal rules that must be followed for a reorganization plan to be confirmed are described in the appendix at the end of this chapter.) Deviations from absolute priority are also common in out-of-court restructurings—which makes sense because the main alternative to restructuring is to file for Chapter 11.[6]

A simple but useful model to use in analyzing the returns to vulture investing is to view the firm as a pie. The size of the pie represents the present value of the firm's assets. The pie is cut into slices, with each slice representing a financial claim on the firm's cash flows (e.g., common stock, bonds, bank debt, trade claims, etc.). A vulture investor purchases one or more slices of the pie and profits if the slice grows larger. Viewed this way, a vulture investor can follow three strategies to earn a positive return on this investment. He or she can:

- Make the entire pie larger by taking an active management role in the firm and deploying its assets more efficiently.
- Make someone else's slice smaller, thereby increasing the size of the investor's slice (even if the total pie does not become any larger).
- Do nothing (buy undervalued, inefficiently priced claims and wait for them to appreciate).

The first two strategies are proactive: The investor has to be able to influence the outcome of the reorganization proceedings and exercise some degree of control over the firm. The third strategy is passive: If the investor has correctly identified an undervalued claim, all he or she has to do after purchasing the claim is wait (until the market discovers its "error"). Of course, some combination of all three strategies is also possible.

PROACTIVE INVESTMENT STRATEGIES

An appealing analogy can be drawn between the market for distressed debt and the market for corporate control. In both markets, proactive investors seek to profit either by redirecting the flow of corporate resources to more highly valued uses or by bargaining for a larger share of those resources. The mechanisms for acquiring and exercising influence in these two markets differ in fundamental ways, however.

Taking Control of the Business

In Chapter 11, there are several ways that an investor can influence how the firm's assets are deployed. He or she can:

---

[6]See Julian Franks and Walter Torous, "A Comparison of Financial Recontracting in Distressed Exchanges and Chapter 11 Reorganizations," *Journal of Financial Economics,* vol. 35, no. 3 (June 1994): 349–370.

■ *Submit a reorganization plan* to be considered and voted upon by the firm's claimholders. The reorganization plan specifies what financial consideration will be delivered to each of the firm's outstanding claims and proposes a business plan for the firm once it leaves Chapter 11. In addition to current management, any person who holds any of the firm's claims is entitled to submit a reorganization plan. The judge in the case can permit more than one plan to be voted upon at the same time. In the Chapter 11 bankruptcy of Revco D.S., a total of five plans were filed during the case, including two by the debtor, one by a coalition of creditors and preferred stockholders, and one each by two competitors (Jack Eckerd and Rite-Aid). Although every claimholder in a Chapter 11 case is entitled to submit a reorganization plan, the judge must approve the plan before it can be put to a formal vote. Toward this end, an investor's credibility with the judge (and creditors) will be enhanced if he or she owns many of the outstanding claims in a class.

■ *Purchase currently outstanding debt claims* with the expectation that these eventually will be converted into voting common stock under the firm's reorganization plan. Owning a large block of common stock will enable the investor to exercise control over the firm's assets after it reorganizes. This strategy has been used successfully by vulture investors Sam Zell and David Schulte through their investment vehicle, the Zell/Chilmark Fund. During the Chapter 11 bankruptcy of Carter Hawley Hale Stores, for example, Zell/Chilmark made a tender offer for the company's bonds and trade claims explicitly for the purpose of becoming the company's majority stockholder once these claims were converted into common stock under the reorganization plan. In the end, Zell/Chilmark controlled 73 percent of the retailer's equity.[7]

■ *Purchase new voting stock (and other securities)* that are to be issued under the firm's reorganization plan. This approach is known as "funding the plan." The recent Chapter 11 reorganization of Continental Airlines was premised on an infusion of $450 million from a group of outside investors, which included Air Canada, in return for a majority of Continental's common stock and a package of notes, warrants, and preferred stock.

---

[7]As Zell remarked at the time, "I clearly have no intention of being a bondholder. . . . If I'm going to make an investment, I'm going to be an owner of equity." See Francine Schwadel; "Zell 'Vulture Fund' Offers Investment in Carter Hawley," *Wall Street Journal* (July 25, 1991).

In each of these cases, the investor's goal is to assume a management or control position in the company and directly influence its investment and operating policies. The investor earns a return by causing the company to be run more profitably, thus increasing the value of its assets (and the value of the financial claims held against those assets).

Outside of Chapter 11, control over the firm's assets can be acquired by purchasing a large block of the firm's equity and waging a proxy contest or forcing management to hold a special stockholders' meeting. In principle, special stockholders' meetings are also possible inside Chapter 11, subject to the judge's approval. One goal of having such a meeting might be to force management to propose a more "stockholder friendly" reorganization plan. Such meetings have been permitted in several high-profile Chapter 11 cases, including Lionel, Allegheny International, and Johns–Manville.

In practice, however, purchasing equity is generally an ineffective way to acquire or exercise control in a financially troubled company. Most bankruptcy judges are reluctant to approve special stockholders' meetings. The Bankruptcy Code already includes a procedure for replacing management (with a "trustee") when management is shown to be guilty of "fraud, dishonesty, incompetence, or gross mismanagement."[8] In addition, under state and federal law, the managers and directors of a Chapter 11 debtor are generally considered fiduciaries of both stockholders and creditors; thus, management may be legally unable to pursue a course of action that favors stockholders over creditors. (In an out-of-court restructuring, these constraints do not apply, but management always has the option of filing for bankruptcy if a proxy fight threatens.)

Finally, prebankruptcy stockholders' interests are often severely diluted by the issuance of new common shares to creditors under the firm's bankruptcy or restructuring plan. Any "control" one has over a financially distressed firm by virtue of being a large stockholder is therefore usually short-lived. Stockholders of Wheeling–Pittsburgh Steel, which spent more than five years in Chapter 11, received less than 10 percent of the reorganized firm's stock. This percentage is fairly typical.

As a rule, more-senior claims in the capital structure receive more-senior claims (debt or cash) in a reorganization or restructuring; more-junior claims typically receive more of the common stock. The trick—if the goal is to emerge from the reorganization as a major equity holder—is to concentrate on buying relatively junior claims, but not so junior that one ends up receiving nothing (i.e., because the firm's assets are worth too little to

---

[8]Section 1104(a) of the U.S. Bankruptcy Code.

support distributions that far down the capital structure). Investors who are better able to value the firm's assets have a clear advantage in trying to achieve this goal.

"Bondmail"

An investor can also increase his or her return by acquiring a sufficiently large percentage of an outstanding debt issue to block the firm's reorganization plan. As described in the appendix, in every Chapter 11 case, the firm's financial claims are grouped into distinct "classes." Each class votes separately on whether to approve the reorganization plan(s) under consideration. A class is deemed to have accepted a plan if at least two-thirds in value and one-half in number of the claimholders in that class who vote, vote affirmatively (the latter criterion is referred to as the "numerosity" requirement). Claimholders who do not vote are not counted. A "consensual" plan of reorganization cannot be approved unless every impaired class votes for the plan (see the appendix).

Thus, an investor needs only slightly more than one-third of the claims in a particular class to block a reorganization plan. In this case, the investor can threaten to hold up the firm's reorganization unless he or she is given a higher recovery—a practice that has come to be known as "bondmail." (To return to the pie analogy, the investor can try to enlarge his or her slice at the expense of other sliceholders.)

Note, however, that an investor who holds a blocking position in a class cannot demand more favorable treatment under a plan than other members of the class. Section 1123(a)(4) of the Bankruptcy Code requires that all holders within any given class be treated identically under a reorganization plan (except for holders who agree to be treated differently). Thus, the practice of "greenmail"—seen in many 1980s-style corporate takeovers—is not allowed in Chapter 11.

In determining whether the numerosity requirement has been satisfied, the courts treat a holder of multiple claims within a class as a single holder if the claims are effectively identical, such as publicly traded debentures or notes. In the case of nonidentical claims—for example, different bank loans grouped within the same class—several recent court decisions suggest that the holder is entitled to one vote for each claim he or she holds in this class.

The distinction is an important one in terms of how much voting control a given-sized block of claims confers on the holder. If an investor holds, say, 35 percent of the outstanding principal amount of a debenture issue representing a single class, he or she can block the class from approving a reorganization plan but cannot force the class to approve a plan: As long as one other holder is represented in the class, the investor cannot account for more than half of all holders. Only by controlling 100 percent of the claims can he or she have complete control over how the class votes. Even if the investor forms a voting coalition with other class members, most judges will treat the coalition as a single "holder" when tallying votes. In contrast, an investor may be able to satisfy the numerosity requirement with less than 100 percent ownership of the claims in a class when the claims are nonidentical (e.g., bank loans, trade claims, etc.).

A blocking strategy is riskier if the investor purchases his or her claims before the firm files for Chapter 11. The reason is that claimholder classes are defined within the reorganization plan. The Bankruptcy Code requires only that a class contains "substantially similar" claims; it does not require that substantially similar claims be put in the same class. Thus, the plan proposer has considerable opportunity to gerrymander claims and reduce the voting power of particular claimholders. One way the investor can preempt this possibility is to propose his or her own plan.

An investor's ability to coerce a higher payment from the firm is also limited by the threat of a bankruptcy "cram-down." As discussed in the appendix, a reorganization plan can be confirmed over the objections of a claimholder class (i.e., "crammed down" on that class) if the present value of the consideration class members are to receive under the plan equals the allowed value of their claims or if no more-junior class receives any consideration. In practical terms, an investor who holds a blocking position in a class can still be forced to accept a low recovery if the firm's assets are worth too little to support any additional payments to that class. Even if the cram-down is never used, the threat of a cram-down can be enough to reduce an investor's recovery drastically. Thus, investors in distressed debt (especially junior debt) need to assess carefully whether the claims they are thinking of buying are "in the money."

Investors who have pursued this proactive strategy include Leon Black; Martin Whitman; Sanford Phelps; Carl Icahn; and, until its dissolution, Goldman Sachs' Waterstreet Corporate Recovery Fund. One invariable byproduct of the strategy is intense conflict among different creditor classes. While Revco D.S. was in Chapter 11, vulture investor Talton Embry of Magten Investments purchased blocking positions in the company's subordinated bonds in an attempt to reduce the recoveries realized by holders of Revco's senior bank debt. Conflicts between junior and senior creditors were also much in evidence in the bankruptcy of Gillett Holdings, in which Apollo Advisors held a blocking position in the company's senior claims and Carl Icahn held a blocking position in its junior bonds.

PASSIVE INVESTMENT STRATEGIES

The explosive growth in the demand side of the distressed debt market has greatly reduced the number of opportunities for buying underpriced claims. Most participants now consider this market to be relatively efficient, and several recent academic studies confirm this view.

These studies consider various buy-and-hold strategies that investors might pursue to exploit possible overreaction in the market for distressed bonds or common stock (data limitations preclude looking at the market for most nonpublic claims). After publicly traded bonds go into default, they typically trade at about 30 percent of their face value; the average discount for more-junior bonds is even larger (see Exhibit 6.3). Market overreaction therefore seems at least plausible. These studies, however, fail to find evidence of abnormal returns (adjusting for risk and transaction costs) to buying portfolios of distressed bonds at the end of the default month, the end of the bankruptcy-filing month, or on other key dates.[9] Systematic abnormal returns also do not appear to be available from buying bankrupt firms' common stock.[10]

Although no comparable empirical studies have been done for trading in bank or trade claims, increasing liquidity in this market makes the existence of profitable trading rules seem unlikely here, too. In the mid-1980s, news of a bank loan default typically might have resulted in the bank's workout department being approached by one or two interested potential buyers. In the current market, a bank's digital trading desk might receive up to a hundred inquiries in the case of a large credit.

Although a passive strategy may be unlikely to yield positive abnormal returns, a number of institutional investors hold large amounts of distressed debt as part of a broader portfolio diversification strategy. Included in this

---

[9]See Alan C. Eberhart and Richard J. Sweeney, "Does the Bond Market Predict Bankruptcy Settlements?" *Journal of Finance,* vol. 47, no. 3 (July 1992): 943–980; and Edward I. Altman, Alan C. Eberhart, and Kenneth Zekavat, "Do Priority Provisions Protect a Bondholder's Investment?" manuscript (1993).

[10]See Dale Morse and Wayne Shaw, "Investing in Bankrupt Firms," *Journal of Finance,* vol. 43, no. 5 (December 1988): 1193–1206. In spite of this evidence, a number of investment funds have specialized in buying common stock in companies that have recently emerged from Chapter 11. The rationale for this strategy is that such stocks are undervalued because (1) few analysts follow them (hence the alternate label "orphan stocks") and (2) these stocks are in oversupply because creditors tend to unload the shares they receive in a bankruptcy reorganization quickly. See Matthew Schifrin, "Reborn and Deleveraged," *Forbes* (August 15, 1994).

group are Trust Company of the West, Foothill, T. Rowe Price, and Cargill, among others. As of late 1994, these investors were estimated to hold more than $10 billion in distressed debt. These investors, of course, retain the option to become actively involved in a bankruptcy or restructuring.

Careful fundamental analysis of an individual firm's situation may still yield opportunities to purchase claims for less than their intrinsic value. Careful scrutiny of the covenants of a bond issue may, for example, turn up a weakness in a subordination agreement. Junior bondholders in the Zale and R. H. Macy bankruptcies realized higher-than-expected recoveries—at the expense of senior creditors—because the bonds were released from the subordination agreement under a special exemption. Often, these kinds of provisions are buried in the indenture document; inspecting only the bond prospectus may be insufficient.[11]

RISKS OF INVESTING IN A DISTRESSED SITUATION

The risks in investing in distressed claims are highly firm specific. Many are legal and institutional in nature, and most can be controlled through careful planning and by conducting adequate due diligence. Having a sound working knowledge of bankruptcy law is important; many successful investors in this market are either former practicing bankruptcy attorneys or have access to legal counsel experienced in bankruptcy matters.

The following list of relevant risk factors is undeniably long, but the large number of risks alone has not prevented investors from earning huge returns in this market, on a par with those earned in many corporate takeover contests of the 1980s. Experience has shown that investors who understand and are adept at managing these risks consistently earn the highest returns from trading in distressed debt.

The "J" Factor

To encourage consensual bargaining among a bankrupt firm's claimholders, the U.S. Bankruptcy Code is designed to be flexible. As a result, the

---

[11]In contrast to these buy-and-hold strategies, some investors alternatively specialize in short selling the common stock of companies that are in or near Chapter 11. Such activity, however, is much more limited in scale than the buy-and-hold approach, and the participants in this market are highly sophisticated. In addition, shares in a firm are generally thought to be more difficult to locate after it files for bankruptcy. Short sellers are known to have made large (multimillion-dollar) returns in such bankruptcies as Circle K, ZZZZ, Best, and LTV.

outcome of any case may significantly depend on prior case law or on how a particular judge rules. The judge's track record should therefore be carefully factored into an investor's purchase decision.

Judges can significantly influence investment returns through their control of the administration of a bankruptcy case. Of particular importance to proactive investors is the judge's prerogative to decide whether a particular claim is allowed to vote on a reorganization plan or is entitled to any recovery, whether a proposed reorganization plan can be put up for a vote, and whether an allowed plan is confirmable. At a critical point in the bankruptcy of Integrated Resources, the judge would not permit creditors to see vulture investor Steinhardt Partners' competing reorganization plan until after they had voted on management's plan—even though management's exclusive right to file a plan had expired.

Judges can also influence investor returns because their approval is required before the debtor can undertake major actions that lie outside the "ordinary course" of its business (such as selling off an operating division or making a major investment in new equipment). Interventionist judges have been known to permit a firm to take actions that are potentially harmful to creditors' interests. In the Eastern Airlines bankruptcy, the judge allowed management to spend almost $200 million of cash that had been placed in escrow for Eastern's unsecured creditors, on the grounds that the "public interest" would be better served if Eastern were to continue flying. (The Bankruptcy Code does not give judges this particular charge, however.)

In some jurisdictions, especially the Southern District of New York, judges are thought to systematically favor the interests of management and stockholders over creditors. One alleged consequence of this bias is that the debtor's "exclusivity period"—during which only the debtor can propose a reorganization plan—is more often extended in this district. This policy allows debtor management to remain in control of the firm longer to the possible detriment of the firm's creditors. To seek a more favorable outcome, some firms go "forum shopping," filing in districts that are believed to be debtor friendly.[12] Eastern Airlines filed for Chapter 11 in the Southern District of New York, even though it was incorporated in Delaware and headquartered in Miami. Eastern accomplished this feat by attaching its bankruptcy filing to that of a small subsidiary headquartered in New

---

[12]See Lynn M. LoPucki and William C. Whitford, "Venue Choice and Forum Shopping in the Bankruptcy Reorganization of Large, Publicly Held Companies," *Wisconsin Law Review,* vol. 1991, no. 1 (1991): 13–63.

York, which had filed for Chapter 11 only six minutes before. The subsidiary was less than 1 percent of Eastern's size by total assets and operated a string of airport travel lounges.[13]

Title Risk and the Mechanics of Transferring Claims

When an investor purchases a claim against a financially distressed firm, a number of steps need to be taken to ensure that the investor is legally recognized as the new owner. In practice, one may encounter various hidden hazards during this process.

Transfers of claims in Chapter 11 are regulated by Federal Bankruptcy rule 3001(e). To understand the application of this rule, it is necessary first to describe the procedure the court follows in identifying the firm's claimholders. Within ten days of filing for Chapter 11, the debtor is required to file a schedule of assets and liabilities with the court clerk, including the name and address of each creditor. The debtor then sets a "bar date." Creditors with disputed or contingent claims must file a "proof of claim" by this date or forfeit their rights to participate in the reorganization plan; all other claimholders are automatically assumed to have filed a proof of claim.[14] (Exhibit 6.4 provides a time line of key dates in a typical Chapter 11 reorganization.)

Under Rule 3001(e), an investor who purchases a claim against a firm after a proof of claim has been filed by the selling creditor is required to provide the court with evidence of the transaction. If after approximately 20 days the seller does not object to the transaction, the judge automatically approves the transfer of ownership. If the transaction takes place before proof has been filed, no formal notification of the court is required and filing a proof of claim becomes the investor's responsibility. In neither case does the investor have to reveal the number of claims purchased or the price paid. Also, Rule 3001(e) does not apply to the purchase and sale of publicly traded securities; here, as in other matters, the Bankruptcy Code defers to relevant securities law.

Prior to August 1991, when the current version of Rule 3001(e) was adopted, more-rigorous disclosure requirements had to be satisfied. In gen-

---

[13]For an analysis of the Eastern Airlines bankruptcy, see Lawrence Weiss, "Restructuring Complications in Bankruptcy: The Eastern Airlines Bankruptcy Case," manuscript (1994).

[14]Generally, it is a good idea for even these creditors to physically file a proof of claim, however, to help resolve any future disputes over title and ownership.

eral, an investor had to disclose the terms of the transaction to the court—including the number of claims purchased and, in some circumstances, the transaction price. The transfer of claims also had to be approved by a court order. In a number of widely cited cases, judges refused to approve claims transfers on the grounds that the sellers were not adequately informed about the value of the claims they were selling.[15] Removing the judge from this process (under revised Rule 3001(e)) has arguably had the effect of increasing liquidity in the secondary market for distressed claims.

Notwithstanding this revision, an investor may still encounter a number of problems in trying to establish title to a claim. For example, the seller may have sold a given claim more than once, creating multiple holders of the claim. Such redundant sales may be purely fraudulent or the result of oversight on the part of larger lenders who inadvertently assigned responsibility for selling the loan to more than one person. Small trade creditors are thought to be especially guilty of this practice, and one prominent vulture investment fund now avoids purchasing trade claims altogether.

An investor can take several measures to reduce the risk of buying a redundant claim.[16] If the seller has already filed a proof of claim or granted the buyer a power of attorney to file a proof of claim in the seller's name, virtually no risk exists, because the court assigns the claim a number. By referring to this number when buying the claim, the buyer can establish himself or herself as the true owner. Short of this arrangement, the buyer can insist that the seller provide him or her with a title guarantee; however, le-

---

[15]For example, in the Chapter 11 reorganization of Revere Copper and Brass, the judge refused to approve vulture fund Phoenix Capital's purchase of unsecured trade debt at 28 cents on the dollar, on the grounds that trade creditors may have mistakenly believed the company was being liquidated, causing them to sell out at too low a price. Evidently, one factor in her decision was a *Wall Street Journal* story published shortly after most of these purchases had been made, which reported that the company's reorganization plan would likely propose creditor recoveries between 65 and 100 cents on the dollar. The judge argued that Phoenix did not provide trade creditors with information that would enable them to make an "informed" decision. She specifically cited Section 1125 of the Bankruptcy Code, which prohibits solicitation of claimholders in regard to a plan of reorganization before they have received a copy of the disclosure statement (which describes the plan terms and related pertinent information). Eventually, as a condition of approving the transfer of claims, the judge required Revere to offer selling creditors a full refund.

[16]The remainder of this section is based on the excellent discussion of claims trading and title transfer issues in Thomas Moers Mayer, "Claims Trading: Problems and Failures," manuscript (1994).

gal costs make this option relatively unattractive for smaller claims. The buyer can also file a proof of claim or notice of transfer of claim with the court, even if he or she is not required to do so. Filing either of these forms creates a physical record of the transaction. Unfortunately, the mere existence of this record does not necessarily preclude another investor from buying the same claim; the original record must first be identified. The court eventually compiles a "master list" of all such records that have been filed in the case, but this process can take several months, which leaves the investor to search physically through the many hundreds or thousands of forms that may have been filed in the case to date.[17]

Finally, title issues are important in "multiple debtor" cases in which related parent and subsidiary corporations have all individually filed for Chapter 11. These cases are often "administratively consolidated," meaning the cases are collectively assigned a single case number and name for administrative convenience—even though each individual case also received its own name and number. Creditors who have debt outstanding at the parent company level that is guaranteed by one or more subsidiaries are generally advised to file proofs of claim for each individual parent or subsidiary case, as well as for the consolidated case.[18] One consequence of this procedure is that the total debt outstanding in a case is often significantly overstated because of temporary double-counting. Total claims in Wheeling-Pittsburgh Steel's bankruptcy started out at $14 billion, even though only $1 billion in actual claims was outstanding.

Risk of Buying "Defective Merchandise"

An investor who purchases distressed debt may inherit certain legal "baggage" or liabilities from the original lenders that the investor had no role in

---

[17]Title problems can also arise as a result of how the court records proofs of claim. In most jurisdictions, the court mails creditors the official notice of the bar date along with a computer-coded proof-of-claim form (based on the debtor's schedule of liabilities). Sometimes, however, creditors choose to substitute their own forms. As a result, the same claim will be recognized twice—once as an entry in the debtor's schedule of liabilities and once as a "new" claim listed on the creditor's personalized proof-of-claim form. Such duplication may not be corrected for several months. In the meantime, the investor may be hindered in asserting his or her claim because the debtor chooses to recognize only the "parallel" claim noted on its schedule of liabilities. See Mayer, "Claims Trading."

[18]See Mayer, "Claims Trading."

creating. These liabilities can be significant and present a major risk to participants in this market.

Fraudulent Conveyance An investor who buys debt in a troubled LBO may become liable for damages under an outstanding fraudulent conveyance suit. Roughly speaking, a fraudulent conveyance occurs when (1) property is transferred from a firm in exchange for less than "reasonably equivalent" value, and (2) as a result, the firm is left insolvent (or it was insolvent when the transfer took place). The first criterion is almost always satisfied by an LBO.[19]

In filing a fraudulent conveyance suit, the debtor attempts to recover the property that was fraudulently transferred. In theory, this course of action may mean trying to recover the payments that were made to the selling shareholders; in practice, such efforts are mainly directed at large, deep-pocketed claimholders, who make attractive targets for litigation. An investor who buys up and consolidates a large number of smaller claims may be especially at risk. If a fraudulent conveyance action is successful, lenders' claims can be subordinated or stripped of their security interest if the debt is secured. Under Section 548 of the Bankruptcy Code, a fraudulent conveyance action can be brought within one year of an LBO.[20]

Avoidable Preferences Chapter 11 allows a debtor to recover certain payments, known as "avoidable preferences," that it made to creditors within 90 days prior to filing for bankruptcy.[21] The point of this provision is to

---

[19]In an LBO, the firm borrows a large sum of money and uses the proceeds to buy out the public stockholders. Under the law, this payout of cash is considered a transfer of assets. Neither the cash received by stockholders nor any appreciation in the value of the firm's assets due to the LBO, however, is included in the calculation of reasonably equivalent value.

[20]Fraudulent conveyance actions can also be brought under various state laws patterned after either the Uniform Fraudulent Conveyance Act or the Uniform Fraudulent Transfers Act. Applicable state laws generally have a longer statute of limitations (up to six years). In practice, fraudulent conveyance suits are almost always settled before going to final judgment, typically for less than ten cents on the dollar. See Jack Friedman, "LBO Lawsuits Don't Pick Deep Pockets," *Wall Street Journal* (January 27, 1993). Such suits, however, are often brought as a negotiating ploy during a Chapter 11 case to induce larger concessions from the LBO lenders (or current holders of LBO debt). These concessions are an additional cost to the investor from a fraudulent conveyance attack.

[21]This period increases to one year if the creditors had an insider relationship with the debtor. Such a relationship might be deemed to exist, for example, if a lending bank is represented on the debtor's board of directors at the time the debtor files for Chapter 11.

discourage insolvent firms from cutting side deals with key creditors.[22] Payments to creditors made in the normal course of business and on normal business terms are not recoverable. Payments on LBO debt, however, may be recoverable, given the unusual nature of the transaction. Grants of additional security to a lender are also generally recoverable.

The Bankruptcy Code's treatment of preferences creates several risks for an investor in distressed debt. If the investor purchases debt in a firm that subsequently files for bankruptcy, he or she may have to return payments that were received on the debt within the 90-day prefiling period. If the debt is purchased after the firm files for bankruptcy, the investor is not directly on the hook. The court, however, could still choose not to recognize the investor's claims until all such preferences are recovered (from the previous owners of the debt).

Equitable Subordination and Lender Liability   In Chapter 11, an investor in distressed debt risks having the debt "equitably subordinated"—made less senior—if the selling creditor is found to have engaged in "inequitable conduct" that resulted in harm to other creditors or gave the selling creditor's claim an unfair advantage in the case. (Of course, the same penalty applies if the investor is found guilty of such conduct.) Equitable subordination invariably reduces the investor's rate of return because more-junior claims almost always receive lower percentage recoveries in bankruptcy.

In determining whether inequitable conduct has occurred, basically the same standards apply as those used to assess lender liability outside of Chapter 11. A bank creditor may be considered guilty of inequitable conduct if it exercises excessive control over a firm's operations as a condition of lending the firm more money or refuses to advance funds under an existing credit line, thus impairing the firm's ability to pay its other creditors. In the bankruptcy of convenience store operator Circle K, unsecured creditors holding claims worth approximately $700 million petitioned the court to equitably subordinate $380 million of senior bank debt on the grounds that the banks had contributed to the bankruptcy by financing an ill-advised acquisition.

Environmental Liabilities   Under the Comprehensive Environmental Response Compensation and Liability Act (CERCLA), lenders can be held liable

---

[22]If preferential payments could not be recovered, creditors might, at the first hint of financial trouble, collectively rush to grab whatever of the firm's assets they could to protect their individual interests, making the firm's problems even worse.

for the costs of cleaning up hazardous substances found on the borrower's property. This liability is assessed based on who currently owns or operates the property rather than on who was responsible for creating the pollution. A lender who has a security interest in certain contaminated property may be considered an "owner" or an "operator" of the property—hence potentially liable under CERCLA—if it forecloses on its security interest or assumes an active role in managing the property.

An investor in distressed debt should investigate whether the seller has engaged in past behavior that might qualify it as an owner or an operator of contaminated property. CERCLA provides secured lenders with an exemption to its definition of property "owner," but the courts have differed on how widely this exemption applies; also, this exemption does not shield a lender from liability under various state environmental laws. As a general rule, lenders do not expose themselves to liability under CERCLA simply by exercising their ordinary right as creditors (e.g., by enforcing covenants, restructuring a loan, foreclosing on a security interest and promptly disposing of the acquired property, etc.).

Protecting Against These Risks   Investors in distressed debt can reduce their exposure to these liabilities by obtaining appropriate representations, warranties, and indemnities from the seller. These protections are especially important in the case of bank, trade, and other nonpublic debt, on which less information is generally available from public sources. Representations and warranties, which effectively operate like put options, give the investor some assurance as to what "nonstandard" liabilities, if any, he or she may inherit as a result of buying the debt (especially those that arise from improper conduct by the seller).[23] As added protection, investors also often ask sellers to indemnify them against potential damages.

Obtaining representations, warranties, or indemnities can be difficult, however, because creditors who sell their claims most often wish to rid themselves of all ties to the firm. Many contemplated bank loan sales have fallen through because banks have been unwilling to grant these protec-

---

[23]Most bank loan sale agreements transfer to the buyer responsibility for the "standard" risks and liabilities that can arise in a distressed (or nondistressed) situation, including the risk that the court will disallow part or all of the claim, the risk that the buyer will realize a lower recovery on the claim than he or she initially expected, and the risk that the buyer may have to lend funds to the borrower under the unfunded portion of any letter of credit.

tions to otherwise willing buyers.[24] This attitude has grown increasingly common among banks as the number of potential buyers of distressed claims has rapidly increased in recent years. Also, trading in the current market for distressed debt is characterized by a higher fraction of retrades (in which the seller is not the original lender) and hence a much shorter average holding period than was true even five years ago. In this environment, representations, warranties, and indemnities generally make less sense for both buyers and sellers.

As a result of these considerations, investors who are more familiar with the borrower's operations and management (e.g., as a result of past business dealings or superior research) have an increasing comparative advantage in assessing these risks and in accurately valuing distressed claims.

Disputed and Contingent Claims

In almost every Chapter 11 case, the status, seniority, or size of some claims is not resolved until well into the case. An investor's recovery in the case and percentage return can be greatly affected by how these disputed claims are resolved, especially if they rank senior or equal to the investor's claim in the firm's capital structure.

Claims can be disputed or contingent for many reasons. For example, creditors sometimes file multiple proofs of claim for the same underlying instrument. Another important source of dispute revolves around the issue of when a particular claim comes into existence. When the Environmental Protection Agency (EPA) has a claim outstanding against a bankrupt firm under CERCLA, for example, the debtor will typically try to argue that the claim arose before it filed its bankruptcy petition (e.g., because the actions that gave rise to the contamination occurred before the filing). The EPA, in contrast, will typically argue that the claim arose after the firm filed for bankruptcy (e.g., because the costs of cleaning up the contaminated site have yet to be actually incurred).

The date on which a claim comes into existence is important because under the Bankruptcy Code all prepetition claims are discharged when the firm leaves bankruptcy (to use an analogy, the debtor's record is wiped clean of all offenses committed before it filed for Chapter 11). If the EPA

---

[24]This happened, for example, in the out-of-court restructuring of Western Union and in the bankruptcies of Coleco Industries and Apex Oil. See Chaim Fortgang and Thomas Moers Mayer, "Trading Claims and Taking Control of Corporations in Chapter 11," *Cardozo Law Review*, vol. 12, no. 1 (1990): 1–115.

loses its case, then its claim will most likely be added to the pool of general unsecured claims, although it may still try to have its claim treated as a higher priority administrative expense (see Exhibit 6.2). Exactly the same issues come up when the Pension Benefit Guaranty Corporation brings a claim against a Chapter 11 debtor for unfunded pension liabilities.

Finally, Chapter 11 allows a firm to reject unfavorable leases and other "executory contracts" (including collective bargaining agreements). Any economic loss the owner of the leased property suffers as a result of such rejection becomes a general unsecured claim against the estate. The owner, however, may dispute the debtor's right to reject the lease or its estimate of losses from the rejection.

Counting Votes

Investors should be aware of certain problems that can arise in connection with how, and whether, they vote their claims in Chapter 11.[25] Acquiring, say, 35 percent of the claims in a class does not always mean the investor commands 35 percent of the votes. The source of this discrepancy differs depending on whether the claims are publicly traded.

For the buyer of a bank, trade, or other nonpublic claim to be considered a "holder of record"—and thus be eligible to vote on the reorganization plan—a "statement of transfer of claim" must be received by the claims-processing agent no later than the official voting record date. The court clerk mails this statement to the claims-processing agent, who is usually located in a different state. With various delays possible, this process can take well over a week. An investor who purchases a claim too close to the record date therefore risks being disenfranchised. This problem was recently an issue in the Hills Department Stores bankruptcy. To guard against this possibility, the purchase agreement could include a provision that requires the seller to transmit his or her ballot to the buyer, although the seller may fail to perform its obligation in a timely enough manner. Even better, the buyer could try to obtain from the seller a power of attorney that gives the buyer the right to vote the claim on behalf of the seller.

Voting rights issues are more complicated—and interesting—in the case of publicly traded bonds or debentures than for nonpublic claims. The indenture trustee for a bond issue maintains a registry of ownership, but it rarely lists the real beneficial owners of the bonds. In practice, most bonds are held in "Street name" at various brokerage firms, which act as custodi-

---

[25]This summary of voting issues is based on Mayer, "Claims Trading."

ans for the real owners. When voting on a plan of reorganization commences, the balloting agent sends both a "master ballot" and a set of individual ballots to the brokerage firms registered as holders of record. Each brokerage firm is supposed to distribute the individual ballots to the actual owners. The owners return their marked ballots to the brokerage firm, which then summarizes the votes on the master ballot. Only the master ballot is returned to the balloting agent—without disclosing the identities or votes of the real owners.

A number of things can go wrong in the process. The broker may miss the deadline for returning the master ballot to the balloting agent. In the recent bankruptcy of Spectradyne, a vulture investor who held a blocking position in a preferred stock class was unable to prevent the class from accepting the plan because his votes were not recorded in time.

Also, because no record is kept of how individual bondholders voted, confusion may ensue if bondholders are allowed to choose between two or more alternative settlements (e.g., an all-cash offer versus an all-stock offer). In particular, there is no way to establish which of the alternative settlements applies to bonds that are purchased after the end of balloting (because the bonds do not physically note which settlement option the holder of record chose). This problem was significant in the recent bankruptcies of E-II Holdings and Zale Credit Corporation.

Another risk facing investors is the potential for abuse of the voting process. A bondholder who holds his or her bonds at more than one brokerage firm (or holds the bonds in more than one account at the same firm) gets to cast a vote for each separate account (recall that the master ballot does not list the names of the voting bondholders). This means the holder can block a plan by ensuring that more than one-half of the voting "bondholders" vote against the plan—even if he or she in fact represents fewer than one-half of all voting bondholders. Such behavior is difficult to prove, although it has been rumored in several prominent cases.

Another potential abuse involves "churning" of bonds. The final tabulation of votes in a Chapter 11 case typically does not occur until about 60 days after the voting record date. During this time, a person could purchase some amount of bonds, keep the ballots (by agreement with the sellers), and immediately resell the bonds sans ballots. By repeating this sequence of transactions, the buyer could accumulate a large number of votes without having to hold as many bonds. Such behavior, although possible in theory, is discouraged by various penalties and sanctions (some criminal). Still, investors should be aware of the risk that their ownership of a class can be significantly diluted by such "vote inflation."

Disqualification of Votes

To profit from a proactive investment strategy, an investor must have some control over the outcome of the bankrupt firm's financial reorganization. In Chapter 11, however, investors who are more aggressive in asserting their interests risk having the judge disqualify their votes.

Events surrounding the bankruptcy of Allegheny International greatly helped define the limits of permissible behavior in this context.[26] Allegheny filed for Chapter 11 in early 1988. In late 1989, the company rebuffed the friendly overtures of New York-based Japonica Partners L.P. In response, Japonica purchased $10,000 of Allegheny's public debentures and filed its own plan of reorganization—even while disclosure hearings were being held on Allegheny's plan. Under its competing plan, Japonica proposed to acquire control of Allegheny, settling creditors' claims with mostly cash.

After balloting had commenced on Allegheny's plan, Japonica started to acquire senior bank debt in the company. It eventually acquired just over 33 percent of the class before the close of balloting, at progressively higher prices ranging from 80 percent to 97 percent of the claims' face value. Japonica was thereby able to block the debtor's plan. Soon after, it purchased an additional claim in this class for only 82 percent of face value.

The judge in the case subsequently granted a motion by the debtor to disqualify Japonica's votes under Section 1126(e) of the Bankruptcy Code, which allows the court to disqualify the votes of "any entity whose acceptance or rejection [of a plan] . . . was not in good faith, or was not solicited or procured in good faith." The judge reasoned that Japonica acted in bad faith because it had an "ulterior purpose": to acquire control of the debtor. According to the ruling, Japonica sought to defeat the debtor's reorganization plan to advance interests that it had other than as a creditor. As evidence of this self-interest, the judge noted that Japonica purchased most of its bank claims after balloting had already begun on the debtor's plan and paid a lower price for them after it had attained a blocking position in the class.

Japonica also purchased senior unsecured claims from some of Allegheny's insurance company lenders for 95 cents on the dollar—after they had already voted against Japonica's plan and for higher consideration than they had been offered under the plan. The judge rejected the insur-

---

[26]See Joy Conti, Raymond Kozlowski, Jr., and Leonard Ferleger, "Claims Trafficking in Chapter 11—Has the Pendulum Swung Too Far?" *Bankruptcy Developments Journal*, vol. 9, no. 2 (1992): 281–355; and Richard Lieb, "Vultures Beware: Risks of Purchasing Claims Against a Chapter 11 Debtor," *The Business Lawyer*, vol. 48, no. 3 (May 1993): 915–941.

ance companies' request to change their ballots, finding again that Japonica had acted in bad faith in what he described as a "naked attempt to purchase votes."

After balloting had commenced on its own plan of reorganization, Japonica made a separate tender offer for the public subordinated bonds of Allegheny and its Chemetron subsidiary—without the approval of the court and at a lower price than it was simultaneously offering to bondholders under its plan. Here, the judge found that Japonica's tender offer was a violation of Section 1123(a)(4) of the Bankruptcy Code, which requires a reorganization plan to treat all holders within a given class identically.

Although the judge's ruling has received mixed reviews from legal scholars, several key lessons emerge from the Allegheny case. An investor is more likely to be "shut down" by a judge if he or she openly proposes to acquire control of the debtor and, to achieve this goal, proposes an alternative reorganization plan to the debtor's and/or acquires a blocking position in one or more classes for the sole purpose of defeating the debtor's plan. One cannot appear to be too aggressive in the eyes of the judge. The risk of vote disqualification will also be greater if an investor does not respect the "sanctity" of a formal plan of reorganization (e.g., by simultaneously trying to buy claims both within and outside a plan). Although the objectives of a proactive investor in Chapter 11 may be the same as those of a hostile acquirer in an conventional takeover contest, the path one must take to acquire control in Chapter 11 is almost always more circuitous, given the involvement of the judge at every step.[27]

Holding Period Risk

The annual rate of return that one realizes buying distressed claims depends on two unknowns: the dollar recovery eventually realized by the claims (as specified in the firm's restructuring or reorganization plan), and the amount of time it takes to be paid this recovery. In the case of distressed debt, the potential dollar return is always "capped," in the sense that the most an investor can receive for the claim is the debt's face value

---

[27]In the end, Japonica's plan was defeated, and under the debtor's largely all-equity plan, it received stock in exchange for the debt claims it had purchased. Japonica was also forced to offer to purchase all the remaining common stock of Allegheny under a "control provision" that management had adopted earlier. Japonica was more than happy to oblige, because it believed—correctly, as things turned out—that the stock was grossly undervalued under current management.

(plus such interest that may accrue on secured debt during a Chapter 11 case).[28] Thus, the investor's annual percentage return is highly dependent on how long it takes the firm to restructure or reorganize. It is not uncommon for investors in distressed claims to seek annualized returns in the range of 25 to 35 percent. As shown in Exhibit 6.5, however, even modest extensions of the investor's holding period can result in substantial erosion of annualized returns, especially in the early years of a reorganization.

Aside from how it impacts the holding period, delay also hurts the investor's return because legal and other administrative costs of bankruptcy generally increase over time. (Professionals' fees in a large Chapter 11 case can easily exceed a million dollars a month.) These costs must be paid before any other claims are settled in Chapter 11, and therefore they directly reduce the recoveries available for the firm's claimholders (especially holders of more-junior claims, who are last in line to be paid). Delay also destroys value because management continues to be distracted from running the business and key customers and suppliers are more likely to defect.

Chapter 11 cases typically run for two to three years, but adverse business developments or breakdowns in the negotiations can cause the proceedings to drag on for much longer. LTV Corporation spent more than six years in bankruptcy court. Cases also tend to take longer in certain jurisdictions (such as the Southern District of New York) where judges are inclined to extend the debtor's exclusivity period.[29] Negotiations will generally be completed in less time when the firm has a less complicated capital structure and/or fewer creditors, because creditors have fewer opportunities to disagree over what the firm is worth or what division of the firm's assets is "fair." Negotiations also typically take much less time and are less costly when firms restructure their debt out of court.[30] Finally,

---

[28]In Chapter 11, interest accrues on secured debt if the debt is overcollateralized, but only up to the value of the excess collateral. As discussed earlier, no interest accrues on unsecured debt while a firm is in Chapter 11.

[29]For a sample of 43 firms that filed for Chapter 11, LoPucki and Whitford, in "Bargaining Over Equity's Share," found that cases held in New York take an average of 2.8 years to complete, compared with 2.1 years for other jurisdictions represented in their sample.

[30]Gilson et al., in "Troubled Debt Restructuring," found that out-of-court restructurings are typically completed in about a year, in contrast to about two years for a typical Chapter 11 case. The authors suggested a number of reasons for this difference: Firms that restructure out of court do not have to work through a judge or observe the strict procedural rules of Chapter 11. They can selectively restructure only a subset of their claims if they choose to, and they tend to be financially more solvent than firms in Chapter 11.

firms that require less extensive restructuring of their basic businesses are generally able to restructure their capital structures more quickly.

Because of the time factor, some institutions that invest in troubled situations specialize in companies whose problems are primarily financial rather than operational in nature (e.g., leveraged buyouts that go bust shortly after inception and/or firms that have solid managements in place). Most, when contemplating an investment in a Chapter 11 situation, also consider the reputation of the bankruptcy judge for expediting cases.

The holding period can also drag on unexpectedly because of delays in distributing cash and new securities to creditors under a confirmed plan of reorganization. Often, several months elapse between the plan confirmation date and the distribution date. Some amount of time is needed to print and physically distribute the new securities. In the case of bonds, the Securities and Exchange Commission (SEC)'s approval of the bond indenture is also necessary. Delays are considered more likely when the new securities are distributed through non-U.S. agents, who have less experience processing Chapter 11 distributions than their U.S. counterparts. In the bankruptcy of Wang Laboratories, the use of non-U.S. agents was a concern of the company's Eurobond holders.[31]

The Strategic Role of Valuation

In every distressed situation, an investor's return depends on two key values: the true value of the firm's assets ("true value") and the value of the firm's assets used in determining payouts to claimholders under the firm's reorganization or restructuring plan ("plan value"). These two values are almost always different, and an investor's returns can be significantly affected by changes in either value.

An investor should be aware that various parties in the case may have a significant financial interest in promoting plan values that differ dramatically from the firm's true value. Junior claimholders (e.g. common stockholders) benefit from a higher plan value because they are last in line to be paid. Conversely, senior claimholders (e.g., secured lenders) prefer a lower plan value because they then receive a larger fraction of the total consideration distributed under the plan (in effect, "squeezing out" more junior interests). These conflicting incentives exist even though both junior and senior claimholders may privately assign the same true value to the firm.

As a simple illustration, suppose that senior creditors are owed 200 and junior creditors are owed 100 (for total debt of 300). Suppose further

---

[31]See Mayer, "Claims Trading."

that the true value of the firm's assets is 260. If this amount is also the plan value, then senior creditors are made whole in the restructuring, leaving only 60 for junior creditors and nothing for stockholders. (To simplify the example, I assume that payouts under the plan follow the absolute priority rule.) Stockholders would clearly prefer the plan value to exceed 300. Senior creditors, on the other hand, benefit when the plan value is less than the true value. For example consider an alternative restructuring plan premised on a plan value of 180. In this case, senior creditors receive consideration nominally worth 180 (in the form of new debt and equity securities and possibly some cash), and junior creditors and stockholders both receive nothing. Because the firm is really worth 260, however, the new claims must eventually appreciate in value by 80 (i.e., 260–180)—a pure windfall to senior creditors.

Disagreement over the plan value can be a major obstacle to reaching a consensus and can result in unexpected extensions of the investor's holding period. In the recent bankruptcy of R. H. Macy, various parties in the case proposed plan values ranging from $3.35 billion to $4 billion. Adding to the usual tension in this case was the fact that a company director held a significant amount of Macy's junior debt and would therefore benefit from a higher valuation.

Any claimholder, of course, is free to vote against a reorganization plan that incorporates an unfavorable plan value. To promote a particular plan value more effectively, an investor may consider proposing his or her own reorganization plan in order to determine the general location of bargaining. At a minimum, the investor should understand which particular claimholder class "controls" the reorganization plan proposal process. In the recent bankrupty of National Gypsum, junior classes alleged that management presented overly pessimistic revenue forecasts to enhance senior creditor recoveries—an allegation that to some is supported by the approximate quadrupling of National Gypsum's stock price that occurred during the following year.[32]

---

[32]Under National Gypsum's reorganization plan (confirmed on March 9, 1993), the firm's common stock was estimated by management to be worth approximately $12 a share; one year later, it was trading at about $40 a share. (Of course, an alternative interpretation is that the firm's business improved after it left Chapter 11 and that this improvement was not anticipated by management.) Accusations of management low-balling have become increasingly common in Chapter 11 cases. See Alison Leigh Cown, "Beware Management Talking Poor," *New York Times* (February 13, 1994).

The above analysis also implies that an investor can earn superior returns by being able to estimate more precisely the firm's actual value. At Fidelity's Capital & Income Fund, for example, fund managers have historically pursued a strategy of buying senior claims in bankrupt firms whose assets they believe are fundamentally sound but currently undervalued in the market. By targeting senior claims, the fund hopes to receive more of the firm's equity—and future upside—under the reorganization plan. Key to this strategy is that the firm leaves Chapter 11 and distributes its new securities before the anticipated business turnaround takes place and the undervaluation is corrected.

Lack of Information about Purchases and Purchasers

Investors in distressed claims generally get to operate in relative secrecy. They do not have to disclose the terms of their purchases—either the number of claims acquired or the price paid—when they transact in Chapter 11, and no such disclosure has to be made in an out-of-court restructuring. This information does have to be reported if an investor files a Schedule 13D or 14D-1 with the SEC. In most situations, however, neither filing will be required (at least until after the firm's restructuring or reorganization plan is completed).[33]

For investors in distressed debt, this lack of disclosure can be a double-edged sword. Because no central record is kept of who holds a firm's debt, an investor may—as a bargaining ploy—be able to claim ownership of a blocking position in a class, when his or her actual holdings are more modest. One prominent vulture investor attempted this strategy in acquiring the bonds of bankrupt MGF Oil; management was able to discover

---

[33]A 13D filing must be made by any person who acquires more than 5 percent of an outstanding voting equity security, within ten days of crossing the 5 percent threshold. A 13D filing is not required when an investor purchases debt securities but may be required later if and when these securities are converted into equity under the firm's restructuring or reorganization plan. A 14D-1 filing must be made within five days of the announcement of an intention to solicit tenders for an equity security or any security that is convertible into an equity security. An investor who makes a tender offer for debt securities may therefore have to file a Schedule 14D-1 if these securities are "convertible" into equity under a contemplated restructuring or reorganization plan. A 14D-1 will not be required if the tender offer is for debt claims that are not "securities" or is formally part of a Chapter 11 reorganization plan. (The SEC has ruled that a debtor's disclosure statement includes enough information to make a 14D-1 filing unnecessary.)

through polling other bondholders that the vulture actually owned only 7 percent of the issue.[34] The same lack of information also makes it more difficult for an investor to know how many claims in a given class he or she should acquire, and at what price, when other investors are simultaneously seeking control.

Knowing who owns a firm's claims clearly provides a huge advantage in this market. Apollo Advisors is thought to be especially well informed about junk bond ownership because most of the principals at Apollo are former employees of Drexel Burnham Lambert and thus were directly involved in either designing or underwriting the bonds. This superior knowledge has been credited with giving Apollo a significant competitive advantage when it bid to acquire the junk bond portfolio of failed insurer First Executive in 1991. Apollo eventually acquired more than $6 billion (face value) of First Executive's junk bonds—most of them Drexel issues—for $2 billion less than their true value, according to one recent estimate.[35]

Liquidation Risk

In a Chapter 7 liquidation, the firm's assets are sold for cash by a trustee and the proceeds are paid to the firm's claimholders according to the absolute priority rule. If the firm is worth more as a going concern than as a source of salable assets, then claimholders can collectively do better by keeping the firm alive and trying to reorganize (either in Chapter 11 or out of court).

An investor in distressed claims needs to be able to assess the risk that a firm will fail to reorganize and be forced to liquidate. As described in the appendix, the judge in a Chapter 11 case must convert the case to a Chap-

---

[34]Matthew Schifrin, "Sellers Beware," *Forbes* (January 21, 1991). To preempt this strategy, firms sometimes engage proxy solicitation firms to gather information on bond ownership.

[35]Apollo's purchase of First Executive's junk bond portfolio is analyzed in Harry DeAngelo, Linda DeAngelo, and Stuart Gilson, "The Collapse of First Executive Corporation: Junk Bonds, Adverse Publicity, and the 'Run on the Bank' Phenomenon," *Journal of Financial Economics*, vol. 36, no. 3 (December 1994): 287–336. Apollo also had access to more financing than competing bidders (it is partnered with Altus Finance, a subsidiary of Credit Lyonnais); hence, unlike most other bidders, it was also able to satisfy the insurance regulators' preference that the portfolio be sold as a whole.

ter 7 liquidation if agreement on a plan of reorganization is impossible.[36] Liquidation is more likely if the firm has "hard" and/or nonspecialized assets that retain most of their value when sold off. Liquidation is also a much more frequent outcome for small firms than for large ones. There are several reasons for the frequency of liquidation among small firms. Legal and other out-of-pocket costs of Chapter 11 exhibit significant economies of scale; the relative burden of Chapter 11 is therefore much greater for small firms. Also, small firms typically derive more of their value from intangible and/or specialized assets (e.g., a patent for a new drug). Finally, most small firms simply do not have the resources or depth of management to cope with a lengthy and complex Chapter 11 reorganization. An investor's losses in a liquidation will in general be smaller if he or she has purchased senior or secured claims or if the firm has relatively more unencumbered assets (i.e., assets hat have not been pledged as collateral against some other loan).

Insider Trading Issues

Investors who trade in a distressed firm's claims may be subject to bankruptcy court or other sanctions if they also have an inside or fiduciary relationship with the firm. The concept of insider trading is not explicitly addressed in the Bankruptcy Code (and is not well defined even in nonbankruptcy law). With respect to the publicly traded securities of a bankrupt firm, investors who trade on the basis of inside information face possible sanctions under Section 10(b) of the Securities Exchange Act—the same as investors in nondistressed securities. An investor who had advance knowledge of the debtor's reorganization plan, for example, would be unable legally to buy or sell the firm's publicly traded bonds. It is less clear whether this investor would also be barred from trading in the debtor's nonpublicly traded claims which do not meet the legal definition of a "security."

Bankruptcy court judges generally take a dim view of trading by fiduciaries and can impose a variety of sanctions. An investor will be considered a fiduciary if he or she is also a professional advisor to some party in the case. Investment banks with large trading operations may find themselves in this dual role. An investor will also be considered a fiduciary if he or she sits on the Unsecured Creditors Committee (UCC). A UCC is appointed by the

---

[36]A firm can also liquidate as part of a Chapter 11 reorganization plan, but that is a much less common vehicle for liquidation than Chapter 7.

judge in every Chapter 11 case. It normally consists of the seven largest unsecured creditors who are willing to serve. The UCC is empowered to investigate all aspects of the firm's business, which gives it access to proprietary company information not normally available to investors.[37]

One way for such investors to avoid court sanctions is to erect a "Chinese Wall" to separate their trading activities from their fiduciary activities (for example, by prohibiting the same employees from serving in both capacities). In Federated Department Stores' bankruptcy, Fidelity Investments obtained the judge's special permission to erect such a wall and trade in Federated debt while simultaneously sitting on the Official Bondholders' Committee. The Chinese Wall, however, can be, and has been, challenged in bankruptcy court.[38] As a result, many institutional investors refuse to sit on the UCC, even though they could make valuable contributions in that capacity.

Tax Issues

The particular strategy an investor follows to acquire control in a distressed firm can have a huge impact on the firm's tax liability, hence the in-

---

[37]In addition, the UCC consults with the debtor on administrative matters related to the case and on formulating a plan of reorganization. The operating expenses of the UCC, including all reasonable legal and advisory fees, are paid by the firm. Committees can also be formed to represent other classes of claims if the judge decides these classes would otherwise be disadvantaged in the case. In out-of-court restructurings, the standard practice is to establish a "steering committee" of creditors that functions like the UCC in Chapter 11. Companies also usually reimburse these committees for reasonable operating expenses incurred. The role of UCCs in Chapter 11 is examined by Lynn M. LoPucki and William C. Whitford, "Bargaining Over Equity's Share in the Bankruptcy Reorganization of Large, Publicly Held Companies," *University of Pennsylvania Law Review*, vol. 139, no. 1 (1990): 125–196.

[38]During the bankruptcy of Papercraft Corporation, a failed LBO, a court-appointed examiner recommended that the trading profits made by two investors in the case—Magten Asset Management and Citicorp Venture Capital Ltd.—be refunded to the debtor and that neither investor be allowed to fully vote its claims. The examiner's recommendation was based on the fact that both investors sat on the UCC and were therefore fiduciaries. Citicorp Venture Capital was also an original investor in the LBO and had the right to elect a director to Papercraft's board. Significantly, it made no difference to the examiner that one investor had disclosed its "insider" relationship to the sellers of the claims or that the other's intention in buying claims was to facilitate the reorganization (as well as to make a profit).

vestor's after-tax return. In general, this tax penalty increases with the percentage of equity that an investor either purchases directly or acquires indirectly through the exchange of stock for debt.

Preservation of Net Operating Losses   If an investor purchases a block of claims in a distressed firm for the purpose of acquiring control, the firm may lose significant tax benefits arising from its net operating loss carryforwards (NOLs). This tax "hit" can severely reduce the investor's return. NOLs are often a distressed firm's largest single asset.[39] Before it emerged from Chapter 11, R.H. Macy had NOLs in excess of $1 billion.

Under Section 382 of the Internal Revenue Code, a firm's ability to use its NOLs can be severely restricted when it experiences an "ownership change." An ownership change takes place when any group of stockholders collectively increases its total percentage ownership of the firm's common stock by more than 50 percentage points during any three-year period.[40] Purchasing a large block of equity or debt prior to the firm's reorganization or restructuring can greatly increase the risk of an ownership change, especially if the debt is exchanged for common stock.

If an ownership change does take place, the restrictions on NOL use are generally less severe if the firm is in Chapter 11. In this case, the least severe restriction applies if more than 50 percent of the firm's stock continues to be held by its prepetition shareholders and creditors (who must have been creditors for at least 18 months before the bankruptcy filing).[41] This condition can easily be violated, however, if an outside investor has acquired control of the firm's equity by purchasing claims. The most severe restriction would then apply: Annual NOL use would be limited to the value of shareholders' equity after the reorganization multiplied by a

---

[39]One recent academic study finds that, for public companies in Chapter 11, NOLs typically exceed the total book value of assets by more than 200 percent. See Stuart Gilson, "Transactions Costs and Capital Structure Choice: Evidence from Financially Distressed Firms," *Journal of Finance* 52: 161–196.

[40]In calculating the percentage ownership change, percentage reductions in ownership by individual stockholders are ignored and all stockholders who individually own less than 5 percent of the stock are collectively treated as a single holder. In addition, convertible securities and warrants are treated as actual common shares. The increase in ownership attributed to each stockholder is determined relative to the lowest percentage of the firm's stock owned by that holder during the three-year test period.

[41]NOLs are reduced by approximately one-half the amount of any debt forgiven in the reorganization (net of any new consideration distributed) plus any interest.

statutory federal interest rate. In practice, this calculation produces a relatively small number, making it unlikely that the firm will be unable to use up its NOLs before they expire.[42] If an ownership change occurs while the firm is restructuring its debt out of court, it can lose its NOLs altogether.[43]

Investors can manage such risks by limiting how much they invest in high-NOL firms or by targeting more-solvent firms that are apt to issue less new equity in a reorganization or restructuring.

Cancellation of Indebtedness Income   If an investor purchases a financially distressed firm's debt at less than face value and later—within two years—becomes "related" to the firm by acquiring more than 50 percent of its equity, the discount may be taxable to the firm as "cancellation of indebtedness" (COD) income. Normally, such income is created whenever a firm repurchases its debt for less than full face value. The risk of creating COD income is greatest for investors who seek to control the firm's operations after it reorganizes.

Exit Strategies and Liquidity Risk

Although the market for distressed claims has become much more liquid and efficient in recent years, it is still less liquid than most organized securities markets. Investors should therefore decide on an exit strategy before they invest in a distressed situation. Exit normally occurs in one of three ways. First, and most common, investors can simply trade out of their positions. Second, they can sell their claims in an initial public offering. This strategy is appropriate when investors acquire a large equity stake in the borrower and the borrower's stock is not publicly traded (e.g., because it went private in an LBO). Third, investors can swap their claims for cash and/or other consideration in a merger. This form of exit was available in

---

[42]In the United States, NOLs can be carried back 3 years and then carried forward for 15. Even if the firm manages to preserve some of its NOLs while in Chapter 11, however, it will forfeit even these if it experiences a subsequent ownership change within two years.

[43]Specifically, if the firm continues in its historic line of business, annual use of NOLs is limited to the value of shareholders' equity before the restructuring is implemented multiplied by the same statutory federal interest rate used in calculating the restriction for firms in Chapter 11. If the firm changes its line of business, however, all of its NOLs are lost.

the recent bankruptcy of R. H. Macy, which was acquired out of Chapter 11 by Federated Department Stores.

Unforeseen declines in market liquidity can substantially reduce an investor's returns by lengthening the holding period and/or reducing the exit price. In a distressed situation, such "liquidity risk" can arise in several ways. First, too many new types of claims may be created under the firm's reorganization or restructuring plan, resulting in an overly complex and fragmented capital structure. This fragmenttion will undermine liquidity if the total dollar amount outstanding of a given claim is too small to support an active market in the issue. In practice, a junk bond issue must be worth at least $100 million (face value) to generate strong interest among institutional investors and analysts.

An investor's ability to trade out of his or her position may also be impaired if he or she signed a confidentiality agreement when the claims were purchased. Such agreements are fairly standard in purchases of nonpublic claims, such as bank debt, in which the original lenders have proprietary knowledge about the borrower's operations. (These agreements also typically prohibit the buyer from contacting the borrower.) If the investor tries to sell these claims without disclosing such material inside information, he or she could run afoul of applicable securities law if the claims are considered "securities." An investor can reduce this risk in Chapter 11 by postponing trades until after the firm files its disclosure statement (which discloses at least as much information as a typical securities offering registration statement).

The liquidity of the firm's common stock will also be impaired if the firm places trading restrictions on its stock in order to reserve its NOLs. Such restrictions reduce the likelihood of an "ownership change," which can cause the firm to lose some or all of its NOLs. After significant amounts of new common stock have been issued in a bankruptcy or restructuring, even modest trading in the stock may trigger an ownership change. To guard against this risk, Allis-Chalmers, which emerged from Chapter 11 with nearly half a billion dollars in NOLs, preempted all trading in its common stock by placing its shares in a special trust—effectively taking itself private. In some other cases, bankruptcy judges have enjoined trading in claims—going against the intent of revised Rule 3001(e)—because of concern over the potential loss of NOLs.

Finally, analysts and investors may lose interest in a firm once it becomes financially distressed (e.g., because trading in the firm's securities is suspended by the listing exchange or the SEC or because the firm ends up significantly smaller). In this case, the investor may have to take a proactive role in restoring liquidity to the market. This happened in the case of

Hills Stores, which emerged from Chapter 11 in October 1993. In the summer of 1995, Dickstein Partners L.P.—which had become a major stockholder in Hills under its reorganization plan—waged a proxy fight against management with the goal of forcing an auction for the firm and increasing its share price. In spite of having shown positive operating performance since the bankruptcy, Hills was followed by relatively few analysts—its debt and equity securities had been closely held since the reorganization—and its stock price had remained flat. Dickstein's initiative has been credited with increasing Hills' stock price by more than 20 percent.[44]

DO VULTURES ADD OR SUBTRACT VALUE IN A REORGANIZATION?

The role of vulture investors in the corporate reorganization process is controversial. The very term "vulture" is pejorative, much like the tag "raider," once used to describe proactive investors in the 1980s' takeover market. Many bankruptcy judges are philosophically opposed to the idea that people can insert themselves into a distressed situation for profit—all while the firm's original lenders and stockholders are being asked to make material financial sacrifices. The news media are often no more sympathetic,[45] and the SEC keeps revisiting the idea of bringing the market for distressed claims under the scope of the insider trading laws.

Such hostility to the activities of vulture investors overlooks the critical role they play in creating value in a restructuring situation. A key point is that trading in distressed claims is voluntary: Sellers only participate in a given transaction when they expect to benefit from doing so. When a firm becomes financially distressed, there are various reasons why the original lenders can benefit from selling their claims even for less than full face value.

Bank lenders may be able to book a profit on a distressed loan sale if, as a result of prior writedowns, the sales price exceeds the current book value of the loan. By disposing of their distressed loans and improving the quality of their loan portfolios, these lenders may also be able to reduce the amount of capital that must be set aside to satisfy statutory risk-based capital guidelines. Finally, some banks prefer to sell off their loans as soon as

---

[44]See Stephanie Strom, "Giving the Pros a Taste of Their Own Medicine," *New York Times* (August 28, 1994); and Letter to Hills Stockholders from Dickstein Partners L.P. (dated June 12, 1995), on file with the author.

[45]See, for example, Laura Jereski and Jason Zweig, "Step Right Up Folks," *Forbes* (March 4, 1991).

they become troubled, rather than actively manage them through a workout department.

Trade creditors can also benefit from selling their claims against a distressed firm. Smaller vendors often cannot afford to wait until the end of a bankruptcy or restructuring for their claims to be settled and would rather receive cash up front. Other vendors may wish to continue doing business with the firm after it solves its financial difficulties and therefore sell their claims rather than risk antagonizing the firm in an adversarial Chapter 11 or restructuring proceeding.

By buying up and consolidating distressed claims, vultures can also facilitate a reorganization by reducing the so-called "holdout problem." Outside of Chapter 11, distressed firms often attempt to restructure their publicly held debt by offering bondholders the opportunity to exchange their bonds for new claims (typically consisting of either equity securities or new debt securities having a lower face value or interest rate than the original bonds). Bondholders who hold only a small fraction of a given issue have little incentive to tender their bonds, because their decision will not have a material impact on the likelihood of a successful restructuring. Moreover, if they retain their bonds and the restructuring goes through anyway, they get to receive the more generous payouts offered by the original bonds without having made any financial sacrifice. If enough bondholders behave this way, however, the restructuring must fail and everyone is worse off.[46] By buying up small holdings and consolidating them into large blocks, vulture investors help reduce the holdout problem and make it easier for firms to restructure their debt.

Vulture investors, as discount buyers, are also less wedded to receiving the full face value of their claims in a restructuring or bankruptcy; even a small (e.g., 30 percent) recovery of face value can produce large investment returns if the claims were acquired for a sufficiently low price. Banks and insurance companies, in contrast, often fiercely resist giving up loan principal or taking equity in the borrower.[47] Lender resistance to principal write-downs can result in firms being saddled with excessive leverage after they come out of a bankruptcy or restructuring, forcing them to restructure

---

[46]The holdout problem is less severe in Chapter 11 because bondholders within a class who hold out can be forced to participate in a reorganization plan as long as a sufficient number of other bondholders (representing at least two-thirds in value and one-half in number of all bondholders represented in the class) vote for the plan.

[47]See Stuart Gilson, "Transactions Costs and Capital Structure Choice: Evidence from Financially Distressed Firms," *Journal of Finance* 52: 161–196.

again in the future. (In practice, approximately one in three firms that reorganizes in Chapter 11 makes a return trip to bankruptcy court as a "Chapter 22" or "Chapter 33.") The presence of vulture investors therefore facilitates restructuring by giving the firm greater flexibility to choose an optimal capital structure.[48]

CONCLUSION

Although the strategies for investing in distressed debt are many and varied, investors who are consistently successful in this market tend to exhibit certain key qualities. First is a superior ability to value a firm's assets. This trait not only means being better at processing information; it also means being better at locating and collecting information. When a firm becomes financially distressed, information about the firm from conventional public sources often dries up or is not sufficiently timely. In its bid to control bankrupt Allegheny International (now Sunbeam–Oster Company), Japonica Partners engaged almost a hundred outside people to help it value the company's assets; it extensively interviewed the company's distributors, customers, and line managers in order to understand its products and markets better; and it relentlessly pressured senior management to provide it with detailed and timely operating and financial data. This approach was fundamental analysis with a vengeance.

The second defining quality of successful vulture investors is superior negotiating and bargaining skill. In large measure, this skill is a function of how accurately one values the firm's assets and of how well the investor understands the firm's capital structure, including the legal rights and financial interests of all other claimholders.

Finally, successful vultures understand the risks of investing in distressed situations. These risks cannot be eliminated, but they can be controlled. Again, careful fundamental analysis of the firm's business and financial condition is critical.

As of this writing, the distressed debt market is already regaining its

---

[48]Empirical evidence on the impact of vultures is limited. One recent study finds that common stock prices of distressed firms increase, on average, when vultures acquire the firms' junior claims and decline, on average, when they acquire more-senior claims. See Edith Hotchkiss and Robert Mooradian, "Vulture Investors and the Market for Control of Distressed Firms," manuscript (1995). The authors provide two possible interpretations of their evidence: (1) The vulture's decision to purchase junior (senior) claims in the capital structure signals that he or she believes the firm has a high (low) value; or (2) vultures purchase senior claims to block the firm's reorganization plan and extract higher payments (at the expense of junior claims).

momentum. During the first half of 1995, there were $4.8 billion of junk bond defaults—seven times the amount reported during the same period in 1994.[49] The year 1995 has also seen the return of the "megabankruptcy": Chapter 11 filings by firms with more than $1 billion in revenues or assets, including Grand Union, TWA, and Bradlees.

The future will bring new opportunities from abroad, especially in Europe and Mexico. In the United Kingdom, in particular, annual trading in distressed bank loans now runs, by some estimates, into the billions of dollars. One reason for this growth is the U.K. banks' increasing willingness to break from traditional relationship banking and sell off their loans when they become nonperforming. As lenders in general become more comfortable with the idea of transacting in secondary markets for distressed debt, there is every reason to expect these trends to continue.[50]

APPENDIX: RULES FOR CONFIRMING A CHAPTER 11 PLAN OF REORGANIZATION

Every proposed plan of reorganization assigns the firm's claimholders to different classes. The Bankruptcy Code requires that each class consist only of claims that are "substantially similar." Confirmation of a plan of reorganization can be either consensual or nonconsensual.

Consensual Plans

Under a consensual plan of reorganization, every impaired class of claims must vote for the plan. Acceptance of the plan by a particular class requires the approval of at least two-thirds of the face value of outstanding claims in that class, representing at least one-half of the claimholders in that class who vote (claimholders who do not vote or fail to show up are not counted). The plan must also satisfy the best-interests-of-creditors test: Each dissenting member of every impaired class must receive consideration worth at least what he or she would receive in a liquidation. To ensure that this requirement is satisfied, the plan sponsor normally includes an estimate of the firm's liquidation value in the official disclosure statement given to creditors prior to the vote. In practice, these reported liquidation values are usually low-ball estimates, set sufficiently low so that the best-interests-of-creditors test is almost sure to be satisfied.

---

[49]Source: Moody's Investors Service.
[50]I am grateful to the Harvard Business School's Division of Research for supporting this project. This article is based in part on a presentation I made at the Spring 1994 Berkeley Program in Finance.

Nonconsensual Plans

Under a nonconsensual plan of reorganization, one or more impaired classes vote against the plan. For such a plan to be confirmed, two additional tests must be satisfied: The plan must not discriminate unfairly, and it must be fair and equitable. If the plan meets these two conditions, then it can be "crammed down" on the dissenting classes. A plan is fair and equitable with respect to a dissenting class if the present value of the cash and securities to be distributed to the class equals the allowed value of the class members' claims or if no more-junior class receives any consideration. Stated differently, a plan is fair and equitable if the absolute priority rule holds for the dissenting class and for all more-junior classes. (More-senior classes are excluded from this determination, and their recoveries need not conform to the absolute priority rule.) The rule is more complicated in the case of secured debt.

Consider the hypothetical example in Exhibit 6.6. In this example, suppose the secured and senior unsecured classes vote for the plan, and the subordinated class votes against the plan (the common stock, which is to receive nothing, is automatically assumed to vote against the plan). The plan can be crammed down on both the subordinated and common stock classes (assuming the earlier best-interests-of-creditors test is also satisfied, as it must be under either type of plan). Note that the proposed distributions to the secured and senior unsecured classes do not conform to the absolute priority rule. Because both of these classes vote for the plan, there is no need to cram the plan down on them.

In practice, cram-downs are uncommon because they require the court to hold a valuation hearing to determine the present value of the cash and securities to be distributed to dissenting classes. These hearings tend to be extremely costly and time consuming, so it is generally in everyone's best interest to avoid them. As a consequence, senior classes often leave something on the table for junior classes, even though they would be entitled to nothing if the absolute priority rule were strictly followed. Thus, the threat of cram-down can have as significant an influence on the outcome as an actual cram-down.

With either type of plan (consensual or nonconsensual), confirmation requires that at least one impaired claimholder class vote for the plan. If this vote is impossible to attain, the judge will convert the case to a Chapter 7 liquidation, under which the firm's assets will be sold off and the proceeds distributed to creditors according to the rule of absolute priority.

The Feasibility Test

Every plan (consensual and nonconsensual) must also be deemed feasible by the judge in order to be confirmed, which means the company will be able to generate sufficient cash flow in the future to avoid a return trip to bankruptcy court. In practice, plan feasibility is assessed by comparing projected annual debt service costs with projected earnings or cash flows (generally over a four- to six-year horizon).

EXHIBIT 6.1 Frequency and Size of Chapter 11 Filings and Other Corporate Restructuring Transactions by Publicly Traded Firms, 1981–94

| | Number of Transactions | | | | Total Value of Transactions ($billions)[a] | | | |
Year	Chapter 11 Filings	Hostile Tender Offers	Leveraged Buyouts	Spin-Offs	Chapter 11 Filings	Hostile Tender Offers	Leveraged Buyouts	Spin-Offs
1981	74	10	14	2	$ 6.0	$ 8.6	$ 2.7	$ 1.3
1982	84	8	15	3	11.3	3.4	2.1	0.2
1983	89	9	47	17	15.4	2.5	3.1	3.6
1984	121	9	113	13	7.9	3.3	18.7	1.3
1985	149	12	156	19	6.9	20.3	18.9	1.5
1986	149	17	238	26	15.9	20.6	56.6	4.4
1987	112	16	214	20	49.5	6.1	51.5	3.5
1988	122	28	300	34	49.9	50.0	66.7	12.8
1989	135	15	305	25	78.0	50.0	82.9	8.0
1990	116	5	201	27	85.7	9.0	18.6	5.4
1991	125	3	193	18	86.1	2.8	7.4	4.8
1992	91	1	223	19	55.4	0.5	8.2	5.8
1993	86	1	176	26	17.1	0.0[b]	10.2	14.4
1994	70	7	159	28	8.3	12.4	8.3	23.4
Total	1,523	141	2,354	277	$493.3	$189.4	$355.8	$90.5

[a]All dollar values are converted into constant 1994 dollars using the producer price index. For a Chapter 11 filing, "Total Value of Transactions" equals the book value of total assets of the filing firm. For a hostile tender offer and for a leveraged buyout, "Total Value of Transactions" equals the total value of consideration paid by the acquirer (including assumption of debt), excluding fees and expenses. For a spin-off, "Total Value of Transaction" equals the market value of the common stock of the spun-off entity evaluated at the first non-when-issued stock price available after the spin-off.
[b]Less than $0.1 billion
Sources: The 1995 Bankruptcy Yearbook and Almanac, and Securities Data Corporation.

EXHIBIT 6.2   Hierarchy of Claims in Chapter 11 from Most Senior to Most Junior

1. Secured claims
2. Superprioritiy claims (e.g., debtor-in-possession financing)
3. Priority claims
    3a. Administrative expenses (including legal and professional fees incurred in the case)
    3b. Wages, salaries, or commissions
    3c. Employee benefit claims
    3d. Claims against facilities that store grain or fish produce
    3e. Consumer deposits
    3f. Alimony and child support
    3g. Tax claims
    3h. Unsecured claims based on commitment to a federal depository institutions regulatory agency
4. General unsecured claims
5. Preferred stock
6. Common stock

EXHIBIT 6.3   Weighted-Average Price of Defaulted Bonds at End of Default Month as Percent of Face Value, January 1, 1977–March 31, 1991

Bond Class	Price/Face Value
Senior secured	54.6%
Senior unsecured	40.6
Senior subordinated	31.3
Subordinated	30.1
Junior subordinated	23.0
All bonds	34.2

Source: Salomon Brothers study (April 18, 1991).

EXHIBIT 6.4 Time Line of Key Events and Dates in a
Chapter 11 Reorganization

Filing of Chapter 11 petition
Filing of schedule of assets and liabilities
Bar date
Filing of plan of reorganization and disclosure statement
Hearing on disclosure statement
Balloting on plan
Plan confirmation hearing
Effective date of plan/distribution of new claims under plan

EXHIBIT 6.5 Annualized Return on Investment for a Hypothetical Purchase of
Distressed Claims for Different Percentage Recoveries and Holding Periods

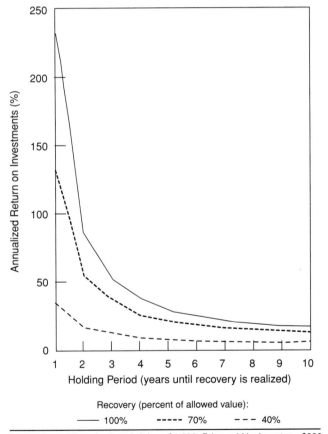

Recovery (percent of allowed value):
——— 100%   ----- 70%   – – – 40%

Assumptions: Allowed value of claim = $1,000, Price paid by investor = $300

EXHIBIT 6.6   Hypothetical Chapter 11 Reorganization Plan

Claim	Allowed Value	Present Value of Consideration	Percent Recovery
Secured debt	100	95	95%
Senior unsecured debt	240	203	85
Subordinated debt	150	90	60
Common stock	—	0	0

Restructuring Shareholders' Claims

This module examines how firms restructure their contracts with shareholders. Such restructuring effectively involves reslicing the equity "slice" of the corporate "pie." Equity is the most junior claim in the firm's capital structure, standing behind debt, employee wages and benefits, payments to suppliers, taxes, and all other fixed and variable expenses of running the business. It is therefore also the riskiest claim. Restructuring equity means changing how the firm's residual cash flows are divided up and distributed among the firm's shareholders, with the goal of increasing the overall market value of the firm's common stock. Managers often consider this kind of restructuring when the firm's stock has failed to perform as well as other similarly risky stocks, despite their best efforts to increase the profitability of the business.

The first two cases in this module highlight alternative methods that can be used to create new classes of publicly traded stock. The third case examines the implications of giving managers of financially troubled firms a significant share of shareholders' equity to reward them for improving company performance.

The most common methods for creating new classes of stock in a restructuring include corporate spin-offs, equity carve-outs, and tracking stock offerings (collectively, "stock breakups"). (See Exhibit I2.1.) Exhibit I2.2 illustrates how these methods work. In a pure spin-off, the company distributes to its shareholders new shares of stock representing 100 percent ownership of a company subsidiary.[1] After the distribution, the subsidiary trades as an independent public company, while the original parent company shares become claims against the firm's remaining assets. There is therefore a complete physical and legal separation of parent and subsidiary operations.

Tracking stock, in contrast, represents a "pure" claim against the profits generated by a specific segment of the firm's operations—but the segment continues to be a part of the consolidated business entity.[2] Most often, firms create tracking stock by simply distributing the shares to their existing shareholders on a pro rata basis (as in a spin-off). These new shares represent a 100 percent claim on the profits of a subsidiary; the parent company shares become a claim on the rest of the business. Alternatively, the new shares can be sold for cash in an initial underwritten offering or issued as payment in an acquisition.[3] Tracking stock therefore produces the same equity structure as a spin-off, but the firm's corporate and organizational structure remains unchanged. There is still only one board of directors, one corporate charter, one borrowing entity, and so forth. Thus management must decide how corporate overhead in allocated between parent and subsidiary, to determine how profits are shared between the two stocks. Management also sets the dividend on each stock.

Finally, in a equity carve-out the firm sells a portion (but not all) of the stock in a subsidiary for cash, usually in a public offering. In the United States, firms usually retain at least 80 percent ownership in the subsidiary, so they can continue to file a consolidated tax return. It also allows them later to spin off the remainder of the subsidiary on a tax-free basis, if they desire complete separation.[4]

---

[1]For convenience, the term "subsidiary" is here loosely defined as any distinct partitioning of the firm's operations, and could also refer to a business division or segment.

[2]Tracking stock is also sometimes called "targeted stock" or "letter stock."

[3]Tracking stock can alternatively be sold to the public for cash, providing the firm with new financing. This was the method chosen by AT&T when it issued tracking stock in its wireless telephony division in April 2000, in what was the largest tracking stock issue ever (net proceeds from the offering were $10.6 billion).

[4]Another, relatively uncommon, form of equity restructuring is a "split-off," in which parent company shareholders are offered the opportunity to exchange their shares for shares in a subsidiary of the company. The exchange is voluntary, but the terms of the exchange are set to offer parent shareholders a premium for tendering.

MANAGEMENT CHALLENGES

Stock Breakups

Selecting an appropriate stock breakup strategy, and implementing that strategy, presents managers with a number of difficult choices and trade-offs.

In a spin-off, prior to separating the parent from the subsidiary, management must allocate corporate overhead between the two entities. This is more than just a simple accounting entry. People and assets must be reassigned and relocated. The allocation decision process must be managed in such a way that neither the parent nor the subsidiary benefits unduly. The managers in charge of this decision will understandably be tempted to send the best people and assets to the entity they expect to join after the spin-off. Controlling these potential conflicts of interest is an important consideration in making the spin-off work. By forcing management to "audit" corporate overhead, the allocation process may also reveal opportunities to reduce unnecessary expenses and eliminate redundancies. These savings can be substantial. However, realizing these savings through layoffs and asset disposals risks disrupting or delaying the spin-off.[5]

If the parent and subsidiary conducted business within one another before the spin-off, it is also necessary to decide how, or whether, that relationship should continue after the spin-off. If either entity has been overly dependent on the other's business, it may have difficulty surviving as an independent concern. A related consideration is what happens when the subsidiary has benefited from receiving business, financial, or other support from the parent, and now stands to gain financially from a spin-off. In this case, do the parent company shareholders have a legitimate claim on some of the value created by the spin-off?[6]

Management must also choose new capital structures for the parent

---

[5]Unprofitable, low-growth firms might be considered especially strong candidates for this benefit of a spin-off. Berger and Ofek (1999) find that the average stock market reaction to conglomerate stock breakups is higher when the firms have higher overhead expenses. However, overhead bloat can also be a problem for profitable high-growth companies. Such companies often have relatively lax internal financial controls, perhaps fearing that such controls could inhibit growth, and also not wanting to take resources away from the growing business.

[6]When General Motors spun off its Electronic Data Systems subsidiary in 1996, EDS agreed to pay GM $500 million. In the previous year, nearly a third of EDS's revenues had come from GM. See Allen Myerson, "Split of Electronic Data and GM Is Set," *New York Times* (April 2, 1996): 11.

and subsidiary entities. The decision can be complicated. In the event of a spin-off, covenants in the firm's debt may require that the debt be refinanced, possibly at unfavorable rates. If one entity is awarded a disproportionately larger share of the assets, while the other entity retains most of the debt, creditors will be left holding more of the firm's risk. If the resulting decline in debt values is large enough, creditors may challenge the spin-off in court as a "fraudulent conveyance," and sue for damages. Or the company may be charged higher rates when it tries to borrow money in the future.

Care must also be taken that the spin-off qualifies as nontaxable. In the United States, this requires that certain stringent tests be met under Section 355 of the Internal Revenue Code. For example, the parent must "control" the subsidiary prior to the spin-off, and the spin-off must have a "valid business purpose." To satisfy the latter test, it is not sufficient to argue that the spin-off will increase shareholder value. Failure to comply with these conditions can result in a huge tax bill—at the corporate and the personal levels.

Equity carve-outs and tracking stocks also present management with some important choices. In carve-outs, management must decide how much of the subsidiary's stock should be sold to the public. Selling more stock may generate a more liquid market and larger analyst following for the stock, both of which should increase the market price. However, as noted above, reducing the parent's ownership below 80 percent can have adverse tax consequences. If the purpose of the carve-out is to improve management incentives by allowing subsidiary managers to be compensated with subsidiary stock, an additional concern is that resulting gaps in what parent and subsidiary managers are paid could fuel resentments and upset the company culture.[7]

With tracking stock, management must be prepared to spend additional resources managing the firm's relations with investors. Although tracking stock has been around for over a decade, it is still controversial.[8] Critics of tracking stock believe it allows entrenched managers to keep control of corporate assets. They also believe it is confusing, because the value of tracking stock depends on management's corporate overhead allo-

---

[7]See Kris Frieswick, "Spin Control: Spinning Off Your E-Business? Make Sure You Aren't Selling Off Your Future," *CFO Magazine* (May 2000): 42–52.

[8]See Robert McGough and Rebecca Buckman, "Tracking Stock, Now the Rage, Has Drawbacks," *Wall Street Journal* (March 1999): C1; and Marcia Vickers, "Are Two Stock Better Than One?" *Business Week* (June 28, 1999): 98–99.

cations. If management is unable to dispel such concerns (for example, by credibly demonstrating there are large synergies between the firm's business units), investors may significantly undervalue the firm.

Management Equity Grants

When a firm is financially troubled, it makes sense to increase senior managers' stock holdings in the firm, so they have stronger incentives to increase the stock price. Professional turnaround managers' compensation often includes large grants of stock or stock options. Creditors or employees who have made concessions to the firm may object to such compensation, however. Paying managers with stock is especially difficult in smaller firms. Such firms may have no publicly traded stock. They are also more likely to be controlled by the founder. If founders hold most of their personal wealth in company stock, they may favor goals (e.g., reducing the firm's risk or maximizing near-term cash flows) that are inconsistent with maximizing the firm's market value. They may also be reluctant to share their equity with an outside manager.

ACADEMIC RESEARCH

Academic research suggests that corporate spin-offs, carve-outs, and tracking stocks significantly increase firms' market values, on average. For example, Schipper and Smith (1983) and Hite and Owers (1983) show that announcements of tax-free spin-offs cause firms' stock prices to increase by approximately 3 to 4 percent, on average (controlling for differences in firms' risk and market movements). Announcements of equity carve-outs are associated with average stock price gains of roughly 2 to 3 percent according to Schipper and Smith (1986); Klein, Rosenfeld, and Beranek (1991). And announcements of tracking stock issues cause issuing firms' stock prices to increase by almost 4 percent, on average, according to D'Souza and Jacob (2000).

Other research suggests several interpretations for these findings. Berger and Ofek (1995) and Comment and Jarrell (1995) show that firms that are more "focused" (i.e., do business in fewer industries) are more highly valued in the stock market than less focused firms, everything else being equal. Managers of focused firms are less distracted and better able to oversee the firm's core business operations. Managers of focused firms also face more financial discipline, because there is less opportunity to subsidize unprofitable divisions using the profits of profitable divisions. And stock breakups make it possible to tie divisional managers' compensation more closely to the performance of the firm's business units, by issuing stock options in the newly created shares. Consistent with the "refocusing" rationale for breakups, Daley, Mehrotra, and Sivakumar (1997) and Desai and Jain (1999) show that the stock price gains associated with spin-off announcements apply *only* to spin-offs where the spun-off entity is in a different industry than the parent company. Moreover, these cross-industry spin-offs later exhibit significant increases in operating performance (measured by return on assets), but same-industry spin-offs do not.

Another interpretation of the stock return evidence is offered by Cusatis, Miles, and Woolridge (1993). They find that firms that are spun off exhibit large positive stock returns over the three years that follow their spin-offs (76 percent, on average). Most of these gains disappear, however, when firms that are subsequently taken over are excluded. Thus the positive average stock price increase around spin-off announcements may reflect the market's expectation of future acquisition activity, rather than any operating improvements from the spin-off per se.

Finally, some research suggests that stock breakups help reduce investor confusion about the firm's operations, making the stocks more valuable. Following a spin-off, for example, each of the resulting firms issues its own set of financial statements, providing greater transparency for investors. Krishnaswami and Subramaniam (1999) show that various measures of investor uncertainty decline after spin-offs. Gilson, Healy, Noe, and Palepu (2000) show that firms created in stock breakups attract greater following by sell-side analysts who are specialists in the firms' businesses. Research by these analysts should be more informative for investors. Consistent with this prediction, Gilson et al. show that analysts' earnings forecast errors decline significantly after stock breakups. Moreover, the improvement in forecast accuracy is greatest for firms that experience the greatest increase in specialist coverage.[9]

Ownership of a company's stock can also change dramatically when managers receive large amounts of stock as an incentive to lead a restruc-

---

[9]Attempts to generalize about the market impact of stock breakups must be made with caution, however, since, as noted earlier, the three types of breakups differ in important ways. For example, an equity carve-out raises cash for the firm, while a spin-off does not. Allen and McConnell (1998) analyze the stock market reaction to equity carve-out announcements, and find that the size of the reaction depends on how the proceeds are used. Firms that use the carve-out proceeds to pay down debt experience almost a 7 percent increase in their stock prices, on average, while firms that retain the proceeds experience a small stock price decline.

turing. Gilson and Vetsuypens (1993) show that financially troubled firms typically grant their chief executive officers (CEOs) large stock or stock option awards. These awards greatly increase the sensitivity of CEOs' compensation to corporate performance—by orders of magnitude relative to nontroubled firms. Stock option awards are largest when the CEO has been recently appointed from outside the firm, suggesting that incumbent managers, who may be held responsible for the firm's difficulties, have less power to negotiate their compensation packages.

CASE STUDIES

This module consists of three case studies. The first case, **Humana Inc.,** concerns a rapidly growing integrated health care provider that operated a large chain of hospitals and a health insurance business (specializing in managed care). By adding the second business, the company hoped to increase occupancy rates in its hospitals, which, like most other hospitals at the time, had significant unused capacity. However, Humana's financial performance and stock market value lagged its competitors'. Management considered a number of options for increasing the stock price, including doing a tax-free spin-off, issuing tracking stocks in the two divisions, doing an equity carve-out of subsidiary stock, repurchasing its stock, or undertaking a leveraged buyout.

The second case study features one of the very first tracking stock issues, by **USX Corporation.** USX, which operated a steel business and an energy business, had received unwanted advances from the corporate raider Carl Icahn. Icahn wanted the company to spin off its steel unit, which he believed had dragged down USX's overall market value. Separating the two businesses, he argued, would allow investors to value each part more accurately. However, management believed there were important synergies and other benefits from keeping the businesses together. It therefore proposed splitting the company's *stock* apart instead, by creating two new classes of stock that would separately track the performance of each business. Icahn did not believe this would solve the company's problems, however.

The final case in the module, **Donald Salter Communications,** describes a private family-owned company that ran into serious financial difficulty and hired a professional turnaround manager as its new CEO. Turnaround managers often receive company stock or stock options, so their compensation is tied to the success of the restructuring. Donald Salter's new manager insisted on being paid this way. However, the company had no publicly traded stock, and the family was unwilling to give up any of its control by issuing new equity. This presented a major dilemma for the board of directors, since failure to provide the CEO with appropriate incentives would put the entire restructuring at risk.

READINGS

Academic Research

Abarbanell, Jeffery, Brian Bushee, and J. Smith Raedy. 1998. "The Effects of Institutional Investor Preferences on Ownership Changes and Stock Prices around Corporate Spin-Offs," Unpublished working paper, Harvard Business School.

Allen, Jeffrey and John McConnell. 1998. "Equity Carve-Outs and Managerial Discretion," *Journal of Finance* 53: 163–186.

Berger, Phillip and Eli Ofek. 1995. "Diversification's Effect on Firm Value," *Journal of Financial Economics* 37: 39–65.

Berger, Phillip and Eli Ofek. 1999. "Causes and Effects of Corporate Refocusing Programs," *Review of Financial Studies* 12: 311–345.

Comment, Robert and Greg Jarrell. 1995. "Corporate Focus and Stock Returns," *Journal of Financial Economics* 37: 67–89.

Cusatis, Patrick, James Miles, and Randall Woolridge. 1993. "Restructuring Through Spin-Offs," *Journal of Financial Economics* 33: 293–311.

Daley, Lane, Vikas Mehrotra, and Ranjini Sivakumar. 1997. "Corporate Focus and Value Creation: Evidence from Spinoffs," *Journal of Financial Economics* 45: 257–281.

Desai, Hemang and Prem Jain. 1999. "Firm Performance and Focus: Long-Run Stock Market Performance Following Spinoffs," *Journal of Financial Economics* 54: 75–101.

D'Souza, Julia and John Jacob. 2000. "Why Firms Issue Targeted Stock," *Journal of Financial Economics* 56: 459–483.

Gilson, Stuart, Paul Healy, Christopher Noe, and Krishna Palepu. 2000. "Analyst Specialization and Conglomerate Stock Breakups," Unpublished working paper, Harvard Business School.

Gilson, Stuart and Michael Vetsuypens. 1993. "CEO Compensation in Financially Distressed Firms," *Journal of Finance* 48: 425–458.

Hite, Gailen and James Owers. 1983. "Security Price Reactions Around Corporate Spin-Off Announcements," *Journal of Financial Economics* 12, 409–436.

Jensen, Michael. 1986. "Agency Costs of Free Cash Flow, Corporate Finance, and Takeovers," *American Economic Review* 76: 323-329.

Jensen, Michael and Kevin Murphy. 1990. "Performance Pay and Top Management Incentives," *Journal of Political Economy* 98: 225–264.

Klein, April, James Rosenfeld, and William Beranek. 1991. "The Two Stages of an Equity Carve-Out and the Price Response of Parent and Subsidiary Stock," *Managerial and Decision Economics* 12: 449–460.

Krishnaswami, S. and V. Subramaniam. 1999. "Information Asymmetry, Valuation, and the Corporate Spin-Off Decision," *Journal of Financial Economics* 53: 73–112.

Nanda, Vikram. 1991. "On the Good News in Equity Carve-Outs," *Journal of Finance* 46: 1717–1737.

Schipper, Katherine and Abbie Smith. 1983. "Effects of Recontracting on Shareholder Wealth: The Case of Voluntary Spin-Offs," *Journal of Financial Economics* 12, 437–467.

Schipper, Katherine and Abbie Smith. 1986. "A Comparison of Equity Carve-Outs and Equity Offerings: Share Price Effects and Corporate Restructuring," *Journal of Financial Economics* 15, 153–186.

Management Books and Practitioner Resources

Blanton, Peter, Adam Perrett, and Eizelle Taino. 2000. "Unlocking Hidden Value: Realizing Value Through Spin-Offs, Carve-Outs, Split-Offs, and Tracking Stock," Credit Suisse First Boston Corporation.

M&A Tax Report. Published monthly by Panel Publishers, New York, NY (1-800-638-8437).

Mergers and Acquisitions: The Dealmaker's Journal. Published 11 times a year by Securities Data Publishing, 40 West 57th Street, New York, NY 10019.

Reed, Stanley and Alexandra Lajoux. 2000. *The Art of M&A (Third Edition)* (Chicago, IL: Irwin).

The Spin-Off Report. Published monthly by PCS Securities, Inc., 55 Liberty Street, Suite 1300, New York, NY 10005 (or online: www. pcssecurities.com/spinoff_report.htm).

EXHIBIT 12.1   Corporate Stock Breakups, U.S. 1980–2000

	Spin-Offs		Equity Carve-Outs		Tracking Stock Issues	
Year	Number of Companies	Stock Market Value ($millions)	Number of Companies	Stock Market Value ($millions)	Number of Companies	Stock Market Value ($millions)
1980	0	$ 0	1	$ 11	0	$ 0
1981	2	982	22	331	0	0
1982	3	219	17	143	0	0
1983	17	2,855	61	1,801	0	0
1984	13	1,134	33	646	1	2,550
1985	21	1,273	37	2,055	1	5,000
1986	28	3,639	68	4,457	0	0
1987	21	2,912	52	3,189	0	0
1988	34	11,220	23	1,504	0	0
1989	28	7,324	23	2,259	0	0
1990	28	5,113	17	1,162	0	0
1991	19	4,576	45	3,846	1	9,581
1992	29	5,716	78	7,045	1	170
1993	36	14,327	116	12,912	2	1,059
1994	31	23,386	73	6,036	1	670
1995	47	51,740	41	7,560	3	19,228
1996	44	87,812	64	12,770	2	2,018
1997	39	24,760	46	7,502	2	12,097
1998	58	88,930	24	9,793	2	6,063
1999	44	38,744	53	15,552	7	13,258
2000	40	98,318	40	16,888	2	68,595
Total	582	474,978	934	$117,461	25	$140,290

Note: For spin-offs, stock market value is the market value of the common stock of the spun-off entity immediately following the transaction; for equity carve-outs it is the market value of common stock sold to the public; and for tracking stock issues it is the market value of the tracking stock immediately after issuance, including the implicit market value of any equity retained by the parent entity.

Source: Securities Data Corporation, Lehman Brothers, Credit Suisse First Boston, *The M&A Tax Report.*

EXHIBIT 12.2 Methods of Stock Breakups

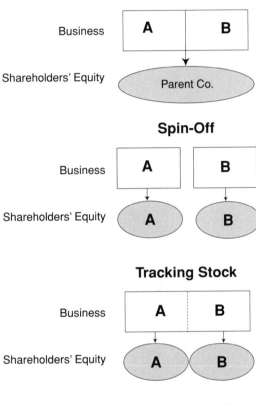

Before Restructuring

Business

Shareholders' Equity

Spin-Off

Business

Shareholders' Equity

Tracking Stock

Business

Shareholders' Equity

Equity Carve-Out

Business

Shareholders' Equity

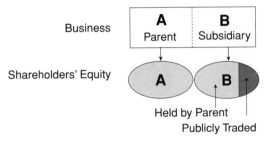

Held by Parent
Publicly Traded

CHAPTER 7

Humana Inc.

Managing in a Changing Industry

In late June of 1992, David Jones—chairman and chief executive officer (CEO) of Humana Inc.—stood looking out the window of his downtown Louisville, Kentucky, office and considered how rapidly events had unfolded over the past year. As the nation's largest integrated health care provider, Humana operated eighty-one acute-care hospitals in nineteen U.S. states, England, and Switzerland, and offered a broad range of managed health care plans to approximately 1.7 million individuals, mainly through health maintenance organizations (HMOs) and preferred provider organizations (PPOs). Since being cofounded by Jones some thirty years earlier, the company had experienced almost uninterrupted growth and profitability. Jones believed that much of this past success was made possible by a corporate culture that encouraged change and innovation; throughout its history, the company had periodically remade itself in response to changes in its marketplace. For example, Humana began in the early 1960s as an operator of nursing homes; in 1972, it shed its original business to focus exclusively on hospital management. And in the early 1980s, the company embarked on its current integrated strategy of managing both hospitals and health plans.

Now, at Jones' urging, Humana was again considering a major change in its strategic direction—in particular, the possibility of modifying or abandoning its integrated strategy. Since early last year, Jones had begun to question whether it still made sense for Humana to jointly operate both

---

This case was prepared by Professor Stuart Gilson, assisted by Research Associate Jeremy Cott. Copyright © 1994 by the President and Fellows of Harvard College. Harvard Business School case 294-062.

hospitals and health plans, given certain emerging trends in the U.S. health care industry. Although at the time there was nothing in Humana's financial performance to warrant serious concern, Jones felt that more information and analysis were needed. An internal review of Humana's strategy and operations (undertaken in late 1991 by certain members of senior management) had considered a number of options for restructuring Humana's business and corporate structure—including the complete separation of the company's hospital and health plan operations.

As the middle of 1992 approached, such a separation was viewed as increasingly likely by financial analysts who followed Humana. Although the company was conservatively leveraged, and was in no immediate danger of defaulting on its debt, it had just reported its steepest quarterly earnings decline in five and a half years, setting the stage for its first annual earnings decline since 1986. In addition, hospital stocks currently traded at historically low price-earnings multiples (about 15× on average for the industry), while multiples for HMO stocks were generally much higher (about 26× on average). Possibly because hospitals accounted for most of Humana's earnings, its recent price-earnings multiple (10× at the end of May) was much more reflective of other hospital stocks than stocks of publicly traded HMOs.[1] This raised concerns among some analysts as to whether Humana's stock price adequately reflected the value of its health plan operations. (See Exhibit 7.1.)

After considerable internal debate and discussion, management had concluded that the company's best long-term interests would be served by abandoning the integrated strategy and separating its two businesses by means of a corporate spin-off. As currently envisioned, the spin-off would be effected by distributing one share of common stock in a new company for each share of Humana stock currently owned. The new company would own and operate all of Humana's hospitals. All health plan operations would remain with the old company, which would retain the Humana name. Management decided to present the spin-off plan to Humana's board in early July.

THE BUSINESS

Change was not new to Humana. The company that was eventually to become Humana was founded in 1962 by two young lawyers, David Jones and

---

[1]In fiscal-year 1991, pretax income from the company's hospitals was $541 million, whereas pretax income from its health plans was only $14 million.

Wendell Cherry, to own and operate a single nursing home in Louisville, Kentucky. By 1968, the company, which was then called Extendicare, operated eight nursing homes. Feeling that its growth prospects were limited by lack of capital, the company made an initial public offering of its stock and acquired its first hospital, located in Alabama. Only four years later, Extendicare had expanded to become the largest operator of nursing homes in the United States, with over forty facilities. Around this same time, Jones and Cherry began to realize that hospitals could be successfully run using the same management techniques that they used to run their nursing home business. Sensing that hospitals would yield higher returns in the long run—Jones liked to point out that the government's daily reimbursement for a flu patient was six times that for a nursing home patient—the company shed all of its nursing homes in 1972 and focused exclusively on hospital management, changing its name to Humana in 1974. A watershed in the company's development occurred in January 1978, when it acquired American Medicorp Inc. of Pennsylvania for $304.5 million in a hostile takeover, in the process almost doubling the number of its hospitals from 59 to 114. Many of Humana's hospitals were located in the South, where population growth rates were high. The geographic distribution of Humana hospitals and hospital beds is shown in Exhibit 7.2.

Humana pioneered a system of measuring the quality and productivity of hospital services, and as a matter of policy distributed questionnaires to patients who stayed in Humana hospitals, giving individual attention to any complaints. Humana was also one of the first firms to make extensive use of centralized computer systems to track and analyze the company's operations. One of the company's main objectives was to become known as a provider of high-quality, state-of-the-art medical care. The company took considerable pride in the fact that the world's second artificial heart transplant took place in one of its hospitals.

In the early 1980s, several developments took place that radically changed the economics of the health care industry. Most significantly, the federal government, responding to rising health care costs, changed how it reimbursed hospitals for treating Medicare patients. Under the new system, a hospital received a *predetermined* payment for each Medicare patient that it treated, based on the patient's particular illness and the estimated costs of treatment (independently of how long the patient actually stayed in the hospital).[2] Hospitals did not receive any extra reimbursement from the government if the actual costs of treating a patient exceeded this fixed

---

[2] Currently, this system classifies illnesses into approximately 500 "diagnostic related groups," or DRGs, and specifies a fixed dollar reimbursement for each group.

payment; however, they were allowed to keep any surplus. At the same time, private health insurance plans were also becoming increasingly aggressive in trying to control costs (for example, by charging their members higher deductibles and copayments).

Coupled with continuing advances in medical technology, these developments resulted in an increasing share of hospital cases being treated on an outpatient rather than an inpatient basis. This shift threatened to undermine hospital profits—first, by reducing hospital occupancy rates, and second, by forcing hospitals to handle the more serious medical cases, which generally required more labor-intensive and costly treatment.

To fight the resulting decline in hospital occupancy rates, Jones and Cherry decided to expand into the health insurance business by offering a broad range of flexible health care plans for employers and their employees. These included managed care plans—health maintenance organizations (HMOs) and preferred provider organizations (PPOs)—and various traditional indemnity plans, including supplemental Medicare insurance for the elderly ("Medicare Supplement").[3] Jones believed that managed health care represented the wave of the future in health care delivery.

Humana marketed its HMO and PPO plans primarily to employers and other groups ("Commercial" plans). In return for offering health care services to a firm's employees, Humana would charge the firm a fixed monthly premium for each enrollee in the plan (some or all of the premium could be passed on to employees as a payroll deduction). Currently, about 57 percent of Humana's health plan premium revenues came from its Commercial HMO and PPO products. Humana also contracted with the Health Care Financing Administration (HCFA) to provide medical benefits to Medicare-eligible individuals ("Medicare Risk") in return for a fixed monthly payment that was set—and revised annually—by HCFA. This business accounted for an additional 39 percent of Humana's premium revenues. The company earned much higher margins on its Commercial business than it did either on Medicare Risk or on underwriting Medicare Supplement policies. Exhibit 7.3 shows the distribution of membership in Humana's health plans by product segment and geographic region. Competition among HMOs was intense. At the end of 1991 there were 581 in-

---

[3]This latter product was a traditional insurance policy that Medicare enrollees could purchase to pay for hospital deductibles, co-payments, and co-insurance that were not covered under either Part A or Part B of Medicare (Part A covers inpatient medical care, while Part B, which requires the payment of a regular premium, covers physician and other hospital services).

dependent HMOs operating in the United States, although continuing industry consolidation had reduced the number of HMOs from a peak of 707 in 1987 (a significant portion of the growth in Humana's health plan business had in fact come from acquisitions).

HMOs and PPOs appealed to employers because they controlled costs more effectively than conventional fee-for-service insurance plans, by assigning responsibility to a particular group for monitoring the cost of treating patients. In a typical HMO, patients were required to meet initially with a primary care physician (or "gatekeeper"), who decided whether they should be referred to more costly specialists. Medical procedures also had to be performed in the most efficient way possible, and only when necessary. Doctors often had to obtain prior authorization before admitting patients to a hospital, and a second opinion before recommending surgery. As a result of such controls, the average hospital inpatient utilization rate among HMO enrollees was, according to some studies, less than two-thirds that for traditional health insurance plans.[4] PPOs combined elements of both HMOs and traditional health insurance, in that they allowed enrollees to choose their own physicians, but also gave them financial incentives to choose from among a group of preferred health care providers who contracted with the PPO to provide medical services at favorable rates.

Some of Humana's HMOs employed their own physicians (who worked in buildings owned by Humana), while others contracted with groups of independent physicians, who would agree to provide certain medical services to the HMO members for a fixed per-member-per-month fee (called a "capitation" payment). This fee did not vary with the type of medical services performed, and thus provided physicians with a direct financial incentive to control costs. Physicians who were directly employed by Humana typically were paid a straight salary. Humana HMOs and PPOs also contracted with Humana hospitals and other hospitals to provide inpatient and outpatient services to Humana plan enrollees at predetermined rates (generally on a per diem basis for inpatient services and on a discounted fee-for-service basis for outpatient services). By mid-1992, Humana owned and operated ten HMOs, which contracted with approximately 22,000 physicians (including 4,600 primary care physicians) and 500 hospitals.[5] In addition, Humana's HMOs directly employed over 400 physicians.

---

[4] A standard measure of hospital inpatient utilization used by health insurance plans is the number of hospital days per year per 1,000 plan enrollees.

[5] Most of these doctors and hospitals were also under contract to provide services to Humana's PPO enrollees.

The attraction of owning both hospitals and health plans was that Humana could use its health plans to feed patients into its hospitals, resulting in higher average (and more stable) occupancy rates. Back in 1983, before it adopted its integrated strategy, Humana's hospitals suffered a critical loss of business when Cigna Corporation unexpectedly pulled out of an agreement to use only Humana hospitals for a large number of its HMO enrollees. An integrated strategy would reduce both the impact and the likelihood of such an episode in the future. In addition, by operating hospitals and health plans jointly, Humana could realize savings in overhead costs (for example, by having both business segments share the same administrative, data processing, and personnel facilities). An integrated strategy had been employed with great success for many years by Kaiser Permanente, which operated largely in California. Kaiser, like Humana, used its health plans (with approximately 6.5 million enrollees) to feed patients into its hospitals (with approximately 7,700 beds); unlike Humana, however, Kaiser largely employed its own physicians, and its hospitals largely treated only enrollees in Kaiser health plans. Exhibit 7.4 presents the historical consolidated financial statements of Humana, and Exhibits 7.5 and 7.6 present selected financial and operating information for other major publicly traded HMOs and hospital companies.

REEVALUATING HUMANA'S INTEGRATED STRATEGY

From the beginning the new strategy had worked extremely well. However, in conducting its internal review of Humana's strategy in late 1991, management identified a number of disturbing recent trends, particularly in the hospitals segment. In addition, the long-term prospects of the firm's two businesses were growing increasingly divergent, causing some to question whether an integrated strategy was still appropriate.

On the one hand, the long-term outlook for managed care providers like HMOs and PPOs looked extremely bright. In 1991, total national enrollment in HMOs was approximately four times as large as it was in 1981, and was expected to increase by 6 to 10 percent annually for at least the next five years. In 1991, HMOs accounted for 29 percent of the persons enrolled in employer-sponsored health plans in the United States, compared to 20 percent the previous year. To many observers—like Professor Alain Enthoven of Stanford University and the other members of the "Jackson Hole Group"—managed care represented the best hope for improving the nation's health care delivery system. Many predicted that any health reform proposal would include incentives to promote greater use of HMOs as a way of controlling health care costs and of extending coverage to the 37 million Americans who were currently without health insurance.

Humana's health plan business appeared to be benefiting from these favorable trends. Pretax income from health plans had grown by 125 percent in fiscal year 1991 (by more than ten times in fiscal year 1990) and was up 16 percent for the nine months ended May 29, 1992. Total enrollment in Humana's health plans had also been growing much faster than the rest of the industry. At fiscal year-end 1991, there were approximately 1.7 million enrollees in Humana health plans (including 339,000 enrollees in three HMOs that Humana had acquired that year), compared to 1.2 million the previous year—a 42 percent increase. In 1990, total enrollment had grown by 26 percent. In sharp contrast, total enrollment increases for the industry were only 5 percent in 1991 and 7 percent in 1990.

On the other hand, there were some signs that high growth was placing the company under increasing financial strain. For fiscal year 1991, Humana's administrative cost ratio (administrative costs as a percentage of total premium income from health plans) was 16.1 percent. Although this ratio was down from 22.6 percent three years earlier, management still considered it to be excessive. Management was also concerned about Humana's high medical loss ratio (the percentage of health plan premiums paid out as direct medical costs). Currently standing at 85.9 percent—up from 84.4 percent for fiscal year 1991—Humana's medical loss ratio exceeded that of all other major HMOs except Maxicare (Exhibit 7.7).

Getting the medical loss ratio down would be difficult because relations between the company and its physicians had become increasingly strained. Many physicians resented the company's recently stepped-up efforts to control costs. The situation was especially severe in the San Antonio market, where, in 1991, the company had tried (unsuccessfully) to extend its capitation payment system to cover specialists, and had recently been forced to replace the entire emergency room staff at one of its hospitals following a dispute over costs. As one physician stated to the press, "We just don't trust those people. . . . Physicians are concerned that patients are not getting the kind of treatment they deserve at Humana hospitals." Physicians were also upset that Humana hospitals generally charged other insurance plans higher rates for hospital services than they charged Humana health plans. (However, comparing these rates was difficult because Humana hospitals were able to treat Humana-insured patients at relatively lower cost than patients enrolled in other, unaffiliated health plans. In addition, changing the rate that was charged for transactions between Humana's two business segments would arguably have little or no impact on the firm's *consolidated* profits or cashflows.)

Compared to the HMO industry, the long-term outlook for the hospital industry was bleak. Although growth in the elderly segment of the population was expected to increase the long-term demand for medical care, reimbursement rates for Medicare and Medicaid had historically failed to keep pace with the rising health care costs. In 1991, 60 percent of all U.S. hospitals operated at a loss on their Medicare patients; meanwhile, the aging population meant that Medicare patient-days had come to represent an increasing share of hospitals' total patient-days. To make a profit, hospitals had to charge higher rates to their insured patients in order to recoup losses on their uninsured and Medicare/Medicaid patients (known as "cost shifting"). To make matters worse, there was a nontrivial risk that the federal government might cut expenditures on Medicare and Medicaid as part of its deficit reduction effort.

Hospital profits were also being squeezed by rapid increases in operating costs and declines in average hospital stays brought about by the growth of competing outpatient surgery centers and home infusion companies. The development of less invasive, more advanced surgical techniques reinforced these trends by allowing many procedures to be performed on an outpatient basis that had formerly required inpatient stays. To compound matters, insurance companies and managed care providers were applying increasing pressure on hospitals to shorten hospital stays and limit price increases. Perhaps most troubling of all, the hospital industry was plagued by severe excess capacity. In 1991, the average occupancy rate for U.S. hospitals was 69 percent, compared to 78 percent in 1981 (although occupancy rates were generally higher for hospitals located in large urban areas). As a result, competition among hospitals for patients was fierce. Some industry observers predicted that nearly one-third of all U.S. hospitals would have to be closed within the next five years.

In addition to having to deal with these industry problems, Humana hospitals had lately been the subject of unfavorable media coverage, including a story that ran in late 1991 on ABC's *Primetime Live* which alleged that Humana hospitals overcharged for their services. Even though Humana argued that its pricing policies were consistent with industry norms, media treatment of the company fueled the perception that Humana hospitals charged more for their services than other hospitals.

The recent financial and operating performance of the company's hospitals business left little room for optimism. Since late 1991, same-store admissions at Humana hospitals had been declining by more than at other hospitals. For fiscal year 1992, total hospital revenues were expected to remain flat. The occupancy rate for Humana hospitals currently stood at only 47 percent, far below the national average of 69 percent.[6] Hospital operating margins had also fallen to historically low levels (to approximately 15 percent for fiscal year 1991 and 14 percent for the most recently ended fiscal quarter, compared to 23 percent for fiscal year 1987). For the nine months ended May 29, 1992, pretax income from hospitals was down 12 percent from the previous year. Adding to the pressure on margins, high-margin private pay patients (i.e., those who belonged to managed care plans other than Humana's or who had traditional health insurance) had come to represent an increasingly smaller share of total patient-days at Humana hospitals; from 1987 to 1991, the percentage of total patient-days accounted for by private pay patients fell from 53 percent to 21 percent. This decline was especially pronounced in markets where the integrated strategy was in effect. Doubts about the effectiveness of the integrated strategy were also raised by the fact that Humana health plans still accounted for only 27 percent of Humana hospitals' total patient-days (and only 11 percent of hospital revenues), while fully a third of the health plans' hospital utilization involved non-Humana hospitals. Exhibits 7.8 and 7.9 present, respectively, selected operating statistics and sources of revenue for Humana hospitals.

RESTRUCTURING ALTERNATIVES

Back in December 1991, management had come up with a range of possible restructuring options for Humana. The list would eventually be narrowed down as further analysis and the passage of time revealed what factors were responsible for the company's problems. One option considered was to somehow effect a division between the hospital and health plan operations, while keeping the basic company structure intact. For example, the business could be reorganized into two separate subsidiaries, to be controlled by a common parent holding company. Another way of achieving such separation would be to issue "tracking stock." Under this proposal, Humana would dividend a new class of common stock to shareholders that would represent a claim only on the cash flows generated by its hospital or health plan opera-

---

[6]Some of this difference was due to differences in how hospitals defined occupancy rates. Occupancy rates reported by Humana were defined as the number of beds in use divided by the number of *licensed* beds (roughly speaking, the total number of beds in a hospital, as determined by regulation). In contrast, most other hospitals defined the occupancy rate as the number of beds in use divided by the number of *staffed* beds (i.e., only those beds that were currently in service).

tions (but not both). All other aspects of the company's corporate structure would remain intact.[7] In the previous year, USX Corporation had successfully used tracking stock as a way of allowing the market to separately value its U.S. Steel and Marathon Oil divisions. Finally, management considered the possibility of selling off only those hospitals that operated in the same geographic markets as its health plans.

A related option was to keep the hospital and health plan operations together, but adopt a new price structure for hospital services, thus removing a major source of the conflict with physicians. Earlier in the month, Humana had lowered the prices of most inpatient and outpatient services offered at some of its hospitals by up to 35 percent in an attempt to woo back physicians and their patients. It was still too early to judge the impact of this experiment.

Another proposed solution involved selling off some or all of the company's hospitals (possibly those that were experiencing the greatest operating and financial difficulties). Recent sales of hospitals had generated proceeds of approximately 6.0× hospitals' earnings before interest, taxes, depreciation, and amortization (EBITDA). However, a drawback to this approach was the fact that Medicare had historically reimbursed hospitals for part of their depreciation. If a hospital was sold for more than its undepreciated book value, the government would likely assert a claim (known as "Medicare recapture") for part of the accumulated depreciation on the hospital. Humana estimated that it would have to pay Medicare recapture of $584 million if it sold off all of its hospitals. The company would also incur a tax liability from selling its hospitals, although Medicare recapture was tax deductible.

Another option considered was to take the company private in a leveraged buyout. Earlier in the year, Hospital Corporation of America (HCA), which did its own leveraged buyout in March 1988, had made an initial public stock offering at a price more than *eight times* what management had paid for the company three years earlier. At the time of the buyout, HCA, like Humana currently, owned approximately eighty hospitals (concentrated in the Southern states) and had annual net operating revenues of approximately $5 billion. One potential drawback to this alternative was that Humana's health plans were by law required to keep a large percentage of their assets in the form of safe, marketable securities. At fiscal year-end 1991 these restricted assets amounted to $523 million

---

[7]All transactions between the two segments, including intercompany pricing and allocation of overhead, would be conducted on an arm's length basis.

(Exhibit 7.4), and would not be available to help pay down debt issued in a leveraged buyout.

Alternatively, Humana could achieve the same capital structure as it would in a buyout—but retain the benefits of being publicly traded—by doing a stock buyback. Some analysts who followed the company felt that some form of stock repurchase made sense, given Humana's relatively low debt-to-capital ratio and the low multiple at which its common stock traded vis-à-vis other health care companies. Historically, firms that repurchased their own stock through a tender offer had seen their stock price rise by 10 to 20 percent in response to the offer.

Other options considered by management included allowing the company's health plan enrollees to seek treatment in non-Humana hospitals, and diversifying into new (albeit related) lines of business. This latter strategy would allow Humana to capitalize on its long experience in providing health care, as well as hedge against some of the risk posed by possible government initiatives in health care regulation. Finally, the company considered whether it should adopt an employee stock ownership plan (ESOP). Such a plan would include participation by Humana physicians, and could be modeled along the same lines as a transaction undertaken in 1987 by Hospital Corporation of America, which sold 104 of its hospitals to a newly formed company that was largely owned by the hospitals' employees through an ESOP.

Although management gave serious consideration to each of these options, by late spring a consensus had started to emerge that Humana's long-term interests would be best served by abandoning the integrated strategy altogether. This would mean completely separating the two sides of the business. This goal could be met in either of two ways: by selling off the company's hospitals or by spinning off one of the two businesses as a free-standing public company. The spin-off option had been under consideration since the management team first met late last year.

THE SPIN-OFF PROPOSAL

As currently envisioned, a spin-off would be effected by issuing one share of new common stock for each share of Humana common stock currently outstanding, representing an equity interest in the company's acute-care hospital operations (henceforth, Hospitals). The old shares would remain outstanding and, after the spin-off, would represent a claim against the company's health plan operations (henceforth, Health Plans), which would continue to operate under the Humana name. Shares in both Hospitals and Health Plans would be traded on the New York Stock Exchange, and Health Plans would become the nation's largest publicly traded HMO.[8]

To minimize any disruption to the two businesses, the plan would provide for substantial continuity of management. David Jones (currently CEO of Humana) would be named CEO and chairman of Health Plans, while Carl Pollard (currently president of Humana) would become the CEO and chairman of Hospitals. There would be no overlap in the boards of directors of the two companies. Hospitals' certificate of incorporation and company bylaws would include a classified board of directors, a super-majority voting provision with respect to the election of directors, a fair price provision, and a prohibition on shareholder consent solicitations. Similar provisions were currently in effect for Humana.

Three critically important issues had to be resolved before the spin-off could take place. First there was the matter of allocating corporate overhead between Hospitals and Health Plans. Currently, both business segments shared the services of a number of departments, including personnel, legal, purchasing, finance and administration, and corporate planning. In addition, there were a number of shared physical assets, such as the company's computer and data processing systems and the corporate headquarters building. Deciding how these resources should be divided between Hospitals and Health Plans would be a complicated endeavor. How overhead was allocated could also significantly affect the reported financial and operating performance of each company, and thus how each was valued in the stock market after the spin-off. For fiscal year 1991, unallocated corporate operating expenses came to $156 million, or 22 percent of the combined pretax operating income of the hospital and health plan segments (since fiscal year 1989, these unallocated expenses had increased by 57 percent, while combined pretax operating income had increased by only 28 percent). Exhibit 7.10 presents recent business segment information for Humana, including unallocated corporate overhead.

The second issue that had to be decided was how to allocate the company's pre–spin-off debt between Hospitals and Health Plans. As of May 31, 1992 (the most recently ended fiscal quarter), total long-term debt owed by Humana (including such debt payable within one year) amounted to $792 million. In making this decision, it would be necessary to consider how the spin-off might affect the debt capacities of the two businesses. It

---

[8]Given the relative significance of the hospital operations, the company would initially report consolidated financial statements for the spun-off hospital business, and account for the health plan business as a discontinued operation.

was senior management's wish that neither business receive a lower credit rating than Humana enjoyed currently.

Finally, it would be necessary to specify the terms of any future business dealings between the two segments. At one extreme, each segment would be free to seek the best competitive terms from its customers and suppliers and would not be obligated to continue doing business with its former partner. At the other extreme, certain pre–spin-off business ties would be maintained, for example, by requiring Hospitals to provide hospital services to Health Plans enrollees at rates in effect before the spin-off, or by requiring Health Plans to contract with Hospitals for some minimum fraction of patients needing inpatient hospital care. Proponents of the latter approach believed that a complete separation would be too disruptive, since each segment currently contributed to the revenues and profits of the other.

In addition the above three decisions, a number of other more technical issues had to be dealt with before the spin-off could be implemented. The company had applied to the Internal Revenue Service (IRS) for a ruling that the spin-off would qualify as a tax-free transaction under Section 355 of the Internal Revenue Code. If the ruling was unfavorable, then the amount by which the fair market value of Hospitals common stock exceeded the company's adjusted tax basis would be considered a taxable capital gain to the company. In addition, each Humana shareholder would be taxed on the difference between the market value of Hospitals stock and his or her allocated basis in the stock. The portion of this gain that represented the shareholder's pro rata share of current and accumulated retained earnings in the company would be taxed as a dividend, and the remainder as a capital gain. Shareholders would be unlikely to approve the spin-off if the company failed to obtain a favorable tax ruling.

It would also be necessary to make certain adjustments to Humana's three management stock options plans. Current and former managers of Humana held options to purchase 3.3 million shares of common stock in the company. Exhibit 7.11 reports beneficial ownership of the company's stock (including options exercisable within sixty days) by Humana management and nonmanagement shareholders. Under the distribution, each outstanding management stock option would be bifurcated into two separately exercisable options, one for each newly formed company. The exercise price of each option would be based on the relative prices of the two underlying shares observed during the twenty trading days following the distribution date. Vesting and termination dates of the options would be amended to provide managers in each company incentives to exercise options held in the other company. Each new option would be a nonqualified stock option for tax purposes. Normally, when such an option is exercised, any option exercise profits represent taxable income to the employee and a tax deduction for the sponsoring company. However, in Humana's case, there was some uncertainty as to whether the IRS would allow either Hospitals or Health Plans to take such a deduction when the options exercised were owned by an employee of the other company; Humana had asked the IRS for a ruling on the matter.

Jones sat down at his desk and began to draft his presentation to the board.

Note: Humana and the Harvard Business School have discussed the description of the transaction, and each recognizes that this case represents a simplification, and therefore is not a complete description of the facts and issues applicable to the company and the transaction.

EXHIBIT 7.1 Humana Common Stock Price and Dividend History

Date	Month-End Stock Price	Per Share Dividend Payout
Jan-90	$25.667	
Feb-90	25.417	17⁵/₁₆¢
Mar-90	25.917	
Apr-90	26.000	
May-90	30.000	17⁵/₁₆¢
Jun-90	32.667	
Jul-90	31.917	
Aug-90	30.667	20¢
Sep-90	29.667	
Oct-90	27.833	
Nov-90	28.750	20¢
Dec-90	28.083	
Jan-91	30.333	
Feb-91	30.250	20¢
Mar-91	32.667	
Apr-91	33.000	
May-91	34.500	20¢
Jun-91	31.917	
Jul-91	33.500	
Aug-91	32.500	22¹/₂¢
Sep-91	30.250	
Oct-91	29.000	
Nov-91	24.125	22¹/₂¢
Dec-91	26.875	
Jan-92	28.125	
Feb-92	25.250	22¹/₂¢
Mar-92	25.000	
Apr-92	24.375	
May-92	21.625	22¹/₂¢

Note: Share data are adjusted for August 1991 3-for-2 stock split.
Source: New York Stock Exchange; Bloomberg Financial Services.

EXHIBIT 7.2 Humana Hospitals: Geographic Distribution and Number of Beds (as of August 31, 1991)

	Number of Hospitals	Number of Beds
Alabama	7	1,241
Alaska	1	238
Arizona	2	441
California	5	930
Colorado	2	400
Florida	18	4,125
Georgia	4	720
Illinois	2	1,364
Indiana	1	150
Kansas	2	510
Kentucky	7	1,897
Louisiana	7	658
Mississippi	1	101
Nevada	1	688
Tennessee	3	422
Texas	10	2,746
Utah	1	110
Virginia	2	400
West Virginia	2	201
Total U.S.	78	17,342
Switzerland	1	242
United Kingdom	2	245
Total international	3	487
Total all regions	81	17,829

Source: Company annual reports.

EXHIBIT 7.3 Humana Inc. Recent Commercial and Medicare Risk Membership

	Commercial		Medicare	
	PPO	HMO	Risk	Total[1]
Chicago, IL	17,600	274,000	19,000	310,600
Corpus Christi, TX	7,800	23,300	5,800	36,900
Daytona, FL	3,200	12,400	17,800	33,400
Kansas City, MO	300	76,000	5,600	81,900
Las Vegas, NV	12,300	11,300	—	23,600
Lexington, KY	39,500	38,800	—	78,300
Louisville, KY	14,300	165,500	3,400	183,200
Orlando, FL	16,800	35,800	20,600	73,200
Phoenix, AZ	1,900	15,600	9,100	26,600
San Antonio, TX	28,000	67,300	10,300	105,600
South FL[2]	48,400	149,000	105,500	302,900
Tampa, FL	31,900	84,300	65,200	181,400
Others	15,200	47,000	—	62,200
Total	237,200	1,000,300	262,300	1,499,800

[1]Excludes approximately 203,900 persons who have purchased Medicare Supplement policies.
[2]Includes Dade, Broward, and Palm Beach counties.
Source: Company annual reports.

EXHIBIT 7.4 Consolidated Financial Statements ($millions)

	Years Ended August 31		
	1991	1990	1989
Assets			
Current assets			
Cash and cash equivalents	$ 74	$ 100	$ 105
Marketable securities	87	55	79
Accounts receivable	789	680	616
Inventories	104	91	81
Other	115	129	134
	$1,169	$1,055	$1,015
Property and equipment, at cost			
Land	230	207	177
Buildings	2,136	1,928	1,760
Equipment	1,576	1,379	1,211
Construction in progress	99	90	58
	$4,041	$3,604	$3,206
Accumulated depreciation	1,468	1,326	1,155
	$2,573	$2,278	$2,051
Investments of health plan and insurance			
subsidiaries	523	453	462
Other	162	150	168
Total assets	$4,427	$3,936	$3,696
Liabilities and Stockholders' Equity			
Current liabilities			
Trade accounts payable	175	147	115
Salaries, wages, and other compensation	139	100	96
Other accrued expenses	335	266	229
Unearned premium revenues	83	64	-
Medical claims reserves	272	246	195
Income taxes	81	117	106
Long-term debt due within one year	20	35	35
	$1,105	$ 975	$ 776
Long-term debt	826	717	1,140
Other liabilities	487	494	453
Common stockholders' equity			
Common stock, $0.1667 par value;			
200,000,000 shares authorized;			
issued and outstanding:			
158,206,059 shares (1991);			
156,469,806 shares (1990);			
147,658,278 shares (1989)	26	26	26
Capital in excess of par value	481	449	234
Other	(3)	(5)	(11)
Retained earnings	1,505	1,280	1,078
	$2,009	$1,750	$1,327
Total liabilities and stockholder's equity	$4,427	$3,936	$3,696
Revenues	5,865	4,852	4,088
Operating expenses	4,794	3,848	3,218
Provision for doubtful accounts	226	226	184
Depreciation and amoritization	256	231	209
Interest expense	97	111	139
Interest income	(63)	(63)	(61)
	$5,310	$4,353	$3,689
Income before income taxes	555	499	399
Provision for income taxes	200	180	143
Income before extraordinary item	355	319	256
Extraordinary loss on early extinguishment			
of debt, net of income tax benefit	—	(9)	—
Net income	$ 355	$ 310	$ 256

Source: Company annual reports.

EXHIBIT 7.5   Major Publicly Traded Health Maintenance Organizations

	1991	1990	1989
Pacificare Health Systems			
Runs group health plans with 726,500 enrollees.			
Beta = 1.20			
Assets ($millions)	322	232	194
Long-term debt ($millions)	2.3	0.3	2.3
Net worth ($millions)	100	75	44
Operating revenues ($millions)	1,242	976	650
EBITDA ($millions)	36	19	11
Net income (loss) ($millions)	26	17	11
Earnings per share ($)	2.20	1.40	0.96
Dividends per share ($)	nil	nil	nil
Common stock price range ($) high/low	42.6/14.6	27.6/12.0	30.4/6.2
Average PE ratio	11.4	12.7	12.7
Average shares outstanding (millions)	11.39	11.38	10.75
United Healthcare			
Runs group health plans with 1,300,000 enrollees.			
Beta = 1.30			
Assets ($millions)	574	293	237
Long-term debt ($millions)	3.4	7.0	58.3
Net worth ($millions)	319	126	60
Operating revenues ($millions)	847	605	412
EBITDA ($millions)	129	66	33
Net income (loss) ($millions)	75	34	14
Earnings per share ($)	2.40	1.20	0.61
Dividends per share ($)	0.02	0.02	nil
Common stock price range ($) high/low	78.3/20.0	24.0/7.9	12.6/4.1
Average PE ratio	19.5	12.5	15.0
Average shares outstanding (millions)	31.47	27.10	19.35
U.S. Healthcare			
Runs group health plans with 1,240,000 enrollees.			
Beta = 1.25			
Assets ($millions)	758	613	414
Long-term debt ($millions)	0	0	0
Net worth ($millions)	347	234	164
Operating revenues ($millions)	1,709	1,330	1,000
EBITDA ($millions)	258	130	53
Net income (loss) ($millions)	151	78	28
Earnings per share ($)	2.09	1.08	0.40
Dividends per share ($)	0.24	0.16	0.10
Common stock price range ($) high/low	45.8/15.9	19.9/6.4	10.3/3.5
Average PE ratio	14.5	10.8	18.9
Average shares outstanding (millions)	70.54	70.43	69.27

Source: Value Line; company annual reports.

EXHIBIT 7.6 Major Publicly Traded Hospital Companies

	1991	1990	1989
Columbia Hospitals			
Runs 11 general hospitals with 2,643 licensed beds and 2 psychiatric hospitals with 172 beds.			
Beta = na			
Assets ($millions)	485	322	
Long-term debt ($millions)	230	172	
Net worth ($millions)	118	41	
Operating revenues ($millions)	499	290	
EBITDA ($millions)	81	46	
Net income (loss) ($millions)	15	10	
Earnings per share ($)	0.90	0.83	
Dividends per share ($)	nil	nil	
Common stock price range ($) high/low	18.8/9.8	15.5/10.0	
Average PE ratio	14.1	14.5	
Average shares outstanding (millions)	16.54	11.82	
Community Psychiatric Centers			
Runs 50 psychiatric hospitals with 5,044 licensed beds.			
Beta = 1.20			
Assets ($millions)	570	552	475
Long-term debt ($millions)	27	29	30
Net worth ($millions)	484	461	387
Operating revenues ($millions)	397	382	331
EBITDA ($millions)	84	83	72
Net income (loss) ($millions)	45	83	72
Earnings per share ($)	1.51	1.80	1.56
Dividends per share ($)	0.36	0.36	0.36
Common stock price range ($) high/low	40.0/10.6	30.6/19.8	35.0/22.3
Average PE ratio	18.7	14.2	18.8
Average shares outstanding (millions)	46.19	46.63	46.82
National Medical Enterprises			
Runs 35 general hospitals with 6,559 beds, 32 rehabilitation hospitals with 2,704 beds, and 82 psychiatric hospitals and related facilities with 6,588 beds.			
Beta = 1.15			
Assets ($millions)	4,060	3,807	3,877
Long-term debt ($millions)	1,140	1,361	1,671
Net worth ($millions)	1,762	1,257	1,101
Operating revenues ($millions)	3,806	3,935	3,676
EBITDA ($millions)	741	681	582
Net income (loss) ($millions)	277	242	192
Earnings per share ($)	1.73	1.52	1.29
Dividends per share ($)	0.40	0.36	0.34
Common stock price range ($) high/low	25.8/12.6	20.1/14.6	19.5/10.7
Average PE ratio	13.0	13.0	9.4
Average shares outstanding (millions)	174.76	157.78	148.74

Note: In 1992, the two largest (other than Humana) publicly traded hospital companies in the United States were HealthTrust, Inc. and Hospital Corporation of America. HealthTrust went public in 1991, and HCA in 1992. Due to their brief trading histories, they are not represented in this table. Columbia Hospitals went public in May 1990.

Source: Value Line; company annual reports.

EXHIBIT 7.7   HMO Medical Loss Ratios (Average of Most Recent Four Quarters), June 1992

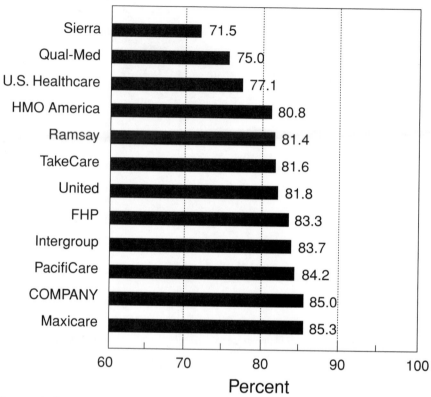

Source: *Pulse*, and company documents.

EXHIBIT 7.8 Selected Operating Statistics for Humana Hospitals

	Fiscal Year Ended August 31			
	1991	**1990**	**1989**	**1988**
Number of hospitals in operation at end of period	81	85	84	83
Licensed	17,830	17,838	17,576	17,323
Weighted average licensed beds	17,700	17,644	17,411	17,573
Patient-days	3,084,100	3,083,600	2,990,300	2,987,900
Occupancy rate (%)	47.70	47.90	47.10	46.50
Health plans patient-days in hospitals:				
Commercial	200,200	172,300	147,300	106,300
Medicare Risk	188,900	131,700	109,100	108,200
Medicare Supplement	365,300	294,100	207,900	103,400
Total	754,400	598,100	464,300	317,900

Source: Company annual reports.

EXHIBIT 7.9 Humana Hospitals' Sources of Revenue (Percent)

	1991	1990	1989	1988
Medicare, including Humana Health Plans Medicare Supplement	26	27	28	28
Medicaid	4	3	3	2
Humana Health Plans Commercial and Medicare Risk	9	7	5	4
All other payers, including unaffiliated HMOs and PPOs, traditional insurance companies, Blue Cross and self-payers	61	63	64	66

Source: Company filings.

EXHIBIT 7.10   Fiscal Year 1991 Business Segment
Information ($millions)

Assets	
Hospitals	$3,540
Health Plans	703
Corporate	184
	$4,427
Long-term debt (including debt currently payable):	
Hospitals	102
Health Plans	22
Corporate	722
	$ 846
Revenues	
Hospitals	
Inpatient	3,046
Outpatient	954
	$4,000
Health Plans	2,233
Hospital revenues paid by Humana health plans	(368)
	$5,865
EBITDA	
Hospitals	904
Health Plans	100
Corporate	(159)
	$ 845
Depreciation and amortization	
Hospitals	210
Health Plans	26
Corporate	20
	$ 256
Net interest expense	
Hospitals	193[a]
Health Plans	(36)
Corporate	(123)
	$ 34
Additions to property and equipment	
Hospitals	396
Health Plans	113
Corporate	77
	$ 586

[a]Includes $169 million in interest on intercompany debt owed to Corporate.
Source: Company documents and annual reports.

EXHIBIT 7.11 Stock Ownership of Management and Large Holders

	Position	Number of Common Shares Beneficially Owned as of 11/1/91	Percent of Class If Greater Than 1.0
K. Frank Austen, M.D.	Director	5,150	
William C. Ballard, Jr.	CFO[1,2]	219,216	
Michael E. Gellert	Director	128,100	
J. David Grissom	Director	82,500	
David A. Jones	Chairman & CEO[1]	3,140,675	2.0%
John W. Landrum	Director	314,333	
Carl F. Pollard	President & COO[1]	415,438	
W. Ann Reynolds, Ph.D.	Director	900	
Wayne T. Smith	Director	191,467	
William T. Young	Director	1,439,181	
All directors and current executive officers as a group, including the above (31 in number)		6,827,566	4.3%

[1]Also a director of the company.
[2]William C. Ballard, Jr., retired on April 30, 1992.
Note: The company knows of no person who owns more than 5% of the outstanding stock as of November 1, 1991.
Source: Company proxy statement, dated November 27, 1991.

CHAPTER 8

USX Corporation

In late 1990, senior managers of USX Corporation were preparing for a board of directors meeting at which a decision would be made about possible restructuring moves. The company was a diversified company, operating in both the steel and energy industries. Steel had been for years a troubled industry, and, while energy had greater growth prospects, it was a volatile industry subject to various forces over which USX had limited control. The company's stock had languished for years. Carl Icahn, the company's largest shareholder, had been pressuring USX management to spin its steel business off from its energy business, believing that the sum of USX's parts was worth more than the whole. The company was no stranger to restructuring: Billions of dollars in company assets had been sold over the previous decade. Charles Corry, the company's chairman and chief executive officer (CEO) since June 1989, was a thirty-one-year veteran of the company but tended to be fairly realistic about the difficulties the company faced. The chief financial officer had, only several months earlier, publicly indicated his expectation that there would be further restructuring on the steel side. The senior vice president–finance and treasurer, Robert Hernandez, had proposed consideration of an innovative financial security called "tracking stock,"

This case was prepared by Research Associate Jeremy Cott and Professor Stuart Gilson. Copyright © 1996 by the President and Fellows of Harvard College. Harvard Business School case 296-050.

which would give the company two distinct classes of common stock to reflect the performance of its two distinct business–segments—would probably run for seats without, however, breaking the company apart as a consolidated entity.

As Charles Corry prepared for the meeting, he had to decide what course of action to recommend to the board.

BACKGROUND

USX had its origins in 1901 as the United States Steel Corporation (U.S. Steel). In one of the legendary episodes of American business history, J.P. Morgan formed U.S. Steel by purchasing Andrew Carnegie's steel holdings and merging them into his own in order to create a vast combine or trust. It was incorporated with a capitalization of $1.4 billion, the first billion-dollar corporation in history. In its early years the company was responsible for two-thirds of all U.S. steel production and operated an enormous, vertically integrated structure that included the company's own supplies of iron ore, limestone, and coal, which were mined and transported to the mills by the company's huge shipping fleet and rail lines. It was, as J.P. Morgan put it, a "rounded proposition."

The company's history was marked by many acquisitions, divestitures, consolidations, and labor disputes. By the 1950s its domestic market share had declined to about 30 percent, as the company faced increasing domestic competition and operating costs. Foreign competition also increased, particularly from Japanese and German mills that were rebuilt and modernized after World War II. U.S. share of world steel production, which was around 20 percent in the early 1970s, dropped below 15 percent in the early 1980s. The steel industry, moreover, not only had excess capacity but at the same time was in need of modernization, particularly in the United States. This required significant capital expenditures. Continuous casting equipment, for example, was expensive, but it provided large savings in energy and labor costs, increased productivity, and yielded a better product. In the early 1980s, the United States produced about 20 percent of its steel with continuous casters, while Europe produced about 45 percent of its steel, and Japan 75 percent, using this kind of equipment. Competition for the steel industry also came from the increasing use of alternative materials such as aluminum and plastics.

RESTRUCTURING

In 1979 David Roderick became chairman and CEO of U.S. Steel[1] and began a difficult, protracted effort to restructure the company. He closed thirteen steel plants, wrote off approximately $3 billion, and sold or leased out various cement, real estate, timber, and mineral properties. In 1982, the company made the biggest diversification move in its history and bought Marathon Oil for $6.2 billion. (Marathon Oil was not one of the majors in the oil industry, like Exxon and Mobil, but was one of a number of intermediate-sized firms, like Phillips Petroleum Company and Unocal Corporation, with substantial oil reserves.) Charles Corry—who was to succeed Roderick as the company's chairman and CEO in 1989—was at that point U.S. Steel's vice president for strategic planning. The company's 1982 annual report referred to both operating and financial benefits from the diversification move. Financially, the diversification move was intended to make the company "less vulnerable to a downturn in any one of our business segments." Steel was a very cyclical business,[2] and, as Robert Hernandez was later to put it, "Steel is usually up when energy is down, and vice versa. It's not perfect, but it works pretty well." Management also expected some operating benefits from the diversification move. As the 1982 annual report put it, Marathon would provide "an energy hedge for our energy-dependent steel business and raw material support for our chemicals business," and the steel business would provide some of the drilling and production equipment for the energy business. (See Exhibit 8.1, which shows financial trends in the steel and oil industries for 1980–1990; Exhibit 8.2, which shows financial trends for USX itself for 1980–1990; and Exhibit 8.3, which shows intersegment sales for USX during the 1984–1990 period.)

There was, moreover, an additional source of strength in USX's diversifi-

---

[1]Roderick had been with the company since 1953. He was an extremely strong proponent of the importance of the manufacturing sector in the United States. "It's the only thing in this country that creates wealth," he stated. "I [also] advise young people not to [move around]. With most careers, it's counterproductive. With continuity, you learn everything about that market and that product. If you keep moving around, that doesn't come very well." (Interview in the *Wall Street Journal*: "For Roderick, the Future Lies in Factories," May 22, 1989.)

[2]The largest individual markets for the steel industry were the automobile and construction industries, which were themselves cyclical industries. Their fortunes tended to rise and fall with the state of the macroeconomy.

cation move. USX's energy business—like most large energy companies—was itself diversified in order to mitigate some of the impact of fluctuating oil prices. There were both "upstream" and "downstream" operations. The upstream operations were the exploration and production of oil and gas; the downstream operations involved their refining, transportation, and marketing (e.g., wholesale and retail outlets). As one of USX's annual reports stated: "The strength of our upstream and downstream operations has given us the ability to earn good returns in different energy environments."[3]

By 1985, Roderick had reduced the company's steel-making capacity by more than 30 percent, cut 54 percent of white-collar jobs, laid off about 100,000 production workers, and sold about $3 billion in assets. In early 1986 he continued the company's diversification program by buying Texas Oil & Gas through an exchange of stock valued at approximately $3 billion.

An Extraordinary Year

But 1986 was to be an extraordinary year for the company in other respects as well. In July the company officially changed its name from U.S. Steel to USX in order to reflect its diversification. It was felt that its old name no longer provided an adequate indication of what it did.

In early August, 44,000 members of the United Steelworkers of America union went out on strike against the company in a dispute over wage and benefit concessions that company management believed were necessary. (As it turned out, the strike lasted for five and a half months and became the longest steel strike in American history.)

A few days after the strike began, the price of the company's stock fell to $14.50, the lowest it had been since 1954.

In early October, Carl Icahn disclosed that he had bought 11.4 percent of the outstanding shares and offered to buy the remainder of the company for $7.19 billion, or $31 a share, subject to various conditions, including the availability of necessary financing. He believed that USX was badly undervalued and in need of further, drastic restructuring. His takeover plan did not pan out, however. In November, the insider trading scandal involving Ivan Boesky and Drexel Burnham Lambert broke, and Drexel, which was Icahn's investment banker, became the object of a federal investiga-

---

[3]For example, when Iraq invaded Kuwait in the summer of 1990 and oil prices soared, earnings in USX's upstream operations improved, while earnings in its downstream operations declined.

tion, thus hampering its ability to finance takeovers. Then, toward the end of December, USX called about $3 billion of its notes, refinancing them with debt that contained a provision requiring its immediate repayment if USX underwent a "change in control." This in effect raised Icahn's cost for financing a takeover from $7.1 billion to over $10 billion, and that, Icahn acknowledged, made it "all but impossible."

The CEO's View

In USX's annual report for 1986, David Roderick stated that "restructuring at USX is based on long-term benefit, not on possible short-term gain; nor is it in response to a particular crisis or development." During the year, he pointed out, the company continued selling "nonstrategic assets." (Total proceeds from asset sales for the year were about $1.1 billion.) It also recorded a $1,457 million restructuring charge, primarily in its steel business, for writing down assets and accruing employee costs related to indefinitely idled facilities. "Restructuring," Roderick stated, "has been an ongoing process at your Corporation since 1980. Indeed, ours may be the most restructured corporation in America."

Nevertheless, 1986 had been a poor operating year for the company, due in part to the effects of the prolonged steel strike but also to "depressed oil and gas prices" and "lower steel demand."

CONTINUED CHALLENGE FROM CARL ICAHN

Icahn continued to urge USX management to spin off or sell its steel business.[4] He believed that the problems of USX's steel business—and the steel industry generally—were depressing the value of its energy business. In 1988, *The Wall Street Journal* reported, USX executives took a secret internal vote on whether to stick with the steel business or try to find a buyer. A merger with Bethlehem Steel Corporation, the country's second largest steelmaker, was considered. David Roderick saw steel as America's backbone, however, and voted to stick with it. In 1988 USX executives also considered selling 20 percent of the steel business in an initial public offering (IPO), but they couldn't get underwriting of an offering at an accept-

---

[4]In 1989 Icahn increased his stake in USX to over 13 percent.

able price. They felt that at another time, when the market for steel equity was better, they might consider an IPO again.[5]

Finally, in the spring of 1990, USX management allowed a formal Icahn proposal to be put to a shareholder vote—although the results of the vote would not be legally binding on the board of directors. Technically, the proposal was that USX spin its steel business off from its energy business; that is, USX shareholders would receive a dividend consisting of U.S. Steel stock, while continuing to hold common stock in USX's energy business. What would be created would be two legally separate corporate entities. Icahn argued that the market values of USX's energy and steel businesses, as stand-alone companies, would be $39 and $9, respectively. (In the spring of 1990, USX stock was trading for about $35 a share.)

Pros and Cons of a Spin-Off

Taxability   Whether spinning off the steel business as a legally separate entity would be tax-free was unclear. Exhibit 8.4 summarizes the IRS requirements regarding this. There were two major stumbling blocks. USX might well have a problem demonstrating that a spin-off was being done for a valid "business purpose." It might also have a problem with the issue of "control." USX management wanted to be able to oversee the resolution of possible environmental liabilities and other contingencies associated with U.S. Steel's operations. "Given the way the environmental . . . liability laws work," as one commentator put it, "there is very little that USX could do to avoid liability for past acts committed by a steel business that was [once] part of the parent corporation. Even if the steel business were sold outright, the government and private plaintiffs could come after the parent for past acts of environmental damage if the steel business or its new owners could not satisfy the claims."[6] It was unclear, however, whether USX would have to retain "practical control" of U.S. Steel (in the form of a significant minority stock position) in order to best resolve this. USX management believed that it would. Carl Icahn believed that it wouldn't.

---

[5]Information in this paragraph is taken from articles in *The Wall Street Journal*: Thomas F. O'Boyle, "Icahn Forces the Issue at USX: Is It Time to Get Out of Steel?" (March 9, 1990); Clare Ansberry, "Icahn's Proxy Fight with USX Is in Its Final Rounds," (May 2, 1990).

[6]Lee A. Sheppard, "USX's Nasty Tax Rumors," in *Highlights & Documents*, March 23, 1990.

If, however, a spin-off became taxable, there would be a double tax—at the USX corporate level as well as at the USX shareholder level. At the USX corporate level, the tax would be on the difference between the fair market value of the net assets of U.S. Steel and the tax basis of those assets (similar to, but not the same thing as, their book value). At the shareholder level, the distribution of U.S. Steel stock would be treated as a dividend and the tax would be based on the initial trading value of U.S. Steel stock.

Incremental Costs   In letters it sent to shareholders, USX management argued that a spin-off would be perilous in other respects as well. They argued that splitting the corporation up into two legally separate entities would involve significant incremental costs. For example, although USX debt instruments contained very few covenant restrictions, they could not be assigned without consent of the lenders. They would have to be refinanced at prevailing market rates and under prevailing market conditions. USX's debt was rated BBB by Standard & Poor's, and, in the spring of 1990, the average yield on industrial bonds rated BBB (irrespective of years to maturity) was around 11.7 percent. USX management also believed that there would be about $30 million per year in additional administrative costs (due to the loss of the economies of scale of a larger, unified corporation); about $20 million per year in additional state and local taxes (primarily because separate business entities would lose the benefit of available net operating losses); and about $15 million per year for the cost of insurance that the company did not carry at present but that lenders to a separate steel company would probably require.

Other Arguments   USX management argued—as they had for years—that if the company were broken up the financial benefits of diversification would be lost. They also argued that a spin-off would be irreversible, and that USX management had been demonstrating for years its commitment to appropriate restructuring.

They also argued that Icahn's estimate of what USX's energy and steel businesses would be worth as stand-alone companies—$39 and $9 per share—was incredible. Among other things, they believed that energy and steel businesses are best valued on the basis of cash flow, earnings, or dividend yield, and that Icahn's reliance on "industry standard values" of oil and gas in the ground was simplistic because it omitted factors like field locations, operating costs, future recoverability, and actual recent transactions. In a letter to shareholders, USX management presented their own analysis, which suggested that if Icahn's methodology were applied to comparable groups of publicly traded, stand-alone energy and steel companies, the values of the energy companies would be, on average, 112 percent higher than their actual market values, and the values of the steel companies would be 90 percent higher than their actual market values. USX management suggested that Icahn had used a methodology to back into an answer that he wanted in the first place.

Icahn argued, on the other hand, that separating the steel and energy businesses would increase their operating efficiency. It would, he believed, make the managers of each business more accountable for their performances. And it would also increase the efficiency with which the investment community would value the two businesses, given their different growth prospects and strategic directions. Energy companies, he argued, traded at higher multiples than steel companies—because they were less cyclical and had better business prospects. But, because USX was not a pure play in either industry, the steel business dragged down the multiple for the entire corporation. There was also a sense that a spin-off could increase a business entity's exposure to the market for corporate control and therefore the possibility of a takeover premium.

The Vote

USX management recommended a vote against Icahn's proxy proposal. At the company's annual meeting in May 1990, however, 42 percent of the shareholders (which included Icahn's 13 percent interest) voted in favor of Icahn's proposal. While the proposal was defeated, even some institutional investors who voted with management were concerned about the lackluster performance of USX stock and wrote to Corry urging major changes at the company. "There will be additional restructuring I'm sure," USX's chief financial officer was quoted as saying, "and a lot will take place on the steel side."

A NEW POSSIBILITY

The pressure to do something was clearly on. In late 1990, USX management was scheduled to meet with the board to present a few restructuring options. Icahn stated publicly that he planned another proxy challenge at the next annual meeting. While his spin-off proposal had been defeated, an unusually large number of shareholders had voted with him and against management's recommendations; and next time he might just win.

Another possibility for USX to consider was a partial IPO of the company's steel operation (an "equity carve-out"). This would raise cash and provide a market for the steel equity.[7] A limitation on any partial move, however, was that under IRS rules USX would have to retain at least 80 percent of the stock representing the steel business in order to maintain the benefit of tax consolidation—and, to the extent that the steel and energy businesses moved in different cycles, that might be an important consideration. USX had also held discussions that autumn with a few foreign steel producers about a possible sale of all or a substantial portion of its steel business.

But Robert Hernandez, who was USX's senior vice president–finance and treasurer, had another thought. "Why," he had long wondered, "did diversified companies get a lot of value in the credit market which wasn't necessarily reflected in the stock market?" Because USX was capital-intensive, pleasing bond holders seemed to him very important. USX executives prided themselves, in fact, on having very few covenants in the company's debt agreements, and virtually none of the debt was secured.

USX executives agreed with Icahn in at least one respect. They agreed that USX's energy and steel businesses were both being undervalued by Wall Street. (Exhibit 8.5 shows operating and market data for a number of comparable energy and steel companies in 1989 and 1990.)

Targeted Stock

So Hernandez came up with another proposal, developed with the help of Ron Gallatin at Lehman Brothers. The proposal would, they believed, maintain the company's credibility with the bond market while propping up the company's value in the stock market. It would involve the issuance of two classes of stock that would be called "tracking stock." (General Motors was the only company to have used a version of the idea before, and did so in the context of an acquisition. General Motors called it "alphabet stock" or "letter stock," referring to the letter designations of different classes of stock that they issued.) Tracking stock would be distinct classes of parent

---

[7]One study has found that, among 76 equity carve-outs completed between 1963 and 1983, parent company shareholders earned, on average, a 1.8 percent abnormal return around the time of a carve-out announcement, compared with a 3 percent average abnormal loss associated with announcements of seasoned equity offerings by publicly traded firms. Often, however, the carve-out is temporary: Many minority stakes are reacquired by the parent; others are spun off completely; and sometimes the subsidiary is sold. (Katherine Schipper and Abbie Smith, "Effects of Recontracting on Shareholder Wealth: The Case of Voluntary Spin-Offs," *Journal of Financial Economics* 12 [1983]).

company common stock that would track the performances of distinct businesses belonging to the parent. The revenues and earnings of those businesses would be reported separately; dividends would be determined based on the separate performances of those businesses; and the assets and liabilities used in those businesses would be formally allocated to them. The allocation, however, would be only for financial reporting purposes and for purposes of making separate dividend decisions. Legal title to the assets and responsibility for the liabilities would not be affected by such allocation. There would be one board of directors and one federal income tax return.

The proposal was for USX to have one class of common stock for its energy business and another class of common stock for its steel business. This would allow stockholders to exercise their investment preferences in terms of specific businesses ("quasi pure plays"). It would give the company greater flexibility in raising capital and the ability to make acquisitions with stock having the higher multiple. It would allow the company to establish executive incentive plans tied to the specific businesses in which people worked. It would also foster greater efficiency and better coverage by investment analysts.

Hernandez was particularly interested in the latter. USX was both an energy company and a steel company, but at one investment house it would be covered by an energy analyst who (it seemed to Hernandez) might not know much about steel, and at another house it would be covered by a steel analyst who might not accord much value to the company's vast energy operations. Tracking stock would solve that problem. Moreover, since tracking stock would involve simply the creation of new classes of parent company stock, its issuance would not be taxable at either the corporate or the shareholder level. (Exhibit 8.6 presents consolidated income statements and balance sheets for USX for 1988–1990, along with financial statements for the Marathon and U.S. Steel Groups that company management put together as an aid to stockholders in voting on the tracking stock proposal, which reflected various allocations.)

Icahn's spin-off proposal meant two companies with two stocks. The tracking stock proposal meant one company with two stocks.

The General Motors (GM) Experience The progenitor of the tracking stock idea was General Motors' issuance of class E and class H shares in 1984 and 1985, when it bought Electronic Data Systems (EDS) and Hughes Aircraft, respectively. The new classes of stock were meant to reflect the performances of the acquired companies, even though they legally became part of General Motors. Ross Perot, the founder of EDS, wanted to have a continuing stake in the business, and he also wanted EDS managers to be rewarded with stock that they directly impacted, rather than with GM stock, over which they would have little influence. Thus the revenues and earnings of those businesses were to be reported separately; dividends were to be determined based on the separate performances of those businesses; and the assets and liabilities used in those businesses were to be formally allocated to them. (See Exhibit 8.7, which shows the performances of these special classes of GM stock from their trading inception up to the end of 1990.)

There were some sensitive nonoperating issues for which General Motors made some formal provisions. For example, voting rights for holders of the class E and class H shares were fixed at the time of their issuance to one-half vote per share. This amounted, at their issuance, to about 10 percent of the total General Motors shareholder vote. Also, if General Motors were to sell substantially all of either EDS or Hughes, the holders of the class E and H shares would receive shares of the parent company stock at a 20 percent premium. That is, the market value of the General Motors common shares that they would receive would be 1.2 times the average market value that their special class of stock had in the twenty-day period before the announcement of the sale.

There were also various uncertainties, not at all formalized, about the way this kind of stock might be handled. There could, for instance, be conflicts of interest among different classes of stockholders. There was no precedent under Delaware law to determine the fiduciary duties of directors of corporations with tracking stock. Case law involving analogous situations, however, suggested the applicability of the "business judgment rule," which means essentially that so long as a decision by a board of directors can be attributed to a rational business purpose and does not provide a clear demonstration of fraud or self-dealing, a court will not presume to substitute its judgment for that of the board. In effect, a board of directors is presumed innocent unless clearly proven guilty. Delaware courts *have* ruled against the directors of corporations in certain cases—they are not necessarily a rubber stamp—but they have tended to grant considerable discretion in matters of corporate governance. Conflicts of interest among different kinds of stockholders may not always be resolved to the satisfaction of all parties. For example, conflicts among different classes of stockholders could arise in connection with merger or recapitalization proposals that seem to favor one class over another, or even in connection with a corporation's internal allocation of investment capital.

Dividend-Paying Capability   The dividend-paying capability of a separate steel company was also a concern, and part of the concern was related to a new accounting standard. In the late 1980s, continuing into 1990, the Financial Accounting Standards Board (FASB), the major rule-setting body for the accounting profession, was considering the adoption of a new standard that would, for the first time, require companies to accrue the full amount of their obligation for retiree health care costs on their balance sheets. In the past, companies had recorded no such obligation; the accounting was done simply on a pay-as-you-go, cash basis. FASB's attention to this was stimulated by the skyrocketing health care costs and a recognition that many companies—particularly older, unionized companies that had made promises to workers to pay most of their health care costs during their retirement—were failing to recognize a substantial liability that they had incurred and were therefore badly overstating their net worth. (The new accounting standard was in fact adopted in December 1990, and FASB required all large corporations to implement it no later than 1993.)

USX management believed that for their energy business the impact of the accounting standard would be immaterial. For the steel business, however, management believed that the present value of the liability would be—as of the end of 1990—between $1.8 and $2.7 billion (pretax). Moreover, for the next couple of years at least, the steel business would probably be on the down side of the steel industry cycle. Under Delaware law, a corporation cannot pay common stock dividends if the fair market value of its net worth is less than zero. Thus, even though recognizing a liability for retiree health care costs would not involve any expenditure of cash, the dividend-paying capability of a separate steel company could be seriously affected.

In this respect, moreover, the sympathies of the still-powerful steelworkers union would probably lie with USX management since a consolidated company—which would include the richer assets of the energy operation—would be better able to support the retiree health care liability than a stand-alone steel company.

THE DIRECTORS' DECISION

USX's directors had a whole host of issues to consider in any possible restructuring decision. To begin with, the immediate prospects for USX's businesses were unclear and potentially very difficult. The U.S. Steel Group was still the largest integrated steel producer in the United States. It had in recent years invested heavily in continuous casting equipment, so that 53 percent of its steel production was now done by this method, and since 1983 it had cut its steel production capacity in half and reduced the number of man-hours needed per ton of steel produced from 11 to 3.6. It was now one of the lowest-cost steel producers in the country. The steel industry remained, however, extremely competitive. A number of its competitors faced serious financial difficulties, and LTV Corporation and others were operating in bankruptcy. Steel prices had declined in 1990 and were expected to decline further in 1991 with the ongoing recession in the United States. In addition, the company faced a possible strike, since its contract with the steelworkers union was to expire at the end of January 1991 and had not yet been renegotiated.

The prospects for the Marathon Group, which was one of the larger oil and gas companies in the country, were very much subject to the volatility in world oil and gas prices as well to the outcomes of its various exploration and production activities. About two-thirds of its oil and gas production, however, took place at domestic sites. Its overseas production was mostly in the North Sea. It had no exploration or production taking place in Iraq, Kuwait, or Saudi Arabia.

Institutional investors, stock analysts, and Carl Icahn were all pressuring the company to improve the performance of its common stock. To increase this pressure, Icahn had formed a paid Shareholders Enhancement Committee, which included a Harvard professor and several others who would probably run for seats on USX's board of directors.

The pros and cons of a full-fledged spin-off had been hotly debated earlier in the year. A partial spin-off would represent one kind of compromise. Selling off the steel operation was another possibility, and would generate cash, but the industry was near a low point in its cycle—1988 had been a cyclical peak—so that selling prices might well be depressed. Tracking stock represented another possibility. It aimed to provide the best of all worlds. If the directors favored this option, however, what provisions could they make in the company's governance to satisfy shareholders? And how could they assess whether choosing this option would indeed increase the company's total equity value?

EXHIBIT 8.1 USX: Industry Trends: Financial Ratios and Common Stock Prices for the Steel and Integrated Domestic Oil Industries, 1980–1990

	1990	1989	1988	1987	1986	1985	1984	1983	1982	1981	1980
Steel											
Return on total assets	(4.9%)	5.4%	7.4%	3.3%	(6.5%)	(2.9%)	(1.3%)	(7.5%)	(8.2%)	5.7%	3.2%
Return on sales	(4.0%)	4.6%	5.8%	3.1%	(7.5%)	(2.7%)	(1.2%)	(7.8%)	(8.1%)	4.7%	2.7%
Debt to total assets	16.0%	16.0%	18.0%	22.0%	30.0%	29.0%	32.0%	32.0%	31.0%	19.0%	21.0%
Dividend yield											
High	4.1%	2.3%	1.2%	0.3%	4.2%	2.4%	3.1%	3.6%	8.7%	7.2%	7.9%
Low	2.8%	1.8%	0.9%	0.2%	2.7%	2.0%	2.0%	2.5%	5.4%	5.2%	5.8%
Common stock price											
High	$ 52.61	$ 60.57	$ 54.73	$ 51.78	$ 38.08	$ 41.38	$ 52.07	$ 49.70	$ 46.29	$ 60.94	$ 51.40
Low	$ 35.47	$ 47.71	$ 40.84	$ 28.62	$ 24.13	$ 33.38	$ 33.56	$ 34.25	$ 28.41	$ 44.33	$ 37.91
Integrated Domestic Oil											
Return on total assets	3.3%	4.5%	3.6%	2.9%	1.5%	3.4%	6.2%	6.2%	6.9%	8.9%	9.3%
Return on sales	3.4%	5.0%	4.5%	3.6%	2.0%	3.3%	6.2%	5.8%	6.1%	7.1%	7.0%
Debt to total assets	29.0%	29.0%	30.0%	30.0%	30.0%	27.0%	19.0%	18.0%	21.0%	19.0%	18.0%
Dividend yield											
High	4.8%	5.3%	5.5%	5.4%	6.6%	6.9%	6.0%	6.2%	7.8%	5.1%	4.6%
Low	4.1%	3.8%	4.5%	3.8%	5.3%	5.4%	4.9%	4.7%	5.3%	3.6%	2.3%
Common stock price											
High	$762.79	$729.18	$568.66	$638.45	$448.98	$469.13	$415.53	$368.06	$325.83	$422.73	$503.96
Low	$648.46	$528.88	$466.50	$446.61	$362.41	$369.30	$339.76	$278.14	$221.06	$295.89	$258.52

Definition of measurements:

- "Return on total assets" means primary earnings from continuing operations, less preferred dividends, divided by total assets.
- "Return on sales" means primary earnings from continuing operations, less preferred dividends, divided by total sales.
- "Debt to total assets" means long-term debt (excluding current portion) divided by total assets.
- "Dividend yield" means common stock dividend divided by stock price
- "Common stock price" refers to a Standard & Poor's index for each industry.

Note: There are about eight companies included in the Standard & Poor's "Steel" index; USX was included through 1986. There are about eleven companies included in the Standard & Poor's "Integrated Domestic Oil" Index; USX was included starting in 1987.

Source: Standard & Poor's Analyst's Handbook (annual editions); some calculations are by casewriter.

EXHIBIT 8.2 USX: Trends, 1980–1990 ($millions, Except Per Share Amounts)

	1990	1989	1988	1987	1986	1985	1984	1983	1982	1981	1980
Total sales	$20,659	$18,717	$16,877	$14,836	$14,938	$19,283	$19,104	$17,523	$18,907	$13,941	$12,492
Total assets	17,268	17,500	19,474	19,557	21,823	18,446	18,989	19,314	19,432	13,316	11,748
Long-term debt	5,330	5,741	5,963	6,618	5,697	5,348	6,261	7,164	6,843	2,340	2,401
Depreciation, depletion, and amortization	1,304	1,336	1,369	1,332	1,559	1,294	1,241	1,169	1,072	571	524
Earnings (losses) from continuing operations	800	907	686	141	(1,925)	288	374	(1,245)	(383)	1,077	505
Common stock dividend	1.40	1.40	1.25	1.20	1.20	1.10	1.00	1.00	1.75	2.00	1.60
Common stock price High	37.50	39.50	34.38	39.38	28.75	33.00	33.25	31.00	30.13	35.25	25.88
Low	29.63	28.88	26.00	21.00	14.50	24.38	22.00	19.63	16.00	23.38	16.25

Note: 1986 and 1983 earnings include pretax restructuring charges of $1,457 million and $1,149 million, respectively. Restructuring charges (credits) in other years are not material. Statistics are presented as reported in each year and do not reflect subsequent restatements.
Source: Company annual reports.

EXHIBIT 8.3   USX: Segment Sales Information ($millions)

	Unaffiliated Customers	Between Segments	Total
Energy			
1990	$14,586	$ 30	$14,616
1989	12,209	55	12,264
1988	9,883	66	9,949
1987	10,015	63	10,078
1986	8,895	68	8,963
1985	11,992	82	12,074
1984	12,209	105	12,314
Steel			
1990	5,465	8	5,473
1989	5,724	6	5,730
1988	5,804	3	5,807
1987	3,663	10	3,673
1986	3,580	128	3,708
1985	5,609	320	5,929
1984	5,507	409	5,916
Diversified businesses			
1990	608	106	714
1989	784	125	909
1988	1,190	399	1,589
1987	1,235	301	1,536
1986	2,463	348	2,811
1985	3,178	653	3,831
1984	3,376	670	4,046
Corporate eliminations			
1990		(144)	(144)
1989		(186)	(186)
1988		(468)	(468)
1987		(374)	(374)
1986		(544)	(544)
1985		(1,055)	(1,055)
1984		(1,184)	(1,184)
Total consolidated			
1990	20,659		20,659
1989	18,717		18,717
1988	16,877		16,877
1987	14,913		14,913
1986	14,938		14,938
1985	20,779		20,779
1984	21,092		21,092

Note: Intersegment sales and transfers are, for the most part, accounted for at commercial prices.
Source: Company annual reports.

EXHIBIT 8.4   Tax Issues Relating to Spin-Off Transactions

A corporate spin-off will be tax-free to both the distributing corporation and the recipient stockholders only if it satisfies numerous statutory and nonstatutory requirements. Many of the statutory requirements are contained in Section 355 of the Internal Revenue Code. Restructuring corporations will often, therefore, be said to be endeavoring to make their spin-off transactions qualify as "Section 355 transactions."

Some of the statutory and nonstatutory requirements are as follows. (To simplify, "P" represents a parent corporation wishing to make a distribution, and "S" represents a subsidiary or division that it wishes to distribute.)

- P must control S immediately before the spin-off. Control generally means possession of at least 80 percent of the outstanding stock.
- P must distribute all of the S stock it held immediately before the distribution or an amount of S stock that constitutes control. If it retains any of the S stock, it must establish to the satisfaction of the IRS that it is not doing so to exercise "practical control" of S.
- P and S must each "actively conduct" a trade or business immediately before the distribution.
- The trade or business that P and S "actively conduct" must have been actively conducted throughout the five-year period ending on the date of the distribution, and must not have been acquired during that five-year period in a transaction in which a gain or loss was recognized.
- P's distribution must not be used principally as a "device" for the distribution of the earnings of either P or S. This is meant to ensure that substantial sales or exchanges of the stock of either entity will not closely follow the distribution. To some extent, however, this is a matter of intent. If stockholders dispose of their P or S stock shortly after the distribution but it can be shown that, at the time of the distribution, they had no intent to do so, they will satisfy the "device" standard; by contrast, if it can be shown that, at the time of the distribution, they already intended to dispose of their stock, they will violate the "device" standard.
- The distribution must be motivated by a valid "business purpose." The IRS views enhancing shareholder value, for example, as a shareholder purpose but not a valid business purpose. Some examples of a valid business purpose would be the following: to separate shareholders who cannot agree on how to manage P or S; to rid P of a subsidiary that a corporation seeking to acquire P cannot take on for regulatory or business reasons; to allow P or S to go public and thus increase its access to the equity or debt markets.
- The predistribution P stockholders must maintain sufficient continuity of interest in both P and S following the distribution. As with the "device" standard, the question of intent is important here—whether stockholders intended, at the time of the distribution, to dispose of their stock.

Source: Material is summarized and abbreviated from Kenneth W. Gideon and Alan S. Kaden (members of the tax department of the law firm of Fried Frank, Harris, Shriver & Jacobson), "Tax Issues Relating to Spin-Off Transactions," and Robert Willens, "Tax and Accounting" memoranda at Shearson Lehman Hutton (4/4/90 and 4/17/90).

EXHIBIT 8.5 USX Financial Data on Comparable Energy and Steel Companies ($millions Except Per Share Data)

	Steel Companies					
	Armco		Bethlehem Steel		Inland Steel	
	1990	1989	1990	1989	1990	1989
Revenues	$1,735	$2,422	$4,899	$5,251	$3,870	$4,147
Restructuring charges	0	43	550	105	0	0
Operating profit	77	116	(443)	267	2	231
EBITDA	117	173	(137)	592	121	362
Net income from continuing operations	(63)	202	(487)	219	(48)	113
Net income including discontinued operations and extraordinary items	(98)	157	(463)	246	(48)	113
Long-term debt (at year-end)	367	423	590	656	692	578
Preferred stock (at year-end)	93	93	308	320	339	339
Per share						
Net income from continuing operations	(0.71)	2.28	(6.45)	2.93	(1.41)	3.15
Net income including discontinued operations and extraordinary items	(1.10)	1.78	(6.45)	2.93	(1.41)	3.15
Dividends on common stock	0.40	0.30	0.40	0.20	1.40	1.40
Common stock						
High	11.250	13.500	21.125	28.500	36.375	48.500
Low	3.875	9.500	10.625	15.375	20.875	31.375
At end of year	5.125	10.750	14.875	18.500	24.75	33.75
Book value per share	9.54	10.98	15.56	22.37	41.27	43.00
# of shares outstanding at year-end (millions)	88.5	88.4	75.9	75.2	30.9	34.7

(Continued)

283

EXHIBIT 8.5 (Continued)

	Energy Companies							
	Amerada Hess		Atlantic Richfield		Phillips Petroleum		Unocal	
	1990	1989	1990	1989	1990	1989	1990	1989
Revenues	$7,081	$5,679	$19,896	$16,815	$13,975	$12,492	$11,808	$11,353
Restructuring charges	0	0	0	0	0	0	0	0
Operating profit	706	618	2,568	2,209	1,435	1,073	625	685
EBITDA	1,450	1,164	4,290	3,957	2,243	2,179	1,649	1,558
Net income from continuing operations	483	476	1,685	1,949	541	219	401	358
Net income including discontinued operations and extraordinary items	483	476	2,008	1,949	779	219	401	260
Long-term debt (at year-end)	2,532	2,348	5,997	5,313	3,839	3,939	4,047	3,887
Preferred stock (at year-end)								
Per share								
Net income from continuing operations	5.96	5.87	10.20	11.26	2.18	0.90	1.71	1.53
Net income including discontinued operations and extraordinary items	5.96	5.87	12.15	11.26	3.13	0.90	1.71	1.11
Dividends on common stock	0.60	0.60	5.00	4.50	1.03	0.94	0.70	0.60
Common stock								
High	56.000	51.875	142.250	114.375	31.125	30.125	34.500	31.250
Low	42.875	31.000	105.500	80.375	22.500	19.125	24.625	18.875
At end of year	46.375	48.750	123.625	111.375	26.125	25.250	26.250	29.750
Book value per share	38.34	31.69	44.83	39.64	10.51	8.74	10.87	9.83
# of shares outstanding at year-end (millions)	81.0	80.8	158.9	164.2	258.7	243.9	234.5	234.0

Note: "Operating profit" excludes interest expense and income, income taxes, income from equity investments, gain or loss on assets sales, and minority interest; it includes, however, restructuring charges.
Source: Company annual reports; Bloomberg.

EXHIBIT 8.6   USX: Balance Sheets, 1989–1990 ($millions)

USX—Marathon Group

	December 31	
	1990	**1989**
Assets		
Current assets		
Cash and cash equivalents	$ 193	$ 490
Receivables	721	5573
Receivable from U.S. Steel Group	—	31
Inventories	1,336	1,2038
Other current assets	107	100
Total current assets	$ 2,357	$ 2,381
Long-term receivables and other investments	385	527
Property, plant, and equipment, less		
accumulated depreciation of $6,614 and $6,995	8,836	9,428
Prepaid pensions	202	161
Other noncurrent assets	151	1254
Total assets	$11,931	$12,629
Liabilities		
Current liabilities		
Notes payable	106	12
Accounts payable	1,601	1,3536
Payroll and benefits payable	72	70
Accrued taxes	293	539
Payable to U.S. Steel Group	240	—
Accrued interest	82	87
Long-term debt due within one year	133	87
Total current liabilities	$ 2,527	$ 2,148
Long-term debt	3,926	4,348
Deferred income taxes	1,480	1,894
Deferred credits and other liabilities	373	550
Total liabilities	$ 8,306	$ 8,940
Stockholders' Equity		
Preferred stock	83	295
Common equity	3,550	3,391
Other equity adjustments	(8)	(4)
Total stockholders' equity	$ 3,625	$ 3,682
Total liabilities and stockholders' equity	$11,931	$12,622

Casewriter Note: The financial statements presented in Exhibit 8.6 are taken from the USX Corporation shareholder proxy statement dated April 10, 1991. These statements therefore reflect additional analysis that the company did after the case decision date.

(Continued)

EXHIBIT 8.6   *(Continued)*

USX—Steel Group

	December 31	
	1990	**1989**
Assets		
Current assets		
Cash and cash equivalents	$ 70	$ 296
Receivables	535	373
Receivable from Marathon Group	240	—
Inventories	696	548
Total current assets	$1,541	$1,217
Long-term receivables and other investments	773	887
Property, plant, and equipment, less		
accumulated depreciation of $5,595 and $5,353	2,748	2,567
Deferred income tax benefits	—	574
Prepaid pensions	454	190
Other noncurrent assets	66	64
Total assets	$5,582	$5,499
Liabilities		
Current liabilities		
Notes payable	32	4
Accounts payable	600	646
Payroll and benefits payable	171	205
Accrued taxes	122	213
Payable to Marathon Group	—	31
Accrued interest	31	31
Long-term debt due within one year	64	47
Total current liabilities	$1,020	$1,177
Long-term debt	1,404	1,393
Deferred income taxes	23	—
Deferred credits and other liabilities	891	874
Total liabilities	$3,338	$3,444
Stockholders' Equity		
Preferred stock	25	87
Common equity	2,228	1,976
Other equity adjustments	(9)	(8)
Total stockholders' equity	$2,244	$2,055
Total liabilities and stockholders' equity	$5,582	$5,499

EXHIBIT 8.6 *(Continued)*

USX Consolidated		
	December 31	
	1990	1989
Assets		
Current assets		
Cash and cash equivalents	$ 263	$ 786
Receivables	1,249	914
Inventories	2,032	1,751
Other current assets	109	100
Total current assets	$ 3,653	$ 3,551
Long-term receivables and other investments	1,158	1,414
Property, plant, and equipment	11,584	11,995
Prepaid pensions	656	351
Other noncurrent assets	217	189
Total assets	$17,268	$17,500
Liabilities		
Current liabilities		
Notes payable	138	16
Accounts payable	2,196	1,983
Payroll and benefits payable	243	275
Accrued taxes	415	752
Accrued interest	113	118
Long-term debt due within one year	197	134
Total current liabilities	$ 3,302	$ 3,278
Long-term debt	5,330	5,741
Deferred income taxes	1,503	1,320
Deferred credits and other liabilities	1,264	1,424
Total liabilities	$11,399	$11,763
Stockholders' Equity		
Preferred stock	108	382
Common equity	269	269
Treasury common stock at cost	(462)	(422)
Additional paid-in capital	3,520	3,512
Net income reinvested in business	2,451	2,008
Other equity adjustments	(17)	(12)
Total stockholders' equity	$ 5,869	$ 5,737
Total liabilities and stockholders' equity	$17,268	$17,500

Note: For the consolidated company, the average number of common shares outstanding in 1990, 1989, and 1988 was 255 million, 257 million, and 262 million, respectively.
Source: Proxy statement, April 10, 1991.

(Continued)

EXHIBIT 8.6 (*Continued*)   USX: Income Statements, 1988–1990 ($millions)

	Marathon Group		
	1990	**1989**	**1988**
Sales	$14,616	$12,264	$9,949
Operating costs			
Cost of sales	10,485	8,507	6,699
Inventory market valuation credits	(140)	(145)	(23)
Selling, general, and administration expenses	383	378	352
Depreciation, depletion, and amortization	1,026	1,029	1,006
Taxes other than income taxes	1,552	1,400	1,291
Exploration expenses	229	165	191
Restructuring credit	—	—	—
Total operating costs	$13,535	$11,334	$9,516
Operating income	1,081	930	433
Other income (loss)	(21)	114	62
Interest and other financial income	34	129	92
Interest and other financial costs	(315)	(602)	(499)
Total income before income taxes	$ 779	$ 571	$ 88
Less provision for U.S. and foreign income taxes	271	146	35
Net income	$ 508	$ 425	$ 53
Dividends on preferred stock	(14)	(41)	(39)
Net income applicable to common stock	$ 494	$ 384	$ 14

Notes:
• The large "other income" figures for 1989 and 1988 were due primarily to gains on disposals of assets.
• Selling, general, and administrative expenses were negative for U.S. Steel because of large offsetting credits from earnings on pension plan assets.
• Corporate general and administrative expenses were $92 million, $93 million, and $76 million in 1990, 1989, and 1988, respectively.
Source: Proxy statement, April 10, 1991, and internal company source.

U.S. Steel Group			USX Consolidated		
1990	1989	1988	1990	1989	1988
$6,073	$6,509	$6,996	$20,659	$18,717	$16,877
5,216	5,378	5,510	15,671	13,827	12,141
—	—	—	(140)	(145)	(23)
(97)	(23)	(45)	286	355	307
278	307	363	1,304	1,336	1,369
201	207	236	1,753	1,607	1,527
—	—	—	229	167	191
—	—	(50)	—	—	(50)
$5,598	$5,869	$6,014	$19,103	$17,147	$15,462
475	640	982	1,556	1,570	1,415
58	292	147	37	406	209
102	93	107	136	222	199
(198)	(238)	(332)	(513)	(840)	(831)
$ 437	$ 787	$ 904	$ 1,216	$ 1,358	$ 992
127	247	201	398	393	236
$ 310	$ 540	$ 703	$ 818	$ 965	$ 756
(4)	(17)	(31)	(18)	(58)	(70)
$ 306	$ 523	$ 672	$ 800	$ 907	$ 686

EXHIBIT 8.7   Comparative Performance of General Motors Class E Stock (Electronic Data Systems)

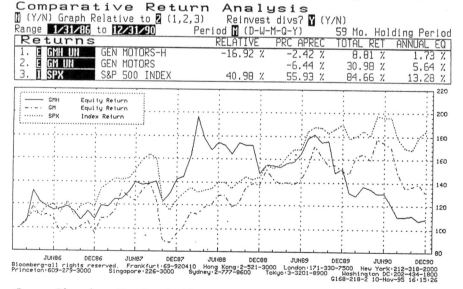

Source: Bloomberg. Reprinted with permission.

Comparative Performance of General Motors Class H Stock (Hughes Aircraft)

Source: Bloomberg. Reprinted with permission.

CHAPTER 9

Donald Salter Communications Inc.

As a late autumn day in 1991 drew to a close, Jim Myers sat in his office at the corporate headquarters of the Donald Salter Communications company, located in downtown Boise, Idaho. Myers had been hired as chief executive officer (CEO) of the company in June 1991. The company was losing money, and 1991 would be the third successive year in which earnings were lower than the year before. This was a company with some special characteristics, however. It was a private, family-owned media business that went back almost a century in the Salter family. The current chairman of the board was a granddaughter of the founder and had run the company for about thirty years. The family had deep roots in the state of Idaho, where its largest and most important business property was located, but the company held a number of media enterprises in six states. Revenues were well over $100 million a year.

Myers had a mandate to stop the short-term hemorrhaging of the company, but he also had a variety of seemingly conflicting longer-term mandates—to invest in the future by breaking out of the box of the mature industries that the company was in, to establish a liquidity mechanism for minority shareholders who might want to sell their principal, and to maintain certain intangible values of product quality and community commitment that were also very important to the family. Myers' base salary and expected annual bonus were somewhat below average for the industry, but a corporate executive long-term incentive plan had just been instituted that would significantly increase the compensation of Myers and his key executives if the company's market value increased substantially over a five-year period. Since the company was privately held, however, determining its market value was itself a problem.

This case was prepared by Research Associate Jeremy Cott and Professor Stuart Gilson. Copyright © 1995 by the President and Fellows of Harvard College. Harvard Business School case 295-114.

As Myers wrestled with these issues, he would sometimes look up at the large oil portrait of Donald Salter hanging on the wall of his office—a pleasant, three-quarter-length figure—and wonder what *he* would have done.

BACKGROUND

The founder of the Salter family's business interests was a man named Josiah Salter, who in the 1890s began publishing, out of Pocatello, Idaho, a monthly magazine called *Health*, primarily as a way of promoting the laxatives he was selling. The magazine became a quick success: Within a few years circulation exceeded half a million. In the 1920s, however, his son, Donald Salter, sold *Health* magazine and used the proceeds to buy several daily newspapers in Idaho. Later, he also acquired AM and FM radio stations in the state. Donald Salter was an energetic, somewhat flamboyant man, and gradually became an influence in political as well as business matters. When he died in 1962, his daughter, Margaret Salter Graham, inherited the control of the family business. She led it for the next thirty years. During much of her career she was considered one of the more powerful women in the state.

By the late 1980s and early 1990s, the family business had become a diversified company generating well over $100 million a year in revenues. It owned thirteen media-related companies in six states, including newspapers, radio and television (TV) stations and broadcasting facilities, a small book publishing operation, and a midsized commercial printer. Its flagship property was the daily newspaper in Boise, Idaho, which had been acquired by Donald Salter in the 1920s. The paper had been for decades— and remained—the only daily newspaper in Boise, which was the largest city in the state; it was thus the largest newspaper in the state, and its most important editorial voice.

The company was a private company, the seventeen shareholders of which were all members of the Salter family. In 1987, however, the company ceased being a regular C corporation and elected S corporation status. S corporations (sometimes called Subchapter S corporations, after the subchapter of the tax code defining this structure) represent a kind of hybrid structure. They have the advantage of limited liability given to regular corporations, yet, like partnerships, they are also able to avoid the burden of double taxation that regular corporations have to live with. S corporations are treated as "pass-through" entities. That is, the corporations themselves are not taxed; instead, they pass through their income or loss to their stockholders, who then report their pro rata share of the corporations' income or loss on their individual tax returns. (There are, however, several restrictions imposed on S corporations, the most important of which is that they can have no more than 75 stockholders.[1]) The Donald Salter company elected S corporation status in 1987 evidently because passage by Congress of the 1986 Tax Act made the corporate tax rate higher than the personal tax rate for the first time in history.[2] This necessarily made pass-through entities superior to regular corporations as a way of minimizing taxes—and thus maximizing after-tax rates of return, all other things being equal.[3] On the other hand, there are various *nontax* advantages of regular corporations,[4] but their chief nontax advantage relative to S corporations—the absence of any limitation on the number of shareholders—did not seem relevant to the Donald Salter company, at least in the late 1980s. It was a family-owned, closely held company.

Family Issues

In the late 1980s, however, some general problems developed in the company. A rift developed between the CEO—who had been with the company since the mid-1970s—and key family members. They talked to each other less and less. In addition, one family member began saying as early as 1988, when the company was still profitable, that it was not being managed well. He himself had been working at another, public newspaper company, and had seen things done differently. The board, however, which included some friends of the CEO, wasn't very sympathetic to management

---

[1]At the time of this case the limit was only 35 shareholders. The limit was later raised to 75, following a change in the law on S corporations enacted in 1996.

[2]Passage of the 1986 Tax Act caused the maximum federal tax rate on corporations to decline from 46 percent to 34 percent, and the maximum federal tax rate on individuals to decline from 50 percent to 28 percent.

[3]Passage of the 1986 Tax Act resulted in a flood of corporations switching to S corporation status. "In 1985, there were approximately 75,000 S-Corporation elections. In the 5 weeks spanning the end of 1986 and the beginning of 1987 [after passage of the Tax Act] there were approximately 225,000 S-Corporation elections." (Myron S. Scholes and Mark A. Wolfson, *Taxes and Business Strategy*, p. 65.)

[4]Compared with partnerships, the most common kind of pass-through business entity, regular corporations have the nontax advantages of limited liability, a larger amount of relevant case law, more certain property rights in various circumstances, and (if the corporations are traded on organized security exchanges) easier access to debt and equity capital. Compared with S corporations, another kind of pass-through business entity, regular corporations have several advantages—for example, not having any limitation on the number of shareholders, which increases their potential liquidity, and being able to have more than one class of stock (although an S corporation can have more than one class of stock provided that the only difference has to do with voting power).

change. Family politics became a larger factor. Margaret Graham arranged to replace some members of the board. She also told the chief financial officer (CFO) that she wanted to sell the radio division, which was losing money, but when a proposal to do so was made at a board meeting, she voted against it, having subsequently changed her mind. (One estimate was that the division could have been sold for $30 million to $35 million at that point. By the early 1990s, with the recession in full force, outside consultants suggested that it might fetch $14 million.)

The family member with outside newspaper experience was an outspoken figure, but his directness got people thinking. The management recruiter who contacted Jim Myers told him that the company's affairs and the family's affairs would be closely intertwined.

In 1989 and 1990 the board decided that a basic change was needed. The company's earnings were sliding, the CEO was going to be retiring, and the board considered selling the company. Instead they engaged an outside recruiter to find a turnaround manager. Jim Myers had spent his entire career in or around the newspaper industry. He had spent eleven years with Knight Ridder, a diversified media company, in a variety of positions; then six years as CFO of the *Dallas Morning News*, one of the more important newspapers in the country; then four years with the Wetstone Company, which published a large number of daily and suburban weekly newspapers. At the Wetstone Company he was involved in asset sales and debt restructuring as the company struggled through a series of financial crises. Knight Ridder and Dallas Morning News were public companies; Wetstone was private. Myers was, however, interested in more than purely financial matters. He was, he admitted, to some extent "a child of the 60s," and the concern that the Donald Salter family had with more than financial matters appealed to him. They were—they made clear to him—interested in producing quality products, making a positive contribution to the community, and really involving company employees in what the company was doing.

Other Family Histories

The history of family-owned media companies is legendary in America. Newspapers had generally been their anchor. Newspapers had for a long time been the most significant mass communications medium in America, an essential part of the enormous economic and demographic expansion in the country in the early part of the century, particularly in cities. By the 1960s, however, due largely to competition from television, their popularity began to decline. (In absolute numbers, newspaper circulation continued to increase somewhat, but relative to population growth it declined.) Their importance was by no means gone, however: In the early 1990s, total daily newspaper circulation in the United States exceeded 60 million. Many of the country's family-owned papers were absorbed by big public companies, sold stock to the public themselves, or simply disappeared. Fierce infighting within old newspaper families became a recurring event. In Louisville, Kentucky, for example, the Bingham family owned the principal newspaper since the early part of the century. Both a father and son had used the paper as a platform for political appointments of some significance. But finally bitter family quarrels and recriminations made the paper ungovernable, and in 1986 it was sold to the public company Gannett, Inc.

In St. Louis, Missouri, the Pulitzer family had owned the principal newspaper since the 1870s—and was responsible for founding the prestigious Pulitzer Prizes. By the 1980s it also owned television and radio stations and a number of other papers. In 1986, however, a bitter family feud erupted. Several minority shareholders, who were family members but not involved in the business as such, wanted to sell their shares for the highest price possible. Terms of the family trust—designed to discourage a hostile takeover—gave the company the option to buy stock being sold by family members at a price equal to the company's book value—which was about $25,000 a share. Morgan Stanley estimated that the company as a whole was worth $113,000 a share, factoring in a control premium. An outside investor offered $91,000 a share for the company, then upped it to $115,000. The majority shareholders, however, who were family members and directly involved in the business—two of them in fact were grandsons and namesakes of the company founder—rejected the outside offer, but, facing a lawsuit from the minority shareholders, finally agreed to buy their shares back at $78,000, an approximation of market value.[5]

In San Francisco, California, the de Young family had owned the principal newspaper since the 1860s, and by the 1980s it also owned television sta-

---

[5]A few months later, the company made a limited public offering of its common stock, for the first time in its history. It appeared that the offering was less an effort to raise capital than a way of establishing for family members a vehicle to sell their shares in the future at market value, if they so wished. The offering represented only about 10 percent of the company's stock, and it would have only 1.6 percent of the voting power in the company because it was designed as a separate class of stock—an arrangement, not uncommon among newspaper companies, that allows effective control to remain within family hands. The offering sold for about $78,000 a share (adjusted for an enormous stock split). In order to comply with Securities and Exchange Commission (SEC) regulations, the offering also involved the disclosure of some previously private family matters.

tions, cable systems, a book publishing operation, and two smaller papers. The company's financial performance had weakened badly, however, and the board finally hired outside managers to replace most of the family people who had been running the operating divisions and evidently tolerating a good deal of waste. The chairman of the board, however, remained the founder's granddaughter, who insisted that the company would not be sold. (One of the operating divisions, however, was put on the block in order to satisfy a few family stockholders who wanted to cash out.) The chairman said that owning a newspaper was not like owning a shoe company. "If we'd inherited a shoe company, it would be hard to be very emotional about that."

Myers' Authority

When Myers accepted the job at the Donald Salter company, he insisted on—and was given in his employment contract—pretty much free rein. He had the right to hire and fire management people, even if they were family members.

Soon after he started, he found that a few key people were defensive and resistant to change (they would say to Myers, "No, you don't understand"). Other managers, however—like the television executives—were more open to the kinds of change that Myers felt were necessary. Myers attributed this in part to the nature of the TV industry, which was a fairly fast-moving, competitive business; in comparison, newspapers tended to be monopolistic and more labor-intensive.

THE ECONOMIC SCOREBOARD

Myers was concerned about the way in which financial performance had historically been measured in the company, particularly as it applied to the incentives that various managers in the company were given. In the past, incentive plans in the Donald Salter company had been based on conventional accounting measures—for example, net income divided by stockholders' equity, as recorded in the books. Myers had had experience working for publicly traded companies, and was concerned about more market-oriented measures, which was what family members were increasingly concerned about as well. "Economics," he wrote in a long memo to operating managers soon after he arrived, "is an increasingly important part of the company's performance criteria," and he described to them "the economic scoreboard to which most of us, myself included, will be held accountable." This, he said, was based on basic business finance, industry standards, and the needs of the owners. "Any property must provide a fair financial return commensurate with its capital value," he said; but "capital value is not usually the same as the investment shown on the balance sheet." In fact, the equity shown on Donald Salter's balance sheet was less than half what the equity was probably worth in the market. So, in the 1980s, what the company reported to managers and owners as its return on investment (book income divided by book equity) tended to be in the high teens, but in market-based terms, in Myers' view, it was nowhere near as good as that.

Exhibit 9.1 shows financial statements for the Donald Salter company for 1989–1991. Exhibit 9.2 shows comparative financial data for 1988–1991 for a group of public companies that, like Donald Salter, were primarily newspaper publishers but were diversified into other media as well. In general, companies that had significant involvement in the newspaper business were hit hard in the late 1980s and early 1990s, as the recession caused a downturn in advertising revenues (which represent about 80 percent of newspaper revenues) and the biggest slump in the newspaper industry since the Depression.

Incentive Plans

In the past, the company's incentive plans had all been based on accounting measures, particularly accounting definitions of income. Myers believed that it was more important to focus on operating cash flow—defined as earnings before interest, taxes, depreciation, and amortization (EBITDA). This, as Myers explained to the company's managers, related to almost all of the company's financial needs—being able to service debt, being able to make appropriate capital expenditures, being able to pay dividends to shareholders. It was also, he pointed out, the primary basis for bolstering the market value of the company or its component parts.

The company's incentive plans were therefore changed. Short-term incentive plans for operating and corporate managers were now based on annual cash flow budgets, and longer-term (five-year) incentive plans for operating and corporate managers were now based on the market value of the company and its component businesses. The short-term plans were of course simpler. But they represented a change not only in focusing on cash flow; they also established higher thresholds for bonuses (previously, the threshold was about 70 percent of budget), and for one operating division (the TV stations) the short-term plan established a matrix whereby two variables, rather than one, would determine executives' bonus awards. Exhibit 9.3 shows a short-term incentive plan for corporate management, and Exhibit 9.4 shows a short-term incentive plan for TV executives. Exhibit 9.5 presents excerpts from the most important plan—the corporate executive long-term incentive plan in effect from July 1, 1991, to June 30, 1996.

Before accepting the job at Donald Salter, Myers went through negotiations with key board members to establish the kind of incentive plan that would apply to him. He was concerned about this. Myers knew very well that changes over time in the market-based value of a company could be, to a fair extent, uncontrollable by the chief executive (for example, changes due to the expansion or contraction of market price/earnings (P/E) multiples, as well as changes due to macroeconomic forces that could sharply lift or depress earnings themselves). Only in the end did he agree to an incentive plan tied to the vagaries of the market and the economy in general, acknowledging that the shareholders were ultimately in the same boat.

Valuation

The long-term incentive plans had some special requirements. Chief among them was that—as the covering letter to an incentive plan for one of the divisional managers stated—"the ending value will be determined either by appraisal or actual sale and *not* by a formula applied to key numbers." The company's stock, after all, was not publicly traded. The company therefore hired a small consulting group that specialized in giving financial advice to closely held corporations to do an annual review of the market value of the Donald Salter company, and to provide advice regarding values to the board.

There was actually an appraisal done in June 1991 because one stockholder wanted to make a gift of stock to another family member. Therefore, an appraisal was needed for tax purposes. Valuation was also important because of the need to provide liquidity for some minority shareholders, who owned as much as 11 percent of the company and who would probably want to sell their shares within the next few years.

Exhibit 9.6 outlines the conceptual framework for three different possible measures of equity value—a "freely traded value," an "illiquid or non-traded value," and a "control premium value." If the company were to redeem minority stockholders' shares—actually paid out cash for what they were worth—there would be a question as to which of these measures of value should be used. Exhibit 9.6 also summarizes the concrete way in which the appraisal of the company's equity value was done in June 1991, using market multiples. The data in the appraisal helped the board establish the beginning value in the five-year incentive plan for corporate managers, and the annual growth rate in the company's appraised equity value would largely determine the awards granted under the incentive plan.[6]

OPERATING TURNAROUND

When Jim Myers began work as CEO in June 1991, the company was in difficult financial circumstances. Pretax operating income, after peaking in 1987, had declined every year since then. The cash flow of the company as a whole was still positive, but it was declining. If it continued to decline, the company risked defaulting on a loan covenant with its main bank, Boise National. Moreover, the company's quarterly dividends to its stockholders had been reduced by almost half at the start of 1991, and then, in the third quarter of 1991, were suspended. The basic tax advantage of S corporations had also been eroded. Dividends and any other distributions paid by an S corporation to its stockholders are tax free to stockholders only so long as a special tax account analogous to retained earnings—that is, an account that accumulates all earnings and losses, less dividends and any other distributions to stockholders—remains positive. In 1991, however, it became negative, and as a result the dividends paid to stockholders in 1991 were taxable.

There were signs of problems in several of the company's businesses. Earlier in the year, the evening edition of the Boise newspaper—which the company had operated since 1925—was closed down.[7] In 1989–1990, the company had spent over $30 million on a new printing facility for the Boise newspaper—by far the company's largest capital expenditure in years. The printing facility employed a new technology called flexography, which, unlike the more common offset printing process, used water-based rather than oil-based inks, was less polluting, and produced sharper color images—and the inks did not easily rub off on a reader's fingers. It was a state-of-the-art facility. When it was built, however, no serious cost–benefit analysis had been done, and Myers felt that a scaled-down facility adequately serving the business's needs could have been built for between $15 million and $20 million. The cost of newsprint—which was generally a newspaper's second largest expense, after salaries—had been rising, but

---

[6]The long-term incentive plan was put together by Towers Perrin (the well-known benefits consulting group) in collaboration with Donald Salter's outside valuation appraisers and the CEO and CFO of Donald Salter itself.

[7]In 1991, total circulation in the United States of morning and evening editions of newspapers was 41.5 million and 19.2 million, respectively; in 1960 it was 24 million and 34.9 million, respectively.

when Myers arrived he found that the company was buying newsprint at about a 20 percent discount from the announced price, when the average in the newspaper industry was about 30 percent.[8] The company published two other daily newspapers in Idaho, each with its own printing and distribution facilities. But they had fairly small circulations of around 20,000 each, and the cities in which they were published were only about 30 miles apart. The problematic radio division was still losing money. The company's biggest money-losing operation, however, was a group of weekly newspapers in Colorado, which the company had bought in 1987—at what one outside analyst regarded as a very inflated price. Competition for advertising revenues had proven more intense than expected. The company put the operation up for sale in 1990, but it was taken off the market in early 1991 when no serious offers emerged. In fact, the newspaper broker who worked on the proposed sale said that more than half of the offerings he was currently handling would probably be taken off the market because prices for newspaper properties were so low. Myers felt, nevertheless, that there were cost-cutting possibilities in the operation that were not being pursued vigorously enough. In general, he impressed on operating managers what the "economic scoreboard" was, to which, he emphasized, both he and they would be held accountable. Some managers did not respond well to this. Others did.

The fortunes of the newspaper and broadcast television industries generally were expected to improve in the next few years as the country came out of the recession, but the long-term prospects for these industries—given, for example, the growth of direct-mail marketing and of cable television, with their natural advantages in segmented marketing—were uncertain. Commercial printing—the other industry that Donald Salter was involved in in a significant way—was a capital-intensive business. Structurally, Myers felt that it was likely to become bimodal: There would be, Myers thought, just a few giant companies (such as R.R. Donnelley & Sons Co. and Arcata Graphics Co.) and various small mom-and-pop operations. Whether Donald Salter should be prepared to increase the size of its own commercial printing company in order to compete was unclear. At the moment, however, its commercial printing

---

[8]The cost of newsprint in Donald Salter's newspaper businesses was about 15 percent of total operating costs (that is, all costs other than interest, taxes, and corporate allocations).

company was doing well by industry standards, and had an excellent manager.

How Myers should manage the company relative to his incentive plan involved some ambiguity. In the company's flagship property, the Boise newspaper, for instance, it was evident that about a million dollars could be saved annually if some of the journalistic staff were eliminated. The short-term finances of the company would improve, but the appeal of the paper over the long term might be weakened. Myers was particularly concerned how the outside appraisers would or would not factor this into their valuation of the company. Although the valuation of the company was being done on the basis of a good many aspects, and involved a judgment about various trends and the relative weights to give them, nevertheless it was centered around multiples of earnings and cash flow, and since Myers' incentive award was based on the increase in the company's value over a five-year period, it would be in his self-interest to maximize earnings and cash flow over the next few years. Exhibit 9.7 shows circulation trends in the Boise newspaper.

Myers needed, in any case, to improve the company's liquidity for its shareholders. In 1991, dividends had been suspended. From 1980 to 1988, however, the annual dividend payout had been fairly consistently around 30 percent of net income. In 1988, the board changed dividend policy to provide more stability and predictability: Annual dividends were thereafter to be 6 percent of beginning-of-the-year stockholders' equity. Then in 1989, the company's net income dropped sharply; it went negative in 1990 and even more negative in 1991, and dividends were suspended. There was, moreover, an additional liquidity problem: One or more minority stockholders were probably going to want to cash out—sell their shares—in the not distant future, and the company's long-term incentive plan deferred payment of plan awards until minority stockholders had been given the chance to do just that.

Myers also had to be concerned with growth and diversification if the company's value for the family was to continue into the next century. When Myers arrived, about half of the company's revenues came from print-based newspaper publishing, about a quarter came from TV and radio stations, and another quarter came from commercial printing. Thus some initial strategic planning documents referred to the need to "break out of the box of mature industries." Myers was concerned that the company's businesses were all at the peak—or even on the beginning of the down side—of their industry cycles. Myers also felt, however, that most of the businesses—even given what they were—could turn in better financial performances, such that the company could show growth in earnings even in declining industries.

A very concrete aspect of this long-term concern expressed itself in terms of the Salter family's generational and legal structure. The senior members of the Salter family were income beneficiaries of the family trust; that is, they received dividends from the company. Once the last member of that generation died, however, the trust would be dissolved and the next generation would inherit the principal. Actuarial estimates were that the youngest member of the senior generation would die around the year 2020, and the members of the next generation were concerned that the company might not be worth anything then. They had, at present, no voting power in the company. But they were able to persuade the older members of the family, as well as Myers himself, to hold back somewhat on the company's dividends so that the company would have adequate funds to invest in the future. They wanted the company to pursue what a later strategic document would call "related diversification":

> *We are seeking small "seedling" companies that are engaged in less mature aspects of the media business. The object will be to gain expertise in new techniques and technologies, to participate in faster growing segments of the media business, and to find opportunities to extend and strengthen our existing media businesses. . . . This "seedling" component of the strategy will require us to be willing to take risks and fail . . . Judging from the performance of venture capital companies, a successful track record out of ten purchases might be five flops, three mediocre performers, one success, and one superstar.*

Myers was familiar with what other, predominantly newspaper companies—like Times Mirror and Knight Ridder—had been doing in terms of investing in less mature aspects of the media business. He knew, however, that Donald Salter couldn't afford most of the big-company tactics; he felt that $5 million to $10 million was probably the maximum that the company should risk in any given venture.

Another concern facing Myers was a lawsuit developing in Texas, where a Hispanic broadcaster, Roberto Martinez, was claiming that Donald Salter's broadcast tower division had breached a service contract, effectively destroying Martinez' TV station. Martinez was suing

Salter, claiming $70 million in damages. Lawyers had been engaged on both sides. Salter had engaged two firms on the case. The local Idaho attorneys thought the case was frivolous, but the Texas trial attorneys advised Myers that, while they probably would win the case, there were weaknesses that did not make a win certain. Myers had met with Martinez once and had come away from a three-hour meeting shaken in his confidence of Salter's case.

THE CHALLENGE

Myers thus found himself facing a host of somewhat conflicting demands. He had to decide which businesses to invest in and which, possibly, to sell off. He had to improve the company's performance in the short term, but also to be mindful of the family's concern for its viability in the long term. The incentive plan allowed him and other key managers to share in the additional wealth that they were able to create in the company, but even measuring what that was involved a fair amount of uncertainty.

EXHIBIT 9.1 Donald Salter Communications: Summary of Operations ($000, Except Per Share Data)

	Net Revenues		
	1989	1990	1991
Newspaper—daily			
Boise, Idaho	$ 47,693	$ 42,992	$ 41,218
Pocatello, Idaho	8,879	8,862	8,513
Idaho Falls, Idaho	9,220	9,176	8,320
Total	$ 65,792	$ 61,030	$ 58,051
Newspaper—weekly			
Colorado Springs, Colorado	15,317	13,632	12,127
Commercial printing			
Lafayette, Colorado	28,152	35,074	37,147
Television			
Boise, Idaho	8,347	7,403	6,445
Spokane, Washington	7,554	8,000	7,217
Green Bay, Wisconsin	6,909	7,252	7,427
Dayton, Ohio	6,368	6,461	6,142
Total	$ 29,178	$ 29,116	$ 27,231
Radio			
Albuquerque, New Mexico	6,153	7,172	7,538
Broadcasting Towers			
Texas	1,174	1,670	1,880
Books			
Salter Books	147	119	67
Other			
Unallocated corporate expenses			
Interest expense			
Elimination of intercompany sales			
Weekly newspaper and commercial printing	(5,057)	(4,363)	(3,560)
Other	(122)	(487)	(478)
Total revenues	$140,734	$142,963	$140,003
Grand total			
Provision for income taxes[b]			
Boise newspaper severance			
Gain on sale of land			
Net income (loss)/cash flow after taxes			
Dividends declared			
Dividends per share			

Source: Company reports.

[a]Cash flow for the individual business units means EBITDA.

[b]The company's election of S status in 1987 meant that it no longer had to pay tax. Instead, individual stockholders pay tax on their pro rata share of the company's income—regardless, however, of the amount of dividends they receive. Coincident, therefore, with its election of S status, the company contractually promised to provide stockholders each year with the cash necessary to meet their tax obligations relevant to the company's income. This was over and beyond whatever dividends the company might pay to stockholders. Hence the "provision for income taxes" (calculated at personal income tax rates) in the above statement.

Income			Cash Flow[a]		
1989	1990	1991	1989	1990	1991
$6,892	($ 387)	($ 365)	$ 8,615	$ 2,797	$4,159
1,205	875	710	1,605	1,298	1,136
625	641	61	956	1,046	497
$8,722	$1,129	$ 406	$11,176	$ 5,141	$5,792
(4,478)	(4,670)	(3,880)	(1,313)	(1,885)	(1,902)
1,008	1,565	1,839	2,906	3,931	4,013
1,715	648	(705)	2,216	1,227	(75)
1,273	1,457	896	1,848	2,090	1,573
1,150	1,339	788	1,878	2,176	1,689
699	1,146	462	2,347	2,309	1,563
$4,837	$4,590	$1,441	$ 8,289	$ 7,802	$4,750
(1,988)	(1,528)	(1,509)	(1,379)	(858)	(797)
708	960	1,064	918	1,266	1,379
(177)	(105)	(199)	(177)	(105)	(199)
105	0	(791)	105	0	(791)
(1,178)	(4,941)	(5,299)	(1,178)	(4,941)	(5,299)
$7,559	($3,000)	($6,928)	$19,347	$10,351	$6,946
2,959	(644)	(2,253)			
$4,600	($2,356)	($4,675)			
	(1,770)				
	480				
$4,600	($3,646)	($4,675)			
3,484	3,543	1,042			
234	238	70			

EXHIBIT 9.2   Comparative Data for Diversified Newspaper Companies

	1988	1989	1990	1991
Comparison Companies				
Earnings as % of sales	10.0%	9.8%	5.2%	5.2%
Cash flow as % of sales	15.6%	15.5%	11.3%	11.6%
Dividends as % of earnings	35.4%	36.9%	73.0%	76.4%
Price (1970 = 10)				
High	112.41	138.38	118.07	112.11
Low	91.60	102.33	78.58	91.12
P/E ratio				
High	15.59	18.26	28.52	27.89
Low	12.70	13.50	18.98	22.67
Donald Salter				
Earnings as % of sales	6.1%	3.3%	-2.1%	-3.0%
Cash flow as % of sales	13.8%	11.6%	7.3%	6.9%

Source: Casewriter's calculations, based on Standard & Poor's "Industry Surveys" and company documents. For Donald Salter Communications, "earnings" figures (which are after-tax) are adjusted to reflect the same effective tax rate paid each year by the comparison companies. The tax rate paid during this period by the sample companies (which are C corporations) was usually higher.

Notes:

- The comparison companies are public companies that are primarily involved in the newspaper business but diversified into other media as well: Dow Jones, Gannett, Knight Ridder, New York Times, Times Mirror, and Tribune Co. The data used for these companies are consolidated data.

- "Earnings" is defined as after-tax income excluding discontinued operations, extraordinary items, and accounting charges, but including gains or losses on asset sales. "Cash flow" is defined as net income plus depreciation and amortization.

EXHIBIT 9.3 Short-Term Incentive Plan for Corporate Management

Percent of Budgeted Cash Flow Achieved	Percent of Bonus Earned
110%	125.0%
109	120.0
109	115.0
107	110.0
106	105.0
105	100.0
104	85.0
103	70.0
102	55.0
101	40.0
100	25.0
99	22.5
98	20.0
97	17.5
96	15.0
95	12.5
94	0.0

Source: Company documents.

EXHIBIT 9.4 Short-Term Incentive Plan for TV Executives: Percent of Bonus Matrix

Percent of Budgeted Net Revenues Achieved	Percent of Budgeted Cash Flow Achieved							
	92%	96%	99%	100%	103%	106%	109%	110%
105%				10%	20%	80%	90%	100%
104				20	33	90	100	105
103				33	55	100	105	110
102			27%	55	65	105	110	110
101		20%	37	65	75	110	110	120
100	7%	27	47	75	85	110	120	125
99	17	37	57	85	95	115	120	125
98	27	47	67	95	105	115	125	135
97	37	57	77	105	115	125	135	
96	47	67	87	115	125	135		
95	57	87	97	125	135			

Source: Company documents.

EXHIBIT 9.5   Long-Term Corporate Executive Incentive Plan: Excerpts

[The text of the incentive plan was 26 pages long. Excerpts from it are as follows.] All defined terms appear at the end of this plan.

1. Objectives and Summary

This plan is established:

- To facilitate recruitment and retention of individuals of exceptional talent in those corporate executive positions benefited by the Plan.
- To provide key corporate executives with an incentive to increase substantially the value of the Company during the Plan Term.
- To permit key corporate executives to receive incentive compensation, provided that a certain threshold level of increased value is reached.
- To defer payment of Plan Awards until the Minority Shareholders have been provided an opportunity to sell or redeem their stock in the Company.

2. Plan Term

The term of the Plan shall begin as of July 1, 1991 (the "Commencement Date"). Awards will be calculated for the period beginning on the Commencement Date and ending on the earlier of June 30, 1996 and the date of final closing of a Sale of the Company (the "Plan Termination Date").

3. Participants

3.1   Those persons holding the following corporate positions with the Company as of the Commencement Date will be participants in the Plan as of the Commencement Date: President; Vice President, Finance; Vice President, Human Resources; Vice President, Television; Corporate Controller.

4. Determination of Value, Subsequent Sale Adjusted Value and Payment Rights Value

4.2   The Committee shall, in its sole and separate discretion, determine the Value of the Company and the Adjusted Value of the Company as at the end of each fiscal year of the Company during the Plan Term . . . after conferring with corporate valuation consultants selected by the Committee.

4.5   [This subsection describes how the value of the company shall be reduced by any infusions of equity capital during the Plan Term and increased by any provision for income taxes shown on the company's books as a liability payable to company stockholders, should there be a gain recorded on the sale of any operating division during the Plan Term. Any such amounts would be adjusted by a discount rate equal to the Growth Rate, compounded annually.]

4.6   In the event that (a) within eighteen (18) months after the Plan Termination Date, the Company or one or more of its stockholders enters into an agreement or agreements with one or more purchasers containing the parties' binding commitment to enter into a Subsequent Sale, followed by (b) the final closing of the transaction described in such agreement, the Subsequent Sale Adjusted Value of the Company shall be established by the Committee . . . after review of an Appraisal as of the date of final closing of the Subsequent Sale prepared by corporate valuation consultants selected by the Committee, which Appraisal shall be adjusted on a good faith basis to exclude the results of all Company activity during the period from the Plan Termination Date to the date of final closing of the Subsequent Sale (including, but not limited to [various items listed]). . . . The

EXHIBIT 9.5 *(Continued)*

purpose of the foregoing adjustments is to cause the Subsequent Sale Adjusted Value to reflect the Adjusted Value of the Company as of the Plan Termination Date based upon the information as to value obtained by reason of the Subsequent Sale, and to disregard any increase in value of the Company attributable to the result of operations during the period from the Plan Termination Date to the date of final closing of the Subsequent Sale.

5. Calculation of Plan Awards

5.2   Awards for each Participant shall be calculated according to the following formula: The Participant's Preliminary Award Maximum shall be equal to the product of the Multiple times the Participant's Target Award times the Participant's Vesting Factor. The Participant's Award shall be the lesser of (a) the Participant's Preliminary Award Maximum and (b) the Participant's Percentage Cap multiplied by the Increased Value. . . .

5.3   The Growth Rate shall be established as follows:

   5.3.1   In the case of calculation of Awards on a Plan Termination Date other than those described in Section 5.3.2 hereof, the Growth Rate shall be established for the period beginning on the Commencement Date (except as otherwise provided in Section 5.8.1 hereof) and ending on the Plan Termination Date, and the Adjusted Value of the Company shall be established as of the Plan Termination Date based upon the Value of the Company as of such date in accordance with the provisions of Section 4.3, with calculation of dividends and distributions (and compounding thereof) to be determined up to (but not including) the Plan Termination Date.

   5.3.2   In the case of calculation of Awards on a Plan Termination Date resulting from the Sale of the company. . . .

5.4   The Multiple shall be established as follows:

   5.4.1   If the Growth Rate is less than 0.10, then the Multiple is 0;

   5.4.2   If the Growth Rate is 0.10 or more, but less than 0.125, then the Multiple is calculated as follows: Multiple = $0.5 + [20 \times (\text{Growth Rate} - 0.10)]$

   5.4.3   If the Growth Rate is 0.125 or more, but less than 0.16, then the Multiple is calculated as follows: Multiple = $1.0 + [28.57142 \times (\text{Growth Rate} - 0.125)]$; and

   5.4.4   If the Growth Rate is 0.16 or more, then the Multiple is 2.0.

5.5   A Participant's Target Award means the amount set forth in [column A of Exhibit 9.5A] labelled "Target Award" for the Participant, as such Exhibit may be amended from time to time.

5.6   A Participant's Vesting Factor means the lesser of (a) the number one (1) and (b) a fraction, the denominator of which is 36 and the numerator of which is the number of full calendar months that a Participant has been employed by the Company in a position covered by the Plan during the period commencing on the later of (x) the Commencement Date and (y) the Participant's Actual Date of Hire through the earlier of the (i) Plan Termination Date and (ii) the Participant's Actual Date of Termination.

(Continued)

EXHIBIT 9.5 *(Continued)*

5.7 A Participant's Percentage Cap means the percentage set forth in [column B of Exhibit 9.5A] labeled "Percentage Cap" for the Participant, as such Exhibit may be amended from time to time. The Percentage Caps for Participants employed as of the Commencement Date have been calculated by (a) multiplying each Participant's Target Award by the number two (2) (the highest Multiple available under the Plan), and (b) dividing the product calculated under clause (a) by [a number representing the maximum Increased Value for which a Participant may be compensated under the Plan]. . . .

7. Payments to Participants

[This section, of roughly 2,200 words, describes specific options and conditions concerning the ways in which Participants would be paid the Plan Awards. It attempts, as much as possible, to defer payment of Plan Awards until the Minority Shareholders have been given the opportunity to sell or redeem their stock in the company.]

9. Miscellaneous

[This section, of roughly 1,000 words, describes various administrative matters, such as the authority of the Committee, the benefits earned by Participants relative to their estate and employment status, and the terms of possible outside arbitration.]

10. Definitions

[This section, running from subsection 10.1 through subsection 10.54, defines or clarifies various terms used in the substance of the Plan document. A few examples follow:]

10.3 *Adjusted Value of the Company* means the Value of the Company as of the date specified in Section 5.3 hereof, increased by the amount of all dividends and distributions (other than payments made for stockholder liability for taxes attributable to Company income) paid to Company stockholders in respect of Company stock from the Commencement Date (except as otherwise provided in Section 5.8.1 hereof) through the date specified in Section 5.3 hereof, and such amounts shall be adjusted from the date of each such payment to the date specified in Section 5.3 hereof at a discount rate equal to the Growth Rate, compounded annually.

10.8 *Beginning Value* means One Hundred Forty Million Dollars ($140,000,000). . . .

10.21 *Growth Rate* means the Adjusted Value as of the date specified in Section 5.3 hereof minus the Beginning Value (except as otherwise specified in Section 5.8.1 hereof), expressed as an annual average compounded rate of increase over the period of measurement; i.e., the rate of growth which would cause the Beginning Value (except as otherwise specified in Section 5.8.1 hereof), if compounded annually, to equal the Adjusted Value as of the date specified in Section 5.3 hereof. For all computations under the Plan, the Growth Rate shall be expressed as a decimal.

10.22 *Increased Value* means the Adjusted Value of the Company as of the date specified in Section 5.3 hereof minus the Beginning Value (except as otherwise provided in Section 5.8.1 hereof).

EXHIBIT 9.5A *(Continued)*

	Column A Target Award	Column B Percentage Cap	Column C Actual Date of Hire	Column D Effective Date of Hire (for Participants Described in Section 3.4 Only)	Column E Value at Effective Date of Hire (for Participants Described in Section 3.4 Only)	Column F Actual Date of Termination (for Participants Described in Section 3.6 Only)	Column G Effective Date of Termination (for Participants Described in Section 3.6 Only)	Column H Value at Effective Date of Termination (for Participants Described in Section 3.6 Only)	Column I Adjusted Value on Effective Date of Termination (for Participants Described in Section 3.6 Only)	Column J Preliminary Award Maximum
President	$XXX	YYY%								
Vice President, Finance	$XXX	YYY%								
Vice President, Television	$XXX	YYY%								
Vice President, Human Resources	$XXX	YYY%								
Corporate Controller	$XXX	YYY%								

EXHIBIT 9.6 Donald Salter Communications: Valuation

Conceptual Framework

One company document stated the following:

> Stock value estimates of non-publicly traded companies such as [this one] involve subjective determinations due, in large part, to the absence of an active and public market for the stock of such companies. Moreover, stock values may differ depending, among other matters, upon the date of the valuation, the block of stock being valued, and the purpose of the valuation.

The document also described three different measures of value:

> *Freely traded value.* This is an estimate of the price at which small blocks of the Company's stock would sell if the Company's stock were publicly listed and traded on an exchange. A buyer would not expect control of the Company but would expect to be able to buy or sell shares at will. Factors considered in establishing freely traded value include historical price-earnings ratios, cash flow ratios, and dividend history.

> *Illiquid or non-traded value.* This is an estimate of value that reflects a discount for lack of marketability of shares from the freely traded value described above in light of the privately held nature of the Company.

> *Control premium value.* This is an estimate of the price that a buyer would be willing to pay in order to purchase a controlling interest in the Company (i.e., over 50% of the Company stock). The control premium value reflects the added value inherent in being able to control the direction and management of an enterprise. The control premium value . . . [is] determined . . . based upon analysis of merger and acquisition data for publicly traded broadcasting companies. The 5-year average control premium paid for [such] companies is 31%.

The 1991 appraisal elaborated on the discount necessary to arrive at an *illiquid or non-traded value* of the company. From time to time, restricted (unregistered) shares of public corporations are sold in private transactions. "These private transactions," the document said, "enable us to compare the prices of shares which may not be immediately traded in public markets with the prices of . . . shares in the same company which may be immediately traded in the established public market." Leaving out various transactions because of special factors (e.g., transactions involving very small companies, unprofitable companies, companies whose stock trades on an established exchange rather than over-the-counter), the analysis found that the median discount for such restricted shares was 29%. Additional factors, however, suggested that the discount for Donald Salter stock should be somewhat greater (e.g., the buyer of restricted stock of a public company can eventually sell the stock in the public market under the so-called "dribble out rule," whereas the hypothetical buyer of Donald Salter stock would have no prospect of being able to sell it in a public market at the full, freely traded value). The analysis thus concluded that the discount from the freely traded value of Donald Salter should be 35%.

EXHIBIT 9.6 *(Continued)*

Summary of June 1991 Valuation

The outside appraisers calculated a freely traded value of the company based on a comparison with a group of freely traded public companies. Like Donald Salter, these companies were all diversified media companies and derived at least 40% of their operating profits from newspaper publishing activities. The companies were Affiliated Publications, Central Newspapers, Gannett Company, Knight Ridder, Lee Enterprises, McClatchy Newspapers, New York Times, Times Mirror, and Washington Post.

The appraisers based their valuation primarily on multiples of earnings and cash flow at which the common stock of the guideline companies was trading in the market. (Cash flow here was defined as net income plus depreciation and amortization.) The earnings and cash flow numbers officially reported by both the guideline companies and the Donald Salter company were adjusted in a few ways; for example, the amortization of intangibles, unusual gains or losses from the sale of assets, effects of accounting changes, one-time charges from workforce reductions, and a few other items were eliminated. In addition, for Donald Salter they eliminated the operating losses associated with several businesses that had been started up or purchased in recent years on the assumption that an investor in Donald Salter would expect management to make them profitable in short order or dispose of them.

Having thus calculated the multiples of earnings and cash flow at which the common stock of the guideline companies was trading in the market, the appraisers then considered some less tangible factors applicable to Donald Salter. For example, the fact that Donald Salter was smaller in size and lacked the same degree of geographic and business diversification as most of the guideline companies was viewed as a negative factor. The fact that Donald Salter's earnings in recent years had been more variable and thus less predictable was also viewed as a negative factor. On the other hand, Donald Salter's balance sheet was somewhat stronger, which was a positive factor. The company's S status was also a positive factor, although the appraisers felt that the effect of this on the company's value was hard to quantify, if just because the company might not be able to continue to satisfy all of the conditions required to retain the S status in the years ahead.

On balance, the appraisers felt that the negative factors outweighed the positive factors, and that this should be reflected in the price that an investor would be willing to pay for a minority interest in the Donald Salter company. They thus reduced the market multiples for the guideline companies by 15% and came up with the following multiples to be used for valuing Donald Salter:

Multiples

- 12.5 times latest five-year weighted average earnings.
- 9.0 times latest five-year weighted average cash flow.

Donald Salter's latest five-year weighted average earnings were $6,899,000, and its latest five-year weighted average cash flow was $15,775,000.

EXHIBIT 9.7   Donald Salter's Boise, Idaho, Newspaper: Circulation Trends

	9/91	9/85	9/81	9/70	9/60
Boise Times					
(morning edition)	66,886	54,912	52,705	50,079	48,203
Boise Tribune					
(evening edition)	—	24,635	27,311	26,707	26,019
	66,886	79,547	80,015	76,785	74,222
Idaho Sunday Times					
(Sunday edition)	129,745	119,884	110,567	100,916	87,935
Boise population data	1990	1980	1980	1970	1960
	census:	census:	census:	census:	census:
	57,922	55,415	55,415	58,604	65,309
	ABC-CZ:	ABC-CZ:	ABC-CZ:	ABC-CZ:	ABC-CZ:
	108,095	102,556	101,610	113,783	107,948

Source: Editor and Publisher Year Book.
Notes:
- Throughout the above period, the Donald Salter newspaper was the only daily newspaper published in Boise. (The three newspapers indicated are only different editions of the same paper. The evening edition was voluntarily closed down in early 1991.)
- The "census" figure is for the city proper. The "ABC-CZ" figure is for a broader "city zone" as reported by the authoritative Audit Bureau of Circulation. (The "city zone" is said to represent the "area described as the corporate city or center or the target area of circulation.")
- In the United States as a whole, total weekday and Sunday newspaper circulation in 1990 was 62 million and 68 million, respectively; in 1960 it was 59 million and 48 million, respectively. The total United States population was 248 million in 1990 and 179 million in 1960.

three

Restructuring Employees' Claims

This module examines how firms restructure their contracts with employees. These contracts differ from the other contracts studied in this volume in several important ways. First, contracts with employees are often informal and unwritten. Until recently, for example, most Japanese companies offered their workers lifetime employment. Such implicit contracts are generally easier to break than explicit written contracts. Second, employees are a critical input in production. Layoffs (Exhibit I3.1) or wage reductions may adversely impact the firm's business because the cuts are made too deeply or employee morale suffers. Finally, employees cannot sell their claims on the firm. Hence, relative to other claimholders, they are less well diversified and a larger fraction of their personal wealth is tied to the fortunes of the firm. They are generally less willing to take risks.

The cases in this module highlight alternative approaches that companies can take to reduce their labor costs. The range of possible approaches can be illustrated by considering the simple representation of labor costs in Exhibit I3.2. By definition, a company's labor costs are equal to the average hourly wage (W) times the average number of hours worked per employee (H) times the number of employees (N). Some companies (e.g., Scott Paper Company) focus on reducing labor costs through layoffs (N), while others (UAL Corporation/United Air Lines) may try to negotiate a reduction in hourly wages or benefits (W). Although relatively uncommon in the United States, another possible approach is to negotiate a reduction in the length of the workweek (H). Recent legislation in France has attempted to do exactly this, by shortening the legal workweek from thirty-nine to thirty-five hours.[1] To decide which approach is best for a company, managers must weigh a variety of factors.

MANAGEMENT CHALLENGES

In every corporate downsizing program, management must confront the following critical questions: How many layoffs are appropriate? How quickly should the layoffs be made? Which employees should be targeted (e.g., factory workers or management)? What severance or retraining benefits should be offered to employees? And what information about the restructuring should be given to investors, analysts, and the news media?

To establish the target number of layoffs, managers (or their consultants) often perform a benchmarking analysis. Various productivity ratios (e.g., annual revenues divided by the number of employees) will be estimated for the company and compared to the ratios of comparable firms in the same industry. Such comparisons only make sense, however, if the comparable firms are truly comparable and they represent best management practice. Benchmarking is of relatively less value when the firm's entire industry is troubled or suffers from excess capacity.

A more thorough approach involves redesigning work processes—how work is actually done—so the firm's activities are organized more efficiently, allowing it to produce the same or greater output with fewer workers. This analysis is more likely to yield permanent job reductions, although it is more costly and time-consuming. It may also require the cooperation of the very people it is designed to replace. Management's decision is further complicated by the fact that layoffs will undoubtedly affect revenues, making it more difficult to forecast the financial impact of downsizing.

Setting a timetable for layoffs also presents management with hard choices. Implementing the plan too quickly may result in too many people, or the wrong people, being laid off ("cutting muscle rather than fat"). On the other hand, prolonging the process and leaving people uncertain about their futures can be devastating to the organization.[2]

Management must also decide how the restructuring should be publicly presented to investors, analysts, and the media. Communicating with these different audiences at once can create difficult conflicts. Disclosing more detailed information about layoff-related cost savings may establish credibility with analysts and help increase the firm's stock price. On the other hand, such disclosures may offend or further demoralize employees.

---

[1]See Suzanne Daley, "A French Paradox at Work: 35-Hour Week May Turn Out to Be Best for Employers," *New York Times* (November 11, 1999): 1.
[2]See Jeff Cole, "Boeing Boosts Number of Jobs It Plans to Cut," *Wall Street Journal* (May 24, 1995): A.3.

They may provide valuable information to the firm's competitors. And they may stimulate critical news media coverage, especially if managers' compensation is linked to the firm's earnings or stock price.[3]

ACADEMIC RESEARCH

Academic research on the financial impact of corporate downsizing has focused on the stock market's reaction to announcements of employee layoffs and plant closings.[4]

Layoffs

Studies by Worrell, Davidson, and Sharma (1991) and Lin and Rozeff (1993) document that when firms announce layoffs, they experience statistically significant stock price declines, on average (controlling for differences in firms' risk and market movements). It is difficult to conclude from this, however, that corporate downsizing per se harms shareholders. Layoffs may be motivated by a decline in company performance (for example, demand for the company's products may have fallen, or the cost of some key input may have increased). Investors may therefore interpret the layoff announcement as bad news about the firm's profitability.

Evidence by Palmon, Sun, and Tang (1997) supports this possibility. They show that layoff announcements cause stock prices to fall by approximately 2 percent, on average, when management blames the layoffs on a decline in demand. In contrast, stock prices typically increase by almost 1 percent when the layoffs are framed as part of a comprehensive restructuring program to improve company efficiency. Nohria and Love (1996) also show that stock prices increase significantly around layoffs that are under-

---

[3]See Molly Baker, "I Feel Your Pain? When the CEO Orders Massive Layoffs, Should He Get a Pay Raise?" *Wall Street Journal* (April 12, 1995): R6; and Dial and Murphy (1995).

[4]In this book, "corporate downsizing" is identified with workforce reductions, however, achieved (e.g., through layoffs, voluntary severance or early retirement programs, etc.). This review therefore excluded transactions like spin-offs and asset divestitures, which cause the company to become smaller, but do not necessarily result in layoffs or related actions. The stock price evidence on spin-offs is summarized in the preceding module of this book. Studies of asset divestitures have generally found that selling company's stock price increases by approximately 1 to 2 percent when the divestiture is announced. See Linn and Rozeff (1984), Jain (1985), Klein (1986), and Hite, Owers, and Rogers (1987).

taken as part of a major strategic repositioning or organizational redesign. They further show that stock prices increase more for firms that have experienced poorer operating performance prior to the layoffs (i.e., firms that can benefit relatively more from the cost reductions).[5] Both studies document significant improvements in profitability (measured by return on assets, return on equity, etc.) in the years that follow layoffs for firms that experience stock price gains at announcement.

In a related study, Houston, James, and Ryngaert (2001) show that the stock price gains realized by shareholders in bank mergers can mostly be explained by management's forecasted cost savings in the merger. Most of these savings are attributable to layoffs. Forecasted revenue enhancements, in contrast, receive little or no credit in stock market merger valuations.

Plant Closings

Studies by Blackwell, Marr, and Spivey (1990) and Gombola and Tsetsekos (1992) show that the stock market reacts negatively to most announcements of plant closings. Companies typically reduce the size of their workforces in the years that follow plant closings (Gombola and Tsetsekos). They also experience a significant improvement in their return on equity (Blackwell et al.).

CASE STUDIES

This module consists of five case studies. The case of **Navistar International** describes that company's attempt to restructure a huge liability for retiree medical benefits. One of the nation's largest manufacturers of heavy-duty trucks, the company had, for years, provided generous retirement benefits to its employees. This included the promise to pay for the future medical expenses of every retired Navistar worker and his or her family. However, due to unexpected increases in medical costs and the number of retirees, the associated liability had grown to $2.6 billion—more than five times Navistar's net worth. A recent accounting rule change would soon require the company to show the liability on its balance sheet,

---

[5]For such firms that are already known to have performance problems, layoff announcements may also convey less *new* negative information about the firm's financial condition.

wiping out shareholders' equity. This prospect, compounded by a downturn in Navistar's markets, meant that it faced possible bankruptcy unless it could persuade retirees to make significant concessions.

The second case features the massive downsizing program at **Scott Paper Company**, under the controversial turnaround manager "Chainsaw" Al Dunlap. Under previous management, the company had reported a series of large losses, and debt had ballooned to twice the industry average. Several attempts to restructure had failed. Soon after joining the company, Dunlap announced that he would cut Scott's worldwide workforce of 34,000 employees by almost a third in less than a year. The resulting potential cost savings, and gains for shareholders, were huge. Scott's senior managers and directors also stood to benefit from their substantial holdings of company stock and stock options. The threat of major labor disruptions and negative media coverage meant the success of the restructuring was far from assured, however.

FAG Kugelfischer is a German ball-bearings manufacturer that faced possible bankruptcy following a severe downturn in its markets and an ill-advised acquisition in former East Germany. Burdened by a heavy debt load and high labor costs, the company hired a German professional turnaround manager to restructure its business. He faced a number of formidable obstacles, however. Compared to the United States, laying off workers in Germany would be expensive. Under German law, workers were entitled to high severance benefits and held seats on the firm's board of directors. Moreover, Kugelfischer, like most German firms, had historically been managed for the benefit of *all* corporate stakeholders, including employees. Any attempt to break this social contract might provoke a severe public backlash. Although one of the executive's primary goals was to increase Kugelfischer's stock price, it was against German custom to compensate managers with stock options.

The case study of **Chase Manhattan Corporation** examines the 1995 merger between Chase Manhattan and Chemical Bank, which produced what was then the largest bank in the United States (and fourth largest bank in the world). Management believed the merger created significant opportunities to cut expenses. Annual savings of $1.7 billion would be realized by laying off 12,000 of the banks' 74,000 employees and closing hundreds of retail bank branches, among other things. Management also believed the merged bank would enjoy important competitive and strategic advantages in its markets, generating major sources of new revenue. Whether these benefits would be fully realized, however, depended on management's ability to successfully integrate the two banks' operations. An important part of this process was deciding how the pain of restructuring should be distributed between the two banks' workforces.

The final case in the module, **UAL Corporation**, examines the employee buyout of United Air Lines, under which United's employees made almost $5 billion in wage and benefit concessions in return for 55 percent of the company's stock. Employees also got to keep their jobs. Thus the company offered what appeared to be a viable alternative to the mass layoffs that were occurring at other major U.S. airlines. Implementing this restructuring posed major challenges, however. Many employees were concerned they had overpaid for their stock. Further, many analysts and investors were initially skeptical about the proposed benefits of the buyout, fearing that once employees were in charge, they would place their interests above those of United's minority public shareholders. Overcoming this skepticism was critical if the buyout was to succeed.

READINGS

Academic Research

Blackwell, David, Wayne Marr, and Michael Spivey. 1990. "Plant-Closing Decisions and the Market Value of the Firm," *Journal of Financial Economics* 26: 277–288.

Cornell, Bradford and Alan Shapiro. 1987. "Corporate Stakeholders and Corporate Finance," *Financial Management* 16: 5–14.

DeAngelo, Harry and Linda DeAngelo. 1991. "Union Negotiation and Corporate Policy: A Study of Labor Concessions in the Domestic Steel Industry during the 1980s," *Journal of Financial Economics* 30: 3–43.

Dial, Jay and Kevin Murphy. 1995. "Incentives, Downsizing, and Value Creation at General Dynamics," *Journal of Financial Economics* 37: 261–314.

Donaldson, Gordon. 1994. *Corporate Restructuring: Managing the Change Process from Within* (Boston: Harvard Business School Press).

Gilson, Stuart. 2000. "Analysts and Information Gaps: Lessons from the UAL Buyout," *Financial Analysts Journal* 56: 82–110.

Gombola, Michael and George Tsetsekos. 1992. "The Information Content of Plant Closing Announcements: Evidence from Financial Profiles and the Stock Price Reaction," *Financial Management* 21: 31–40.

Hite, Gailen, James Owers, and Ronald Rogers. 1987. "The Market for Interfirm Asset Sales: Partial Sell-Offs and Total Liquidations," *Journal of Financial Economics* 18: 229–252.

Houston, Joel, Christopher James, and Michael Ryngaert. 2001. "Where Do Merger Gains Come From? Bank Mergers from the Perspective of Insiders and Outsiders," *Journal of Financial Economics* (forthcoming).

Jain, Prem. 1985. "The Effect of Voluntary Sell-Off Announcements on Shareholder Wealth," *Journal of Finance* 40: 209–224.

Jensen, Michael. 1993. "The Modern Industrial Revolution and the Challenge to Internal Control Systems," *Journal of Finance* 48: 831–880.

Klein, April. 1986. "The Timing and Substance of Divestiture Announcements: Individual, Simultaneous, and Cumulative Effects," *Journal of Finance* 41: 685–697.

Lin, Ji-Chai and Michael Rozeff. 1993. "Capital Market Behavior and Operational Announcements of Layoffs, Operation Closings, and Pay Cuts," *Review of Quantitative Finance and Accounting* 3: 29–45.

Linn, Scott and Michael Rozeff. 1984. "The Corporate Sell-Off," *Midland Corporate Finance Journal* 2: 17–26.

Nohria, Nitin and Geoffrey Love. 1996. "Adaptive or Disruptive: When Does Downsizing Pay in Large Industrial Corporations?" Unpublished working paper, Harvard Business School.

Palmon, Oded, Huey-Lian Sun, and Alex Tang. 1997. "Layoff Announcements: Stock Market Impact and Financial Performance," *Financial Management* 26: 54–68.

Worrell, Dan, Wallace Davidson III, and Varinden Sharma. 1991. "Layoff Announcements and Stockholder Wealth," *Academy of Management Journal* 38: 662–676.

Management Books and Practitioner Resources

Downs, Alan. 1995. *Corporate Executions* (New York: American Management Association).

Dunlap, Albert. 1996. *Mean Business* (New York: Times Business).

Mass Layoff Statistics. Published by the Bureau of Labor Statistics at the U.S. Department of Labor, available online at stats.bls.gov/mlshome.htm.

EXHIBIT I3.1   Corporate Layoffs, United States, 1989–2000

Year	Permanent Staff Cuts Announced by U.S. Corporations
1989	111,285
1990	316,047
1991	555,292
1992	500,000
1993	615,186
1994	516,069
1995	439,882
1996	477,147
1997	434,350
1998	677,795
1999	675,132
2000	613,960
Total	5,318,186

Source: Challenger, Gray and Christmas, Inc.

EXHIBIT I3.2   Calculation of Labor Costs

Annual Labor Costs	=	W	×	H	×	N
		Hourly wage		Number hours worked/ year		Number of employees

CHAPTER 10

Navistar International

In the fall of 1992, James C. Cotting—chairman and chief executive officer (CEO) of Navistar International—was, for the second time in his thirteen-year career at Navistar, faced with a major financial crisis that threatened the company's very survival.

Navistar was a company with a legendary history. It was what was left of the company known as International Harvester—once one of the largest corporations in America and the largest manufacturer of agricultural harvesting equipment in the world. During the mid-1980s the company had lost a huge amount of money, had teetered on the edge of bankruptcy, and had gone through an enormous downsizing that was painful to both workers and managers.

Navistar had historically provided generous benefits to its workers. Because of the enormous downsizing, however, the company no longer had the revenue and asset base to continue to provide the full range of benefits—most notably, health care benefits—to all of the company's active and retired workers. The company had been losing money for three years, and a new accounting standard was soon going to require the company to record in its financial statements, for the first time, its actual liability for employee health care costs. Management estimated this liability at $2.6 billion—more than five times its current stock market capitalization of $500 million. Management believed that unless the unions agreed to reduce this liability by giving up a significant fraction of their previously promised health care benefits, the company would have no choice but to file for Chapter 11—an alternative that would make everyone worse off.

This case was prepared by Research Associate Jeremy Cott and Professor Stuart Gilson. Copyright © 1994 by the President and Fellows of Harvard College. Harvard Business School case 295-030.

Earlier in the year, Navistar had initiated legal action against the unions in an attempt to force them to accept an 80 percent reduction in the health care benefit liability (to $500 million). Soon afterward, the unions filed a countersuit. By October, with no obvious resolution in sight, both sides agreed to try to settle their differences out of court. Cotting and other senior managers involved in the negotiations had to come up with a proposal for reducing this liability that would be considered reasonable and fair by both sides. Even if the liability could be scaled down, moreover, it would still be necessary to decide how remaining future health care benefits should be funded. Since the memory of Navistar's 1980s downsizing was still painfully etched in the minds of many workers and recent relations between management and the unions had been acrimonious, it was unlikely that the unions would give ground easily.

BACKGROUND

Navistar International was an old company with an important place in American economic history. It had its roots in Cyrus McCormick's invention, in 1831, of the first practical mechanical reaper, a farm machine that cut grain and that led to the development of a variety of harvesting machines that contributed, over time, to the extraordinary increase in agricultural productivity. In 1902 the McCormick Harvesting Company merged with four other struggling companies to form International Harvester; the new entity controlled 85 percent of the U.S. harvester market. By 1908 the company had 75,000 employees, and in the early part of the century it diversified its product line significantly and sold its products through more than 36,000 dealers in thirty-eight countries. It was the fourth largest corporation in the United States. In 1907 it introduced a new piece of farm equipment called the "auto wagon," a rough, high-wheeled vehicle designed to carry a farmer, his family, and his produce over rutted mud roads to the marketplace. Thus was the truck born. By the late 1980s, it was to represent the company's core business.

During the period of general economic recovery after World War II, International Harvester experienced growing problems. It lost market share with most of its products. And it developed a reputation for conservatism; for example, it didn't modify organizational structures when it expanded, promotions were strictly in-house, and there was a failure to introduce genuinely innovative products. (Competitors claimed that the company merely redesigned existing machines rather than made new ones.) Management's relationship with labor also changed. Fiercely antiunionist for almost a century, the company now negotiated master contracts with the

United Auto Workers (UAW) and made regular, liberal concessions on work rules. Employee benefits were unusually generous. In the context of the postwar economic boom, keeping production going—by avoiding strikes—was deemed paramount. One salaried worker who came to the company from Xerox Corporation was struck by the effect of all this:

> *The total benefit package for all Harvester employees—the dental, medical, and eye care and all of that—was really superior to anything anybody had anywhere else. I couldn't believe it when I first saw it! It was a consequence of the union getting all of those benefits and the culture that flowed through the company.*[1]

In 1955, for the first time, the company sold more trucks than agricultural equipment, and soon afterward Deere and Company took the lead in the agricultural equipment market. In the construction equipment market, International Harvester lagged well behind Caterpillar Inc. In the view of one observer, the company "[fell] prey to the myth of its own historical greatness"[2]: It tried to be all things to all people, and overdiversified into a variety of capital-hungry businesses. It sold off some product lines and closed a number of inefficient plants. In the early 1980s, however, the recession, combined with a six-month strike by the United Auto Workers largely over work rules, pushed the company to the edge of bankruptcy. (After recording net income of $370 million in 1979 on sales of $8.4 billion, the company had net losses of $397 million in 1980, $393 million in 1981, and $1.6 billion in 1982; the total three-year loss of $2.4 billion was, at the time, the highest for any corporation in American history.) Restructuring, the company laid off tens of thousands of workers and sold off businesses that were losing money. It sold the construction equipment business to Dresser Industries in 1982. And in 1985 it sold the agricultural equipment business to Tenneco Inc.—along with the "International Harvester" name.

The impact, both tangible and intangible, was enormous. Not only did tens of thousands of people lose their jobs with the company; a whole history and culture was broken. Among workers as well as customers, there were many families in which successive generations of people had fundamental attachments to International Harvester. Some people had virtually married the company. During the period of traumatic downsizing in the

---

[1]Barbara Marsh, *A Corporate Tragedy: The Agony of International Harvester Company* (Garden City, NY: Doubleday, 1985), pp. 131–132.
[2]Ibid., p. 130.

early 1980s, one plant manager recounted a meeting with a Harvester veteran who was terminated after twenty-four years with the company: "His wife divorced him and he claimed the divorce was because he'd put in so much time at work he never had time to take care of his family. He sat there and cried and said, 'I gave up my family for you and now you don't want me. What am I going to do with my life? . . . I don't know anything but Harvester.' "[3]

REBORN

In 1986, however, the directors declared the company reborn. It was renamed "Navistar," which was meant to convey a futuristic, high-technology outlook. It was now a smaller company: Its core business was the manufacture and marketing of medium and heavy-duty trucks, which accounted for about 75 percent of its revenues. It also produced diesel engines, both for its own medium trucks and for other vehicle manufacturers (principally Ford); this represented about 10 percent of its business. Replacement parts represented another 15 percent of its business.[4] Like the Big Three automakers—General Motors (GM), Ford Motor Company, and Chrysler Corporation—Navistar also maintained a finance subsidiary, which was wholly owned, to provide financing for its customers.

Because of the enormous losses that it had experienced and the massive downsizing that it had gone through, Navistar's capital structure had also changed significantly. The company lost over $3 billion from 1980 through 1985, and had taken on a lot of debt and preferred stock to provide needed cash along the way. In the process of restructuring, however, it converted a fair amount of debt to common stock—most dramatically in early 1987, when it redeemed over $500 million in high-coupon debt primarily with the proceeds from the issuance of common stock. This reduced the ratio of long-term debt to total capitalization for the manufacturing operation from 93 percent at the end of fiscal year (FY) 1986 to 23 percent at the end of FY 1987. In the course of the 1980s, the number of common shares outstanding increased more than sevenfold. (See Exhibit 10.1, which gives stock data for the company for fiscal years 1980–1992.)

Navistar's business was closely tied to cycles in the overall economy. It

---

[3]Ibid., p. 289.

[4]The average prices that Navistar received for its heavy-duty trucks, medium trucks, and diesel engines were $40,000, $30,000, and $4,000, respectively.

was particularly sensitive to the industrial sector, which generated a significant portion of freight tonnage hauled. (The company was not involved in the production of lighter-weight pickup trucks, which were oriented to the more general consumer.) The medium and heavy-duty truck industry was a mature industry, intensely competitive, and had excess production capacity. This made price competition keen and placed tremendous pressure on margins. Moreover, all of Navistar's principal competitors in this industry—with only one exception, a company named Paccar Inc.—were (or were part of) larger corporations with greater financial resources. In the heavy truck market, Navistar's main competitors were Freightliner Corporation (which was owned by the German industrial giant Daimler-Benz, the maker of Mercedes-Benz automobiles), Volvo-GM, Mack Trucks (which was owned by Renault), Ford, and Paccar; in the medium truck market, its main competitors were Ford and GM. Paccar, the one standalone company among its competitors, was largely nonunionized.

To some extent, the problems of the industry were a consequence of its own success. The productivity of its products had increased. For example, a heavy-duty Navistar truck that in 1980 hauled 72,000 pounds at 55 miles per hour had a fuel economy rating of five miles a gallon. In the early 1990s, a similar truck could carry 80,000 pounds at 60 to 65 miles per hour, getting seven miles a gallon. Yet, since the mid-1980s, prices on heavy trucks had moved up very little.

Despite these problematic aspects of the industry, however, and despite the painful downsizing that Navistar had gone through in the 1980s, the company had some competitive strengths. For over ten years—beginning in 1981 and continuing into the 1990s—Navistar held North American market share leadership for medium and heavy-duty trucks; its market share was close to 30 percent. It had a reputation for producing durable, economical products. It had considerable product line breadth, which allowed it to address virtually any volume purchaser's specific needs. (In the late 1980s, contravening some of its past habits, it actually redesigned 85 percent of its product line.) It also had the largest dealer network in North America; this network of close to a thousand independent dealers was largely exclusive to Navistar, although in recent years a number of them had begun to sell other companies' trucks as well. This dealer network was valuable to Navistar not only in making sales but also in providing service and making replacement parts available. (One analyst suggested that, although Navistar probably hadn't made any money in the heavy truck market for at least a decade, it had gross margins of close to 50 percent on its replacement parts.) Through its finance subsidiary, Navistar was also able to provide financing to both its wholesale and retail customers.

THE HEALTH CARE PROBLEM

In the early 1990s, the company faced another serious problem that again threatened it with bankruptcy. The recession was damaging. Total retail sales of medium and heavy trucks in the North American market peaked at 350,000 units in 1988 but by 1991 declined to 229,000 units, the lowest level since 1983. (See Exhibit 10.2.) Although Navistar made modest profits in 1987, 1988, and 1989, it began losing money again in 1990. (Exhibit 10.3 shows income statements, statements of financial condition, and cash flow statements for 1990–1992.) Analysts from Merrill Lynch and Duff & Phelps, commenting on this in late 1991 and early 1992, said the company was suffering from "weak truck demand." In its 1991 annual report, however, the company gave serious attention to another problem:

> *While 1991 financial results reflect truck industry sales at the lower end of historic demand cycles, improvements in manufacturing margins, as demand recovers, will not alone be sufficient to achieve an adequate return to shareowners and to provide for long-term reinvestment and growth in the business. To achieve adequate returns, significant progress must be made in the near-term to address the escalating costs of providing health care and pension benefits to active and retired employees.[5]*

The problem that Navistar had was affecting many older industrial companies that had a lot of retirees and that had made promises to them for postretirement health care coverage in union contracts. In the 1950s the Big Three automakers, for example, had 4 to 5 active workers for every retiree; by the early 1990s, they had only 1 to 1.5 active workers for every retiree. Navistar's situation was far worse. It now had, for every active worker, 3.3 retirees. (It had about 13,000 active workers and over 40,000 retirees; and the retirees along with their dependents, who were also covered in the health care plans, numbered 63,000.) This situation had developed because of the enormous downsizing that Navistar went through in the 1980s. (Exhibit 10.4 shows the number of Navistar employees from 1979 to 1992, and Exhibit 10.5 shows the ratio of retired to active employees in 1992 for Navistar and several comparable or near-comparable companies.)

Navistar reported that "substantially all active employees may become eligible for [health care and life insurance] benefits when they retire." The company provided free health care to retirees who had been represented dur-

---

[5]Navistar International Corporation, *Annual Report 1991*, pp. 2–3.

ing their work career by unions (that is, there were no deductibles, hospital co-payments, or required contributions to insurance premiums), and the health care plans for all employees were based on traditional fee-for-service, as opposed to managed-care, arrangements. The company had, in the late 1980s, made some effort to raise the consciousness of employees about the problem of escalating health care costs. Voluntary wellness programs were established, and nonunion workers were asked for the first time to share in the cost of health care through deductibles and co-payments. There was, however, considerable resistance to these changes. For example, the company was hit with a number of suits in federal and state courts. All of the suits were ultimately settled on varying terms, but the litigation dragged on for two years.

To some extent, Navistar's retiree health care benefits were not unusual. In the late 1980s, a federal government agency survey found that, in medium to large companies, close to half of employees who participated in company-sponsored health care plans were promised free or highly subsidized health insurance upon retirement. The Big Three automakers—General Motors, Ford, and Chrysler—all provided free health insurance to their workers and retirees.

In 1991 and 1992, however, Navistar felt itself facing a growing liquidity problem. It factored $58 million in receivables. It deferred pension plan contributions of $27 million. It reduced its capital expenditures to $77 million and $55 million in 1991 and 1992, respectively, compared with a five-year historical average of $112 million. The manufacturing operation obtained special dividends of $40 million from the finance subsidiary. The company also adopted several measures with health care providers that reduced annual increases in retiree health care costs to around 9 percent, which the company said was lower than the experience of most corporations. The company also contacted as many as two hundred potential lessors in an effort to sell and lease back its diesel engine manufacturing facilities, but those efforts were unsuccessful. Moreover, because of its financial difficulties in the 1980s, the company was already on extended payment terms with most of its suppliers—it paid in fifty-five to sixty days, compared with industry norms of twenty to thirty days. Navistar's end-of-fiscal-year cash balance had been declining for a few years, but, in addition, the seasonality of its business caused the low point of its cash balance during the year to be between $107 and $175 million lower than the end-of-year balance.

A NEW ACCOUNTING STANDARD

There was another factor that had galvanized Navistar into trying to do something about the problem of retiree health care costs. In December

1990 the Financial Accounting Standards Board (FASB), the major rule-setting body for the accounting profession, issued its Statement of Financial Accounting Standards No. 106 (FAS 106). This new standard required companies to accrue the full amount of their obligation for retiree health care costs on their balance sheets. Previously, companies recorded no such obligation; the accounting was done simply on a pay-as-you-go, cash basis. In effect, FASB was requiring companies to account for retiree benefits other than pensions in the same way that it required companies to account for pensions—on the basis of the actuarially determined present value of those future benefits. Companies now had to accrue the cost of those benefits when they were earned, not when the cash for them was paid out.

In the past, FASB had not applied this principle to retiree health care benefits. For one thing, the money involved was considered immaterial. In recent years, however, the costs of health care had been skyrocketing, and retiree benefits were, in effect, indexed to those skyrocketing costs because companies promised to pay for certain benefits, regardless of what they cost. (This made the obligation very different from traditional defined-benefit pension plans, which promised retirees annually an absolute amount of dollars, regardless of what inflation might do to the value of those dollars.)

Another reason was that, unlike pension plans, which were government-regulated and in which employees were formally vested, the promises that companies made to workers for postretirement health care were considered by management to be revocable. Whether they were in fact revocable was unclear. Federal law did not govern the administration of companies' health care plans. Rather, this was dependent on the interpretation of the relevant contracts between management and workers, and a raft of lawsuits were now being filed throughout the country that hinged on how explicit companies' promises to workers had been in the past. Navistar management, for instance, believed that its collective bargaining agreements with the unions—going back as far as the 1950s—clearly and consistently allowed it to modify or terminate its health care benefits during a "window period" of one month prior to the end of each three-year union contract.[6] The Navistar unions, on the other hand, believed that em-

---

[6]A "Duration of Agreement" provision in the contracts stated that during the window period "each party shall be at liberty . . . to give notice of termination of the program or to request such changes, amendments or additions by specifying the same in writing to the other party." [Exhibit D (affidavit of James P. Gats), in "Defendants' Motion for a Stay of Litigation," entry date 9/14/92, U.S. District Court for the Southern District of Ohio (Dayton), case *Shy et al. v. Navistar International Corp. et al.*]

ployee health care benefits were guaranteed for life, and cited as evidence of this a typical letter sent by Navistar management to a worker upon his retirement from the company (see Exhibit 10.6).

Analysts estimated that American companies' accumulated liability for retiree health care benefits, as now required to be reported under FAS 106, was between $500 billion and $2 trillion. Retired employees, it was now observed, sometimes had a claim on a corporation equal to its total net worth. FASB gave companies the choice of recognizing the liability through a one-time charge or amortizing it over twenty years. Many large companies—particularly in older, employee-intensive industries with historically generous benefits packages—were opting for the former, evidently desiring to get the pain behind them. General Motors took the largest charge, an after-tax charge on its 1992 income statement of $20.8 billion ($33.1 billion pretax), which wiped out most of the book value of its equity. For some companies, the reduction of equity resulting from these charges would put them in violation of debt covenant agreements.[7]

Navistar management estimated that its liability for retiree health care costs, if unchanged, would be $2.6 billion.

In February 1992 Navistar management approached the United Auto Workers, the principal union, and stated that retiree health care costs were threatening the company's solvency. During a series of meetings over the next several months, Navistar management made detailed presentations about the company's financial condition and the level of retiree health care benefits that it believed the company could afford. Initially skeptical, the UAW insisted on being able to retain outside financial advisors who could provide them with an independent assessment of the company's financial condition. Navistar agreed. The company's financial condition and recent financial performance in relation to comparable or near-comparable companies is shown in Exhibit 10.7.

Looking ahead, Navistar estimated that in 1994, in the absence of any change, retiree health care benefits would cost $160 million under the current pay-as-you-go, cash method of accounting; under the new accrual method of accounting required by FASB, the company would have to record an expense of $270 million (if it chose to recognize its liability through a one-time charge) or $410 million (if it chose to amortize the liability over twenty years). The liability at that point would have grown to $2.8 billion. If Navistar were able to reduce the liability, each $100 million reduction would

---

[7]The Financial Accounting Standards Board required all large corporations to implement FAS 106 no later than their fiscal year beginning after December 15, 1992.

decrease its annual cash-basis expense by about $5.3 million, and decrease its annual expense under the accrual method of accounting required by FASB by about $9.7 million (assuming immediate recognition of the liability).

POSSIBLE CHANGES

There were two basic ways in which companies could potentially reduce their liabilities for retiree health care costs—redesign the health care plans and/or prefund them. Companies could redesign the plans and keep their basic structure but insist that employees pick up a greater share of their cost through premiums, deductibles, or co-payments. In addition, they could encourage employees to use managed-care plans, like health maintenace organizations (HMOs), rather than the traditional fee-for-service plans, which were more expensive. More radical would be to change the very structure of retiree health care coverage: In effect, companies could shift from a defined benefit structure—which was what almost all companies used—to a defined contribution structure. This would parallel what was increasingly happening with pension plans: Greater emphasis was being placed on 401(k) plans in which companies matched, with company stock, a certain amount of the money that employees themselves contributed to a retirement savings vehicle. Some of the investment risks and benefits would thus be transferred to employees. Procter & Gamble and the Gillette Company were setting up retiree health care plans along these lines. Moreover, the reporting requirements of FAS 106 would not apply to defined contribution plans of this sort because companies' obligations would be satisfied simply by their contribution to the account; there was no promise as to whether the account would be sufficient to provide certain benefits in the future.

Companies could also choose to prefund their retiree health care plans (just as they prefunded their pension plans).[8] This would, by definition, reduce their net liability; it would also reduce their annual expense in the future because earnings on the assets invested would offset the annual increase in projected benefits. Moreover, there were some tax advantages to prefunding. One option, for example, was the formation of

---

[8]This involves essentially making periodic tax-deductible contributions to a fund managed by an independent agent, like an insurance company. The fund is set up to be legally distinct from the main operations of the company, and the agent invests the money in the fund to achieve reasonable long-term returns. Navistar prefunded its pension plans, as it was legally required to, but, like almost all American corporations, had never provided any prefunding for other retiree benefits.

a Voluntary Employee Benefits Association (VEBA), an investment trust established technically as a separate company with the specific purpose of paying for retiree benefits; at least some of the contributions to it by the parent company would be tax-deductible, and most of the earnings would accrue tax-free. One drawback of VEBAs, however, was that if Congress passed national health care legislation, contributions that companies had already made to VEBAs might be less valuable because, under U.S. tax law, assets of a VEBA cannot, under any circumstances, revert to the employer.

LITIGATION AND NEGOTIATIONS

Beginning in February 1992 and continuing into the summer, Navistar management and the UAW held many meetings and discussions. Due to the complexity of the problem, they also established a number of subcommittees to discuss specific issues and to attempt to reach agreement on them. On July 28, however, without any agreement having been reached, Navistar announced the termination of its existing retiree health care benefits and the creation of a new program. This would reduce the company's health care liability from $2.6 billion to $550 million; the company would be able to terminate the program at will; and there was no provision for any prefunding. Navistar simultaneously filed suit in a federal district court seeking a declaratory judgment (essentially a "declaration of rights") that it was entitled to unilaterally modify or terminate its retiree health care benefits. Discussions with the UAW stopped.

Navistar management explained in court that the reason for seeking a declaratory judgment had to do, in effect, with efficiency. The problem they were dealing with involved 63,000 retirees and their spouses, plus all of the active workers, 25 different unions with whom the company had negotiated agreements over the years (although the UAW was the principal union), and 230 union locals. In seeking a declaratory judgment, the company was designating retirees as an entire class, to whom the judgment would apply as a whole. In the absence of this, the company felt that it could be hit with lawsuits from retirees all around the country, and the company could be put in a situation of prolonged legal and financial uncertainty, which it felt it could not afford.

A month later, however, in August 1992, the UAW and other unions filed a countersuit (in another district court) contending that Navistar had no right to unilaterally modify or terminate its retiree benefits. The secretary/treasurer of the UAW issued an angry statement: "Individuals who gave decades of dedicated and loyal service to the company have been forced by Navistar's harsh and unilateral actions to seek court protection of the retiree health benefits that they toiled for and were promised."[9]

The very location of possible court proceedings was a source of contention. Navistar management filed its initial suit in Chicago because, in its view, that's where it logically belonged: The company's headquarters had been in Chicago for over a century; the greatest concentration of Navistar retirees lived in Illinois; and that's where all of the thousands of relevant documents were located. The UAW filed its countersuit in Ohio, in a different district court, because—Navistar's lawyers claimed—it was "forum shopping." Although Navistar operated a major production plant in Ohio, and some of the union members lived there, the court there had a reputation for being more sympathetic to unions than the court in Illinois.

In October, however, the two sides agreed to negotiate again, out of court. The UAW served as lead negotiator for all employees. At the end of fiscal year 1992, approximately 9,940 of Navistar's 13,945 active employees were represented by unions, and the UAW represented the large majority of the union people. Nationally, however, the UAW's primary strength came from its representation of workers at the Big Three automakers, where it represented 413,000 people. Moreover, the same health care issues and accounting standards applied to GM, Ford, and Chrysler, and, although none of them had yet formally recognized their retiree health care liabilities in their financial statements, their combined pretax health care liabilities were estimated to be around $54 billion.

As the months passed, Navistar management had additional concerns. The public debt and preferred stock issued by the company and its subsidiaries and carrying a face value of about $900 million were being downgraded by debt-rating agencies. For example, in February, Standard & Poor's had lowered its ratings for the company's senior debt from BBB– to BB, and Moody's Investors Service had lowered its ratings from Baa3 to Ba2. In December these ratings were lowered yet again. Moody's cited the "heightened risk" to security holders on account of the negotiations going on between Navistar management and the UAW over a possible restructuring of health care benefits. Those negotiations, Moody's said, "may entail a sacrifice on the part of the fixed-income security holders." (Exhibit 10.8 gives information about the company's short-term and long-term debt.)

One immediate consequence of the downgrading of the company's

---

[9]*Journal of Commerce*, August 26, 1992, p. 2B.

debt was that it restricted the company's ability to place commercial paper and short-term debt securities. One recent Securities and Exchange Commission (SEC) regulation, for example, prohibited money market mutual funds from investing more than 5 percent of their portfolios in low-grade commercial paper, down from 25 percent previously. As a result, the finance subsidiary increased its borrowings under its long-term bank revolving credit facility.

An additional concern—for both Navistar management and the unions—was the uncertainty over the possible outcome of the dispute if it were ultimately decided in court. Retired workers generally had received a boost from Congress' passage, in 1988, of an amendment to the federal Bankruptcy Code entitled the "Retiree Benefits Bankruptcy Protection Act" (formally, section 1114 of the Bankruptcy Code). Passage of the Act occurred in reaction to LTV Corporation's termination of retiree medical benefits when it filed for Chapter 11 bankruptcy in the summer of 1986. The LTV filing represented, at the time, the largest bankruptcy case in the history of the United States, and LTV's termination of retiree medical benefits suddenly left 78,000 former employees without coverage, and caused a media outcry. The Retiree Protection Act increased the priority of retiree claims for medical benefits in a bankruptcy proceeding: They were now to be senior to general unsecured creditors and junior only to secured creditors. In effect, they had the same status as administrative claims (such as bankruptcy-related legal and accounting fees). Thus the Act required that a company going through a Chapter 11 reorganization continue to pay for retiree medical benefits—unless doing so could be shown to threaten its survival, in which case the judge could order a reduction in the company's obligation. (And any such reduction would become an unsecured claim along with other unsecured claims.)

But there was an even more basic uncertainty. Although Congress' formulation was not entirely clear on this, courts generally interpreted the Act to protect only retiree benefits that were valid under nonbankruptcy law— that is, if there were seen to be a valid contract between a company and its employees that required payment of retiree medical benefits irrespective of bankruptcy. (In other words, if a company had a right to reduce or terminate its payment of benefits, it could do so whether or not it was in bankruptcy.) Here the judgment of the courts could vary a good deal. The Sixth Circuit, in which the Navistar unions filed their countersuit, had a greater tendency than other courts to find ambiguity in the written words of benefit plan documents and seemed more willing to allow the introduction of extrinsic evidence (such as oral representations and informal written communications to employees) to assess the intent of the parties involved.

THE DECISION

These concerns came to a head when, in October 1992, Navistar and the unions sat down to try to settle their differences out of court. Management's stated view was that unless the unions made material concessions on health care benefits, the company this time might have no choice but to file for Chapter 11. Cotting and the other senior managers involved in the discussions had to convince the unions that such concessions were truly necessary for the company's survival. To this end, the company presented union negotiators with extensive financial and operating data. (Exhibit 10.9 presents cash flow forecasts for Navistar, assuming no change in its retiree health care benefits.) It would be necessary to agree on a specific dollar reduction in Navistar's $2.6 billion employee health care liability, that both sides would consider reasonable and fair. It would also be necessary to decide whether the liability should be prefunded, and if so, how.

Throughout the fall of 1992, both sides met in literally hundreds of meetings. The negotiations were, according to one key UAW lawyer, "long, difficult, and adversarial."

EXHIBIT 10.1   Selected Common Stock Data

Fiscal Year	Market Price Range		Number of Common Shares Outstanding at October 31 (Millions)
	Low	High	
1992	$ 1³/₄	$ 4¹/₈	254
1991	2	4¹/₈	250
1990	2¹/₈	4⁷/₈	250
1989	3³/₄	7	251
1988	3¹/₈	7³/₈	253
1987	3⁵/₈	8³/₄	251
1986	5³/₄	11⁵/₈	109
1985	6¹/₈	11¹/₄	63
1984	5¹/₈	14³/₄	58
1983	3	14⁵/₈	41
1982	2³/₄	8⁵/₈	33
1981	7¹/₄	31¹/₂	33
1980	23	40¹/₂	32

Source: Company annual reports and 10-Ks.

EXHIBIT 10.2 Industry and Company Volume Trends (Thousands of Units)

	1992	1991	1990	1989	1988	1987	1986	1985	1984
North American Industry Retail Truck Sales[1]									
Medium trucks	118.3	120.1	149.8	162.8	187.3	169.2	165.1	162.9	154.6
Heavy trucks	125.2	109.0	139.0	172.2	163.5	150.4	135.6	154.2	135.4
Total	243.5	229.1	288.8	335.0	350.8	319.6	300.7	317.1	290.0
Navistar Retail Truck Sales									
Total	69.3	67.2	78.6	90.9	93.3	82.3	81.4	80.5	75.4
Gross profit margin of Manufacturing[2]	4.8%	4.2%	8.2%	9.6%	12.3%	13.5%	12.3%	13.6%	NA

[1]1988 and 1979 were the peak years of the two most recent industry cycles, and 1991 sales were the lowest since 1983.
[2]Net of retiree expenses.
Source: Company 10-Ks.

EXHIBIT 10.3A   Income Statements for the Years Ended October 31 ($millions, Except Per Share Data)

	Consolidated		
	1992	**1991**	**1990**
Revenues			
Manufacturing	$3,685	$3,259	$3,643
Financial services	190	201	211
Total revenues	$3,875	$3,460	$3,854
Expenses			
Cost of sales	3,254	2,885	3,144
Postretirement benefits			
Pension expense	109	101	80
Health/life Insurance	146	138	123
Total	$ 255	$ 239	$ 203
Engineering expense	92	88	85
Marketing and administrative	248	245	249
Interest	99	108	121
Financing charges on sold receivables	12	24	28
Insurance claims and underwriting	62	54	49
Provision for losses on receivables	21	26	22
Interest (income)	(17)	(28)	(45)
Other (income) expense, net	(6)	(19)	5
Total expenses	$4,020	$3,622	$3,861
Income (loss) before income taxes			
Manufacturing	—	—	—
Financial Services	—	—	—
Income (loss) before income taxes	($ 145)	($ 162)	($ 7)
Taxes on income	2	3	4
Income (loss) of continuing operations	($ 147)	($ 165)	($ 11)
Loss on discounted operations	(65)	—	—
Net income (loss)	($ 212)	($ 165)	($ 11)
Net income (loss) applicable to common stock	($ 241)	($ 194)	($ 40)
Net income (loss) per common share	(0.95)	(0.77)	(0.16)

[1]In the supplemental information, "Manufacturing" includes the reporting of finance subsidiaries under the equity method of accounting. Transactions between Manufacturing and Financial Services are eliminated from the "Consolidated" columns.

Source: Company annual reports.

Supplemental Information[1]

Manufacturing			Financial Services		
1992	1991	1990	1992	1991	1990
$3,685	$2,259	$3,643	—	—	—
—	—	—	230	242	250
$3,685	$3,259	$3,643	$230	$242	$250
3,254	2,885	3,144	—	—	—
108	100	79	1	1	1
146	138	123	0	0	0
$ 254	$ 238	$ 202	$ 1	$ 1	$ 1
92	88	85	—	—	—
226	223	230	22	22	19
12	11	6	87	97	115
52	65	67	—	—	—
—	—	—	62	54	49
18	20	18	3	6	4
(17)	(28)	(45)	—	—	—
(9)	(21)	4	3	2	1
$3,882	$3,481	$3,711	$178	$182	$189
(197)	(222)	(68)	—	—	—
52	60	61	—	—	—
($ 145)	($ 162)	($ 7)	$ 52	$ 60	$ 61
2	3	4	20	23	22
($ 147)	($ 165)	($ 11)	$ 32	$ 37	$ 39
(65)	—	—	—	—	—
($ 212)	($ 165)	($ 11)	$ 32	$ 37	$ 39

EXHIBIT 10.3B   Statements of Financial Condition as of October 31 ($millions)

	Consolidated		
	1992	1991	1990
Assets			
Cash and cash equivalents	$ 335	$ 295	$ 275
Marketable securities	171	220	313
Receivables, net	1,479	1,316	1,627
Inventories	365	332	343
Prepaid pension assets	122	123	105
Property and equipment, net	582	604	628
Equity in Financial Services subsidiaries	—	—	—
Investments and other assets	203	149	125
Intangible pension assets	370	404	379
Total assets	$3,627	$3,443	$3,795
Liabilities and Shareowners' Equity			
Liabilities			
Accounts payable	637	474	574
Accrued liabilities	401	330	306
Short-term debt	114	341	699
Long-term debt	1,291	865	682
Other long-term liabilities	305	319	335
Losses reserves and unearned premiums	102	119	112
Pension liabilities	439	418	272
Total liabilities	$3,289	$2,866	$2,980
Shareowners' Equity			
Preferred stock	245	245	245
Common stock and warrants	508	522	521
Retained earnings[2]	(400)	(158)	81
Accumulated foreign currency transition adjustments	(4)	—	(1)
Common stock held in treasury, at cost	(11)	(32)	(31)
Total shareowners' equity	$ 338	$ 577	$ 815
Total liabilities and shareowners equity	$3,627	$3,443	$3,795

[1]In the supplemental information, "Manufacturing" includes the reporting of finance subsidiaries under the equity method of accounting. Transactions between Manufacturing and Financial Services are eliminated from the "Consolidated" columns.
[2]Balances accumulated after the reclassification of the deficit as of October 31, 1987, of $1,968 million; this amount was moved from retained earnings to common stock and warrants. The reclassification did not change shareowners' equity as a whole and had no effect on the carrying value of the assets or liabilities of the company.
Source: Company annual reports.

Supplemental Information[1]

	Manufacturing			Financial Services	
1992	**1991**	**1990**	**1992**	**1991**	**1990**
$ 222	$ 252	$ 281	$ 113	$ 43	$ 25
28	70	147	143	150	166
131	42	103	1,348	1,283	1,532
365	332	343	—	—	—
121	122	104	1	1	1
563	586	622	19	18	6
240	237	279	—	—	—
168	104	81	35	45	44
370	404	379	—	—	—
$2,208	$2,149	$2,393	$1,659	$1,540	$1,774
581	398	493	56	83	87
368	296	274	33	36	34
15	9	12	99	332	718
172	145	152	1,119	720	530
295	306	321	10	13	14
—	—	—	102	119	112
439	418	272	—	—	—
$1,870	$1,572	$1,524	$1,419	$1,303	$1,495
245	245	245	—	—	—
508	522	521	178	190	193
(400)	(158)	81	62	48	84
(4)	—	(1)	—	(1)	2
(11)	(32)	(31)	—	—	—
$ 338	$ 577	$ 815	$ 240	$ 237	$ 279
$2,208	$2,149	$2,339	$1,659	$1,540	$1,774

EXHIBIT 10.3C   Cash Flow Statements for the Years Ended October 31 ($millions)

	Consolidated		
	1992	**1991**	**1990**
Cash Flow from Operating Activities			
Net income (loss)	($212)	($165)	($ 11)
Depreciation and amortization	77	73	67
Equity in earnings of Financial Services net of dividends received	—	—	—
Allowance for losses on receivables and dealer loans	24	27	23
Provision for loss of discontinued operations	65	—	—
Other, net	(49)	(16)	4
Change in operating assets and liabilities[2]	74	357	29
Cash provided by (used in) continuing operations	($ 21)	$276	$112
Cash Flow from Investing Activities			
Purchase of retail notes and lease receivables	(659)	(619)	(564)
Principal collections on retail notes and lease receivables	409	310	307
Sale of retail receivables	249	236	264
Acquisitions (over) under cash collections of wholesale notes and accounts receivable	—	—	—
Purchase of marketable securities	(248)	(867)	(518)
Sales or maturities of marketable securities	283	958	484
Capital expenditures	(55)	(77)	(182)
Special dividends from Financial Services	—	—	—
PBGC settlement—discontinued operations	(20)	—	—
Other investment programs, net	(30)	9	9
Cash provided by (used in) investing activities	($ 71)	($ 50)	($200)
Cash Flow from Financing Activities			
Principal payments on long-term debt	(170)	(102)	(13)
Net decrease in short-term debt	(184)	(413)	(270)
Issuance of term debt and notes	8	118	287
Proceeds from bank revolving credit facility	507	220	—
Dividends paid	(29)	(29)	(29)
Repurchase of common stock	—	—	(7)
Cash provided by (used in) financing activities	$132	($206)	($ 32)
Cash and cash equivalents			
Increase (decrease) during the year	40	20	(120)
At beginning of the year	295	275	395
At the end of the year	335	295	275

[1]In the supplemental information, "Manufacturing" includes the reporting of finance subsidiaries under the equity method of accounting. Transactions between Manufacturing and Financial Services are eliminated from the "Consolidated" columns.

Supplemental Information[1]

	Manufacturing			Financial Services		
	1992	**1991**	**1990**	**1992**	**1991**	**1990**
	($212)	($165)	($ 11)	$ 32	$ 37	$39
	74	71	66	3	2	1
	(15)	1	(4)	—	—	—
	19	21	19	5	6	4
	65	—	—	—	—	—
	(41)	(10)	9	(6)	(7)	(7)
	159	34	39	(17)	(3)	8
	$ 49	($ 48)	$118	$ 17	$ 35	$45
	—	—	—	(659)	(619)	(564)
	—	—	—	409	310	307
	—	—	—	249	236	264
	—	—	—	(66)	330	(13)
	(120)	(549)	(366)	(128)	(318)	(152)
	162	626	357	121	332	129
	(55)	(77)	(182)	—	—	—
	—	40	—	—	—	—
	(20)	—	—	—	—	—
	(14)	20	11	(17)	(11)	(3)
	($ 47)	$ 60	($180)	($ 91)	$260	($32)
	(11)	(12)	(13)	(159)	(90)	—
	—	—	—	(184)	(44)	(277)
	8	—	—	—	118	287
	—	—	—	507	220	—
	(29)	(29)	(29)	(20)	(81)	(37)
	—	—	(7)	—	—	—
	($ 32)	($ 41)	($ 49)	$144	($277)	($27)
	(30)	(29)	(111)	70	18	(14)
	252	281	392	43	25	39
	222	252	281	113	43	25

(Continued)

EXHIBIT 10.3C   *(Continued)*

²The following provides information related to the "Change in operating assets and liabilities" included in "Cash provided by (used in) continuing operations":

	1992	1991	1990
Manufacturing			
(Increase) decrease in receivables	($111)	$ 45	($ 2)
(Increase) decrease in inventories	(37)	13	(6)
(Increase) decrease in prepaid and other current assets	(9)	—	(1)
Increase (decrease) in accounts payable	190	(100)	11
Increase in accrued liabilities	126	76	37
Manufacturing change in operating assets and liabilities	$159	$ 34	$39
Financial Services			
(Increase) decrease in receivables	8	(3)	6
Increase (decrease) in accounts payable and accrued liabilities	(25)	—	2
Financial Services change in operating assets and liabilities	($ 17)	($ 3)	$ 8
Eliminations/reclassifications	(68)	326	(18)
Change in operating assets and liabilities	$ 74	$357	$29

"Acquisitions (over) under cash collections" relating to Navistar Financial's wholesale notes and accounts have been included on a consolidated basis as a change in operating assets and liabilities under cash flow from operations. This differs from the Financial Services classification in which net changes in wholesale notes and accounts are classified as cash flow from investment programs. In 1991, this amount included $300 million of proceeds from Navistar Financial's initial offering of pass-through certificates backed by certain wholesale notes receivable.

Source: Company annual reports.

EXHIBIT 10.4 Changes in Size of Workforce

Year	Number of Employees
1992	13,945
1991	13,472
1990	14,071
1989	14,118
1988	15,719
1987	14,918
1986	14,997
1985	16,836
1984	31,104
1983	32,445
1982	43,290
1981	65,640
1980	87,162
1979	97,660

Notes to Navistar's 10-K reports indicate the following:

1981: Sold turbine engine business, which employed 3,900.

1982: During 1982, the workforce "declined by 22,350, of which approximately 40% relates to declines in reduction volume and approximately 60% is the result of cost reductions and of some small divestures."

1983: Sold construction equipment business, which employed 1,200, to Dresser.

1985: Sold agricultural equipment business, which employed 12,500, to Tenneco. "Obligations [for] all employee benefit plans . . . will be assumed by Tenneco."

Source: Company 10-Ks.

EXHIBIT 10.5 Ratio of Retired to Active Employees

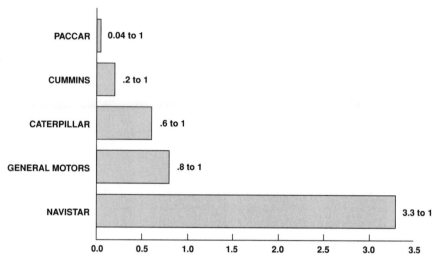

RATIO OF RETIRED TO ACTIVE EMPLOYEES

Source: Exhibit C, in "Defendant's Motion for a Stay of Litigation," entry date 9/14/92, U.S. District Court for the Southern District of Ohio (Dayton), case *Shy et al. v. Navistar International Corp. et al.*

EXHIBIT 10.6   Letter from Navistar to Retiree

Navistar International   401 North Michigan Avenue
Transportation Corp.   Chicago IL 90811
                             312-838-2000

6-15-89

Re: After Retirement Insurance Coverage

NAVISTAR

Dear *Mr. Shy* :

We are pleased to advise you that effective *7-1-89* you and your spouse are insured for lifetime medical coverage in conjunction with your retirement from the Company.

In order for our department to maintain the records of your coverage, we must have the enclosed enrollment form completed where checked and returned to our office in the enclosed envelope as soon as possible.

Your medical coverage is in accordance with the benefits described in the enclosed booklet. If you need any claim forms you should write to AEtna Life & Casualty Company, P.O. Box 5367, Rockford, IL 61125 or call toll free 1-800-435-2969.

Enclosed is a statement of After-Retirement Life Insurance provided for you by Navistar International Transportation Corp. under Group Policy 52000 issued by the AEtna Life & Casualty Company. This form provides information concerning your After-Retirement life insurance coverage including Accidental Death and Dismemberment Benefits and Supplemental Survivor Benefits where applicable. This statement should be retained as your evidence of continued coverage as indicated.

Any questions concerning your benefits may be directed to the writer.

Sincerely,

Frantz R. Cook
Employee Insurance Plans Analyst

Enclosures

gs

INTERNATIONAL

Source: Exhibit A, in "Complaint for Class Action," entry date 8/21/92, U.S. District Court for the Southern District of Ohio (Dayton), case *Shy et al. v. Navistar International Corp. et al.*

EXHIBIT 10.7 Comparative Data ($millions)

Date	Unfunded OPEB	Net Worth	Sales	EBIT	EBIT as Percent of Sales	Pension Expense	OPEB Expense	Pension Expense as Percent of Sales	OPEB Expense as Percent of Sales
Navistar									
Oct. 87			$ 3,530	$ 128	3.6%	$ 56	$100	1.6%	2.8%
Oct. 88			4,080	201	4.9%	84	108	2.1%	2.6%
Oct. 89			4,023	42	1.0%	70	115	1.7%	2.9%
Oct. 90			3,643	(62)	-1.7%	80	123	2.2%	3.4%
Oct. 91			3,259	(211)	-6.5%	101	138	3.1%	4.2%
Oct. 92	$2,600	$ 338	3,685	(185)	-5.0%	109	146	3.0%	4.0%
Average through 1991					0.5%			2.1%	3.2%
Paccar[1]									
Dec. 87			2,427	163	6.7%	4	0	0.2%	0.0%
Dec. 88			3,122	244	7.8%	6	0	0.2%	0.0%
Dec. 89			3,341	254	7.6%	10	0	0.3%	0.0%
Dec. 90			2,601	94	3.6%	11	0	0.4%	0.0%
Dec. 91			2,195	39	1.8%	8	0	0.4%	0.0%
3rd qtr. 92	15	1,044	1,862	39	2.1%	NA	NA	NA	
Average through 1991					5.8%			0.3%	0.0%
Caterpillar[2]									
Dec. 87			8,180	651	8.0%	16	54	0.2%	0.7%
Dec. 88			10,255	1,091	10.6%	6	63	0.1%	0.6%
Dec. 89			10,882	785	7.2%	56	75	0.5%	0.7%
Dec. 90			11,103	477	4.3%	68	86	0.6%	0.8%
Dec. 91			9,838	(65)	-0.7%	43	101	0.4%	1.0%
3rd qtr. 92	3,750	3,868	7,196	(4)	-0.1%	NA	NA	NA	NA
Average through 1991					5.8%			0.4%	0.8%

Cummings[3]							
Dec. 87	2,767	86	3.1%	(5)	9	-0.2%	0.3%
Dec. 88	3,310	54	1.6%	(1)	11	0.0%	0.3%
Dec. 89	3,520	72	2.1%	4	11	0.1%	0.3%
Dec. 90	3,462	(35)	-1.0%	0	14	0.0%	0.4%
Dec. 91	3,406	(3)	-0.1%	3	16	0.1%	0.5%
3rd qtr 92	2,733	93	3.4%	NA	NA	NA	NA
Average through 1991	388	774	1.1%			0.0%	0.4%
General Motors[4]							
Dec. 87	101,781	3,636	3.6%	715	983	0.7%	1.0%
Dec. 88	110,288	6,438	5.8%	544	1,131	0.5%	1.0%
Dec. 89	112,533	7,117	6.3%	811	1,067	0.7%	0.9%
Dec. 90	110,797	1,718	1.6%	369	1,199	0.3%	1.1%
Dec. 91	109,156	(1,620)	-1.5%	1,520	1,356	1.4%	1.2%
3rd qtr 92	86,673	829	1.0%	NA	NA	NA	NA
Average through 1991	34,688	31,444	3.2%			0.7%	1.1%

Notes:

- OPEB stands for "other post-employment benefits," that is, retiree benefits other than pension benefits; these include mainly life insurance and health coverage.
- In general, sales and EBIT numbers are as reported in 10-Ks, excluding finance subsidiaries. All EBIT figures exclude restructuring charges and equity earnings, and include other or interest income where disclosed. Unfunded OPEB figures are estimated pretax figures.

[1] Paccar is a truck manufacturer. 1990 EBIT excludes $7.6 million restructuring charge.

[2] Caterpillar is a construction equipment manufacturer. 1991 EBIT excludes $262 million provision for plant closings.

[3] Cummings is a diesel engine manufacturer. 1988 and 1990 EBIT figures exclude $50 million and $62.9 million in unusual charges.

[4] General Motors is a diversified vehicle manufacturer. 1990 and 1991 EBIT figures exclude restructuring charges of $3.3 billion and $2.8 billion, respectively.

Source: Exhibit A in affidavit of Robert E. Kiss, in "Joint Motion," entry date 4/5/93, U.S. District Court for the Southern District of Ohio (Dayton), case *Shy et al. v. Navistar International Corp. et al.*, modified by casewriter.

EXHIBIT 10.8   Short-Term and Long-Term Debt, October 31, 1991, and 1992 ($millions)

	1992	1991
Short-Term Debt		
Manufacturing		
Notes payable and current maturities of long-term debt	$ 15	9
Financial Services		
Commercial paper	—	144
Bank borrowings	—	40
Current maturities of long-term debt	99	148
Subtotal	$ 99	$332
Total short-term debt	$ 114	$341
Long-Term Debt		
Manufacturing		
$8^5/_8\%$ sinking fund debentures, due 1995	15	22
$6^1/_2\%$ sinking fund debentures, due 1998	14	14
9% sinking fund debentures, due 2004	83	84
8% secured note, due 2002	37	—
Capitalized leases	19	21
Other	4	4
Subtotal	$ 172	$145
Financial Services		
Senior debentures and notes		
$7^5/_8\%$, due 1993	—	60
$7^1/_2\%$, due 1994	75	75
9.07% to 9.9% medium-term due 1993–1996	222	272
Bank revolver, variable rate, due Dec. 1994	727	220
Subordinated debentures, 11.95%, due Dec. 1995	100	100
Unamortized discount	(5)	(7)
Subtotal	$1,119	$720
Total long-term debt	$1,291	$865

Notes:

- Manufacturing's 8% secured note, due 2002, is secured by certain plant assets.
- At October 31, 1992, Navistar Financial had $1,327 million of committed credit facilities, including a $727 million bank revolving credit facility, scheduled to expire in December 1994, and a $600 million retail notes receivable purchase facility available until August 23, 1993. Unused commitments under these facilities were $497 million which, when combined with unrestricted cash and cash equivalents, made $568 million available to fund the general business purposes of Navistar Financial.
- Navistar Financial's $727 million bank revolving credit facility included various covenants, such as the following: (1) Navistar Financial shall maintain debt ratings from Moody's and Standard & Poor's at or above Baa3 from Moody's and BBB– from Standard & Poor's; if it does not, its dividends to the parent company cannot exceed 50% of its net income. (2) The tangible net worth of Navistar Financial shall not at any time be less than the higher of $150 million or a percentage of assets that involves a complicated calculation, but that, at the end of FY 1992, amounted to about $180–$190 million.

Source: Company 10-Ks and annual reports.

EXHIBIT 10.9 Projections ($millions)[1]

	1993	1994	1995	1996
Income Statement				
Sales				
Medium trucks	$1,566	$1,686	$2,042	$2,071
Heavy trucks	1,759	1,597	1,481	1,551
Engines	477	529	546	574
Replacement parts	625	663	663	683
Total sales	$4,427	$4,475	$4,732	$4,879
Gross profit	571	636	656	741
Postretirement benefits	265	278	290	302
Marketing and administrative expense	229	216	222	226
Engineering expense	94	99	100	103
Receivables loss provision	10	10	12	10
Operating income	(27)	33	32	100
Interest expense	12	12	8	7
Other expense (income)	37	37	34	32
Pretax income	(76)	(16)	(10)	61
Pretax finance sub income	59	52	67	70
Provision for taxes	(6)	14	22	50
After-tax income	(11)	22	35	81
Cash Flow Statement				
Operating activities				
After-tax income	(11)	22	35	81
Depreciation and amortization	72	95	100	105
Deferred income taxes	0	14	22	50
Finance subsidiary income in excess of dividends	(18)	(16)	(20)	(21)
Accounts receivable	20	(11)	(6)	(26)
Inventories	(45)	39	(4)	13
Accounts payable and accruals	13	(10)	55	(11)
Other	10	10	12	10
Net cash provided	41	143	194	201
Investing activities				
Capital expenditures	(120)	(120)	(120)	(120)
Net cash provided	(120)	(120)	(120)	(120)
Financing activities				
Preferred dividends	0	(58)	(29)	(29)
Net cash provided	0	(58)	(29)	(29)
Net change in cash	(79)	(35)	45	52

[1]Above statements are for the Manufacturing operations, with results for the Finance subsidiary presented in one-line consolidations or as special items. Figures in income statement for "Postretirement benefits" are presented, for comparative purposes, as they would be prior to FAS 106; that is, health care expenses are recorded on a cash basis.

(Continued)

EXHIBIT 10.9   *(Continued)*

Annual maturities and sinking fund requirements for long-term debt are as follows:

Year	Manufacturing	Finance Subsidiary	Total
1994	21	80	101
1995	23	826	849
1996	18	218	236
1997	17		17
Thereafter	93		93

As of 10/31/92 Navistar has the following NOL carryforwards to reduce future taxable income:

Year of Expiration	NOLs
1994–1995	1
1997–1998	712
1999–2000	335
2001–2002	190
2004–2005	238
2006	128
2007	26
	1,630

Sources: Duff & Phelps company analysis, modified by casewriter; company annual reports.

CHAPTER 11

Scott Paper Company

Scott should be making money for its shareholders. It's a sin to lose money, a mortal sin.

—Albert J. Dunlap

On a sunny day in late June 1994, Albert Dunlap, chairman and chief executive officer (CEO) of Scott Paper Company, looked out his office window at the surrounding expanse of Scott's Philadelphia headquarters complex. The size of the complex offered an ironic reminder of the challenge that he now faced. Dunlap was a corporate turnaround specialist, and less than two months ago he had been brought in by Scott's board of directors to orchestrate a turnaround of the troubled 115-year-old company.

Scott Paper was the largest producer of consumer tissue products in the world, and employed over 30,000 people. However, it had, for the past four years, performed poorly. For 1993, Scott had reported a net loss of $277 million for its consolidated operations (including restructuring charges). For 1988, in contrast, it had reported a near-record profit of $401 million. Over this same four-year period, Scott's share price had remained virtually unchanged, while U.S. forest-products companies and the S&P 500 had each gained approximately 10 percent in value. And in January 1994, Standard & Poor's had downgraded Scott's public bonds. Although Scott's debt was still rated investment grade quality, Dunlap believed the company could lose this distinction if measures were not quickly taken to address Scott's problems.

This case was prepared by Research Associate Jeremy Cott and Professor Stuart Gilson. Copyright © 1996 by the President and Fellows of Harvard College. Harvard Business School case 296-048.

Previous management had been unable to stop the company's slide, despite having attempted several restructurings involving employee layoffs and asset sales. Over 1990 to 1993, Scott's official head count fell from 30,800 to 25,900. Special restructuring charges of $167 million and $249 million had been taken in 1990 and 1991, respectively. In early 1994, prior to Dunlap's arrival, an additional restructuring charge of $490 million was announced, and Scott's head count was reduced by an additional 3,000. Further layoffs and asset sales were planned; however, Scott's stock price stubbornly remained at around $38 a share.

COMPANY AND INDUSTRY BACKGROUND

The Scott Paper Company was founded by brothers Irvin and Clarence Scott in Philadelphia, in 1879. Initially it produced coarse paper products, like bags and wrapping paper. With the introduction of domestic bathroom plumbing in the late nineteenth century came a market for toilet tissue, which Scott produced and sold through hundreds of private labels. Victorian mores, however, prevented the company from launching any significant advertising campaign. Only later did the company develop its own brand-name products. During the Depression of the 1930s, in fact, Scott was the largest advertiser in its industry, and its sales remained as high as ever. Starting in the late 1920s the company became vertically integrated, acquiring timberlands and pulp mills. Eventually it was to operate some of its own energy facilities as well, to power its mills.

In time the company developed a whole range of tissue products (e.g., toilet paper, facial tissue, paper towels, baby wipes, table napkins), and some of its products became well-known brand names (e.g., ScotTissue, ScotTowels, Cottonelle, Waldorf, Viva, Baby Fresh).

In the 1960s the company began to diversify outside its core business of consumer tissue products. Its largest diversification move was its acquisition, in 1967, of S.D. Warren, an old company involved primarily in the manufacture of coated printing papers. S.D. Warren's paper products were known for their fine quality, and were used, for example, in magazines, textbooks, catalogs, and corporate annual reports.[1]

---

[1]Printing papers represented about 80 percent of Warren's sales; the remainder involved sales of various kinds of specialty papers such as pressure-sensitive base materials sold to electronic data processing (EDP) label manufacturers.

The Paper Industry

In 1993 the paper industry in the United States was a $131-billion-a-year industry with several distinct segments (see Exhibit 11.1). Printing papers include both uncoated papers used for office and copier supplies, envelopes, and forms, and coated papers used for such things as glossy magazines, textbooks, and corporate annual reports. Newsprint is the thin paper used for newspapers. Tissue paper represents a variety of consumer and commercial products like bathroom and facial tissue, paper towels, and napkins. Packaging paper includes things like the heavy brown paper used for grocery bags and the linerboard for corrugated boxes. Paperboard—which is somewhat distinct from the other paper segments—is used for things like folding cartons, milk cartons, and disposable cups and plates.

Most paper products are commodity products that allow for little product differentiation. Most of the industry, too, is extremely capital intensive (particularly the commodity-oriented parts of it). A new machine at Champion International, for example, was one of the largest industrial machines in existence at the time. It took two years to build, cost about $400 million, and was higher than a five-story building and a third longer than a football field. Much of the paper industry, however, is cyclical, and—given its generally capital-intensive character—tends to do very well when the economy is healthy but very badly when the economy is in a recession.

Scott's business was roughly three-quarters in the tissue segment of the industry and one-quarter in the coated printing papers segment. Exhibit 11.2 shows segment data for Scott for 1991–1993, and Exhibit 11.3 gives an eleven-year summary of financial and operating data for the company. Scott owned more than two dozen manufacturing facilities in the Americas (of which five produced coated printing paper products) and approximately two dozen additional facilities in Europe and the Pacific region.

Scott was the eighth largest paper company in the United States. (International Paper Company was the largest.) In the tissue segment of the industry, however, Scott was the second largest U.S. producer, after Procter & Gamble; and in the total world market for tissue, it was the largest, with an approximately 15 percent market share. Moreover, countries' consumption of tissue products tended to vary in direct relation to per capita wealth. So, although North America and Western Europe together accounted for about 70 percent of world tissue consumption, markets in other parts of the world offered greater possibilities for growth in the years ahead. (Scott in fact had full or partial ownership of tissue operations in twenty-one countries around the world.)

Scott's S.D. Warren subsidiary, which accounted for about one-quarter of the company's sales, was the largest producer of coated printing papers in the country. (Champion International and Consolidated Papers were the next largest.) Printing papers are a commodity-type, cyclical business. For example, the demand for coated magazine papers depends on the fortunes of the magazine business, which is largely dependent for its revenues on space advertising. But in the economic recession of the early 1990s, ad revenues fell significantly, and therefore the demand for and prices for coated papers declined as well.

Analysts in the investment community generally evaluated Scott Paper in the context of the paper and forest products industry along with companies like International Paper, Champion International, Georgia-Pacific Corporation, and Consolidated Papers. Exhibit 11.4 shows financial and operating data for a number of comparable paper companies for 1992–1993.

Corporate Culture at Scott

Management in the paper industry tended to consist of insiders. In key positions like chairman, CEO, or board director, a half-dozen firms were still connected by blood to their founders, going back in some cases over a hundred years.

Scott Paper was one of the oldest and most famous paper companies. Since the company's founding, corporate headquarters had been located in Philadelphia, and the grounds, on the outskirts of the city, were extensive, with walking paths, fountains, and ponds stocked with geese. The company was, as *The Wall Street Journal* said, "known for attracting and retaining loyal employees." About 1,500 people worked at the Philadelphia headquarters. Secretarial support staff was generous. There was a sense of a proud tradition in the company, which was nationally and internationally well known.

The management style followed at Scott had traditionally been a consensus style. Many people tended to be involved in decisions—through meetings and the distribution of reports—before decisions were made. There were a lot of controls in the operation.

RECENT HISTORY

In 1979 the company hired a former R.J. Reynolds executive as president, chief operating officer, and heir apparent to the CEO position. He left a year and a half later, however. Observers believed at the time that he had failed to penetrate Scott's corporate culture. A new CEO was appointed in

1982 named Philip Lippincott, who had been with the company since the late 1950s.

Lippincott greatly expanded Scott's tissue business overseas. He also sold off a number of ancillary businesses like casual furniture and lighting and foam liners for carpets. In 1989 and 1990 the company made huge capital investments (totaling $700 million) in S.D. Warren, which, in the long run, was necessarily a more capital-intensive business than Scott's tissue business. The timing, however, was not good, as the economy fell into a recession in 1990, competing companies also expanded their capacity, and commodity-paper prices fell. Loyal S.D. Warren customers, however, generally appreciated the service they got. "We [know] they wouldn't let us run out of paper," said the head of manufacturing at Condé Nast, one of the country's premier magazine publishers. The manager of direct marketing at Saks Fifth Avenue, which bought a lot of paper from S.D. Warren for its catalogs, said, "Often they delivered paper earlier than I needed it because they were running out of warehouse space."

In 1988 Scott reported record consolidated after-tax net income of $401 million (including Scott's share of earnings in its international equity affiliates). Since then, however, its financial situation had steadily deteriorated. In 1990, net income had declined to $148 million, and in 1991 Scott reported a $70 million loss (see Exhibit 11.3). Lippincott acknowledged that the company had made certain mistakes. In early 1991 he said, "I guess we overestimated our people's capabilities and took on too many projects at once."

The company recorded substantial restructuring charges in 1990 and 1991 for $167 million and $249 million, respectively. These charges were meant to cover the cost of workforce reductions and the sale of a number of assets that the company considered "nonstrategic." From 1990 to the end of 1993, the company's official head count declined from 30,800 to 25,900.[2] Two of the assets earmarked for sale were sold (a food-service container business and a bulk nonwovens business), but in 1993 the specialty papers business that was part of S.D. Warren's operation was taken off the market.

Throughout 1993, however, no evidence of a turnaround was forthcoming. In November, Philip Lippincott announced that he would be re-

---

[2]The company's official head count did not equal the number of people employed in all of the company's operations. At the end of 1993 the company's consolidated operations employed approximately 25,900 people, but its unconsolidated affiliates in Canada and Mexico employed an additional 6,600 people. Those affiliates were unconsolidated because Scott's ownership interest in them was only 50 percent.

signing as chairman and CEO. He would leave the company by the following April, assuming a replacement had been found. Full-year results for 1993 showed an operating loss of $154 million, compared with a profit of $414 million the year before, and net income of negative $277 million compared with $167 million the year before. Exhibit 11.5 presents detailed income statements, balance sheets, and cash flow statements for Scott Paper for 1991 to 1993.

On January 26, 1994, the company announced yet another substantial restructuring charge, this time for $490 million. This was to cover the cost of further workforce reductions and plant shutdowns. The company's worldwide workforce was to be cut by 25 percent, or 8,300 people.[3] (3,800 would be cut in the United States). Two of S.D. Warren's four specialty paper machines would be shut down, and a few of the older, inefficient tissue facilities in the United States and Europe would be closed.

The company also indicated that it planned to increase workforce productivity by 5 percent annually. This effort would be closely based on a new financial measurement system recently adopted by the company called Economic Value Added (EVA). Under this system, the profitability of a business or project was evaluated based on the returns it generated *in excess of* the opportunity cost of the capital used to generated these returns. Recently an increasing number of prominent U.S. companies had adopted the EVA approach to measuring performance.

This restructuring plan was to be implemented over a three-year period.

The steady downturn in Scott's financial performance, together with the company's increasing reliance on borrowed funds, was not well received by the bond ratings agencies. On January 27, 1994, one day after the latest restructuring plan was announced, Standard & Poor's lowered its rating on Scott's senior debt from BBB+ to BBB. Exhibit 11.6 shows Scott's long-term debt outstanding at the end of 1993.

ARRIVAL OF ALBERT DUNLAP

On April 19 the board of directors announced the appointment of Albert Dunlap as chairman and CEO. Upon assuming his duties, Dunlap immedi-

---

[3]The announced head count reduction of 8,300 referred to all of Scott's operations, both consolidated and unconsolidated. Of the 8,300 people to be let go, 1,900 were employed by the company's unconsolidated Mexican affiliate, in which Scott held a 50 percent equity interest. The cost of the workforce reductions was estimated at roughly two-thirds of the total restructuring charge.

ately bought $2 million of the company's stock, with his own money, on the open market. (Later, in June, he purchased an additional $2 million of Scott stock, bringing his total personal investment in the company to $4 million.) Exhibit 11.7 gives a summary of Dunlap's employment agreement with Scott.

On the day the company announced its restructuring plan, January 26, the price of the company's stock increased 5 percent, from $43.375 to $45.50. By April 18, however, the day before the announcement of Dunlap's appointment, the price had fallen back to $37.75. (Exhibit 11.8 compares the performance of Scott's common stock with the S&P 500 from January 25 to April 18, 1994.)

Dunlap was known as a turnaround specialist. He was the first chief executive hired from outside Scott in its 115-year history.

"A perpetual-motion machine with a bulldozer voice and a caustic wit," as one reporter described him, Dunlap had already lived in seventeen states in the United States and on three continents. A graduate of West Point, where he earned a degree in engineering, Dunlap began his business career in 1963 in the manufacturing operation at Kimberly-Clark Corporation, one of the largest and oldest tissue companies in the country (responsible, for example, for Kleenex facial tissue). In the years following, he occupied managerial positions at numerous companies, most of them in the paper goods industry, but some in other fields as well. As chairman and CEO of Lily-Tulip, the paper-cup maker, in the mid-1980s, he slashed costs, cut debt, and saw the company's stock double when it went public. (While at Lily-Tulip, Dunlap was also instrumental in developing the co-extruded trophy cup.)

Following his tenure at Lily-Tulip, Dunlap was chosen by English billionaire investor Sir James Goldsmith to serve as chairman and CEO of Goldsmith's global holdings, and Dunlap was credited with turning around Diamond International and Crown Zellerbach Corporation. His most recent position had been as CEO of one of Australia's largest corporations, Consolidated Press Holdings, which was involved in television, magazine publishing, and chemical and agricultural operations. In two years Dunlap sold off about a hundred divisions and eliminated most of the corporation's debt.

He was a complicated person. He was resented by some employee groups for what they regarded as his slash-and-burn tactics, but Dunlap said that he sympathized with the pain of workers who sometimes lost their jobs as a result of his restructuring actions. "I come from a working-class family," he would point out, "and lots of times my father [who was a shop steward at the Hoboken, New Jersey, shipyards] was out of work due to no fault of his own." When Dunlap arrived in Australia to turn around Consolidated Press Holdings, he insisted on visiting the company's plants, even though his corporate host thought that was a waste of time. According to one person who had worked with Dunlap in a few business settings, Dunlap believed that corporate headquarters are worthless, that "the money is made by the guy in the plant."

Publicly, he often argued that the importance given to various stakeholders in a corporation was misguided. A corporation, he would say, was not a social experience. Everything should be done to maximize shareholders' interests. Dunlap's employee agreement with Scott, in fact, included a very large stock-based incentive package (see Exhibit 11.7).

Management-Labor Relations

Historically the paper industry had had a lot of labor-management problems. The United Paperworkers Union represented about 250,000 workers in the United States and Canada; about 5 percent of them worked for Scott. Up until the late 1980s, Scott Paper had possibly the most adversarial relations with unions in the industry. It had repeatedly been the object of strikes. In 1989, however, a new director of employee relations, John Nee, helped set up a joint advisory committee that included senior-level people from both management and the union. The purpose of the "jointness" effort, as it was called, was to work out a more cooperative relationship between the two sides. Production workers in the mills were involved more in decision making and given more responsibility, and fewer supervisors were therefore needed. Workers generally responded well to this. Absenteeism, insurance premiums, and the filing of grievances decreased. And management began sharing more information with workers, including financial information.

The paper industry, contrary to popular perception, was one of the higher-paying manufacturing sectors in the United States. At Scott's unionized mills, employees earned over $15 an hour in straight time, and average earnings were over $40,000 a year.

Dunlap had to consider labor-management relations very carefully. When the company announced the large restructuring charge earlier in the year, it acknowledged that it continued to have "high labor density at numerous sites, and several of its production facilities have relatively complex process flows and older equipment." The downward price pressures in the industry in recent years made the company's overall cost structure increasingly important. Dunlap hired a consulting firm with which he had worked before to help him evaluate this. Some of their suggestions were drastic.

Consulting firms often target the number of employee layoffs necessary in a company based on certain comparative ratios—for example, how a given company's sales-to-employee ratio compare with others in the same industry. Scott's consultants argued that simply laying off people would not be adequate. In the mills, they suggested, fundamental redesign of much of the work was needed. They carried out extremely concrete analyses. They did some time-and-motion kinds of studies, and examined work flows and factory organization. They noted that there continued to be a lot of "jurisdictional barriers" on the factory floor. For example, the people who did maintenance on machines were different from the people who actually operated them. If a paper machine broke down and no one was on shift who was authorized to make the repairs, it would be necessary to call someone in and pay him or her overtime—even if some other employee currently on shift could do the job. A good deal of idle time resulted, but to some extent that was part of the shop floor culture.

The amount of salaried administrative support (measured in terms of hours per ton of paper product) was, in several of Scott's plants, 15 percent or more of total labor input and was twice the amount of administrative support utilized in the mills of benchmark and median competitors. The consultants also found that maintenance costs in Scott's European plants were 40 to 50 percent lower than they were in the United States. They argued that the company's U.S. mills could get the same amount of work done with 20 percent fewer people. This would involve laying off about 2,400 people.

What the Company Should Be Doing

Dunlap, however, wanted all aspects of the company's operation to be examined. What should the company be doing and what should it not be doing? The argument was made that many functions should be outsourced—benefits and payroll administration, almost all of management information systems (MIS), some of technology research, medical services, some of telemarketing, all of the security guards, and more. Many of these functions had long been carried on at headquarters. The estimate, however, was that by outsourcing these functions their quantifiable cost could be reduced from $35 million to about $20 million annually. About 450 Scott employees would be affected (see Exhibit 11.9).

Various people, in both headquarters and the plants, were interviewed about what they did. For example, the consultants would ask the investor relations manager what he did, and then they would ask the chief financial officer (CFO, to whom the investor relations manager reported) what the chief financial officer wanted from investor relations, and there was often a mismatch. The chief financial officer, for example, really wanted less than what the department reporting to him was doing. This represented another opportunity for cost cutting.

Of the approximately 1,500 employees at headquarters, it was argued that outsourcing and streamlining could reduce that number to about 450, and an additional 240 should be located off-site. That would leave about 210 in headquarters—but, of that number, about 80 would really be involved in activities related to specific business units.

All sorts of other controllable expenses were examined. Literally dozens of very concrete expense items were looked at. It was argued that annual savings on individual expense items ranging from as much as $17 million (for travel and entertainment) to as little as $340,000 (for promotional printing) could probably be achieved. (For example, a comment attached to the recommendation to reduce travel and entertainment expense noted: "Video conf. has 25% utilization rate." The projected annual savings on promotional printing carried the descriptor line: "Eliminate 11% of expenses through consolidation of print shops.") Some expense savings, it was believed, would derive from others. For example, $3 million in office, computer, and other supplies could be saved annually through the reduction of salaried and hourly workers. It was argued that the prices of various services provided by outside firms should be "renegotiated." The pension plan, it was suggested, should be switched from a traditional defined-benefit plan to a defined-contribution plan, which would, at the very least, reduce an administrative expense. Dues and membership fees should be reduced from $2.8 million to $1 million. "Expats" should be reduced from forty-five to about twenty-two.[4] Total controllable expenses of this sort, it was argued, could be reduced from $206 million annually to $114 million (see Exhibit 11.10).

All such analysis, however, was complicated. Many managers at other companies that had downsized targeted reductions in selling, general, and administrative expense based simply on a comparison of this expense as a percent of sales with competing companies.

The consultants also identified $165 million in additional annual sav-

---

[4]"Expats" were American expatriates in managerial positions who worked and lived abroad and were customarily paid American-level wages. In their place the company could hire local people who could be paid less and who would know the local markets better. This, however, would counter the customary multinational corporate practice of moving managers around to give them international experience.

ings in operating costs that could be realized through better process management, work redesign, and the breaking down of jurisdictional barriers within Scott.[5]

Scott's operations had, for years, been integrated backwards to a considerable extent. Under Dunlap's direction, this strategy was also critically scrutinized.

In North America, Scott owned approximately 2.5 million acres of timberlands, and had long-term cutting rights (or lease or purchase rights) on approximately 350,000 additional acres. The annual harvest from these timberlands supplied about 30 percent of the raw material needed for Scott's pulp-manufacturing operations. In turn, Scott's pulp-manufacturing operations produced about 85 percent of the pulp needed in its papermaking operations. The rest was purchased at market prices from numerous suppliers under long-term contracts. (In other countries, the figure was about 50 percent.)

In addition, the company's North American pulp-manufacturing and papermaking operations generated about 75 percent of their energy requirements by burning various waste materials. A few facilities had distinct energy complexes that generated electricity not only for the company's own use but also for sale to electric utilities.

In 1994, with the improvement in the economy, market prices for pulp had been increasing. Exhibit 11.11 shows representative pulp prices for the prior seventeen years, as well as yearly estimates of how Scott's profitability had been affected by the integration of pulp manufacturing in its operations.

Potential Labor Savings

The possible labor savings were estimated, based on the average cost of wages and benefits among different categories of employees. The layoffs envisioned were as follows: in the United States, about 3,000 salaried employees costing about $65,000 annually, and about 2,200 hourly employees costing $55,000 annually; in Canada, about 400 employees costing $45,000 annually; in Europe, about 2,400 employees costing $16,000 annually; in the Pacific region, about 700 employees costing $9,000 annually;

---

[5]These estimated cost savings reflect improvements in the following specific areas: asset dedication and rationalization ($41 million), maintenance effectiveness ($24 million), administrative support ($7 million), customer support and material flow effectiveness ($18 million), system material flow and work redesign ($63 million), inventory carrying costs ($5 million), and effective use of fiber ($7 million).

and in Mexico, about 2,500 employees costing $8,000 annually. Exhibit 11.12 presents a breakdown of potential labor force reductions at Scott.

In place of the 450 or so people whose jobs would be outsourced, however, the company would be paying about $20 million annually to outside firms to do that work. Also, only half of the total projected savings in Canada and Mexico would be realized by Scott, since Scott held only a 50 percent equity interest in those operations. The possible savings in the S.D. Warren operation itself (included in the above figures) would be about $80 million annually.

And what would all the employee layoffs cost the company? The terms of the union contracts capped involuntary severance payments at six weeks of pay.

DECISIONS TO MAKE

Dunlap believed that to successfully implement any corporate restructuring program, it was necessary to achieve certain key goals.

One goal was to choose the right management team. Dunlap had, in his view, largely met this goal soon after arriving by firing several of the highest-ranking executives in the company and hiring three executives—Russ Kersh in finance and administration, John Murtagh as general counsel, and Jack Dailey in purchasing and logistics—with whom he had worked before. Dunlap's management team also included the two most senior executives to remain at Scott—Basil Anderson, who continued as treasurer and chief financial officer, and Newt White, who continued as head of Scott's Worldwide Away-from-Home Products business. As Dunlap put it, "You must get rid of the people who represent the old culture, or they will fight you. And you have to get rid of all the old symbols."

Another goal was to achieve a low cost structure and a strong balance sheet. Since arriving at Scott, Dunlap's team had extensively analyzed the company's operations from the ground up, and had investigated every aspect of the business that might yield real improvements in operating efficiencies. Dunlap knew that he also had to act decisively in addressing the company's mounting debt burden. He was afraid that Scott was in jeopardy of losing its investment grade rating on its bonds. Further downgrading of Scott's credit rating would hurt the shareholders by raising the company's borrowing costs and reducing its financial flexibility.

Another goal was to decide on a clear, focused strategy for the company. One challenge that Dunlap faced was to build on Scott Paper's core competencies and make sure the restructuring produced long-term benefits. Scott essentially operated two paper products businesses: consumer tissue products and coated printing papers. The coated printing papers business (at S.D. Warren) was expected to be entering the up part of its industry cycle, and it represented a significant part of the company's revenues. At the end of 1993, the book equity value of S.D. Warren was approximately $1.6 billion. Exhibit 11.13 presents stand-alone financial projections for S.D. Warren, and Exhibit 11.14 presents historical and projected prices for some of S.D. Warren's coated paper products. In Scott's tissue business, downward pressure on prices due to intense competition was expected to continue, but Scott's product lines included a number of products that had high brand value in the marketplace.

A final goal was to execute the restructuring plan decisively, and follow through on the plan once it was announced. Dunlap expected to publicly announce the specific terms of his restructuring plan by the end of summer or early fall.

Dunlap believed strongly that the interests of key executives and directors of a company should be consistent with the interests of shareholders, and for that reason he wanted to make a greater amount of the compensation to key executives and directors dependent on the value of the company's stock. When Dunlap arrived at Scott, officers and directors held under 2 percent of the company's common stock on a fully diluted basis (including stock options). Directors were paid an annual retainer of $20,000, and in addition they were paid for serving on committees, chairing committees, and even taking part in telephonic meetings. Dunlap, of course, had invested $4 million of his own money in Scott Paper stock since joining the company in April. Exhibit 15 gives a summary of the stock-based compensation that Dunlap wanted to institute at Scott.

The final restructuring plan would provide answers to a number of difficult questions that Dunlap had had to grapple with in seeking a solution to Scott's problems: Which, if any, of Scott's assets should be sold, and which should be retained (or grown)? How many of Scott's employees should be laid off, and where? What timetable should be set for implementing the restructuring? How should the restructuring be presented to shareholders, analysts, the media, and employees? And how would the various planned cost savings and operating changes affect Scott's share price?

EXHIBIT 11.1 Financial Results and Segments of the Paper Industry

	1993	1992	1991	1990	1989
Financial Results					
Sales ($billions)	131	127	123	116	114
Net income to sales (%)	(0.15%)	0.94%	1.76%	4.23%	6.20%
Return on stockholders' equity (%)	(0.45%)	2.52%	4.45%	10.62%	15.44%
Paper Industry Segments: Production (in Thousands of Tons)					
Printing papers	23,891	23,394	22,064	22,371	
Newsprint	7,068	7,082	6,841	6,610	
Tissue paper	6,008	5,784	5,669	5,802	
Packaging and other papers	4,608	4,713	4,509	4,576	
Total paper	41,575	40,973	39,083	39,359	
Paperboard	43,213	41,968	40,416	39,423	
Total paper and paperboard	84,788	82,941	79,499	78,782	

Source: Standard & Poor's "Industry Surveys."

EXHIBIT 11.2   Business Segment Information, 1991–1993 ($millions)

1993	Sales	EBIT	Identifiable Assets[a]	Capital Expenditures	Depreciation and Cost of Timber Harvested
Personal care and cleaning	$3,584.9	$ (48.4)[b]	$3,760.7	$371.3	$174.7
Printing and publishing papers	1,164.0	(29.6)[c]	1,851.8	75.1	102.6
Total business segment	4,748.9	(78.0)	5,612.5	446.4	277.3
Corporate restructuring	—	(25.4)	—	—	—
Corporate	—	(50.2)	1,012.6	11.4	3.8
Interest expense	—	182.0	—	—	—
Other income and (expense)	—	4.2	—	—	—
Consolidated total	$4,748.9	$(331.4)	$6,625.1	$457.8	$281.1

[a]Includes investments in and advances to other equity affiliates of: Personal care and cleaning: $57.3; Corporate: $26.8.
[b]Includes $353.6 million in restructuring charges.
[c]Includes $110.3 million in restructuring charges.

1992	Sales	EBIT	Identifiable Assets[a]	Capital Expenditures	Depreciation and Cost of Timber Harvested
Personal care and cleaning	$3,856.0	$374.7	$3,780.5	$269.2	$172.4
Printing and publishing papers	1,235.3	90.8[b]	1,842.2	56.5	172.4
Total business segment	5,091.3	465.5	5,622.7	325.7	260.4
Corporate	—	(51.3)	676.9	4.0	5.4
Interest expense	—	205.1	—	—	—
Other income and (expense)	—	11.2	—	—	—
Consolidated total	$5,091.3	$220.3	$6,299.6	$329.7	$265.8

[a]Includes investments in the advances to other equity affiliates of: Personal care and cleaning: $65.3; Corporate: $22.8.
[b]Includes extraordinary income of $12.5 million.

1991	Sales	EBIT	Identifiable Assets[a]	Capital Expenditures	Depreciation and Cost of Timber Harvested
Personal care and cleaning	$3,793.4	$ 216.2[b]	$3,917.0	$266.6	$209.5
Printing and publishing papers	1,165.9	18.0[c]	1,836.7	45.5	119.4
Total business segment	4,959.3	234.2	5,753.7	312.1	328.9
Divestments and corporate restructuring	—	(141.0)	—	—	—
Corporate	—	(42.7)	738.9	2.5	5.8
Interest expense	—	238.5	—	—	—
Other income and (expense)	—	67.2	—	—	—
Consolidated total	$4,959.3	$(120.8)	$6,492.6	$314.6	$334.7

[a]Includes investments in the advances to other equity affiliates of: Personal care and cleaning: $65.9; Corporate $2.1.
[b]Includes $124.2 million in restructuring charges.
[c]Includes $25.3 million in restructuring charges.

Source: Company annual reports, company documents.

EXHIBIT 11.3 Eleven-Year Financial Summary, 1983–1993 ($millions)

	1993[a]	1992[b]	1991[cd]	1990[cd]
Sales	$4,748.9	$5,091.3	$4,959.3	$5,168.6
Cost and expenses				
Production costs	3,578.0	3,799.2	3,754.5	3,873.6
Marketing and distribution	598.7	631.2	597.3	585.0
Research, administration, and general	232.2	250.1	251.4	256.4
Restructuring, divesture, and other	493.6	(3.4)	305.6	161.9
	4,902.5	4,677.1	4,908.8	4,876.9
(Loss) Income from operations	(153.6)	414.2	50.5	291.7
Interest expense	182.0	205.1	238.5	199.4
Other income and (expense)	4.2	11.2	67.2	25.8
(Loss) Income before taxes	(331.4)	220.3	(120.8)	118.1
Income taxes	(64.0)	58.5	(20.7)	7.9
Share of (loss) earnings of international equity affiliates	(21.7)	5.4	30.2	37.8
(Loss) Income before cumulative effect of accounting change and early extinguishment of debt	(289.1)	167.2	(69.9)	148.0
Extraordinary loss due to extinguishment of debt, net	(9.6)	—	—	—
Cumulative effect of change in accounting for income taxes	21.7	—	—	—
Net (loss) income	$ (277.0)	$ 167.2	$ (69.9)	$ 148.0
Total assets at year-end	$6,625.1	$6,299.6	$6,492.6	$6,900.5
Long-term debt at year-end	2,366.2	2,030.6	2,333.2	2,454.9
Capital expenditures	457.8	329.7	314.6	814.8
Depreciation and cost of timber harvested	281.1	265.8	334.7	327.4
Dollars per common share				
(Loss) Earnings	$ (3.75)	$ 2.26	(.95)	$ 2.01
Dividends	.80	.80	.80	.80
Market price—High	41	46	46⅝	51³/₈
Low	31	34½	29½	30
Average common shares outstanding (millions)	74.0	73.9	73.7	73.6
Number of common shareholders (thousands)	37.7	37.9	39.5	40.7
Number of employees (thousands)	25.9	26.5	29.1	30.8

[a]Loss per share included net special items of $5.33. Excluding these items, earnings per share were $1.58.

[b]Reflects the adoption of FAS 106, Employers' Accounting for Postretirement Benefits, and the revision of estimated useful lives for depreciable assets, which increased net income by $35.3 million and earnings per share by $.48.

[c]Certain accounting reclassifications (not affecting net income) have been made to present more clearly the results of operations.

[d](Loss) Earnings per share for 1991 and 1990 include net charges of $2.49 and $1.36, respectively, for special items related to the company's business improvement program. Excluding special items, earnings per share for 1991 and 1990 were $1.54 and $3.37, respectively.

1989[cc]	1988[cf]	1987[c]	1987[cg]	1985[c]	1984[c]	1983[c]
$4,894.9	$4,549.4	$3,976.9	$3,313.1	$2,934.0	$2,747.4	$2,615.5
3,633.7	3,246.7	2,827.9	2,376.9	2,123.3	2,003.2	2,021.3
545.2	515.7	484.7	423.7	358.1	312.6	290.1
245.4	247.5	206.3	157.5	146.1	127.3	117.1
(165.6)	(192.8)	15.5	(13.4)	10.3	(1.9)	(18.0)
4,258.7	3,817.1	3,534.4	2,944.7	2,637.8	2,441.2	2,410.5
636.2	723.3	442.5	368.4	296.2	306.2	205.0
157.9	147.5	139.0	122.0	81.4	64.2	42.4
31.4	16.9	8.6	28.7	14.4	43.2	3.9
509.7	601.7	312.1	275.1	229.2	285.2	166.5
165.2	237.8	117.1	106.3	75.4	104.2	66.4
31.0	37.0	38.8	17.7	47.3	6.0	23.6
375.5	400.9	233.8	186.5	201.1	187.1	123.7
— —	—	—	—	—	—	
— —	—	—	—	—	—	
$375.5	$ 400.9	$ 233.8	$ 186.5	$ 201.1	$ 187.0	$ 123.7
$5,746.3	$5,156.3	$4,480.5	$3,939.4	$3,517.2	$3,313.3	$2,846.3
1,677.6	1,450.3	1,381.9	1,412.3	1,379.1	640.4	562.5
776.9	508.7	380.1	420.7	514.2	285.8	225.3
297.0	271.5	2436.8	202.8	167.3	158.8	149.6
$ 5.11	$ 5.23	3.05	$ 2.48	$ 2.26	$ 1.91	$ 1.29
.80	.755	.68	.635	.605	.56	.50
52½	42¾	43½	33⁵/₁₆	26⅛	17⁷/₁₆	16⅛
38⅜	32⅜	27½	24	16¹¹/₁₆	12⅝	9⁵/₁₆
73.4	76.6	76.5	75.0	88.8	96.4	91.0
41.4	44.2	44.5	27.5	52.4	55.9	59.1
29.4	27.0	25.4	24.9	22.2	20.6	20.9

[e]Earnings per share for 1989 included a net gain of $1.00 for special items, which include the sale of timberlands in Washington State net of charges for asset restructuring and other items. Excluding special items, earnings per share for 1989 were $4.11.

[f]Earnings per share for 1988 included a net gain of $1.22 for special items, which include the sale of Scott's interest in Brunswick Pulp and Paper Company net of charges for asset restructuring and other items. Excluding special items, earnings per share for 1988 were $4.01.

[g]Reflects the adoption of FAS 87, Employers Accounting for Pension, for U.S. plans, which reduced 1986 pension cost and thereby increased net income by $10.6 million and earnings per share by $.14.

Source: Company annual report.

EXHIBIT 11.4 Scott Paper: Comparable Paper Companies ($millions Except Per Share and Employee Data)

	Procter & Gamble		International Paper		Georgia-Pacific	
	1993	1992	1993	1992	1993	1992
Sales	$ 30,433	$ 29,362	$13,685	$13,598	$12,330	$11,847
Gross profit	12,750	12,038	3,494	3,461	2,516	2,450
SG&A expenses	9,589	9,171	1,633	1,610	1,190	1,170
Restructuring charge	2,705	0	0	370	0	0
EBIT	456	2,867	810	453	536	491
EBITDA	1,596	3,918	1,708	1,303	1,359	1,339
Net income	269	1,872	289	86	(18)	(60)
Earnings per share	0.25	2.62	2.34	0.71	(0.21)	(0.69)
Total assets	24,935	24,025	16,631	16,516	10,545	10,912
Long-term debt	5,824	5,735	3,779	3,195	4,214	4,276
Preferred stock	1,969	1,986	0	0	0	0
Common stock						
Price—High	55.75	53.50	69.88	78.50	75.00	72.00
Low	45.25	38.88	56.63	58.50	55.00	48.25
No. shares, year-end	681.8	678.8	123.9	122.7	90.3	88.1
Number of employees	103,500	106,000	72,500	73,000	50,000	52,000

Source: Companies' annual reports.

Note: Net income and EPS figures exclude extraordinary items, discontinued operations, and effects of changes in accounting principles. EBIT and EBITDA figures are net of restructuring charges. Long-term debt figures include current portion.

Approximate business breakdown for each company:

Procter & Gamble	Personal care products (53%; e.g., tissue and towels, beauty care), laundry/cleaning products (33%), food and beverages (10%), pulp and chemicals (4%)
International Paper	Printing papers (28%), distribution services (22%), paperboard and packaging products (22%), miscellaneous wood products (12%), special products (16%)
Georgia-Pacific	Building products (58%; e.g., wood panels, lumber), packaging paper (15%), printing papers (10%), tissue products (6%), other things (11%)

	Kimberly-Clark		Champion International		James River		Consolidated Papers	
	1993	1992	1993	1992	1993	1992	1993	1992
	$ 6,973	$ 7,091	$ 5,069	$ 4,926	$ 4,650	$ 4,728	$ 947	$ 904
	2,391	2,557	359	362	792	752	175	146
	1,597	1,763	293	288	678	702	62	61
	0	250	0	0	0	112	0	0
	793	543	66	73	114	(62)	113	85
	1,089	832	509	484	472	294	213	174
	511	345	(134)	14	0	(122)	64	50
	3.18	2.15	(1.75)	(0.15)	(0.40)	(1.82)	1.46	1.15
	6,381	6,029	9,142	9,381	5,851	6,336	1,467	1,487
	1,063	1,107	3,403	3,312	2,040	2,367	171	221
	0	0	300	300	454	454	0	0
	62.00	63.25	34.63	30.25	23.38	23.38	54.25	44.75
	50.63	54.00	27.13	23.50	16.25	17.00	37.50	36.00
	160.9	160.8	93.0	92.8	81.6	81.6	44.0	43.8
	42,100	42,900	25,300	27,300	35,000	38,000	4,900	4,900

Kimberly-Clark	Consumer products (80%; e.g., Kleenex tissue, towels, disposable diapers), newsprint and cigarette papers (15%), airline (5%; "Midwest Express")
Champion International	Printing papers (52%), various wood products (25%), packaging and other papers (16%), and newsprint (7%)
James River	Consumer products (49%; e.g., tissue and paper towels), food and consumer packaging (43%; e.g., cereal boxes, potato chip bags), and printing papers (19%)
Consolidated Papers	Mostly coated printing papers

EXHIBIT 11.5 Consolidated Statement of Income ($millions)

	1993	1992	1991
Sales	$4,748.9	$5,091.3	$4,959.3
Costs and expenses			
Product costs	3,578.0	3,799.2	3,754.5
Marketing and distribution	598.7	631.2	597.3
Research, administration, and general	323.2	350.1	251.4
Restructuring and divestments	489.6	—	300.2
Other	4.0	(3.4)	5.4
	$4,902.5	$4,677.1	$4,908.8
(Loss) Income from operations	(153.6)	414.2	50.5
Interest expense	182.0	205.1	238.5
Other income and (expense)	4.2	11.2	67.2
(Loss) Income before taxes	(331.4)	220.3	(120.8)
Income taxes	(64.0)	58.5	(20.7)
(Loss) Income before share of (loss) earnings of international equity affiliates, extraordinary loss and cumulative effect of accounting change	(267.4)	161.8	(100.1)
Share of (loss) earnings of international equity affiliates	(21.7)	5.4	30.2
(Loss) Income before extraordinary loss and cumulative effect of accounting change	(289.1)	167.2	(69.9)
Extraordinary loss on early extinguishment of debt, net of income tax benefit of $5.2	(9.6)	—	—
Cumulative effect of change in accounting for income taxes	21.7	—	—
Net (Loss) income	$ (277.0)	$ 167.2	$ (69.9)
Per share:			
(Loss) Income before extraordinary loss and cumulative effect of accounting change	$ (3.91)	$ 2.26	$ (.95)
Extraordinary loss on early extinguishment of debt	(.13)	—	—
Cumulative effect of change in accounting for income taxes	.29	—	—
(Loss) Earnings per share	$ (3.75)	$ 2.26	$ (.95)
Dividends per share	$ .80	$ .80	$ .80
Average common shares outstanding	74.0	73.9	73.7

EXHIBIT 11.5 *(Continued)* Consolidated Balance Sheet ($millions)

	December 25, 1993	December 26, 1992
Assets		
Current assets		
Cash and cash equivalents	$ 133.6	$ 141.7
Receivables	600.3	647.1
Inventories	523.7	537.2
Deferred income tax assets	277.9	—
Prepaid items and other	74.4	65.5
	$1,609.9	$1,391.5
Plant assets, net of depreciation	4,023.9	3,968.5
Timber resources, at cost less timber harvested	113.0	111.7
Investment in international equity affiliates	223.8	246.2
Investments in and advances to other equity affiliates	84.1	88.1
Construction funds held by trustees	87.1	2.1
Notes receivable, goodwill, and other assets	483.3	491.5
Total	$6,625.1	$6,299.6
Liabilities and Shareholders' Equity		
Current liabilities		
Payable to suppliers and others	$891.5	$998.1
Accruals for restructuring programs	639.0	207.8
Current maturities of long-term debt	180.2	255.3
Accrued taxes on income	59.1	54.3
	$1,769.8	$1,515.5
Long-term debt	2,366.2	2,030.6
Deferred income taxes and other liabilities	913.4	728.6
	$5,049.4	$4,274.7
Preferred shares	7.1	7.1
Common shareholders' equity		
Common shares	450.4	445.1
Reinvested earnings	1,358.1	1,708.3
Cumulative translation adjustment	(227.5)	(121.6)
Treasury shares	(12.4)	(14.0)
Total	$6,625.1	$6,299.6

(Continued)

EXHIBIT 11.5 *(Continued)*   Consolidated Statement of Cash Flows ($millions)

	1993	1992	1991
Cash Flows from Operating Activities			
Net (loss) income	$(277.0)	$ 167.2	$ (69.9)
Adjustments to reconcile net (loss) income to net cash from operating activities:			
Cumulative effect of accounting change	(21.7)	—	—-
Share of loss/earnings of affiliates, net of distributions	29.0	16.0	(17.1)
Depreciation, cost of timber harvested and amortization	300.3	291.0	353.0
Deferred income taxes	(93.9)	(2.9)	(73.7)
Extraordinary loss on extinguishment of debt, net of taxes	9.6	—	—
(Gains) Losses on asset sales	(5.7)	(12.9)	33.8
Other postretirement benefits, deferred expenses	33.6	14.7	—
Changes in current assets and current liabilities net of effects from businesses divested:			
Decrease (Increase) in receivables	7.5	(9.3)	109.9
(Increase) Decrease in inventories	(9.5)	(4.1)	118.7
(Increase) Decrease in prepaid items and other	(10.3)	(10.5)	(3.8)
(Decrease) Increase in payable to suppliers and others	(78.9)	43.4	29.2
Increase (Decrease) in accruals for restructuring programs	429.1	(95.4)	145.0
Increase (Decrease) in accrued taxes on income	6.6	17.7	(43.1)
Net cash provided by operating activities	$318.7	$ 414.9	$ 582.0
Cash Flows from Investing Activities			
Investments in plant assets, timber resources, and other assets	(457.8)	(329.7)	(314.6)
Proceeds from businesses divested and asset sales	5.7	103.9	70.7
Investment in construction funds	(85.0)	—	3.9
Advances to affiliates, net	(2.3)	(6.6)	(13.4)
Other investing	11.0	(11.8)	29.7
Net cash used for investing activities	$(528.4)	$(244.2)	$(223.7)
Cash Flows from Financing Activities			
Dividends paid	(59.5)	(59.4)	(59.6)
Net increase in short-term borrowings	(143.7)	(192.6)	(158.9)
Proceeds from issuance of long-term debt	815.4	403.7	386.8
Repayments of long-term debt	(389.3)	(363.8)	(477.6)
Other financing	(15.4)	.9	25.9
Net cash provided by (used for) financing activities	$ 207.5	$(211.2)	$(283.4)
Effect of exchange rate changes on cash	(5.9)	(2.4)	(4.5)
Net (Decrease) Increase in cash and cash equivalents	(8.1)	(42.9)	70.4
Cash and cash equivalents at beginning of year	141.7	184.6	114.2
Cash and cash equivalents at end of year	$ 133.6	$ 141.7	$ 184.6

EXHIBIT 11.6 Long-Term Debt ($millions)

	Average Rate[a]	Payable Through	Dec. 25, 1993	Dec. 26, 1992
Debentures	9.16%	2023	$1,095.4	$ 924.1
Revenue bonds	3.88	2023	493.5	391.8
Notes	8.27	2009	468.0	433.3
Commercial paper	3.49	Various	154.8	—
Capital leases	6.23	Various	12.9	15.1
Other currencies	7.84	2007	157.4	275.6
			$2,382.0	$2,039.9
Less unamortized discount			(15.8)	(9.3)
			$2,366.2	$2,030.6

[a]At December 25, 1993.

Scheduled maturities of long-term debt and sinking fund payments, in $millions, at December 25, 1993, are:

1995	$ 81.3
1996	196.9
1997	213.8
1998	78.9
1999	9.6
2000–2023	1,785.7

Source: Company annual reports.

EXHIBIT 11.7 Summary of Employment Agreement of Albert J. Dunlap, April 19, 1994

The company has agreed to employ Mr. Dunlap as chairman of the Board and chief executive officer, and Mr. Dunlap has agreed to serve in such capacities, for an initial period of five years ending April 18, 1999, and for successive one-year renewal periods unless six months advance notice of termination is given by either party.

Under the agreement, Mr. Dunlap will be paid a base salary at an annual rate of $1,000,000. The Management Development and Executive Compensation Committee of the Board of Directors may increase Mr. Dunlap's base salary for any year after 1994, but may not reduce it after such increase. The Agreement also provides for the payment to Mr. Dunlap of a special bonus for 1994 of $333,333 within 30 days after the date of the Agreement. The sum of Mr. Dunlap's base salary in 1994 and the special bonus may not exceed $1,000,000.

Mr. Dunlap agreed to invest $1,000,000 in shares of the Company by purchasing 26,316 shares from the Company at a price of $38.00 per share, effective as of the date of the Agreement. The last sale price of the Company's shares on that date, as reported in *The Wall Street Journal*, New York Stock Exchange—Composite Transactions, was $37.75.

STOCK OPTION GRANT

Subject to approval by the Company's shareholders at the Meeting, Mr. Dunlap received a one-time grant effective as of April 19, 1994 of options (the "Options") to purchase 750,000 shares at a price of $38.00 per share, on the terms that would apply if the Options were granted under the 1994 Long-Term Incentive Plan, except to the extent specifically modified by the Agreement. The term of the Option is ten years, and they will vest at the rate of 20% on each of the first, second, third, fourth, and fifth anniversaries of the grant date.

To avoid increasing dilutive effect of options on the Company's shareholders because of the grant to Mr. Dunlap, the Board of Directors has amended the 1994 Long-Term Incentive Plan to reduce the maximum number of shares with respect to which options may be granted from 3,600,000 to 2,850,000.

ANNUAL INCENTIVE BONUS

Subject to approval by the Company's shareholders at the Meeting, Mr. Dunlap will receive, in lieu of participation in any annual incentive plan of the Company, an annual incentive bonus for each Company fiscal year after 1994 if he is employed during the entire fiscal year. The amount of the bonus would equal 1.25% of the Company's net income for the year in excess of 10% of the average of the Company's shareholders' equity at the beginning and end of the year. The bonus would be payable in cash in the first quarter of the following year.

If the incentive bonus provision of the Agreement had been in effect for any of the years 1991, 1992, or 1993, no incentive bonus would have been payable for those years.

EXHIBIT 11.7 *(Continued)*

TERMINATION BONUS

Subject to approval by the Company's shareholders at the Meeting, Mr. Dunlap will receive a termination bonus for any fiscal year after 1995 in which his employment terminates, if the termination is due to death or disability, if it is by the Company other than for "cause," or if it is by Mr. Dunlap for "good reason" (including a change in control of the Company). No termination bonus would be payable if the termination is by the Company for "cause" or by Mr. Dunlap other than for "good reason."

The amount of the termination bonus would be determined by the Committee, but could not be less than the annual incentive bonus payable for the prior year, prorated for the number of days employed during the year of termination. The bonus would be payable in cash within 60 days after termination.

ALTERNATIVE COMPENSATION AGREEMENTS

If the shareholders do not approve the stock option and bonus provisions of the Agreement, the Company and Mr. Dunlap have agreed to negotiate in good faith mutually acceptable alternative compensation arrangements. The terms and conditions of any such alternative compensation arrangement have not been determined.

OTHER BENEFITS

Mr. Dunlap will be eligible to participate in the 1994 Long-Term Incentive Plan if it is approved by the Company's shareholders at the Meeting and he will be required to purchase performance shares on the same terms as other corporate officers. Mr. Dunlap will also be eligible to participate immediately in the other benefit plans available generally to employees or other senior executives of the Company. However, he will not be eligible to participate in any other annual incentive plan, the Retirement Plan for Salaried Employees or the Termination Pay Plan.

In the Agreement, the Company has agreed to purchase Mr. Dunlap's current home in Florida at its cost to him, $3,268,000, in order to facilitate his relocation to Philadelphia, and to provide certain other benefits. The Company intends to sell the home.

Source: 1994 shareholder proxy statement of Scott Paper Company, May 3, 1994.

EXHIBIT 11.8 Comparison of Scott Paper Stock to the S&P 500 (January 25 to April 18, 1994)

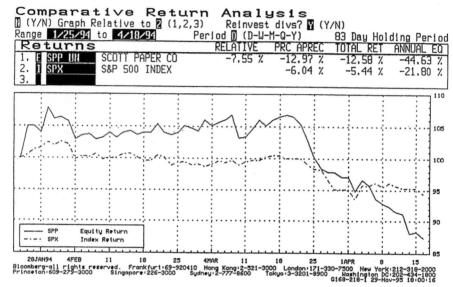

Source: Bloomberg. Reprinted with permission.

EXHIBIT 11.9 Summary of Potential Cost Savings from Greater Outsourcing, U.S. Operations ($millions)

Work Outsourced	Employees Avoided	Cost Avoided	Outsource Cost
Compensation and benefits administration and payroll	130 HR and payroll employees	$ 8.4	$ 3.8
Medical services at corporate	13 medical employees	0.91	0.43
Sales and marketing resource center; coupon redemption and promotion	13 SRMC employees	0.65	0.35
Logistic third-party export customer service	35 logistics employees	2.1	0.45
Medical services for all plants	11 medical employees	0.8	0.3
Security for all plants	60 guards at all plants	3.6	1.9
Information systems data center/operations and technical services	120 MIS employees	14.0	10.3
Consumer customer inquiry on Scott products/graphic design	7 inquiry operators and 4 graphics designers	0.7	0.5
AFH telemarketing services and dispenser installation	36 sales employees	2.5	1.25
Technology research from university; fiber research	25 technology employees	1.75	0.5
	454 employees	$35.4	$19.8

Source: Company documents.

EXHIBIT 11.10 Summary of Potential Cost Savings from Controllable Expense Reductions ($millions)

	1993 Spending	Projected Spending	Savings
Contract maintenance	$ 36	$ 31	$ 5
Project workers	21	2	19
Professional services	24	9	15
Travel, meetings and training	25	8	17
General miscellaneous	14	10	4
Rents, leases	14	11	4
Warehouses	14	11	3
Computer lease, software	10	7	3
Voice communication	8	6	3
Supplies	8	5	3
Expatriates	6	3	3
Moving expenses	4	2	2
Safety, security equipment	3	2	1
Purchased office energy	3	2	1
Contributions	3	1	2
Dues and memberships	3	1	2
Furniture, office equipment	3	1	2
Postage	2	1	1
Bank, service charges	2	2	1
Additional employee benefits	3	1	2
Total	$206	$114	$92

Source: Company documents.

EXHIBIT 11.11 Impact of Fiber Integration on Baseline Earnings, 1977–1993 (Earnings in $millions)

Year	Price of NSWK Pulp (per Ton)	Earnings with Integration	Earnings without Integration
1977	$390	$ 27.8	$ (9.8)
1978	340	35.3	73.9
1979	435	49.6	52.2
1980	535	22.4	11.7
1981	545	38.2	47.2
1982	480	44.6	111.0
1983	415	89.2	180.5
1984	525	146.7	196.4
1985	400	132.1	258.1
1986	470	172.3	293.6
1987	600	215.1	271.7
1988	730	270.8	262.7
1989	830	226.3	189.4
1990	810	212.6	229.9
1991	570	147.1	274.2
1992	550	178.7	290.7
1993	425	125.9	318.1

Source: Company documents.

EXHIBIT 11.12 Summary of Potential Head Count Reductions at Scott Paper

	Oct. 1, 1993	Head Count Reduction	Final
U.S. Operations			
Printing and publishing papers	4,900	(1,200)	3,700
Tissue products and other U.S. operations			
Hourly employees	7,600	(1,700)	5,900
Salaried employees	4,300	(2,300)	2,000
Total	11,900	(4,000)	7,900
Total U.S. operations	16,800	(5,200)	11,600
International Operations			
Wholly owned subsidiaries			
Europe	6,600	(2,400)	4,200
Pacific	2,800	(700)	2,100
Costa Rica	1,200	0	1,200
Total	10,600	(3,100)	7,500
Equity interests			
Canada	2,200	(400)	1,800
Mexico	4,900	(2,500)	2,400
Total	7,100	(2,900)	4,200
Total international operations	17,700	(6,000)	11,700
Total U.S. and international	34,500	(11,200)	23,300

Source: Company documents and casewriter estimates.

EXHIBIT 11.13 Financial Projections for S.D. Warren as a Stand-Alone Entity, July 1994 (Net Sales, EBITD, Depreciation, and Capital Expenditures in $millions)

	1989	1990	1991	1992	1993
Company Projections					
Total sales tonnage	1,076	1,083	1,091	1,184	1,131
Coated average net price/ton	$1,160	$1,144	$1,055	$984	$ 968
Net sales	$1,241	$1,220	$1,148	$1,189	$1,122
EBITD	240	204	176	181	195
Depreciation	92	103	121	90	91
Capital expenditures	295	341	48	60	67
Base Case Projections					
Total sales tonnage	1,076	1,083	1,091	1,184	1,131
Coated average net price/ton	$1,160	$1,144	$1,055	$984	$ 968
Net sales	$1,241	$1,220	$1,148	$1,189	$1,122
EBITD	240	204	176	181	195
Depreciation	92	103	121	90	91
Capital expenditures	295	341	48	60	67
Low-Volume Projections					
Total sales tonnage	1,076	1,083	1,091	1,184	1,131
Coated average net price/ton	$1,160	$1,144	$1,055	$984	$ 968
Net Sales	$1,241	$1,220	$1,148	$1,189	$1,122
EBITD	240	204	176	181	195
Depreciation	92	103	121	90	91
Capital expenditures	295	341	48	60	67

Source: Independent investment banking analysis and company data.

(Continued)

EXHIBIT 11.13 *(Continued)*

	1994	1995	1996	1997	1998
Company Projections					
Total sales tonnage	1,161	1,180	1,230	1,278	1,324
Coated average net price/ton	$ 932	$1,045	$1,169	$1,251	$1,165
Net sales	$1,141	$1,327	$1,568	$1,788	$1,754
EBITD	160	361	529	659	554
Depreciation	93	96	100	104	107
Capital expenditures	68	128	178	113	61
Base Case Projections					
Total sales tonnage	1,161	1,180	1,230	1,278	1,324
Coated average net price/ton	$ 932	$ 997	$1,1044	$1,091	$1,035
Net sales	$1,141	$1,259	$1,409	$1,569	$1,556
EBITD	160	298	380	452	367
Depreciation	93	96	100	104	107
Capital expenditures	68	128	178	113	61
Low-Volume Projections					
Total sales tonnage	1,161	1,130	1,129	1,143	1,150
Coated average net price/ton	$ 932	$ 994	$1,040	$1,086	$1,031
Net Sales	$1,141	$1,206	$1,292	$1,387	$1,330
EBITD	160	276	334	378	287
Depreciation	93	96	100	104	107
Capital expenditures	68	128	178	113	61

EXHIBIT 11.14   Historical and Projected Coated Paper Prices, 1987–1997

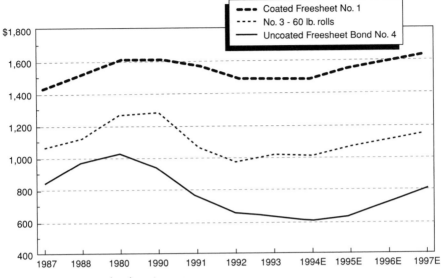

Source: Investment bank estimate.

EXHIBIT 11.15   Summary of Stock-Based Compensation That Albert Dunlap Wanted to Implement at Scott

COMPENSATION TO BOARD DIRECTORS

All nonemployee directors would be compensated solely with shares of the company's stock. They would each receive 1,000 shares annually. All other forms of compensation—in the form of fees, committee bonuses, retirement arrangements, and so on—would be terminated.

STOCK OPTIONS TO KEY EXECUTIVES

As part of his employment agreement (see Exhibit 11.7), Albert Dunlap was awarded 750,000 stock options, exercisable at the price of the company's stock when he began employment with the company ($37.75). These options would vest at the rate of 20% per year. However, if there were a "change in control" of the company, all of his unvested options would vest immediately. Dunlap wanted to grant stock options to five other executives in 1994—including Russ Kersh and John Murtagh, former colleagues whom he had recently hired at Scott. He wanted to grant them 170,000 stock options each. Most of their options would also vest at the rate of 20% per year. Their exercisability would also be accelerated in the event of a "change in control."

The company had awarded stock options to certain employees in the past, but the program that Dunlap now wanted to implement would "front-load" the awards to a greater extent: the magnitude of the awards would be greater than usual, but they would be in lieu of annual grants over a multiyear period. (For example, the executive who headed Scott's "commercial" tissue business, and who had been with Scott for over twenty years, had been granted 18,000 stock options in each of the previous two years, and had been granted 20,000 options in early 1994. Dunlap wanted an additional 150,000 options to be granted to him this year.)

RESTRICTED STOCK TO KEY EXECUTIVES

Dunlap wanted restricted shares to be awarded to twenty-two senior executives in the company, including himself. The restricted shares would be awarded annually if a "performance goal" for the company were achieved—namely, if the total return on Scott Paper's stock during a given year exceeded the total return on the Standard & Poor's 500 Index by at least one percentage point. The award would be a "matching" award: each executive would receive three common shares for each share that the executive bought on his own, on the open market, during a given year. (The minimum number of shares that an executive would have to buy each year in order to qualify would be 500.) The restricted shares would vest at the rate of 20% per year. However, if there were a "change in control" of the company, all of the restricted shares would vest on the date of the "change in control" or six months after the date when the shares were granted, whichever came later.

The company had awarded restricted stock to certain employees in the past, but the program that Dunlap now wanted to implement was more extensive.

Source: Shareholder proxy statement of Scott Paper Company, March 10, 1995.

CHAPTER 12

FAG Kugelfischer

A German Restructuring

Karl-Josef Neukirchen, a famous—in some quarters infamous—manager of businesses in West Germany, was again in the hot seat. It was January 1993. He had been asked to help solve the problems of an old German industrial company, FAG Kugelfischer, that had an important place in Germany's history and its present economic situation. Kugelfischer was the largest producer of ball bearings in Germany, and the second largest in Europe.

Over the last several years the company had come under increasing financial strain. The bearings industry was experiencing the worst recession in half a century. The long-dreamed-of reunification of West and East Germany was finally occurring, and, along with it, massive financial investment in the East. Kugelfischer had purchased East Germany's largest ball bearings maker soon after the Berlin Wall fell, but the acquisition had created unexpected problems. The process of reunification was causing a lot of dislocation of economic and social relationships. There had been strikes in both the private and public sectors of the country the previous spring.

Kugelfischer's banks were putting pressure on Neukirchen to do something. But the economic and social culture of Germany was very different from what it was in the United States, and U.S.-style restructurings, which typically involved a downsizing of operations and a laying off of

This case was prepared by Research Associate Jeremy Cott and Professor Stuart Gilson, assisted by Research Associate Cedric Escalle and doctoral student Matthias Vogt. Copyright © 1998 by the President and Fellows of Harvard College. Harvard Business School case 298-046.

significant numbers of employees, were very uncommon in Germany. Still, Neukirchen knew that the problems facing him were not likely to go away on their own.

COMPANY BACKGROUND

The origins of FAG Kugelfischer could be traced to 1883, when a man named Friedrich Fischer invented a new technology for producing round steel balls to precise specifications. Prior to this, Fischer had been manufacturing and repairing bicycles and sewing machines, which used ball bearings. He was importing the bearings from England, and his frustration over their high price and low quality provided the impetus for his invention. He soon built a facility to manufacture his own bearings in the German city of Schweinfurt, which was to become the company's headquarters and an important industrial center. Fischer's ball bearings were widely used in the manufacture of bicycles, and he came to be known by his nickname, Kugel-Fischer (literally translated, "Ball-Fischer"). When he died in 1899, his company employed almost four hundred people. Not long afterward, however, the company ran into financial problems, and it was purchased in 1909 by a man named Georg Schäfer. The acquired company was merged into Schäfer's own company and successfully restructured. The new company was named FAG Kugelfischer (FAG was an abbreviation of "Fischer AG").[1] (In 1992, the company was still headed by a member of the Schäfer family.)

Georg Schäfer believed that the bearings business had enormous potential. Germany was in the midst of an industrial revolution, and he saw a whole range of possible commercial uses for bearings. Through the beginning of World War I, Kugelfischer prospered, largely on the strength of the rapidly growing automobile industry, which was the largest consumer of bearings. Moreover, the company exported a large amount of its production to Western European countries and the United States.

By the time Schäfer died in 1925, the company employed 2,000 people, and had recaptured much of its foreign business that had been lost in

---

[1]AG stands for *Aktiengesellschaft*, which literally means stock company or corporation. It is the standard designation for a business corporation in Germany, analogous to Inc. (for "incorporated") in the United States and PLC (for "public limited company") in England. (Thus, for example, Daimler-Benz AG, Siemens AG, Volkswagen AG.)

the economic and social turmoil following World War I. In his last will and testament, Schäfer wrote: "The Kugelfabrik Fischer is today, in our ruined Germany, an industrial firm of extraordinary importance, for it employs 2,000 people. Including the employees' wives and children, it has to earn bread for more than 4,500 people. The Kugelfabrik Fischer must be preserved for the purpose of standing up for the German community, to serve and fight for this community, and to save the lives of these 4,500 people." This last will of Georg Schäfer became the maxim of all his heirs.

Over the next decade, competition in the German bearings industry was intense. Many German bearings manufacturers either filed for bankruptcy or were acquired by foreign companies. The Swedish bearings manufacturer SKF Group acquired seven major plants and companies in Germany during this period. At the end, only two major bearings producers remained in Germany—Kugelfischer and SKF.

Ball bearings were used extensively in military hardware, and the German bearings industry therefore became strategically important during World War II. Most of the German bearings production was concentrated in Schweinfurt, which was bombed repeatedly by the Allies. By the end of the war the city lay in ruins. With help from the Marshall Plan, however, Kugelfischer—along with much of West Germany—was able to rebuild.

In the 1960s the company undertook aggressive efforts at growth, acquiring or building production facilities throughout Europe, as well as in the United States, Canada, and Brazil. It also diversified into a number of new businesses involving industrial engineering. In 1978 its legal status was changed from that of a general partnership to that of a limited partnership. Then in 1985, because of a need for additional financing, it became a "corporation-partnership" (*Kommanditgesellschaft auf Aktien,* or KGaA): Just under half of its shares, which carried limited liability, were publicly traded, while the general partner—a member of the Schäfer family—retained personally liability, along with control over management. (The "corporation-partnership" was a special sort of German corporate structure that protected the dominant family's interests. By the early 1990s, however, the equity analyst at Morgan Stanley, for instance, felt that Kugelfischer was "now more concerned than the average German company with the outside investor" and communicated fairly well with stock analysts.)

After it went public in 1985, the company pursued an acquisitions program that was meant to further diversify its holdings and thus help insulate it from the cyclical nature of the bearings industry. Its various industrial engineering products—most of which had different markets from the bearings industry as such—grew from 18 percent of sales in the early 1980s to 25 percent of sales by the end of the decade. One equity analyst said that the company's strategy was to increase the proportion of its industrial engineering sales to about one-third of the total. There were separate divisions for sewing technology, textile machine accessories, abrasives, hydraulic brakes, industrial gauging and control systems, radiation measuring technology, die castings, and other things. The most important part of the industrial engineering group was sewing technology—sophisticated, industrial-strength machines sold largely to the textile industry—but other components of the group, while possessing small market shares, were felt to have considerable development potential. Profit responsibility for these businesses, however, remained with management at Schweinfurt. (See Exhibits 12.1 and 12.2, which show balance sheets, income statements, and other financial and operating data for Kugelfischer from 1988 to 1992.)

THE BEARINGS INDUSTRY

As products, bearings lack a certain romantic appeal, but they are essential to the functioning of the world economy. Bearings—representing the idea of "bearing" or supporting a weight—are rolling or sliding machine elements, usually made from a specially treated steel, that reduce the friction between the moving parts of a machine. Bearings are thus essential to the functioning of almost all mechanical systems, like consumer appliances, cars, drilling equipment, and aircraft. Many bearings are commodity-type products, but some have to be customized for particular needs, and in any case they have to perform well in conditions of varying pressures and temperatures. Although bearings themselves are generally not expensive, their unexpected breakdown in industrial settings can lead to significant financial losses. They require great precision in their manufacture; acceptable tolerances are often a tiny fraction of the width of a human hair.[2]

Because their use is so widespread, the demand for them tends to track industrial activity in general. It is a cyclical business. (For Kugelfis-

---

[2]The two most commonly used bearings are spherical (thus the well-known ball bearings) or cylindrical (roller bearings).

cher, the most recent cyclical peaks had occurred in 1984 and the summer of 1990.) This cyclicality is reinforced by customers' purchasing practices. At the beginning of an economic expansion, customers typically order many more bearings than they actually need, to build up stocks of replacements and avoid costly production shutdowns. At the start of an economic downturn, by contrast, customers often cancel large outstanding orders for bearings, even though production of the bearings might have already commenced. The customers' large size allows them to cancel these orders with impunity.

In the developed industrial world, the bearings industry is also a fairly low-growth business. Partly for this reason, major players in the industry had been making additional investments in some of the emerging Asian economies, through either wholly owned ventures or joint ventures.

In the early 1990s, one analyst characterized the industry—and Kugelfischer's place in it—in the following way:

> *The bearings business is a cumbersome one. Production runs are generally small, and there is a high labor content—40–45% of the cost of goods sold. The final customer needs not only a product but a package of services—speedy delivery, engineering assistance, quality control, and often special product design. . . .*
>
> *Improved bearing design tends to reduce demand. The cost and size of the appropriate bearing for a given application has shrunk some 30% over the past decade. . . .*
>
> *Bearing makers compete on two fronts—direct product cost and efficiency of service. In the former category, Kugelfischer has no advantage, at least against the Japanese producers. Sales of commodity products are important to spread out overhead costs, but the bulk of Kulgelfisher's bearing profits come from specialized products, for which service is crucial.[3]*

European bearings producers in particular had a special relationship with the automobile industry. Bearings were a key input in the manufacture of automobiles. At a very early stage of the product development cycle for new car models, an automobile manufacturer would typically give

---

[3]Morgan Stanley, "FAG Kugelfischer: Company Report," January 8, 1991.

detailed product plans to its bearings suppliers to ensure that they were able to supply what was needed. The bearings producers were also involved in the highly confidential design process for new automobile models, giving local suppliers a competitive advantage over foreign suppliers, as their trustworthiness was perceived to be higher.

Kugelfischer was known for the high quality of its bearings products. It was also one of the few manufacturers to offer a full line of products. It produced 320,000 different kinds of bearings.

Competitors

There were several major players in this industry. The Swedish company SKF had long held the largest share of the world bearings market. Up through the late 1980s, Kugelfischer had the second largest market share. At the end of 1992, SKF still had the largest share of the world bearings market (18% to 20%). Two Japanese companies, Nippon Seiko (NSK) and NTN Corporation, however, each had market shares of 10 percent to 11 percent; Kugelfischer had a market share of about 9 percent, although it was the largest bearings producer in Germany and the second largest in Europe. An American manufacturer, the Timken Company, was next, with a market share of 7 percent to 8 percent, although it held the largest share of the market in the United States. Exhibit 12.3 provides comparative data for Kugelfischer and these other companies.

All of these companies were multinational in scope; they all had plants or sales offices in numerous countries. Market leader SKF, for example, generated roughly 20 percent of its business in its home country of Sweden, but its largest manufacturing operation was actually in West Germany, where roughly 25 percent of its employees worked and roughly 25 percent of its sales were generated. (Its German operation was in fact headquartered in Schweinfurt.)

Important Factors of Production

Research and development (R&D) was vital to the bearings industry, as it was to various industrial engineering businesses. Kugelfischer carried on a broad range of very sophisticated R&D activity. It received patents for some of its work. (The work involved things like melting technologies, corrosion resistance, radiometric quality control, a central clutch release for motor vehicles, a thread-tension measuring system, computer-based customization of clothing, and joint development projects with universities.)

Capital expenditures were also important. Exhibit 12.4 provides information about capital expenditures and R&D expenditures by Kugelfischer and its competitors from 1990 to 1992.

Germany had the highest labor costs in the world, but its design skills, product innovativeness, a highly trained and literate workforce, and an efficient national infrastructure often made up for the high costs. The 1980s, for example, had been a period of almost uninterrupted economic growth in the country.

Company Culture

The constitution of the government of West Germany said something very distinct. It said: "Ownership is an obligation." The Schäfer family seemed to take this seriously. The company was in some respects run like a traditional family business. Although shares in it had been publicly traded since 1985, the legal structure made Fritz Schäfer, the general partner, personally liable. The family had historically shown a strong commitment to employee welfare, and job security, good wages, and generous benefits were considered standard. (Exhibit 12.5 shows wages and benefits in the main business component of the company in 1991 and 1990.) A centennial booklet published in 1983 boasted of the company's strike-free history. Some managers, however, felt that Kugelfischer's culture "did not allow a fair discussion of different opinions," and there was a perceived tendency toward risk aversion.[4]

The equity of the company consisted of 3.3 million common shares and 1.18 million nonvoting preferred shares. The Schäfer family owned 52 percent of the outstanding common stock. The rest was publicly traded—as was the preferred stock. The preferred stock, however, was unlike most preferred stock in the United States. It paid a regular dividend, but the dividend was not fixed in either percentage or dollar terms. Rather, the dividend was stipulated to be (on an annual basis) one deutsche mark (DM) more than whatever the common dividend was. Thus if the common dividend was DM 5 per share, the preferred dividend had to be DM 6 per share. If there was no common dividend, there would be no preferred dividend—but there was a "cumulative minimum dividend" on the preferred of DM 2 per share. Thus in 1990 and 1991 the dividend yield on the com-

---

[4]*Manager* Magazine, No. 12, 1993.

mon stock was between 3 percent and 4 percent, while the dividend yield on the preferred was between 4 percent and 5 percent. The recent market performance of Kugelfischer's common and preferred shares is shown in Exhibit 12.3.

The Schäfer family was involved in more than just business. It owned the most important private collection of nineteenth-century German art in the world. It had also amassed a huge collection of antique manuscripts and books. Almost all of this the family planned to donate to a special foundation, which would be open to the public. This was meant to help stimulate a tourist industry in the company's home town of Schweinfurt.

EXPANSION INTO EAST GERMANY

On November 9, 1989, the Berlin Wall fell. A German privatization agency, Treuhand Anstalt, (literally translated, "Trust Agency"), was set up to arrange for the sale of thousands of East German companies. This created a unique opportunity for many West German firms. They felt that they could extend the use of their technological and marketing expertise, while the East German companies could contribute their knowledge about eastern markets. Some East German companies were snapped up by western firms with "near gold-rush ferocity" (in the words of the *Financial Times* of London). A large Swedish-Swiss electrical engineering group, for example, was one of the acquirers of East German firms.

On July 1, 1990, Kugelfischer acquired, for DM 69 million, East Germany's largest ball bearings manufacturer, Deutsche Kugellagerfabriken Leipzig (DKFL), from the Treuhand. Kugelfischer stated in its annual report:

> *The acquisition of DKFL was a decision of great importance. It was made because we see an attractive medium-term potential in East Germany and Eastern European [markets] and also because we felt that we had the responsibility to contribute to the maintenance and development of industrial facilities in the new German states.*

The company also said that it expected it would have to make various adjustments in DKFL's operation in order to raise quality and productivity to world market levels. "The necessary adjustments," it said in its 1990 annual report, "will inevitably cause losses in the first few years, but these losses have been taken into account in the valuation of the acquisition and will therefore not have a negative effect on [Kugelfischer's] earnings position. For this reason, the pro-rata reorganization losses of DKFL . . . in the stub period from July 1 to December 31, 1990 did not affect the earnings of [Kugelfischer] in the past fiscal year." At year-end 1990, Kugelfischer's balance sheet showed a special reserve for losses from DKFL in the amount of DM 198 million. (See Exhibit 12.1.)

Following the fall of the Berlin Wall in 1989, a burst of economic activity related to the reunification of the country (the "unification boom") shielded Germany, to some extent, from the recession elsewhere. Soon after, however, the economic slowdown also hit Germany. Germany was particularly vulnerable because its production costs were high relative to those of many foreign competitors. An increase in taxes imposed by the government in order to help pay for the reunification effort also had an impact. In the spring of 1992, the umbrella union for 4,250,000 metalworkers—the country's largest private-sector union—began strikes at selected sites because of a dispute with a federation of businesses that it was negotiating with. The workers wanted a 9.5 percent pay hike, while the employers were offering 3.3 percent. The largest public-sector union then went out on strike as well, with similar wage demands.[5] In many cities, public transportation, garbage collection, and postal service came to a halt. Although this was the first strike by the public-sector union since 1974, Chancellor Helmut Kohl warned against giving in too easily to union demands. Eventually both private-sector and public-sector unions settled on 5.4 percent wage increases.

In May 1992, Kugelfischer announced a sharp reduction in its dividends and forecast a net loss for the year. The downturn was not affecting Kugelfischer alone. It also affected the market leader, SKF, badly, as well as other competitors. This was to be the steepest downturn in the bearings industry in a half century.

Kugelfischer did have special problems, however, with the East German company it had acquired. Prior to 1990, DKFL's sales had been running about DM 400 million a year. When Kugelfischer took the company over, it planned to reduce DKFL's workforce from 7,500 to 4,000 by 1995. In the months following the German currency union of July 1,

---

[5]In Germany, collective bargaining agreements between management and labor were negotiated on a countrywide level, rather than company by company.

1990, however, DKFL's eastern European business largely disappeared as customers were unable to make payments in hard currency. Kugelfischer also found that DKFL's manufacturing facilities were quite outdated. The company was kept going largely because Kugelfischer diverted orders to it from its other businesses, worth about DM 80 million in annual sales. Kugelfischer management believed that the subsidiary would be profitable in the long run and provide important access to the potentially huge East German and eastern European bearings markets. By the end of 1991, however, the workforce was reduced to 3,000 and three of the company's eight plants were closed. For 1991, DKFL recorded a loss of DM 142 million on sales of DM 113 million. In late 1992 Kugelfischer announced plans to close an additional DKFL plant in Berlin, which would involve about 500 layoffs.

For the first time, Kugelfischer also found itself facing a cyclical downturn in both its bearings markets and sewing technology markets.

Kugelfischer's banks became very concerned. (As Exhibit 12.1 shows, DM 2,069 million of Kugelfischer's debt was owed to banks as of the end of 1992.) A group of them asked Kajo Neukirchen for advice about the situation.

KAJO NEUKIRCHEN

Karl-Josef ("Kajo") Neukirchen was a well-known business executive in Germany. He had developed a reputation as a highly skilled professional turnaround manager, after having led successful turnarounds at several troubled West German firms, including Klockner-Humboldt-Deutz (KHD), a tractor and diesel engine producer, and Hoesch AG, a major steel producer.

By background and temperament Neukirchen was well suited to the bearings industry. From 1981 to 1987 he had served as chairman of the managerial board of SKF's operation in West Germany. He had a master's degree in economics and a doctorate in operations research from the University of Bonn, but he had a keen interest in engineering. He loved to explain the arcane technical aspects of ball bearings to anyone who would listen.

Neukirchen was a controversial figure in Germany. The companies that hired him often suffered from excess capacity and low labor productivity, and he had ordered the layoffs of many workers. He also believed that the success of a turnaround could be measured by the value he created for stockholders. His views and deeds were immensely unpopular among German politicians, labor leaders, and the general public. The German press often referred to him in such terms as Rambo, Jobkiller, and Man with the Bushknife. Even the conservative newspaper *Frankfurter Allge-meine Zeitung* editorialized: "Indeed, did he wipe out forty, fifty, or even seventy thousand jobs? This man must be a monster, a tyrannosaurus of German industry."[6]

Neukirchen had the reputation of being a tough manager. "His man-agement style is rude, to put it mildly," said a former colleague. But Neukirchen argued that desperate situations sometimes required unpopu-lar solutions. He explained that, in a business, "you can't have the goal of being loved."[7]

He was also known as a decisive and energetic practitioner, who did everything at high speed. One business magazine speculated that he pre-ferred to be known by his nickname "Kajo"—an abbreviation of his first two names—because it saved time. Although he had advanced graduate-level education, he liked to point out that he grew up in a working-class family. He wanted to be known as more than just a job cutter. While at Hoesch, for example, he developed a strategic restructuring plan called "Hoesch 2000," which was an ambitious proposal for growing the com-pany's businesses into the next century.

In late 1992, Kugelfischer's banks strongly recommended that Neukirchen be appointed the new chairman of Kugelfischer's supervisory board and, in that capacity, carry out a restructuring of the company. The Schäfer family accepted the recommendation, though (as one Euro-pean press account put it) only "grudgingly." Neukirchen began his new job in January.

THE GERMAN CONTEXT FOR RESTRUCTURING

In recent years, there had been an enormous wave of restructuring of publicly traded corporations in the United States. U.S.-style restructurings, involving a downsizing of operations and the laying off of significant numbers of employ-ees, were, however, very uncommon in Germany. Some of the reasons for this were embedded in the very nature of these countries' capital markets, their accounting practices, and financial reporting. (See Exhibit 12.6.)

---

[6]*Frankfurter Allgemeine Zeitung*, September 30, 1994.
[7]*Business Week*, July 4, 1994, p. 58.

Stakeholder Capitalism

In the United States, the idea of maximizing shareholder value was revered, and laws protecting workers were fairly limited. In Germany, by contrast, "stakeholder capitalism" generally commanded greater support than purely "shareholder capitalism." The interests of the country as a whole were generally understood to be at stake in the workings of private enterprise. There was a long tradition of cooperation between labor and management. Laws protecting workers were extensive. For example, Germany had a system called "codetermination" (*Mitbestimmung*) whereby employees were legally required to hold one-third to one-half of the seats on a large company's supervisory board (roughly equivalent to the board of directors in the United States). In Kugelfischer's 1992 annual report, in fact, 10 of the 24 members listed on its supervisory board were representatives of rank-and-file workers' groups.[8] With the increase in global competition, there were stirrings in Germany to implement a rougher kind of corporate management. As the *Financial Times* commented, however, "Such moves are not without wider costs. The sense of community in the German workplace creates valuable social capital which has contributed to its competitiveness in world markets."[9]

Laws Regarding Restructuring

There were actual laws in Germany regarding corporate restructuring. If a company wanted to undertake a restructuring (*Betriebsanierung*)—involving, for example, a significant number of layoffs, the closure of a plant, or the introduction of completely new working practices—it was generally required to inform the workers' council of what it wished to do and the reasons why it wished to do it. A workers' council (*Betriebsrat*) existed in most large companies. It consisted of elected representatives of the employees of individual plants (though it was not part of any union as such). Ultimately, a workers' council had no right to prevent a restructuring; it could only delay it with legal challenges, with a possibly negative impact on productivity. For its part,

---

[8]This was one of several features of codetermination (essentially, the right given to employees to participate in some of the important decision making in a company). Legislation establishing codetermination was passed by the German parliament in 1951, 1952, 1965, and 1976. Its origins in the aftermath of World War II are attributed by some observers to the need to win over human capital at a time when much of the country's physical capital had been destroyed.
[9]*Financial Times*, April 9, 1996

company management was said to have "an obligation to attempt" to reach an agreement with the council. Outside mediation by a labor court judge was sometimes used.

When a restructuring was decided on, company management was then required to negotiate with the workers' council a "social plan" (*Sozialplan*)—essentially, severance payments for people being laid off, along with terms of possible assistance in finding new employment and provisions for retraining. Again, despite its legal formality, this constituted a mostly good-faith procedure—although an outside conciliation board could ultimately make a binding ruling about it, taking into consideration the economic condition of the employer. No specific formulae existed to determine what the severance compensation should be. In small companies, however, the compensation typically ranged from one-fourth to one and a half times the product of the number of years of an employee's service and his or her gross monthly salary. In large companies, the age of the employee and his or her family status (married or unmarried, number of children) would often be factored in as well.

German laws made certain kinds of dismissal illegal. However, "rationalization" measures, lack of orders, or relocation or closure of a business constituted valid legal grounds for the dismissal of workers. The sale of an entire plant or business, on the other hand, was treated differently. In such a situation all contracts of employment were legally transferred to the acquirer.

Formal laws or guidelines regarding corporate restructuring existed to some extent in all European Community countries. In some countries—like Spain, France, and Italy—the laws were roughly as demanding as those in Germany, while in others—like England, Ireland, and Denmark—they were much less demanding.[10]

THE COURSE TO FOLLOW

There was a great deal at stake at Kugelfischer—for employees, for shareholders, for the Schäfer family, and for Neukirchen as well. But there was also possibly a geopolitical matter at stake. The former chief executive officer of an important bearings manufacturer in England had expressed his

---

[10]The sources for much of the information in this section are Gerhard Roder, "Labor Law Implications of the Restructuring of Enterprises in the Federal Republic of Germany," in *International Lawyer* (an American Bar Association publication), Summer 1994; and Hilary Barnes et al., "Ground Rules for the Firing Squad: Variations in the Ways European Countries Protect Workers," in *Financial Times*, February 15, 1993.

views about some of this in a letter to the *Financial Times* a few years earlier. (See Exhibit 12.7.)

What Neukirchen might think should be done was not necessarily what he could do. He knew that even the chancellor of Germany, Helmut Kohl, couldn't carry out all of the steps toward restructuring an important German business that either or both of them might rationally think appropriate.

REFERENCES

Charny, David. 1998, "The German Corporate Governance System," *Columbia Business Law Review* 1998, 145–166.

Ordelheide, Dieter and Dieter Pfaff. 1994, *Germany* (London: Routledge).

EXHIBIT 12.1 Kugelfischer: Balance Sheets (Fiscal Years Ending December 31) (DM millions)

			Preliminary		
	1988	1989	1990	1991	1992
Assets					
Intangibles	7.8	11.6	16.4	17.5	16.4
Tangibles					
Land and buildings	459.5	502.3	710.2	823.5	871.6
Plant and machinery	398.5	492.0	733.1	773.0	802.7
Other facilities and equipment	160.3	199.3	239.3	240.9	247.6
Advances to suppliers	168.0	200.4	205.7	185.4	75.7
Financial assets	32.7	26.3	223.2	23.6	33.7
Current assets					
Inventories	1,391.8	1,469.6	1,845.9	1,820.2	1,705.8
Receivables	623.6	682.8	708.9	718.3	629.1
Other assets	38.6	170.7	350.8	243.1	149.6
Marketable securities	11.6	37.6	34.3	31.3	6.9
Cash	131.1	126.2	98.9	95.7	54.2
Deferred taxes	0.0	15.6	9.4	7.6	1.2
Prepaid expenses	10.0	11.7	10.6	13.1	15.6
Total	3,433.5	3,946.1	5,186.7	4,993.2	4,610.1
Equity and Liabilities					
Equity					
Common shares	165.0	165.0	165.0	165.0	165.0
Nonvoting preferred shares	31.0	59.9	59.0	59.0	59.0
Additional paid-in capital	490.3	602.3	602.3	602.3	602.3
Retained earnings	251.4	263.8	243.1	58.4	21.5
Other	59.7	67.7	61.6	28.0	20.8
	997.4	1,157.8	1,131.0	912.7	868.6
Reserves and provisions[a]					
Special reserves	138.7	189.6	236.1	223.2	0.0
Special reserve for losses from acquisitions	0.0	0.0	198.0	58.9	0.0
Provisions for pensions	857.2	852.9	903.2	887.8	909.1
Other provisions	162.5	257.4	292.9	330.6	200.1
	1,158.4	1,299.9	1,630.2	1,500.5	1,109.2
Liabilities					
Bonds	1.0	19.8	22.7	22.3	22.8
Bank borrowings	667.0	722.2	1,643.7	1,866.0	1,768.8
Bills and notes payable (to banks)	145.1	207.7	200.1	216.0	299.7
Accounts payable	211.6	269.5	256.6	193.4	210.4
Advances from customers	18.0	19.4	8.9	16.6	18.2
Other liabilities	231.3	244.7	287.3	258.6	305.4
Deferred income	3.7	5.1	6.2	7.1	7.0
	1,277.7	1,488.4	2,425.5	2,580.0	2,632.3
Total	3,433.5	3,946.1	5,186.7	4,993.2	4,610.1
Average exchange rate for DM	$0.53	$0.57	$0.62	$0.60	$0.64

[a]The company does not distinguish clearly between equity and liabilities. The "provisions" are clearly liabilities, but the company indicates in its annual reports that it considers some of the "reserve" amounts equity and some of the "reserve" amounts liabilities.
Source: Company annual reports.

EXHIBIT 12.2 Kugelfischer: Income Statements and Other Financial and Operating Data (Fiscal Years Ending December 31) (DM Millions Except Number of Employees)

			Preliminary		
	1988	1989	1990	1991	1992
Sales	3,502.0	3,895.1	4,048.0	3,885.2	3,562.8
Increase in inventories of finished goods and work-in-process	29.1	111.7	220.2	0.1	8.4
Company-produced additions to plant and equipment	55.0	59.1	70.0	42.9	67.0
Other operating income[a]	75.9	111.2	172.4	284.9	172.5
Output	3,662.0	4,177.1	4,510.6	4,213.1	3,810.7
Cost of materials	(1,107.4)	(1,334.7)	(1,424.1)	(1,241.7)	(1,125.2)
Personnel expenses	(1,690.5)	(1,814.7)	(1,998.3)	(2,011.4)	(1,968.6)
Depreciation and amortization	(203.5)	(232.6)	(285.1)	(329.8)	(205.3)[b]
Other operating expenses	(462.8)	(536.0)	(584.9)	(494.9)	(455.3)
Operating income	197.8	259.1	218.2	135.3	56.3
Equity income	0.0	0.2	0.0	0.5	0.0
Income from other investments and loans	26.5	48.3	54.9	35.7	34.7
Write-downs of financial assets and marketable securities	(1.2)	(3.0)	(3.3)	(1.4)	(1.5)
Interest expense	(64.7)	(87.4)	(137.3)	(201.1)	(205.1)
Results from ordinary activities	158.4	217.2	132.5	(31.0)	(115.6)
Extraordinary income	0.0	39.5	25.6	15.0	226.6[c]
Extraordinary expense	(9.2)	(39.5)	(25.6)	(58.3)	(61.7)[c]
Taxes on income	(62.2)	(92.9)	(41.8)	16.9	(9.9)[c]
Other taxes	(23.7)	(22.4)	(32.1)	(23.3)	(23.9)
Net income	63.3	101.9	58.6	(80.7)	15.5
"Value added"[d]	1,904	2,119	2,268	2,165	1,978
Gross cash flow[e]	374	490	449	225	47
Capital expenditures[f]	352	489	486	404	274

	Preliminary				
	1988	1989	1990	1991	1992
Average number of employees[g]	30,218	30,823	35,535	37,746	32,294
Average exchange rate for DM	$0.53	$0.57	$0.62	$0.60	$0.64

[a]"Other operating income" consists of various things. In 1991 and 1992, it includes amounts of DM 139 million and 59 million, respectively, drawn from the specific reserve that the company set up for losses it anticipated in the East German company DKFL, which it acquired in 1990. The yearly release of those reserve amounts corresponds to DKFL's losses; hence it involves no net increase in earnings. "Other operating income" also includes the release of other reserves (amounting to about DM 30 a year in 1990, 1991, and 1992), as well as charges for services to employees, gains from currency translation, rental receipts, and reductions in the provision for bad debts.

[b]The company decided that, in 1992, the estimated depreciable lives of certain fixed assets would be extended: for office and factory buildings, from 25 years to 50 years; for various plant and equipment by 4 to 7 years. A footnote to the annual report would say something like: "These changes, which raised the company's net earnings by DM 110 million, were made because of the strained earnings situation." This is already reflected in the above numbers for 1992.

[c]Extraordinary income in 1992 consists largely of the release of general reserves. Extraordinary expense in 1992 consists primarily of restructuring expenses related to the announced closing of the DKFL plant in Berlin (about DM 30 for severance pay and DM 13 million for asset write-downs.) The income tax figure for 1992 derives from subsidiaries' individual income statements.

[d]See Exhibit 12.6 for an explanation of "value added."

[e]Kugelfischer—like German corporations generally—doesn't provide a cash flow statement. The "gross cash flow" number that it discloses is a not very well defined number that represents pretax income, excluding extraordinary items, plus depreciation and amortization, and other adjustments having to do with reserves.

[f]Capital expenditures shown above exclude acquisitions.

[g]The large increase in the number of employees in 1990 and 1991 was due mainly to the addition of the East German company DKFL.

Source: Company annual reports.

EXHIBIT 12.3 Kugelfischer and Comparable Bearings Companies: Selected Financial and Operating Data (DM millions except stock prices, number of common shares outstanding, and number of employees)

	Kugelfischer		SKF	
	1992	1991	1992	1991
Sales	3,563	3,885	7,195	7,233
Cost of goods sold	2,800[a]	3,000[a]	5,453	5,275
Operating profit	56	135	(320)[b]	(15)[b]
EBITDA	261	465	276[b]	306[b]
Net income	16	(81)	(460)[b,d]	(324)[b]
Total assets	4,610	4,993	8,833	8,986
Total inventories	1,706	1,820	2,547	2,592
Total liabilities	3,986[e]	3,799[e]	6,422	6,147
Total interest-bearing debt	2,092	2,104	2,634	2,591
Total short-term interest-bearing debt	1,548	1,621	880	1,369
Common/preferred stock price (DM)				
High	256.1/185.7	271.6/221.3	32.9	33.6
Low	80.1/66.2	186.4/143.5	16.2	18.4
Beginning of year	191.0/143.5	213.4/188.9	25.7	18.4
End of year	87.6/67.6	191.0/143.5	20.0	26.1
Average during year	188.6/141.4	237.5/190.4	25.4	27.5
Number of common/preferred shares				
outstanding at year-end (millions)	3.3/1.18	3.3/1.18	113.0	113.0
Number of employees at year-end	30,847	34,675	45,151	52,469
Location of headquarters	Schweinfurt, Germany		Goteborg, Sweden	

Approximate sales breakdown for each company:
Kugelfischer   Bearings (76%), various industrial engineering products (24%)
SKF   Bearings and seals (84%), special steels (9%), tools (7%)
NSK   Bearings (60%), automotive components (31%), precision machine parts and mechatronics products (7%), other (2%)
NTN   Bearings (70%), other (30%; e.g. precision processing equipment, automated production equipment, automotive equipment)
Timken   Bearings (71%), steel (29%)

[a]Casewriter's estimate. Kugelfischer does not specifically disclose its "cost of goods sold." Per Exhibit 12.2, its income statement shows "Cost of materials" and "Personnel expenses," and the latter represents wages and benefits for all employees in the company.
[b]In 1992 and 1991, SKF recorded pretax restructuring charges—having to do mostly with employee layoffs—of DM 296 million (Kroner 1,100 million), and DM 261 million (Kroner 950 million), respectively.
[c]In 1991, Timken recorded a DM 68 million ($41 million) pretax restructuring charge.
[d]SKF's 1992 net income includes a DM 58 million (Kroner 214 million) extraordinary charge, net of tax, for discontinued operations.
[e]Kugelfischer's total liabilities are calculated to include "provisions" but to exclude "reserves."
[f]NTN: number of employees is casewriter's estimate.
General note: Financial data for SKF (in kroner), NSK (in yen), and Timken (in dollars) were converted into deutsche marks based on the average exchange rates during 1992 and 1991. The deutsche mark was worth, on average, $.64 and $.60 in 1992 and 1991, respectively.
Source: Companies' annual reports; Bloomberg.

NSK		NTN		Timken	
1992	1991	1992	1991	1992	1991
5,182	5,508	3,873	4,010	2,571	2,742
4,390	4,566	3,162	3,231	2,031	2,181
37	180	60	129	77	(2)[c]
400	567	398	473	299	179[c]
9	77	59	77	6	(60)
8,156	8,316	5,796	5,833	2,722	2,929
961	937	1,310	1,224	487	533
5,233	5,361	3,717	3,781	1,179	1,234
3,566	3,479	2,315	2,215	501	453
1,520	942	1,202	721	230	230
767.5	1,056.8	785.0	1,030.8	47.0	49.7
574.1	667.4	499.2	679.8	37.2	34.5
698.9	859.0	767.5	883.7	37.2	35.2
610.3	692.2	581.6	760.1	41.5	39.5
673.9	873.9	605.3	852.8	42.0	42.8
557.2	557.1	463.1	463.1	30.5	29.9
10,129	9,975	8,000[f]	8,000[f]	16,729	17,740
Tokyo, Japan		Osaka, Japan		Canton, Ohio (U.S.)	

EXHIBIT 12.4 Kugelfischer and Comparable Bearings Companies: Capital Expenditures and Research and Development (DM millions)

	1990	1991	1992
Kugelfischer			
Capital expenditures	486	404	274
Research and development	"3% to 14% of sales"[a]	"3% to 14% of sales"[a]	N.A.
SKF			
Capital expenditures	435	489	303
Research and development	146	148	128
NSK			
Capital expenditures	481	571	426
Research and development	137	146	140
NTN			
Capital expenditures	—[b]	—[b]	—[b]
Research and development	N.A.	N.A.	N.A.
Timken			
Capital expenditures	188	233	213
Research and development	65	68	66

Notes:
[a]Kugelfischer did not disclose the actual amounts of money it spent on R&D. In its 1990 and 1991 annual reports, however, it said that R&D expenditures "remain high. During the year under review, these outlays amounted to between 3% and 14% of sales, depending on the product division."

[b]NTN's capital expenditures varied enormously during the late 1980s and early 1990s.

General note: Financial data for SKF (in kroner), NSK (in yen), and Timken (in dollars) were converted into deutsche marks based on the average exchange rates during 1992, 1991, and 1990.

Source: Companies' annual reports.

EXHIBIT 12.5 Kugelfischer: Wages and Benefits

	1991 In Millions of DM	1991 As % of Basic Wages and Salaries	1990 In Millions of DM	1990 As % of Basic Wages and Salaries
Basic wages and salaries	638.4	100.0%	682.2	100.0%
Paid downtime, of which:	256.9	40.2%	248.9	36.5%
Paid vacation (collectively negotiated)	109.3		100.6	
Additional vacation pay (collectively negotiated)	51.3		50.4	
Holiday pay	43.5		42.7	
Continuation of wages and salary payments in case of illness	42.1		44.6	
Recreation time and other hours not worked	10.7		10.6	
Statutory social welfare contributions, of which:	171.3	26.8%	171.9	25.2%
Social security contributions	161.0		162.0	
Contributions to workmen's compensation insurance	9.6		9.7	
Contributions to Pension Guarantee Fund	0.7		0.2 / 171.9	
Extra payments, of which:	61.4	9.6%	71.8	10.5%
Christmas bonuses and similar allowances	50.4		60.8	
Payments under the Law Promoting Capital Formation by Employees	11.0		11.0	
Education and training	24.1	3.8%	23.3	3.4%
Employee services, including cafeteria	14.8	2.3%	13.8	2.0%
Less amounts included more than once	(5.9)	−0.9%	(4.6)	−0.7%
Separation benefits	34.9	5.5%	0.0	0.0%
Pensions and welfare expense	28.9	4.5%	88.3	12.9%
Total personnel expenses	1,224.8	191.9%	1,295.6	189.9%

Note: The above information—which pertains to the largest business component of the company—is the only information of this sort made public. It is, however, representative of the company as a whole.
Source: Company annual reports.

EXHIBIT 12.6   Some Differences between Germany and the United States in Capital Markets, Accounting, and Financial Reporting

- By international standards, German capital markets were fairly small. For example, in the mid-1980s, when Kugelfischer went public, the total market value of publicly traded German companies was only about 14 percent of the country's gross domestic product; in the United States, Japan, and the United Kingdom, it was 50 percent or more. Only one-tenth of one percent of German businesses were publicly traded. Many were family controlled. There were historical reasons for this:

  > In a country twice destroyed by crippling world wars, the German investor had naturally been a cautious one, keener on bonds and bank savings than on volatile and vulnerable stakes in business. The German businessman, for his part, carefully building an enterprise out of nothing after the devastation of the early 1940s, relied on the security of his immediate family to manage his business, and on the relationship with his friendly banker to finance it.[1]

  With a healthy economy, a healthy stock market, and a new generation of investors in the 1980s, however, changes in the German equity market were (in one banker's words) "slow but steady."

- Banks generally played a more significant role in the financing and governance of corporations in Germany than they did in the United States. Corporations borrowed much more money from banks than they did by issuing bonds. Moreover, a greater proportion of debt tended to be short-term than was the case in the United States; it was fairly common for 20 to 30 percent of a major corporation's interest-bearing debt to be due within one year. Although many people believed that banks controlled corporate Germany, that was not true in terms of direct equity holdings. Banks did hold a fair amount of equity in German companies, but their influence derived more from their financing role and from the practice of "proxy voting," whereby banks cast votes on behalf of dispersed shareholders who deposited their shares with them.

- The market for corporate control had historically been much more limited in Germany than it had been in the United States. Through the early 1990s, hostile takeovers in Germany were virtually unheard-of.

- Using accounting to "smooth income" from one year to the next went on to a considerably greater extent in Germany than it did in the United States. The general presumption is that income smoothing reduces the volatility of earnings and thus the perceived riskiness of a company's stock. The generally accepted accounting principles (GAAP) of some European countries, however, "actually encouraged income smoothing by companies as a way to stimulate a long-term view of companies' operations and to encourage overall confidence in the nation's economy."[2] The well-known

EXHIBIT 12.6   *(Continued)*

use of "reserves" in German accounting contributed to this. Additions to reserves (that is, charges against income) could be taken in good years, and the reserves could be "drawn down" in bad years (thus increasing income). This practice went well beyond the recording of "loss contingencies" in U.S. accounting.[3]

- Whereas in the United States financial reporting and tax reporting were quite different things, in Germany extremely little difference between them was permitted. For example, if you used accelerated depreciation for tax purposes, that's what you also had to use for financial reporting. The opening sentence of the auditors' report indicated whether or not a company's financial statements "comply with the legal regulations."

- Accounting standards in the United States required diversified companies to report the sales, operating profits, total assets, depreciation, and capital expenditures of distinct business segments. In Germany, they did not. Accounting standards in the United States also required companies to provide a cash flow statement, organized into "operating," "investing," and "financing" activities. In Germany, they did not. (Thus Kugelfischer did not make public any business segment information other than sales and also did not provide any cash flow statement.) The use of "reserves" in Germany, however, was meant to provide some protection for bank creditors.

- German corporations provided, in their annual reports, far more information about employees than American corporations did. American corporations typically indicated their year-end head count, their compliance with certain basic labor laws, what their relationship with unions was, and that's all. German corporations provided not only information of that sort but also information about things like wages, benefits, educational background of employees, training programs, and age distribution. Some German companies, like Kugelfischer, also provided—on a voluntary basis—a "value added" statement. (This had nothing to do with the concept of Economic Value Added, or EVA, which measures financial returns to shareholders in excess of the cost of capital.) The "value added" statement represented a kind of social reporting. It indicated how much wealth the corporation had produced for society as a whole. Mathematically, "value added" represented total "output" minus the cost of all goods and services purchased from sources outside the company. (Per Kugelfischer's income statements shown in Exhibit 12.2, "output" included not only sales but also changes in inventories of finished goods and work-in-process, company-produced additions to plant and equipment, and other income.) The resulting number was then shown—in a pie chart, for example—broken down among the various groups who derived financial benefit from the company's existence—employees, governmental entities, creditors, shareholders, and the company itself (in terms of earnings

(Continued)

EXHIBIT 12.6   *(Continued)*

---

retention). The "value added" statement served, among other things, to highlight the very large proportion of "value added" that was distributed to employees.

- Whereas in the United States, publicly traded companies had to disclose total compensation paid to each of its board members and top executives, in Germany they didn't. German companies were required to disclose only the amount paid to board members in aggregate and the amount paid to top executives in aggregate. Moreover, in the United States, the large majority of publicly traded companies awarded stock options to senior managers. In Germany, although bonuses were often paid to senior managers, stock options were rare.

---

[1] *Euromoney Corporate Finance*, January 13, 1987.

[2] Gerhard G. Mueller, *Accounting: An International Perspective (4th edition)*, New York: Richard D. Irwin, 1996, p. 27.

[3] A dramatic example of this occurred in 1993 when Daimler-Benz—the maker of Mercedes-Benz cars and the largest industrial corporation in Germany—listed its stock on the New York Stock Exchange. In order to comply with U.S. securities laws, Daimler-Benz submitted financial statements that reconciled its net income as reported in Germany with net income as defined by U.S. accounting standards. Under German GAAP, the company's net income in 1993 was DM 615 million (about $373 million); under U.S. GAAP, its net income was a *loss* of DM 1,839 million (about $1,114 million). The primary reason for the difference was the use of accounting reserves in Germany that were not permitted in the United States. The chief financial officer of Daimler-Benz said at the time: "There is a big gap between German accounting standards and U.S. principles. U.S. accounting discloses so much more and tells you what is really happening in a company" (*Wall Street Journal*, October 5, 1993).

EXHIBIT 12.7   Letter to the *Financial Times* of London, January 23, 1990

Sir:

The purchase last week by Japan's largest ball-bearing manufacturer [NSK] of Britain's [largest] ball-bearing company (RHP) . . . is an example of the patient determination of the Japanese to dominate strategic industries.

Your article [on January 18, 1990] accurately describes how RHP was formed under pressure from the British Government in 1969 to [prevent] the existing three British firms [from falling] under the control of the Swedith SKF company [and] to maintain a British capability in this essential strategic product. No vehicles, aircraft, or machinery can function without ball bearings, which are precision products manufactured from specialist alloy steel.

I was chief executive and chairman of RHP from its formation until 1977. After pyaing off the initial government loans in 1971, we went ahead to modernise the factories and rationalise the product lines. We organised joint ventures in some lines with European Community competitors. The company became an effective international competitor. . . .

[He describes how, in the early 1970s, several Japanese companies, including NSK, exported a lot of low-priced bearings into the British market and paid heavy anti-dumping fines for doing so, but achieved "considerable market penetration" in the process.]

In 1973 the [British] government, after talks with Prime Minister Tanaka of Japan, said it would welcome inward investment from Japanese manufacturers, and NSK got approval to build a greenfield new factory at Peterless, Durham, to make popular, high-volume sizes only. RHP protested vigorously against this because it already had adequate capacity to supply the British market. From Peterlee, NSK was able to supply bearings "Made in Britain" and expoert them to the [European Community]. The Japanese are content with a lower return on capital than can be accepted by a British plc, and price pressures on popular sizes caused RHP later to reduce capacity, and a relatively modern plant in Durham was eventually closed.

Now 15 years later, with great patience, NSK has achieved its objective of dominating the UK market.

With a deplorable lack of patience the financial institutions and venture capitalists have taken a fat profit. . . . As a result, management shareholders will receive cash beyond their dreams and retain their jobs—at least for the time being.

The City will doubtless regard this as a successful financial foray. Our financial institutions often claim they are real investors, but many cannot resist the temptation of as hort-term gain, and industry cannot rely on their loyalty.

As the Government seeks inward investment, it will probably not bat an eyelid. The supply of high technology bearings for aero-engines for the RAF and Rolls-Royce now all depends on foreign-owned companies, as do the bearings for all our vehicles and machinery, but current industrial policy, or lack of one, accepts this type of situation.

So why worry? I worry because I see the progressive weakening of Britain's industrial manufacturing and with it a long-term threat to our economic strength, and the sale of RHP to a Japanese company is a significant further step in the wrong direction.

William Barlow
Third Floor
Devonshire House,
Mayfair Place, W1

Source: Financial Times, January 23, 1990. Reprinted with permission of William Barlow and the *Financial Times*.

CHAPTER 13

Chase Manhattan Corporation

The Making of America's Largest Bank

In mid-August 1995, Walter Shipley, chairman and chief executive officer (CEO) of Chemical Banking Corporation, was preparing to leave the bank's Manhattan headquarters building after a long day. For the past four weeks he and other senior Chemical managers had been in intensive negotiations with their counterparts at Chase Manhattan Corporation, including that bank's chairman and CEO Thomas Labrecque. At issue was whether the two banks would agree to merge in a friendly transaction. If completed, the merger would produce the largest commercial bank in the United States, and the fourth largest bank in the world, with total assets of nearly $300 billion and over 74,000 employees.

Shipley believed the merger would create value in two ways. First, it would allow the banks to realize substantial savings in operating and overhead costs. The banks' businesses overlapped in many areas, and they both maintained extensive retail branch networks in the Downstate New York area. In addition, both banks were headquartered in Manhattan, and maintained elaborate trading floors in both Manhattan and London. Cost savings of up to $1.5 billion were deemed possible, but this would require reducing the banks' combined workforce by 12,000 employees and closing over 100 branches.

The second benefit of the merger, in Shipley's view, was that as a larger bank with significant product and market leadership positions, Chemical-Chase would enjoy significantly higher revenue growth. Larger banks with

---

This case was prepared by Professor Stuart Gilson, assisted by Research Associate Cedric Escalle. Copyright © 1997 by the President and Fellows of Harvard College. Harvard Business School case 298-016.

leadership positions in each business could more easily enter new markets and develop new products; they could better satisfy the complex needs of large corporate customers; and they could better afford the large-scale investments in new technology that would be required to take a financial services firm into the twenty-first century.

Important issues had to be resolved before the merger could proceed. It would be necessary to set an exchange ratio for the transaction—the number of shares of Chemical stock that would be swapped for each share of Chase stock. It would also be necessary to decide how, and by whom, the new entity would be managed, as well as how the two complex organizations would be integrated.

Shipley also had more fundamental concerns. Chemical was currently profitable, and was under no immediate pressure to merge or change its present course. And less than four years earlier, Chemical had merged with Manufacturers Hanover to form the second-largest bank in the United States, with combined shareholders' equity of $7.3 billion. The full integration of these two banks had only recently been completed. This raised a number of important questions. Did a merger with Chase—or any bank—make sense at this time? If the merger did go forward, would it be possible to achieve the proposed cost savings without damaging the bank's long-term competitiveness, or its ability to keep up with the rapid pace of change in the financial services industry? And would the stock market give the bank full credit for the value created by the merger?

CHEMICAL BANKING CORPORATION

The Chemical Banking Corporation was founded in 1824 by three New York City merchants as a division of a chemical manufacturing company. Twenty years later, the chemical business was liquidated and the company was reincorporated as a bank. Over the next century, the bank rapidly expanded and developed a reputation for sound, conservative management. During the 1930s, Chemical's business prospered and its deposits rose by 40 percent, even while 8,000 other banks failed.

The postwar era was a period of spectacular growth for Chemical. From 1946 to 1972, the bank's assets increased from $1.35 billion to $15 billion. It aggressively acquired other banks, and expanded into a variety of new product and geographic markets. Starting in the late 1950s, Chemical greatly expanded its international business, forming numerous overseas subsidiaries and opening up its first full-service branch in London in 1959. Over the next two decades the bank established offices in key financial centers around the world, including Frankfurt, the Bahamas, Zurich, Brussels,

Paris, Tokyo, Milan, Taiwan, and Singapore. As part of this growth, the bank also diversified into a variety of different banking products and services, and decentralized its organizational structure. It had two objectives in doing this: to increase the proportion of its earnings that were derived from fee-based service businesses (thereby reducing its exposure to fluctuations in interest rate spreads) and to acquire a reputation for being innovative.

Still lacking a clear niche in the industry, however, and with its financial performance lagging, starting in the early 1980s Chemical restructured its nonconsumer banking businesses, and undertook a series of aggressive acquisitions. In 1982 Chemical secured a future presence in the profitable Florida market by acquiring a stake in Florida National Banks. In 1986 it entered into a deferred merger agreement with New Jersey-based Horizon Bancorp (the merger was consummated in 1989). And in 1987 it acquired Texas Commerce Bankshares (TCB) in what was then the largest interstate bank merger in U.S. history. These acquisitions were made either in anticipation of or in response to agreements between various states to allow interstate banking, which had previously been prohibited. In the banking industry as a whole, the number of such acquisitions increased dramatically in response to these regulatory changes.

Although Chemical continued to grow in size, by the late 1980s and early 1990s its financial performance began to suffer under the strain of a U.S. recession, mounting real estate losses, and increasing loan defaults by sovereign borrowers, especially in Latin America. In 1991, $1 billion of loans in Chemical's $6.7 billion real estate portfolio were in default.

Merger with Manufacturers Hanover

In late 1991 Chemical Banking Corporation merged with Manufacturers Hanover Corporation. This transaction was the first major bank merger "among equals." (At the time Chemical and Manufacturers Hanover were, respectively, the sixth and ninth largest banks in the United States.) With total assets of $135 billion, the bank was second largest in the United States, after Citicorp.

The chief executives of the two banks—Walter Shipley at Chemical and John McGillicuddy at Manufacturers Hanover—conceived the merger as an opportunity to realize substantial cost savings, through approximately 6,000 employee layoffs and the closing of 80 branches (especially in the New York City area where both banks were headquartered). To reflect the costs of merger-related workforce reductions and back office consolidations, Chemical took a pretax restructuring charge of $625 million in 1991 (later, in 1993, it took an additional charge of $158 million). Also, in January 1992—less than one month after the 1991 merger became effective—the bank sold 57.5 million shares of new common stock in a massive public offering, netting proceeds of $1.52 billion. The issue was, at the time, the largest equity offering ever by a U.S. bank.

The merger was subsequently judged a success by Chemical management and most market analysts. By 1995, management believed, the merger had enabled the bank to reduce its pretax noninterest expense by almost $750 million a year. This amount represented 36 percent of Manufacturers Hanover's total noninterest expense, or 19 percent of the two banks' combined noninterest expense, before the merger. Annual corporate overhead expense alone had been reduced by nearly 30 percent since the merger. Chemical's efficiency ratio, which stood at 75 percent in 1990, had been reduced to 58 percent by 1993.[1]

Despite the financial benefits of the merger, however, by late 1994 the bank had fallen to fourth place in terms of total size, as the U.S. banking industry was consumed by a wave of merger activity and other huge banks were formed. And near the end of 1994, Chemical launched a major initiative aimed at reducing expenses and selectively investing for revenue growth, called the "Margin Improvement Program." Under this initiative the bank would seek an additional $440 million in annual expense reductions by restructuring and rationalizing its operations; and it would reinvest about half of these savings in selected areas, including its national consumer and investment banking businesses. In 1994 Chemical took a pretax restructuring charge of $308 million for the costs of implementing the program. The program was fully implemented by mid-1995.

CHASE MANHATTAN CORPORATION

Chase Manhattan Corporation was formed in 1955 as the merger of two New York–based banks, Chase National Bank and the Bank of Manhattan. Both of these banks had colorful histories. The company that was to become the Bank of Manhattan was formed in 1799 to supply water to New York City residents during a yellow fever epidemic, but its real purpose was to be a bank, and in less than a year this is what it became. By 1955 the bank had grown to become one of the nation's most profitable

---

[1]The efficiency ratio, a standard measure of operating efficiency used in the banking industry, equals total noninterest expense per dollar of revenue, where revenue is defined as the sum of (1) noninterest income and (2) *net* interest income (i.e., gross interest income *minus* gross interest expense).

and well-regarded regional banks. Most of its business was in retail banking, and it operated 67 branches in New York City. Chase National Bank was one of the largest banks in the world, following decades of high growth. This growth was fueled both by acquisitions (during the 1920s and 1930s it had acquired seven of the largest banks in New York City) and by aggressive development of new markets and products (especially in corporate banking). The bank had extensive international operations, and it was the first bank to open up branches in Germany and Japan after World War II.

A driving force behind the merger was David Rockefeller, and he became chairman of Chase in 1969. The Rockefeller family was one of the most important families in American business and politics. Rockefeller traveled extensively, and he developed close ties to business and government leaders around the world. Through size and political connections, Chase became a major power broker in international affairs. By the end of the 1970s, Chase was the third largest bank in the United States, with 226 branches in New York City. It was truly a global bank: Two-thirds of its income came from foreign operations, and it operated thirty-four subsidiaries outside the United States.

In the 1980s, however, Chase encountered significant difficulties. The bank found itself holding hundreds of millions of dollars in bad real estate loans; and it had one of the largest exposures to defaulted Third World debt of any U.S. bank. In May 1987 Chase added $1.6 billion to its loan loss reserves, and for the year it reported a record loss of $895 million; for 1989 and 1990 it had a combined loss of one billion dollars.

The bank's response to this crisis was to reduce its workforce by 10 percent between 1986 and 1988 and to replace the chairman and CEO, Willard Butcher, with Thomas Labrecque (David Rockefeller had retired in 1981). Labrecque had started with Chase as a trainee in 1964, and had steadily advanced through the management ranks. Under Labrecque, Chase took further steps to address its problems. By the end of 1991 the workforce was reduced by another 6,000, and several subsidiaries were sold. The bank scaled back its foreign operations by eliminating many of its overseas branches. And it eliminated all of its domestic branches that were located outside the New York area. Going forward, Chase would focus its energies in three areas: regional banking in the New York/New Jersey/Connecticut Tri-State region; national consumer operations (e.g., credit cards, home mortgages, and automobile loans); and international investment banking.

These initiatives seemed to work, and Chase returned to profitability in 1991 when it reported net income of $520 million. Earnings continued to be positive for the next three years, reaching $1.1 billion in 1994. The bank's stock price remained weak, however, and many analysts felt that Chase was vulnerable to being taken over by a stronger bank.

Takeover speculation intensified in April 1995, when money manager Michael Price acquired a 6.1 percent stake in Chase and became its largest shareholder. Price, who had a reputation as a shareholder activist, publicly called on Chase management to consider ways to increase the stock price. He especially favored actions that would allow the bank to achieve greater business focus, including divestitures or spin-offs of noncore businesses. He told the press: "Chase's activities are so sprawling that Wall Street is having trouble evaluating the bank's worth."[2]

Chase management agreed that the bank was undervalued, but believed the problem was not in being too diversified; indeed, it felt that "the company's large reach was the very essence of its value."[3] In June 1995, the bank responded by announcing a restructuring program that was code-named "Focus." Under this program the bank would reduce its workforce by an additional 3,000 to 6,000 people, and, by 1997, reduce its annual noninterest costs by $400 million (pretax). One banking analyst, however, commented that "Chase's biggest problem isn't one of expense reduction but revenue growth. In an era of rapid bank consolidation, product innovation and cutthroat competition, Chase hasn't been aggressive enough in pursuing new business opportunities."[4] Major initiatives under the program had not yet started when final merger negotiations with Chemical commenced in mid-July 1995.

RESTRUCTURING IN THE BANKING INDUSTRY

Merger and Consolidation

The 1990s witnessed a number of significant changes in the U.S. banking industry. Having worked through most of its problems in 1990 and 1991, the industry entered a period of record profitability. Between 1991 and 1995, U.S. commercial banks experienced a near quadrupling of their total pretax earnings from about $20 billion to $80 billion. This growth represented a dramatic turnaround from the late 1980s, which had seen a record number of bank failures.

---

[2]*New York Times*, April 7, 1995, p. D1.
[3]Ibid.
[4]*Wall Street Journal*, June 27, 1995, p. 3.

There had also been a dramatic upsurge in bank mergers. During 1988–1990 the total value of bank equity acquired in acquisitions had been $4.5 billion a year on average; since 1991 the average had been over $15 billion—$25.5 billion for the first eight months of 1995 alone.[5] This trend reflected both an increase in the number of transactions as well as an increase in average transaction size; the most recent mergers had been of unprecedented size (Exhibit 13.1). One consequence of this merger activity was a decline in the number of banks. In 1980 there were 15,300 commercial banks in the United States; by 1995 there were fewer than 10,000. The banking industry had also become more concentrated, with the top fifty banks now holding 65 percent of total bank assets, up from 53 percent in 1985.

Bank industry analysts recognized two distinct types of bank mergers: in-market mergers and market extension mergers. In an in-market merger, the acquiring bank and target bank did business in the same geographic markets. Elimination of duplication and overlap between the banks' activities allowed them to realize potentially significant savings in operating and overhead expenses. A market extension merger, in contrast, was a merger between banks that did business in distinct, nonoverlapping markets. These mergers produced fewer expense reduction opportunities, but also more opportunities to enter new markets, diversify income streams, and grow revenues. Both types of mergers allowed banks to achieve scale economies in certain back office operations—for example, those that supported a credit card or mortgage servicing business.

The 1991 merger of Chemical and Manufacturers Hanover had been an in-market merger, as was the February 1995 merger between New England–based Fleet Bank and Shawmut Bank. In-market mergers typically produced pretax cost savings equal to 30 to 40 percent of the target bank's total noninterest expense before the merger.

In contrast, the June 1995 merger of First Union (based in Charlotte, North Carolina) and First Fidelity (based in Newark, New Jersey) was a market extension merger. With a value of $5.4 billion, this was the largest bank merger to date; the resulting bank was the sixth largest in the United States, with $124 billion in assets and 1,970 branches located all the way from Florida to Connecticut. The banks' branch networks overlapped only in Maryland, so cost savings were expected to be relatively modest (5

---

[5]*Source:* Investment banking analysis prepared for Chemical Bank (excludes transactions under $35 million).

percent of the two banks' combined noninterest expense).[6] Exhibit 13.2 shows the principal geographic markets served by a sample of the largest U.S. banks.

Forces for Change

According to some observers, the high level of restructuring by commercial banks could be traced to powerful economic forces that were dramatically altering the profitability and structure of the entire financial services industry.[7]

Traditionally, government regulation had imposed severe limits on the product and geographic markets in which a given financial institution could legally do business. For example, the 1933 Glass Steagall Act prohibited commercial banks from underwriting corporate securities, and the 1927 McFadden Act and the 1956 Bank Holding Company Act restricted interstate branch banking. As a result, the financial services industry tended to be organized along institutional lines, with different financial institutions—commercial banks, savings and loans, insurance companies, mutual funds, and pension funds—each providing a distinct set of products and services.

With the recent trend towards degregulation of the financial services industry, however, many of these barriers were breaking down. For example, in 1994 Congress passed the Riegle-Neal Interstate Banking and Branching Efficiency Act, which provided for nationwide banking by October 1995. And since the late 1980s, commercial banks had, on a restricted

---

[6]One analysis of bank mergers showed that average cost savings varied substantially across different functional areas of the bank. For market extension mergers, cost savings relating to the merging banks' branch networks were found to be roughly equal to 5 percent of the acquired bank's total noninterest expense, on average. For cost savings related to staff and to systems and operations, the corresponding percentage was 20 percent. These percentages were significantly higher for in-market mergers: 35 percent for branch networks and 40 percent for staff and systems/operations. (*Source:* Mitchell Madison Group.)

[7]The following section draws heavily on Robert C. Merton, "The Financial System and Economic Performance," *Journal of Financial Services Research,* December 1990; Dwight B. Crane and Zvi Bodie, "Form Follows Function: The Transformation of Banking," *Harvard Business Review,* March–April 1996, pp. 109–117; and Dwight B. Crane et al., *The Global Financial System* (Boston: Harvard Business School Press, 1996).

basis, been allowed to underwrite certain corporate securities.[8] More recently, banks had received the right to sell mutual funds, in direct competition with mutual fund complexes like Fidelity and Vanguard.

While these trends clearly benefited banks, deregulation had also given nonbank financial institutions increased access to the banks' traditional markets. For example, mutual fund companies could now offer their shareholders check-writing privileges, providing the banks' customers with a direct substitute for bank checking accounts. As a result of these and related developments, U.S. households had allocated an increasing fraction of their savings to nonbank institutions. In 1994, for example, only 35 percent of households' financial assets were held in conventional bank deposits, down sharply from 49 percent in 1980. Exhibit 13.3 shows market share information for selected products and services offered by commercial banks.

These trends were reinforced by the sharp decline in the cost of computing technology. This development enabled nonbanks to develop a cost advantage in providing certain products and services through increased specialization, and to compete directly with banks in their traditional markets. In corporate lending, institutions like General Motors Acceptance Corporation and General Electric Credit Corporation now provided U.S. businesses with hundreds of billions of dollars of financing (much of it secured by certain specialized assets). In the consumer credit card business, nonbank institutions now accounted for 40 percent of all credit card balances outstanding, up from 25 percent in 1992. And the mortgage servicing business was now dominated by nonbank institutions, although some banks—including Chemical and Chase—continued to have a significant presence in this market.

The impact of technology was not one-sided, however. Advances in technology and computing power, while allowing nonbank institutions to intrude on the banks' traditional businesses, also provided banks with their own opportunities to develop new markets and products. One potentially promising area was online or home banking. Some expected the growth of this market to be huge (Exhibit 13.4). Significant investments in new technology would be necessary to develop this business, however. And growth

---

[8]Following a Supreme Court ruling in July 1988, commercial banks were permitted to conduct nonbanking activities such as securities underwriting and trading through a special ("Section 20") subsidiary. As of August 1995, revenue from the underwriting business was legally capped at 10 percent of the subsidiary's gross revenue, but many industry observers expected this percentage—and the list of securities banks could underwrite—to grow.

in home banking could be limited by the increasing availability and popularity of automated teller machines (ATMs). (In 1990 there were 80,200 ATMs installed in the United States; by 1995 there were 122,700.)

Taking all of these factors into account, the current level of profitability in the U.S. banking sector might therefore be difficult to sustain. For 1995, total pretax earnings for all U.S. banks were expected to be around $75 billion, implying a return on shareholders' equity of 14.7 percent.[9] But increasing competition for banks' traditional businesses from nonbank institutions—which could provide the same products and services at lower cost—meant that banks had to find ways to cut their costs if they were to avoid future declines in profitability or market share. Exhibit 13.5 reports relative interest rates earned or charged by banks and competing financial institutions.

RESTRUCTURING ANALYSIS

The decision to pursue a merger of Chemical and Chase was the product of a lengthy, much more general debate that had been proceeding independently at each bank for several years. Management at each bank was keenly aware of the powerful forces that were reshaping the financial services industry, potentially threatening the long-term profitability of commercial banks.

A merger with a bank or other financial institution represented one important option for dealing with these pressures, but the issues here were complicated. Under a traditional in-market merger, elimination of redundant retail branch offices and other hard assets made it possible to achieve significant reductions in operating expenses. Participants in this debate recognized, however, that it was becoming increasingly difficult to measure the extent of a bank's retail business in terms of "bricks and mortar." For many products—for example, credit cards and consumer mortgage loans—the relevant markets were national in scope, yet a merger of these businesses could also create significant expense reduction opportunities.

A market extension merger, which would allow a bank to grow revenues and enter new markets, represented another competitive response. This option also raised a number of difficult questions. As with in-market mergers, market extension mergers could be differentiated by the closeness of the

---

[9]This figure includes a deduction for banks' aggregate loan losses, which in 1995 were equal to 30 basis points on total bank assets of $4.2 trillion. This was below the previous ten-year average loan loss rate of 55 basis points.

merging banks' businesses. Both Chemical and Chase management recognized that a market extension merger could be used either to strengthen and grow existing product lines or to acquire new products and enter entirely new businesses. (An example of the latter option would be a merger between a bank and a full-service brokerage house, although such a combination would not have been permitted under then-existing regulations.)

Other issues were debated as well. One was the mix of retail and wholesale business that was most appropriate for each bank; this mix would clearly be affected by the choice of merger partner. Another issue was whether it made more sense to expand in multiple markets at once by acquiring a multiline bank or instead to concentrate on growing certain selected businesses individually—for example, by acquiring a consumer credit card company. Chemical and Chase had both recently acquired, or were in the process of acquiring, consumer mortgage loan companies.

A critical consideration in any merger decision would be the opportunity to realize economies of scale and scope by expanding the size of the bank, thereby strengthening the market and product positions of the combined institutions. At Chemical, Shipley felt strongly that larger institutions with market leadership enjoyed a distinct competitive advantage.

For one thing, larger banks could better afford the massive investment in new information technology that was needed to provide the level of service and breadth of product offerings that retail and corporate customers were increasingly demanding. Chemical believed it would have to invest billions of dollars in new technology over the next few years to respond to these pressures.

Shipley had argued this point several years earlier when Chemical merged with Manufacturers Hanover:

> If it's important for the United States to have large, globally competitive automobile companies, globally competitive chemical companies, globally competitive computer companies, it's important to have large globally competitive banks as well. There is a certain point where the scale of your operations does become important, in terms of profitability and ability to serve your customers efficiently and effectively, and your ability to invest in new products and services. It is very hard for a small bank to keep up with the technology development expenses.[10]

---

[10]*The Record*, September 8, 1991, p. B1.

Shipley also perceived scale economies in the discretionary outlays that Chemical would have to make in its various businesses over time to stay competitive, as new products were introduced and existing products were improved. For example, a new innovation in the credit card business might require an up-front investment of $100 million, regardless of the number of credit cards issued or the dollar value of card receivables managed by the bank.

Finally, Shipley believed that larger banks enjoyed a distinct comparative advantage in attracting new business, especially from corporate clients. If a company needed bank financing for a new investment or acquisition, for example, a large bank would be better positioned to underwrite the loan and provide the needed funds. A large bank would also have the depth of management and the financial wherewithal to offer a broad range of products and services to its corporate clients, in essence offering them "one-stop shopping." Being larger, and better capitalized, would also make a bank more competitive in derivatives market-making. Finally, some banking industry observers reckoned that treasurers and chief financial officers at larger (e.g., Fortune 500) firms preferred to conduct their business with larger banks, which as large institutions themselves better understood the needs of a large corporation.

Summing up these arguments, Shipley noted:

Market leadership across the board [will] materially [enhance] our ability to deploy resources for maximum return. We will be able to finance our growth businesses, including nationwide consumer products and services, private banking, trading, securities underwriting, and information and transaction services, without penalizing other businesses that are solid, but where the potential for growth is not as large. We will have the resources to create new and better products, build closer linkages among our products and provide greater convenience and choice for customers, leading to above average revenue growth.[11]

Chemical management believed that the 1991 merger with Manufacturers Hanover had produced material revenue enhancements and scale economies, resulting in additional revenues in the range $150 million to $200 million a year since the merger. Management believed this increase was in large part made possible by the bank's $1.52 billion equity issue immediately following the merger, which significantly improved its credit quality.

---

[11]*Source:* Company 1995 annual report to shareholders.

Not all bank executives shared Shipley's vision of the industry, however. A number of banks appeared to have developed profitable niches in relatively narrow or specialized product lines. For example, Boston-based BayBank had achieved success by emphasizing consumer banking and small business lending, building an extensive branch-ATM network and emphasizing convenience for the customer. Ohio-based Banc One had also chosen to focus on traditional retail banking and middle-market corporate lending (although its markets were much broader geographically). At the other extreme, State Street Bank & Trust Company specialized in providing financial services like asset custody and investment management for institutions and wealthy individuals, and had little presence in traditional banking activities like deposit-taking or lending. Similarly, New York–based J.P. Morgan had grown to become one of the largest banks in the United States largely on the strength of its wholesale banking business, which included corporate lending and securities underwriting, financial derivatives, and sales and trading; it did not operate retail bank branches or have a presence in any national consumer lending business (such as credit cards or mortgage loans). Bankers Trust also had completely exited from retail banking.

More generally, in recent years scores of industrial companies had chosen to increase their business focus and become much smaller, through downsizing, spin-offs, and asset divestitures—effectively undoing the diversification programs they had pursued years before. Such increases in focus were often rewarded with an increase in the firm's stock price; one study, for example, estimated that firms announcing spin-offs increased their stock price by 3 percent, on average.[12]

Benefits of a Chemical/Chase Merger

At Chemical, a more focused inquiry into the benefits of merging with another bank began in early 1995. This effort, like the more general strategic discussion that preceded it, was initially led by a small group of senior managers that included the three members of the office of the chairman, supported by Peter Tobin and Dina Dublon (respectively, the chief financial officer and corporate treasurer of Chemical). The group's goal was to think broadly about the kinds of combinations that might make sense for the

---

[12]See Patrick J. Cusatis, James A. Miles, and J. Randall Woolridge, "Restructuring Through Spinoffs: The Stock Market Evidence," *Journal of Financial Economics*, vol. 33, 1993, pp. 293–311.

bank. A long list of potential merger partners was considered that included Chase, BankAmerica, NationsBank, First Union, Banc One, and J.P. Morgan, among others. Exhibit 13.6 shows financial and descriptive information for these banks. Exhibit 13.7 shows estimates of the potential cost savings that might be achieved if Chemical were to merge with these banks, based on the experience of recent bank mergers.

As the analysis moved forward and the bank's choices were vigorously debated, a consensus began to emerge that the interests of Chemical would be best served through a merger with Chase.

From Chemical's perspective, Chase was an attractive merger partner for several reasons. It had a globally recognized brand name. It had strong wholesale businesses, and was a leading provider of foreign exchange products. These product lines were complemented by the bank's state-of-the-art trading operations. It was the largest custodian in the world (with $1.8 trillion in total trust and custody assets) and a leader in the international money transfer business. Chase also had competitive strengths in private banking, credit cards, and mortgage banking. Finally, it was a leading provider of retail and middle market corporate banking services in New York State (especially in Downstate New York, which included Manhattan and the nearby metropolitan areas).

A merger of Chemical and Chase would also create significant expense reduction opportunities. Chemical and Chase operated in a number of common businesses. Geographically, the retail and middle-market banking activities of both banks were concentrated in the Tri-State area (New York, New Jersey, and Connecticut). Both banks were headquartered in Manhattan, and both maintained technologically sophisticated sales and trading operations in Manhattan and London.

Management's analysis showed that a Chemical-Chase merger could eventually produce $1.5 billion of annual cost savings. Implementing the merger "saves" would take time, however, so in the first and second year after the merger, anticipated savings would be $600 million and $1.05 billion, respectively. Exhibit 13.8 shows a breakdown of anticipated expense reductions under the merger.

To achieve these cost savings, it would be necessary to close redundant retail branch offices, reduce the size of the banks' combined workforces, and otherwise eliminate excess capacity that would be created by the merger. For example, it would make sense to keep only one trading floor in operation in Manhattan. As many as 100 retail branches might have to be closed. Exhibit 13.9 shows the location of Chemical and Chase retail bank branches in the Downstate New York area.

It would also be necessary to let go of approximately 12,000 employees. The banks hoped to achieve up to two-thirds of these workforce reductions, or saves, through through retirements and attrition, with the rest coming from layoffs. The reductions would be staged over several years.

While announcements of in-market bank mergers were generally well received by the stock market, some observers felt that aggressive cost cutting entailed certain risks. As one bank executive commented: "Once you get [a bank's efficiency ratio] down much further than 55%, what I am afraid happens is that you get a tradeoff for service. And if your service slips, that's going to impact your revenue side."[13]

Beyond the anticipated cost savings, the merger would also produce a much larger bank and therefore allow shareholders to realize the potential benefits of increased scale and scope that Shipley envisioned. A merged Chemical-Chase would be the largest commercial bank in the United States, and the fourth largest bank in the world. On a pro forma basis, as of June 30, 1995, the banks would have combined total assets of $297.3 billion (surpassing Citicorp with $257 billion in assets) and a total stock market capitalization of $22.9 billion (book value of $20 million). Chemical-Chase would have total loans outstanding of $148.9 billion and total deposits of $163.2 billion.

Shipley's goal was for the merged bank to become the leader in nearly every business in which it operated, including credit cards, mortgage banking, branch banking, national consumer banking, syndicated loan financing, and global capital markets. Exhibit 13.10 shows 1995 revenue forecasts for the two banks by line of business. The benefits of increased size, he believed, would eventually translate into higher revenues, especially in the bank's operating services, global wholesale banking, and international private banking businesses. Given the many factors and events that could affect revenues, however, coming up with a precise estimate of the potential revenue enhancements would be extremely difficult. Based on an extremely conservative analysis, the bank estimated that revenues could increase by $20 million in the second year of the merger and $120 million a year thereafter—but actual revenue increases could be substantially higher than this.

A number of analysts who had recently speculated about a possible Chemical-Chase merger also believed that the merged bank's increased size and diversity would enable it to get a better credit rating, thus lowering the cost of borrowing. Currently Chemical and Chase were each rated A by

---

[13]Gerry Cameron, CEO of U.S. Bancorp, quoted in *The American Banker*, January 8, 1996, p. 6a.

Standard & Poor's, but the analysts believed a merger might raise this to at least AA–.

Over the short term, however, management recognized that the merger would place some stress on the banks' combined earnings. Revenues would decline to some extent due to overlap of the banks' businesses and client bases in some areas, such as credit cards, deposits, and middle market and corporate lending. Revenue could also be adversely affected by the disruptions that would occur as the banks undertook to integrate their computer systems and ATM networks, temporarily inconveniencing customers. Management estimated that the incremental negative impact of these factors on revenue could be $125 million in the first year of the merger.

In addition, the merged bank would incur a one-time restructuring charge. Management estimated that the total charge would be $1.5 billion. This included $550 million for severance payments, $550 million for real estate–related restructuring costs, and $400 million for other costs. Employees who were laid off would be paid severance equal to three weeks' salary for each year of service, plus an additional twenty-six weeks of pay if they had been with the bank for more than twenty-five years. Each departing employee would also receive a $2,500 grant to pay for retraining programs.

Ultimately, to justify the merger it would be necessary to show that the banks' stockholders would be made better off. Given the size and complexity of the banks' operations and the massive changes that were still taking place in the industry, valuing the merger could be difficult. Wall Street analysts currently valued commercial banks using a price-earnings multiple of about eight times, although a higher multiple could be justified for banks with above-average growth prospects. Exhibit 11 presents stand-alone financial projections for Chemical and Chase.

CHALLENGES

The new bank would be called the Chase Manhattan Bank, to capitalize on the stronger name recognition that Chase enjoyed internationally. Actually making the merger work presented a number of significant challenges.

Setting the Merger Terms

Chemical planned to finance its merger with Chase by swapping its common stock for Chase's at a predetermined ratio, as it had also done in its 1991 merger with Manufacturers Hanover. Choosing an appropriate exchange ratio—the number of shares of the acquiring bank offered in exchange for each share of the target bank—involved certain trade-offs. In bank mergers where the acquiring bank was clearly dominant, the exchange ratio would typically be set to give a 30 percent premium to target bank shareholders (that is, target bank shareholders would be given stock in the acquiring bank worth 30 percent more in market value than the shares they gave up). In some recent mergers involving a dominant bank the premium had reached 40 percent. In its recent merger with First Fidelity, First Union had paid a 32 percent premium above market value to acquire First Fidelity's shares.

In contrast, the premium paid in a "merger of equals" was generally much smaller—as low as 5 percent—although the acquiring bank would be less well off in the sense of having to relinquish more management control to the target bank. In merging with Manufacturers Hanover, Chemical had paid a premium of only 10 percent above Manufacturers Hanover's pre-merger announcement stock price.

In the current merger negotiations, setting the exchange ratio turned out to be a complicated, and emotional, issue. The desire of senior management at both Chemical and Chase was to structure the deal so that shareholders and employees of the two banks would share equally in both the rewards and the risks of the merger. Shipley believed that a lower acquisition premium made it easier for management to be objective in deciding which people and assets to retain when the banks were put together; it would also facilitate more equitable sharing of management control.

In general, the exchange ratio in a bank merger was the product of negotiation between the merging banks. The healthier and better capitalized bank, or the bank that made the greater contribution to the merger benefits, would be negotiating from a position of greater strength. The exchange ratio would therefore likely reflect a number of characteristics of the two banks, including size, profitability, asset quality, and the contribution to total cost savings or revenue growth projected under the merger. Exhibit 13.12 shows the stock price history of Chemical and Chase, and Exhibit 13.13 shows ten-year financial summaries for the two banks.

Merger Integration

The task of integrating the two banks would pose a major challenge. First, it would be necessary to decide which of the two banks' distinct systems and technologies should be retained for the merged bank. For example, each bank's retail branch network had its own particular check clearing system, but only one of these systems could be used once the two branch networks were merged. Similar choices had to be made with respect to deposits systems, bank statements, ATMs, and literally hundreds of other systems. The integration of these systems would have to proceed smoothly to avoid inconveniencing the banks' customers. (The bank adopted the motto: "This is our merger, not our customers' merger.")

It would also be necessary to decide how the planned layoffs, branch closings, back office eliminations, and asset disposals should be divided between the two banks. The decision was complicated. On the one hand, the goal of producing a more competitive bank would be best served by retaining only the best people and the best assets. On the other hand, one bank could not appear to be dominant in this process if this were truly to be a "merger of equals," and in many cases the choice would not be obvious (as, for example, when a Chase branch and a Chemical branch both occupied the same city block). Shipley believed it would be very difficult to cut costs and grow revenues according to plan if employees of the acquired bank felt inferior or second-class.

The integration would be overseen by Chemical's senior vice-chairman, Ed Miller, with the primary support of the bank's chief administrative officer, Joseph Sponholz. The process would take place in several stages, starting with the formation of "mapping" teams—groups of managers from both banks who would collect information necessary to plan the integration. The integration process would be tracked closely using a computer software program called the Merger Overview Model (MOM). This model would provide a precise timetable for implementing the proposed merger saves and system integrations.

MOM was extraordinarily complex. Each key event or milestone that was planned as part of the integration was precisely noted on a time line that stretched from August 1995 through December 1998. MOM contemplated more than 3,300 major milestones in all, and planned to complete three-quarters of them by the end of 1996. MOM also explicitly recognized the thousands of interdependencies that were present in the integration plan. For example, the banks' ATM machines could not be fully integrated until a single software system was adopted for processing ATM transactions. Similarly, retail branch offices could not be combined until the banks agreed on a uniform check clearing system. Given such interdependencies, if a single milestone were missed, the entire integration schedule could be disrupted. Exhibit 13.14 shows a condensed graphical representation of MOM.

It would also be necessary to integrate senior management of the two banks. Shipley would be appointed chairman and chief executive officer of the new bank, while Labrecque would become president and chief operating officer. Other senior management appointments also had to be decided.

Some industry observers felt that merging Chemical and Chase would be more challenging than merging Chemical and Manufacturers Hanover had been. Chemical and Chase had been competitors for over 200 years and they had distinct corporate cultures.

Impact on Employees

The merger could create morale problems. Both banks had downsized their workforces over the past three years, and the prospect of additional workforce reductions could generate anxiety and ill will among employees.

A merger would affect the well-being of Chemical and Chase employees in another important way. In 1994, both banks had adopted broadbased stock option plans for all of their full- and part-time employees. Approximately 20 million options had been granted initially under Chemical's plan at an exercise price of $40.50, and 32.5 million such options were outstanding at the end of 1994, with exercise prices ranging from $30.77 to $40.50. Under Chase's option plan, 13.2 million options were outstanding at the end of 1994, with exercise prices ranging from $32.00 to $38.50. These two plans would have to be integrated somehow if the banks merged.

Given the size of the merger and the public's interest in corporate downsizing, it was likely that any layoffs would be very closely scrutinized by the news media.

Other Issues

There were a number of other issues that had to be addressed as well.

If the merger cost savings and revenue enhancements materialized as forecasted, the bank would accumulate significant cash in excess of regulatory capital requirements over the next few years. Management therefore had to decide what to do with this cash. One possibility was to finance a stock buyback program.

If management wished to account for the merger as a nontaxable "pooling" transaction, however, Securities and Exchange Commission (SEC) rules limited the number of shares that could be repurchased (by Chemical or Chase) in the two years prior to the merger and 180 days after the merger. Management estimated that the merged bank could repurchase up to 10 percent of the shares issued in the deal without violating pooling rules. If the merger did not qualify for pooling treatment, then it would have to be accounted for as a "purchase" transaction, and the difference between the acquisition price and the book value of Chase stock acquired would have to be amortized over twenty-five years as "goodwill."

The merger would have to be approved by various regulatory agencies, including the Federal Reserve Board and the New York State Banking Department.

The merger could also meet with resistance from some community activists. Under the 1977 Community Reinvestment Act, banks were required to meet the credit needs of the communities that they served. Some community activist groups were critical of Chase's lending record with low-income and minority customers, and could seek to legally block a merger. To meet the concerns of these groups, Chemical and Chase were prepared to commit up to $20 billion for community investment if they merged.

Finally, it was necessary to decide what information about the anticipated merger benefits should be disclosed to Wall Street analysts and investors. In the earlier merger with Manufacturers Hanover, management had provided a fairly detailed breakdown of anticipated expense reductions and revenue enhancements by product line and business. At the time, it had been management's hope that by providing this level of disclosure, the benefits of the merger would be reflected more quickly (and accurately) in the bank's stock price.

THE DECISION

Shipley believed that a Chemical-Chase merger made good strategic sense, but the stakes involved were enormous, and he was prepared to call the merger off if an acceptable set of deal terms could not be reached. Intensive negotiations between the two banks had been going on for several weeks. Even though both banks had considerable experience in bank mergers, the decisions that had to be made were complicated.

As he drove home, Shipley reviewed the many questions that had come up during the day's discussions. How should the exchange ratio be set? Were the targeted cost savings achievable? How would the layoffs, branch closings, and other expense reductions impact the two banks? How would the merger affect the banks' combined stock prices—and what could the banks do to ensure that Wall Street understood the value that the merger would create?

More fundamentally, was Chase truly the best merger partner for Chemical? From Chemical's perspective, one option was simply to wait. The bank was not under any immediate pressure to cut costs, and its recent financial performance had been solid. Moreover, the task of implementing the earlier merger with Manufacturers Hanover had, over the past four years, placed nontrivial demands on management's time and on the bank's resources. Undertaking a new merger at this time—on a much larger scale than the first—might impose a significant strain on the organization. Finally, the pace of merger activity and consolidation in the U.S. banking industry had been quite high during the past year, and this had put upward pressure on acquisition premiums paid in bank mergers.[14] On the other hand, as more and more large banks were acquired, fewer attractive merger opportunities would remain for Chemical if it chose to wait. Chase might even merge with some other bank if Chemical did not proceed with its own bid; recently, the chief financial officer of NationsBank had publicly expressed some interest in Chase as a potential merger partner.

[14]In 1995, the average price paid to acquire one share of common stock in a target bank was about 15.7 times the bank's earnings per share for the most recent twelve months, up from 14.4 times in 1994.

Note: For expositional purposes this case study portrays events surrounding the merger mainly from the perspective of Chemical Bank's management, and therefore does not fully reflect the active involvement and participation of Chase management in the design and execution of the merger.

EXHIBIT 13.1 Major Bank Mergers Announced in 1995 (through August)

Acquiror/Acquiree	Transaction Value ($billions)	Price to Book	Price to Market[a]	Buyer Rationale	Seller Rationale
First Union/First Fidelity	5.4	1.9×	1.3×	Geographic expansion Revenue enhancements	Limited growth prospects Margin compression 30% shareholder
First Chicago/NBD	5.3	1.5	1.1	Merger of equals—defensive move Achieve scale Preserve Chicago headquarters Preserve name	Achieve scale Consolidate Midwestern position
Fleet/Shawmut	3.7	1.8	1.5	Achieve size Market consolidation Cost reduction	Limited growth prospects Margin compression Limited acquisition opportunities Weak stock price Defensive move
PNC/Midlantic	3.0	2.0	1.3	Strengthen New Jersey franchise Revenue enhancements Cost savings	Importance of size/scale Weak competitive position
US Bancorp/West One	1.6	2.0	1.4	Geographic expansion Achieve scale	Achieve scale Attractive social issues
NAB/Michigan National	1.5	1.9	1.2	Market entry vehicle Opportunities for further acquisitions	Defensive move
Boatmen's/Fourth Financial	1.2	1.8	1.1	Strong position in Oklahoma and Kansas Achieve scale	Limited growth prospects Margin compression Limited acquisition opportunities

[a]Based on price one day prior to announcement.
Source: Company documents.

EXHIBIT 13.2　Banks by Region, with Branch Offices

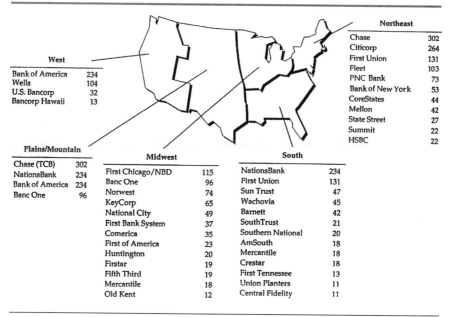

Northeast

Chase	302
Citicorp	264
First Union	131
Fleet	103
PNC Bank	73
Bank of New York	53
CoreStates	44
Mellon	42
State Street	27
Summit	22
HSBC	22

West

Bank of America	234
Wells	104
U.S. Bancorp	32
Bancorp Hawaii	13

Plains/Mountain

Chase (TCB)	302
NationsBank	234
Bank of America	234
Banc One	96

Midwest

First Chicago/NBD	115
Banc One	96
Norwest	74
KeyCorp	65
National City	49
First Bank System	37
Comerica	35
First of America	23
Huntington	20
Firstar	19
Fifth Third	19
Mercantile	18
Old Kent	12

South

NationsBank	234
First Union	131
Sun Trust	47
Wachovia	45
Barnett	42
SouthTrust	21
Southern National	20
AmSouth	18
Mercantile	18
Crestar	18
First Tennessee	13
Union Planters	11
Central Fidelity	11

Source: Mitchell Madison Group.

EXHIBIT 13.3 Comparative Market Share Data: Tri-State Regional Banking (Top Five Rankings for 1994)

| | Downstate New York Middle Market | | | | New York Nine-County Consumer Share | | |
| | Relationship Share | | Lead Share | | Deposit Share | | |
	Rank	Share[a]	Rank	Share	Branches	Rank	Share
Chemical	1	55%	1	29%	282	1	14%
Chase	3	30%	2	12%	184	3	6%
Citicorp	4	29%	4	7%	212	2	13%
Bank of New York	2	31%	5	7%	237	4	4%
NatWest	N.R.	N.R.	3	7%	131	5	3%
Merrill Lynch	5	23%	N.R.	N.R.	N.R.	N.R.	N.R.

[a]Gives credit for each banking relationship and therefore adds to more than 100%.
N.R. = not ranked in top five.
Source: Claritis, The Nilsson Report, *National Mortgage News*, Lipper Analytical Services, Inc., Loan Pricing Corporation Gold Sheets.

(Continued)

EXHIBIT 13.3 *(Continued)* Comparative Market Share Data: National Consumer Business (Dollar Amounts in $billions)

Top Credit Card Issuers (1994)	Rank	Cards (millions)	Balances Outstanding
Citibank	1	34.0	$39.0
Discover Card	2	42.6	20.9
MBNA	3	16.0	17.6
AT&T Universal	4	22.0	12.3
First Chicago	5	18.3	12.2
First USA	6	8.8	11.0
Household Bank	7	15.0	10.8
Chase	8	13.3	10.4
Chemical	9	9.8	8.9
American Express	10	25.3	8.1

Mortgage Originations (First Half 1995)	Rank	Originations	Share
Countrywide	1	$13.1	4.5%
Norwest	2	12.3	4.2
Prudential	3	5.7	2.0
Fleet	4	5.5	1.9
Chase	5	5.3	1.8
Chemical	6	4.9	1.7
NationsBank	7	4.1	1.4
Great Western Bank	8	4.0	1.4
BankAmerica	9	3.9	1.3
GMAC Mortgage	10	3.3	1.1

Mortgage Servicing (June 30, 1995)	Rank	Servicing
Countrywide	1	$121.2
GE Mortgage	2	109.4
Norwest	3	100.5
Fleet	4	99.8
Prudential	5	77.8
NationsBank	6	77.5
Chase	7	73.6
BankAmerica	8	57.1
Chemical	9	51.9
Home Savings	10	49.5

EXHIBIT 13.3 *(Continued)* Comparative Market Share Data: Other Businesses (Dollar Amounts in $billions)

Bank Mutual Fund Assets under Management (March 31, 1995)	Rank	Servicing
Mellon	1	$68.0
PNC Bank	2	22.4
NationsBank	3	14.7
Wells Fargo	4	10.6
Chase	10	7.0
Chemical	13	5.7

Loan Syndications—Agent Only (First Half 1995)	Rank	Agent Volume	Number of Deals	Share
Chemical	1	$132	162	24%
J.P. Morgan	2	68	73	12
Citicorp	3	56	101	10
BankAmerica	4	52	115	9
Chase	5	46	94	8
NationsBank	6	27	94	5
First Chicago	7	22	62	4
Bank of New York	8	22	38	4
Bankers Trust	9	22	59	4
Bank of Nova Scotia	10	11	20	2

EXHIBIT 13.4   Projected Growth in Online Banking

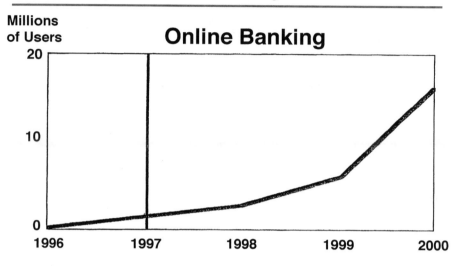

EXHIBIT 13.5   1995 Interest Rate Comparisons

	Aggregate Amount Outstanding for Banks ($billions)	Average U.S. Rates Paid or Charged	
		Banks	Main Competitors
Deposit rate[a]	$453	2.71%	5.05%
Credit card loan rate	240	16.0%	14.0%
Small business loan rate spread[b]	300	6.0%	3.0%

[a]Represents money market demand accounts for banks, and money market mutual funds with check-writing privileges for main competitors.
[b]Spread for "Main Competitors" represents estimated future spread given the likely impact of increasing competition in this market.
Source: Mitchell Madison Group; FDIC; analyst reports.

EXHIBIT 13.6 Comparables Analysis, December 31, 1994 (Dollar Amounts in $millions)

	Chemical	Chase	BankAmerica	NationsBank	First Union	Banc One	J.P. Morgan
Income Statement Data							
Interest income	$ 9,088	$ 8,134	$ 12,384	$ 10,529	$ 5,095	$ 6,437	$8,379
Noninterest income	3,597	3,053	4,147	2,597	1,159	1,420	3,536
Interest expense	4,414	4,445	4,842	5,318	2,061	2,249	6,398
Noninterest expense[a]	5,509	4,472	7,512	4,942	2,677	3,847	3,692
Net income	1,294	1,205	2,176	1,609	925	1,005	1,215
Earnings per share	4.64	5.87	5.33	6.12	5.22	2.42	6.02
Performance Ratios							
Return on average assets	0.78%	1.01%	1.08%	1.02%	1.27%	1.15%	0.70%
Return on average common equity	12.32%	15.79%	13.20%	16.10%	17.04%	13.35%	12.90%
Efficiency ratio	63.00%	66.33%	64.27%	62.54%	62.47%	64.60%	66.92%
Nonperforming assets as % of total assets	0.66%	0.60%	1.03%	0.67%	0.72%	0.52%	0.14%
Balance Sheet Data							
Total assets	$171,423	$114,038	$215,475	$169,604	$77,314	$88,923	$154,917
Total loans	78,767	63,038	137,222	103,371	53,051	61,096	20,949
Total deposits	96,506	69,956	154,394	100,470	58,958	68,090	43,085
Total liabilities (total debt)	160,711	105,679	196,584	158,593	71,916	81,358	145,349
Risk-based capital ratio—Tier 1	8.20%	8.30%	7.27%	7.43%	7.76%	9.93%	9.60%
Total	12.35%	12.78%	11.69%	11.47%	12.94%	13.33%	14.20%
Market Data							
Common stock price—High	42.13	40.00	50.25	57.38	47.63	44.73	79.38
Low	33.63	30.38	38.38	43.38	39.38	24.13	55.13
Number shares, year-end (in millions)	244.5	181.2	371.2	276.4	176.0	396.9	187.7
Market value/share	35.88	34.38	39.50	45.13	41.38	25.38	56.13
Book value/share	37.88	39.28	42.63	39.43	30.66	18.43	46.73
Market-to-book ratio	94.72%	87.51%	92.66%	114.44%	134.95%	137.71%	120.10%
Other							
Headquarters (city/state)	New York, NY	New York, NY	San Francisco, CA	Charlotte, NC	Charlotte, NC	Columbus, OH	New York, NY
Employees	42,130	35,774	98,600	61,484	31,858	48,800	17,055

[a]Noninterest expense reported in this exhibit includes nonrecurring charges; noninterest expense net of nonrecurring charges for Chemical and Chase is reported in Exhibit 13.11.
Source: Companies' annual reports.

EXHIBIT 13.7 Estimated Impact of Merger between Chemical and Selected Banks

Target Bank	Estimated Reduction in Noninterest Expense		Chemical's Ownership at Current Market Price of Common Stock[a]	Impact on Chemical's EPS[b]	Impact on Target's EPS[b]
	$Millions	As percent of Target's Premerger Expenses			
Chase	$1,500	34%	59%	31%	44%
BankAmerica	655	13	40	8	12
NationsBank	539	10	45	9	10
First Union[c]	185	7	60	3	7
Banc One	350	10	51	(1)	18
J.P. Morgan	587	15	50	(2)	34

[a]Assumes Chemical's common stock price is $53.50.
[b]1995 pro forma full-year impact of expense reductions based on consensus analyst EPS forecasts.
[c]Shown before consolidation of First Fidelity.
Source: Casewriter estimates.

EXHIBIT 13.8 Targeted Merger Saves, Pretax (Dollar Amounts in $millions)

Business Unit	Planned Saves as Percent of Combined Expense Base[a]	Forecasted Dollar Savings	Reduction in FTEs[b]
Global bank	19%	$ 560	3,600
Global services	12%	$ 150	1,400
Tri-State regional	16%	$ 250	2,600
National consumer	16%	$ 280	2,700
TCB (Texas)	0%	0	0
Total regional and national consumer business	13%	$ 530	5,300
Central information technology and operations	25%	$ 240	1,000
Corporate functions	29%	$ 190	1,200
Miscellaneous		$ 30	
Total	18%	$1,700[c]	12,500
Saves as percent of smaller base (Chase)	38%		
One-time pretax restructuring charges		$1,650	
Related expenses		$ 250	
Total		$1,900	

[a]Combined expense base equals the sum of total noninterest expense for Chemical and Chase.
[b]Stands for full-time equivalent employees.
[c]This figure reflects a $200 million positive adjustment that management later made to the initial $1.5 billion estimate of merger savings.

EXHIBIT 13.9 Locations of Chemical and Chase Branches before Merger

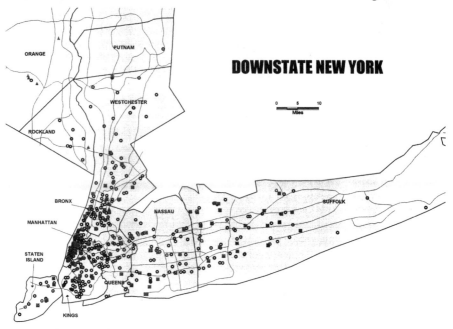

EXHIBIT 13.10 1995 Forecast Revenues by Business Line

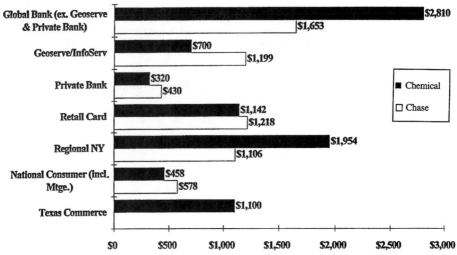

Source: Company documents.
Casewriter note: Geoserve and InfoServ offer operational and information technology support services to wholesale customers.

EXHIBIT 13.11 Stand-Alone Financial Projections: Chemical ($millions, Except Per Share Amounts)

	1994	1995	1996	1997	1998	1999	2000
Total Revenues	$ 8,272	$ 8,404	$ 8,800	$ 9,394	$ 9,936	$ 10,510	$ 11,119
Expenses excluding Other Real Estate (ORE)	5,159	4,959	4,943	5,185	5,433	5,689	5,953
Income before Provision	3,113	3,445	3,858	4,209	4,503	4,821	5,166
Provision	550	500	650	750	800	850	900
Other Real Estate (ORE)	41	(12)	17	17	17	17	17
Net Earnings Before Taxes (NEBT)	2,522	2,957	3,191	3,442	3,686	3,954	4,249
Taxes	1,046	1,141	1,244	1,343	1,438	1,542	1,657
Operating Income	1,476	1,816	1,946	2,099	2,248	2,412	2,592
Extraordinary	(180)	(11)	0	0	0	0	0
Reported Income	1,296	1,805	1,946	2,099	2,248	2,412	2,592
Preferred dividends	138	100	100	100	100	100	100
Net Income Applicable to Common	$ 1,158	$ 1,705	$ 1,846	$ 1,999	$ 2,148	$ 2,312	$ 2,492
Common equity[a]	$ 9,262	$ 10,730	$ 11,930	$ 13,229	$ 14,626	$ 16,128	$ 17,748
Period-end assets	171,423	178,655	188,655	198,655	208,588	219,017	229,968
Period-end loans	78,767	88,000	94,000	102,000	106,774	111,780	117,016
Average shares[a]	249.3	260.9	260.9	260.9	260.9	260.9	260.9

Source: Casewriter analysis based on various analysts' estimates.

[a]Assumes constant fully diluted shares of 261 million and no dividend reinvestment plan.

(Continued)

EXHIBIT 13.11 (*Continued*) Stand-Alone Financial Projections: Chase ($millions, Except Per Share Amounts)

	1994	1995	1996	1997	1998	1999	2000
Total Revenues	$ 6,659	$ 6,525	$ 7,014	$ 7,434	$ 7,880	$ 8,351	$ 8,856
Expenses excluding Savings and Other Real Estate (ORE)	4,308	4,457	4,600	4,768	4,943	5,124	5,313
Focus savings	0	0	(400)	(400)	(400)	(400)	(400)
Net expenses	4,308	4,457	4,200	4,368	4,543	4,724	4,913
Income before Provision	2,351	2,068	2,814	3,067	3,336	3,627	3,943
Provision	500	360	450	500	525	546	567
Other Real Estate (ORE)	7	(30)	0	0	0	0	0
Net Earnings Before Taxes (NEBT)	1,844	1,738	2,364	2,567	2,811	3,081	3,376
Taxes	589	695	945	1,026	1,124	1,234	1,351
Operating Income	1,255	1,043	1,419	1,542	1,687	1,847	2,025
Extraordinary	(50)	(240)	0	0	0	0	0
Reported Income	1,205	803	1,419	1,541	1,687	1,847	2,025
Preferred dividends	127	123	123	123	123	123	123
Net Income Applicable to Common	$ 1,078	$ 680	$ 1,296	$ 1,419	$ 1,564	$ 1,724	$ 1,902
Common equity[a]	$ 6,959	$ 7,649	$ 8,491	$ 9,413	$ 10,430	$ 11,550	$ 12,787
Period-end assets	114,038	127,007	134,992	142,462	150,385	158,777	167,674
Period-end loans	63,038	66,639	70,446	74,471	78,725	83,222	87,977
Average shares[a]	183.6	189.9	189.9	189.9	189.9	189.9	189.9

Source: Casewriter analysis based on various analysts' estimates.

[a]Assumes constant fully diluted shares of 261 million and no dividend reinvestment plan.

EXHIBIT 13.12 Common Stock Price Histories

Month-End	Chemical	Chase
Jan 94	$39.500	$36.130
Feb 94	37.250	32.630
Mar 94	36.380	32.250
Apr 94	34.750	34.000
May 94	38.380	37.750
Jun 94	38.500	38.250
Jul 94	38.380	36.880
Aug 94	38.750	37.750
Sept 94	35.000	34.630
Oct 94	38.000	36.000
Nov 94	36.380	35.630
Dec 94	35.880	34.380
Jan 95	39.000	33.130
Feb 95	40.130	35.880
Mar 95	37.750	35.630
Apr 95	41.750	43.750
May 95	46.130	46.250
Jun 95	47.250	47.000
Jul 95	51.630	53.630

Source: Company documents.

EXHIBIT 13.13 Chemical, Ten-Year Financial Summary, 1985–1994 (Dollar Amounts in $millions)

	1994	1993	1992	1991[a]
Income Statement Data				
Interest income	$ 9,088	$ 8,403	$ 9,148	$ 11,282
Noninterest income	3,597	4,024	3,026	2,846
Interest expense	4,414	3,767	4,550	7,169
Noninterest expense	5,509	5,293	4,930	5,324
Provision for loan losses	550	1,259	1,365	1,345
Net income	1,294	1,604	1,086	154
Restructuring charge	308	158	0	6250
EPS (including extraordinary income and charges)	4.64	5.63	3.90	0.11
Performance Ratios				
Return on average assets	0.78%	1.11%	0.78%	0.11%
Return on average common equity	12.32%	16.66%	12.36%	0.33%
Efficiency ratio	63%	58%	61%	65%
Nonperforming assets as % of total assets	0.66%	2.35%	4.36%	4.43%
Balance Sheet Data				
Total assets	$171,423	$149,888	$139,655	$138,930
Total loans	78,767	75,381	82,010	84,237
Total deposits	96,506	98,277	94,173	92,950
Total liabilities (total debt)	160,711	138,724	129,084	131,649
Market Data				
Common stock price, year-end	35.88	40.13	38.63	21.258
Other				
Employees	42,130	41,567	39,687	43,169

Source: Company annual reports.
n.m. = ratio is not meaningful because earnings are negative
n.a. = data are not available
[a]Chemical merged with Manufacturers Hanover in December 1991. Financials for prior years shown in the exhibit have not been restated for the effects of the merger.

1990	1989	1988	1987	1986	1985
$ 6,511	$ 6,823	$ 6,220	$ 5,470	$ 4,520	$ 4,883
1,456	1,404	1,424	1,285	968	768
4,460	4,806	3,913	3,500	2,850	3,311
2,623	2,740	2,460	2,476	1,708	1,532
537	1,135	364	1,492	439	281
291	(482)	754	(854)	402	390
52	0	11	135	0	0
2.38	(8.29)	12.02	(16.68)	7.57	7.33
0.37%	n.m.	0.99%	n.m.	0.70%	0.70%
7.08%	n.m.	27.74%	n.m.	14.22%	15.06%
75%	80%	66%	76%	65%	65%
4.50%	4.59%	n.a.	n.a.	n.a.	n.a.
$73,019	$71,513	$67,349	$78,189	$60,564	$56,990
45,131	44,512	41,590	49,800	39,425	39,096
48,951	50,151	47,966	55,509	39,055	34,505
69,112	67,808	63,382	75,186	63,382	75,186
10.75	29.88	31.00	21.38	42.25	45.38
26,689	29,139	27,225	28,597	20,993	19,691

(Continued)

EXHIBIT 13.13 *(Continued)*   Chase, Ten-Year Financial Summary, 1985–1994 (Dollar Amounts in $millions)

	1994	1993	1992	1991
Income Statement Data				
Interest income	$ 8,134	$ 8,468	$ 8,705	$ 9,638
Noninterest income	3,053	2,949	2,420	2,202
Interest expense	4,445	4,605	5,141	6,293
Noninterest expense	4,472	4,520	3,939	3,818
Provision for loan losses	500	1,561	1,220	1,085
Net income	1,205	966	639	520
Restructuring charge	0	205	0	0
EPS (including extraordinary income and charges)	5.87	4.79	3.46	3.12
Performance Ratios				
Return on average assets	1.01%	0.94%	0.64%	0.52%
Return on average common equity	15.79%	14.59%	11.14%	10.49%
Efficiency ratio	66.33%	66.35%	65.83%	68.83%
Nonperforming assets as % of total assets	0.6%	1.0%	4.0%	4.4%
Balance Sheet Data				
Total assets	$114,038	$102,103	$95,862	$98,197
Total loans	63,038	60,493	62,558	67,785
Total deposits	69,956	71,509	67,224	71,517
Total liabilities (total debt)	105,679	93,981	89,298	92,820
Market Data				
Common stock price, year-end	34.38	33.88	28.50	17.25
Other				
Employees	35,774	34,390	34,540	36,210

n.m. = ratio is not meaningful because earnings are negative.
n.a. = data are not available.
Source: Company annual reports.

1990	1989	1988	1987	1986	1985
$11,572	$ 11,959	$10,112	$ 8,839	$ 7,717	$ 8,418
2,100	1,945	2,252	1,906	1,743	1,316
8,384	8,934	6,850	5,858	4,721	5,669
4,119	3,702	3,431	3,455	3,301	2,732
1,300	1,737	750	2,150	595	435
(334)	(665)	1,059	(895)	585	565
220	38	48	63	30	0
(3.31)	(7.94)	11.55	(11.56)	6.63	6.39
n.m.	n.m.	1.11%	n.m.	0.65%	0.65%
n.m.	n.m.	27.75%	n.m.	13.29%	13.64%
77.89%	74.49%	62.22%	70.69%	69.65%	67.21%
4.6%	3.6%	4.2%	4.3%	2.0%	2.3%
$98,064	$107,369	$97,455	$99,206	$94,838	$87,685
74,727	76,692	69,602	67,979	66,220	61,931
70,713	69,073	64,057	68,578	66,003	61,353
93,279	102,371	92,495	95,220	89,822	83,227
10.50	34.75	28.63	22.13	35.63	36.31
38,470	41,610	41,570	42,390	47,480	46,450

EXHIBIT 13.14   Merger Overview Model

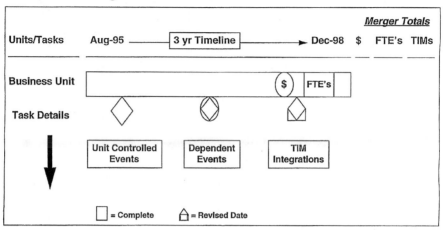

Source: Company documents.

CHAPTER 14

UAL Corporation

On the evening of December 21, 1993, Douglas Hacker, senior vice president of finance for UAL Corporation, was putting together a final batch of documents in preparation for a special board of directors meeting that was to take place the following day. At issue was a possible massive restructuring of United Air Lines—which was a wholly owned subsidiary of the UAL Corporation and comprised almost all of UAL's revenues and assets. United was about to complete its third unprofitable year in a row, and the airline industry as a whole was in turmoil. During the four years 1990–1993, the industry had lost $12.8 billion, five important carriers had filed for Chapter 11, and three had been liquidated. Deregulation of the industry in 1978 had led to increasing price competition, but most of the older airlines—like United—were now in financial trouble because their cost structures were, to a large extent, left over from the pre-deregulation era when increased costs could usually be recouped through higher fares. Airline unions were powerful and were generally resistant to concessions on wages and benefits. (Exhibit 14.1 shows UAL's income statements, balance sheets, and cash flow statements for 1991–1993.)

During the past half year, management and union leaders at United had carried on extensive negotiations over the possibility of cost reductions that United management believed were necessary in order for the company to remain viable. The tentative plan they agreed to was radical: in exchange for significant concessions, employees would be given, over a number of years, 53 percent of the common stock of the company, and UAL would therefore become the largest employee-owned company in the United States. Hacker had been involved in the negotiations, knew that the very structure of the company was at stake, and wondered how the twelve members of the board would vote.

This case was prepared by Research Associate Jeremy Cott and Professor Stuart Gilson. Copyright © 1995 by the President and Fellows of Harvard College. Harvard Business School case 295-130.

BACKGROUND

United Air Lines was, in terms of traffic volume, the largest airline company in the United States (see Exhibit 14.2). It was also one of the oldest. Formed in the early 1930s, it had "united" a consortium of independent airlines and had, over the years, often taken a lead on safety and technological issues in the industry. In 1967 it became the first airline company to surpass $1 billion in annual revenue.

Beginning in 1970 United pursued a strategy of being more than simply an airline; it attempted to become an integrated, full-service travel conglomerate. Thus, in 1970, the company bought Westin Hotels and named Westin's president as its new chief executive officer (CEO) the following year. Resort properties in Hawaii were acquired in the late 1970s in an effort to take advantage of the tourist business in the company's most popular destination. In 1979 another hotelier became CEO, and he bought the Hertz car rental company (in 1985) and Hilton Hotels (in 1987). This diversification strategy—which resulted in a failure to invest in the airline business—was not successful, however. In 1985 the company lost its number one ranking in traffic volume to American Airlines, and in 1987 the company's largest shareholder, Coniston Partners, threatened a proxy fight to oust the board and CEO and to liquidate the company, believing that the whole of United was worth less than the sum of its parts. The CEO and several other board members were forced out. The new CEO, Stephen Wolf, was a veteran of the airline industry. Under his direction, United sold off its hotel and car rental businesses, as well as 50 percent of its computer reservation system.

The company's diversification strategy was something that its unions had also become unhappy with. In 1985 the pilots—who were by far the mostly highly trained and highly paid employees—went out on a twenty-nine-day strike, partly over wage issues, but also over concern with the company's diversification strategy. Roger Hall, who was then chairman of the United division of the pilots union (and who held that position again in 1993) recalled sitting in a meeting during the strike with the lawyer F. Lee Bailey. Bailey suggested that the union try to acquire a majority stake in the company so that it could have a say in blocking other strategies that it considered misguided. "About the only way you're ever going to solve these long-term problems," Bailey said, "is to buy the company."[1]

---

[1]After the strike was over, the company borrowed against the airline to buy Hertz rent-a-car and Hilton hotels, and the pilots felt betrayed. The CEO, as one of the pilots said, "was using the airline as a cash cow to buy hotels instead of airplanes, and pilots don't fly hotel rooms" (Michael Peltz, "Takeovers to the Rescue," *Institutional Investor*, October 1994).

On a few occasions, the pilots tried—either on their own or in concert with various partners. In 1989 an attempted takeover by an outside investor led to a management and union buyout bid, but that failed when the necessary bank financing couldn't be obtained. Another attempted union buyout failed the following year for the same reason, as Iraq's invasion of Kuwait heightened the public's fears about airline travel, caused fuel prices to rise, and thus depressed the whole airline industry.

DEREGULATION

Quite apart from the problems specific to United, however, the airline industry as a whole was changing. In 1978 Congress largely deregulated the industry, which led to increasing price competition. During the 1983-1993 period, for example, airline fares didn't even remotely keep pace with inflation (see Exhibit 14.3).

The older airlines therefore found themselves facing problems with their cost structures. One of them had to do with salaries and benefits, which represented between 35 percent and 40 percent of total costs. Prior to deregulation, the major airlines were often willing to acquiesce to union demands for salary and benefit increases because the increased costs could usually be passed on by way of higher fares. After deregulation, the airlines had to absorb a larger share of these cost increases.

The wave of low-fare service sweeping the airline industry was being led by Southwest Airlines. Founded in the early 1970s, Southwest was profitable every year from 1972 through 1993. It had a highly focused, low-cost, low-fare strategy. (See Exhibit 14.4, which shows benchmark revenue and cost data for the airline industry and for the major carriers.)[2] Southwest provided only point-to-point, short-haul service (flights of less than two hours) in markets with high traffic volumes. It took only twenty minutes to turn its aircraft around between flights (much faster than the industry average). It used only one aircraft type. It provided minimal onboard amenities. And its wage costs were lower than those of most of its

---

[2]The data in Exhibit 14.4 involve one significant adjustment. Travel agent commissions were an important part of airlines' cost structures, but on international flights travel agents typically passed on a large fraction of their commissions to the passengers in the form of fare discounts. Most airlines had historically accounted for these discounts as an additional commission expense—but they were really reductions in revenue. In Exhibit 14.4, therefore, these international fare concessions are excluded from commission expense and instead are netted out of revenues. For United in 1993, for example, this reduces commission expense by about $1.1 billion.

competitors. They were much lower than United's, even though Southwest's workforce was far more unionized than United's. (In 1993, 83 percent of Southwest's workforce was unionized, compared to 64 percent at United.) Exhibit 14.5 shows a comparison of wage rates for three main job categories at Southwest and United.

Southwest eventually outgrew its niche player status—in 1993 it had revenues of $2.2 billion and was the eighth largest airline in the country. In 1988 it competed with United Air Lines on about 8 percent of United's routes; by 1993, however, it competed with United on 16 percent of its routes. In California, the most heavily traveled air corridor in the country, United's market share had grown from 14 percent in 1988 to 26 percent in 1993; over the same period, Southwest's market share had grown from 2 percent to 47 percent. Industry analysts expected Southwest to continue growing about 15 percent a year to the end of the decade.

When a low-cost airline like Southwest entered a short-haul market that United was already servicing, it typically did so with lower fares and was thus able to both stimulate demand and grab market share. What United had generally done in such situations was to match the competitor's lower fares even though doing so resulted in operating losses on those flights. United did this because the short-haul flights often fed into United's longer-haul, connecting flights, many of which were profitable. United's international route network, for example, was considered by many people the strongest of any American company, and represented 37 percent of its total operating revenues. In that segment of its business, too, United had some protection, since many international routes were restrictively regulated by bilateral treaties. (Southwest had no international flights.) On its long-haul domestic flights, United's full-service capability appeared to provide at least some competitive advantage. However, maintaining unprofitable short-haul flights to feed into longer-haul flights was only making the best of a bad situation. (Exhibit 14.6 shows United's revenues, operating profits, and unit costs by business segment, as estimated in the summer of 1993.)

In the late 1980s and early 1990s, the industry went into a tailspin. Iraq's invasion of Kuwait discouraged passenger travel and caused fuel prices to double within three months.[3] The American economy went into recession. And fare wars intensified. As mentioned earlier, in the four years

---

[3]The cost of fuel represented about 15 percent of total costs for airlines but was largely uncontrollable by them. A one-cent change in the cost of fuel increased or decreased operating profits for the industry by over $100 million a year. For United, based on 1993 consumption levels, it would have about a $25-million-a-year impact.

1990–1993, the industry as a whole lost $12.8 billion. Among the major carriers, only Southwest continued to be profitable. Pan Am, Continental, America West, Midway, and Trans World Airlines all filed for Chapter 11 bankruptcy protection in 1991–1992; in 1991, Eastern Airlines, Pan Am, and Midway went out of business. Costs were cut: Companies laid off thousands of workers, abandoned unprofitable routes, and canceled some of their new aircraft orders.

A few carriers that were faced with financial distress went further: They began arranging with their employees significant concessions-for-equity swaps. Faced with the possibility of bankruptcy, Northwest Airlines in 1993 obtained wage and work rule concessions from employees valued at $886 million over a three-year period in exchange for stock options ultimately worth 37 percent of the company's equity. TWA emerged from bankruptcy in 1993 by obtaining employee concessions valued at $600 million annually in exchange for 45 percent of the company's equity.

THE MOVE BY UNITED MANAGEMENT

United Air Lines management believed that the trend toward low fares represented a permanent, long-term change in the industry.

United's balance sheet was still strong, but the company had lost $749 million in 1991 and 1992 ($1,289 million including the effect of accounting changes), and its bonds had junk-bond status. When the 1993 budget was put together, the numbers did not look good. Thus in early 1993 the company announced a $400 million cost reduction program, which involved subcontracting certain maintenance services, laying off 2,800 employees, and negotiating substantial price reductions from suppliers; it also reduced its capital spending commitments for new aircraft through 1996 by $6.2 billion. But United's CEO, Stephen Wolf, believed that would not be enough:

> *As we analyzed our options, we found only two available to us that could effectively achieve our objective of lowering costs to ensure UAL's long-term viability: We could pursue a significant change in our labor costs in a cooperative effort with our union representatives, or we could undertake a unilateral restructuring of our business by selling assets and outsourcing work to third parties.*[4]

---

[4]UAL Corporation, *1993 Annual Report*, p. 2.

The cooperative option was nicknamed, by an outside financial advisor, Project Yuletide; the radical restructuring option was nicknamed Project Seminole. The first option was seen as far preferable, and management therefore proposed that all U.S.-based employees agree to a program that included salary reductions, work rule changes, partial contributions to their medical insurance, and participation in a profit-sharing program. United's unions, however, wouldn't buy it. United then announced its intention to undertake certain kinds of unilateral restructuring. (Stephen Wolf later commented that this would have meant "the loss of tens of thousands of jobs and a great deal of disruption to the airline.")

In 1993 the total workforce of UAL numbered 83,400, of which 64 percent were unionized. There were three main union groups: the Air Line Pilots Association (ALPA), which represented 8,022 pilots; the International Association of Machinists and Aerospace Workers (IAM), which represented 26,984 machinists and other service people; and the Association of Flight Attendants (AFA), which represented 17,330 flight attendants.

Since the pilots' strike in 1985, the company's relations with its principal unions had been, by the company's own admission, often "discordant." Stephen Wolf, hired as CEO in 1987 to return United to its core business of airline travel, was an accomplished airline executive with experience turning around unprofitable companies, but he was not liked by the unions. During the series of union buyout efforts in the late 1980s and early 1990s, he had received the support of the UAL board, but he also antagonized the company's unions in the process. "It's wholly consistent with Wolf's modus operandi," commented a leader of United's pilots group at the time, "to try and split labor groups. . . . He is about to learn a lesson in labor relations." Thus, in 1990, the UAL board was expressing its "unanimous support" for Wolf, while the unions determined that Wolf would have to go if a union buyout were ever to be successful.

Not long after United announced its intention to undertake certain kinds of unilateral restructuring, however, the unions reacted. "Based upon Steve Wolf's past history in the airline industry," commented a leader of the pilots union, "when he says he's going to do something, he does it." In April 1993, a coalition of the three principal unions sent a letter to the UAL board indicating their interest in working out a "shared solution" to the company's problems, and from June to December the unions and UAL management carried on intense, sometimes acrimonious negotiations, involving proposals and counterproposals from each side. In late September, the flight attendants dropped out of the negotiations because of the company's decision to open a flight attendant domicile in Taiwan, thus effectively moving a certain number of jobs overseas, and because of the company's refusal to eliminate employee weight restrictions.

In December, however, the pilots and machinists reached a tentative agreement with the company that would give them, along with management salaried employees, 53 percent of UAL's stock in exchange for wage, benefit, and work rule concessions valued, in present value terms, at $4.9 billion (pretax). The stock would be distributed through an employee stock ownership plan (ESOP). The restructuring would also involve setting up a new low-cost, short-haul service to compete with Southwest. And it would involve a substantial recapitalization that would dividend out to existing shareholders over $2 billion in cash and/or new securities. Exhibit 14.7 outlines the terms of the restructuring plan and some of the key underlying assumptions. The plan was subject to approval by the UAL board, unionized employees, and shareholders. The vote by the UAL board was scheduled for December 22.

THE COMPANY'S OPTIONS

During the summer and fall of 1993, the board had considered three possible management options other than the proposed concessions-for-equity swap.

Status Quo

One was to maintain the status quo, that is, not to undertake any extraordinary actions. The positive elements of this were that it would maintain labor peace and would preserve the possibility of carrying out a fallback strategy later on. The negative elements were that it did not address the company's fundamental cost and competitive problems, it would lose a window of opportunity before labor contracts expired (both the pilots' and mechanics' contracts expired on December 1, 1994), and the price of the company's stock would probably decline. Exhibit 14.8 shows a month-by-month record of UAL's stock price during 1993.

Exhibit 14.9 presents a status quo scenario developed by company management for the years 1994–2000. This scenario assumed medium unit revenue growth (other scenarios had better and worse outcomes) based on assumptions of a recovering worldwide economy in the next few years, and slower revenue growth in the long term due to slower economic growth and the addition of domestic airline capacity, particularly from low-cost carriers. This scenario did not assume any wage increases other than for promotion and seniority or for what had already been contractually agreed to. On the other hand, it also assumed that there would be no more significant fare wars (such as occurred in the summer of 1992), no significant oil price shocks, and a relatively constant consumer propensity to spend on air travel.

"Enhanced Status Quo"

Another possibility was referred to as the "enhanced status quo," which would involve an extensive amount of unilateral restructuring, stopping short, however, of a fundamental change in the company's business structure. This would call for outsourcing all sorts of service activities (such as food preparation, equipment maintenance, cleaning and janitorial work, and data processing) that could be provided at lower cost by other companies; a reduction in certain employee benefits; and the spinning off of short-haul flying on the West Coast to a lower-cost, nonunion carrier with which United would have a close alliance. United felt particularly vulnerable to the challenge from Southwest on the West Coast. As mentioned earlier, California was the most heavily traveled air corridor in the country, and, although United's market share in California had grown from 14 percent in 1988 to 26 percent in 1993, Southwest's market share had grown from 2 percent to 47 percent. The positive element of this option was that it would improve the company's financial performance. The negative elements were the potential labor disruption in the workplace, the possibility of adverse media and political attention, and the lack of sufficient improvement in financial performance. It would also involve laying off thousands of workers. The investment banking firm Credit Suisse (CS) First Boston, which had been hired by UAL as a financial advisor, estimated in August 1993 that the "enhanced status quo" scenario would yield a value per share for the company of $150 to $180.

Radical Restructuring

Another possibility was a radical restructuring, which would involve a fundamental change in the company's business structure. This would, in a sense, take the unilateral restructuring idea of the "enhanced status quo" to its logical extreme. Under this scenario, United would get out of short-haul flying altogether and would continue to operate only long-haul domestic and international flights. United would transfer its short-haul domestic operations to four nonunion regional airlines in exchange for most of their common stock. Under a "scope clause" in United's labor union contracts, employees at these other airlines would automatically be covered under the same contracts—that is, they would effectively be unionized—if UAL owned the airlines' common stock. To get around this, UAL would arrange to have the stock passed directly to its shareholders. It would, however, effectively control the operations of these regional carriers through tightly structured marketing and code-sharing agreements, thus leveraging the strengths it had in managing a large network.[5]

United's advisors estimated that the short-haul carriers could save $780 million to $980 million annually in operating costs, when compared with United's current short-haul operation. This would be accomplished through the kinds of savings that United specified in the agreement it eventually reached with its own employee groups in December (that is, improved asset utilization, more limited reservation and food service, and lower travel agent commission expense), as well as through the large labor savings possible in nonunion operations. Among the alliances that United considered, in fact, were alliances with America West Airlines and Continental Airlines, both of which had been in bankruptcy for a few years, were nonunion and therefore had lower labor costs, but lacked the revenue strengths that United had.

There would, however, be various problems with a radical restructuring. There would probably be some loss of feed revenue from connecting flights (since the relationship between United and the short-haul carriers would not be completely seamless), some loss of revenue due to lower short-haul fares, and some increased costs from a less efficient management of United's aircraft (which would be partly disbursed to the new short-haul entities). All in all, United's advisors estimated that the operating profits of the several entities combined would be $500 million to $700 million higher. CS First Boston estimated in August 1993 that the "fundamental restructuring" scenario would, if successful, yield a value per share for the company of $183 to $253.

It might not be successful, however. In plain operational terms, it could be very difficult to implement. In addition, it would almost certainly generate intense opposition from United's employees, who—when they learned of management's deliberations—estimated that over twenty thousand jobs would be lost. They would probably fight it in the courts, charging that the arrangement was a violation of labor and antitrust law as well as of certain provisions in United's union contracts (such as a prohibition on the establishment of "alter ego" carriers). This could cause enormous disruption in

---

[5]"Code sharing" is a kind of alliance whereby two airlines operating as independent entities share flight codes on connecting flights, thus making it more likely that passengers will book with these, rather than other connecting flights that have different codes.

the workplace and extremely adverse media and political attention. The credibility of the famous marketing slogan that United had used for years—"Fly the friendly skies of United"—might be greatly diminished. If the plan were not successful and the company pursued the "enhanced status quo" as a fallback strategy, CS First Boston assumed that the company would have already absorbed the transition expenses and labor disruption costs (which could run as high as $2 billion), and the value per share for the company would be $108 to $158.

UNION ISSUES AND POLITICAL REALITIES

At one point in the fall of 1993, negotiations between United management and employees appeared to come to an end. In early November, United management, finding the latest proposal from employee groups inadequate, announced its intention to follow through on one of its "unilateral restructuring" options, to sell its flight kitchens. This would put roughly 5,200 union employees out of work but realize considerable annual savings for the company. (See the line "Flight kitchen sale savings" in Exhibit 14.9.) The unions were enraged. A telephone message recorded by the machinists' union for their members referred to United management's "reckless, ruthless, greedy, union-busting course." They threatened strikes as well as public demonstrations against the company's directors.

In the background of the negotiations at United, moreover, was a dispute that was erupting at American Airlines, the second largest airline in the country. On November 18, shortly before the busy Thanksgiving holiday period, the flight attendants at American went out on strike. Management was demanding more stringent work rules from them. The flight attendants, on the other hand, were demanding pay hikes exceeding the 12 percent increase over four years that management was offering. Their current salaries ranged from $14,988 to $38,420 and averaged around $25,000, which was about a fifth of what the average American Airlines pilot earned.

Union issues in the airline industry were complicated. Not only were there (in many companies) serious tensions between unions and management; historically there was also a good deal of animosity among the union groups themselves. Pilots were the most highly trained and by far the most highly paid airline employees (at the four largest airlines, namely United, American, Delta, and Northwest, their salaries topped out at $180,000 to $200,000 and averaged over $100,000 a year); they were mostly men; and they were regarded by some as bearers of large egos (they had long carried the nickname "flying vice presidents"). Flight attendants were the lowest paid; were mostly women; and, despite the traditionally glamorous, jet-setting image of their jobs, often regarded themselves as simply working-class people who, despite certain attractive features of their jobs, had to put up with the indignities of rigid dress and weight codes and lectures from management on how to be nice. They had the most direct contact with customers.

On November 22, 1993, three days before Thanksgiving, President Clinton publicly sided with the striking flight attendants at American, pressuring management and the union to submit to binding arbitration, which was what the union had favored. It was evident that the unions had sympathy in Washington. Just a few weeks before the strike at American, United's machinists union warned Clinton's political advisor and members of the National Economic Council that "there would be labor chaos at the airline if the negotiations [then going on at United] collapsed, according to sources familiar with the meeting."[6]

THE CEO-IN-WAITING

By now, United's unions had become sophisticated and hardened from their multiyear effort to gain control of the company. They had, for example, a CEO-in-waiting. In June 1990, during one of their earlier buyout efforts, they hired away from Chrysler an enormously respected executive who, they felt, had the financial stature to help get the bank financing they needed, but who was also sympathetic to workers, and who was designated to become the CEO and chairman of UAL if and when the employee buyout was successful. This was Gerald Greenwald. (As it turned out, the 1990 effort was unsuccessful, but Greenwald was still the unions' choice in 1993.)

Greenwald had spent almost his entire career in the auto industry. As the chief financial person at Chrysler during its famous turnaround in the late 1970s and early 1980s, he had convinced hundreds of bankers to lend money to Chrysler, and later had helped reorganize the company's operations—so that there was, for example, greater coordination between the sales and manufacturing operations. (By 1990 he was vice-chairman of Chrysler and heir apparent to Lee Iacocca.) He was known as a strong advocate of team approaches to corporate problem solving. One of the union leaders at United said of him, "He knows how to work with workers." The son of immigrants, he had attended Princeton University on scholarship and worked one summer in St. Louis as an organizer for the garment

---

[6]Richard M. Weintraub and Frank Swoboda, "Union-UAL Talks Said to Enter 'Critical' Phase," *Washington Post*, October 22, 1993.

workers' union. "If you had asked me then to name my top ten heroes," he said, "half of them would have been labor leaders."

The challenges he would face at United, however, would be truly diverse. He had to be sympathetic to workers. At the same time, close to half of the company's common stock would still be publicly traded if the reorganization went through, and the company's debt and preferred stock would probably still have junk-bond ratings. When Greenwald first signed up with the UAL unions in 1990, he stated publicly that he accepted the possible United position only after he was assured that employee ownership of the airline would not interfere with management's goal of making it profitable. The unions "will be investors but not managers," he said, and UAL "will be run like any other company, . . . for profits and cash flow." As negotiations proceeded in 1993, however, he also indicated that he would have to deal with all sorts of bad habits in the corporate culture. He said he would like to "reverse the agendas of many conversations at the company, which focus about 80 percent on internal machinations and about 20 percent on how to better serve passengers."

RISKS WITH THE PLAN

The board and management of United knew that the plan had various shortcomings. To begin with, it would damage UAL's balance sheet. UAL's cash balance would be reduced by over $600 million (assuming that the $25.80 cash component of the consideration offered to existing shareholders were taken from the company's existing cash), and the company's long-term debt and preferred stock would increase by about $1.5 billion (representing the remaining components of the consideration). As a result, UAL's shareholders' equity would become negative. Future earnings would be difficult to forecast and evaluate since a circular relation would exist between the company's annual ESOP accounting charge and its stock price. This was because the stock price would largely determine the size of the ESOP accounting charge, and the ESOP accounting charge would reduce reported earnings per share which, in turn, might affect the stock price. Moreover, reported earnings would be depressed in early years due to the mismatch between the term of the employee concessions (some of which would last twelve years) and the term of only five years and nine months over which ESOP accounting charges would be made.

The terms of the plan were, by the company's own admission, very complicated—so much so that (as one company document said) "it is possible that the equity research community and investors may find the company difficult to evaluate, which may have the effect of reducing the trading price" of the company's stock.

The restructured company would, at best, take some time to get up to full speed. The new "airline-within-the-airline," for example, would probably not begin until the fall of 1994, and some of its performance targets (like turning planes around in only twenty minutes between flights) could be difficult to achieve in the first year.

There were more intangible issues as well. Although leaders of the employee groups had reached agreement in principle on the plan with United management, there were indications that large minorities of the pilots and mechanics were unhappy with the deal. The flight attendants, of course, had, at least as of December, refused to participate in the plan altogether. Moreover, because of job security provisions in the plan involving restrictions on things like layoffs, subcontracting of work, transfer of jobs abroad, and asset sales, future management might find its flexibility limited in dealing with changes in a volatile industry.

Competition was not likely to abate. Just a couple of months earlier, on October 1, Continental Airlines had begun a low-fare, short-haul service in the Eastern half of the United States called CALite. Continental had been losing money in one of its hubs, Denver; felt it had to move a lot of its aircraft elsewhere; and wanted to be able to offer a Southwest-like service. In general, the barriers to entry in the airline industry were fairly low. Aircraft, skilled labor, and gates at most airports were readily available— partly because of the various bankruptcies and downsizing that had occurred in recent years—and new carriers were typically able to start off with lower cost structures. Only some of the old, major carriers like United, however, were able to maintain hub and spoke networks.

The members of the UAL board recognized that their upcoming decision was momentous but that, in some sense, UAL's situation was not desperate. The company had one of the strongest balance sheets in the industry and was nowhere near bankruptcy. Was a restructuring of this magnitude necessary? Would existing shareholders be getting enough in exchange for the majority stake that they would be giving up? And would the two participating unions' rank-and-file members vote to approve the plan?

EXHIBIT 14.1 Income Statement ($millions)

	Year Ended December 31		
	1993	1992	1991
Operating revenues:			
Passenger	$12,841	$11,524	$10,296
Cargo	962	796	704
Contract services and others	708	570	663
	$14,511	$12,890	$11,663
Operating expenses:			
Salaries and benefits	4,760	4,562	4,057
Commissions	2,516	2,231	2,046
Aircraft fuel	1,733	1,699	1,674
Rentals and landing fees	1,505	1,342	1,085
Purchased services	983	936	784
Depreciation and amortization	764	726	604
Aircraft maintenance	385	330	363
Food and beverages	317	342	292
Personnel expenses	263	271	239
Advertising and promotion	163	215	208
Other	859	774	805
	$14,248	$13,428	$12,157
Earnings (loss) from operations	263	(538)	(494)
Other income (expense):			
Interest expense	(358)	(328)	(210)
Interest capitalized	51	92	91
Interest income	98	69	85
Equity in earnings (loss) of affiliates	(30)	42	7
Miscellaneous, net	(71)	7	13
	$ (310)	$ (118)	$ (14)
Loss before income taxes, extraordinary item, and cumulative effect of accounting changes	(47)	(656)	(508)
Provision (credit) for income taxes	(16)	(239)	(176)
Loss before extraordinary item and cumulative effect of accounting changes	$ (31)	$ (417)	$ (332)
Extraordinary loss on early extinguishment of debt, net of tax	(19)	—	—
Cumulative effect of accounting changes:			
Accounting for postretirement benefits, net of tax	—	(580)	—
Accounting for income taxes	—	40	—
Net loss	$ (50)	$ (957)	$ (332)

Source: UAL annual report.

EXHIBIT 14.1 (*Continued*) Balance Sheets ($millions)

	December 31	
	1993	1992
Assets		
Current assets:		
Cash and cash equivalents	$ 437	$ 522
Short-term investments	1,391	961
Receivables	1,095	1,066
Aircraft fuel, spare parts, and supplies	278	324
Refundable income taxes	26	64
Deferred income taxes	124	33
Prepaid expenses	362	328
	$ 3,713	$ 3,298
Operating property and equipment:		
Flight equipment	7,899	7,790
Advances on flight equipment	589	710
Other property and equipment	2,673	2,100
	$11,161	$10,600

	December 31	
	1993	1992
Liabilities and Shareholders' Equity		
Current liabilities:		
Short-term borrowings	$ 315	$ 450
Long-term debt maturing within one year	144	116
Current obligations under capital leases	62	54
Advance ticket sales	1,036	1,068
Accounts payable	599	646
Accrued salaries, wages, and benefits	943	911
Accrued aircraft rent	893	715
Other accrued liabilities	904	885
	$4,896	$4,845
Long-term debt	2,702	2,801
Long-term obligations under capital leases	827	812

(*Continued*)

EXHIBIT 14.1 *(Continued)*   Balance Sheets ($millions)

	December 31	
	1993	1992
Accumulated depreciation and amortization	(4,691)	(4,205)
	$ 6,470	$ 6,395
Postretirement benefit liability	1,058	960
Operating property and equipment under capital leases:		
Flight equipment	1,027	959
Other property and equipment	104	101
	$ 1,131	$ 1,060
Accumulated amortization	(395)	(344)
	$736	$716
Other assets:		
Intangibles	866	907
Deferred income taxes	590	589
Other	465	352
	$ 1,921	$ 1,848
Total Assets	$12,840	$12,257

	December 31	
	1993	1992
Other liabilities and deferred credits:		
Deferred pension liability	571	576
Deferred gains	1,400	1,430
Other	148	127
	$ 3,177	$ 3,093
Minority interest	35	—
Shareholders' equity:		
Preferred stock: issued, 6,000,000 shares; million aggregate liquidation value	30	—
Common stock: issued, 25,489,745 shares in 1993 and 25,284,670 shares in 1992	127	126
Additional capital invested	932	341
Retained earnings	249	332
Other	(70)	(19)
Treasury stock: 920,808 shares in 1993 and 1,046,188 shares in 1992	(65)	(74)
	$ 1,203	$ 706
Total Liabilities and Shareholders' Equity	$12,840	$12,257

Source: UAL annual report.

EXHIBIT 14.1 *(Continued)* Cash Flow Statements ($millions)

	Year Ended December 31		
	1993	1992	1991
Cash and cash equivalents at beginning of year	$ 522	$ 449	$ 221
Cash flows from operating activities:			
Net loss	(50)	(957)	(332)
Adjustments to reconcile to net cash provided by operating activities:			
Extraordinary loss on early extinguishment of debt	19	—	—
Cumulative effect of accounting changes		540	—
Deferred postretirement benefit expense	89	75	—
Deferred pension expense	242	165	75
Depreciation and amortization	764	726	604
Foreign exchange (gains) losses	20	(2)	20
Gain on disposition of property	(3)	(32)	(49)
Provision (credit) for deferred income taxes	(67)	(146)	22
Undistributed (earnings) losses of affiliates	42	(27)	(4)
Decrease (increase) in receivables	11	(133)	1
Decrease (increase) in other current assets	24	(67)	(91)
Increase (decrease) in advance ticket sales	(31)	183	40
Increase (decrease) in accrued income taxes	8	164	(254)
Increase (decrease) in accounts payable and other accrued liabilities	(163)	142	353
Amortization of deferred gains	(83)	(82)	(82)
Other, net	36	26	35
	$ 858	$ 575	$ 338
Cash flows from investing activities:			
Additions to property and equipment	(1,496)	(2,519)	(2,122)
Proceeds of disposition of property and equipment	1,165	2,367	1,281
Decrease (increase) in short-term investments	(414)	(238)	248
Acquisition of intangibles	—	(150)	(358)
Other, net	5	3	—
	$(740)	$ (537)	$(951)
Cash flows from financing activities:			
Issuance of convertible preferred stock	591	—	—
Proceeds from issuance of long-term debt	99	198	687
Repayment of long-term debt	(695)	(115)	(67)
Principal payments under capital lease obligations	(55)	(50)	(31)
Proceeds from issuance of common stock	—	—	247
Increase (decrease) in short-term borrowings	(135)	1	1
Cash dividends (preferred)	(27)	—	—
Other, net	19	1	4
	$(203)	$ 35	$ 841
Increase (decrease) in cash and cash equivalents	(85)	73	228
Cash and cash equivalents at end of year	437	522	449

EXHIBIT 14.2   The Largest U.S. Passenger
Airlines: 1993

Revenue Passenger Miles (millions)[a]	
United	100,992
American	97,061
Delta	82,862
Northwest	58,032
Continental	39,858
USAir	35,220
Trans World	22,664
Southwest	16,715
America West	11,188
Alaska	5,447
Industry total	489,137
Operating Revenues ($millions)	
American	$14,737
United	14,353
Delta	12,375
Northwest	8,447
USAir	6,623
Continental	5,085
Trans World	3,094
Southwest	2,067
America West	1,331
Alaska	698
Industry total	$73,000[b]

[a]"Revenue passenger miles" is the standard measure of passenger volume in the airline industry. It
represents the number of seats occupied by revenue passengers multiplied by the number of miles
those seats are flown.

[b]Industry total for revenues is approximate. It excludes airline companies like Federal Express and
UPS that are not primarily passenger airlines.

Source: Air Transport Association, "The Annual
Report of the U.S. Scheduled Airline Industry."

EXHIBIT 14.3 Average Airline Fares and Inflation

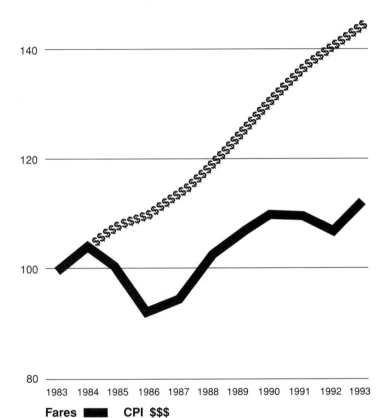

FARES vs CONSUMER PRICES
1983=100

Source: Air Transport Association, "The Annual Report of the U.S. Scheduled Airline Industry."

EXHIBIT 14.4 Benchmark Cost and Revenue Data for Airline Industry, 1991–1993

	"Unit Cost" (Operating Expense per Available Seat Mile) (Cents)	"Yield" (Revenue per Revenue Passenger Mile) (Cents)	"Load Factor" (Capacity Utilization)	"Unit Revenue" (Operating Revenue per Available Seat Mile) (Cents)
Airline Industry				
Average				
1993	10.68	13.07	63.5%	10.87
1992	10.70	12.50	63.6%	10.38
1991	10.75	12.72	62.6%	10.51
Major Airlines				
United				
1993	8.54	11.61	67.1%	8.74
1992	8.86	11.27	67.4%	8.50
1991	9.02	11.50	66.3%	8.62
American				
1993	8.81	13.28	60.4%	9.16
1992	8.95	12.25	63.7%	8.90
1991	9.11	13.11	61.7%	9.13
Delta				
1993	9.51	13.67	62.3%	9.30
1992	9.48	13.33	61.3%	8.85
1991	9.26	13.91	60.4%	9.02
Northwest				
1993	9.23	12.60	66.7%	9.60
1992	9.22	11.86	65.3%	8.88
1991	9.30	12.22	65.8%	9.22
Continental				
1993	8.06	11.42	63.3%	8.03
1992	7.90	10.77	63.5%	7.62
1991	8.24	11.24	62.6%	7.84
USAir				
1993	11.28	17.27	59.2%	11.07
1992	11.01	16.49	58.8%	10.38
1991	10.67	16.67	58.6%	10.33
TWA				
1993	9.31	11.35	63.5%	8.62
1992	8.74	10.22	64.7%	7.92
1991	9.00	10.42	64.7%	8.22

EXHIBIT 14.4   *(Continued)*

	"Unit Cost" (Operating Expense per Available Seat Mile) (Cents)	"Yield" (Revenue per Revenue Passenger Mile) (Cents)	"Load Factor" (Capacity Utilization)	"Unit Revenue" (Operating Revenue per Available Seat Mile) (Cents)
Southwest				
1993	7.16	11.92	67.5%	8.29
1992	6.98	11.78	64.5%	7.83
1991	6.77	11.25	61.1%	7.10
America West				
1993	7.04	11.08	65.4%	7.75
1992	7.15	10.32	61.4%	6.76
1991	7.39	10.15	63.6%	6.88

Source: Department of Transportation Form 41.

- "Available seat miles" represents the number of seats on an aircraft, whether or not they are occupied, multiplied by the number of miles those seats are flown. It is thus a measure of capacity. Total "available seat miles" in the airline industry in 1993 was 770 billion. For United alone it was 150 billion.
- "Unit cost" represents total operating expenses divided by available seat miles. "Unit revenue" represents total operating revenues divided by available seat miles.
- "Revenue passenger miles" represents the number of seats occupied by revenue passengers multiplied by the number of miles those seats are flown. "Load factor" is simply the number of revenue passenger miles divided by the number of available seat miles. It is thus a measure of capacity utilization.
- "'Yield' is a measure of average fares charged, expressed as the average amount received for flying a passenger one mile. The obvious trade-offs between load factor and passenger yeld are synthesized in a more meaningful measure—revenue per available seat mile" (American Airlines, "1993 Annual Report").
- The Department of Transportation defines "major airlines" as airlines with more than $1 billion in annual operating revenues.
- America West filed for Chapter 11 bankruptcy in June 1991; as of the end of 1993 it was still in Chapter 11. Continental filed for Chapter 11 in December 1990 and emerged in April 1993. TWA filed for Chapter 11 in January 1992 and emerged in November 1993.
- The airline industry as a whole recorded net losses in 1993, 1992, 1991, and 1990 of $2.1, $4.8, $1.9, and $3.9 billion, respectively.

EXHIBIT 14.5   Wage Comparison: United versus Southwest (1993)

	United		Southwest	
	Average Annual Wage	Average Number of Flight Hours Worked per Month	Average Annual Wage	Average Number of Flight Hours Worked per Month
Pilots[a]	$109,000	49	$99,000	71
Mechanics	44,000		Similar to United	
Flight attendants	31,000		Similar to United	

[a]Average for captain and first officer, with six years of experience.
Source: UAL internal documents.

EXHIBIT 14.6   United's Revenues, Operating Profits, and Unit Costs by Segment in 1993 (Estimated)

	Operating Revenues		Operating Profits ($millions)	"Unit Cost" (Operating Expense per Available Seat Mile)
	Dollars ($millions)	Percent of Total		
International	$ 5,301	37%	($ 53)	10.0 cents
Long-haul domestic	5,285	37	290	7.9
Short-haul domestic				
West coast	849	6	(62)	11.5
East coast	456	3	(120)	11.8
Midwest	1,557	11	59	11.4
Central	690	5	(52)	10.5
Total short-haul domestic	$ 3,552	25%	($175)	
Total domestic	8,837	63	115	
Total	$14,138	100%	$ 62	9.4 cents

Source: UAL internal documents.

EXHIBIT 14.7 Terms and Assumptions of the Tentative Restructuring Plan

A. EMPLOYEE INVESTMENT

Three employee groups will make concessions on wages, benefits, and work rules carrying an estimated present value of $4.9 billion (pretax). These concessions are referred to as the employee "investment."

The plan contains no guarantee that, at the end of the investment period, employee wages and benefits will "snap back" to what they were before. The employee investment includes the startup of a new short-haul "airline-within-an-airline" (to be referred to as "U2").

The plan contains extensive job security provisions, involving restrictions on layoffs, subcontracting of work, transfer of jobs abroad, and asset sales.

Exhibit 14.7A shows the estimated savings from labor concessions generally and from particular operating features of the short-haul operation. Exhibit 14.7B shows the projected changes from the status quo due to the restructuring plan.

Wages and Work Rules

ALPA Investment (Pilots) Systemwide savings will last for five years, nine months and will include a wage reduction of 15.7% and a reduction in the company's contribution to the defined contribution retirement plan from the current 9% of wages to 1% of reduced wages. There will be no pay raise during the first three years other than existing seniority and promotion increases. In years 4 and 5 there will be the possibility of wage increases under an arbitrated settlement, based on the company's profitability and industry wage trends ("potential midterm increase"). Additional savings will come from the new U2 operation and will remain in force for twelve years; they will include an additional wage reduction of 7.1% and adjustments in work rules (for example, the U2 pilots will fly more hours each month). However, most of the 7.1% reduction should be recovered through the longer hours, and the trips will be scheduled more efficiently, which should enable the U2 pilots to be home most nights. Benefits under the company's defined benefit pension plan, disability plan, and life insurance plan will continue to be based on existing wage levels. There will also be some "contract improvements" (such as higher expense allowances when pilots are out of town).

IAM Investment (Mechanics) Savings will last for six years and will include a 9.7% wage reduction and the elimination of the contractually promised May 1, 1994 wage increase of 5%. There will be no pay raise during the first three years other than existing seniority and promotion increases. In years 4 and 5 there will be the possibility of wage increases under an arbitrated settlement, based on the company's profitability and industry wage trends ("potential midterm increase"). Work rule changes (in lieu of creating a separate U2 work force) will last for

(Continued)

EXHIBIT 14.7 *(Continued)*

twelve years and will include things like eliminating the half-hour paid lunch period and allowing the outsourcing of up to 20% of maintenance work. On the other hand, pension benefits will increase, and there will also be some "contract improvements" (such as larger reimbursements for moving expenses and severance payments for over 5,000 employees being laid off due to the sale of the flight kitchens).

Salaried and management investment   Savings will last for five years, nine months and will include an 8.25% wage reduction and the elimination of 127 management positions. There will be no pay raise during the first three years other than existing seniority and promotion increases. In years 4 and 5 there will be the possibility of wage increases, based on the company's profitability, industry wage trends, and increases given to other employee groups. In lieu of creating a separate U2 work force, a two-tier wage system will be established, which will involve "market-based" compensation for nonmanagement new hires (40%–55% lower wages, 25% payment by employees of medical costs, and a reduction in some other benefits). Work rule changes will also include things like eliminating the half-hour paid lunch period on overtime. Benefits under the company's defined benefit pension plan, disability plan, and life insurance plan will continue to be based on existing wage levels.

Airline-within-the-Airline (U2)

This operation will offer, like Southwest, low-cost, low-fare, low-frills, high-frequency flights of up to 750 miles. It will be marketed as a branded product feature of United, and initially will operate mainly in California. U2 will realize savings from three sources (per Exhibit 14.7A):

- *Improved utilization.* United intends to turn planes around between flights in 20 minutes, compared with its current 40–45 minutes, and to increase average daily utilization of aircraft from 9.5 to 11 hours. The increased utilization should allow more trips to be flown by the same fleet of aircraft.
- *Limited product.* On-board amenities, such as meals, will be reduced; reservation and airport check-in procedures will be streamlined.
- *Reduced distribution expense.* By offering consistently low fares and high-frequency service, United expects to reduce customers' use of travel agents and increase direct airline-to-customer ticketing. This should reduce "commission" expense.

On the other hand, United will differentiate its U2 operation from other low-cost carriers in a few ways. For example, it will offer assigned seating; make first-class seats available to help retain high-yield connecting traffic in

EXHIBIT 14.7 *(Continued)*

United's hubs; and allow U2 customers to participate in United's extensive frequent-flier program.

There are also some constraints placed upon the operation by the pilots' group. During the first five years, total flight hours cannot exceed 20% of United's entire system, which translates to approximately 130 aircraft.[1] (After year five, those limits will be increased.) The operation cannot fly between United's hubs and/or international gateways other than San Francisco and Los Angeles (thus excluding flights between Denver, Chicago, Washington, D.C., and New York).

Assumptions Made in Valuing the Employee Investment (Exhibit 14.7A)

- The $4.9 billion (pretax) employee investment is valued using a discount rate of 10%. (This rate is what the company estimated its weighted average cost of capital would be after the restructuring. The employee groups had initially argued for a 9% discount rate, and an outside analyst calculated a WACC closer to 11%. The company acknowledged that a higher discount rate would be appropriate if there were less assurance that the projected cost savings would be realized.)
- "Labor Savings" are measured against current wage levels. (Some people argued that pay hikes historically tended to occur even in tough times, such that the "baseline" against which labor savings were measured really should be higher wage levels that employees would normally achieve. The company said that it intended not to grant any future wage increases. However, if future wage increases would have averaged 3% annually, the after-tax present value of forgone wage hikes would have been $1.3 billion.)
- Wages and benefits return to current levels ("snap back") after the investment period. However, there is no guarantee in the restructuring plan that this will happen.
- The employees get all of the credit for the "Short-Haul Savings." (The work rule concessions that employees would be making for the U2 operation were necessary to achieve the "Improved utilization." Some participants in the negotiations argued that employee concessions would *not* be directly responsible for the "Limited product" and "Reduced distribution" savings, however. In principle, they said, the company could achieve these unilaterally, and therefore they should not be counted as part of the employee investment. Others argued that all of these things went together, and that the company would probably not market a new kind of short-haul operation unless all of these savings were in place.)

(Continued)

EXHIBIT 14.7 *(Continued)*

B. RECAPITALIZATION CONSIDERATION

The holder of each existing share of common stock ("old share") will receive one-half of a new share of common stock *plus* an $88 dividend consisting of $25.80 in cash; either $31.10 principal of two series of debentures (with an estimated interest rate of 9.35%) or the cash proceeds from their sale by UAL; and either $31.10 liquidation preference of preferred stock (with an estimated dividend rate of 10.25%) or the cash proceeds from their sale by UAL.

C. EMPLOYEE EQUITY AND COMPANY GOVERNANCE

The three employee groups making concessions will receive, in the form of an employee stock ownership plan (ESOP), 53% of the new shares of common stock; but if, during the first year after the establishment of the restructuring plan, the average stock price exceeds $170, additional shares will be issued to the ESOP up to a maximum of 63% of the new shares of common stock.[2]

The stock will be issued to the ESOP in the form of convertible preferred stock, the fair market value of which will be recorded as a charge mostly to compensation expense. The projections assume a 14% compound annual growth rate for the market price of the common stock and a purchase price premium for the preferred stock in excess of the market price of the common that would initially be 38%, declining in subsequent years. (This premium reflects the additional value of the preferred dividend.) In all instances, however, the fair market value of the preferred stock will be determined by negotiation between UAL and an outside ESOP trustee. The stock will formally be sold to the ESOP in seven tranches over a period of five years and nine months (which corresponds roughly to the period of the system-wide concessions by employees).

Virtually all of the ESOP charges will be deductible for federal income tax purposes.

Participating employees are immediately vested. However, their shares can only be sold if they leave the company, retire, or die.

Shares will be allocated to individual accounts of employees in accordance with both "agreed percentages" (roughly 46% for ALPA members, 37% for IAM members, and 17% for salaried and management employees) and employees' relative compensation (or, in the case of IAM members, their relative wage concession). The employees will vote the entire 53% of the shares immediately, regardless of how many have been allocated.

Because the preferred stock held by the ESOP trustee cannot remain outstanding indefinitely and is convertible to common stock, it will be considered a common stock equivalent for accounting and voting purposes.

EXHIBIT 14.7 *(Continued)*

The employee groups' control of seats on the board, however, will be limited. Even though they will hold 53% of the company's common stock, they will directly control only three out of the twelve seats on the UAL board; the other seats will be voted on by the other common stockholders or a subgroup of "independent" directors. On the other hand, the employee groups will be given veto power over certain extraordinary courses of action—such as mergers, material investments outside the airline business, and asset sales greater than $200 million. They will also be given veto power over certain proposed replacements on the board. And they will hold this power (and the 53% voting power) until the "sunset"—that is, when they hold less than 20% of the common stock. According to actuarial estimates, this will occur around the year 2016.

On the effective date of the reorganization (tentatively set at July 1, 1994), the current chairman and CEO of the company (Stephen Wolf), along with two other key executives, will be required to leave. The new chairman and CEO will be Gerald Greenwald.

[1]At the end of 1993 United operated a total of 544 aircraft; Southwest operated 178.
[2]The number of fully diluted "old shares" was 28,926,185. After the recapitalization, they would become $28,926,185 \times \frac{1}{2} = 14,463,093$ new shares. Since the employee groups would hold 53% of the equity of the recapitalized company, the total number of "new shares" would be $14,463,093/.47 = 30,772,538$.

EXHIBIT 14.7A   Total Labor Savings ($millions)

	Year 1	Year 2	Year 3	Year 4	Year 5	Year 6
Total Labor Savings						
Salary reduction	$388	$408	$427	$443	$470	$424
Benefit reductions	127	134	144	154	165	144
Potential midterm increase	0	0	(16)	(61)	(105)	(102)
Work rule changes	32	56	87	111	127	136
Contract improvements	(60)	(47)	(42)	(45)	(47)	(44)
Total	$487	$551	$600	$601	$611	$558
Short-Haul Savings						
Improved utilization	28	43	62	75	81	83
Limited product	26	42	60	72	78	80
Reduced distribution	24	37	53	65	70	72
Total	$ 78	$122	$174	$212	$228	$235
Summary of Savings						
Labor savings	487	551	600	601	611	558
Short-haul savings	78	122	174	212	228	235
Total	$564	$673	$774	$813	$838	$793

- Net present values (NPVs) were based on a discount rate of 10%. However, cash flows are assumed to occur evenly over the course of each year—which approximates the midpoint of each year. Therefore the NPVs arrived at via conventional means (which discount cash flows as if they were at the end of the year) are multiplied by 105% [= 1 + (10%/2)] in order to reach the higher NPVs shown.

Year 7	Year 8	Year 9	Year 10	Year 11	Year 12	Total	NPV
$ 52	$ 64	$ 79	$ 96	$115	$130	$3,095	$2,150
42	49	56	63	71	76	1,222	801
(3)	(3)	(3)	(3)	(3)	(4)	(302)	(189)
143	151	157	162	168	173	1,501	792
(9)	(9)	(9)	(9)	(9)	(9)	(337)	(240)
$225	$252	$279	$309	$342	$366	$5,179	$3,313
90	99	109	121	134	143	1,066	557
87	96	106	117	129	138	1,028	538
77	85	94	104	115	123	917	478
$254	$280	$309	$342	$377	$404	$3,011	$1,573
225	252	279	309	342	366	5,179	3,313
254	280	309	342	377	404	3,011	1,573
$479	$531	$588	$651	$719	$770	$8,190	$4,886

- Year 1 is assumed to begin July 1, 1994, and all subsequent years are assumed to begin on July 1.
- All figures are pretax.

EXHIBIT 14.7B Projected Changes from Status Quo Due to Restructuring ($millions):

Assuming Market Price of Common Stock Just Prior to Recapitalization of $164

	Year 1	Year 2	Year 3	Year 4	Year 5	Year 6
Employee investment savings	$564	$673	$774	$813	$838	$793
ESOP accounting charge	(619)	(630)	(642)	(662)	(689)	(532)
Change in operating income	$(55)	$43	$132	$151	$149	$262
Provision for income taxes	21	(16)	(50)	(57)	(57)	(99)
Changes in net income	$(34)	$27	$82	$94	$92	$162
Add back: noncash ESOP accounting charge	619	630	642	662	689	532
Deferred taxes	(71)	(54)	(38)	(32)	(29)	41
Change in cash flow	$514	$603	$686	$724	$753	$734

Assuming Market Price of Common Stock Just Prior to Recapitalization of $132

	Year 1	Year 2	Year 3	Year 4	Year 5	Year 6
Employee investment savings	$564	$673	$774	$813	$838	$793
ESOP accounting charge	(386)	(391)	(392)	(395)	(401)	(302)
Change in operating income	$178	$283	$382	$418	$437	$492
Provision for income taxes	(68)	(107)	(145)	(159)	(166)	(187)
Changes in net income	$110	$175	$237	$259	$271	$305
Add back: noncash ESOP accounting charge	386	391	392	395	401	302
Deferred taxes	9	30	51	63	75	81
Change in cash flow	$505	$595	$680	$717	$746	$687

Notes:
- The provision for taxes assumes statutory income tax rate.
- The changes shown do not factor in the effect of the new debentures and preferred stock.
- Year 1 is assumed to begin July 1, 1994, and all subsequent years are assumed to begin on July 1.

EXHIBIT 14.8 UAL: Stock Prices in 1993

Date	Price
1/4/93	$125\frac{3}{4}$
2/1/93	$124\frac{7}{8}$
3/1/93	$117
4/1/93	$126\frac{1}{8}$
5/1/93	$138\frac{3}{8}$
6/1/93	$136\frac{5}{8}$
7/1/93	$123\frac{1}{2}$
8/2/93	$142\frac{1}{2}$
9/1/93	$146\frac{1}{4}$
10/1/93	$139\frac{7}{8}$
11/1/93	$154
12/1/93	$151

Source: Daily stock price record.

EXHIBIT 14.9 Status Quo Scenario ($millions)

	1994	1995	1996	1997	1998	1999	2000
Income Statement							
Operating revenue	$14,725	$15,794	$16,970	$17,840	$18,760	$19,684	$20,649
Operating expense	(14,487)	(15,427)	(16,480)	(17,319)	(18,299)	(19,159)	(20,028)
Flight kitchen sale savings	27	49	60	60	56	59	61
Operating income	$ 265	$ 416	$ 550	$ 581	$ 517	$ 584	$ 682
Interest expense	(318)	(302)	(288)	(273)	(259)	(243)	(232)
Interest capitalized	51	33	42	27	18	15	15
Interest income	73	74	96	118	157	193	236
Other, net	(10)	10	44	52	60	79	41
Pretax income	$ 61	$ 231	$ 444	$ 505	$ 493	$ 628	$ 742
Provision for income taxes	(23)	(88)	(169)	(192)	(187)	(239)	(282)
Net income	38	143	275	313	306	389	460
Cash Flow Statement							
Net income	38	143	275	313	306	389	460
Depreciation	745	756	812	872	942	974	1,023
Noncash pension expense	(10)	29	137	129	112	83	78
Deferred taxes	(17)	14	61	70	77	78	95
Change in working capital	346	206	226	169	178	180	188
Other	(12)	(23)	(44)	(46)	(39)	(26)	22
Funds from operations	$ 1,090	$ 1,125	$ 1,467	$ 1,507	$ 1,576	$ 1,678	$ 1,866

Aircraft capital expenditures	(682)	(1,052)	(869)	(1,278)	(672)	(183)	0
Nonaircraft capital expenditures	(700)	(700)	(700)	(700)	(700)	(700)	(700)
Sale/leaseback proceeds	569	1,382	766	1,539	825	255	0
Capitalized interest	(51)	(33)	(42)	(27)	(18)	(15)	(15)
Existing preferred dividends	(37)	(37)	(37)	(37)	(37)	(37)	(37)
Flight kitchen sale	111	0	0	0	0	0	0
Other	72	0	31	24	26	48	0
Funds from financing	$ (718)	$ (440)	$ (851)	$ (479)	$ (576)	$ (632)	$ (752)
Free cash flow	372	685	616	1,028	1,000	1,046	1,114
Debt repayments	(204)	(189)	(184)	(191)	(204)	(138)	(125)
Net cash flow	$ 168	$ 496	$ 432	$ 837	$ 796	$ 908	$ 989
Cumulative cash	$1,996	$2,492	$2,924	$3,761	$4,557	$5,465	$6,454

Notes:
• The provision for taxes assumes the statutory income tax rate.
• Aircraft capital expenditures represents expenditures only on aircraft that the company was committed to take, as of late 1993.
• The cash balance at the end of 1993 was $1,828.

483

Closing the Value Gap

A Simple Framework for Analyzing Corporate Restructuring

Since the materials in this volume cover a wide range of topics and situations, the reader may find it helpful to have a framework for analyzing the cases. An obvious place to start is to ask, what is corporate restructuring? The term "restructuring" is widely used, but has many different meanings.

In this book, the definition of restructuring takes its cue from the influential work of Michael Jensen and William Meckling.[1] They argue that a company can be viewed as a collection of contracting relationships among individuals—a "nexus of contracts." These contracts are what make it possible for the company to conduct business. The parties to these contracts include shareholders, creditors, managers, employees, suppliers, and customers—in other words, anyone who has a claim on the firm's profits and cash flows.[2]

Applying this perspective to the case studies in this book, restructuring is the process by which firms change these contracts. What usually drives firms to restructure is some opportunity to increase their market value.[3] Restructur-

---

[1]Michael Jensen and William Meckling, 1976, "Theory of the Firm: Managerial Behavior, Agency Costs and Ownership Structure," *Journal of Financial Economics* 3: 305–360.

[2]Contracts can be either explicit or implicit in nature. An example of an implicit contract is an informal unwritten promise by a company to its workers that it will employ them throughout their working lives, or grant them regular wage increases.

[3]Formally, the firm's market value is the value that the capital market places on all the firm's outstanding financial claims, including debt and common and preferred stock. The value of these claims reflects investors' current expectations about the firm's ability to generate business profits and cash flows, which are the source of all dividends, interest payments, and other distributions of capital. Appendix B provides a precise definition of "cash flows" for use in corporate valuation.

ing can be very costly, however, so the value gap must be large enough to make it worthwhile.

The cases in this volume highlight three reasons why companies restructure:

1. *Address Poor Performance.* For some firms, restructuring is a way to address losses in market value caused by poor performance or financial distress. Such losses may or may not be management's fault. Management may have overdiversified into too many businesses or borrowed too aggressively. On the other hand, the firm's problems could be caused by an economic recession or adverse change in currency exchange rates.

2. *Pursue Strategic Opportunities.* A second reason firms restructure is to take advantage of a new strategic or business opportunity. A firm may have been managing its business perfectly well, but to exploit the opportunity it must first restructure a contract with some claimholder. An obvious example is a company that has the opportunity to make a profitable investment in a new factory, but the capital expenditure would violate a bank loan covenant.

3. *Correct Valuation Errors.* A third goal of restructuring is to correct a mistake in how investors value the firm. At any point in time, investors may significantly undervalue or overvalue the business. Managers may be unwilling to eliminate such discrepancies by publicly disclosing more information, since this could benefit their competitors. Valuation errors could be quite large for diversified conglomerates, for example. Shareholders of these firms may only understand a subset of the firms' activities. A corporate spin-off or tracking stock issue can reduce such errors by making the performance of the separate business divisions more transparent and easier to value.

WHY DOES RESTRUCTURING MATTER?

Although no two restructurings are ever exactly alike, every restructuring impacts the firm's market value for the same reason: There are certain market frictions or institutional rigidities that make it difficult for the firm to recontract. Such frictions—called "market imperfections" by economists—include transaction costs, agency costs, information costs, and taxes.

Transaction costs include all costs—both out-of-pocket costs and forgone opportunities—that firms incur when they restructure. Examples include legal and investment banking fees in a bankruptcy reorganization and severance payments to employees laid off in a downsizing program.

Agency costs include the loss in market value when managers take actions that benefit themselves but harm shareholders (for example, buying too many corporate jets). These costs also include the costs to shareholders of trying to prevent managers from behaving this way.[4] Note that when these conflicts exist, managers may benefit from restructuring the firm even though the firm's market value falls.[5]

Information costs include the costs to investors of acquiring and processing information about the firm's activities and opportunities.[6] In practice, these costs can be lowered by the activities of financial analysts, who provide expert commentary and analysis about companies to investors. But as noted earlier, sometimes analysts are also unable to determine what a firm is actually worth.

Finally, taxes—both corporate and personal—are a critical concern in almost every restructuring. If a firm wishes to rid itself of a business division (e.g., for strategic reasons), a corporate spin-off can avoid the onerous tax liability created by an outright cash sale. A firm that reorganizes in Chapter 11 may choose to keep its debt level relatively high, because issuing new stock may limit its ability to use its net operating loss carryforwards.

Understanding how these factors can impact market value in a particular situation is critical for successfully managing the restructuring process, addressing the firm's problems, and creating value.[7]

---

[4]For a comprehensive discussion of agency costs, see Oliver Hart, *Firms, Contracts, and Financial Structure* (New York: Oxford University Press, 1995).

[5]Agency costs arise in a variety of other contexts that are relevant to corporate restructuring. For example, managers, acting as agents for the firm's shareholders, may invest too heavily in high-risk opportunities, which increases the market value of the firm's stock but reduces the value of its debt. See Dan Galai and Ronald Masulis, 1976, "The Option Pricing Model and the Risk Factor of Stock," *Journal of Financial Economics* 3 (1/2): 53–81.

[6]See Stephen Ross, 1977, "The Determination of Financial Structure: The Incentive Signaling Approach," *Bell Journal of Economics* 8: 23–140; and Stewart Myers and Nicholas Majluf, 1984, "Corporate Financing and Investment Decisions When Firms Have Information That Investors Do Not Have," *Journal of Financial Economics* 13: 187-221.

[7]In a seminal study, Professors Merton Miller and Franco Modigliani demonstrated that when there are no transaction costs, agency costs, information costs or taxes (i.e., when markets work seamlessly and perfectly) altering the terms of the firm's financial contracts has no impact on its market value, holding its real investment decisions constant. Merton Miller and Franco Modigliani, 1958, "The Cost of Capital, Corporation Finance and the Theory of Investment," *American Economic Review* 48: 261–297.

AN EXAMPLE

The restructuring of USX Corporation illustrates this perspective. In the early 1990s the company received a challenge from the investor Carl Icahn, who wanted management to split the company apart into its two main business divisions, Steel and Energy. Icahn proposed doing this through a corporate spin-off, which would have created two independent public companies. Management instead favored issuing tracking stocks in each division. Each tracking stock would be a claim only on the profits and dividends of the division it tracked; the company's business and corporate structure would otherwise remain unchanged.

The choice between the two types of restructuring presents several trade offs. Under tracking stock, the company could continue to pool profits and losses of the two divisions, potentially reducing the present value of corporate taxes that it paid (taxes). Keeping the divisions together in the same company would also preserve any operating synergies between them. And tracking stock would reduce total administrative expenses relative to a spin-off, because it would be unnecessary to have two corporate treasury or human resources departments, two corporate headquarters buildings, and so on (transaction costs).

On the other hand, value could be lower under the tracking stock alternative if management's only motive for keeping Steel and Energy together was to run a bigger company (agency costs). And with tracking stock, reported profits for each division would reflect management's allocation of corporate overhead and interest expense. Relative to a pure spin-off, this could produce a noisier measure of performance for each business, confusing investors (information costs).

So deciding what is best for the company means assessing each of these trade-offs, and, to the extent possible, quantifying the benefits and costs of each alternative. All of the cases in this volume can be analyzed using this approach. Since restructurings are almost all very complex, with many things happening at once, having a simple analytical framework like this can be extremely helpful.

Valuing Companies in Corporate Restructurings

Technical Note

When planning, negotiating, and executing a restructuring, one of the most important considerations is how the restructuring is likely to affect the value of the firm as an ongoing concern (its "enterprise value"). The change in firm value affects the wealth of the firm's shareholders and other claimholders, and therefore whether they will support or oppose the restructuring. The change in firm value also provides claimholders with important information about management's abilities and motives. When a restructuring is negotiated or determined by a vote, disputes over what the firm is worth can be costly by delaying agreement on a restructuring plan, or by preventing any agreement from being reached. Corporate managers, investors, and others affected by a restructuring can therefore greatly benefit from knowing how to estimate value, and knowing which of the different methods available is likely to work best in a given situation.

This note illustrates how enterprise value can be estimated using alternative discounted cash flow techniques and market value multiples for comparable companies or transactions. Specific numerical examples are used to show how the methods differ and to highlight the relative strengths and weaknesses of alternative approaches in the context of corporate restructuring. A list of selected references on valuation appears at the end of the note.

This note was prepared by Professor Stuart Gilson. Copyright © 2000 by the President and Fellows of Harvard College. Harvard Business School case 201-073.

DISCOUNTED CASH FLOWS

Discounted cash flow models measure enterprise value as the discounted present value of all expected future cash flows available to the firm's stockholders and creditors ("cash flows to capital"). Exhibit B.1 highlights three alternative discounted cash flow valuation models: the adjusted present value (APV) method, the capital cash flow (CCF) method, and the weighted average cost of capital (WACC) method. Under all three methods, there are two primary sources of enterprise value:

1. Cash flows generated by the firm's assets and operations (its "business").
2. Cash flows generated by various tax shields, principally interest expense and net operating loss carryforwards (NOLs).

The methods differ in how they mechanically calculate cash flows for discounting purposes and in what discount rate(s) they use to calculate the present value of the cash flows.

Discount Rate

In general, the discount rate is estimated using the Capital Asset Pricing Model (CAPM), which provides a formula for calculating the expected rate of return on a risky asset.[1] For any asset ("j"), the expected rate of return is:

$$Rj = Rf + Bj(Rm - Rf) \qquad (1)$$

which is the sum of the expected rate of return on a risk-free asset, Rf, and a "risk premium," Bj(Rm − Rf). The risk premium represents the additional return that the marginal investor requires as compensation for holding the asset and taking on additional risk.

The risk of the asset is measured by its "beta" (Bj), which reflects the correlation between the value of the asset and the value of a portfolio consisting of all risky assets (the market). Beta represents risk that cannot be diversified away. An asset with a beta of 1.0 has the same risk as the market. In practice, the beta of an asset is estimated as the slope of the statisti-

---

[1]For detailed discussions of the firm's cost of capital, see Ehrhardt (1994) and Pratt (1998).

cal regression line showing the "best fit" relationship between historical rates of return on the asset and on the market.

The term (Rm − Rf) represents the "market risk premium," or the amount by which the market is expected to outperform the risk-free asset. In practice, Rm is approximated by the return on a broad stock market index like the S&P 500, and Rf is measured as the promised return on a long-term U.S. government bond. The market risk premium has historically been about 7.5 percent on average, although academic estimates of the *ex ante* premium range from 0.5 percent to 12 percent.[2]

The CAPM can be used to calculate appropriate discount rates for both financial and nonfinancial assets. In the case of non-financial assets, which often are not traded or are traded only infrequently, the price data needed to estimate betas might not exist. In the APV and CCF discounted cash flow methods described below, it is necessary to know the beta of the firm's assets, which usually are not actively traded. However, the asset beta (Ba) can be estimated indirectly by exploiting the relationship:

$$Ba = (D/V)^*Bd + (E/V)^*Be \qquad (2)$$

where D and E denote the market value of the firm's debt and equity, respectively, and V denotes the firm's enterprise value (= D + E). Ba can therefore be estimated once one has estimates of the firm's debt and equity betas, Bd and Be.

In practice, to simplify the calculations, it is often assumed that Bd equals zero. In some types of restructuring, however, this assumption may be unwarranted. For example, companies that emerge from bankruptcy reorganization typically have higher than normal amounts of leverage; see Gilson (1997). In these cases, it may be more sensible to assume a positive value for Bd. In this regard, one reasonable value for Bd is 0.25, the estimated beta for risky high-yield bonds; see Cornell and Green (1991).

Adjusted Present Value (APV) Method

In the APV method,[3] total cash flows to capital are allocated to three "buckets," and a separate discount rate is used to estimate the present value represented by each bucket. The three buckets are (1) cash flows generated by the business, (2) cash flows from using interest tax shields, and

---

[2]For example, see Merton (1980), Mayfield (1999), and Welch (2000).
[3]This method is also described in Grinblatt and Titman (1998).

(3) cash flows from using NOL carryforwards. This partitioning of cash flows is illustrated in Exhibit B.1.

To calculate cash flows generated by the business, represented by the first bucket, one estimates earnings before interest and after taxes (EBIAT) and then makes various cash flow adjustments (CFA) for all business-related sources and uses of cash (summarized by the term CFA). EBIAT represents what the firm's accounting earnings hypothetically would be if it had no debt, and therefore had no interest expense. CFA includes an add-back for noncash charges like depreciation or amortization, a deduction for cash expenditures on new capital equipment and net working capital, and credit for cash proceeds from asset sales or any excess cash that the firm holds.[4] Under the APV method, these cash flows are discounted at the expected rate of return on the firm's assets, Ra, which reflects the inherent risk of these cash flows.

(Note that in calculating business-related cash flows, one does not want to deduct interest expense because cash flows to capital represent the sum total of all cash flows available to both stockholders *and* creditors.)

The second bucket of cash includes the tax savings from deducting interest expense. In any year, these savings are equal to annual interest expense ("I" in Exhibit B.1) multiplied by the marginal corporate tax rate (t). If the tax rate is fixed, then any variation in these cash flows over time must be due to changes in interest expense. Thus, under the APV method these cash flows are discounted at the expected rate of return on the firm's debt, Rd, which captures the risk inherent in the firm's interest expense.

The third bucket of cash includes the tax savings from using NOLs. For companies that have to restructure because of poor operating performance, NOLs can be very large, and a potentially important source of value.[5] Tax rules in the United States and many other countries impose limits on how much of a company's NOLs can be used to shield income in a given year, however. In the United States, Section 382 of the Internal Revenue Code imposes a severe annual cap on NOLs in companies that experience a significant change in their equity ownership; in extreme circumstances the NOLs can be eliminated altogether; see Gilson (1997).

The annual impact on cash flows is equal to the amount of NOLs used to

---

[4]Excess cash is literally cash that the firm does not need to conduct its business. Thus it should be possible to pay the excess cash to creditors or shareholders without affecting in any way the firm's future revenues, expenses, and profitability.

[5]For example, for a sample of firms that emerged from Chapter 11 bankruptcy, Gilson (1997) reports that NOLs were equal to 243 percent of the book value of assets for the median sample company.

shield taxable income ("N" in Exhibit B.1), multiplied by the marginal corporate tax rate (t). Until the company's NOLs are exhausted, the amount of NOLs that it uses in any year will equal the lesser of (1) its taxable income and (2) the statutory annual limit on NOL usage. Companies often design a restructuring to avoid running up against the statutory limit. Therefore, unless this limit has been triggered, cash flows from using NOLs will be directly correlated with the firm's taxable income. Since taxable income is received by the firm's stockholders, it is therefore appropriate to discount these cash flows using the expected rate of return on the firm's equity, Re. (If the statutory limit has been triggered, however, then a lower discount rate is warranted.)

Exhibit B.2 presents a specific example of a valuation using the APV method. The example features a company that has provided financial projections for the next five years. Such detailed projections are almost always issued publicly when a company reorganizes under Chapter 11 of the U.S. Bankruptcy Code.[6] Much less information is generally disclosed in other kinds of restructurings, such as corporate equity spin-offs or downsizing programs (although financial analysts may publish their own financial projections). In corporate mergers, the bidder and target companies' investment banking advisors typically produce internal financial projections with the help of management.

In panel A, cash flows generated by the business ("free cash flows") are shown on line 15. Assuming the firm will continue to operate after year 5, the value of free cash flows expected after the projection period must also be estimated. This "terminal value" is calculated using the formula for a growth perpetuity, assuming that free cash flows after year 5 will grow at a constant annual 3 percent rate. (line 16). This terminal value, and free cash flow in years 1 to 5, is then discounted at the expected rate of return on assets, assumed to be 12 percent. The total present value of free cash flows is therefore 615.3 (lines 17–19).

Notice that the terminal value contributes disproportionately to the total present value, accounting for 84 percent (=515.0/615.3) of the total. This is a fairly common situation for firms that are emerging from bankruptcy; see Gilson, Hotchkiss, and Ruback (2000). Although the bankruptcy may have allowed the firm to repair its capital structure, additional time—possibly several years—may be required to turn around its operations. Thus, the

---

[6]By law, the company is required to publish financial projections and an estimate of its enterprise value in a disclosure statement that presents the reorganization plan to creditors. Most companies' projections cover at least four years, with four to five years being typical; see Gilson, Hotchkiss, and Ruback (2000).

free cash flows for such a company may be relatively "back end loaded." Given the formula for the present value of a growth perpetuity,

$$\text{Terminal year cash flow} \times (1 + g)/(Ra - g) \qquad (3)$$

relatively small changes in the assumed growth rate, g, can have a very large impact on estimated enterprise value.

Panel B of Exhibit B.2 shows the present value of cash flows from interest tax shields. This example assumes that the firm's debt stays at a constant level of 300 over time. (The implications of allowing debt to change are considered in the next exhibit.) At a discount rate of 8 percent (the expected rate of return on the debt, Rd) these interest tax shields have a present value of 102 (line 26).

Finally, panel C shows the present value of the cash flows from using NOLs. The calculation assumes there is no statutory limit on using the NOLs. Because the NOLs run out before the end of the projection period, it is not necessary to calculate a terminal value for them. Discounted at the expected rate of return on equity, Re, the NOL tax shield has a present value of 31.4 (line 31).[7]

Total enterprise value assuming constant debt is therefore 748.7 (panel D).

Exhibit B.3 illustrates how the APV method can easily accommodate a changing debt level. The financial projections and assumptions are identical to those in Exhibit B.2, except it is now assumed that the company uses all available cash flows to pay down its debt through year 5, after which debt is maintained at a constant level. Panel A derives the company's new debt level for years 1 to 5. Since free cash flows generated by the business are calculated before deducting interest expense, the first bucket of cash flows is unchanged from the previous example. The present value of interest tax shields is now lower, however, due to the lower debt level (from panel B, interest tax shields are now only worth 76.4, compared to 102 before). On the other hand, the present value of the NOL tax shield is now somewhat higher (31.5 from panel C, versus 31.4 before), since the reduction in interest expense leads to higher taxable income, so the NOLs are

---

[7]This calculation is complicated by the fact that future changes in the company's enterprise value will cause its leverage ratio to change (even though the *dollar* level of debt is fixed), thereby changing Be and thus Re (see equation 2 above). In the Exhibit B.2 calculations, enterprise value is reestimated annually, allowing Be and Re to be updated each year during the projection period until the NOLs expire. In practice, the impact of omitting this adjustment is probably second-order for most companies.

used up more quickly. Overall, the firm's enterprise value falls to 723.2, from 748.7 under the constant debt assumption.

Capital Cash Flow (CCF) Method

The CCF method[8] recognizes the same three buckets of value as the APV method, but the different sources of cash flow are consolidated, and a single discount rate—the expected rate of return on the firm's assets, Ra—is used to calculate the present value of the cash flows. As illustrated in Exhibit B.1, there are several alternative versions of the CCF method, but they differ only in the computational steps taken to calculate cash flows. Total cash flows are the same in each case. Moreover, total cash flows under the CCF method are identical to total cash flows under the APV method.

To justify using the rate Ra to discount interest tax shields, the CCF method assumes that the firm maintains its leverage ratio (D/V) at some constant level over time; see Ruback (2000). If the firm continuously issues or repays debt to keep D/V unchanged whenever V changes, then variation in D over time (and variation in interest expense) is entirely driven by changes in V. Thus the riskiness of the interest tax shield is appropriately captured by the expected rate of return on the firm's assets.

Which valuation method one chooses—CCF or APV—should in part depend on what assumption is being made about the firm's debt policy. Using the CCF method is preferable when the firm has a stable long-run target leverage ratio. However, if large changes in the leverage ratio are planned in the short to medium term, the APV method, or some combination of the two approaches, may be preferable.

The CCF method is also preferable when the firm's effective tax rate differs materially from the statutory marginal rate (e.g., due to tax credits or foreign tax payments). Under the APV method, the firm's tax payments have to be estimated using the statutory rate ("t" in Exhibit B.1). If this rate is inappropriate, under the CCF method one can simply begin with reported net income, which reflects actual taxes paid.

Exhibit B.4 shows how the CCF method can be used to estimate enterprise value using the example from the previous exhibit. The firm is again assumed to use all available cash flow to pay down its debt until year 5. After that it is assumed to grow the debt at the same rate as total cash flows to capital, and thus total enterprise value, consistent with the assumption of a con-

---

[8]This method is developed and explained in Ruback (2000). For applications of this method, see Kaplan and Ruback (1995) and Gilson, Hotchkiss, and Ruback (2000).

stant leverage ratio. The exhibit shows how two versions of the CCF method yield exactly the same estimate of enterprise value, 711.1 (lines 12 and 25).[9]

This estimate is lower than the estimate of 723.2 reported in Exhibit B.3 using the APV method. In general, the two methods will always produce different valuations because they make different assumptions about discount rates and possibly the firm's debt policy, although in practice the difference in valuations is usually modest. In general, the CCF method places a higher value on NOL tax shields because it discounts them at a lower rate (Ra instead of Re), but it places a lower value on interest tax shields because it discounts them at a higher rate (Ra instead of Rd). In the current example, the APV valuation assumes that debt remains constant in dollar terms after year 5, while the CCF valuation assumes that debt grows at 3 percent a year, thereby producing larger dollar interest deductions after year 5. However, the higher discount rate used to value the interest tax shields under the CCF method (12 percent instead of 8 percent) more than offsets the larger dollar tax savings from interest in this case.

Weighted Average Cost of Capital (WACC) Method

The WACC method is perhaps the most widely taught and used approach for valuing cash flows. As shown in Exhibit B.1, the definition of cash flows under this method excludes the tax savings from deducting interest expense. The present value of these tax savings is captured indirectly, however, by discounting remaining cash flows by a single rate—the weighted average cost of capital—which includes an adjustment for the tax deductibility of interest:

$$WACC = (D/V) \times Rd \times (1 - t) + (E/V) \times Re$$

But for the term $(1 - t)$, this discount rate is equivalent to the expected rate of return on the firm's assets (Ra), used to discount cash flows under the CCF method. The WACC method assigns full value for the interest tax shields by using a discount rate that reflects the *after*-tax cost of debt finance. By discounting cash flows at this lower rate, this method inflates the firm's estimated value by exactly the present value of the interest tax shields.

---

[9]This would not necessarily happen if the firm's effective tax rate differed from the statutory marginal rate, since the earnings before interest and taxes (EBIT) version of the model (panel B) assumes that the firm pays taxes at the statutory rate.

The WACC discount rate depends on the firm's leverage ratio (D/V), however. If this ratio changes over time, then the discount rate must be continually recalculated. In practice, leverage often changes dramatically after a company is restructured. For example, most companies that take on significant debt in a leveraged buyout or leveraged recapitalization subsequently pay down the debt. The independent companies that are created by a corporate spin-off may not start out with optimal capital structures, necessitating the subsequent issuance or retirement of debt. And financially distressed companies that reorganize in bankruptcy or restructure their debt out of court may initially retain too much debt for tax or other reasons—see Gilson (1997)—and contemplate a follow-up restructuring or equity issuance.

MARKET VALUE MULTIPLES

Using market value multiples to value a company, one assumes that the capital market values each dollar of profit earned by the company the same as it values the profits of other similar companies (i.e., companies that make the same products, use the same technology, have the same cost structure, face the same business risks, etc.). The capital market's valuation can either be determined by reference to the trading value of other firms' debt and equity securities (the "comparable companies" approach) or by reference to the amounts paid for such companies in corporate acquisitions (the "comparable transactions" approach). In either case, the accuracy of the valuation depends on how closely these other companies match the company being valued.

Exhibit B.5 illustrates how the comparable companies approach can be used to value a firm. The firm, Allied Industries, has issued forecasts of earnings before interest and taxes (EBIT) for the next five years. Companies A, B, and C are considered comparable to Allied. All three companies are publicly traded, so the enterprise value of each company simply equals the market value of its debt and equity (D + E = V).[10] A market value multiple is calculated for each company relative to some year's projected EBIT (in this example, year 1 EBIT).[11] For Company A, for example, the ratio of enterprise value to year 1 EBIT is 9.8. To estimate the enterprise value of Allied Industries, the average market value multiple

---

[10]If some of the debt is not publicly traded, for example a bank loan, it is standard practice to substitute the face value of the debt.

[11]If no projections are available, EBIT for the year just ended can be used instead.

(12.9) is multiplied by Allied's projected year 1 EBIT (32.0), yielding an estimated value of 412.8.

To check the robustness of this estimate, the analysis could be repeated using a different definition of profits—for example, earnings before interest, taxes, depreciation, and amortization (EBITDA) or EBIAT. If profits in the industry are generally negative, it is also possible to compare enterprise values to revenues or some other (positive) measure of activity.

Although this approach is relatively easy to implement, it can produce upward- or downward-biased estimates of enterprise value for companies that have recently completed, or are considering, some kind of restructuring.

One potential problem in using the comparable companies approach arises when the firm is in the early stages of an operating turnaround. Such a firm may have significant future growth potential, and profitable growth should be positively valued in the capital market. However, if the comparable companies are operating in "steady state," the value of such growth will not be reflected in their market values, producing a downward-biased market multiple. This situation is illustrated in Exhibit B.5. Allied Industries is forecasting compound annual EBIT growth of 38.5 percent over the next five years. Corresponding EBIT growth for the three comparable companies, however, ranges from only 6.1 to 19.6. In the example, Allied's estimated enterprise value using the CCF discounted cash flow method is 711.1, so the market multiple approach undervalues the firm by 298.3. Valuation consultants sometimes try to compensate for this problem by using the market value multiple to value projected profits in some later year, after the turnaround has occurred, but this adjustment is ad hoc.

Another potential problem with using market multiples to value a company in need of restructuring arises when the company's entire industry is financially troubled. In this case there may be no external benchmark to which the company can refer to gauge how it will be valued once its financial difficulties are over.

Finally, using comparable transactions multiples to estimate a company's value may be problematic if the company has just completed a restructuring and it used the restructuring to reduce its costs (e.g., through employee layoffs). The price paid in most acquisitions generally includes a premium above the acquired entity's preacquisition market value. One reason the acquirer can afford to pay this premium is that it plans to lay off workers or otherwise cut costs in the acquired company after it takes control. If the company being valued has already realized these cost savings, however, then estimated value based on comparable transactions will be too high.

REFERENCES

Copeland, Tom, Tim Koller, and Jack Murrin. 1994. *Valuation* (New York: John Wiley & Sons, Inc.).

Cornell, Bradford. 1993. *Corporate Valuation: Tools For Effective Appraisal and Decision Making* (New York: Business One Irwin).

Cornell, Bradford and Kevin Green. 1991. "The Investment Performance of Low-Grade Bond Funds." *Journal of Finance*, vol. 46, no. 1: 29–48.

Damodaran, Aswath. 1994. *Damodaran on Valuation* (New York: John Wiley & Sons, Inc.).

Ehrhardt, Michael C. 1994. *The Search for Value* (Boston: Harvard Business School Press).

Gilson, Stuart. 1997. "Transactions Costs and Capital Structure Choice." *Journal of Finance*, vol. 52, no. 1: 161–196.

Gilson, Stuart, Edith Hotchkiss, and Richard Ruback. 2000. "Valuation of Bankrupt Firms." *Review of Financial Studies*, vol. 13, no.1: 43–74.

Grinblatt, Mark and Sheridan Titman. 1998. *Financial Markets and Corporate Strategy* (New York: Irwin/McGraw-Hill).

Kaplan, Steven and Richard Ruback. 1995. "The Valuation of Cash Flow Forecasts: An Empirical Analysis." *Journal of Finance*, vol. 50, no. 4: 1059–1093.

Mayfield, Scott. 1999. "Estimating the Market Risk Premium." Harvard Business School working paper.

Merton, Robert C. 1980. "On Estimating the Expected Return on the Market: An Exploratory Investigation." *Journal of Financial Economics*, vol. 8, no. 4: 323–361.

Patterson, Cleveland S. 1995. *The Cost of Capital: Theory and Estimation* (Westport, CT: Quorum Books).

Pratt, Shannon P. 1998. *Cost of Capital* (New York: John Wiley & Sons, Inc.).

Ruback, Richard. 2000. "Capital Cash Flows: A Simple Approach to Valuing Risky Cash Flows." Harvard Business School working paper.

Welch, Ivo. 2000. "Views of Financial Economists on the Equity Premium and Other Issues." *Journal of Business*, vol. 74, no. 3: 501–537.

EXHIBIT B.1 Comparison of Alternative Discounted Cash Flow Valuation Methods

Definitions of symbols:

R   Revenues
C   Cost of goods sold and selling, general, and administrative expenses
D   Depreciation
I   Interest expense
N   Taxable income shielded by net operating loss carryforwards
t   Marginal corporate tax rate

CFA (cash flow adjustments) =   + Depreciation
                                − Capital expenditures
                                − Investment in net working capital
                                + Excess cash
                                + Proceeds from asset sales

VALUATION METHOD	CALCULATION OF CASH FLOWS
Adjusted Present Value Method	$\underbrace{(R - C - D) \times (1-t)}_{\text{EBIAT}} + \text{CFA} + \underbrace{I \times t}_{\substack{\text{Interest} \\ \text{tax shield}}} + \underbrace{N \times t}_{\substack{\text{NOL} \\ \text{tax shield}}}$
Capital Cash Flow Method A. Net Income Version	$\underbrace{(R - C - D - I) \times (1-t) + N \times t}_{\text{Net Income}} + \text{CFA} + I$
B. EBIT Version	$\underbrace{(R - C - D)}_{\text{EBIT}} - \underbrace{(R - C - D - I - N) \times t}_{\text{Taxes Payable}} + \text{CFA}$
C. EBITDA Version	$\underbrace{(R - C)}_{\text{EBITDA}} - \underbrace{(R - C - D - I - N) \times t}_{\text{Taxes Payable}} + \text{CFA} - D$
Weighted Average Cost of Capital (WACC) Method	$\underbrace{(R - C - D) \times (1-t)}_{\text{EBIAT}} + \underbrace{N \times t}_{\substack{\text{NOL} \\ \text{tax shield}}} + \text{CFA}$

Note: Assume that the firm maintains its debt at a constant dollar level over time.

Initial debt	$300
Initial net operating loss carryforwards (NOLs)	$140
Expected rate of return on debt (Rd)	8.0%
Expected rate of return on equity (Re), initial value[a]	14.8%
Asset beta (Ba)	0.8
Long-term U.S. government bond rate (Rf)	6.0%
Market risk premium (Rm – Rf)	7.5%
Expected rate of return on assets (Ra), where	
Ra = Rf + Ba(Rm – Rf)	12.0%
Long-term annual growth rate (g)	3.0%
Marginal corporate tax rate	34.0%

Panel A. Free cash flows generated by the business

	Year				
Line #	1	2	3	4	5
1 Revenues	$800.0	$860.0	$925.0	$950.0	$1,020.0
2 Cost of goods sold	(720.0)	(774.0)	(786.3)	(807.5)	(816.0)
3 Selling, general, and administrative expenses	(48.0)	(51.6)	(50.9)	(52.3)	(40.8)
4 EBIT	32.0	34.4	87.9	90.3	163.2
5 Interest expense	(24.0)	(24.0)	(24.0)	(24.0)	(24.0)
6 Profit before tax	8.0	10.4	63.9	66.3	139.2
7 Taxes (@34%)	(2.7)	(3.5)	(21.7)	(22.5)	(47.3)
8 Net income	$ 5.3	$ 6.9	$ 42.2	$ 43.7	$ 91.9
9 EBIAT	21.1	22.7	58.0	59.6	107.7
10 + Depreciation	90.9	93.0	98.0	105.0	112.0
11 – Capital expenditures	(95.0)	(96.0)	(105.0)	(115.0)	(120.0)
12 – Investment in net working capital	(16.0)	(17.2)	(18.5)	(19.0)	(20.4)
13 + Excess cash	8.0	0.0	0.0	0.0	0.0
14 + Proceeds from asset sales	3.0	1.0	0.0	0.0	0.0
15 Free cash flows	$ 11.1	$ 3.5	$ 32.5	$ 30.6	$ 79.3
16 Terminal value[b]					$ 907.7
17 Present value of year 1–5 cash flows	$100.3				
18 Present value of terminal value	515.0				
19 **Total present value (discounted at Ra)**	$615.3				

[a]Based on the firm's initial enterprise value of 748.7. Over time, Re is expected to decline due to forecasted increases in the firm's enterprise value, which will reduce its financial leverage (= debt/enterprise value). In panel C, the present value of cash flows from using NOLs is calculated using a different estimate of Re each year, based on updated estimates of the firm's enterprise value and financial leverage. Re is estimated using the capital asset pricing model: Re = Rf + Be*(Rm – Rf). Be, the beta of the firm's equity, is derived from the relationship: Ba = (D/V)*Bd + (E/V)*Be, where V denotes enterprise value, and Bd is assumed to equal 0.25; see Cornell and Green (1991).

[b]Valued using the growth perpetuity formula: Terminal year cash flow * (1 + g)/(Ra – g).

(Continued)

EXHIBIT B.2 *(Continued)*

Note: Assume that the firm maintains its debt at a constant dollar level over time.

Panel B. Cash flows from interest tax shields

Line #	Year				
	1	2	3	4	5
20 Debt	$300.0	$300.0	$300.0	$300.0	$300.0
21 Interest expense	24.0	24.0	24.0	24.0	24.0
22 Tax savings (@34% tax rate)	8.2	8.2	8.2	8.2	8.2
23 Terminal value[a]					102.0
24 Present value of year 1–5 cash flows	$32.6				
25 Present value of terminal value	69.4				
26 **Total present value (discounted at Rd)**	$102.0				

[a]Valued using simple perpetuity formula: Terminal year cash flow/Rd.

Panel C. Cash flows from using net operating loss carryforwards (NOLs)

Line #	Year				
	1	2	3	4	5
27 Profit before tax	$8.0	$10.4	$63.9	$ 66.3	$139.2
28 NOLs used	8.0	10.4	63.9	57.7	0.0
29 Cumulative NOLs used	8.0	18.4	82.3	140.0	140.0
30 Reduction in taxes paid[a]	2.7	3.5	21.7	19.6	0.0
31 **Total present value (discounted at Re)**	$31.4				

[a]Equals NOLs used each year × the marginal corporate tax rate (34%).

Panel D. Total enterprise value

Source of Cash Flow	Present Value
Free cash flows generated by the business	$615.3
Cash flows from interest tax shields	102.0
Cash flows from using net operating loss carryforwards (NOLs)	31.4
Total	$748.7

EXHIBIT B.3 Adjusted Present Value (APV) Method: Declining Debt Level

Note: Assume that the firm uses all available net cash flows (= free cash flows – after-tax interest expense) to pay down debt each year through year 5, then maintains debt at a constant level thereafter.

Initial debt	$300
Initial net operating loss carryforwards (NOLs)	$140
Expected rate of return on debt (Rd)	8.0%
Expected rate of return on equity (Re), initial value[a]	14.8%
Asset beta (Ba)	0.8
Long-term U.S. government bond rate (Rf)	6.0%
Market risk premium (Rm – Rf)	7.5%
Expected rate of return on assets (Ra), where	
Ra = Rf + Ba(Rm – Rf)	12.0%
Long-term annual growth rate (g)	3.0%
Marginal corporate tax rate	34.0%

Panel A. Pro forma debt projection

	Year				
Line #	1	2	3	4	5
1 EBIT	$32.0	$34.4	$87.9	$90.3	$163.2
2 Interest expense	(24.1)	(24.5)	(23.4)	(20.3)	(16.1)
3 Profit before tax	7.9	9.9	64.5	69.9	147.1
4 Taxes (@34%)[b]	0.0	0.0	0.0	(4.2)	(50.0)
5 Net income	7.9	9.9	64.5	65.8	97.1
6 + Depreciation	90.0	93.0	98.0	105.0	112.0
7 – Capital expenditures	(95.0)	(96.0)	(105.0)	(115.0)	(120.0)
8 – Investment in net working capital	(16.0)	(17.2)	(18.5)	(19.0)	(20.4)
9 + Excess cash	8.0	0.0	0.0	0.0	0.0
10 + Proceeds from asset sales	3.0	1.0	0.0	0.0	0.0
11 Net cash flow	$ (2.1)	$(9.3)	$39.0	$36.8	$ 68.7
12 Beginning-of-year debt	300.0	302.1	311.4	272.4	235.6
13 End-of-year debt	302.1	311.4	272.4	235.6	166.9

[a]Based on the firm's initial enterprise value of 723.2. Over time, Re is expected to decline due to forecasted increases in the firm's enterprise value and forecasted reduction in its debt, which will reduce its financial leverage (= debt/enterprise value). In panel C, the present value of cash flows from using NOLs is calculated using a different estimate of Re each year, based on updated estimates of the firm's enterprise value and financial leverage. Re is estimated usign the capital asset pricing model: Re = Rf + Be*(Rm – Rf). Be, the beta of the firm's equity, is derived from the relationship: Ba = (D/V)*Bd + (E/V)*Be, where V denotes enterprise value, and Bd is assumed to equal 0.25; see Cornell and Green (1991).
[b]Reflects utilization of net operating loss carryforwards (NOLs).

(Continued)

Note: Assume that the firm uses all available net cash flows (= free cash flows – after-tax interest expense) to pay down debt each year through year 5, then maintains debt at a constant level thereafter.

Panel B. Cash flows from interest tax shields

Line #	Year				
	1	2	3	4	5
20 Debt	$302.1	$311.4	$272.4	$235.6	$166.9
21 Intereset expense[a]	24.1	24.5	23.4	20.3	16.1
22 Tax savings (@34% tax rate)	8.2	8.3	7.9	6.9	5.5
23 Terminal value[b]					68.4
24 Present value of year 1–5 cash flows	$29.8				
25 Present value of terminal value	46.6				
26 **Total present value (discounted at Rd)**	$76.4				

[a]Interest expense is based on the average amount of debt outstanding during the year.
[b]Valued using simple perpetuity formula: Terminal year cash flow/Rd.

Panel C. Cash flows from using net operating loss carryforwards (NOLs)

Line #	Year				
	1	2	3	4	5
27 Profit before tax	$7.9	$9.9	$64.5	$69.9	$147.1
28 NOLs used	7.9	9.9	64.5	57.7	0.0
29 Cumulative NOLs used	7.9	17.8	82.3	140.0	140.0
30 Reduction in taxes paid[a]	2.7	3.4	21.9	19.6	0.0
31 **Total present value (discounted at Re)**	$31.5				

[a]Equals NOLs used each year × the marginal corporate tax rate (34%)

Panel D. Total enterprise value

Source of Cash Flow	Present Value
Free cash flows generated by the business (from Exhibit B.1)	$615.3
Cash flows from interest tax shields	76.4
Cash flows from using net operating loss carryforwards (NOLs)	31.5
Total	$723.2

EXHIBIT B.4 Capital Cash Flow (CCF) Method

Note: Assume that the firm uses all available net cash flows (= free cash flows – after-tax interest expense) to pay down debt each year through year 5, and thereafter grows debt at the same rate as total capital cash flows (and total enterprise value).

Initial debt	$300
Initial net operating loss carryforwards (NOLs)	$140
Expected rate of return on assets (Ra)	12.0%
Long-term annual growth rate (g)	3.0%
Marginal corporate tax rate	34.0%

Panel A. Net income version

		Year			
Line #	1	2	3	4	5
1 Net income[a]	$ 7.9	$ 9.9	$ 64.5	$ 65.8	$ 97.1
2 + Depreciation	90.0	93.0	98.0	105.0	112.0
3 – Capital expenditures	(95.0)	(96.0)	(105.0)	(115.0)	(120.0)
4 – Investment in net working capital	(16.0)	(17.2)	(18.5)	(19.0)	(20.4)
5 + Excess cash	8.0	0.0	0.0	0.0	0.0
6 + Proceeds from asset sales	3.0	1.0	0.0	0.0	0.0
7 + Interest expense	24.1	24.5	23.4	20.3	16.1
8 Capital cash flows	$22.0	$15.2	$ 62.4	$ 57.1	$ 84.8
9 Terminal value[b]					970.3
10 Present value of year 1–5 cash flows	$160.6				
11 Present value of terminal value	550.6				
12 **Total present value (discounted at Ra)**	$711.1				

Panel B. EBIT version

		Year			
Line #	1	2	3	4	5
13 EBIT	$32.0	$34.4	$ 87.9	$ 90.3	$163.2
14 Taxes (@34%)[a]	0.0	0.0	0.0	(4.2)	(50.0)
15 EBIAT	32.0	34.4	87.9	86.1	113.2
16 + Depreciation	90.0	93.0	98.0	105.0	112.0
17 – Capital expenditures	(95.0)	(96.0)	(105.0)	(115.0)	(120.0)
18 – Investment in net working capital	(16.0)	(17.2)	(81.5)	(19.0)	(20.4)
19 + Excess cash	8.0	0.0	0.0	0.0	0.0
20 + Proceeds from asset sales	3.0	1.0	0.0	0.0	0.0
21 Capital cash flows	$22.0	$15.2	$ 62.4	$ 57.1	$ 84.8
22 Terminal value[b]					$970.3
23 Present value of year 1–5 cash flows	$160.6				
24 Present value of terminal value	550.6				
25 **Total present value (discounted at Ra)**	$711.1				

[a]Reflects utilization of net operating loss carryforwards (NOLs).
[b]Valued using growth perpetuity formula: Terminal year cash flow $* (1 + g)/(Ra - g)$

EXHIBIT B.5   Valuation Using Comparable Company Multiples

Estimate of Allied Industries' enterprise value using enterprise value/EBIT multiple derived from comparable companies A, B, and C.

	EBIT in Year					Enterprise Value	Enterprise Value/ Year 1 EBIT	Five-Year CAGR in EBIT
	1	2	3	4	5			
Allied Industries	$32.0	$34.4	$87.9	$90.3	$163.2			38.5%
Company A	366.0	398.2	423.8	484.7	546.4	$3,581.5	9.8	8.3%
Company B	48.0	48.3	55.0	55.3	64.4	783.7	16.3	6.1%
Company C	25.8	25.9	49.6	56.2	63.1	321.2	12.4	19.6%
Average (enterprise value/EBIT) multiple of comparable companies								12.9
Allied Industries' forecasted year 1 EBIT								32.0
Estimated enterprise value using comparable company multiple								$412.8
Estimated enterprise value using discounted cash flow method (Exhibit B.4)								$711.1

index